D1810201

The complete book of

Children's Clothes

The complete book of

Children's Clothes

Wendy James

COLLINS
GLASGOW & LONDON

The Publishers wish to thank the following for permission to reproduce their designs:

Angela Puppo Designs
BBB Wools
Butterick Publishing Company
CCC Designs
Gatio Wools
Grignasco Wools
Phildar Wools
Schaffhouse Wools
Singer Sewing Machine Company

Front cover photographs
Mulled wine and mulberry pullover: knitted in Patons Double Knitting (instructions page 160)
Navy blue corduroy top with trim: knitted in Listers Motoravia Double Knitting "Cherry" (instructions page 206)
Cotton towelling beach robe (instructions page 24)
Pramsuit (instructions page 94)
Dungarees and check shirt (instructions pages 31-35)

Back cover photographs
Yellow ciré anorak (instructions page 70)
Lipstick red bib and brace: knitted in Patons Trident DK (instructions page 101)
Turquoise party dress: knitted/crocheted in Lister Nylon Courtelle crepe (instructions page 114)

Front flap photograph
Short-sleeved cotton dress (instructions page 60)

First published 1979 by William Collins Sons & Company Limited, Glasgow and London
Printed in Italy by Stabilimento Grafico della Fratelli Fabbri Editori, Milan
Filmset by Tradespools Limited, Frome, Somerset

Designed by Youé and Spooner Limited
Photographs on the cover and on pages 33, 36, 46-50, 60, 73, 115, 116, 135, 185, 206 specially taken by Brock

© English language text and illustrations on the cover and on pages 33, 36, 46-50, 60, 73, 115, 116, 135, 185, 206 William Collins 1979
Il Filo partwork originally published in Italy, colour illustrations copyright 1973 Fratelli Fabbri Editori, Milan

ISBN 0 00 434611 4

Contents

Introduction

A book like this is quite an undertaking mainly because
fashion, like melting snow, doesn't stand still. One thing, however,
does remain constant and that's classic shapes – and we feel that's just
what we've found. This collection, from top European designers,
has that little something that helps
to bridge any fashion gap.
Right from newborn baby up, the garments are as modern
as you want to make them. All you have to do is to choose the
colours and materials that are "in", adding or removing any decoration
according to the dictates of the moment. The hooded battle jacket
shown here is a clever example – in brightly-coloured,
showerproof ciré it has a sporty summer air yet if you turn to
page 71 you'll see how warm and cosy it can be in velour or
fleecy-backed jersey, for boy or girl. The jacket which can also be called
an anorak or blouson, would also look splendid in crushed
velvet or satin. Now that you have the pattern,
there are many possibilities open to you.
That's the message behind all the clothes in this book:
the basic ideas are here for all the family, whatever their needs,
however fast they grow. As well there's lots of advice on altering patterns
so that you can make for smaller or larger sizes, plus what to
watch out for in the making so that the end result
will be successful every time.
This book could not have been accomplished without the
skills and expertise of Shelagh Hollingworth, Frances Rogers, Felicity Murray,
Valerie Barrett, Christine Parsons and Caroline McDonald-Haig. Their
achievement is to present you with a family fashion book that
old and young, beginners and experienced alike,
can rely on for many, many years.

Wendy James

*Wendy with daughters Danielle and Sally,
and son Christopher*

Sewing

For high days or holidays, formal or casual occasions you'll find just what you want in this section for children from very new to nearly adult.

This collection of designs gives you the shapes that go on being popular. By making them yourself, by altering, adding or taking away various elements you can be assured of being able to produce clothes for children from tiny to teenage. Some of the garments are so simple that you can make them for any size – very helpful for mother and daughter outfits, for instance.

As with all the designs in the book, the age guide can only be a guide. The most important thing in all sewing is getting the measurements right (see the diagrams for those that are needed). Make a record of them, so that even if the child isn't there when you're making the garment (or if it's to be a surprise) you can see where the pattern needs to be altered.

Choosing fabrics

If you can't find the width suggested in the fabric you like, ask at the store for how much more you will need to make the garment. In some cases you might have to choose a different type of fabric for a larger size, especially if you want to save money. For example with velvet, because of the nap problem, there could be a lot of wastage if you bought a longer length to make a larger size. You could, of course, try and buy upholstery velvet which is wider but that too can be expensive.

With all fabrics you will need more if you intend matching a design. This can be tricky and you must remember to place all pattern pieces so they're facing in the same direction, and to take extra care at seams, shoulders and waist so that when the garment is sewn, the seams disappear into the overall design.

Although we give pattern layouts on fabric, they won't necessarily apply if you're enlarging a pattern, or if you're using up some leftover fabric or remnants. It just takes common sense and patience to keep arranging the pattern pieces till you cover the material with as little wastage as possible. In a couple of the designs, the wastage has been put to good use as scarves, so perhaps with a little more rearranging you will be able to make something else with the leftover piece – there might be enough for a pochette, or to add a frill or extra pockets if you like.

Apart from the pleasure you get from making clothes for children, it makes money sense and you can cut your costs even further if you save your old clothes. Patterns and designs have more than one day, or even year, in fashion – its more likely to be the style that alters. You'll build up a good store if you unpick seams, darts etc, and wash and iron the pieces. Old worn jeans are always handy to keep (not, of course, if they're paint spattered or permanently marked) as they can so easily be re-used – see page 30 for how to make new from old. Zips and buttons are also worth removing from clothes you're discarding – little things can mean a lot if you constantly have to buy them.

Fabric is usually sold in these widths:	
69/70cm	27 in
90cm	35/36 in
115cm	44/45 in
120cm	48 in
140cm	54/56 in
150cm	60 in

Perfect finish

The finishing touches are as important as any other stage of sewing – in fact, if a garment looks home-made it's usually because the pressing, clipping and tidying up have been hurried or ignored. The inside should not be littered with hanging threads or unravelling edges.

Hems are quite often the giveaway about who made the garment. If a dress or skirt is too long, don't just turn up a deep hem. It is much better to alter at the waist or to take two tucks about two thirds of the way down. These can look very attractive and so long as the fabric doesn't fade or wear, they can be let out as the child grows. With any home sewing, encourage yourself to take a professional attitude to the look of the garment. This way you'll be proud of your handiwork and so will the children.

In fact, once you've gained confidence by making up some of these designs, you can create your own patterns. In our knitting and crochet sections, for example, there are clear diagrams showing the garment's shape. Once you've mastered using squared paper you can add the child's measurements and make in fabric and thread what you can with yarn and needles. This book should stand you in good stead for making clothes for children for many years.

Pattern pieces

You make your own patterns from our diagrams using squared paper (1 square = 5cm), either bought or home-made: join newspaper or tissue together with clear sticky tape and mark the squares in yourself. Even though we do give the imperial conversion in the instructions, 5cm is a fraction more than 2in and, as it can add up to quite a

LENGTHENING A PATTERN

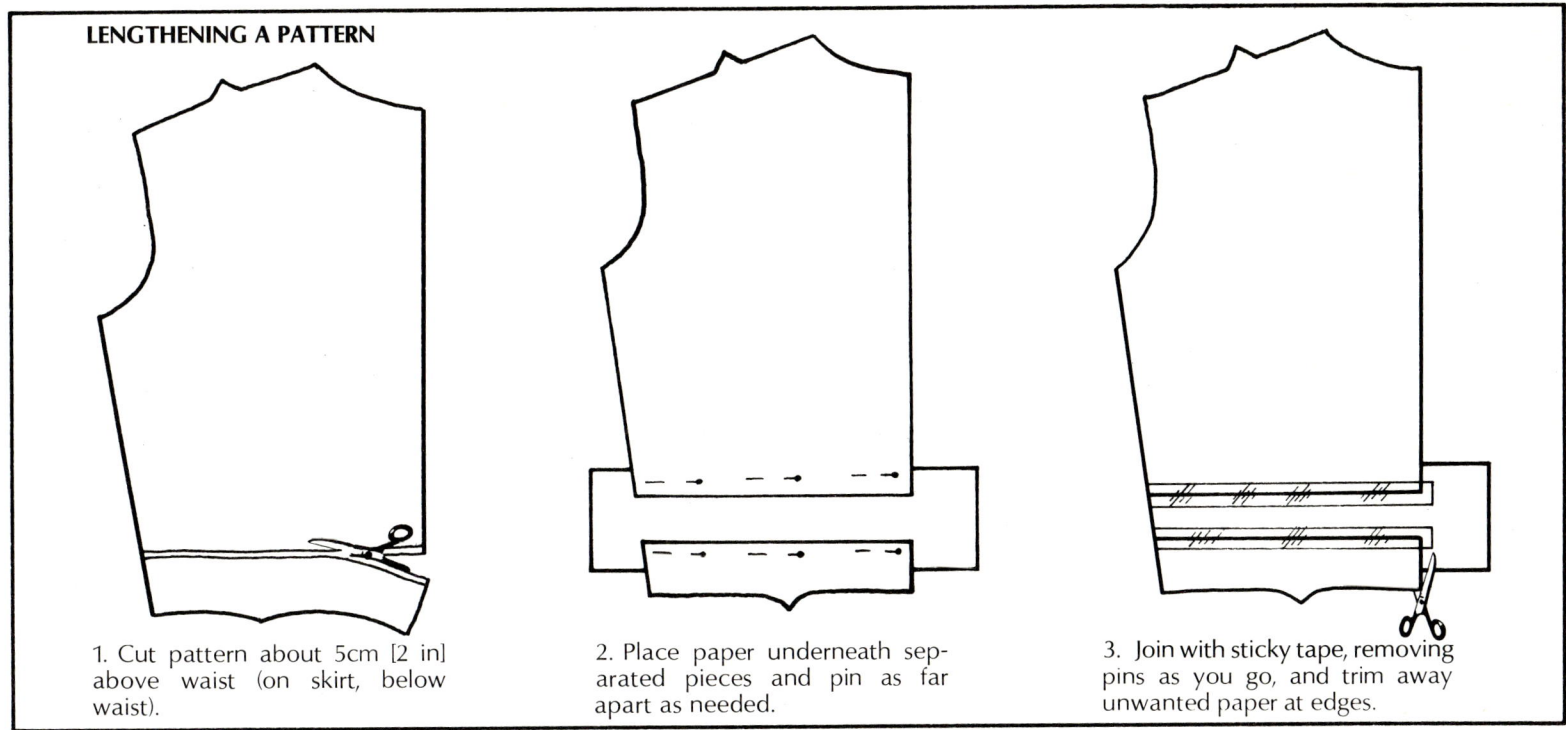

1. Cut pattern about 5cm [2 in] above waist (on skirt, below waist).

2. Place paper underneath separated pieces and pin as far apart as needed.

3. Join with sticky tape, removing pins as you go, and trim away unwanted paper at edges.

difference over a length, it's better to stick to the metric measurements on the diagrams and adjust the pattern later.

Because very few children have the same proportions at the same age (they're shorter or taller, fatter or thinner) do make certain that you apply the known measurements of the child to the pattern and adjust it before any cutting out is done. It is much more sensible to make changes on a piece of paper than it is to try and alter an ill-fitting garment made of expensive material.

With most of the patterns you can add up to 2cm [$\frac{3}{4}$ in] to each seam to widen; sleeves can be lengthened at the upper arm muscle, or shortened midway between wrist and elbow. Shorten a bodice about 5cm [2 in] up from the waist – take a tuck half as much of the amount you are shortening by. To lengthen a bodice or skirt (the point of adjustment is usually 5–7.5cm [2–3 in] from the waist) cut the pattern across and place the separate pieces on another piece of paper, pinning them in position as far apart as you want. Cut away the unwanted edges (see the diagrams above).

Throughout the book, unless otherwise stated, all seams are 15mm [$\frac{5}{8}$ in] and in most of the patterns this allowance must be added when cutting out. Read instructions carefully before beginning in case allowance is different.

THE MEASUREMENTS YOU NEED TO TAKE AND RECORD
1. shoulders
2. back neck to waist
3. chest or bust
4. waist
5. hips
6. front shoulder to waist
7. waist to hem
8. round shoulder from underarm
9. bent arm from shoulder to wrist

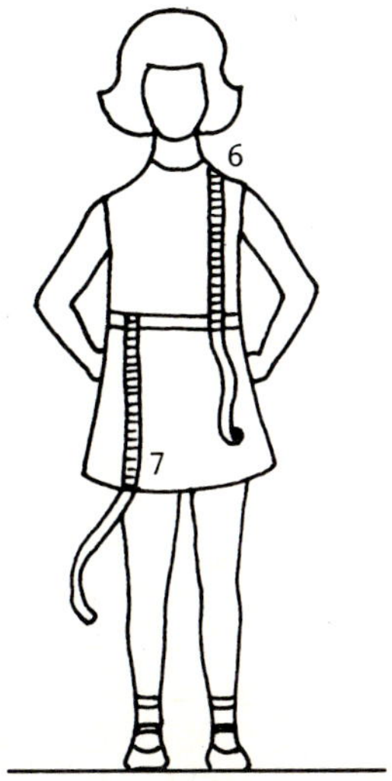

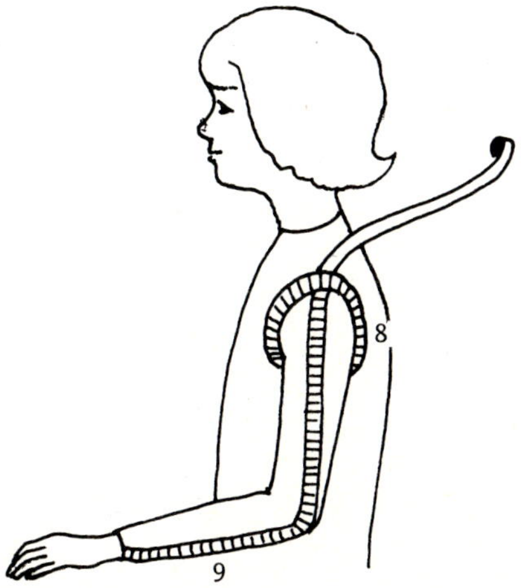

Baby wrap

Newborn to 18 months

A wrap-around to keep the head warm after the bath or on the beach. A splendid idea for a new baby or a toddler.

Materials 65cm × 65cm [25½ in × 25½ in] of cotton towelling; triangle of towelling with two sides measuring 30cm [12 in] (see diagram below); 4m [4½ yd] folded braid 2.5cm [1 in] wide; matching machine twist.

TO SEW

1. Neaten the longest side of the triangle with braid: lap braid over edge of fabric, pin, tack and machine in position close to inner edge.
2. Tack the triangle to one corner of the square as shown in diagram. Neaten all sides with braid as for triangle.
3. Cut two openings for the hands where marked in diagram. Edge the slits with braid. Make decorative triangles using small pieces of braid at each end of slits on both sides of fabric. Pin, tack and machine triangles in place, covering raw ends of braid on sides of slits.

BABY WRAP: PATTERN

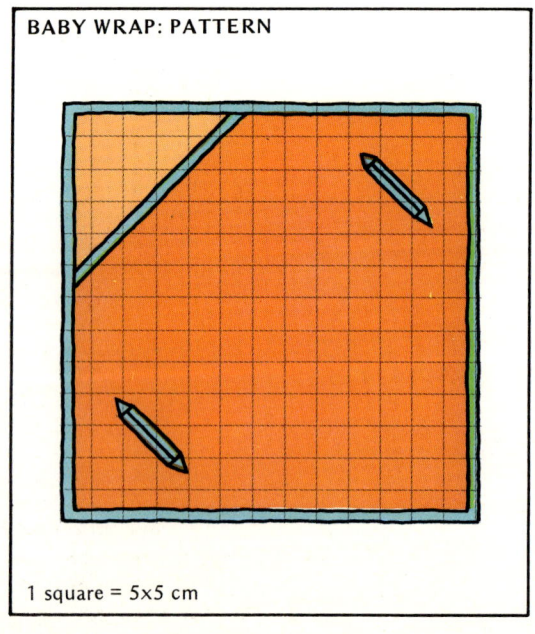

1 square = 5×5 cm

Dresses for special occasions

Classic-shaped dresses that go on being popular. The styles are suited to babies as well as toddlers – the only difference is the length, and you can alter that as you like.

Sun dress

6 months to 5 years

Materials 40cm [16 in] of 90cm [35½ in] wide fabric; 1.60m [1⅓ yd] of 2cm [¾ in] wide broderie anglaise; spool of shirring elastic; matching machine twist.

Measurements To fit 41 (46)cm [16 (18) in] chest. For sizes 1 to 5 years: measure the length (from chest to knee, or longer) and the chest size. Double this last measurement as shirring reduces the fabric by about half. To calculate how much fabric you will need, double both these measurements, then add an extra 20cm [8 in] for the straps. The amount of broderie anglaise you need will be four times the child's chest measurement.

Note All seams are 15mm [⅝ in]. Square brackets contain imperial measurements.

TO SEW

1. Cut two 40cm [16 in] squares.
2. With right sides together, stitch squares together along one side. Press seam open.
3. Pin, tack and machine a length of broderie anglaise to top and bottom, turning under raw edges. Press seams towards centre, slip stitching in place on wrong side.
4. With shirring elastic in the bobbin, and machine twist on the machine, a loose tension and long stitch, sew nine rows of shirring along top of dress 12.5mm [½ in] apart.
5. Right sides together make second seam by stitching along other side, neaten raw edges, turn through to right side.
6. To make shoulder ties, cut 4 pieces 25cm × 2.5cm [10 in × 1 in] from remaining fabric. Right sides together, fold each strap in half lengthways. Stitch down long edge, turn through to right side and press. Neaten short ends by turning in and over-sewing edges together. Stitch straps to dress at front and back 4cm [1½ in] in from sides.

Below: the Sun Dress with its elasticated top
Right, below: the front and back views of the Christening Dress

Christening dress
8 to 18 months

Materials 55cm [21½ in] of 120cm [48 in] wide fabric; 2.5m [3 yd] of double-edged lace; shirring elastic 51cm [20 in] matching bias binding; 1 small button or press-stud if preferred; matching machine twist.

Measurements to fit 41–51cm [16 to 20 in] chest loosely.

Note All seams are 15mm [⅝ in]. Working diagrams are on page 12. Square brackets contain imperial measurements.

TO SEW

1. Cut pattern using squared paper (1 square = 5cm) following Diagram 1. Place on folded fabric and cut out (see Diagram 2), allowing extra 15mm [⅝ in] all round each piece for seams. At centre back of dress, cut down a 10cm [4 in] slit for back opening.
2. Turn up a 2cm [¾ in] hem at bottom of dress on both front and back, and catch-stitch in place on wrong side.
3. Pin, tack and sew 7 rows of lace, equal distance apart, across dress front, stitching bottom row level with edge of dress.
4. With right sides together, pin, tack and machine shoulder and side seams. Press open, turn through to right side.
5. Neaten neck and back opening with bias binding: right sides together, pin, tack and machine binding, starting and finishing at base of neck opening. Turn binding to wrong side and hem in place.
6. On head of each sleeve, sew two rows of running stitches, 15mm and 6mm [⅝ in and ¼ in] from edge. Draw up gathers to fit armhole.
7. Turn up a 2cm [¾ in] hem at bottom of each sleeve, catch-stitching in place on wrong side. Pin, tack and sew lace to sleeve edges.
8. With shirring elastic in the

Continued on next page

The picture above shows the Sun Dress being worked on. On the gate is the Lace-topped Dress (see page 13). In the foreground, left, is the Christening Dress (instructions above) and right, folded, is the Simple Summer Dress (see page 12)

Children's Clothes

Christening dress . . . continued
bobbin, and machine twist on the machine, a loose tension and long stitch, sew 1 row of shirring elastic at lower edge of each sleeve 2.5cm [1 in] from edge. On wrong side of dress, pin, tack and machine sleeves in place adjust gathers evenly.

9. With right sides together, pin, tack and machine underarm seams of each sleeve. Press seams open, turn through to right side.

10. At top of back opening, stitch button to left side. Make corresponding buttonhole on right side (or sew on press-studs if preferred).

Below: pattern diagrams and cutting guide for the Christening Dress.
Right: the finished Sun Dress (see page 10). At her feet is the Christening Dress and Lace-topped Dress (see opposite)

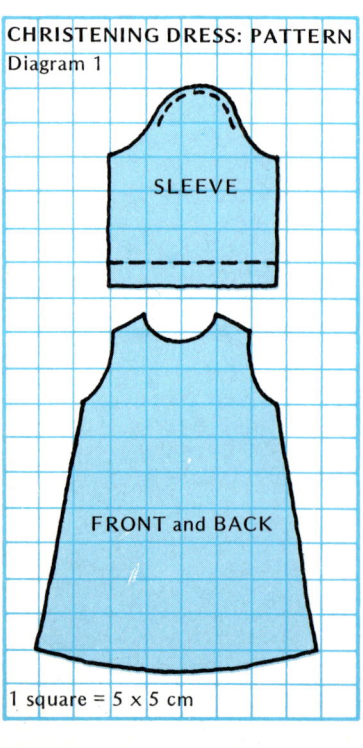

CHRISTENING DRESS: PATTERN
Diagram 1

SLEEVE

FRONT and BACK

1 square = 5 x 5 cm

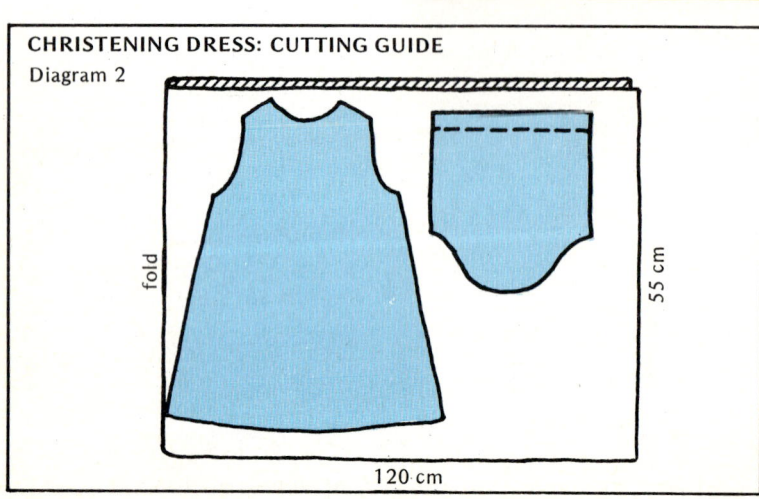

CHRISTENING DRESS: CUTTING GUIDE
Diagram 2

fold

55 cm

120 cm

Simple summer dress

9 to 18 months

Materials 55cm [21½ in] of 90cm [35½ in] wide fabric; 2.5m [3 yd] double-edged broderie anglaise (with eyelet holes for ribbon); 1.5m [2⅔ yd] 3mm [⅛ in] wide ribbon; 6 small buttons or press-studs; matching machine twist.

Measurements 46 (51)cm [18 (20) in] chest.

Note All seams measure 15mm [⅝ in]. Square brackets contain imperial measurements.

TO CUT OUT
Make pattern on squared paper following Diagram 1 (1 sq = 5cm) see first column opposite. Follow dotted lines for larger size. Fold fabric in half (selvedge to selvedge) and cut two body shapes (one front and one back).

TO SEW
1. At top edge of both pieces, turn down 3mm [⅛ in] to wrong side. Turn down a further 6mm [¼ in]; pin, tack and machine

Lace-topped dress

10 to 18 months

Materials 95cm [37½ in] × 90cm [35½ in] piece of fabric; 3m [3¼ yd] 2cm [¾ in] wide broderie anglaise; packet of matching bias binding; 3 small buttons; matching machine twist.

Measurements To fit 51cm [20 in] chest loosely; 46cm [18 in] length. For a larger size, add more to length of skirt if necessary, and 12.5mm [½ in] to all sides of other pieces.

Note All seams are 15mm [⅝ in]. Square brackets contain imperial measurements.

TO SEW

1. Cut out pattern using squared paper following Diagram 1 (1 square = 5cm). **Note:** Bodice front and skirt front and back are cut on fold.

2. Stitch six rows of lace on bodice front as shown, equally spaced.

3. Right sides together, pin, tack and machine bodice front to backs at shoulders and sides.

4. For back opening, turn back and tack 3cm [1¼ in] to wrong side on both back bodices (see dotted line on pattern piece, Diagram 1).

5. With right sides together, stitch front skirt to back skirt at sides.

6. Sew two rows of running stitches round top edge of skirt, 15mm and 6mm [⅝ in and ¼ in] from edge. Draw up gathers to fit bottom of bodice.

7. Right sides together, pin, tack and machine skirt to matching seams, and lapping left back bodice over right bodice by 15mm [⅝ in].

8. To neaten bottom of dress, with right sides together, stitch a length of lace to dress. Press seam up and catch-stitch in place on wrong side.

9. Trim the armhole and neck edges with bias binding: right sides together, starting and finishing at back opening, pin, tack and machine a length of binding to neck edge. Turn bias over to wrong side and hem in place. Neaten ends of binding by turning under and stitching. Neaten armholes in same way, starting and finishing at underarm seam.

10. Make 3 buttonholes on left back bodice where marked on pattern. Stitch buttons to correspond on right back bodice.

Left: front view of the Simple Summer Dress plus the one pattern piece that you'll need Below: front and back views of the Lace-topped Dress, and the pattern diagrams and guide for cutting out the fabric

SUMMER DRESS: PATTERN
Diagram 1

FRONT and BACK

1 square = 5 x 5 cm

in place, close to inner edge.

2. Cut two lengths broderie anglaise so that each will fit from front hem to back neck edge at a slant (as shown) including 20cm [8 in] for shoulder straps. Thread a length of ribbon through each piece of broderie anglaise. Pin, tack and machine lengths to dress front 15mm [⅝ in] in from armhole edges, slanting strips as shown.

3. With right sides together, stitch front and back at sides. Neaten raw edges and press seams open.

4. To neaten armholes, turn under a small hem and stitch in place on wrong side.

5. To neaten lower edge of dress, turn up a 2cm [¾ in] hem and stitch in place on wrong side. Turn dress through to right side. Pin and tack remaining broderie anglaise round hem, with eyelet holes 3mm [⅛ in] above bottom edge. Stitch broderie anglaise to dress just above eyelet holes so that when you press top half down it will look like two rows of lace.

6. Neaten end of each shoulder strap by turning under a small hem to wrong side. Stitch on press-studs or three buttons to end of each strap, equally spaced. Make six corresponding buttonholes on back of dress.

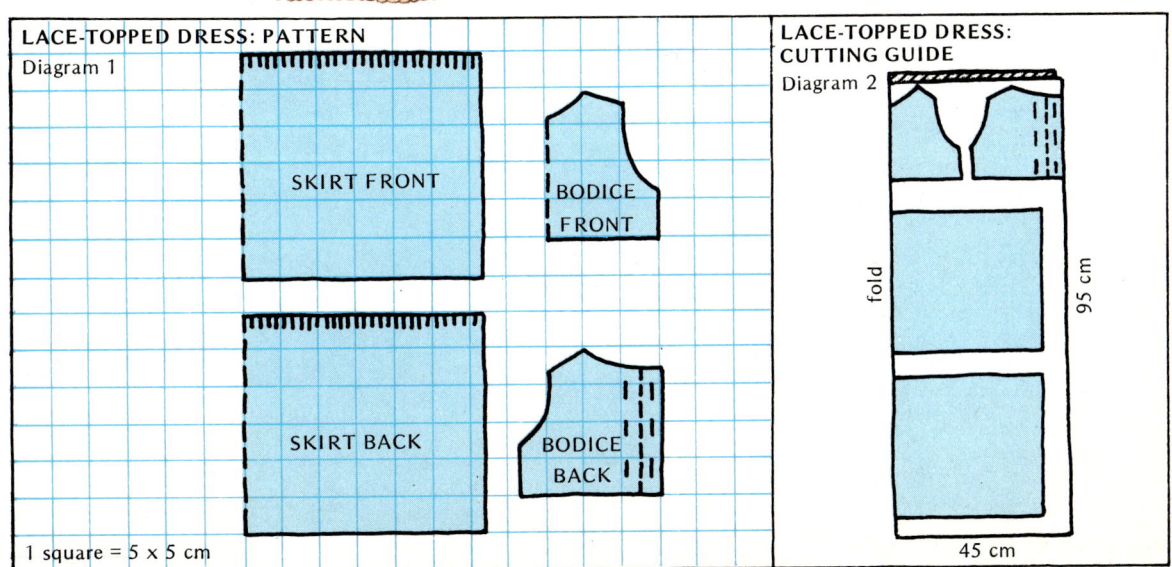

LACE-TOPPED DRESS: PATTERN
Diagram 1

SKIRT FRONT

SKIRT BACK

BODICE FRONT

BODICE BACK

1 square = 5 x 5 cm

LACE-TOPPED DRESS: CUTTING GUIDE
Diagram 2

fold

95 cm

45 cm

Children's Clothes

Party dress

10 to 18 months

A sweet and simple pinafore-style that has a back opening to show off pretty petticoats. If you prefer to knit it, you'll find the pattern for larger sizes on page 114.

Materials 55cm [21½ in] of 90cm [35½ in] wide fabric; 55cm [21½ in] of 90cm [35½ in] wide lining; 50cm [19½ in] of 3cm [1¼ in] wide double edged lace (with eyelet holes for ribbon); 50cm [19½ in] of narrow ribbon; 1.5m [59 in] of 2cm [¾ in] wide satin ribbon; matching machine twist.

Measurements: to fit 40–46cm [16–18 in] chest.

Note All seams measure 15mm [⅝ in]. Square brackets contain imperial measurements.

TO CUT OUT
Make pattern from squared paper (1 square = 5cm) following the diagram below. Cut one skirt and one bodice piece from both main fabric and lining, allowing an extra 15mm [⅝ in] round each piece for seams.

TO SEW
1. Turn up 2cm [¾ in] to wrong side on lower edge of skirt and lining and hem in place.
2. Right sides together, pin, tack and stitch skirt and lining together at side seams. Turn through to right side and press.
3. Tack through both thicknesses along top edge. Sew two lines of running stitches along top edge of skirt between marks A and B, 6mm [¼ in] and 15mm [⅝ in] from edge. Draw up gathers until skirt measures 44cm [17½ in] across and fit bodice between marks A and B.
4. With right sides together, pin, tack and stitch bodice pieces together round all edges but leaving opening between A and

B. Clip seams on curves, turn through to right side and press.
5. Right sides together, pin, tack and stitch skirt to main fabric of bodice only, matching A's and B's. On bodice lining, turn in 15mm [⅝ in] on free edge and hem in place on wrong side covering 1st row of stitching.
6. Make one buttonhole on right-hand side of bodice where marked on pattern.
7. Thread the narrow ribbon through lace, then cut lace in half. To make shoulder straps, stitch lace between dotted lines at centre of bodice and between marks half way along bodice on top edge.
8. Cut satin ribbon in half. Stitch one length to each end of bodice. One end is threaded through the buttonhole and brought to the front and tied to the other length (see back and front views).

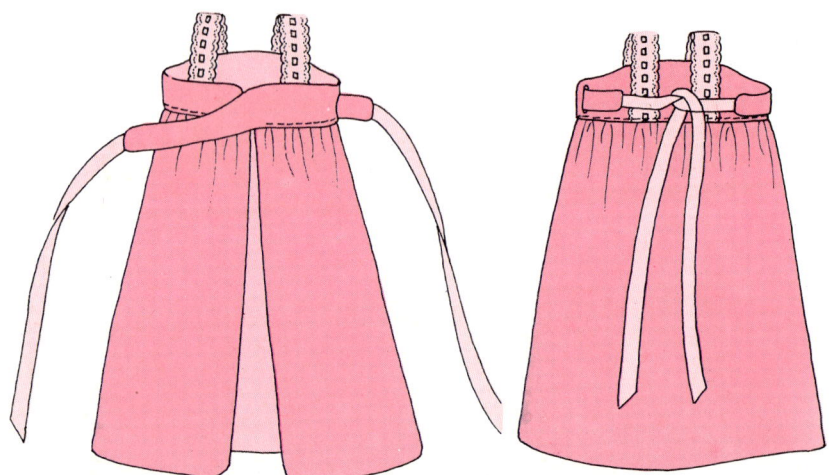

Above: back and front views of the Party Dress. One ribbon is threaded through a buttonhole on the bodice so both ribbons can tie at the front.
Right: the simple shapes of the bodice and skirt. Use this diagram as a guide for the larger version which is knitted (see page 114)
Opposite page: bright and cheerful playsuit with a zip-up front that makes for easy changing of nappies

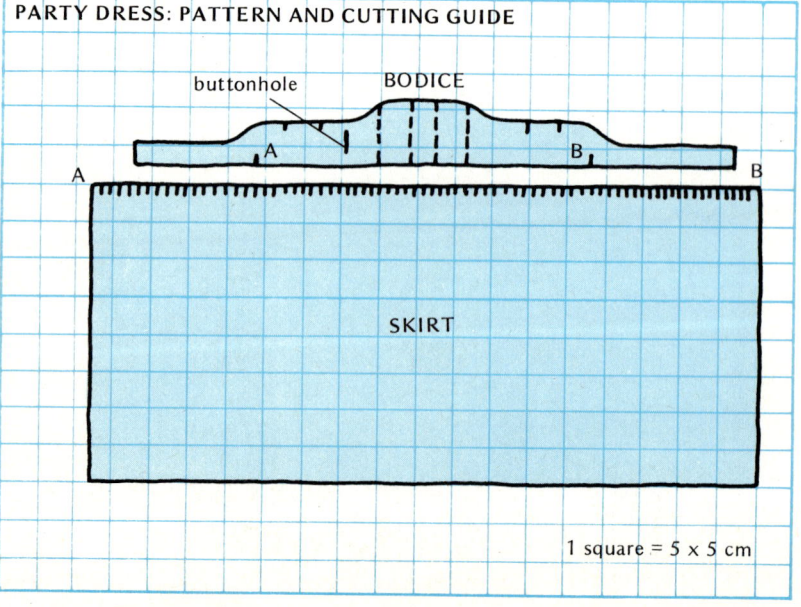

PARTY DRESS: PATTERN AND CUTTING GUIDE

buttonhole   BODICE

A   B

SKIRT

1 square = 5 x 5 cm

Rainbow playsuit

8 to 15 months

Green, red and indigo stripes on sunshine yellow makes a jolly little playsuit. Made in soft wool or a fleecy jersey, it's a perfect wrap-up for out of doors.

Materials In yellow: 1m [39½ in] of 90cm [35½ in] wide fabric or 70cm [27½ in] of 140cm [55 in] wide fabric. In red, blue and green: 20cm [8 in] of 90cm [35½ in] wide fabric; machine twist in each of fabric colours; 38cm [15 in] long nylon zip.

Measurements 40–46cm [16–18 in] chest. For a larger size add 2cm [¾ in] to side and sleeve seams, 4cm [1½ in] to wrist and ankle edges, 12·5mm [½ in] to shorter sides of wrist and ankle bands.

Note All diagrams are on pages 16 and 17.

TO MAKE THE PATTERN
Rule 5cm [2 in] squares on to a sheet of paper, or use graph paper to that scale, then reproduce the pattern exactly as shown in Diagram 1.
The front and back are the same except for the stripes. Cut out following the broken lines for the front stripes and the solid lines for the back stripes.
Detach sleeve from front and back playsuit along line AB. Mark point C with a notch. Also cut out the collar, ankle band and wrist band, as shown.

TO CUT OUT
1. Fold yellow fabric in half lengthways (see Diagram 2A) and place centre back of playsuit to the fold and centre front 3cm [1¼ in] in from selvedge edges (this makes the front facing). Place sleeve along straight grain. Place collar on the cross grain on a single layer of remaining fabric.
2. Fold red fabric in half lengthways (Diagram 2B) and place back stripe No 1 to the fold and No 1 front stripe 3cm [1¼ in] in from selvedge edges (to correspond with centre front facings). Place ankle band on straight grain.
3. Fold blue fabric in half lengthways (Diagram 2C) and place No

Continued on page 16

Rainbow playsuit . . . continued

RAINBOW PLAYSUIT: PATTERN
Diagram 1

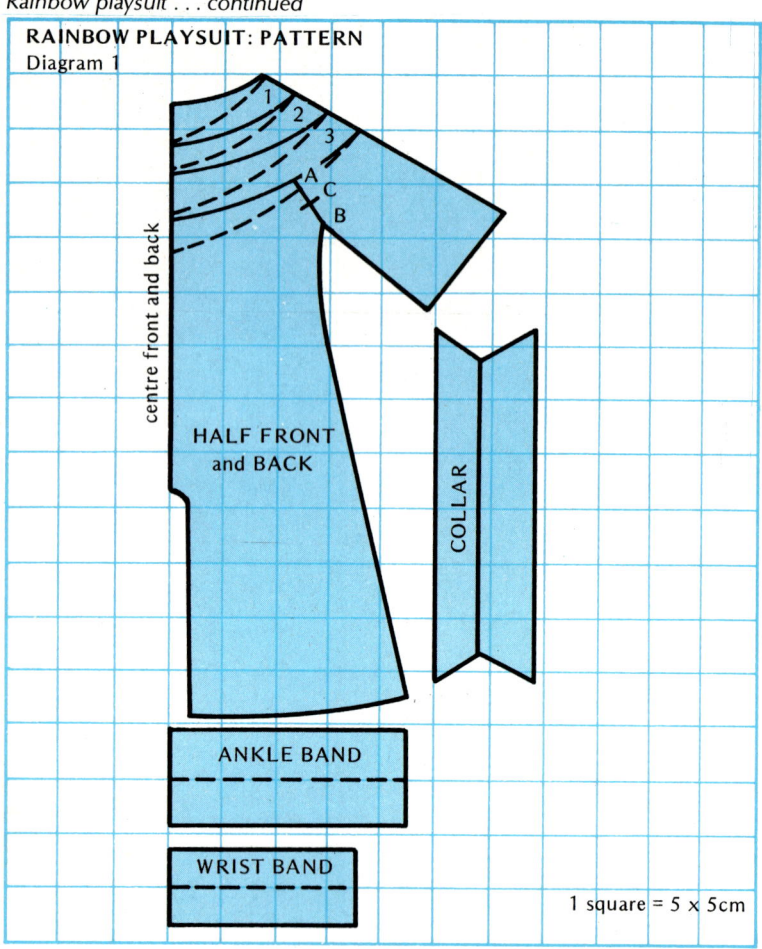

centre front and back

HALF FRONT and BACK

COLLAR

ANKLE BAND

WRIST BAND

1 square = 5 x 5cm

YOKE, ANKLE and WRIST BANDS: CUTTING GUIDE

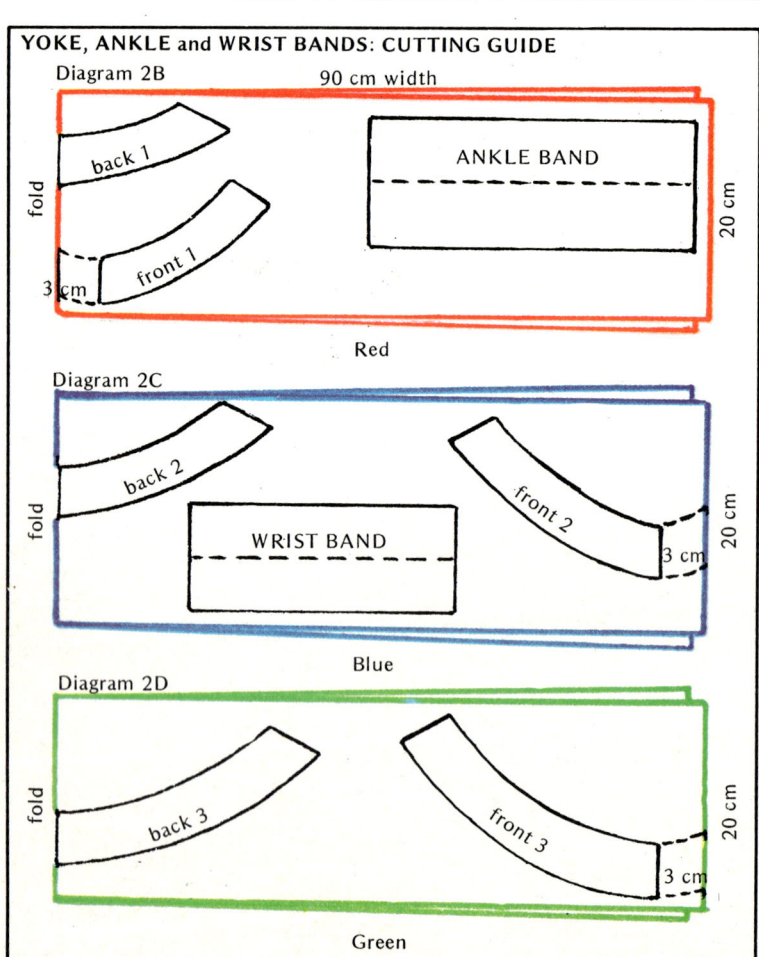

Diagram 2B — 90 cm width

fold
back 1
front 1
3 cm
ANKLE BAND
20 cm

Red

Diagram 2C

fold
back 2
WRIST BAND
front 2
3 cm
20 cm

Blue

Diagram 2D

fold
back 3
front 3
3 cm
20 cm

Green

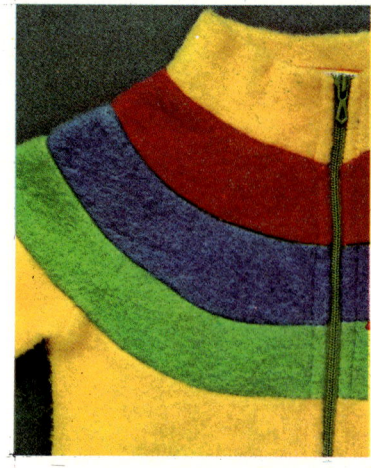

Left: a close-up of the rainbow effect around the yoke of the playsuit. The diagrams on this page give you the patterns and fabric cutting guides
Opposite: how the rainbow is sewn into the playsuit

PLAYSUIT: MAIN CUTTING GUIDE
90 cm width · Diagram 2A

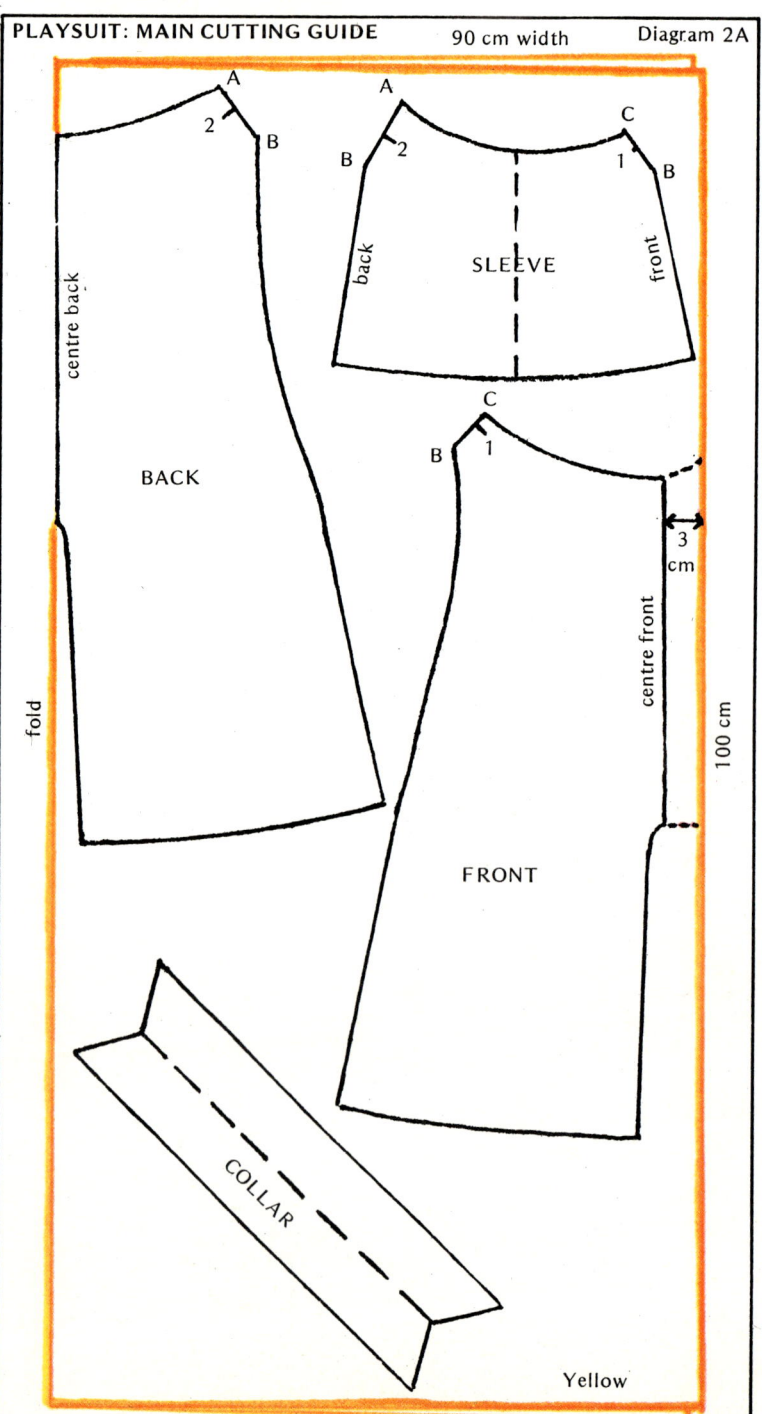

centre back

fold

BACK

A 2 B

B 2 A

C 1 B

back SLEEVE front

C

B 1

3 cm

centre front

FRONT

100 cm

COLLAR

Yellow

2 back stripe to fold and No 2 front stripe 3cm [1¼ in] in from selvedges. Place wrist band on straight grain.

4. Fold green fabric in half lengthways (Diagram 2D) and place No 3 back stripe to the fold and No 3 front stripe 3cm [1¼ in] in from selvedges.

5. Cut out each of the pattern pieces adding 6mm [¼ in] seam turnings and remembering to add on the curves (shown by dotted lines). Mark notches and centres. Oversew raw edges.

TO SEW

1. With right sides together stitch sleeves to fronts and back along short armhole seams AB and CB. Press seam turnings open.

2. With right sides together, stitch front stripes to back stripes at shoulders, matching colours. Press seam turnings open.

3. Turn lower curved edge of each stripe 6mm [¼ in] to wrong side. Tack. Press.

4. Overlap and slip-stitch No 3 stripe to playsuit fronts, back and sleeves. Overlap and pin No 2 over No 3 stripe and No 1 over No 2 stripe. Slip-stitch stripes together (Diagram 3). Press seam turnings open, clipping where necessary (Diagram 4).

5. Run a row of gathering stitches 6mm [¼ in] in from wrist edge of sleeve. With right sides together, tack wrist band to sleeve, adjusting gathers evenly to fit. Stitch. Press turnings towards band.

6. With right sides together, stitch sleeve and side seams (Diagram 4). Press turnings open.

7. Fold remaining raw edge of wrist band 6mm [¼ in] to wrong side and slip-stitch to inside of sleeve over previous stitches.

8. Run a row of gathering stitches 6mm [¼ in] in from ankle edges. With right sides together tack ankle bands to legs, adjusting gathers evenly to fit. Stitch. Press seam turnings towards band.

9. With right sides together stitch collar to neck edge (Diagram 5).

10. Stitch centre front seam for 5cm [2 in] from crotch. Press turnings open. Press centre front facings to wrong side. Tack.

11. Insert zip by pinning, tacking then stitching in place.

12. Turn under remaining raw edges of collar and slip-stitch to previous line of stitching on inside of neck edge and to tapes on zip (Diagram 6).

13. With right sides together, stitch inside leg seams. Finish ankle bands as for wrist bands.

Diagram 3

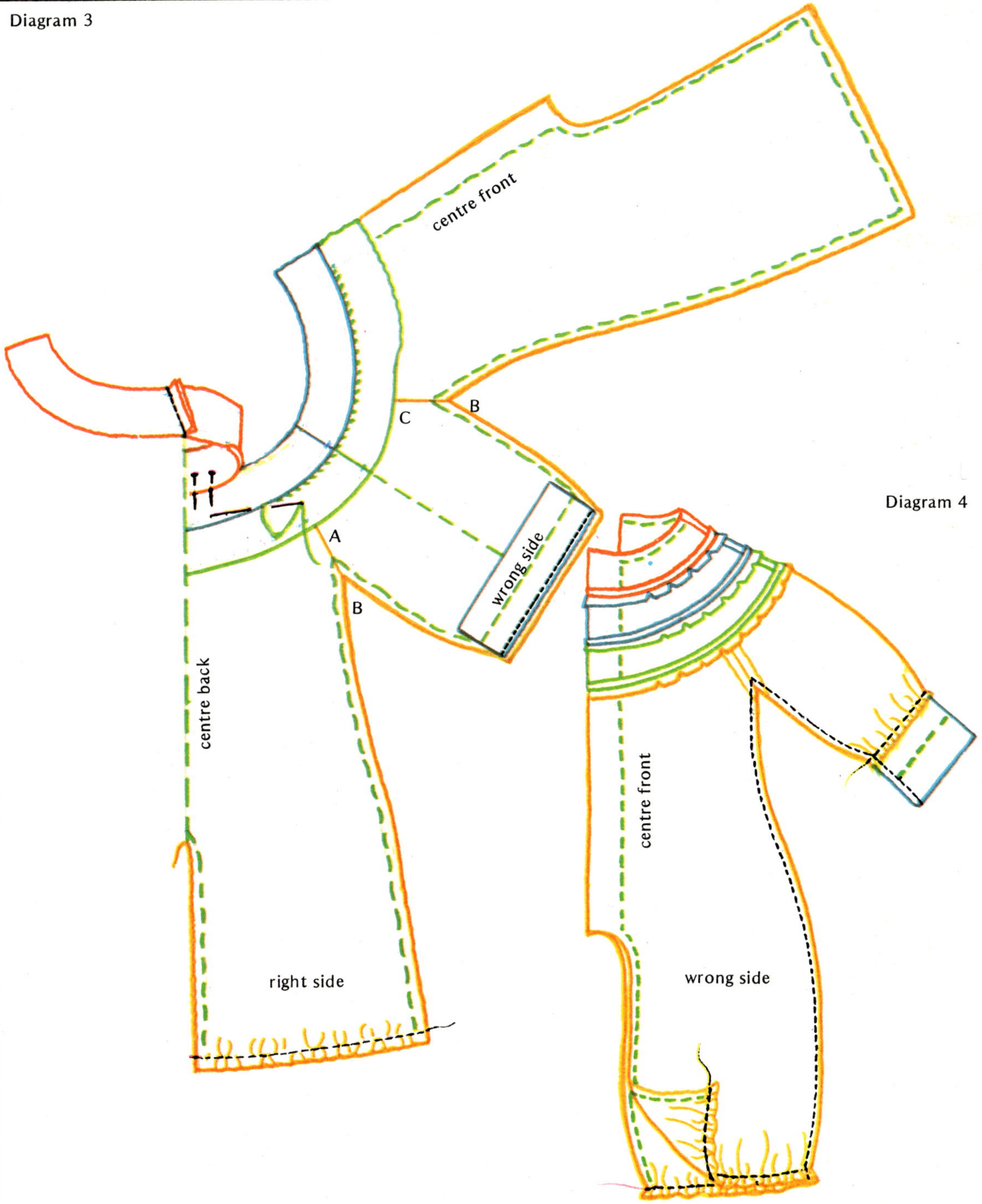

centre front

B

C

A

B

wrong side

centre back

right side

Diagram 4

centre front

wrong side

Diagram 5

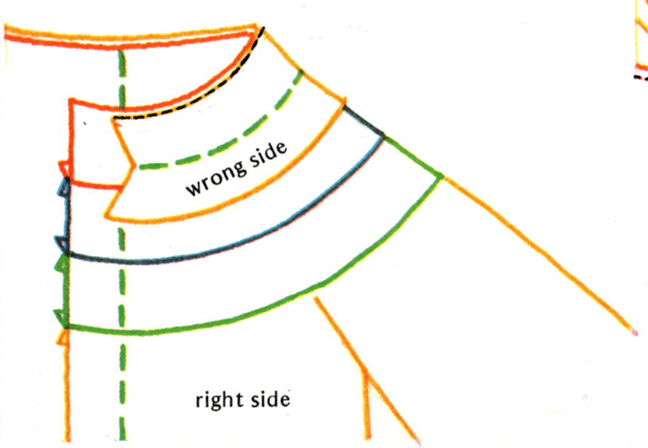

wrong side

right side

Diagram 6

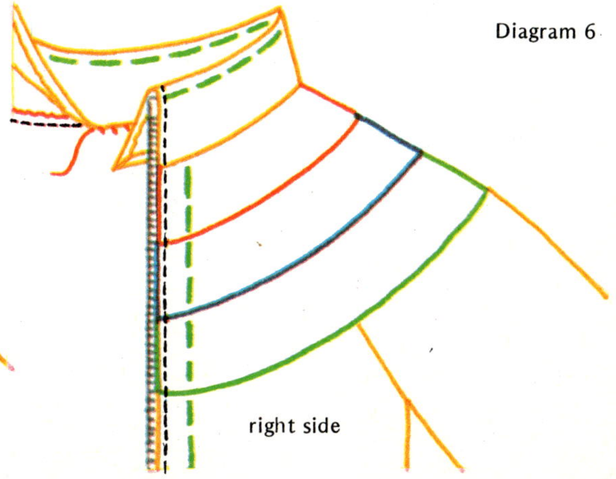

right side

Baby carrier

Not for the newest of new babies (there's not enough support for the neck and back) but this carrier is a splendid way of keeping the strong-headed baby with mum or dad when a pram or pushchair would be inconvenient. When the baby's older and can sit up, the carrier can be used as a makeshift restrainer on an ordinary chair if a a high chair's not available (when you're on holiday, for example).

Materials 3.50m × 60cm [140 in × 23½ in] of washable, strongly woven fabric; matching machine twist.

Note Square brackets contain imperial measurements.

TO MAKE

1. Using newspaper joined together with Sellotape make patterns for central panel and straps (see Diagrams 1 and 2). To make the pointed ends on the straps, fold rectangle 255cm × 27cm [100½ in × 10¾ in] in half lengthways and mark the centre of the short side. Measure in 13.5cm [5⅓ in] along each long side from ends. From these points, draw in lines to the marks on the short sides. Cut out the points. To make the curves on the central panel: mark the centre along each short edge. From this point, measure in 15mm [⅝ in] towards the centre. Draw in each curve freehand from this point to the two outside edges.
2. Place patterns on material and cut two central panels and two straps (Diagram 3).
3. Right sides together, fold each strap piece in half lengthways. Pin, tack and stitch round the outside edges from the pointed ends, leaving an opening between A and B (Diagram 4). Turn each strap through to right side and press.
4. Right sides together, pin, tack and stitch central panel pieces together along two curved edges. Turn through to right side and press. Top stitch along two curved sides, close to outer edge.

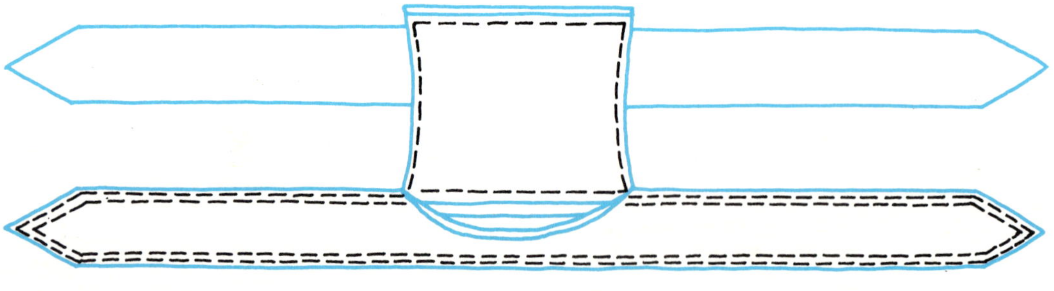

5. Place the two straight sides of panel between openings on each strap piece (Diagram 5). Pin and tack in place.
6. Top-stitch all round each strap close to outer edge, stitching through central panel at the same time. Sew a second line of top stitching 1.5mm [1/16 in] in from the first to strengthen the carrier.

To use the carrier Place the two top straps over the shoulders, cross them at the front then tie them at the back waist. The curved sides of the panel will fit snugly round the baby's back and under the bottom. Tie the other two straps securely but comfortably at front waist.

If in doubt about the shrink-ability of any fabric, wash and iron it before you cut it.

BABY CARRIER: PATTERN
Diagram 1

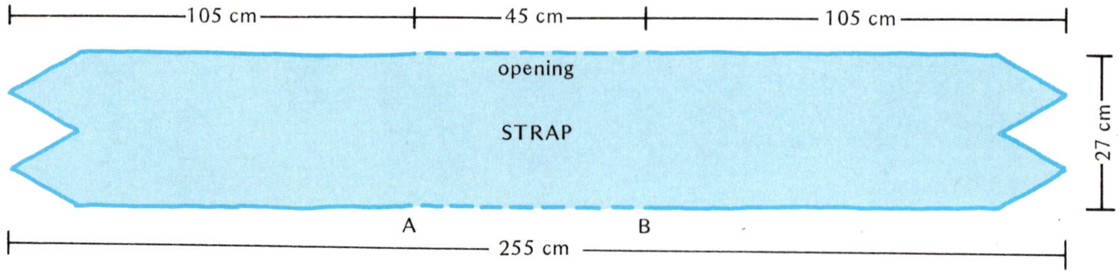

105 cm — 45 cm — 105 cm
opening
STRAP
27 cm
A   B
255 cm

Diagram 2
47 cm
PANEL
wrong side
36 cm

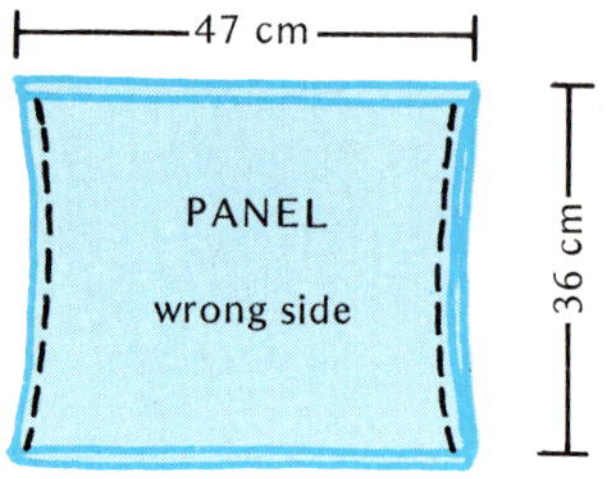

BABY CARRIER: CUTTING GUIDE
Diagram 3

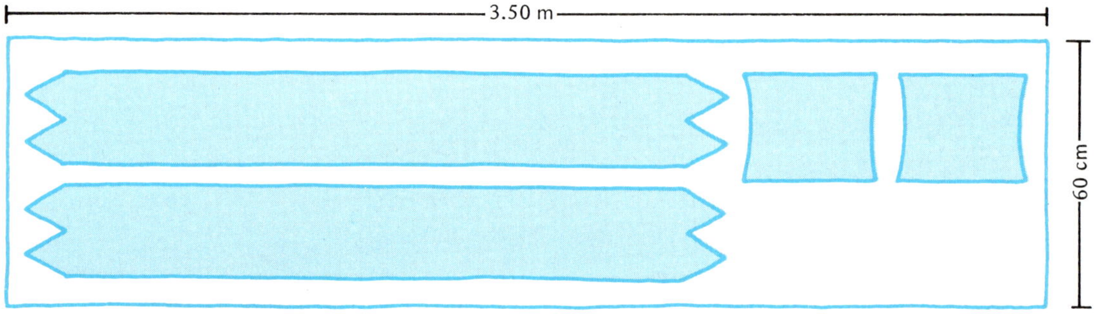

3.50 m
60 cm

HOW TO ASSEMBLE
Diagram 4

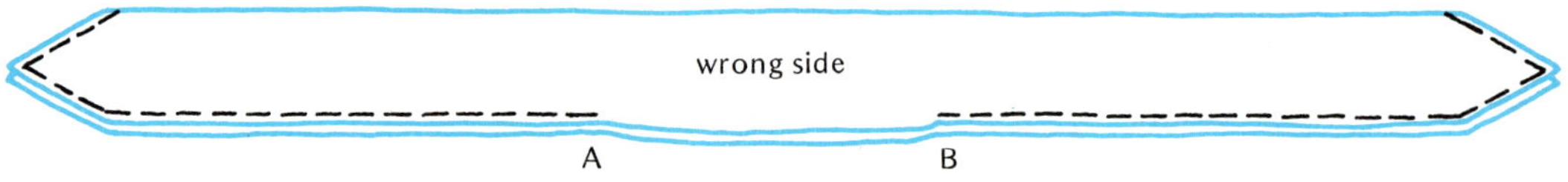

wrong side
A   B

Diagram 5

Gathered blouses

1 year to teenage

Simple and pretty gathered "peasant style" blouses that will suit girls of all ages.

Materials 1.9m of 90cm-wide [75 in × 35½ in] fabric for a girl size 12; 90cm [35½ in × 35½ in] for a 3 year old; 70cm [28 in × 35½ in] for a baby. For all sizes: shirring elastic; matching machine twist; squared pattern [1 sq = 5cm].

Measurements There are three patterns for three sizes: 12 months; 3 years; and adult size 12 [32 in bust].

TO MAKE YOUR PATTERN
Using squared paper reproduce pattern pieces exactly as shown for the chosen size in Diagram 1. Mark positions for rows of elastic with dotted lines. Cut out pattern pieces.

POSITIONING THE PATTERN ON THE FABRIC
See Diagram 2, cutting guides. For the largest size, size 12, fold the fabric in half lengthways, wrong sides together. Place the back and front pattern pieces to the fold, as shown, and the sleeve lengthways on the straight grain. For the 2 smaller sizes cut the material in half so you have 2 pieces of 45cm [17¾ in] and 2 pieces of 35cm [13¾ in]. Fold one piece of fabric, wrong sides together, so that the selvedges meet in the centre of the fabric. Place front and back pieces to the folds. Fold 2nd piece of fabric in half and place the sleeve on the straight grain.

TO CUT OUT
Chalk around the edge of each pattern piece. Cut out allowing 6mm [¼ in] hem allowance on lower edges of sleeves and front and back blouse pieces, and 15mm [⅝ in] seam turnings on all other edges. Mark dotted lines with tailor's tacks.

TO SEW
For all sizes With the shirring elastic in the bobbin and machine twist on the top, stitch two or three rows 3mm [⅛ in] apart along the gathering lines marked on all pieces (*note* the smallest size

has no gathering at the waist).

For size 12 1. With right sides together, stitch side and sleeve seams. Press seam turnings open. 2. Stitch the shoulder seams, right sides together. Press seam turnings open. Insert sleeves with right sides together, matching underarm seams, and easing fullness to fit.

For the two smaller sizes 1. With right sides together, stitch sleeves to front and back blouse pieces at shoulders. Press seam turnings open. 2. With right sides together stitch side and sleeve seams. Press seam turnings open.

For all sizes Make a rolled hem at the neck edge, and at lower edges of sleeves and blouse.

Above and right: the Gathered blouses, plus the patterns and cutting out guides

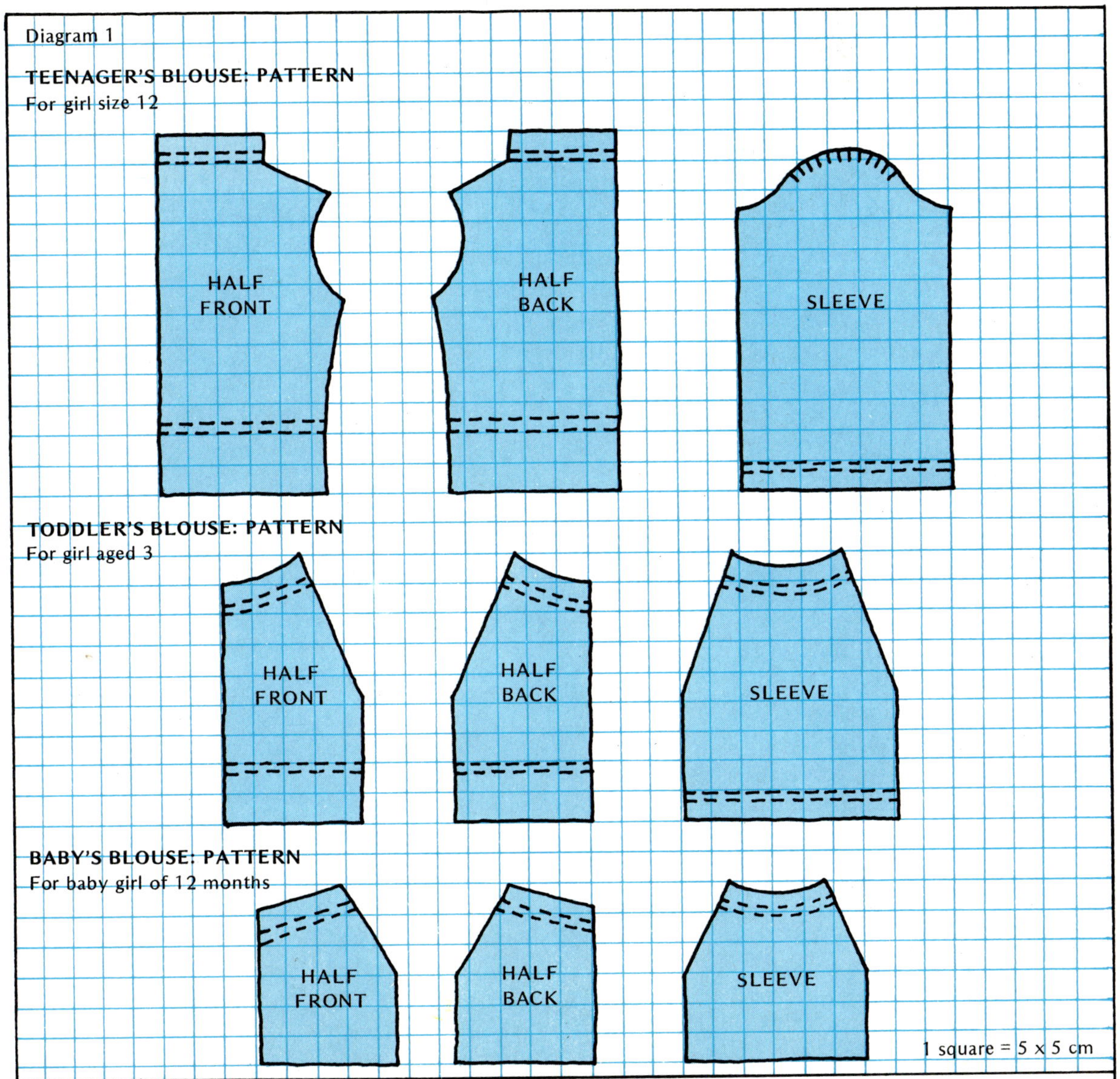

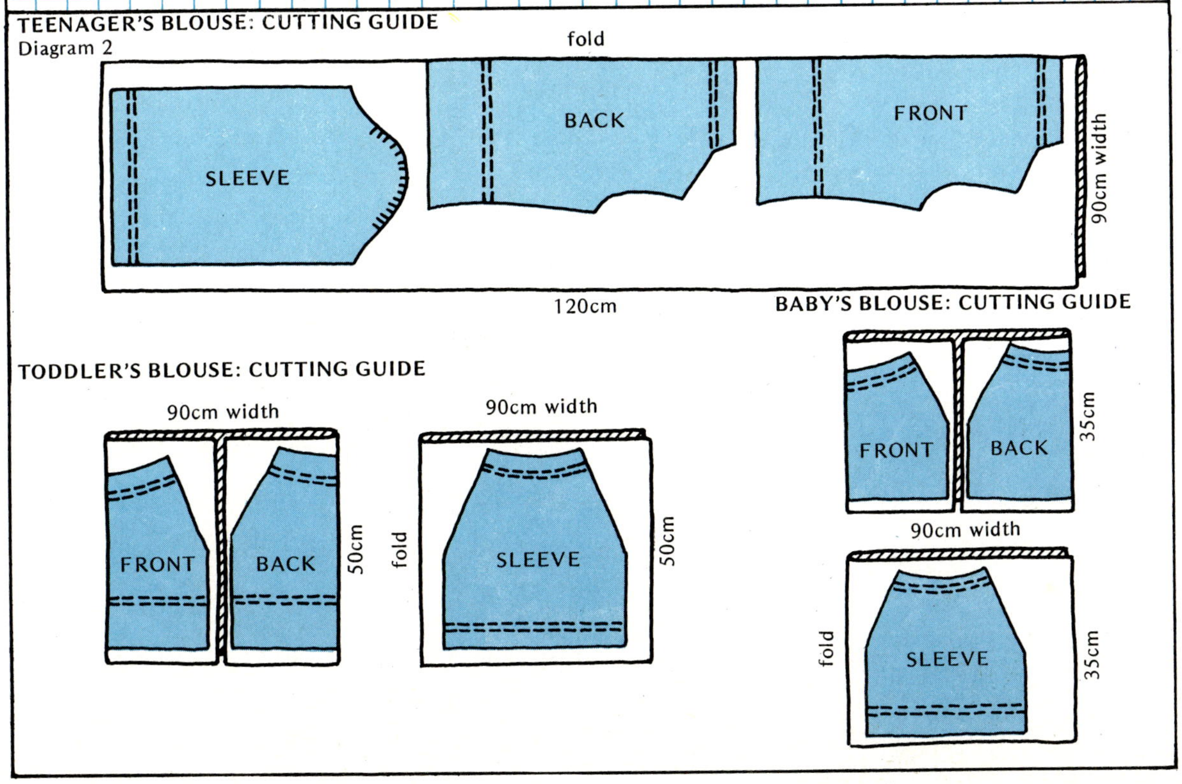

Cap-sleeved popovers
Toddler to teenage
Illustrated overleaf

These simple aprons make attractive cover-ups for large and small – no patterns are needed and there's very little sewing involved. Choose a fairly hard-wearing and washable plain or printed cotton (do remember that small patterns are best for tiny clothes – polka dots, stripes or little flowers).

Materials Teenager: 120cm [48 in] of 90cm [35½ in] wide fabric, 2 metres [79 in] of narrow piping or coloured cord; 1.25 metres [49 in] bias binding in a contrasting colour. **Toddler:** 50cm [19¾ in] of 90cm [35½ in] wide fabric, 120cm [48 in] piping or cord; 80cm [32 in] bias binding. **Baby:** 35cm [14 in] of 90cm [35½ in] wide fabric; 100cm [40 in] bias binding. **All:** matching machine twist; oddments of fabric for pockets and motifs.

Please note Square brackets contain imperial measurements. All diagrams are on pages 22 and 23.

Measurements The popovers are roomy so the large one will fit adult sizes 12 to 16; the small versions will fit a baby or a toddler.

TO CUT OUT
Large size (see Diagram 1). Fold a rectangle of fabric 120cm × 90cm [47¼ in × 35½ in] in half widthwise, then in half again: this gives you a rectangle of 30cm × 90cm [12 in × 35½ in]. Along the double fold, A B, measure 21.5cm [8½ in] from the top to C, and from C, 13cm [5 in] to E. From C measure 10cm [4 in] to D parallel with top edge of fabric. Join D and E with a curve. Cut along curved line through all thicknesses of fabric. This gives you the armholes and cap sleeves.
Small size (see Diagram 2). Start with a rectangle of fabric measuring 90cm × 50cm [35½ in × 19¾ in] and fold as above to give you a rectangle of 22.5cm × 50cm [9 in

Continued on next page

Diagram 1

TEENAGER'S BLOUSE: PATTERN
For girl size 12

HALF FRONT — HALF BACK — SLEEVE

TODDLER'S BLOUSE: PATTERN
For girl aged 3

HALF FRONT — HALF BACK — SLEEVE

BABY'S BLOUSE: PATTERN
For baby girl of 12 months

HALF FRONT — HALF BACK — SLEEVE

1 square = 5 × 5 cm

TEENAGER'S BLOUSE: CUTTING GUIDE
Diagram 2

fold

SLEEVE — BACK — FRONT

90cm width

120cm

BABY'S BLOUSE: CUTTING GUIDE

FRONT — BACK
35cm

90cm width

SLEEVE
35cm

fold

TODDLER'S BLOUSE: CUTTING GUIDE

90cm width

FRONT — BACK
50cm

fold

90cm width

SLEEVE
50cm

CAP-SLEEVED POPOVERS: CUTTING GUIDES

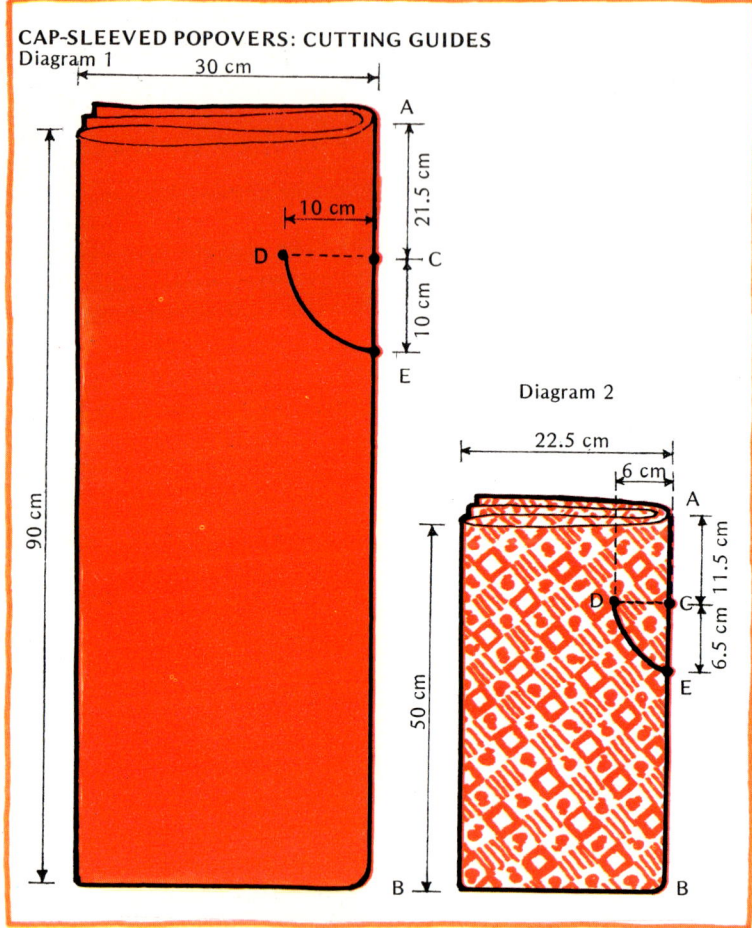

Diagram 1

Diagram 2

×19¾ in]. Along the double fold AB measure 11.5cm [4½ in] from the top to C, and from C, 6.5cm [2½ in] to E. From C measure 6cm [2¼ in] to D parallel with top edge of fabric. Join D and E with a curve. Cut along curve through all thicknesses to give you the armholes and cap sleeves.

TO SEW

1. Bind armholes and cap sleeves: fold bias binding in half and stitch one edge to the right side of the fabric, matching the fold in the binding with the fabric edge. Slip-stitch remaining edge of binding over previous line of stitching on wrong side. If you start and finish the binding at the underarm, E, the join will not be seen.

2. Fold centre back edges under 2cm [¾ in] to wrong side. Turn under raw edges 6mm [¼ in]. Stitch (see Diagram 3).

3. Turn up hem at lower edge (amount adjustable). Turn under raw edges 6mm [¼ in]. Stitch.

4. Fold top edge 4cm [1½ in] to wrong side. Turn under raw edges 6mm [¼ in] and stitch. Stitch another row 3mm [⅛ in] from top folded edge to form a casing for the draw-cord.

5. Thread cord through casing with the help of a safety pin (see Diagram 4). Knot ends for a neat finish.

HOW TO ADD THE POCKETS AND MOTIFS

Pouch pockets Cut four rectangles in different prints each 18cm × 26cm [7 in × 10 in]. Stitch together down longer sides to make one large rectangle (see Diagram 5). Press seams open. Turn side and lower edges 6mm [¼ in] to wrong side and tack in place. Fold top edge 3cm [1¼ in] to wrong side, turn under raw edges 6mm [¼ in] and stitch. Stitch pocket to apron with the lower edge of the pocket level with the hem of the apron. Divide pocket into four compartments by stitching to apron along seamlines. Remove tacking stitches.

Patch pockets Cut 2 rectangles of fabric 15cm × 18cm [6 in ×7 in]. Fold side and lower edges 6mm [¼ in] to wrong side and tack in place. Fold top edge 3cm [1¼ in] to wrong side, turn under raw

Below: the popovers for all sizes
Left: the cutting guide you'll need
Right: how the popovers are sewn

edges 6mm [¼ in] and stitch. Position pockets on popover at equal distances from centre front and hem. Stitch in place along side and lower edges. Remove tacking stitches.

Flower and fruit motifs In a contrasting print cut out a flower shape (use the edge of a glass to make circular petals). Trace the shape of a fruit from a child's book or cut it freehand from contrasting print fabric. Tack flower or fruit to popover, turning under raw edges 6mm [¼ in]. If you have a swing-needle sewing machine, attach the flower or fruit to the apron with a satin stitch. Otherwise slip-stitch or machine in place. Remove tacking stitches.

Bathing beauty

1 to 3 years

A jacket-style robe that can be made to fit any size – just alter the measurements (back, front, length and armholes) to suit.

Materials 70cm × 45cm [27½ in × 18 in] cotton towelling; 3m [3½ yd] folded braid; scraps of red and checked cotton fabric; matching machine twist.

Note All seams are 15mm [⅝ in].

Continued on next page

Right and below: the simple bathing robe plus the rooster pattern and cutting guide. Sewing instructions are on page 24

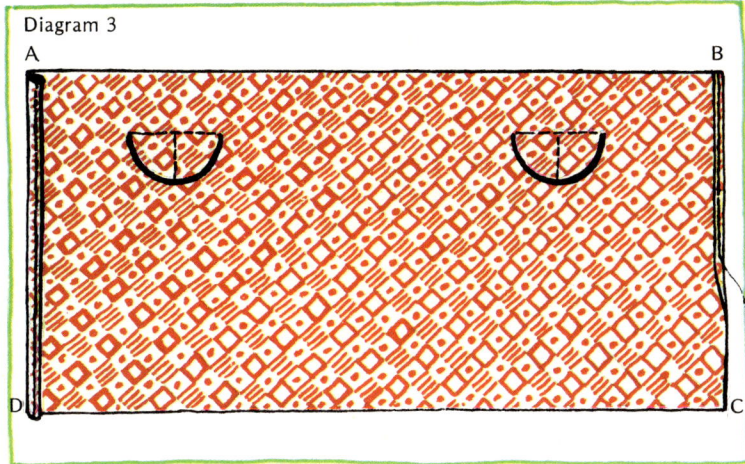

Diagram 3

Diagram 4

Diagram 5

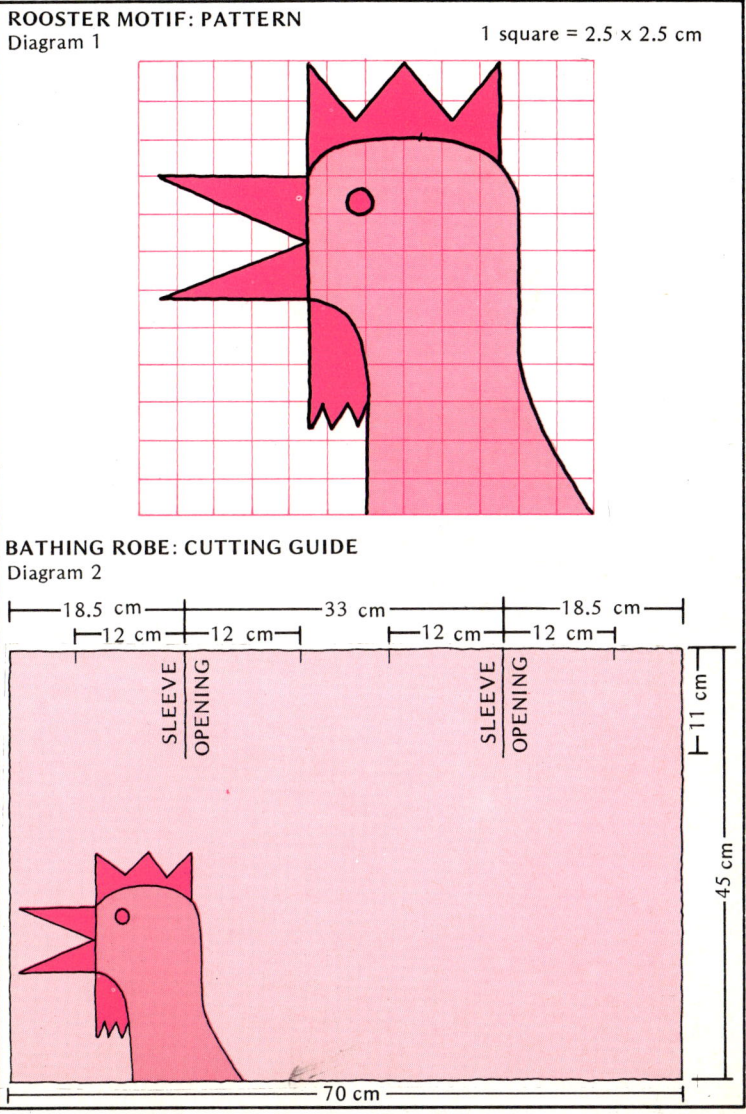

ROOSTER MOTIF: PATTERN
Diagram 1

1 square = 2.5 × 2.5 cm

BATHING ROBE: CUTTING GUIDE
Diagram 2

18.5 cm   33 cm   18.5 cm

12 cm   12 cm   12 cm   12 cm

SLEEVE OPENING   SLEEVE OPENING

11 cm

45 cm

70 cm

Bathing beauty ... continued

TO SEW

1. Following Diagram 1 (previous page) make the pattern for the rooster motif on squared paper (1 square = 2.5cm) and cut out pieces from fabric scraps.

2. Pin, then tack the pieces to the towelling where shown in Diagram 2. Machine motif to bathrobe using satin stitch or turn under a small hem and sew very close to edge.

3. Cut the sleeve openings: 11cm [4¼ in] deep, 18.5cm [7¼ in] from outside edges (see Diagram 2). Mark in the 12cm [4¾ in] marks for shoulder stitching.

4. Neaten sleeve openings with folded braid: lap braid over edge of fabric, pin, tack and machine in position close to inner edge of braid.

5. Neaten all outside edges of bathrobe with braid in the same way.

6. With right sides together, fold the two outside edges towards the centre, matching at 12cm [4¾ in] marks. Stitch shoulders between marks with overcasting stitches. Turn robe to right side. If liked, a press-stud can be sewn at the neck to close the front.

When making any garment remember to check the child's measurements against the pattern and make any alterations to the paper before cutting out the fabric.

Star attraction

1 to 3 years

A little something to slip into after bathing, whether on the beach or at home – see how it looks on an older child on the front cover.

Materials up to 18 months: 1m × 80cm [39½ in × 31½ in] cotton towelling; 3m [3½ yd] folded braid; scraps of cotton fabric in contrasting colours (for clouds and stars), matching machine twist.

Note All seams measure 15mm [⅝ in]. To make larger size: add 2cm [¾ in] to all edges – you'll need extra fabric and braid.

TO SEW

1. Make patterns for bathrobe and motifs on squared paper following diagram, right (1 square = 5cm), adding to length or sleeves if required.

2. Cut bathrobe and hood from towelling adding an extra 15mm [⅝ in] to side and underarm edges for seams. Cut star and cloud motifs from fabric scraps.

3. Pin then tack the motifs in position where shown in diagram. Machine motifs to robe using satin stitch.

4. With right sides together, stitch underarm and side seams in one, pivoting at underarm. Clip corner at underarm, press seams open and turn robe

*Left: the simple but sensible bathing robe for a toddler
Right: the shape of the robe
Below: the pattern which also shows where to place the stars and clouds*

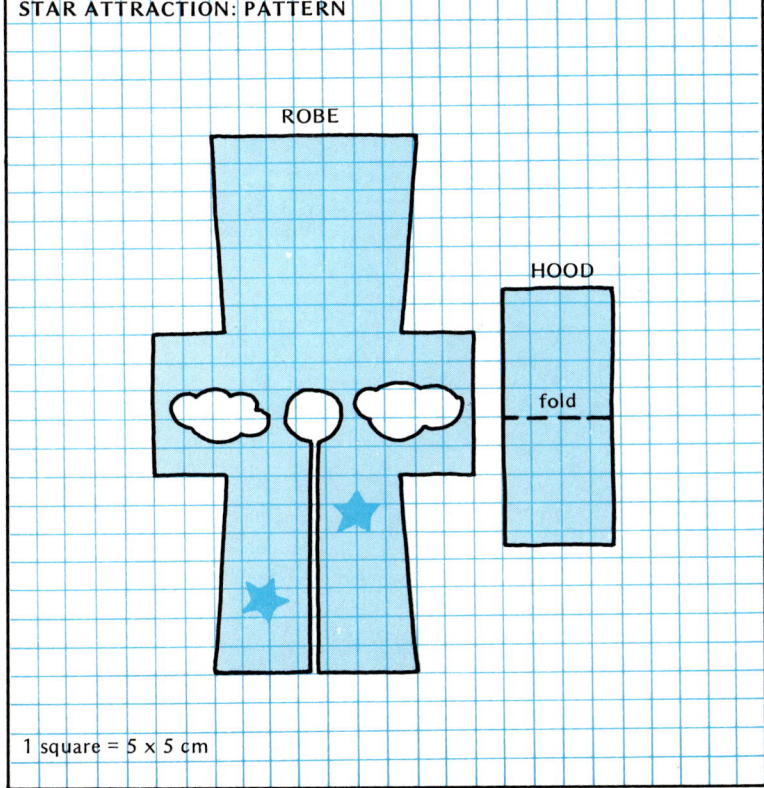

STAR ATTRACTION: PATTERN

ROBE

HOOD

fold

1 square = 5 x 5 cm

Quilted jackets
1 to 4 years

These Oriental-style padded jackets make a bright and cheerful wind break. They need to be very roomy so make them bigger than a child's normal chest measurement. The patterns are simple, the quilting easy – it's done on the machine. Instructions for making the socks and hats begin on page 97.

Note Use either ready-quilted fabric or quilt it yourself (see instructions page 27).
To make larger sizes cut patterns 2cm [¾ in] or 4cm [1½ in] larger on side seams and at shoulders. Also add to length as required. On the front opening version don't forget to cut the facings bigger to match. With the pull-on versions cut the neck deeper at front and back, and if you alter the sleeve measurement, add to the cuff measurement to match.

Measurements To fit 46–61cm [18–24 in] chest. To make larger sizes, see note above.

One-colour pull-on style

Materials 75cm [29½ in] of 140cm [55 in] wide fabric each in top fabric, lining and wadding; 60cm [23½ in] of matching bias binding; matching machine twist.

TO CUT OUT
1. Make pattern from squared paper (1 square = 5cm) following Diagram 1 (see page 26).
2. Quilt fabric (see instructions page 27).
3. Fold material in half and following cutting layout (Diagram 2, page 26) cut one body piece and two sleeves adding an extra 15mm [⅝ in] all round each piece for seams.

TO SEW
1. With right sides together, pin, tack and stitch sleeves to body along dotted line at shoulder only. Turn in seam allowance on

sides of sleeves, pin and tack as far as side edges on body piece. Using zig-zag stitch, top stitch along sleeve seams and across shoulders.
2. Right sides together, pin, tack and machine underarm seams on sleeves. Press seams open, turn through to right side.
3. Turn up 2cm [¾ in] to wrong side on bottoms of sleeves and lower edge of jacket, and hem in place.
4. Neaten neck opening with bias binding: right sides together, pin, tack and machine bias to opening. Turn bias over on to wrong side and hem in place.
5. Neaten all seams inside by trimming back wadding and oversewing (use bias binding, if liked).

Two-colour pull-on style

Illustrated overleaf

Materials 75cm [29½ in] of 140cm [55 in] wide fabric in main colour; 35cm [14 in] of 140cm [55 in] wide fabric in contrast; 1.10m [43½ in] of 140cm [55 in] wide lining fabric and wadding; 60cm [23½ in] of matching bias binding; matching or contrasting machine twist for both main and contrast fabrics.

TO SEW
1. Quilt main part and contrast (see instructions page 27).
2. Make patterns from squared paper (1 square = 5cm) following Diagram 1. Cut out fabrics as shown in Diagram 3 (below, right) adding an extra 15mm [⅝ in] all round each piece for seams.

Continued on next page

through to right side.
5. Right sides together, fold hood in half along dotted line. Stitch along one long edge. Press seam open. Neaten long edge of hood with braid; lap braid over edge of fabric, pin, tack then machine in position close to inner edge.
6. With wrong sides together, matching front edges of hood and robe, pin, tack and stitch hood to neck opening.
7. Neaten bottom and front edges of robe with folded braid continuing round neck opening: pin, tack and machine braid as

far as neck edges. Around neck, fold braid in half to outside edge of bathrobe only – do not lap over fabric. Stitch in place. Lap free edge of braid over on to hood to cover raw edges. Pin, tack and machine in position, close to folded edge.
8. Neaten cuffs with braid in the same way as for hood.

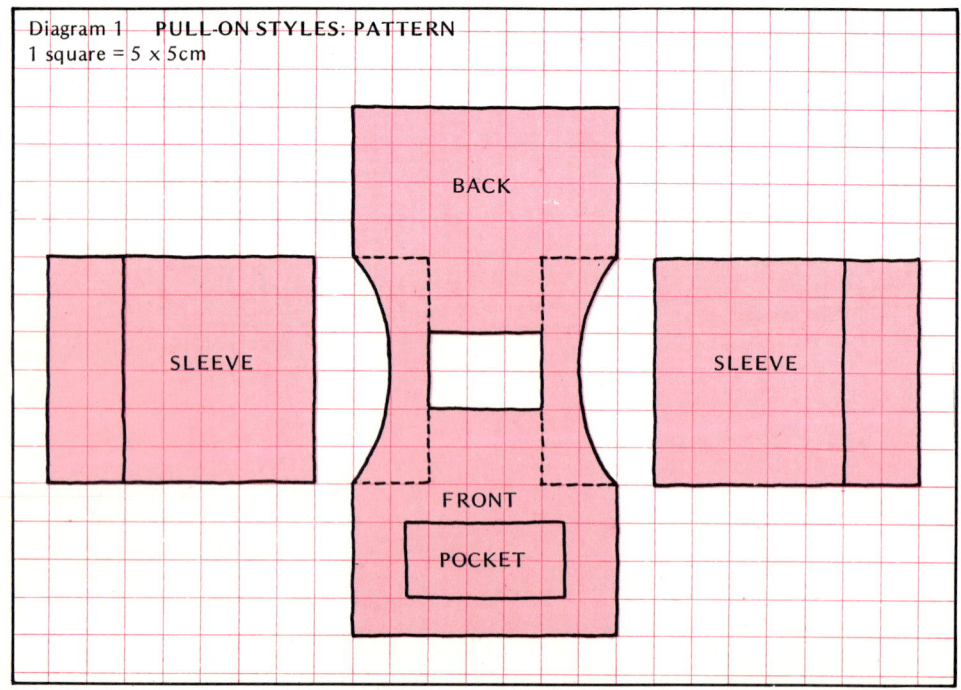

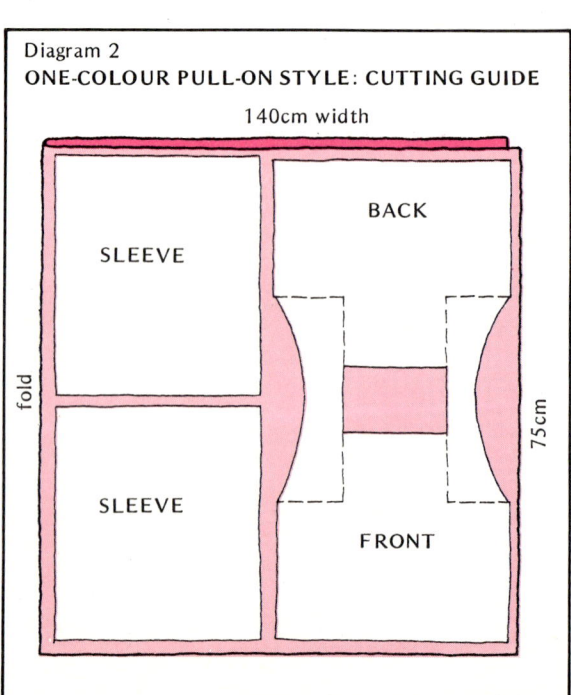

Two-colour pull-on . . . continued

3. Right side of facing to wrong side of sleeve, pin tack and stitch facing to lower edge of sleeves. Press seam up. Turn down 15mm [$\frac{5}{8}$ in] on free edge of facing; pin, tack and top stitch facing in place to sleeve, close to edge.

4. Stitch sleeves to body as for ONE-COLOUR PULL-ON.

5. Stitch underarm seams. Press seams open.

6. Turn up 2cm [$\frac{3}{4}$ in] to wrong side on lower edge of jacket and hem in place.

7. Trim neck edge as for ONE-COLOUR PULL-ON.

8 To make pocket: turn down 2cm [$\frac{3}{4}$ in] to right side of pocket on top edge. Stitch down at sides. Turn this facing through to right side. Top-stitch facing down across top edge. Turn in 15mm [$\frac{5}{8}$ in] along other three sides. Position pocket on front of jacket (see dotted lines Diagram 3). Pin, tack and top stitch in place around sides and bottom.

9. Neaten all seams inside by trimming back wadding and over-sewing (you can use bias binding if liked).

Left: all the Quilted jackets on display. The pull-on versions are worn by the children front left and top right

Diagram 1   PULL-ON STYLES: PATTERN
1 square = 5 x 5cm

BACK

SLEEVE

SLEEVE

FRONT

POCKET

Diagram 2
ONE-COLOUR PULL-ON STYLE: CUTTING GUIDE

140cm width

fold

SLEEVE

SLEEVE

BACK

FRONT

75cm

Front-opening jackets

Materials (for either) 1.10m [43½ in] of 70cm [27½ in] wide fabric in main colour; 45cm × 40cm [18 in × 16 in] in contrast fabric; same size lining and wadding for both fabrics; matching machine twist; 2 frog fastenings.

TO SEW

1. Quilt main part and contrast (see instructions below right).
2. Make patterns from squared paper (1 square = 5 cm) following pattern in Diagram 4. Lay out pieces on fabrics as shown in Diagram 5. From main fabric cut the back (on fold), 2 fronts and 2 sleeves. From the contrast fabric, cut 2 front facings, 1 back facing (on fold), and 2 sleeve facings. Add an extra 15mm [⅝ in] round all pattern pieces for seams.
3. Right sides together, pin, tack and stitch fronts to backs at side and shoulders. Press seams open.
4. Right sides together, pin, tack and stitch back facing to front facings at shoulders. Press seams open.
5. Stitch facings to jacket: with wrong side of jacket to right side of facing, pin, tack and stitch facing round front opening. Press seam towards sides. Turn in 15mm [⅝ in] on free edge of facing. Fold facing on to right side of jacket, with 1st line of stitching on foldline. Pin, tack and top stitch facing around opening on to jacket close to edge.
6. Stitch sleeve facings to lower edge of sleeves as for TWO-COLOUR PULL-ON (step 3).
7. Within seam allowance run row of gathering stitches on crown of sleeve. Draw in gathers gently. Right sides together, pin, tack and stitch sleeve seams. Press seams open.
8. Right sides together, pin, tack and stitch sleeves into jacket, matching underarm seams.
9. Turn up 2cm [¾ in] to wrong side at lower edge of jacket and hem in place. Neaten all seams inside by trimming back wadding and oversewing (you can use bias binding if liked).
10. Overlapping fronts at centre, stitch frog fastenings securely to front of jacket.

Above: detail of the front-opening jackets which you can see opposite worn by the children in the top left and bottom right of the picture

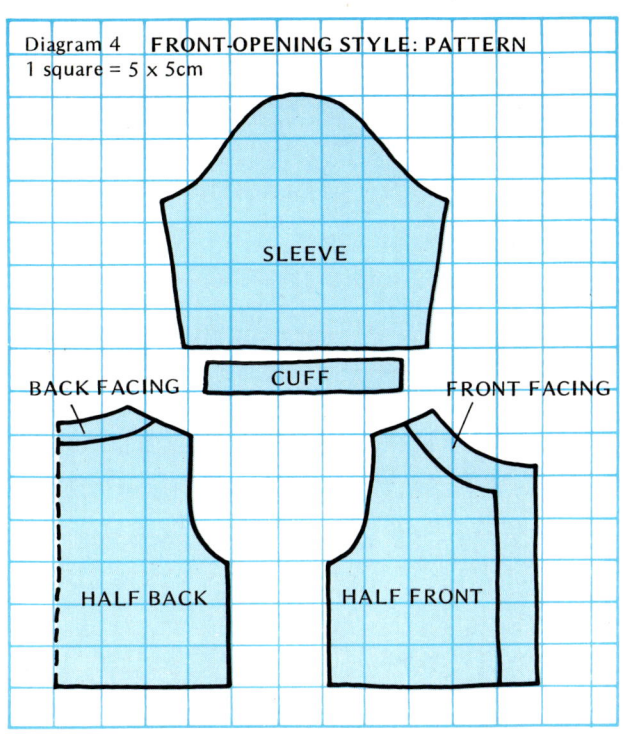

Diagram 4 **FRONT-OPENING STYLE: PATTERN**
1 square = 5 x 5cm

SLEEVE

BACK FACING   CUFF   FRONT FACING

HALF BACK   HALF FRONT

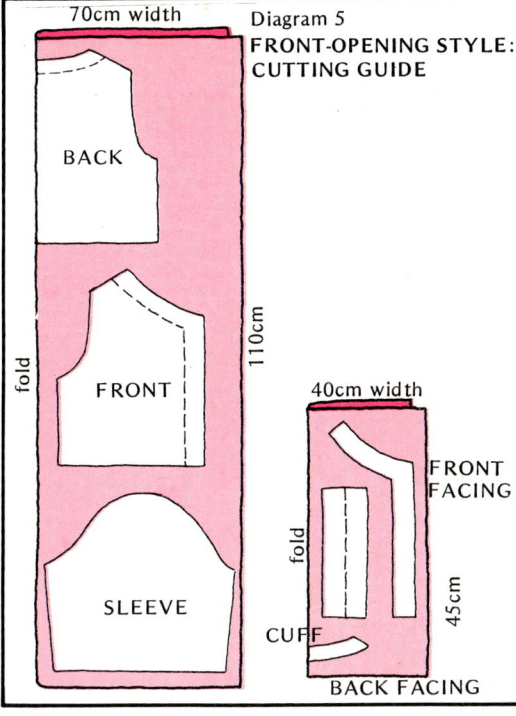

70cm width
Diagram 5
FRONT-OPENING STYLE: CUTTING GUIDE

BACK

fold

FRONT

110cm

SLEEVE

40cm width

FRONT FACING

fold

45cm

CUFF

BACK FACING

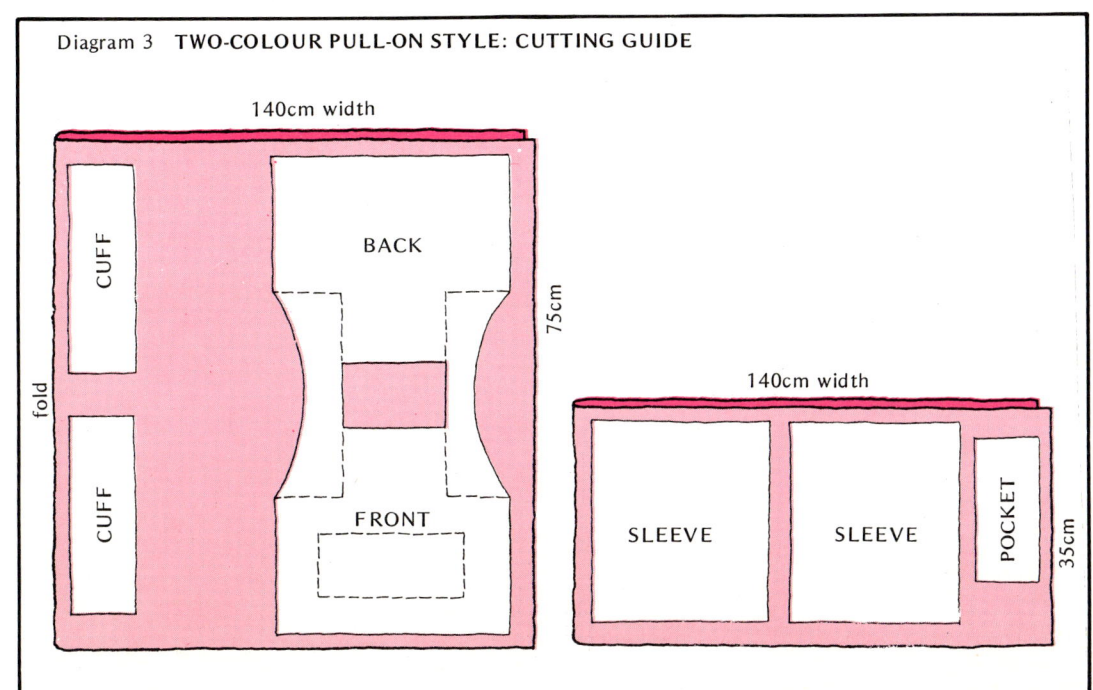

Diagram 3 **TWO-COLOUR PULL-ON STYLE: CUTTING GUIDE**

140cm width

CUFF   BACK   CUFF

fold   75cm

FRONT

140cm width

SLEEVE   SLEEVE   POCKET   35cm

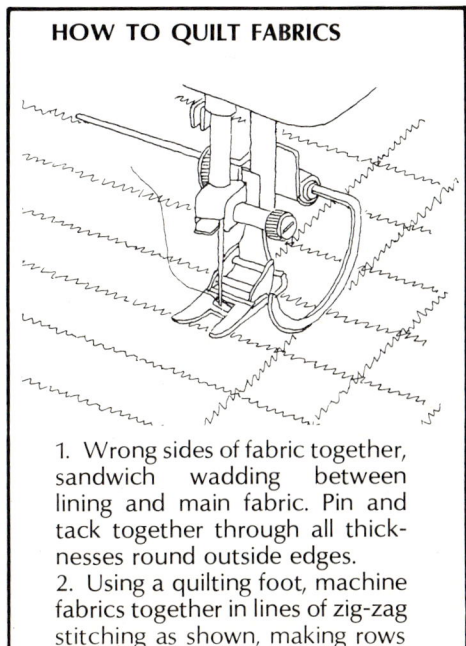

HOW TO QUILT FABRICS

1. Wrong sides of fabric together, sandwich wadding between lining and main fabric. Pin and tack together through all thicknesses round outside edges.
2. Using a quilting foot, machine fabrics together in lines of zig-zag stitching as shown, making rows 2.5cm [1 in] apart.

Rabbit threesome

16 to 20 months

A cheerful motif is used to decorate this set for a small child.

Overalls

Materials 70cm [27½ in] of 90cm ½[35½ in] wide stretch fabric; 25cm × 25cm (10 in × 10 in] square of felt or contrasting fabric; matching machine twist; 2 small buckles.

Measurements to fit 40–50cm [16–20 in] chest

Note All seams are 15mm [⅝ in] Square brackets contain imperial measurements.

TO MAKE
1. Make patterns on squared paper (1 square = 5cm) following Diagram 1. Fold fabric in half as shown in Diagram 2, and cut out 2 bibs, 2 legs, 2 straps, and 2 strap fastenings, allowing an extra 15mm [⅝ in] all round each piece for seams.
2. Following Diagram 3, make pattern of rabbit motif on squared paper (in this case 1 square = 2.5cm). Cut motif from felt or contrasting fabric.
3. Right sides of leg pieces together stitch sides marked front and back. Press seams open.
4. Rearrange leg pieces so that seams are at centre front and centre back then stitch inner leg seams. Press seams open. Turn up hem at bottom of each leg and catch-stitch in place. Turn to right side.
5. Turn in seam allowance of top and curved sides of bib and hem. Right sides together join front and back bib at short sides. Press seams open.
6. Right sides together join bib to trousers at waist. Neaten seam by oversewing. Turn to right side.
7. Pin rabbit motif centrally on overall and sew in position all round with satin stitch.
8. Fold straps right sides together and stitch along long edge and pointed shaping with a 6mm [¼ in] wide seam. Turn through to right side and press.
9. Fold in raw edges then stitch each strap to wrong side of back bib.
10. Right sides together, pin and stitch buckle fastenings along long edge with a 6mm [¼ in]

seam. Turn through to right side and press.
11. Stitch one end of buckle fastening to each side of front bib on wrong side. Thread buckle on to fastening, fold over and stitch other end of fastening in place on wrong side of bib.

Quilt

Note All seams are 15mm [⅝ in].

Materials Two pieces of fabric 90cm × 108cm [35½ in × 42½ in] same size piece of wadding; 35cm × 30cm [13¾ in × 11¾ in] piece of red felt and same size in blue felt; matching sewing threads.

Measurements (finished size) 87cm × 105cm [34¼ in × 41¼ in].

TO MAKE
1. Make pattern for rabbit motif on squared paper (1 square = 5cm) following Diagram 3. Cut 2 motifs from felt fabrics. Position

motifs on one piece of main fabric where shown in Diagram 2. Pin, tack and sew motifs in place using machine satin stitch.
2. Right sides together, pin and tack main fabrics together round sides, leaving a 20cm [8 in] gap. Pin and tack wadding to one side of main fabric. Stitch fabrics together through all thicknesses. Turn through to right side and press. Turn in seam allowance and close opening using overcast stitches.
3. Following pattern in Diagram 4, first pin, then tack diamond-shaped quilting through all thicknesses. Stitch by machine and remove tacking stitches.

Cushions

Materials For each cushion: 95cm × 90cm [37½ in × 35½ in] piece of fabric; 35cm × 30cm [14 in × 12 in] piece of felt or contrasting material; cushion pad; matching machine twist; press-studs, Velcro or a zip.

Note All seams are 15mm [⅝ in] unless otherwise stated.

TO MAKE
1. Make pattern of rabbit from squared paper (1 square = 5cm] following Diagram 3. Cut out rabbit motif from felt or contrasting material.
2. Fold cushion fabric in half widthways and mark centre with a line of tacking stitches. Position motif centrally on one half of fabric. Pin, tack and, using machine satin stitch, sew in place.
3. With right sides together, pin, tack and stitch along two sides of cushion, leaving one side open for filling. Turn through to right side and press.
4. Insert cushion pad into cover and close opening with press-studs, Velcro or a zip.

Right: the rabbit makes a splendidly cheerful motif for overalls, quilt and cushions

OVERALLS: PATTERN — Diagram 1

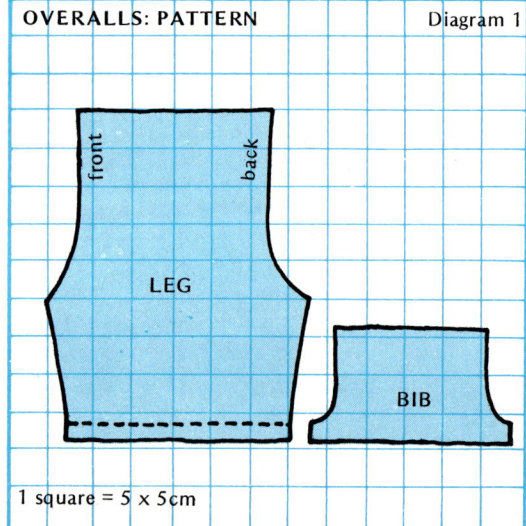

1 square = 5 x 5cm

RABBIT MOTIF: PATTERN — Diagram 3

1 square = 5 x 5cm (for quilt and cushions)
1 square = 2.5 x 2.5cm (for overalls)

OVERALLS: CUTTING GUIDE — Diagram 2

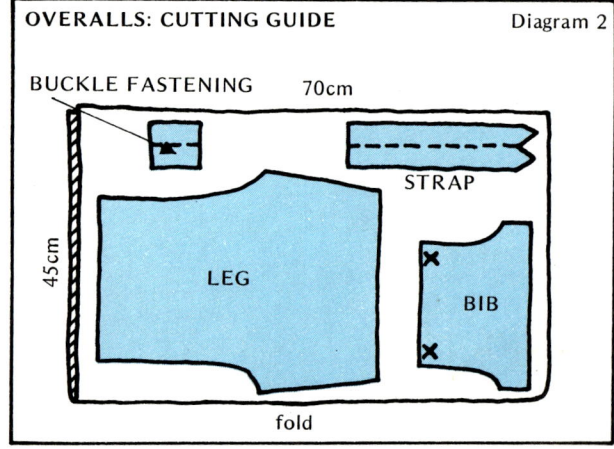

BUCKLE FASTENING   70cm
STRAP
45cm   LEG   BIB
fold

QUILT: DIAMOND-SHAPED PATTERN — Diagram 4

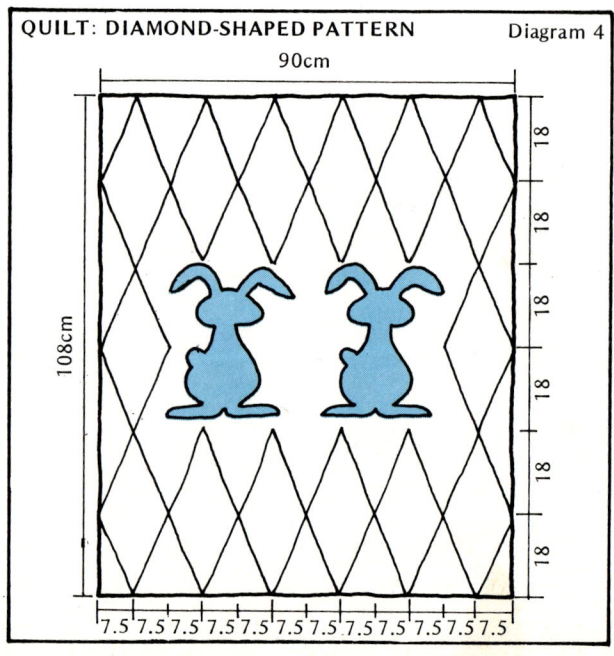

90cm

108cm

18 18 18 18 18 18

7.5 7.5 7.5 7.5 7.5 7.5 7.5 7.5 7.5 7.5 7.5 7.5

Children's Clothes

Dungarees from old . . .

2 to 3 years

Using cast-off jeans is a very economical way of making child-size dungarees.

Materials An old pair of adult's jeans or trousers in virtually any fabric – denim, corduroy, velvet, or jersey; matching machine twist; heavy-duty zip 23cm [9 in] long; 1.5m [59 in] bias binding (not needed if you use a jersey fabric).

Measurements To fit 56–58cm [22–23 in] chest; 102cm [40 in] height. If your jeans are wide enough and long enough, you can make a larger size by adding 2cm [¾ in] plus seam allowance to side and hem edges.

> As jeans rarely wear evenly all over, make sure you cut the two backs and two fronts from similarly coloured material.

TO MAKE THE PATTERN
Rule squares of 5cm [2 in] on to a sheet of paper, or use graph paper of that scale, then reproduce the pattern exactly as shown in Diagram 1. Mark notch for position of zip and fold line on pocket. Cut out pattern pieces.

POSITIONING THE PATTERN ON THE JEANS
Unstitch the jeans at crotch and inner leg seams. Position Dungaree front on the two front leg pieces laid one on top of the other, right sides together. Similarly, place Dungaree back on back leg pieces (see Diagram 2). Place pocket on any remaining single-layer jeans fabric. Pin pieces in place and cut out adding 15mm [⅝ in] seam allowances and 4cm [1½ in] hem.

TO SEW
1. With right sides together, stitch side, shoulder and crotch seams, leaving a gap from notch to neck edge in centre front seam for the zip.
2. Tack zip in position. Stitch.
3. Stitch bias binding to neck and armhole edges. Turn to wrong side and clip seam turnings where necessary. Slip-stitch inside edge of binding in place.

4. Fold top edge of pocket to wrong side. Stitch. Turn under remaining raw edges, tack. Position and stitch pocket to dungarees. Remove all tacking.

5. Turn up hem and slip-stitch on wrong side. Press.
6. If liked, you can top-stitch the new/old dungarees for extra smartness (see Diagram 3).

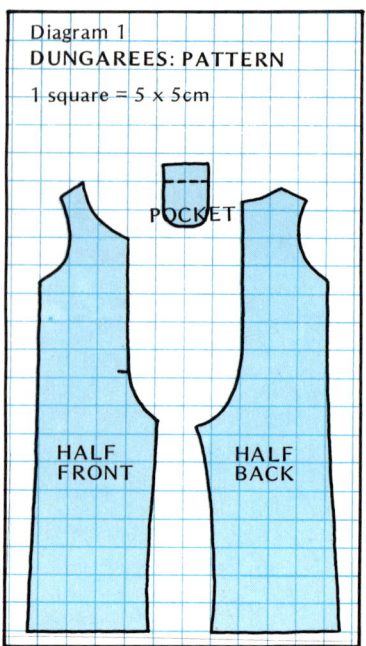

Diagram 1
DUNGAREES: PATTERN
1 square = 5 x 5cm

POCKET
HALF FRONT
HALF BACK

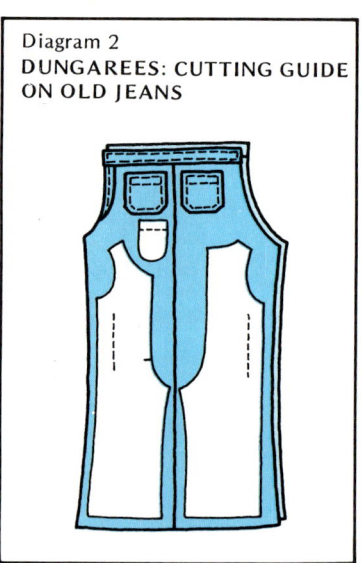

Diagram 2
DUNGAREES: CUTTING GUIDE ON OLD JEANS

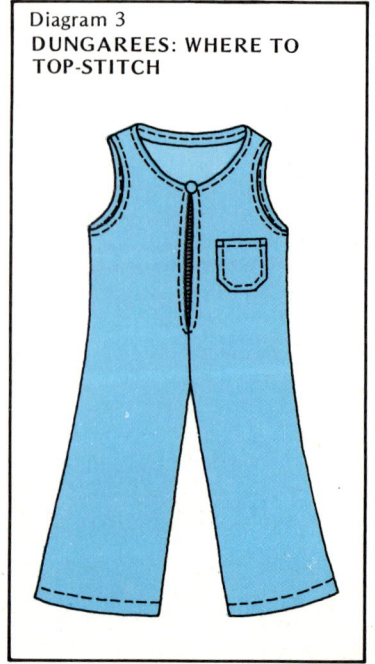

Diagram 3
DUNGAREES: WHERE TO TOP-STITCH

Dungarees from new . . .

2 to 6 years

Dungarees, bib and brace, overalls – whatever you call them children enjoy wearing them. From this pattern you can make either rough and tumble denims like these or the corduroy ones (see page 33) that co-ordinate with a tartan shirt.

Materials (measurements for larger sizes given in brackets) 80 (90, 100)cm [31½ (35½, 39½) in] of 140cm [55 in] wide fabric OR 130 (160, 180)cm [51 (63, 71) in] of 90cm [35½ in] wide fabric; 30–35cm [12–14 in] of 2.5cm [1 in] wide elastic; 2 buttons or overall buckles; matching machine twist.

Measurements To fit either waist 52cm [20½ in], chest 56cm [22 in], crotch 20cm [8 in] and inside leg 53cm [21 in]; OR waist 54cm [21½ in], chest 62cm [24½ in], crotch 22cm [8½ in] and inside leg 62cm [24½ in]; OR waist 56cm [22 in], chest 68cm [27 in], crotch 24cm [9½ in] and inside leg 70cm [27½ in].

TO MAKE THE PATTERN

Note All diagrams are overleaf. Rule squares of 5cm [2 in] on to a sheet of paper, or use graph paper to that scale, reproduce the pattern exactly as shown in Diagram 1 following the appropriate lines for the size you require. Check carefully that the crotch seam is the correct length for your child. If necessary lengthen or shorten at the line indicated.

TO CUT OUT

Fold fabric in half lengthways, right sides together, and place pattern pieces on the straight grain as shown in Diagram 2. Cut out each piece adding 2cm [¾ in] seam allowance at sides, 6cm [2½ in] at hem, and 15mm [⅝ in] at all other edges. Mark all guide lines with tailor's tacks.

Continued on next page

Left and right: dungarees, the most popular kids' wear. Make them from your old – or jumble-sale – jeans (see left) or in any fabric you like (see above)

Dungarees from new . . . continued

TO SEW .

1. With right sides together, stitch centre front and centre back crotch seams (Diagram 3). Clip seam turnings and press open, or if desired, strengthen seam by pressing turnings to one side and top-stitching close to seam line.

2. With right sides together, stitch one bib piece to front waist edge (Diagram 4A). Press seam turnings towards bib. If making the corduroy co-ordinates, sew on pockets and patches at this stage (see right).

3. With right sides together, stitch 2nd bib piece to 1st bib piece at curved side edges and across top (Diagram 4B). Clip seam turnings at curves. Turn bib right side out.

4. With right sides together, stitch trouser side seams incorporating sides of bib (Diagram 5A). Press turnings open.

5. Fold back waistband to wrong side. Turn under raw edges and stitch along waistline to form a casing for the elastic. Run a second row of machine stitches close to top folded edge. (Diagram 5B).

6. Cut elastic 2cm [¾ in] shorter than the child's back waist measurement. Insert elastic into casing and stitch ends securely to side seams (Diagram 5B).

7. Turn under remaining raw edge of bib and slip-stitch over seam turnings at front waist edge of trousers (Diagram 5A). Stitch inner leg seam (see Diagram 6) and press open.

8. Fold straps in half lengthways, right sides together. Stitch across square end and down length 15mm [⅝ in] in from raw edges. Turn straps right side out and press flat. Oversew remaining raw edges together. If desired top-stitch long sides of straps 3mm [⅛ in] in from edges. Make buttonholes at square ends or attach buckles (Diagram 7).

9. Position angled strap ends to inside back waist of trousers. Secure by stitching over previous lines of stitching (casing for elastic) – Diagram 8.

10. Turn up hems on trouser legs. If desired, top-stitch top and side edges of bib. Sew buttons to bib.

Dungarees patches and pockets

a. Cut out patches and pockets using Diagram 1 on page 34 in check and cord fabric (there is no seam allowance).

b. Fold top edge of square pockets 15mm [⅝ in] to wrong side. Turn under raw edges 3mm [⅛ in] and stitch in place. Turn under remaining raw edges and tack in place. Position pockets on trousers and stitch in place close to folded side and lower edges.

c. Slip-stitch binding over raw edges of heart patches and half moon pocket. Position on dungarees and stitch in place along line of inner edge of binding.

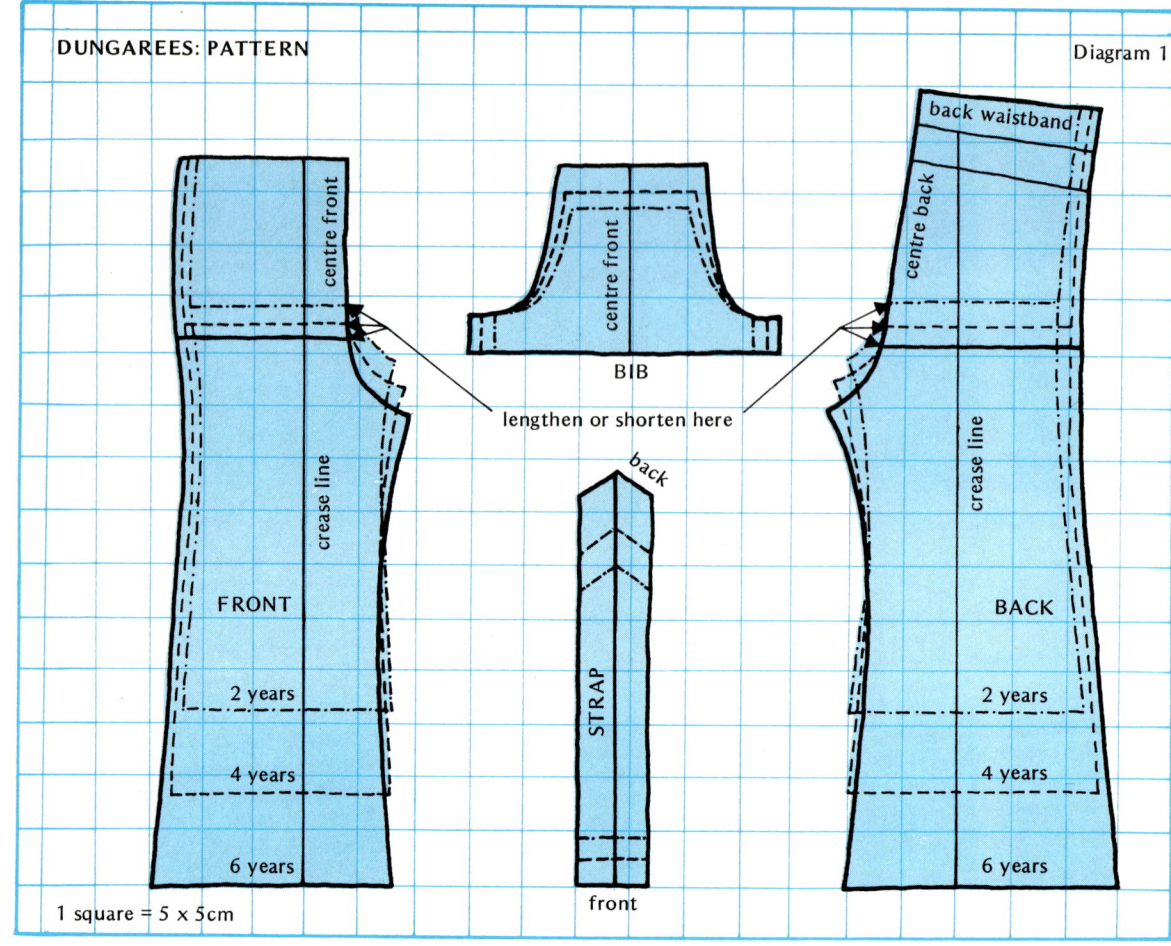

DUNGAREES: PATTERN — Diagram 1

BIB — centre front — centre front — back waistband — centre back — lengthen or shorten here — crease line — FRONT — BACK — crease line — STRAP — back — front — 2 years — 4 years — 6 years

1 square = 5 x 5cm

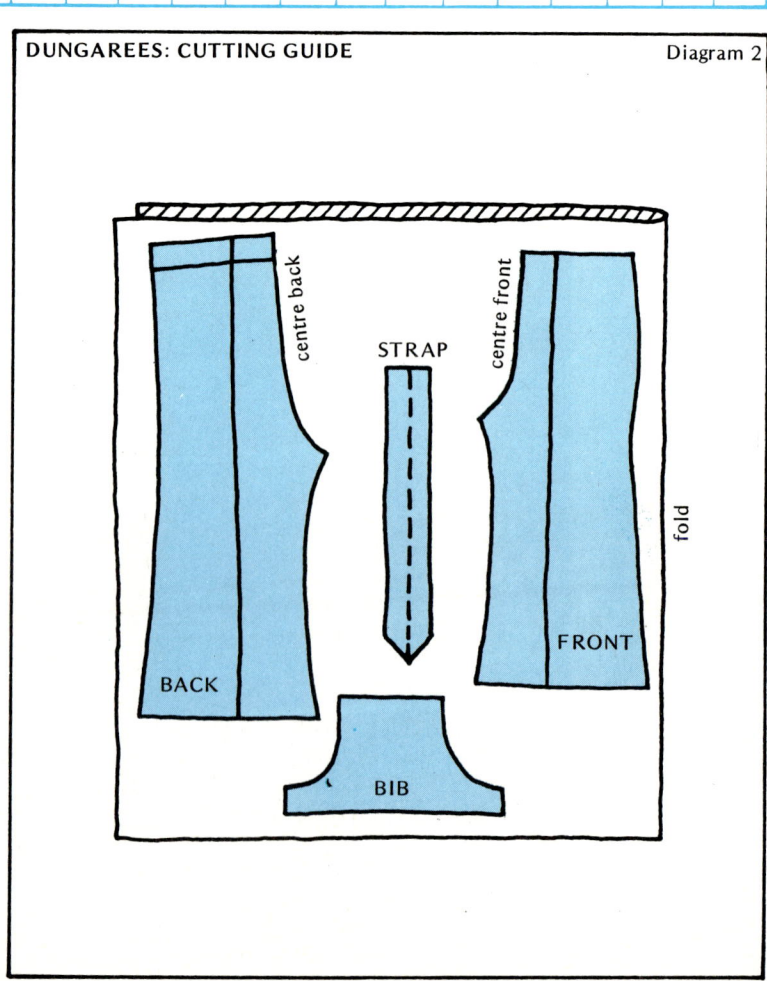

DUNGAREES: CUTTING GUIDE — Diagram 2

centre back — STRAP — centre front — BACK — FRONT — BIB — fold

Above and right: the pattern and cutting out guide for dungarees
Opposite page: how the dungarees look made up in corduroy with contrasting tartan patches and pockets. Follow all the different diagrams to give the garment a truly professional finish
On page 34 you'll find instructions for the tartan shirt

DUNGAREES: HOW TO SEW

Diagram 3

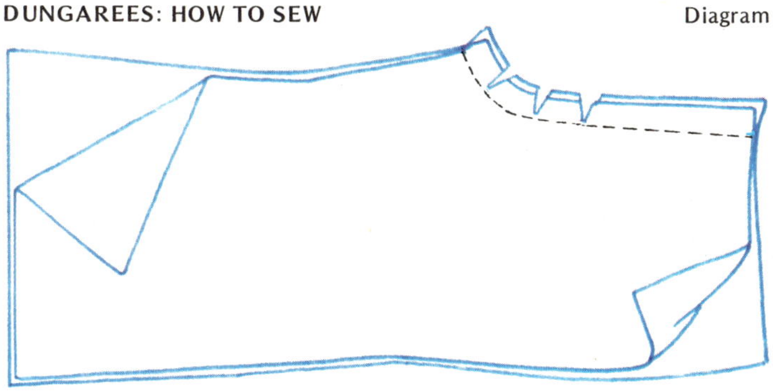

Diagram 5B

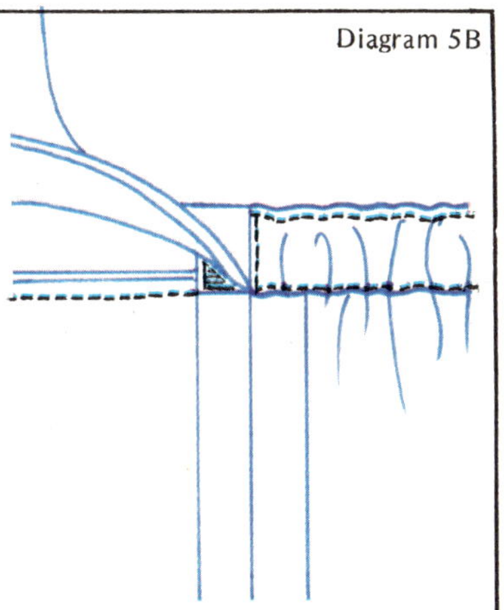

Diagram 4A

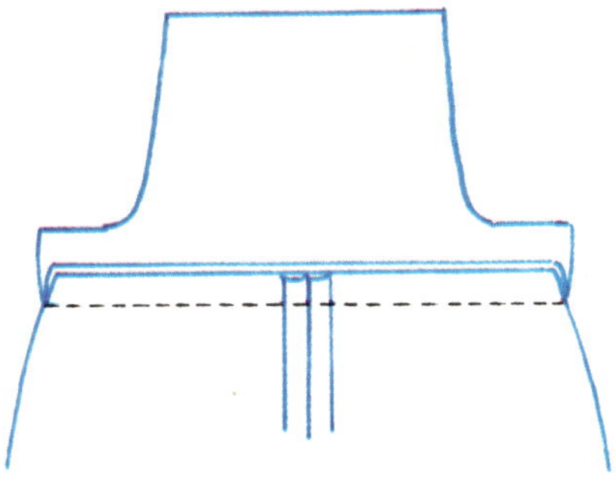

Diagram 4B

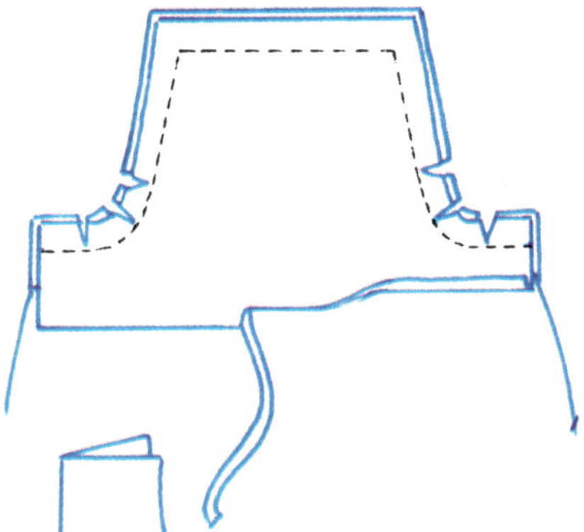

Diagram 6

Diagram 5A

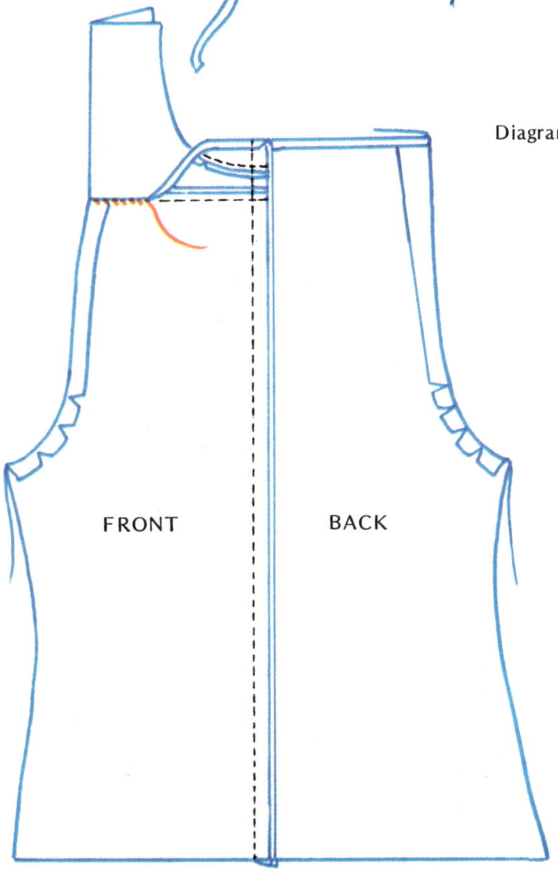

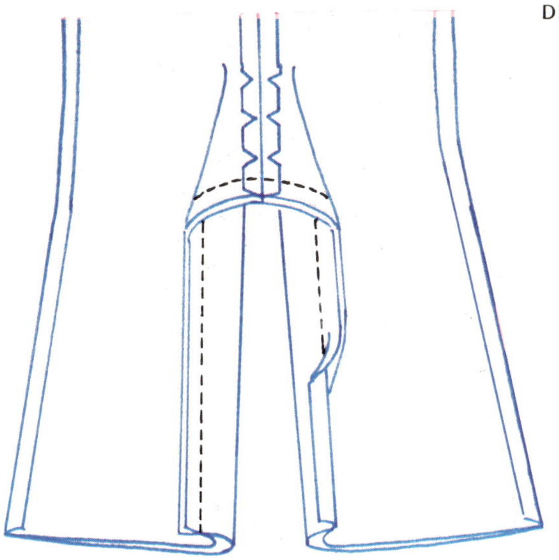

Diagram 7

Diagram 8

FRONT   BACK

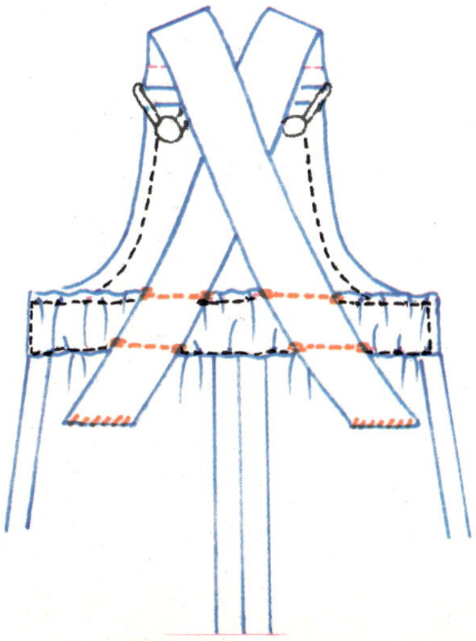

Children's Clothes

Check shirt

4 to 6 years

This attractive shirt teams well with dungarees – or with trousers (reverse the front opening and the shirt becomes a co-ordinate for a little girl as well). There are lots of diagrams to help you achieve a professional finish.

Measurements To fit 64–68cm [25–27 in] chest.

Materials 1.20m [47¼ in] of 90cm [35½ in] wide check fabric or 90cm [35½ in] of 140cm [55 in] wide fabric (use either a brushed cotton or viscose); an odd scrap of plain fabric in a matching colour for the elbow patches, (optional); matching machine twist; 7 buttons.

TO MAKE THE PATTERN
Rule 5cm [2 in] squares on to a sheet of paper, or use graph paper to that scale, then reproduce the pattern exactly as shown in Diagram 1. Mark guide lines.

TO CUT OUT
Fold fabric in half lengthways, right sides together, and place shirt centre back to the fold and collar centre back to the fold twice. Place shirt front to selvedges and place cuff, pocket and patch (these 2 to be used on dungarees, see previous page) on straight grain (Diagram 2).
Cut out adding 15mm [⅝ in] seam turnings to each piece. Mark all guide lines with tailor's tacks.

TO SEW
1. With right sides together, stitch shirt fronts to shirt back at shoulders and sides. Press seams open.
2. Optional elbow patches: turn under raw edges of each patch. Position on sleeves where shown and slip-stitch all round. Alternatively machine stitch close to folded under edges.
3. Run 2 rows of gathering stitches within the seam allowance over crown of each sleeve.
4. With right sides together, stitch sleeve seams.
5. Pin sleeve into armhole, right

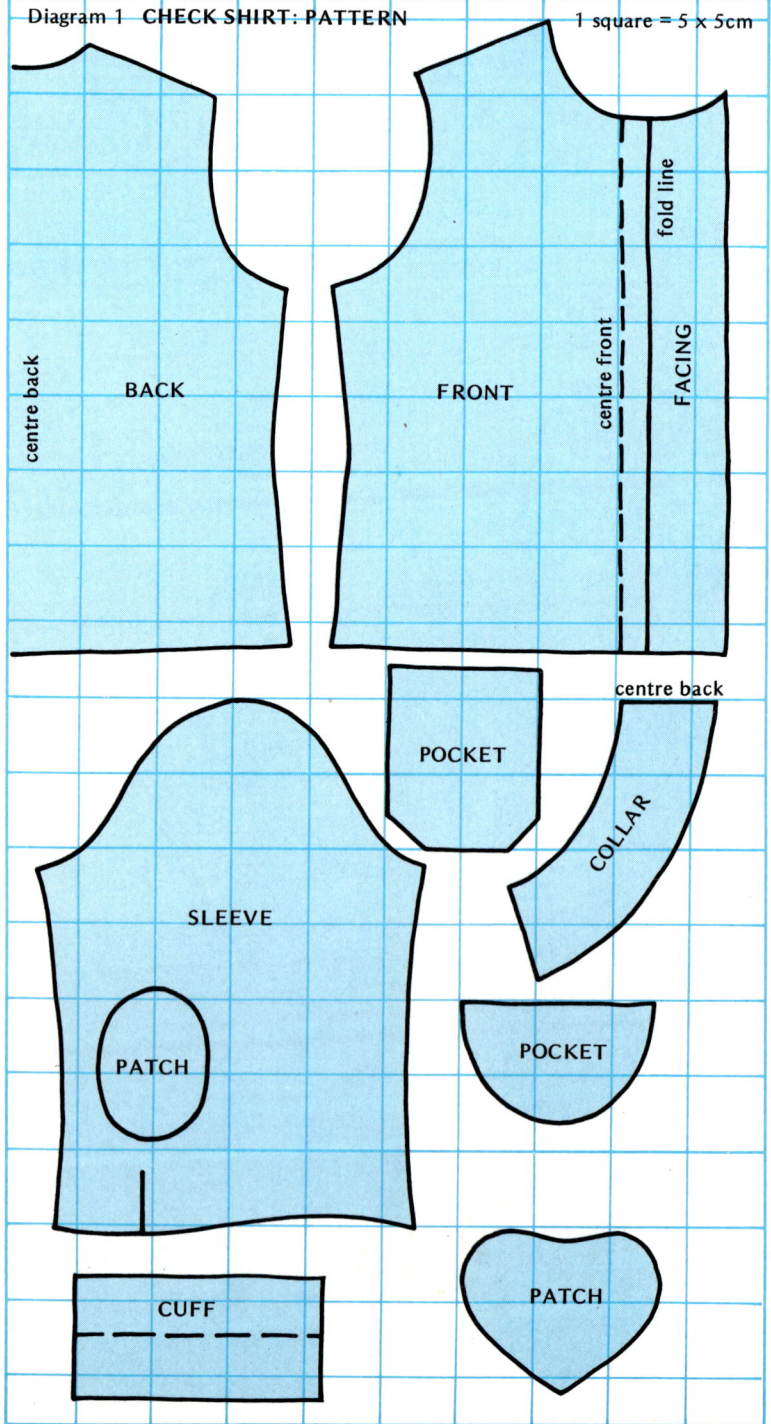

Diagram 1 **CHECK SHIRT: PATTERN**   1 square = 5 x 5cm

sides together and raw edges level, matching underarm seams and easing fullness to fit. Tack. Stitch and press seam turnings towards sleeve.

6. Fold front facings on to right sides of fronts and stitch from fold line to centre front line at neck edge (Diagram 3). Clip seam turnings to fold facing to wrong side. Press and tack close to folded edges (Diagram 4).

7. With right sides together, stitch collar pieces around outer edge and across ends (Diagram 5). Trim seam turnings, turn right side out. Press.

8. With right sides together and raw edges level, stitch one raw edge of collar to neck edge of shirt (Diagram 4). Press seam turnings towards collar.

9. Turn under remaining raw edge of collar and slip-stitch over previous line of stitching on inside of neck edge.

10. Cut a piece of facing fabric 7cm × 5cm [3 in × 2 in]. Turn raw edges 6mm [$\frac{1}{4}$ in] to wrong side on both long sides and across top. Stitch. With right sides together and raw edges level place facing centrally over cutting line at wrist edge of sleeve. Stitch 3mm

[$\frac{1}{8}$ in] either side of line tapering to a point at the top (Diagram 6). Cut through sleeve and facing and turn facing through to wrong side of sleeve. Press and top stitch close to fold edges of opening (Diagram 7).

11. With right sides together fold cuff in half and stitch across ends and for 2cm [$\frac{3}{4}$ in] along wrist edge (Diagram 8). Clip into seam turnings and turn right side out. Press.

12. Run 2 rows of gathering stitches at wrist edge of sleeve within seam allowance.

13. With right sides together pin

one raw edge of cuff to sleeve so that overlap on cuff extends FRONT sleeve opening edge. Stitch, easing gathers to fit. Press seam turnings towards cuff. Turn under remaining raw edge of cuff and slip-stitch over previous line of stitching inside sleeve.

14. Open out front facings at lower edge of shirt and make a small machined hem. Fold back facings and catch-stitch in place.

15. Make 5 evenly spaced buttonholes in left front and one in each cuff extension. Sew on buttons to correspond. Remove all tacking stitches. Press.

Diagram 2
CHECK SHIRT: CUTTING GUIDE

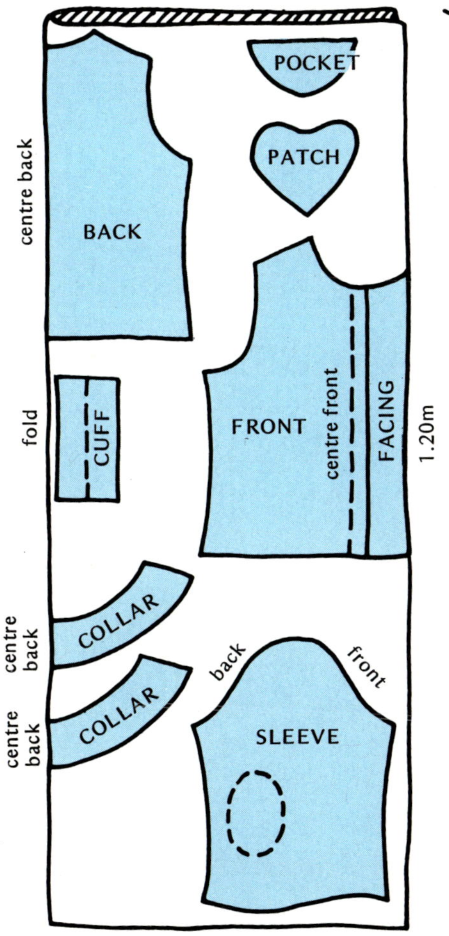

POCKET

PATCH

centre back

BACK

fold

CUFF

centre front

FRONT

FACING

1.20m

centre back
centre back

COLLAR

centre back

COLLAR

back

front

SLEEVE

90cm width

Diagram 3

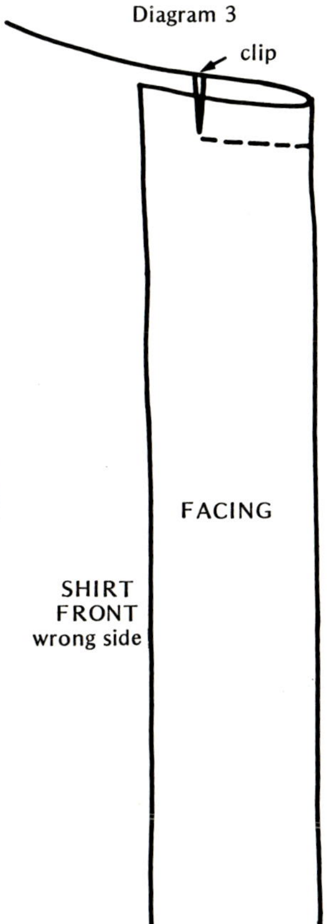

clip

FACING

SHIRT FRONT wrong side

Diagram 4

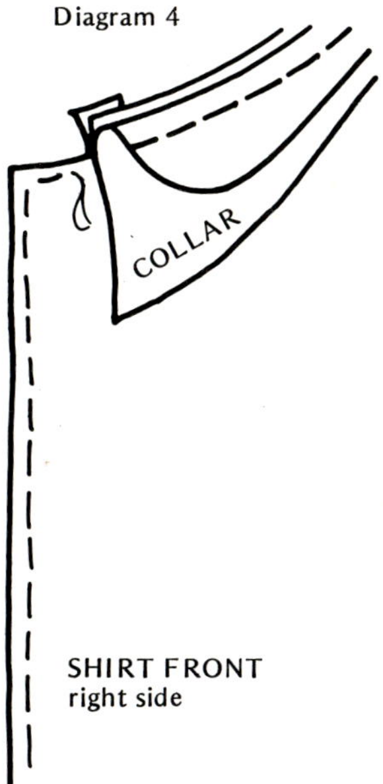

COLLAR

SHIRT FRONT right side

Diagram 6

Diagram 7

Diagram 5

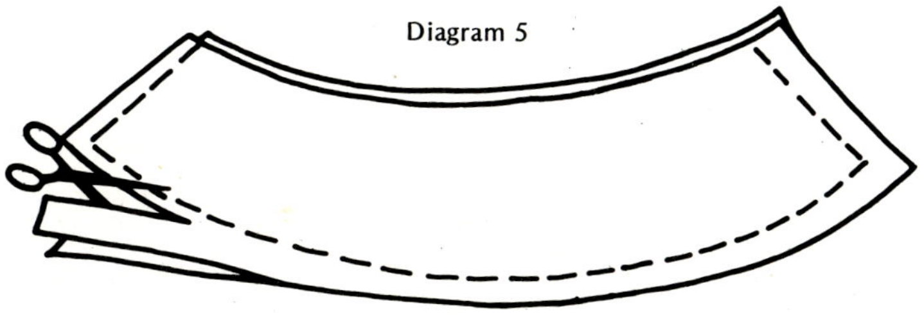

Diagram 8

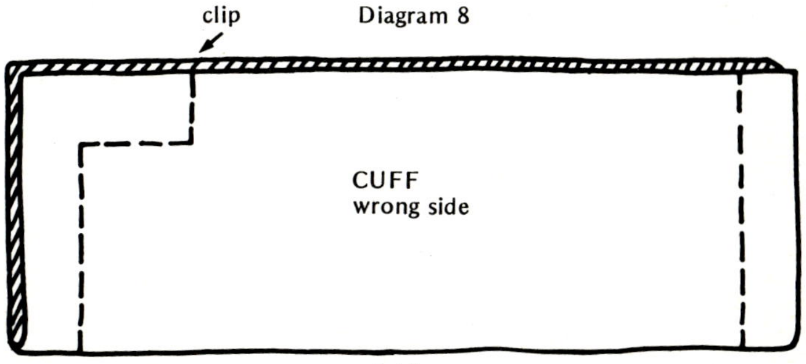

clip

CUFF wrong side

fold

Culottes

4 to 6 years

Culottes are fashionable and practical and have a place in every little girl's wardrobe. Make them in velvet for best or in tweed or corduroy for sporty everyday wear. The instructions for the quilted waistcoat are on page 136.

Measurements To fit 48cm [19 in] waist; length from waist to hem 41cm [16 in]. For smaller size deduct 2cm [¾ in] from all edges except crotch.

Materials 1m [39½ in] of 90cm [35½ in] wide fabric; 25cm of 15mm [⅝ in] wide elastic; 15cm [6 in] zip fastener; 1 hook and bar fastening or 1 button; matching machine twist.

Note All seams measure 15mm [⅝ in]. Square brackets contain imperial measurements.

The width of the velvet restricts the size of these culottes. If you buy furnishing velvet in a wider width to make a larger size do remember to make sure the nap is going the same way. To make larger sizes you will need to alter the crotch, waist, hip and length measurements. If you use a wide tweed or cotton without a design you won't have to worry about the nap.

TO MAKE THE PATTERN

Rule 5cm [2 in] squares on to a sheet of paper or use graph paper to that scale. Reproduce pattern exactly as shown in Diagram 1.

TO CUT OUT

Fold fabric in half lengthways, right sides together and place pattern pieces on fabric as shown in Diagram 2. Place front and back skirt piece twice on straight grain, and waistband to fold. Cut out adding 5cm [2 in] to hem edge and 15mm [⅝ in] seam allowance to all other edges. Mark all guide lines with tailor's tacks.

TO SEW

1. With right sides together, stitch front and back crotch seams. Stitch centre front and centre back seams, following guide lines for 12cm [4¾ in] from waist edge. Press in pleats (Diagram 3).
2. With right sides together tack left side seam. Stitch to within 16.5cm [6½ in] of waist edge. Press seam turnings open.
3. Position closed zip face down over centre of turnings with head 15mm [⅝ in] from top waist edge.
4. Tack then stitch in position (using a zipper foot attachment) 1.5mm [1/16 in] either side of teeth. Remove tacking.
5. With right sides together stitch right side seam. Press seam turnings open.
6. With right sides together, stitch inner leg seams. Clip into seam turnings around curves. Press turnings open.
7. Using a stretch stitch if possible, stitch elastic to wrong side of waistband from centre back to within 6cm [2¼ in] of one end. Keep one edge of elastic on line with centre fold line and stretch elastic as you stitch (Diagram 4).
8. Fold waistband in half lengthways, right sides together, and stitch across short ends. Turn band to the right side.
9. With right sides together, pin then stitch outer raw edge of waistband to waist edge of skirt, extending one end of band 4cm [1½ in] past back edge of zip opening as an overlap. Press turnings towards waistband.
10. Turn under remaining raw edge of waistband and slip-stitch over previous row of stitches on wrong side. Slip-stitch together lower edges of overlaps.
11. Sew on hook and bar fastening or work buttonhole and sew on corresponding button.
12. Turn up hem 5cm [2 in] or more if necessary. Over-sew raw edges and blind-stitch in place.

Opposite page: culottes look stylish made in velvet but you can use any fabric you like
This page: the pattern, cutting guide and diagrams you'll need to make the culottes

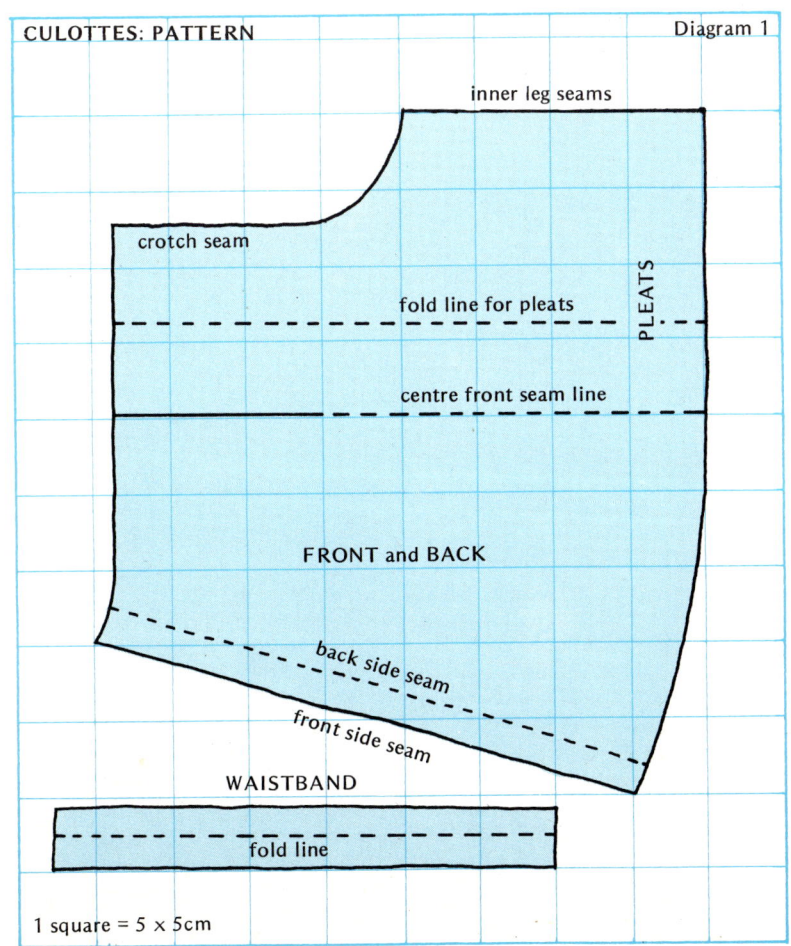

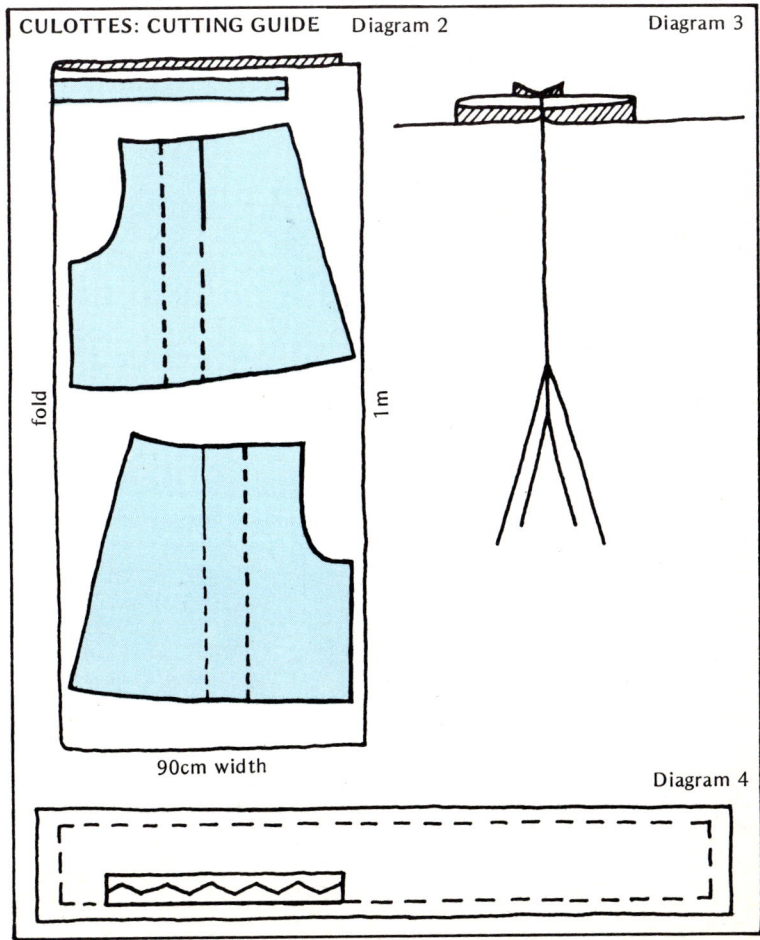

Quilted waistcoat knitted in Lister's Motoravia 4ply, colour "Fisherman"

Pin-tucked dresses

4 to 6 years

Dresses for a special occasion – they look "different" because of the smart pin tucks on the bodice and sleeves.

Pin tucks can be made in various ways but the secret of success lies in getting the tucks straight and parallel with the grain of the fabric. It's advisable to press the lines first so you can be accurate when you sew. Sewing by hand (see Diagram 3) might take longer but you have more control over the stitches and can get them close to the fold. For some machines you can buy a special attachment for tucks and chinese cording.

Materials 1.80m [71 in] of 90cm [35½ in] wide fabric; 1m [39½ in] bias binding; matching machine twist.

Measurements To fit chest 68cm [27 in]; waist 60cm [23½ in] and length 60cm [27½ in].

Note All seams measure 15mm [⅝ in]. Square brackets contain imperial measurements.

TO MAKE

1. Cut out pattern pieces using squared paper following Diagram 1 (1 square = 5cm). Mark dart positions, buttonholes.
2. Fold fabric lengthways and lay on pattern pieces as shown in Diagram 2. Cut out the bias strips (3.5cm/1⅜ in wide) and back skirt and front skirt, adding 15mm [⅝ in] all round for seams and 6cm [2½ in] for hem.
3. Lay front bodice, back bodice and sleeve patterns on the remaining doubled fabric but do not cut out (see step 5). On the bodice fronts, mark in the areas not to be tucked – the white areas on the pattern. Cut roughly round the pattern pieces, leaving a wide margin all round and add an extra 8cm [3 in] width across each front bodice, add 8cm [3 in] extra on back bodice, and add 9cm [3½ in] extra

PIN-TUCKED DRESS: PATTERN

Diagram 1

1 square = 5 × 5cm

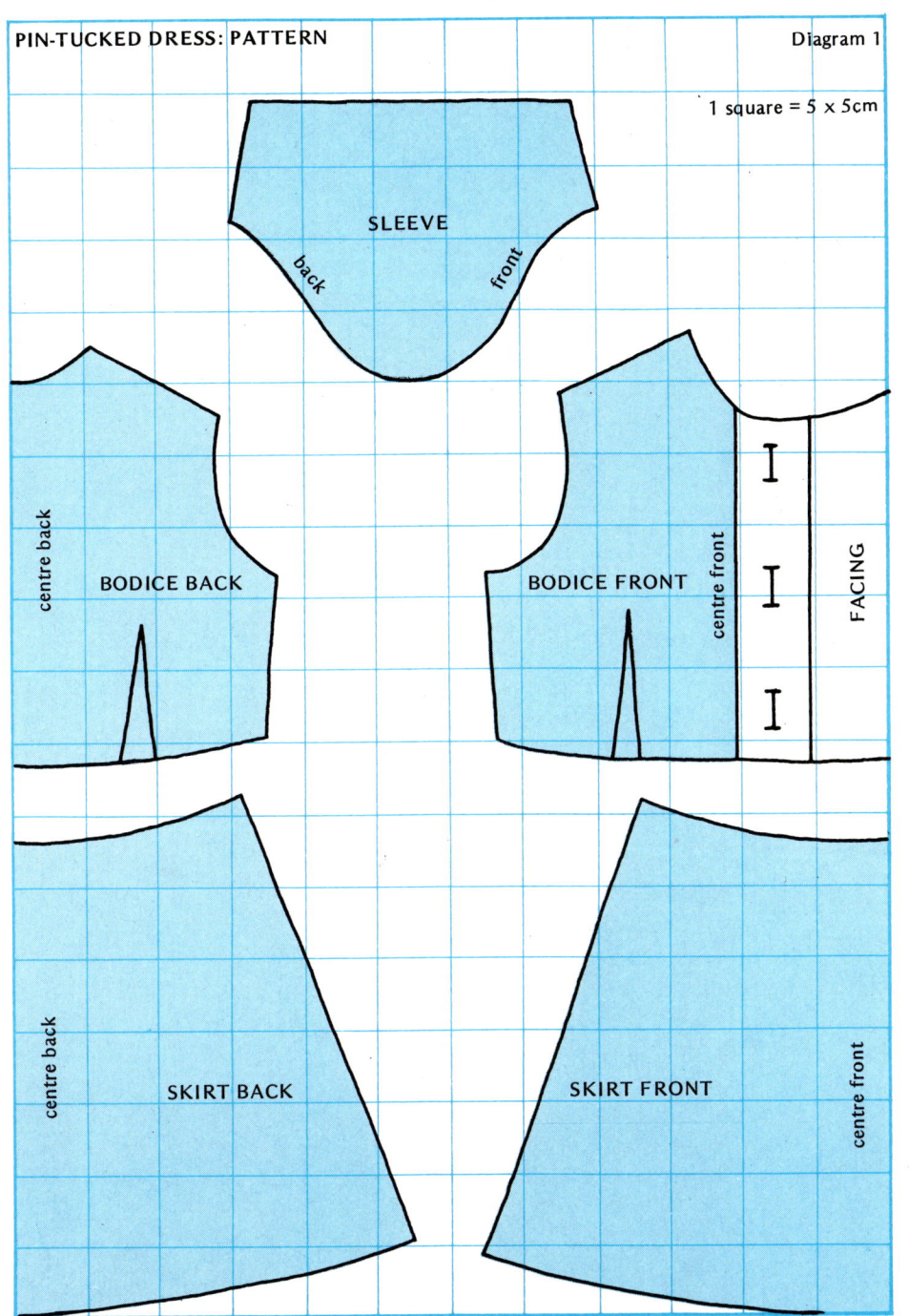

PIN-TUCKED DRESS: CUTTING GUIDE

Diagram 2

90cm width

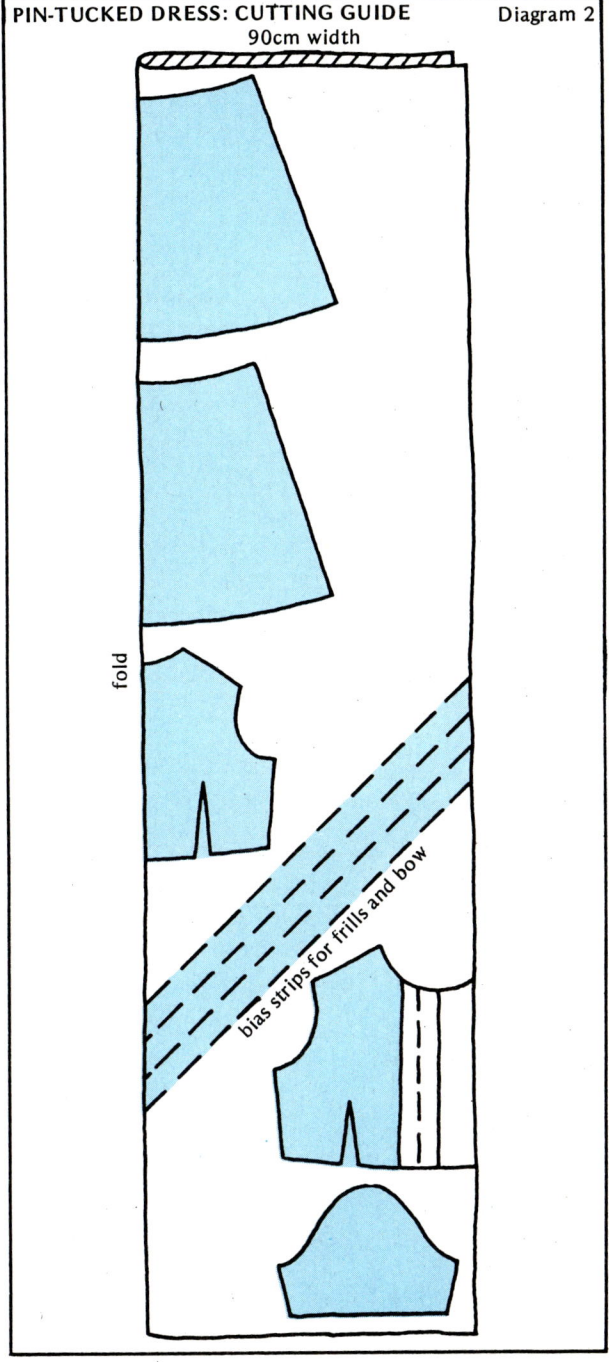

1.80m

width across the sleeves – all the extra will be taken up by the pin tucks.

4. To make the pin tucks press folds in the fabric 15mm [⅝ in] apart and by hand or machine (see box) make tiny running stitches 1.5mm [1/16 in] in from the fold (as shown in Diagram 3 on page 40).

5. When all tucks have been made in bodice back, 2 bodice fronts and 2 sleeves, place the bodice and sleeve patterns correctly over the tucked and plain areas positioning back bodice on the fold, and cut out.

6. Right sides together, stitch darts at waist on front and back

bodices. Press towards centre. Right sides together and raw edges level, stitch back bodice to fronts at shoulders. Press seams open.

7. Right sides together and raw edges level, stitch front and back bodices together at side seams. Press seams open, turn through to right side.

8. To make the frills, join the bias strips to make one long length – cut off 40cm [15¾ in] for the bow to be made later. Along one long edge of the strip, make a rolled hem. On the other edge, sew a line of running stitches, 3mm [⅛ in] in from edge. Pull up stitches to make gentle gathers and

secure. At one short end of the frill, turn under a small hem and catch-stitch on wrong side.

9. With right side facing, match hemmed short end of frill up to fold line at centre front of right bodice front. Pin and tack the length of frill around neck opening. Pin and tack a length of bias to neck opening over frill. Fold each bodice front facing over on to right side (see Diagram 4, page 40) and tack close to neck edge. Machine round neck opening through all thicknesses. Neaten seams, clip where necessary and turn facing through to wrong side and press. On wrong side carefully catch-stitch bias

binding with tiny stitches.

10. On right front facing make 3 equally spaced buttonholes (see Diagram 5, page 40). On right side of both facings sew a line of running stitches 1.5mm [1/16 in] in from all but waist edge. Sew buttons on left facing.

11. Trim lower edge of each sleeve piece with a length of frill and bias as for neck opening (step 9). Right sides together, stitch each underarm sleeve seam. Press open, turn through to right side.

12. Run a line of gathering stitches around the crown of each sleeve. Pull up gathers to fit armhole opening. Right sides together,

Continued on next page

39

Pin-tucked dresses . . . continued

matching underarm and side seams, stitch sleeves into arm-holes.

13. Right sides together, stitch skirt front to skirt back at side seams. Press seams open, turn through to right side.

14. Right side of skirt to wrong side of frill, pin and tack a length of frill all round waist edge.

15. Lap right front bodice over left matching at centre front. Tack together close to waist edge. Right sides together, pin and tack bodice to skirt, matching seams and sandwiching frill between. Stitch through all thicknesses. Neaten seam on wrong side by oversewing all fabric together. Press.

16. Make the bow from the 40cm [15¾ in] length of bias strip; fold

the strip in half lengthways and stitch along the long edge and across one short edge. Turn through to right side. Neaten short edge and press strip. Tie into a bow and stitch securely to front of dress.*

17. Turn up hem and carefully catch-stitch in place on wrong side so stitches don't show on right side (or use special iron-on hemming tape).

*To make a more professional bow, cut the doubled and stitched length into four so you have two tails, and two pieces to make loops. Make the loops and join together, covering the join with a scrap of leftover material. On the wrong side of the loops, sew on the two tails securely.

Checked co-ordinates

4 to 8 years

You can make this cheery bias-cut smock dress quickly and easily but without any of the usual fabric wastage – from the extra you can sew natty shorts for younger brother or sister and still have enough fabric left over for a triangular shawl or scarf.

Materials 1.85m [73 in] of 140cm [55 in] wide wool plaid; 45cm [17¾ in] of 15mm [⅝ in] wide elastic; 2 large press-studs; 50cm [20 in] of 4cm [1½ in] wide bias binding for trouser pockets; matching machine twist; hook and bar.

Measurements Dress: chest 69–74cm [27–29 in], height 132–145cm [52–57 in]. Trousers: waist 56–58cm [22–23 in], height 117–127cm [46–50 in].

TO MAKE THE PATTERNS
Rule squares of 5cm [2 in] on to a sheet of paper, or use graph paper to that scale, then reproduce the pattern exactly as shown in Diagram 1. The front and back patterns for the dress are super-imposed as they are almost the

---

HOW TO MAKE PIN TUCKS BY HAND   Diagram 3

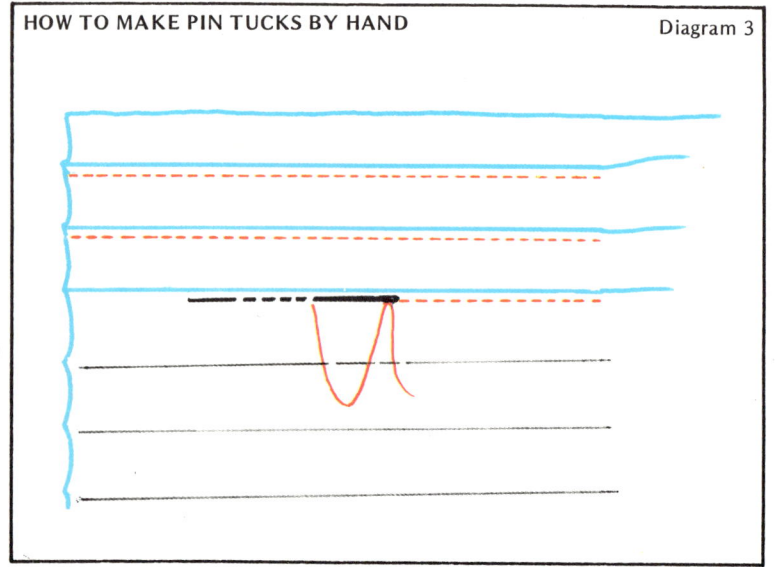

PUTTING ON THE NECK FRILL

Diagram 4   Diagram 5

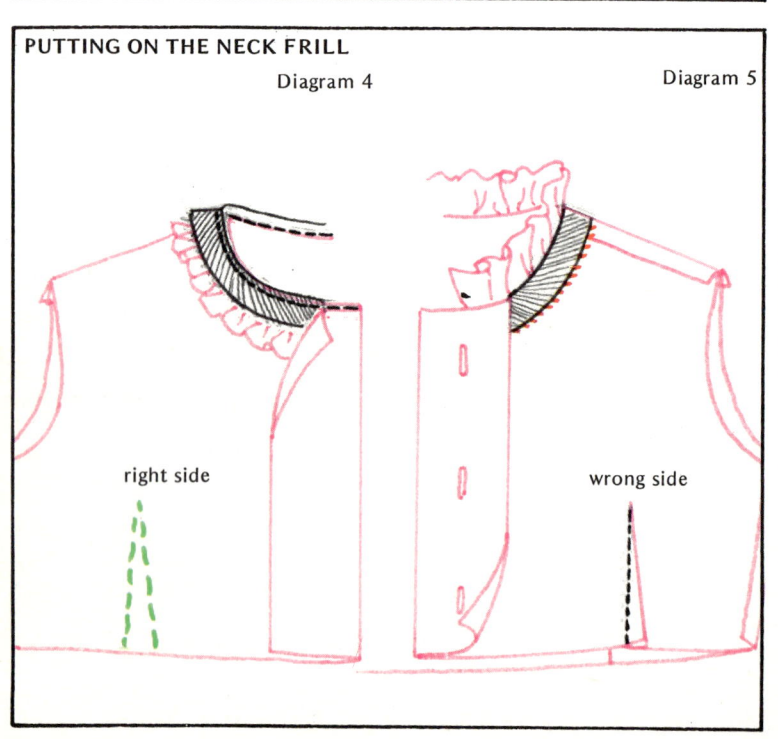

right side   wrong side

same; follow the outer dotted line when cutting the dress front and follow the solid line when doing the back.

TO CUT OUT DRESS AND TROUSERS

1. Cut fabric into 2 lengths – 45cm [17¾ in] and 140cm [55 in].
2. Fold the shorter piece in half lengthways with right sides together and place dress yoke to fold and trouser back on straight grain (see Diagram 2A).
3. Take the 140cm [55 in] square of fabric and fold it corner to corner to find the bias. Mark the diagonal fold with a line of tacking stitches.
4. Align the centre line on the front and back dress pieces with the line of tacking stitches (see

Diagram 2B, page 42). Place collar also on bias.
5. From remaining fabric cut 2 trouser fronts, 2 trouser pockets, 2 dress pockets, dress left placket and dress right placket; the remaining material can be hemmed to make a triangular shawl or scarf.
6. Mark all notches and guide lines with tailor's tacks. Cut out each piece adding 15mm [⅝ in] seam allowances, 2.5cm [1 in] for hems and 3cm [1¼ in] for casing at waist of trousers.

TO SEW THE DRESS

1. Fold top edges of pockets to wrong side and stitch. Turn under side and lower edges of pockets and stitch in position on dress front.

2. Run two rows of gathering stitches 6mm [¼ in] and 15mm [⅝ in] in from top edge of front and back pieces.
3. Cut through front yoke 2cm [¾ in] left of centre line (see Diagram 3A).
4. With right side of placket to wrong side of yoke, stitch placket to right front yoke at neck and front opening edges.
5. Turn placket to right side, clipping into seam allowance at neck edge. Turn under inner edge and top-stitch close to all 3 folded edges of placket (see Diagram 3B).
6. With right sides together, stitch left front placket to left front yoke. Press seam turnings open. Fold facing part of placket on to right side of yoke and stitch across

Continued on next page

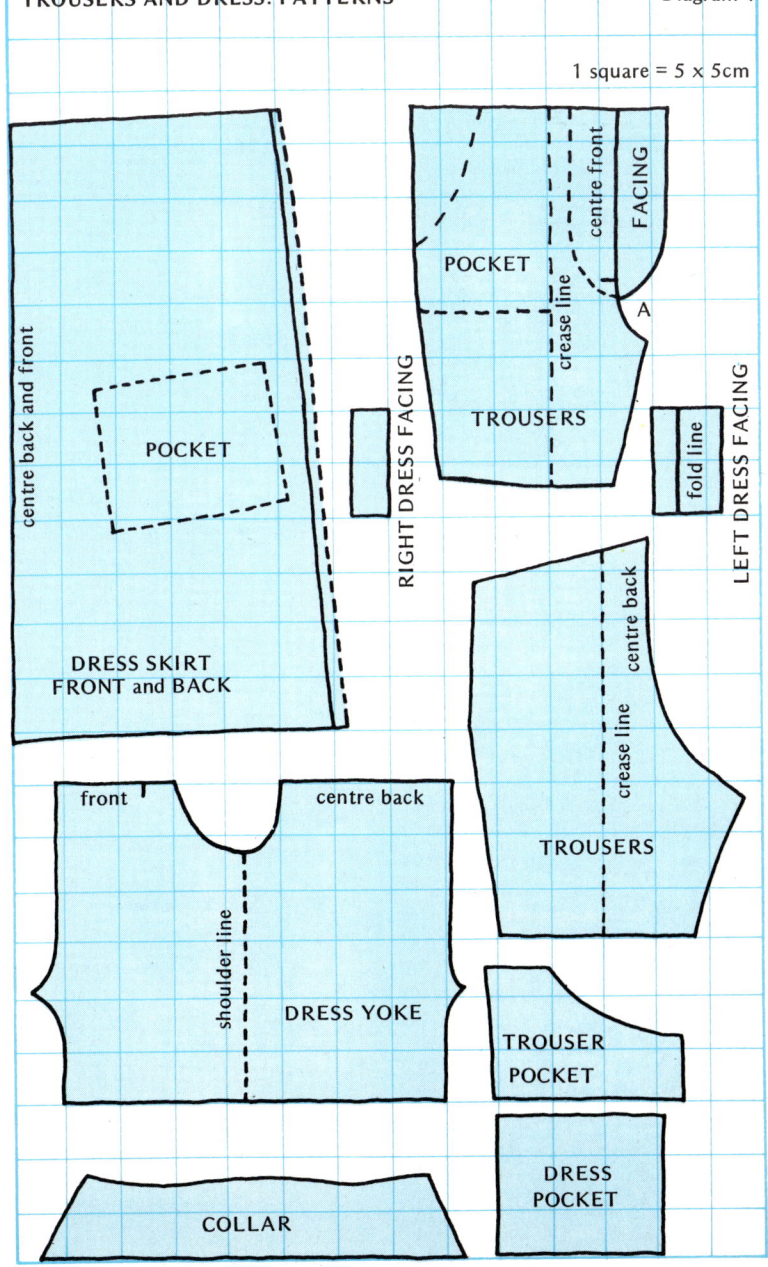

TROUSERS AND DRESS YOKE: CUTTING GUIDE   Diagram 2A

front · centre back · shoulder line · DRESS YOKE

centre back

fold line · TROUSERS BACK

1.40m

45cm

TROUSERS AND DRESS: PATTERNS   Diagram 1

1 square = 5 x 5cm

centre back and front · POCKET · DRESS SKIRT FRONT and BACK

RIGHT DRESS FACING · LEFT DRESS FACING

POCKET · FACING · centre front · crease line · A · TROUSERS

fold line

centre back · crease line · TROUSERS

front · centre back · shoulder-line · DRESS YOKE

TROUSER POCKET

COLLAR · DRESS POCKET

Checked co-ordinates . . . continued
neck edge. Clip into seam allowance at neck edge and turn
facing to wrong side. Press flat.
Top-stitch placket close to seam
lines. Over-sew inner raw edge
of facing and catch-stitch in
place.

7. Fold collar in half lengthways
with right sides together. Stitch
ends. Turn right side out. Press.

8. With right sides together stitch
one raw edge of collar to neck
edge of dress. Press seam turnings towards collar. Turn under
remaining raw edges of collar
and slip-stitch over previous row
of stitching.

9. With right sides together, stitch
front and back yoke pieces to
front and back dress pieces,
overlapping front opening
plackets and drawing up gathers
evenly to fit.

10. With right sides together,
stitch side and sleeve seams.

11. Hem lower edge and sleeve,
slip-stitching on wrong side. Sew
on press-stud fastening to front
placket opening.

TO SEW THE TROUSERS

1. Bind the curved opening edges
of the two pockets with the bias
binding.

2. Fold under lower and longer
side edges of pockets and stitch
in position on trouser fronts.

3. With right sides together, stitch
side and inner leg seams.

4. With right sides together, stitch
crotch from back waist to notch
A on fronts. Press seam turnings
open, clipping where necessary
on curves. Fold right front facing
to wrong side and stitch down
following line of curve.

5. Fold left front opening facing
to wrong side. Top-stitch in place
following line of curve and catching in the lower curved edge of
right front facing. Over-sew raw
edges.

6. Turn waist edge 3cm [1¼ in] to
wrong side. Turn under raw edges
15mm [⅝ in]. Stitch close to inner
edge to form a casing for the
elastic leaving a 2cm [¾ in] gap
near seam.

7. Cut elastic approx 5cm [2 in]
smaller than waist measurement
and insert into casing through
gap.

8. Secure ends of elastic in
position with several rows of
machine stitching. Turn in
remaining raw edges of casing
and slip-stitch to close.

9. Sew on hook and bar fastening
at waist and press-stud half way
down front opening. Press.

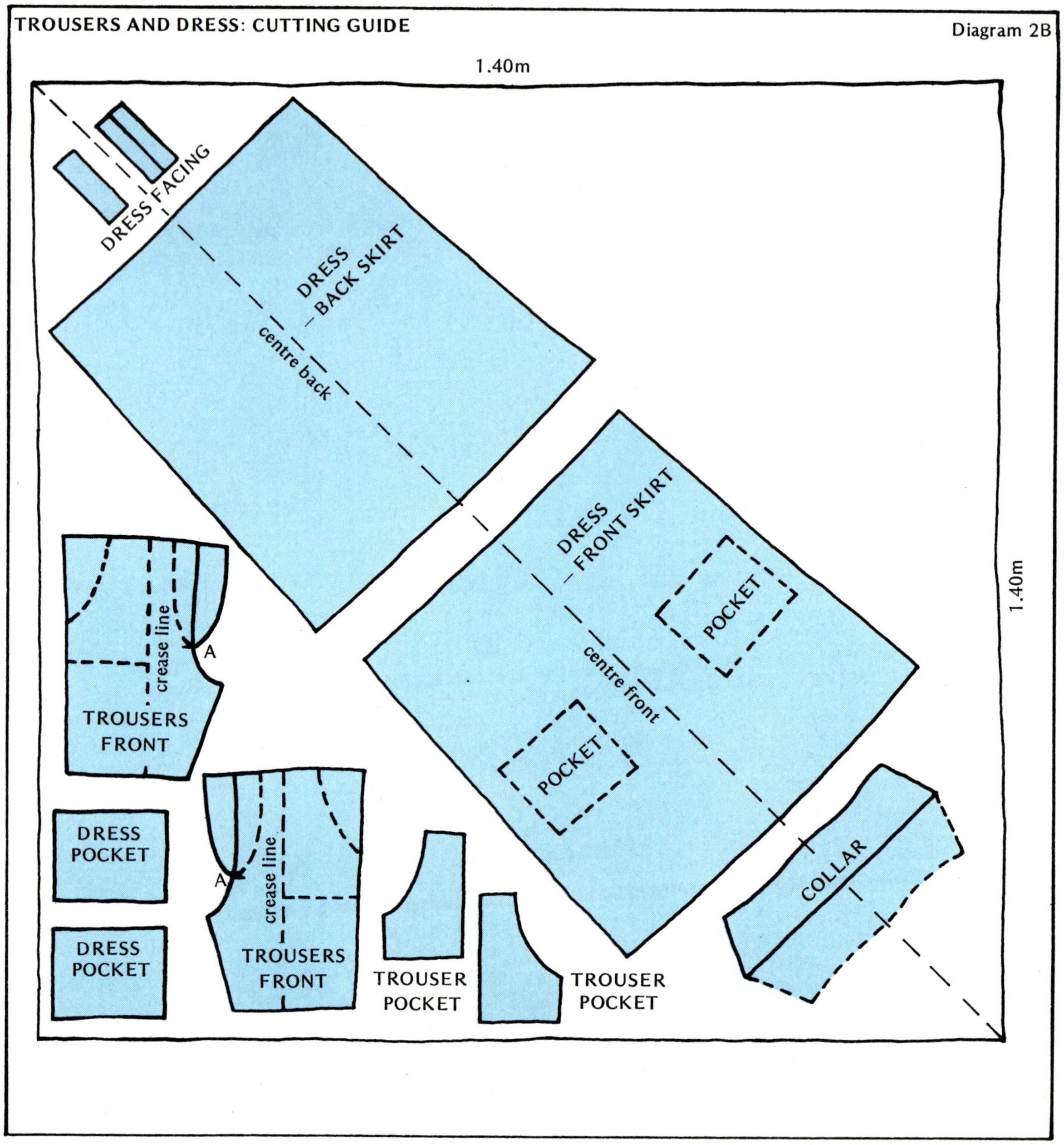

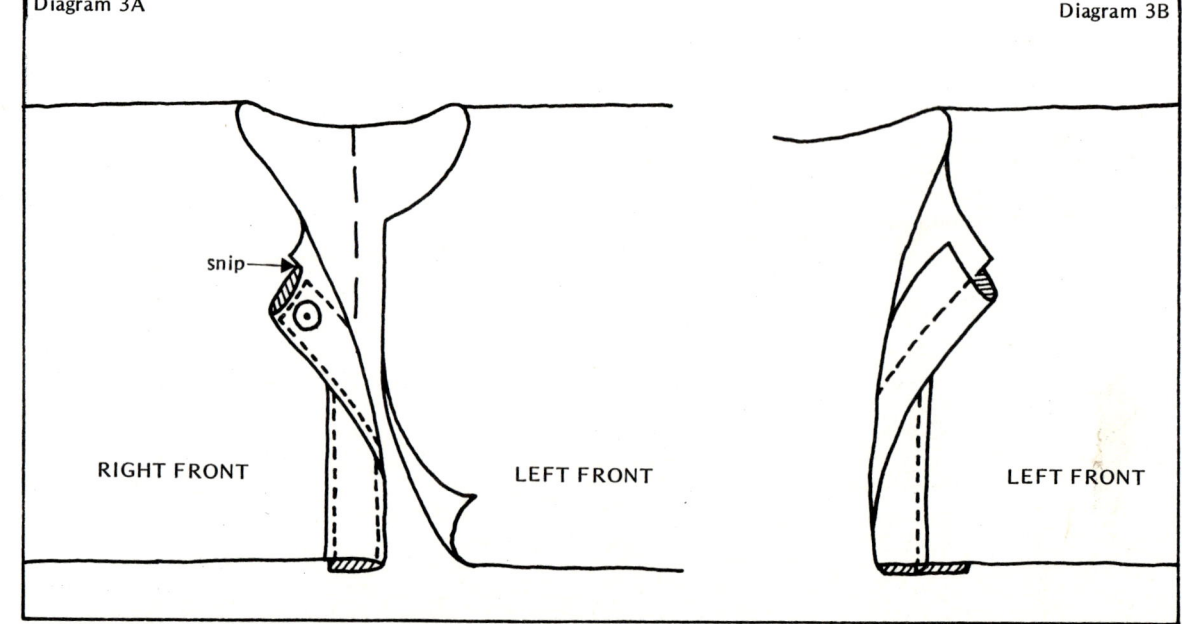

TROUSERS AND DRESS: CUTTING GUIDE — Diagram 2B

1.40m

DRESS FACING

DRESS BACK SKIRT — centre back

DRESS FRONT SKIRT — centre front

POCKET

POCKET

TROUSERS FRONT — crease line — A

DRESS POCKET

DRESS POCKET

TROUSERS FRONT — crease line — A

TROUSER POCKET

TROUSER POCKET

COLLAR

1.40m

Diagram 3A — Diagram 3B

snip

RIGHT FRONT

LEFT FRONT

LEFT FRONT

Painting smocks

5 to 10 years

The perfect answer to playtime – easy to clean, colourful smocks, with or without sleeves, in lightweight PVC, Ciré or glazed cotton. Ideal, too, for art classes at school. The yoke, puffed sleeves and hem are attractively top-stitched in a contrasting colour and the back is fastened by ties on the yoke.

Materials 140 (170)cm [55 (67) in] of 130cm [51 in] wide fabric for the smock WITH sleeves; 90 (120)cm [36 (47) in] for the smock WITH-OUT sleeves; for both smocks, matching machine twist and contrasting buttonhole thread for top-stitching; sheet of paper approx 102 (116)cm × 65 (85)cm [40 (46) in × 26 (34) in] – newspapers Sellotaped together will do; narrow elastic for cuffs; 60cm [24 in] of tape for ties.

Measurements 66 (76)cm [26 (30) in] chest.

Note All measurements for larger size are given in ordinary brackets – the smaller size is printed in blue on Diagram 1. Square brackets contain imperial measurements. All diagrams are on pages 44 and 45.

TO MAKE YOUR PATTERN

1. Fold paper in half widthways then with the fold on your left (see Diagram 1) mark the top left hand corner B and the top right hand corner A.
2. Following the measurements given, mark points N, D and C along the fold line and points G and H along the top edge BA.
3. Rule lines NO, DE and CF parallel to BA. Mark position of M along DE.
4. Join H and M. Mark J 2cm [¾ in] from H along line HM. Join G and J, continuing line to I.
5. Rule IK at right angles to GJI.
6. Join K to E.
7. Cut along lines to separate pattern pieces for yoke, skirt and sleeve, cutting through fold of skirt and fold of yoke. Mark points M and E with notches.

NB The pieces you now have do not allow for seam turnings, hems, gathers or facings. These are added on the cutting-out guide, see Diagram 2.

POSITIONING THE PATTERN ON THE FABRIC

1. Lay fabric right side uppermost on a flat surface.
2. Fold one selvedge edge 30cm [12 in] towards the centre of the fabric, then fold the remaining edge over so selvedges meet.
3. Place back skirt on the wider side of folded fabric adding 10cm [4 in] to the right of centre back for gathers and facing, and 8cm [3 in] to lower edge for hem.
4. Place front skirt on other side with centre front 5cm [2 in] in from folded edge to allow for gathers; add 8cm [3 in] for hem.
5. Position yoke pieces twice on both sides of fabric, as shown in Diagram 2, with centre front edge ND to fold and shoulder edges GJ meeting.
6. When pattern pieces are in position, cut fabric so you have another piece 50cm × 130cm [20 in × 51 in]. Fold (see Diagram 2) and place sleeve patterns in position allowing 8cm [3 in] be-tween each piece for gathers and adding 7cm [2¾ in] for the hem.

TO CUT OUT

1. Chalk around the edge of each pattern piece and then cut out allowing 12.5mm [½ in] for seam turnings all round. In cutting the side edges of the hems (skirt and sleeves) go in slightly from the line of the pattern (see dotted lines in Diagram 2).
2. On the wrong side of the fabric use tailor's chalk to mark hem lines, centre front and centre back fold lines, facing fold lines and notches.

Continued on next page

Above: a close-up of the top-stitching which gives an attractive look to the yoke of the smock. This is the sleeved version but if you turn back to page 43 you can see the version without sleeves

TO SEW

1. Take one yoke piece and, using contrasting buttonhole thread, run 6 rows of topstitching 6mm [¼ in] apart starting first row 2cm [¾ in] in from neck edge. Chalk a line from O to N as a turning point guide at the corners if necessary.

2. Place remaining yoke piece (yoke facing) on to stitched yoke, right sides together, and stitch neck and armhole (no-sleeve version only) edges leaving MDM open for later insertion of skirt. Stitch centre back yoke edges DN encasing 2 tapes approx 3.5cm [1½ in] apart (see Diagram 3).

3. Turn yoke right side out (the tapes should now be on the outside for tying). Press.

4. Fold back skirt facings to wrong side along centre back fold line. Over-sew along both fold lines.

No-sleeve version only Sew back skirt pieces to front at sides. Sew

Diagram 1 PAINTING SMOCKS: PATTERN

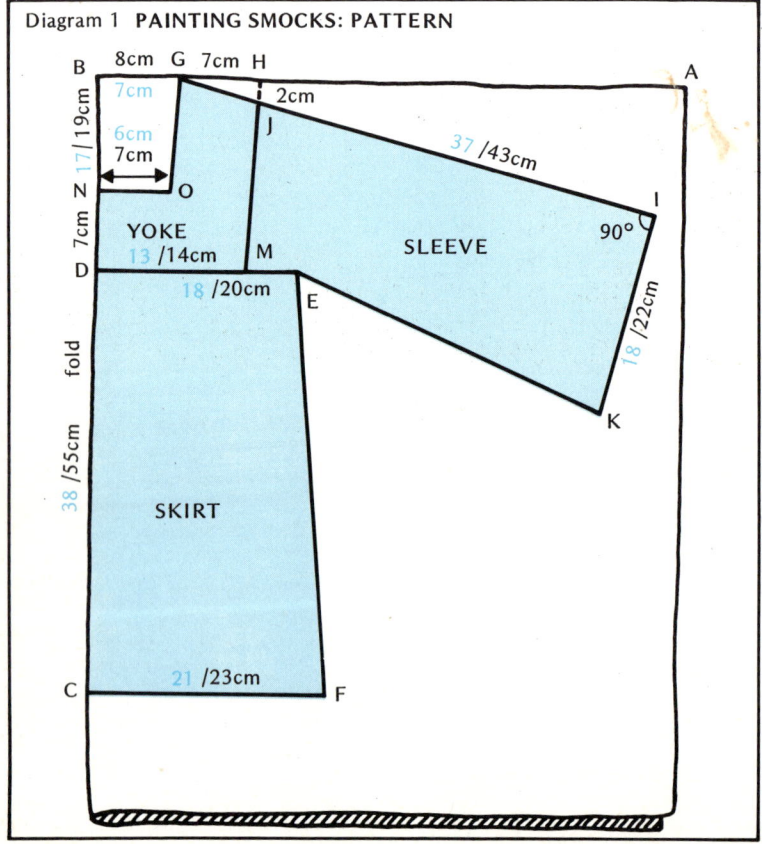

Diagram 2 PAINTING SMOCKS: CUTTING GUIDES

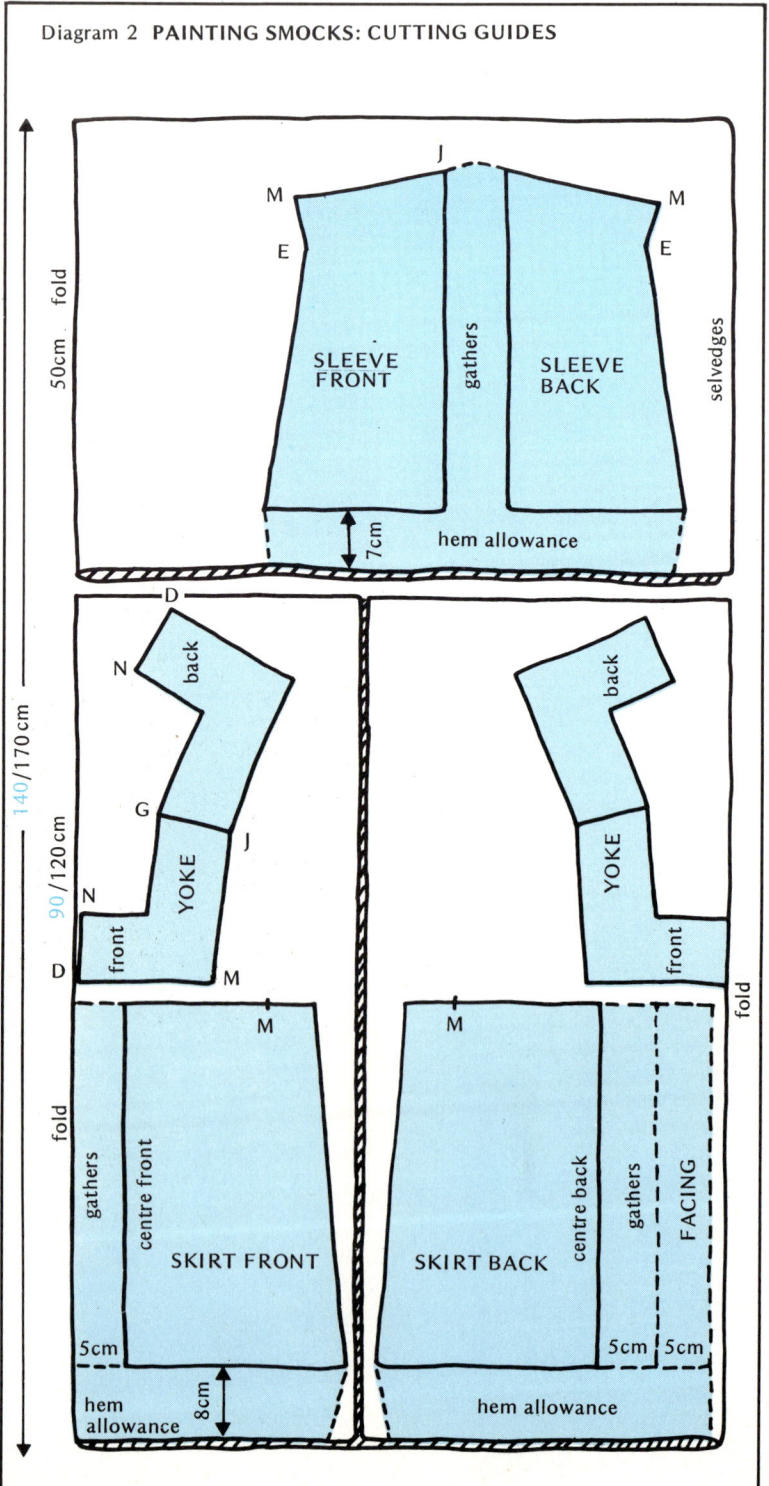

two rows of gathering stitches along top edge of skirt.

With right sides facing, insert gathered edges of skirt inside yoke opening, drawing gathers evenly to fit (Diagram 4). Pin and stitch. Press turnings towards facing.

Turn under remaining raw edge of yoke facing on wrong side and slip-stitch to previous line of stitching.

Sleeved version only Sew two rows of gathering stitches along

top edges of sleeves between points M and M. Adjust gathers to fit then stitch sleeves to front and back skirt pieces between M and E (see Diagram 5). Turn under remaining raw edge of yoke facing on wrong side and slip-stitch to previous line of stitching. Turn up hem on sleeve and run 6 rows of top-stitching 6mm [$\frac{1}{4}$ in] apart, leaving a gap of 2cm [$\frac{3}{4}$ in] in row of stitching near folded edge.

With right sides together, stitch

sleeve and side seams K to E to F. Press seam turnings open. Insert elastic and stitch ends to secure at sleeve seam. Close gap in top-stitching.

Both versions Open out centre back facing at lower edge and turn up hem. Fold back facings and slip-stitch in place.

Run 6 rows of top-stitching 6mm [$\frac{1}{4}$ in] apart around hem edge.

The diagrams on this page show you how the smocks are put together. Diagram 3 shows how the yoke is sewn on the wrong side to incorporate the ties; Diagram 4, how the skirt is sewn to the yoke; and Diagram 5, how the sleeved-version looks (wrong side) before the side seams are sewn. If making the no-sleeve version, the yoke and skirt side seams are sewn in a different way, so read the instructions carefully before you start

Diagram 3

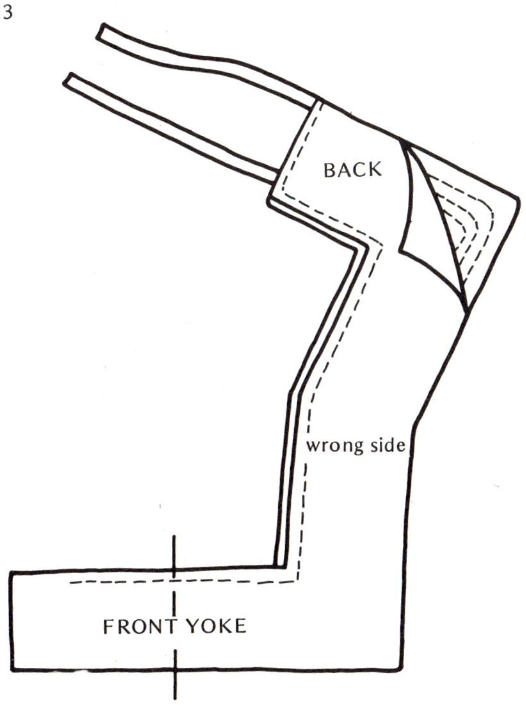

BACK

wrong side

FRONT YOKE

Diagram 4

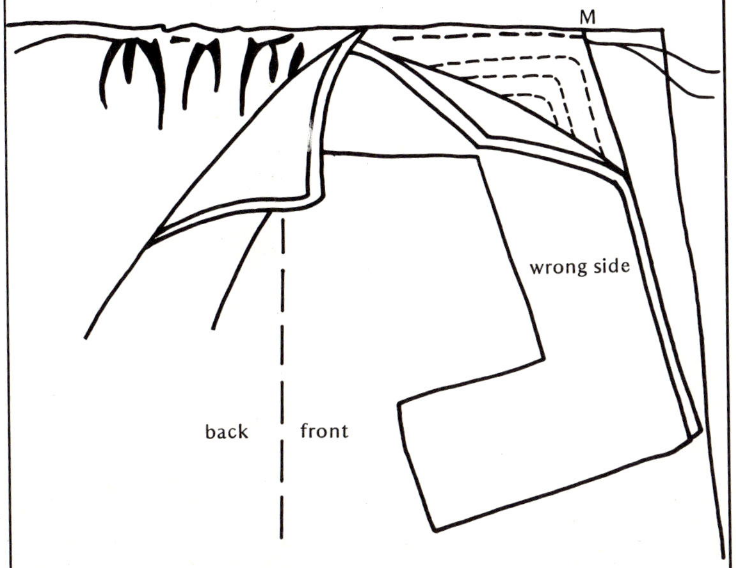

M

wrong side

back   front

Diagram 5

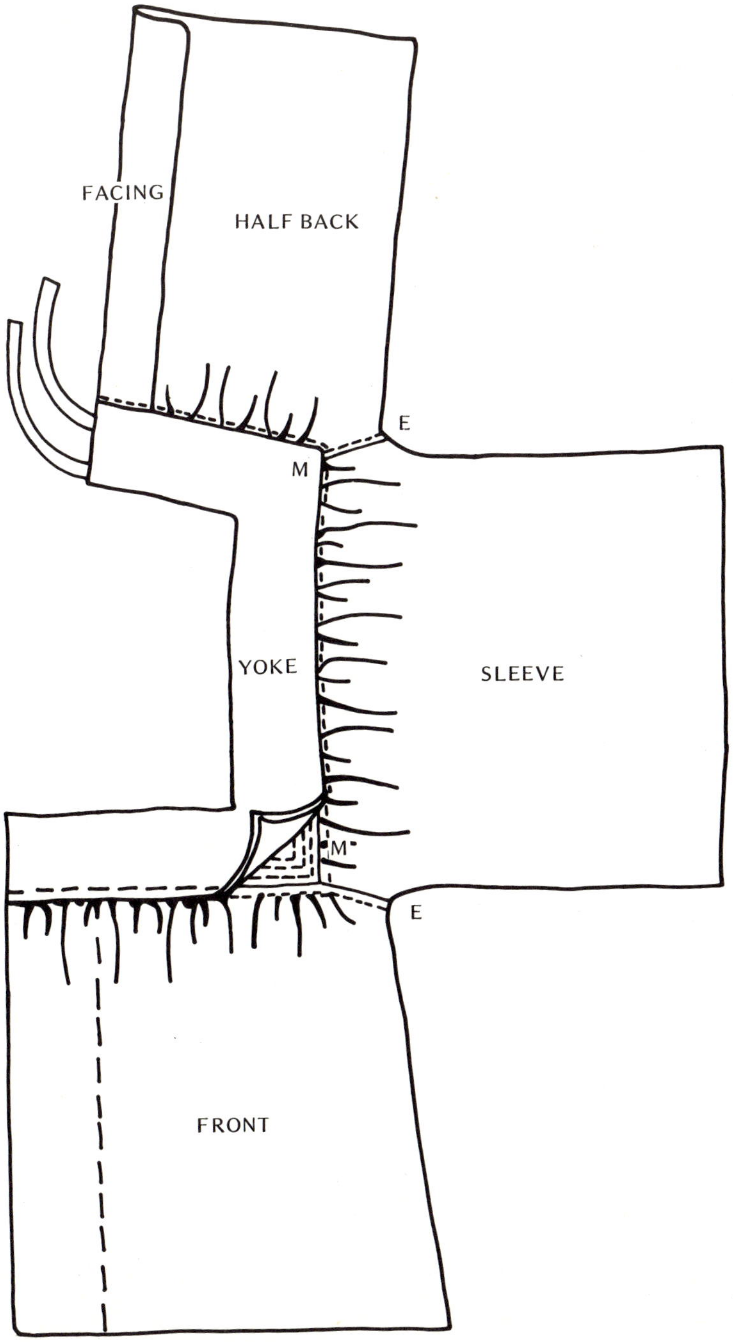

FACING

HALF BACK

E

M

YOKE

SLEEVE

M

E

FRONT

Set for the summer

Simple makes from towelling are easy to wear and easy to care for.

Beach top

6 to 12 years

The T-shirt shape, simply made from three pieces of fabric, suitable for either a girl or boy.

Materials 70cm [27½ in] stretch towelling 98cm [38½ in] wide; matching machine twist. You will need 10cm more (80cm/37½ in) for larger size.

Measurements To fit 66cm [26 in] and 81cm [32 in] chest loosely.

The shape's easily adapted to any size. You'll see from Diagrams 1 and 2 that you can get two different sizes from almost the same amount of fabric, though the sleeves of the larger one are shorter. Stretch towelling usually only comes in one width but other fabrics are less restrictive and the pieces can be cut to fit any measurements.

TO MAKE

1. Open out the material and cut an oblong 98cm × 32cm [38½ in × 12½ in] and two squares 38cm × 38cm [15 in × 15 in] (Diagram 1).*
2. Fold the oblong in half lengthways. Measure in 37cm [14½ in] from each edge along the fold. Cut the central 24cm [9½ in] to make a slit for the head (adjust if necessary). All round neckline turn under a 6mm [¼ in] hem (no need for two turns if using stretch towelling – it doesn't fray). Pin, tack and stitch, preferably using zig-zag stitch.
3. With right sides together, pin, tack and stitch front and back to top using 15mm [⅝ in] seam allowance (Diagram 3).
4. With right sides together, pin and tack sleeve and side seams using 15mm [⅝ in] seam allowance. Stitch all in one go, curving the stitching at underarms (Diagram 4). Clip at curves and trim excess.
5. Turn up small hems at bottom edge and sleeves and secure with a zig-zag stitch, or by hand. Remove tackings, turn to right side.

*For larger size, cut an oblong 98cm × 38cm [38½ in × 15 in] and two squares 40cm × 40cm [15¾ in × 15¾ in] (Diagram 2). Cut slit 28cm [11 in] for head (see step 2).

Left: the towelling makes for sunny summer days. The shorts' instructions are on page 48; bikini on page 50.
Below: diagrams for the Beach Top – easy enough for beginners
Opposite: the simple Beach Top

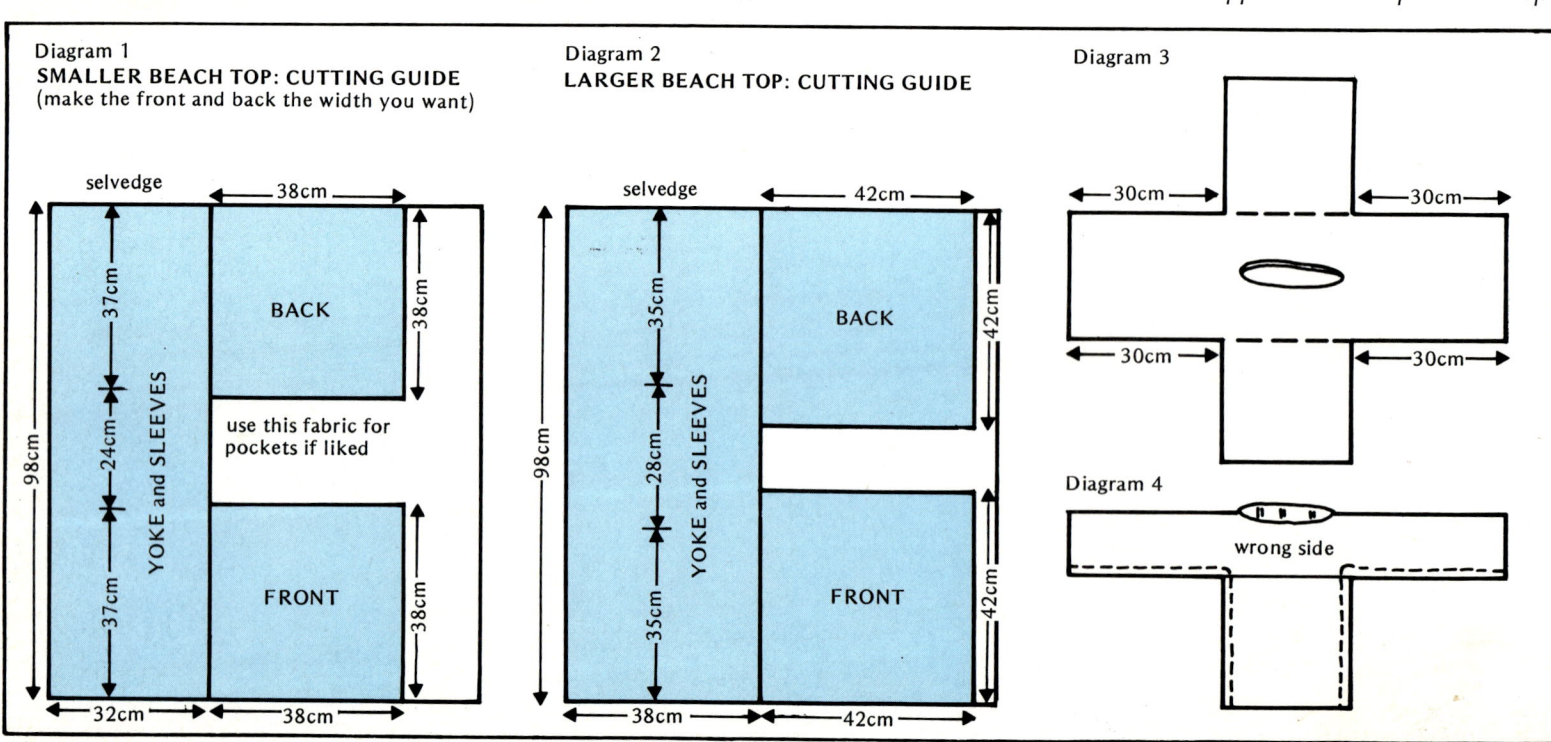

Diagram 1
SMALLER BEACH TOP: CUTTING GUIDE
(make the front and back the width you want)

selvedge
38cm
37cm
BACK
38cm
98cm
24cm
YOKE and SLEEVES
use this fabric for pockets if liked
37cm
FRONT
38cm
32cm
38cm

Diagram 2
LARGER BEACH TOP: CUTTING GUIDE

selvedge
42cm
35cm
BACK
42cm
98cm
28cm
YOKE and SLEEVES
35cm
FRONT
42cm
38cm
42cm

Diagram 3
30cm
30cm
30cm
30cm

Diagram 4
wrong side

Children's Clothes

Shorts

6 to 9 years

Very easy to make little shorts that you can adjust at the side and waist to fit several ages – good swimming trunks for boys, play shorts for girls.

Materials 50cm [20 in] fabric, 90cm [35½ in] wide; machine twist; elastic 2cm [¾ in] wide.

Measurements To fit up to 53cm [21 in] waist.

Note Seams are 15mm [⅝ in].

TO MAKE

1. Using squared paper make pattern pieces following Diagram 1 (1 square = 5cm).
2. Fold the fabric in half, right sides together and selvedges meeting. Pin pattern pieces on fabric then cut out (Diagram 2).
3. Right sides together, pin, tack and stitch centre front seam. For extra strength stitch again over first stitching. Clip curves. Right sides together, pin, tack and stitch centre back seam (stitch again for extra strength). Clip curves.
4. Right sides together stitch front to back at side seams (adjust here if necessary). Press all seams open.
5. Pin, tack and stitch inner leg seam. Press seam open.
6. For waistband, make a 6mm [¼ in] turning on to wrong side, then another turning of 2.5cm [1 in] to form casing. Pin and tack then stitch close to casing edge leaving a gap of 2m [¾ in] at a side seam. Cut length of elastic slightly less than child's waist measurement and thread through the casing with a safety-pin. Stitch ends of elastic together. Close the gap in the casing.
7. Turn up hems at leg edges and stitch by machine or hand.

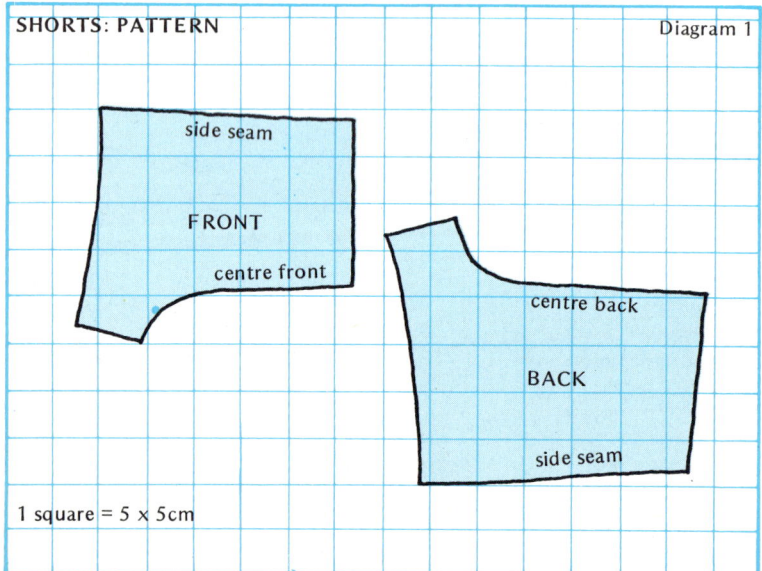

SHORTS: PATTERN — Diagram 1

side seam
FRONT
centre front
centre back
BACK
side seam

1 square = 5 x 5cm

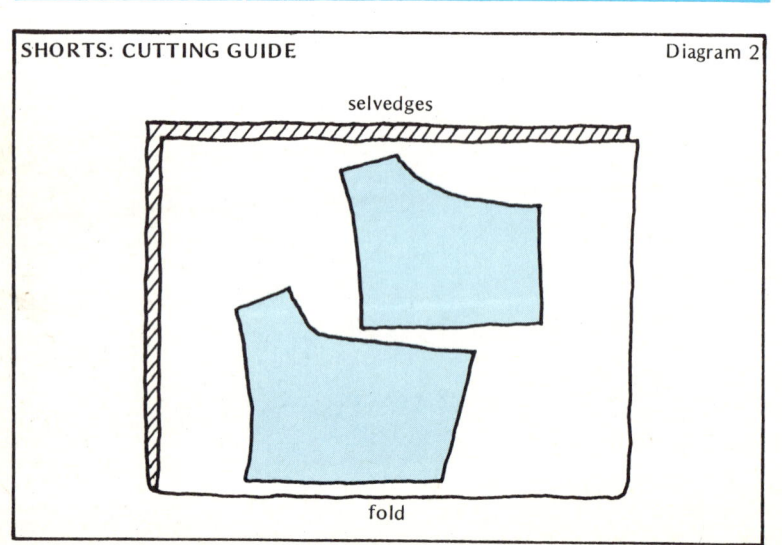

SHORTS: CUTTING GUIDE — Diagram 2

selvedges

fold

Bikini and scarf set

6 to 16 years

Even the kids could make this set it's so simple! The little scarf, made with leftover fabric, can be worn round the shoulders when the sun gets too hot.

Materials 60(70)cm [23½(27½) in] stretch towelling 98cm [38½ in] wide; matching machine twist; packet elastic 6mm [¼ in] wide.

Note Larger size ·is in brackets. Square brackets contain imperial measurements. All seams are 15mm [⅝ in].

> For sizes between ages 6 and 12, cut your pattern halfway between the two, and adjust the elastic at waist and legs.

TO MAKE

1. Using squared paper make patterns from Diagram 1 (1 square = 5cm) for bikini pants.
2. Fold fabric as shown in Diagram 2 and cut out pants, top (Diagrams 3A and 3B) and tab. Cut two bias strips 2cm × 84cm [¾ in × 33 in] long. From remaining fabric cut a triangle as shown for scarf.
3. To make pants, place right sides together and pin, tack and stitch side seams. Stitch again close to first seam for extra strength. Trim seam close to second stitching. Stitch crotch as for side seams.

4. To form casings, turn waist and leg edges under 6mm [¼ in], then turn over a further 12.5mm [½ in]. Stitch close to edge of casing leaving small gaps. Cut length of elastic slightly smaller than hip measurement and insert into casing. Stitch ends together, and close gap. For leg edges cut two pieces of elastic 41(46)cm [16(18) in] long and insert into casings. Adjust to fit comfortably, then stitch ends together. Close gaps. Remove all tackings.
5. Cut one end of each bias strip at an angle. With right sides together join as shown in Diagrams 4A and 4B. With right sides together stitch along the length of the strip as close to the edge as possible. Turn strip inside out to form a rouleau.
6. Make small turning all round tab and stitch.

7. To make the top, turn under 6mm [¼ in] along both edges and machine stitch using a zig-zag. To make the casing at the sides, turn under 6mm [¼ in] then a further 15mm [⅝ in] and stitch by hand. Wrap tab round centre of top so that it draws it in and then sew ends together at back. Insert rouleau through casings (Diagram 5). Adjust length, trim off any excess and sew ends neatly.
8. Turn under 6mm [¼ in] all round scarf. Sew with a zig-zag stitch.

Opposite page: the easy-to-make bikini and scarf for two sizes
This page: the pattern, cutting guide and diagrams you'll need

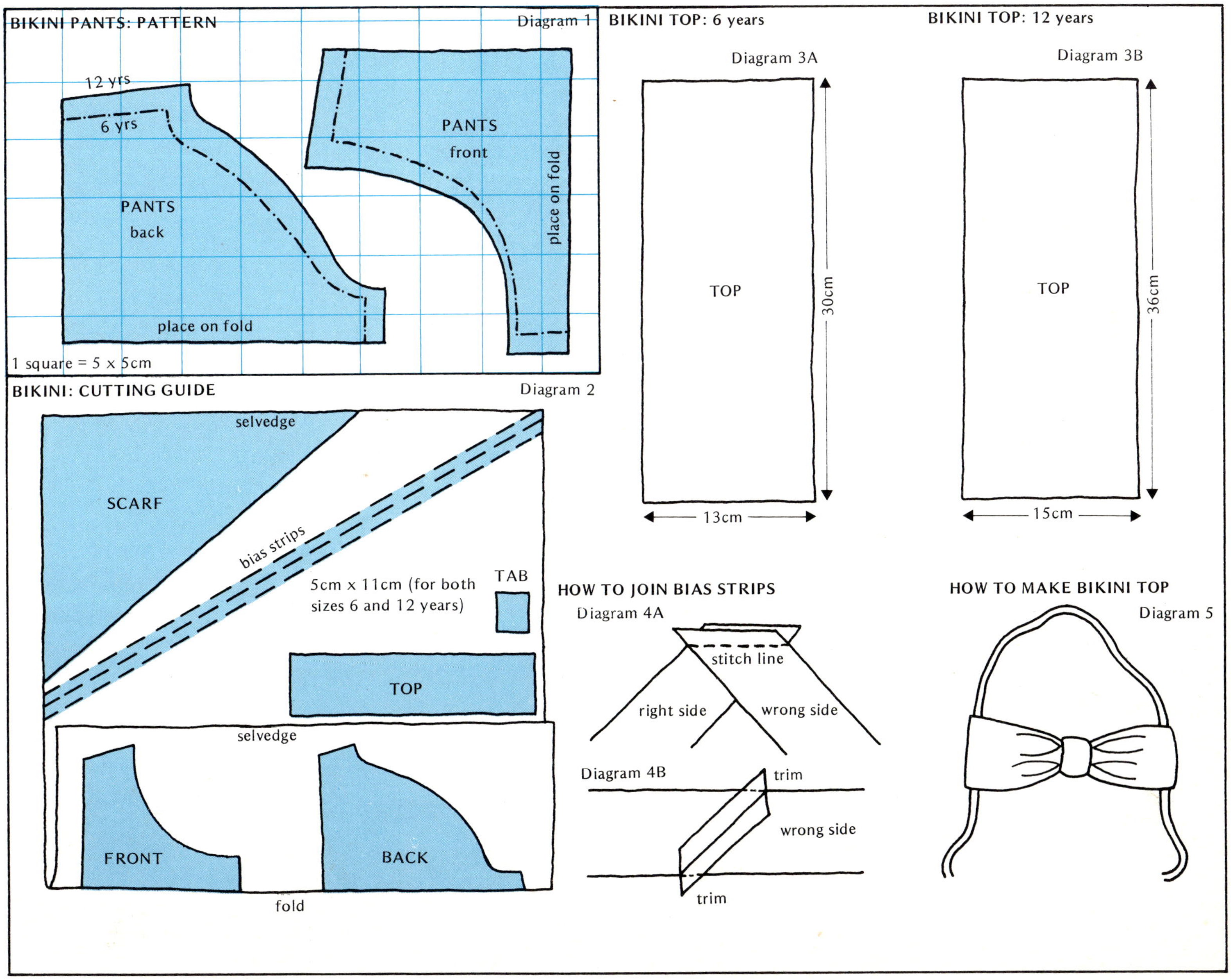

BIKINI PANTS: PATTERN   Diagram 1

12 yrs
6 yrs
PANTS back
place on fold
PANTS front
place on fold
1 square = 5 x 5cm

BIKINI: CUTTING GUIDE   Diagram 2

selvedge
SCARF
bias strips
5cm x 11cm (for both sizes 6 and 12 years)
TAB
TOP
selvedge
FRONT
BACK
fold

BIKINI TOP: 6 years   Diagram 3A

TOP
30cm
13cm

BIKINI TOP: 12 years   Diagram 3B

TOP
36cm
15cm

HOW TO JOIN BIAS STRIPS   Diagram 4A

stitch line
right side
wrong side

Diagram 4B
trim
wrong side
trim

HOW TO MAKE BIKINI TOP   Diagram 5

Children's Clothes

Ruched skirt

5 years to teenage

Here is a quick-to-sew pretty skirt that's made in a summery border print cotton. You could make a warmer version in perhaps a lightweight brushed rayon for winter. It's not a style that's restricted to 5 year olds so we've included measurements for a larger version.

Materials 1 metre [39½ in] of 90cm [35½ in] wide fabric, with or without borders (for the larger size 1 metre of 130cm [51 in] wide border design fabric, or 150cm [59 in] of 90cm [35½ in] wide fabric WITHOUT a border design); 90cm [35½ in] of contrasting bias binding (180cm [71 in] for larger size); a reel of shirring elastic; matching machine twist; squared pattern paper.

Measurements To fit waist size 48/53cm [19/21 in]. For a larger size that will fit sizes 8–12 (56–66cm [22–26 in] waist), measure a rectangle 32cm wide × 60cm [12½ in × 23½ in] long. To shape the side seams, take 5cm [2 in] off either side of the top (waist) edge. Curve the hem edge very slightly as shown for child's size. Make the waistband 44cm × 12cm [17½ in × 5 in] – this will be cut twice.

TO MAKE YOUR PATTERN
The skirt is in four equal pieces. Transfer shapes in Diagram 1 on to squared paper and cut out.

POSITIONING THE PATTERN ON THE FABRIC
Fold fabric in half lengthways, selvedges meeting and with borders on top of each other. With a border design fabric place the skirt panels twice widthways so that the lower edge is 4cm [1½ in] (hem allowance) from the selvedges (see Diagram 2). On plain fabric, or fabric without a border design, place the skirt panels twice lengthways on the straight grain. Place the waistband to the fold, as shown (place to the fold twice for the larger sizes).

TO CUT OUT
Chalk around the edge of each pattern piece.
Cut out pattern pieces allowing

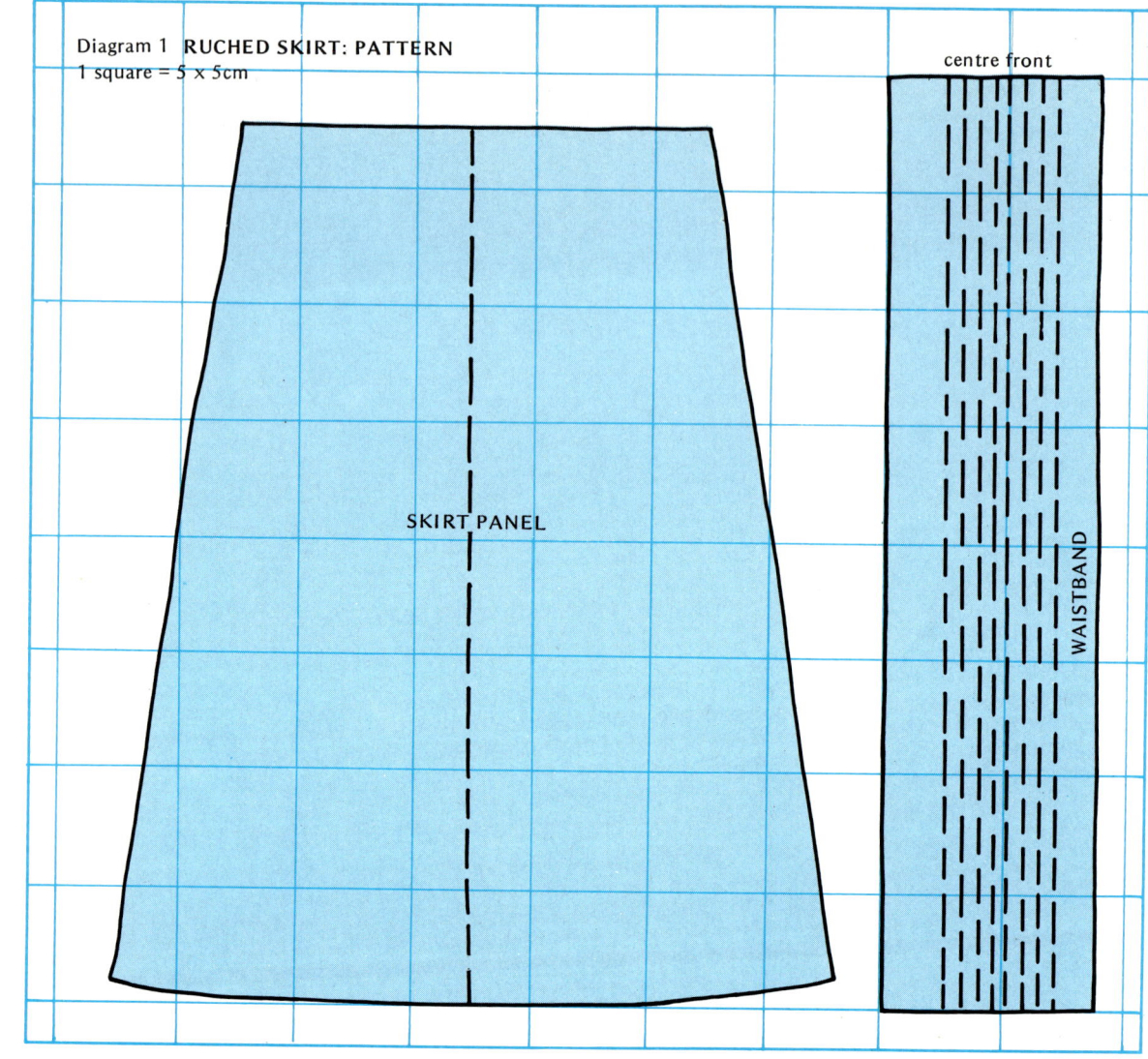

Diagram 1 RUCHED SKIRT: PATTERN
1 square = 5 × 5cm

SKIRT PANEL

centre front

WAISTBAND

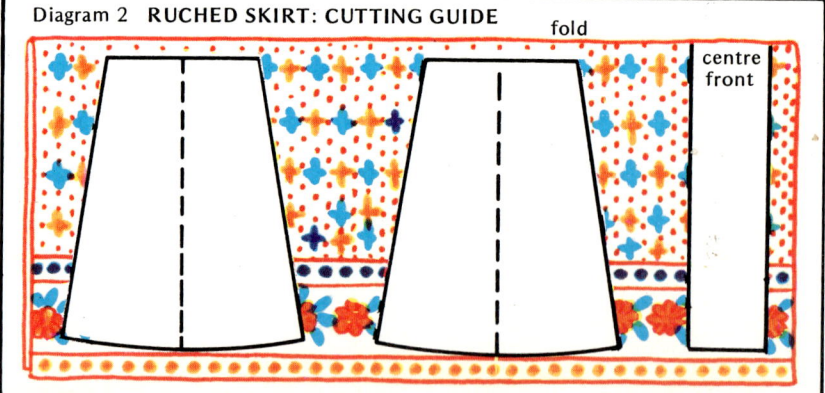

Diagram 2 RUCHED SKIRT: CUTTING GUIDE

fold

centre front

Right: the finished Ruched Skirt made from a flower-scattered border fabric Above and left: pattern and cutting guide

6mm [¼ in] extra for seam turnings at skirt side and waist edges, and at waistband ends. Mark centres.

TO SEW
1. With right sides together, stitch three of the four skirt seams. Over-sew raw edges to neaten. Press seam turnings open.
2. Join the two waistband lengths for larger size.
3. Fold ribbon in half lengthways, wrong sides meeting, and bind both long edges of waistband.
4. Chalk a line 2cm [¾ in] in from lower bound edge of waistband. With wrong side of waistband to right side of skirt, pin waistband to skirt along chalk line.
5. With the shirring elastic in the bobbin of your machine and machine twist on the top, stitch waistband to skirt along chalk line.
6. Continue to stitch a further 7 rows (11 for larger sizes), to gather waistband. If necessary draw up

elastic threads at the end of each row to tighten. Tie all ends to secure.
7. With right sides together, stitch remaining skirt seam from top waistband edge to hem. Over-sew raw edges to neaten.
8. Turn up hem and catch-stitch in place.

Pinafore dress

6 to 8 years

This practical, loose-fitting pinafore dress in hardwearing denim makes a very useful everyday dress for any young girl. You can either decorate it with a machined zig-zag stitch in a contrasting colour or a long straight stitch using contrasting buttonhole thread.

Measurements To fit midriff 70cm [27½ in]; length 57cm [22½ in]. To make a larger size add 15mm [⅝ in] to side seams when making the pattern.

Materials 85cm [33½ in] of 140cm [55 in] wide denim fabric or 160cm [63 in] of 90cm [35½ in] wide fabric; matching machine twist and contrasting thread.

TO MAKE THE PATTERN

First check your child's measurements against the pattern, eg, length and underarm. Add or subtract 15mm [⅝ in] at side seams where necessary. Rule 5cm [2 in] squares on to the sheet of paper, or use graph paper to that scale, then reproduce the pattern exactly as shown in Diagram 1, below.
Cut 1 dress front and 1 dress back. From sheet of tissue paper cut the facings (1 front neck facing, 1 back neck facing, 1 front armhole facing and 1 back armhole facing) by following the lines for the neck and armhole edges of the dress and the corresponding dotted lines.

TO CUT OUT

With Sellotape join patterns of front and back armhole facings at the shoulders edge to edge. Fold fabric in half lengthways with right sides together. Place front neck facing to the fold and remaining pieces on the straight grain as shown (Diagram 2).
Cut out each piece adding 15mm [⅝ in] allowance to neck, armhole, centre front, centre back and side edges, and 6cm [2½ in] to hem edge (or more if preferred). Mark notches.

TO SEW

1. With right sides together, stitch centre front dress seam. Press seam turnings open and work decorative stitch either side of seamline.
2. With right sides together, stitch front to backs at shoulders.
3. With right sides together, stitch front neck facing to back neck facings at shoulders.
4. With right sides together and matching shoulder seams, centre fronts and centre back edges, stitch neck facing to neck.

5. With right sides together and raw edges level, stitch armhole facings to armholes (Diagram 3).
6. Over-sew inner curved raw edges of neck and armhole facings. Turn all facings to wrong side, overlap at shoulders and press (Diagram 3). Catch stitch at shoulders if liked.
7. With right sides together stitch side seams incorporating armhole facings and pockets as shown in Diagram 4. Clip into seam turnings at corners of pockets. Press pockets towards dress front. Press side seam turnings open.
8. Secure pockets in position by pinning then stitching seam allowance to dress front with two rows of decorative stitches (see photograph).
9. With right sides together, stitch centre back seam incorporating back neck facings.
10. Catch-stitch inner edges of neck and armhole facings to underarm, centre back and centre front seam turnings.
11. Finish neck and armhole edges with decorative stitching.
12. Repeat decorative stitching either side of back seam as for front if liked.
13. Turn up hem. Press.

Opposite: contrasting topstitching adds a bright touch to this practical but pretty pinafore

Diagram 2 PINAFORE DRESS: CUTTING GUIDE

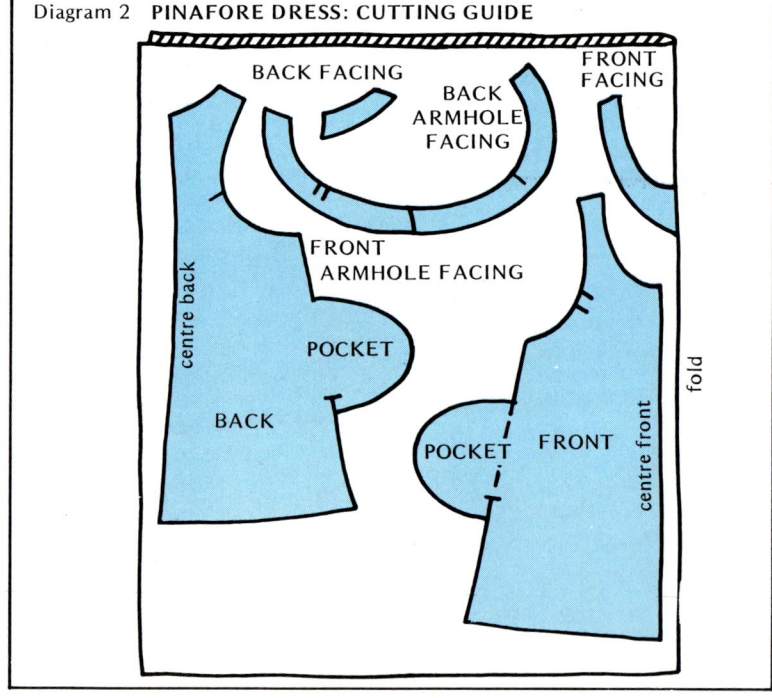

Diagram 1 PINAFORE DRESS: PATTERN
1 square = 5 x 5cm

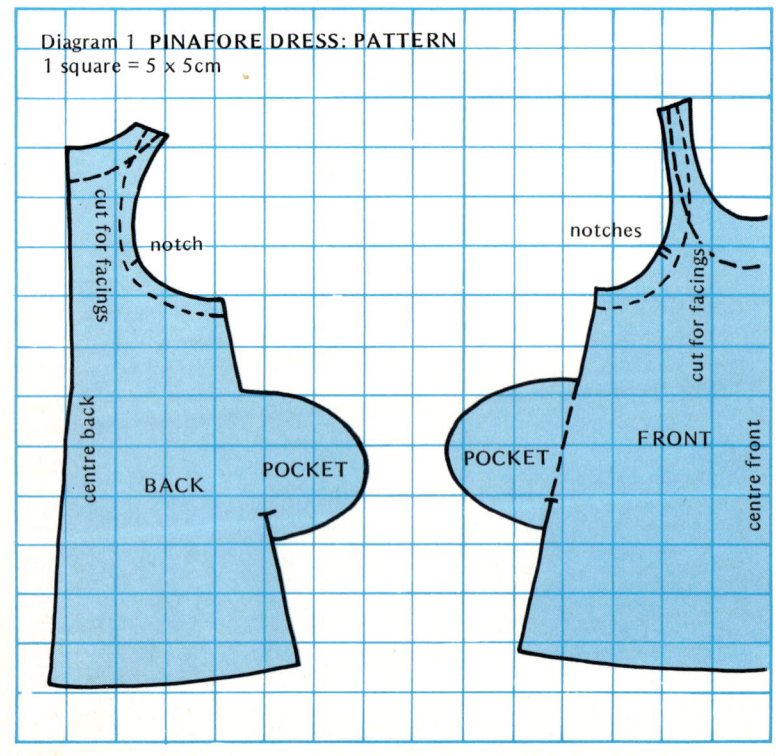

Diagram 3

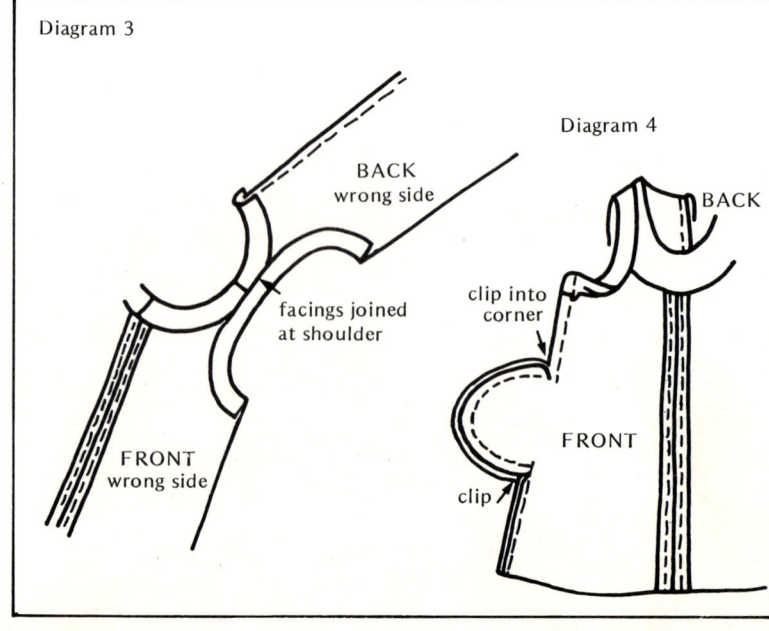

Dressing gown

7 to 9 years

A traditional garment that goes on being appreciated and the style suits light wool, cotton or towelling. Do remember that it should fit loosely – see Measurements for how to make a little larger.

Materials 2.30m [90½ in] of 140cm [55 in] wide fabric; matching machine twist.

Measurements Actual size chest 94cm [37 in]; length 97cm [38 in]. If you want to make it bigger you can add up to 5cm [2 in] to the centre back but add the same amount to seams AC on the front pieces and facings.

TO MAKE

1. Make patterns on squared paper (1 square = 5cm) following Diagram 1. You will need to make extra patterns of the front facing, the pocket and the belt.
2. Fold fabric in half lengthways and cut out pieces as shown in Diagram 2, adding 15mm [⅝ in] extra on all edges for seams (more if you like at the hem) and placing back piece to the fold. When cutting extra belt form "V" at one end. If using checked material place pockets (4 needed) at an angle so you have a contrast. Place the front facing so it has the same check pattern as the front piece.
3. Right sides together, pin, tack and stitch facings of front pieces together across seam AC (Diagram 3) and pin, tack and stitch fronts to back piece at shoulder seams. Clip corner where shoulder seam meets facing. Press seams open.
4. Right sides together, pin, tack and stitch fronts to back at side seams. Press seams open.
5. Fold facing so right sides are meeting and sew across back neck seam (Diagram 4).
6. Turn under seam allowance all round back belt and tack. Position centrally on dotted line (Diagram 4). Pin, tack and stitch in place along two long sides, leaving short ends open.
7. Right sides together, pin, tack and stitch underarm seam in each sleeve. Press seams open,

turn sleeves to right side.

8. Right sides together, matching underarm seams to side seams, pin, tack and stitch sleeves to armhole openings, easing fabric if necessary. Neaten seams, press.

9. Right sides together, pin, tack and stitch seam AC on front facings. Right sides together stitch front facings to fronts round outer edge matching centre back seams. Turn facing to inside and tack around outer edge to flatten. Turn under 15mm [⅝ in] all round free edge of facing and stitch.

10. Turn up hem at bottom edge cutting away bulk under facings at corners if necessary. Catch-stitch hemmed free edge of facing to give a neat look covering first seam at back neck as you sew. Remove tacking. Press.

11. Fold front ties in half, right sides together, then pin, tack and stitch along long edges and angled ends. Turn through to right side and press.

12. Join one front belt to each end of back belt by slipping square end of front ties into short ends of back belt. Top-stitch through all thicknesses. Sew a second row of stitching to secure front ties. Remove tacking.

13. To make pockets, take 2 pieces and, right sides together, sew round one short and two long sides. Turn to right side. Do same with second two pieces. Position pockets one on each front where shown in Diagram 1 (DE) with open edges towards hem. Turn in seam allowance and pin. Top-stitch pockets down sides and across bottom, stitching close to outer edge. Stitch a second row at bottom edge.

14. Turn up hem at lower edges of sleeves and hem in place on wrong side. Press garment well.

To give your work a professional finish, always press each piece as you go. After making seams, pink or hem them before pressing. Always remember to cut off threads and to remove tackings so the inside looks as tidy as the outside.

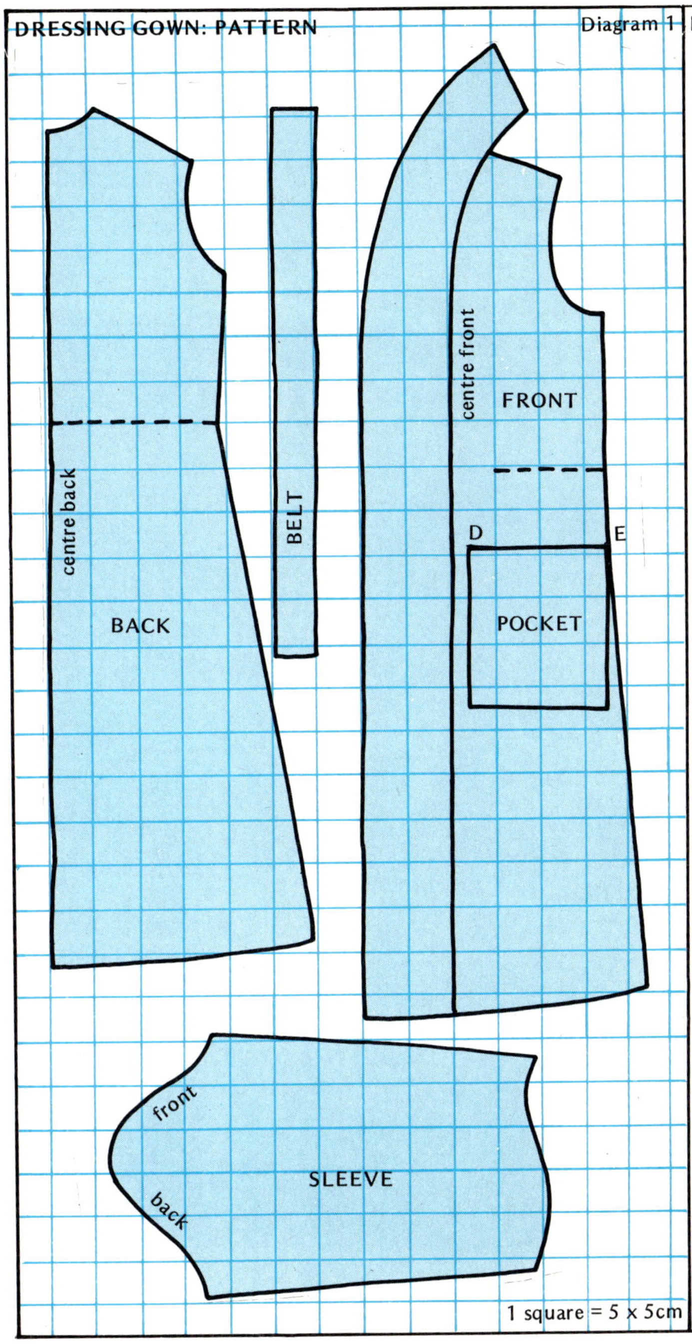

DRESSING GOWN: PATTERN   Diagram 1

centre back
BACK
BELT
centre front
FRONT
POCKET
D   E
front
back
SLEEVE

1 square = 5 x 5cm

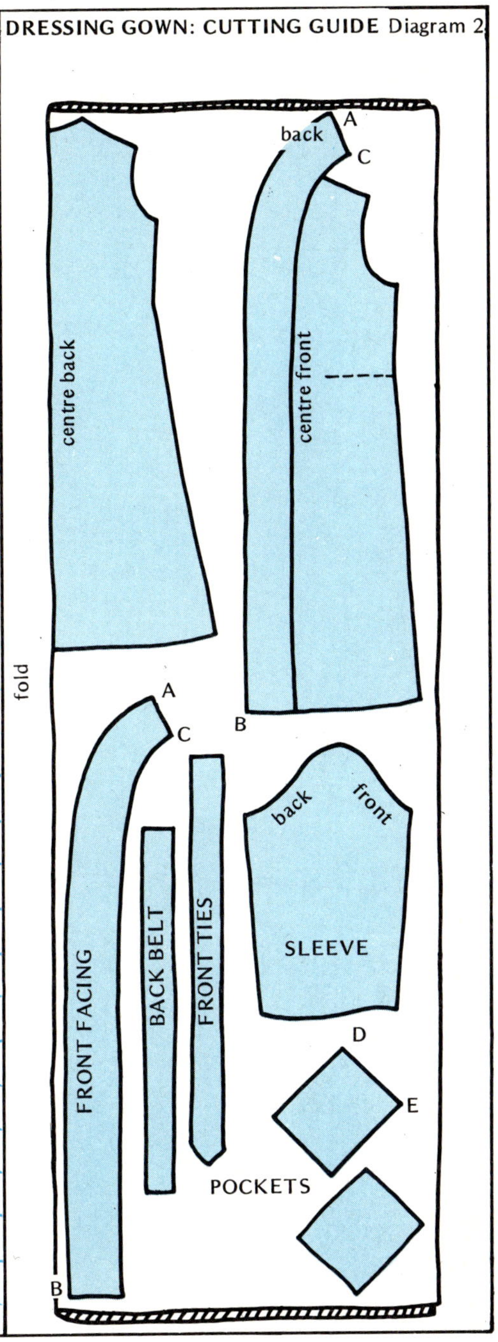

DRESSING GOWN: CUTTING GUIDE Diagram 2

back A
C
centre back
centre front
fold
A
C B
FRONT FACING
BACK BELT
FRONT TIES
back front
SLEEVE
D
E
POCKETS
B

Diagram 3   Diagram 4

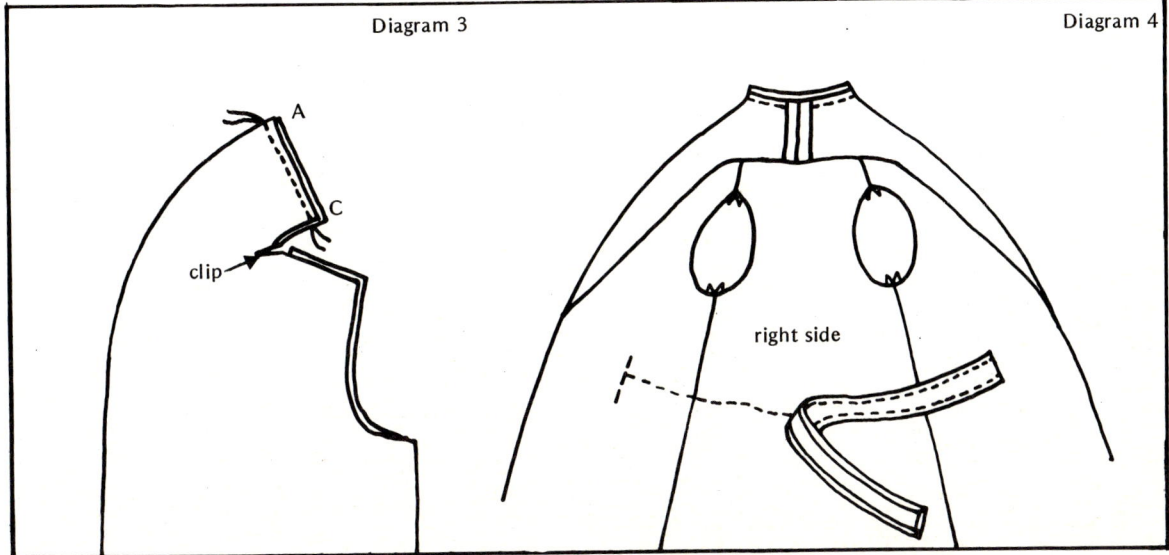

A
C
clip
right side

Dress and hooded coat

7 to 9 years

Make them to match if she'd like an ensemble or make them as separate garments. The dress can be short sleeved, and if you like you can add decorative edging such as braid or ricrac (see how pretty it looks in the picture on page 60).

Materials Coat: 1.80m [71 in] of 140cm [55 in] wide fabric; 2.30m [90½ in] of 90cm [35½ in] wide fabric for lining; 60cm [24 in] open-ended zip; matching machine twist for both fabrics. Dress: 2m [79 in] of 90cm [35½ in] wide fabric; 40cm [16 in] long zip; matching machine twist; 2 small buttons.

Measurements Coat: actual size 88cm [34½ in] chest, 75cm [29½ in] length. Dress: actual size 74cm [29 in] chest, 75cm [29½ in] length. Both hem length and sleeve length are adjustable. To make one size larger add 15mm [⅝ in] to all seams.

Note All seams measure 15mm [⅝ in] and must be added when cutting out. Square brackets contain imperial measurements.

TO MAKE COAT

1. Using squared paper (1 square = 5cm) make patterns following Diagram 1.
2. Fold main fabric in half length-ways and cut out patterns (Diagram 2) adding 15mm [⅝ in] extra on all edges for seams, plus 8cm [3 in] to lower edges of front and back pieces, and 3cm [1¼ in] to lower edges of sleeves. Place back piece to fold when cutting out.
3. Right sides together, pin, tack and stitch back to fronts at side seams. Press open.
4. Right sides together, pin, tack and stitch each front sleeve to one back sleeve, matching at points A. Press seams open. Right sides together, pin, tack and stitch each underarm seam in sleeve pieces. Press seams open. Turn up 3cm [1¼ in] to wrong side at lower edge of each sleeve. Pin and tack in place. Turn sleeves through to right side.

5. Right sides together, pin, tack and stitch each sleeve into each armhole opening (making sure back sleeves face to back and front sleeves face to front) and matching at points B and C. Neaten seams and press open.

6. Right sides together, pin, tack and stitch front facings to centre fronts, stitching down front and across facing at neck edge, pivoting stitching at corner. Neaten seam and turn facings through to wrong side. Cut down into seam at top edges where facings end, so that edges of neck lie flat. Press.

7. Turn up hem cutting away bulk under facing if necessary. Slip-stitch in place.

8. Right sides together, pin, tack and stitch darts in each hood piece. Right sides together, pin, tack and stitch hood pieces together around curved edges. Neaten seam and press open. Turn hood through to right side. Turn under 15mm [$\frac{5}{8}$ in] to wrong side round face edge of hood and catch-stitch in place.

9. Right sides together, pin, tack and stitch neck edge of hood to neck edge of coat, matching front edge of hood to front sleeve seams. Neaten seams and press open.

10. Using patterns for Coat (omit front facings throughout) cut out lining pieces following Diagram 3, adding 15mm [$\frac{5}{8}$ in] extra for seams all round (including centre back at fold).

11. Make up lining in the same way as Coat. Turn in 15mm [$\frac{5}{8}$ in] to wrong side on lower edges of sleeves, up fronts and around hood; pin and tack in place.

12. Turn coat through to wrong

Continued on next page

Opposite page: the coat zipped up against the chilly winds
Right: the lining makes a nice contrast at the front of the hood

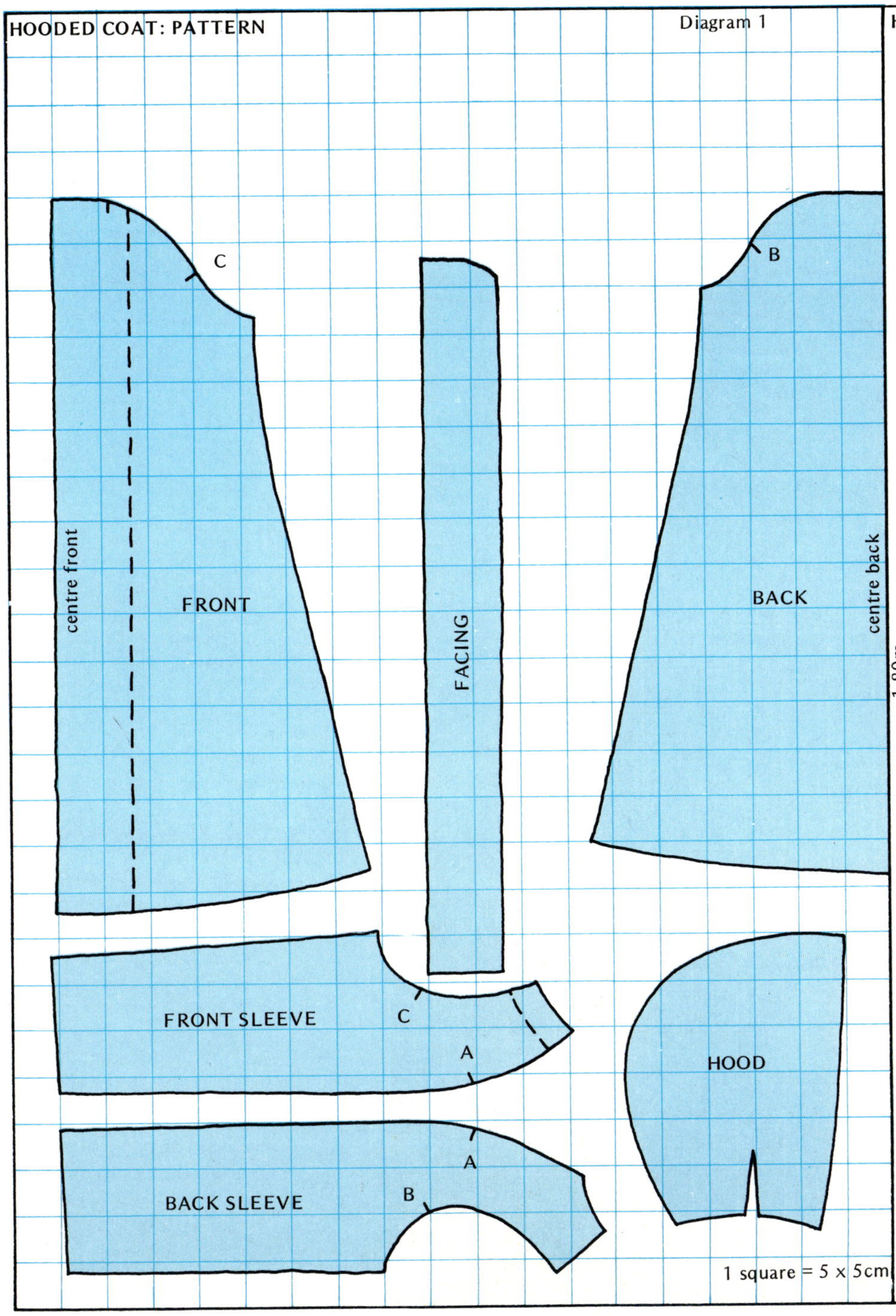

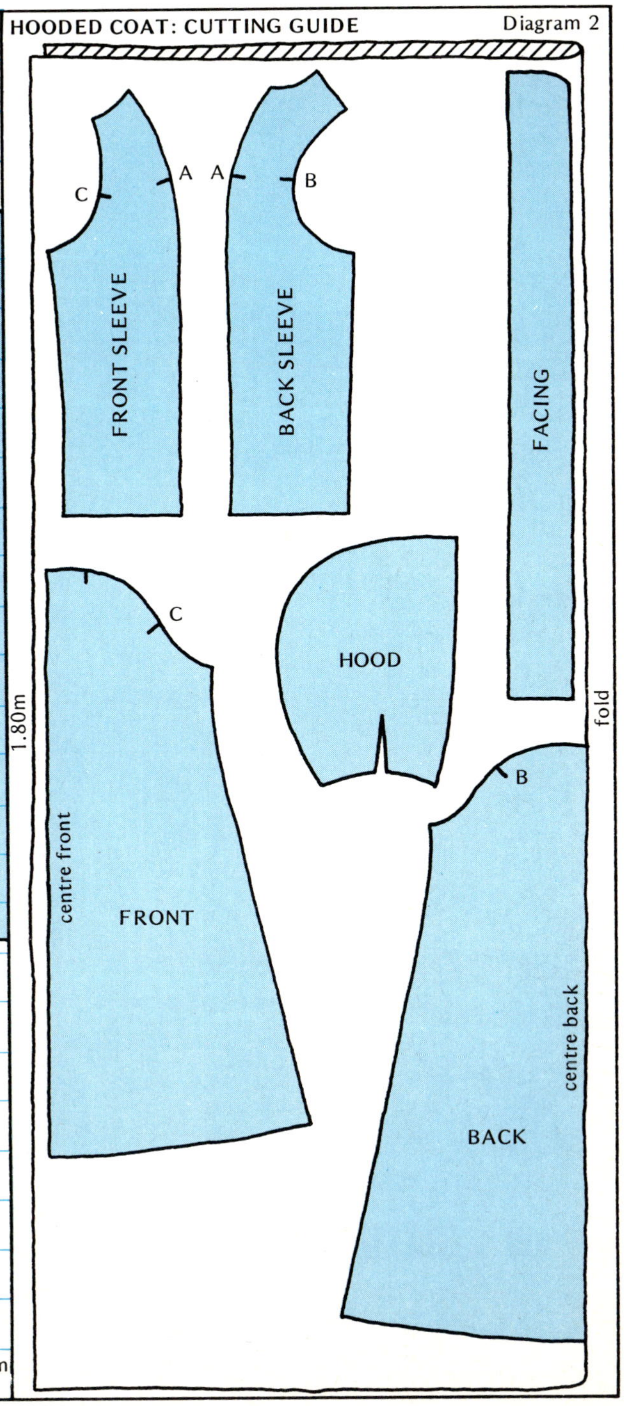

HOODED COAT: PATTERN — Diagram 1

centre front
FRONT
C
FACING
BACK
centre back
B
FRONT SLEEVE
C
A
BACK SLEEVE
A
B
HOOD

1 square = 5 x 5cm

HOODED COAT: CUTTING GUIDE — Diagram 2

C A A B
FRONT SLEEVE
BACK SLEEVE
FACING
C
HOOD
1.80m
centre front
FRONT
B
centre back
BACK
fold

Hooded coat . . . continued

side and lining to right side. Pull lining on over coat (Diagram 4). Pin and tack lining in place at lower edges of sleeves, up front facings and around hood then slip-stitch in place by hand. Turn up and stitch hem at lower edge of lining. Turn coat to right side.
13. Pin, tack and stitch open-ended zip in place between centre fronts matching top of zip to neck edge. Press.

HOODED COAT LINING: CUTTING GUIDE   Diagram 3

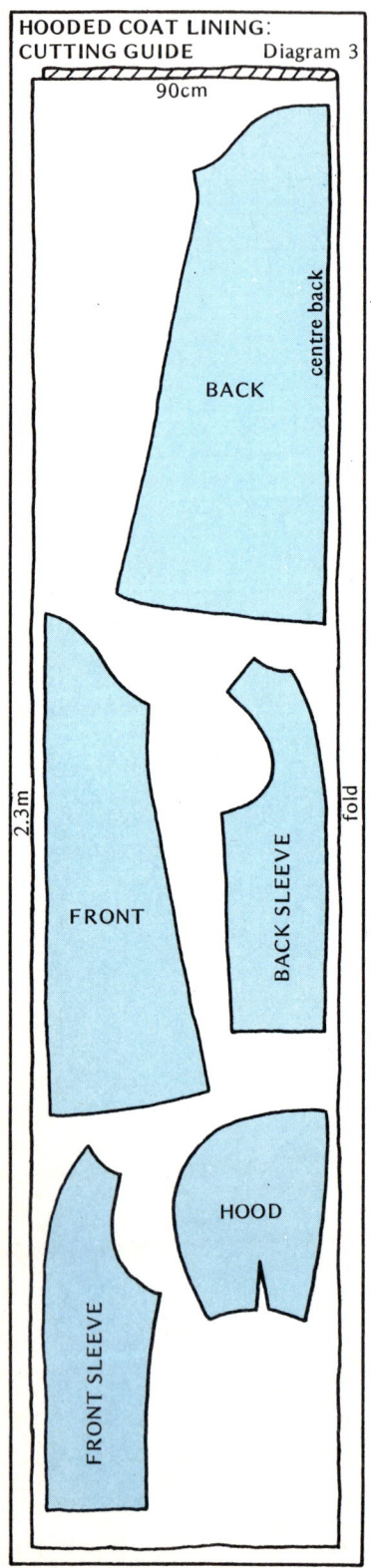

90cm

BACK

centre back

FRONT

BACK SLEEVE

fold

2.3m

FRONT SLEEVE

HOOD

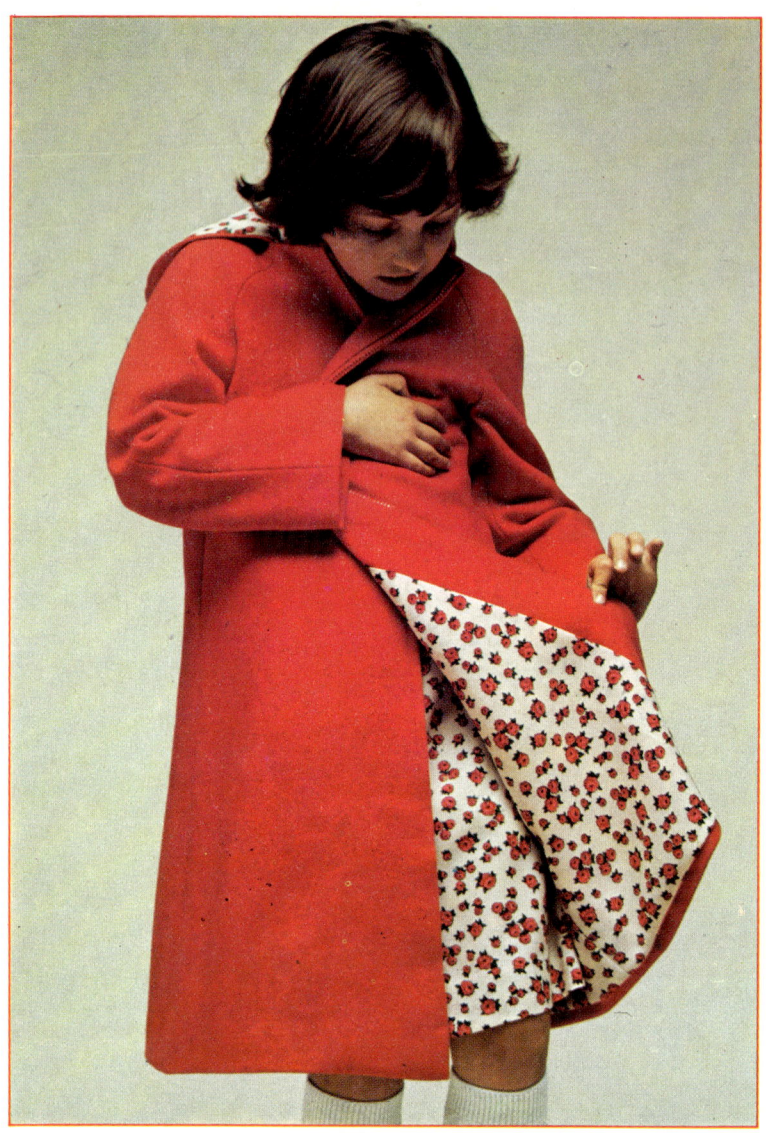

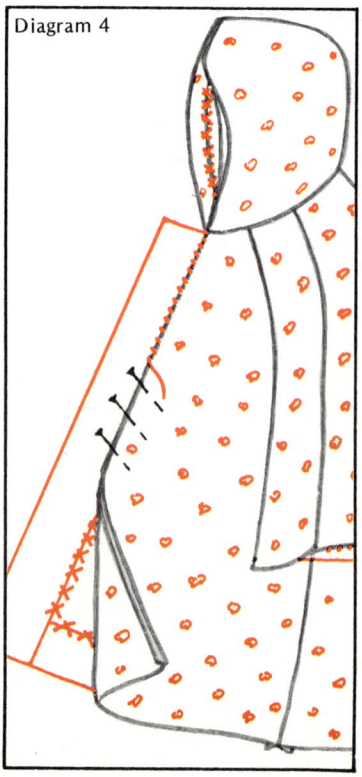

Diagram 4

Below: short-sleeved version is trimmed at neck and cuff
Right: the long-sleeved dress

DRESS: CUTTING GUIDE
Diagram 6

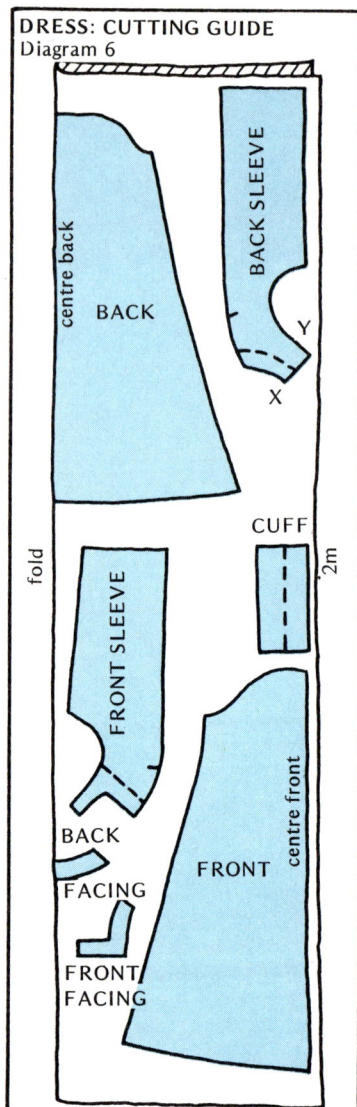

centre back

BACK

BACK SLEEVE

Y

X

fold

FRONT SLEEVE

CUFF

2m

BACK FACING

FRONT

centre front

FRONT FACING

TO MAKE DRESS

1. Make patterns on squared paper (1 square = 5cm) following Diagram 5. For short sleeves cut where indicated and add 5cm [2 in] to cuff length (make this larger or smaller according to the child's upper arm measurement).
2. Fold fabric in half lengthways and cut out pieces as shown in Diagram 6, adding 15mm [⅝ in] on all edges for seams plus 8cm [3 in] to lower edges of front and back pieces for hems. Place back piece and back facing to fold when cutting out.
3. Right sides together, pin, tack and stitch back to fronts at side seams. Press seams open.
4. Right sides together, pin, tack and stitch each front sleeve to one back sleeve at underarm and top but leave 5cm [2 in] open at cuff edge of top seams (long *and* short sleeves). Turn sleeves through to right side then right sides facing, join them together at the back, at seam XY. Press open.

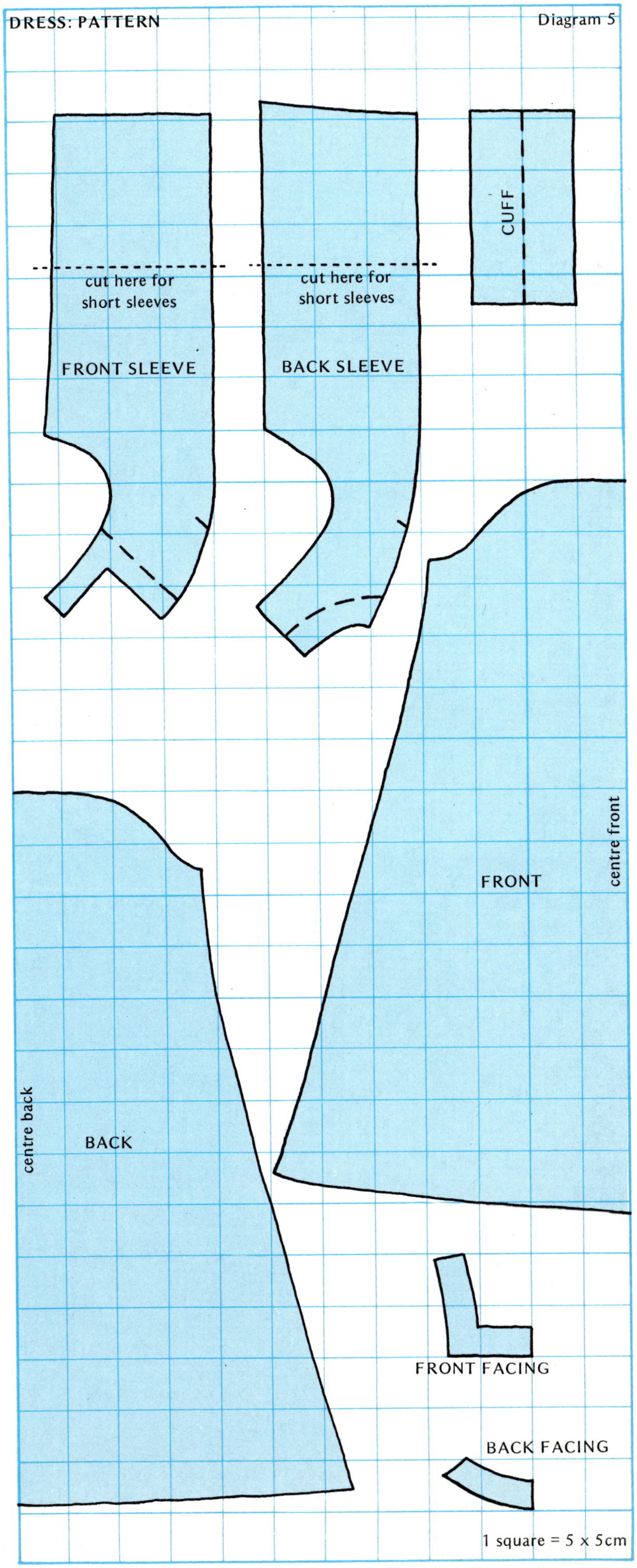

DRESS: PATTERN   Diagram 5

CUFF

cut here for short sleeves   cut here for short sleeves

FRONT SLEEVE   BACK SLEEVE

centre front

FRONT

centre back   BACK

FRONT FACING

BACK FACING

1 square = 5 x 5cm

5. Right sides together, pin, tack and stitch sleeves (now in one piece) to fronts and backs easing or gently stretching fabric where necessary to fit at curves. Clip seams then press open.

6. Right sides together, pin, tack and stitch back facing to front facings at shoulders. Press seams open.

7. *Wrong* sides together, pin, tack and stitch facings to neck edge of dress, matching seams and pivoting stitching at corners. Neaten seam then turn facings over to right side of dress on seam line and press.

8. Turn under 15mm [$\frac{5}{8}$ in] to wrong side on free edges of facings; pin and tack to dress. Top-stitch facings to dress round outer edges, close to fold and pivoting stitching at corners. Sew on braid or ricrac if liked. Press.

9. Right sides together, stitch centre front seam up 40cm [$15\frac{3}{4}$ in] from lower edge (adjustable). Turn in seam allowance on rest of open edges of centre fronts and

press. Matching top of zip to neck edge, pin, tack and stitch zip to centre fronts.

10. Fold each cuff piece in half lengthways. Pin, tack and stitch across two short ends. Turn cuffs through to right side and press. Neaten open edges of top seams of sleeves on wrong side. Run a line of gathering stitches round lower edges of sleeves and gather to fit cuffs (allowing a 2.5cm/1 in overlap).

11. Right sides together, pin, tack and stitch each cuff to sleeve through one thickness only. Press seams up. Turn free edge of cuff under 15mm [$\frac{5}{8}$ in] and slip-stitch in place on wrong side, carrying through to close over-lap. Make buttonhole on overlap and sew button to correspond at other end of cuff.

12. Turn up hem at bottom edge of dress and catch-stitch in place on wrong side. Press.

Four-hour coat

7 years to teenage

An attractive yet economical sports coat that can be made in just one afternoon from a tartan travelling rug or ex-army blanket. Half your work's done for you because the sleeves and hem are finished by the fringe or blanket-stitching already there.

Materials An attractive soft rug or blanket with fringed or blanket-stitched edges; approx 2 metres [2¼ yds] of 2cm-wide [¾ in] wool braid in matching or contrasting colour for binding neck and front opening edges; matching machine twist; newspaper or tissue for pattern.

Measurements Because of the loose shape of the coat the measurements we've given will fit many sizes. For sizes 10–14 follow the measurements given in Diagram 1. For sizes 16–18 add 2cm [¾ in] all round (if you're not very tall do check your sleeve and breast-to-hip lengths first to see if you need the extra). Alongside the adult's measurements in Diagram 1, in blue, are those for a child aged 7–8 years.

> The front of the coat is open, cape style, and you can use a brooch to join the neck edges. If you'd prefer to wear it closed, either insert an open-ended zip (see instructions on page 64) or sew on toggles and loops.

TO MAKE YOUR PATTERN

Draw up your paper pattern following the measurements given in Diagram 1. There are 3 pieces: yoke, coat, and sleeve.

1. Yoke: Draw a rectangle and label each corner ABCD as shown, mark E (the centre between B and C). Consider BE as the centre front of the yoke and CE the centre back. From E measure depth of neckline back and front, and width along shoulder line. Join these points with a curve, as shown.

2. Coat: Draw a second rectangle, ABCD, and measure points E and F 5cm [2 in] apart along AB. Measure depth of armhole and join with 2 curves from E and F.

3. Sleeve: Draw a third rectangle, ABCD, and measure depth of curve as shown. To cut an accurate curve, fold the paper in half lengthways (A to B, D to C) and cut through both halves together. Mark top centre point of sleeve with a notch.

POSITIONING THE PATTERN ON THE FABRIC

1. Fold blanket in half lengthways, see Diagram 2.
2. Put coat pattern piece with centre back, BC, to the fold, and hem edge, DC, to finished edge of blanket. Pin in place.
3. Position yoke with centre front and back edges, CB, to fold. Pin in place.
4. Put sleeve with hem edge to remaining finished edge of blanket. Pin in place.

TO CUT OUT

Cut out each pattern piece adding 15mm extra all round for seams. Mark notches and centres.

TO SEW

1. Run two rows of gathering stitches, 3mm [⅛ in] apart, within the seam allowance of the top edges of the coat section. On the back edge you may find it necessary to break your rows equally in two at the centre back to avoid the threads snapping.
2. Cut through centre front fold

Continued on page 64

Right: the snazzy pattern of a travelling blanket makes a bright cover-up for winter. The diagrams you'll need are below and overleaf

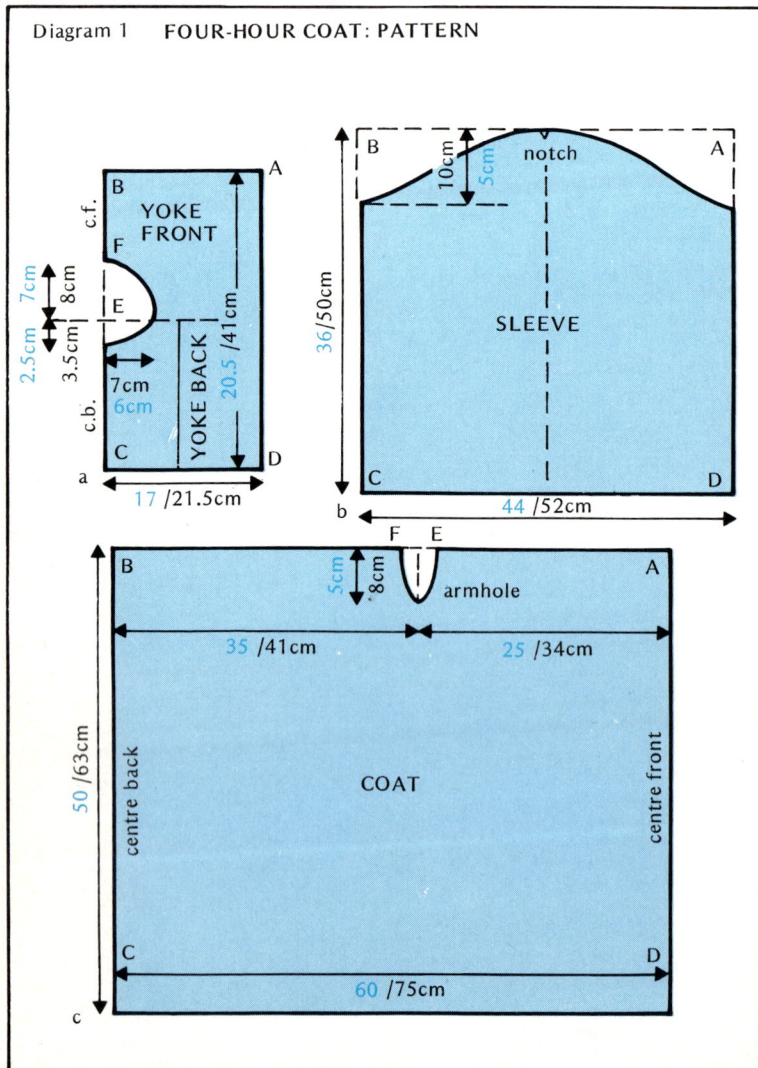

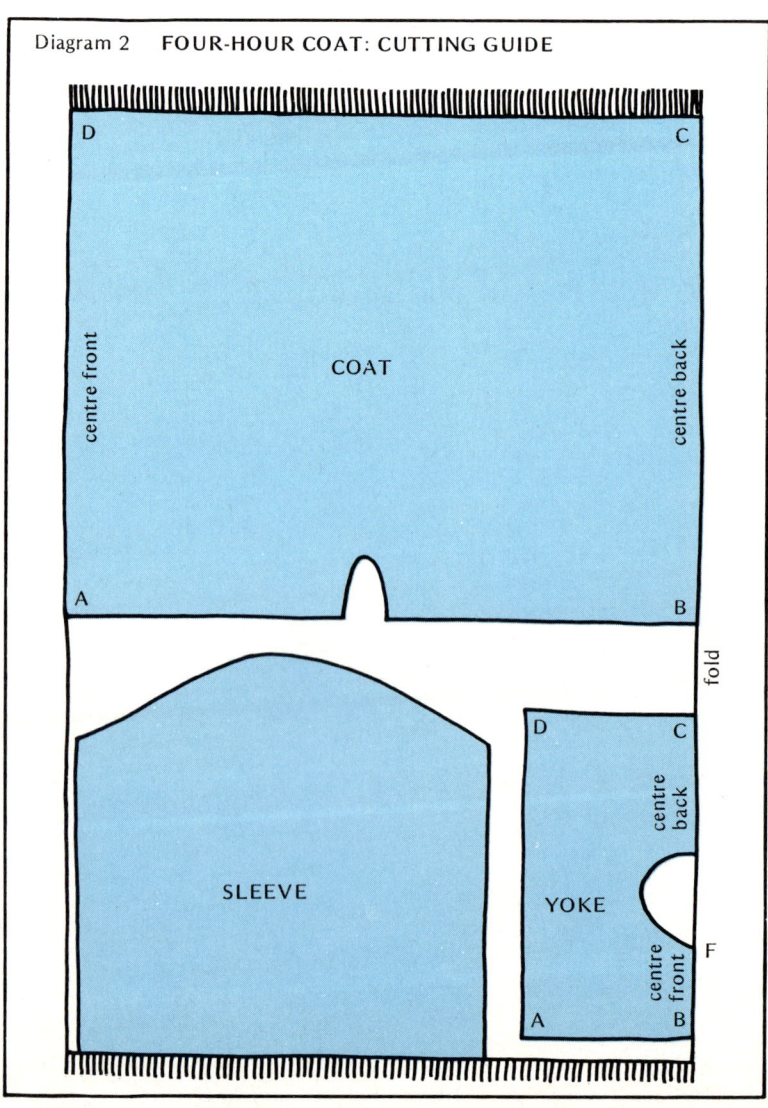

Four-hour coat . . . continued
line of yoke, FB.

3. With right sides together, pin back yoke, DCD, to coat back, matching centres. Draw gathers evenly to fit. Stitch (see Diagram 3).

4. With right sides together, pin yoke fronts, BA, to coat fronts, matching yoke B to coat A and yoke A to coat E. Draw gathers evenly to fit. Tack in place, then machine.

5. Press seam turnings towards yoke. On right side top-stitch seam-turnings in place 6mm [¼ in] from seamline (see Diagram 4). Oversew raw edges together.

6. Fold braid for binding in half lengthways, wrong sides together. Pin braid to cover raw edges of neck and front opening. Tack in place, then slip-stitch outer edge folding corners neatly as shown in Diagram 5. Slip-stitch inner edge of braid to wrong side of coat (see Diagram 6). Remove tacking from right and wrong sides.

7. With right sides together stitch sleeve seams, BC to AD.

8. Run two rows of gathering stitches, 3mm [⅛ in] apart and within the seam allowance, across the head of each sleeve, B to A.

9. With right sides together, insert sleeves matching notches to shoulder lines and underarm seams to base of armholes. Draw gathers evenly to fit. Stitch (this may be done more easily by hand).

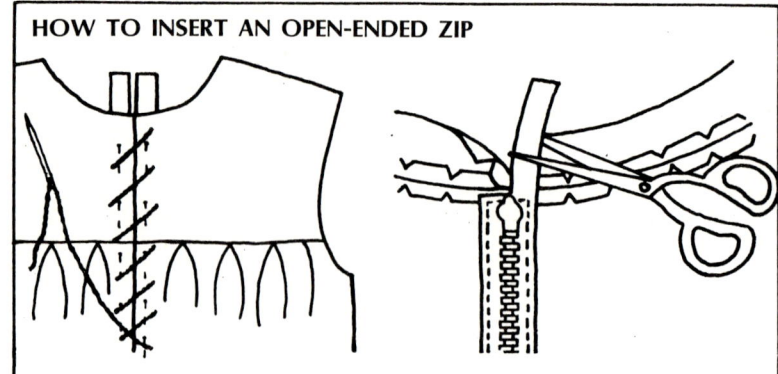

HOW TO INSERT AN OPEN-ENDED ZIP

Pin zip in position. With thick needle and wool, over-sew opening so it is tightly closed. Tack in zip and remove pins

On wrong side, sew in zip by machine or by hand. Secure the webbing with extra stitching at top and bottom of zip. Cut off surplus, remove tacking

Diagram 3: the body of the coat is gathered, then pulled in to fit the yoke which is then stitched on the wrong side
Diagram 4: unless you have a machine that will take the thickness the top-stitching is best done by hand
Diagram 5: a thick contrasting braid is used to bind the neck and front opening of the coat – again, something that's best done by hand
Diagram 6: on the wrong side, slip-stitch inner edge of braid so that it lies flat and gives a neat look to the inside of the coat

Diagram 3

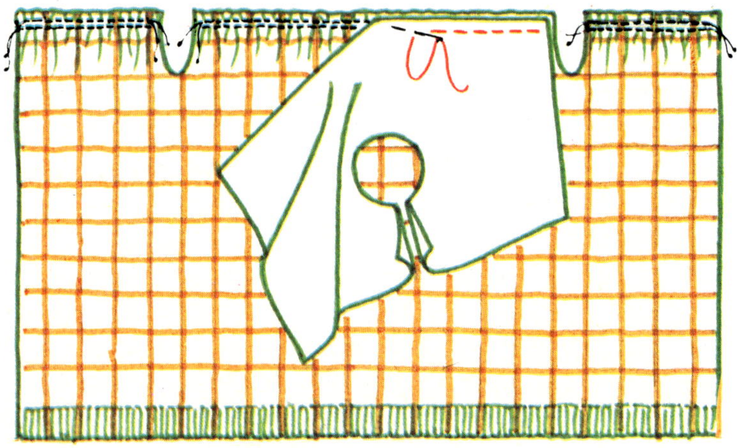

Diagram 4

Diagram 5

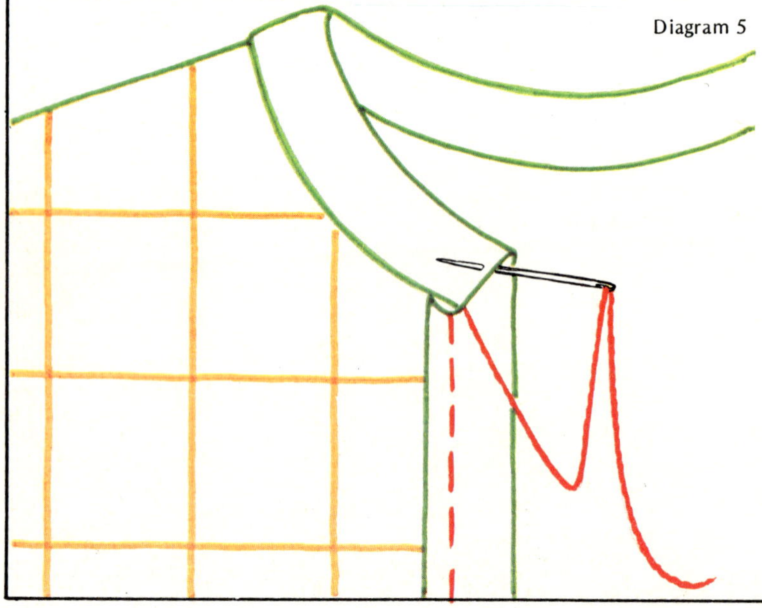

Diagram 6

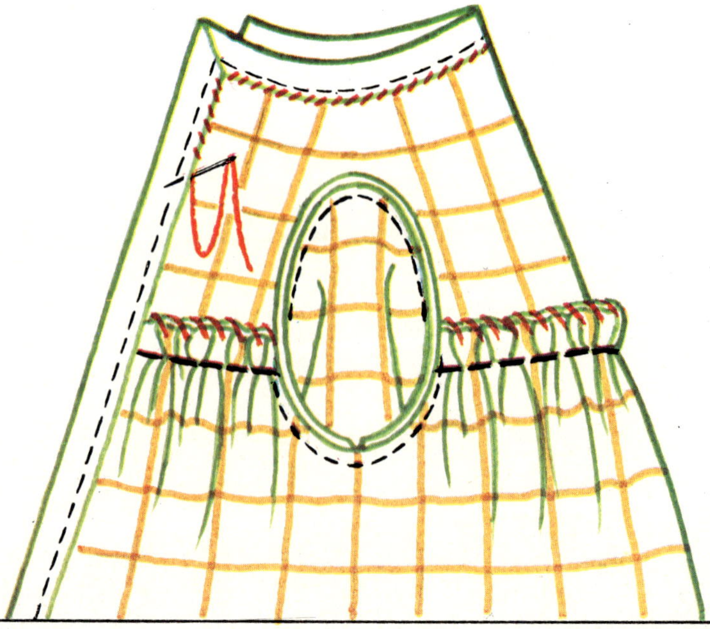

Two-colour dress

8 to 12 years

A rather smart dress that can be made in different ways – in light or heavy fabric, with blanket-stitch edging or without.

Materials 2.2m [86½ in] of 90cm [35½ in] wide fabric in main colour (2m [79 in] for smaller size); 85cm [33½ in] of 90cm [35½ in] wide fabric in contrasting colour; 30cm [12 in] of 90cm [35½ in] wide iron-on interfacing; seven 15mm [⅝ in] wide buttons; matching machine twist; contrasting embroidery thread (optional); bought belt to match.

Measurements Actual size 80cm [31½ in] chest, 73cm [28¾ in] length. For smaller size do not add extra to sides and hem when cutting out unless required.

Note All seams measure 15mm [⅝ in]. Square brackets contain imperial measurements. All diagrams are on pages 66 and 67.

TO CUT OUT

1. Using squared paper (1 square = 5cm) make patterns following Diagram 1. Mark darts, centres.
2. Fold main colour fabric in half lengthways and place pattern pieces as shown in Diagram 2: back piece is placed on the fold, front piece 6mm [¼ in] in from edge. When cutting for ages 10 and 12, _add_ extra 6mm [¼ in] to the front _plus_ 8cm [3¼ in] on lower edges of front and back pieces for hem; 2cm [¾ in] on side and shoulder seams; and 6mm [¼ in] extra at lower edges of sleeves and around crown of sleeve. Mark darts, centres.
3. Fold contrasting colour fabric in half lengthways and cut out pieces as shown in Diagram 3. For ages 10 and 12 _add_ an extra 6mm [¼ in] around collar, yoke, inside edge of front facing, and inside edge of back facing. Also _add_ 8cm [3¼ in] to bottom edge of front facing for hem. Mark centres, buttonholes. _Note_ Cut one back facing only.

TO SEW

1. Turn in 15mm [⅝ in] on lower edges of front yoke pieces. Place wrong side of each yoke to right

Continued on next page

65

Two-colour dress . . . continued

side of each dress front, over-lapping the seam allowance (Diagram 4, top). On both fronts pin, tack and top-stitch close to folded edge of yoke, pivoting at centre point. Sew a second row of stitching 3mm [⅛ in] in from folded edge (Diagram 4, bottom).

2. Following solid lines either side of buttons on pattern for front facing, cut 2 strips of interfacing (adding 8cm [3¼ in] for hem) and iron on to wrong side of each facing with a hot iron.

3. Right sides together, place each front band to corresponding dress front; pin, tack and stitch together (Diagram 5). Press seams towards centre.

4. Right sides together, pin, tack and stitch darts at shoulders on back piece.

5. Right sides together, pin, tack and stitch fronts to backs at shoulders. Press seams open.

6. Using collar pattern, cut one piece of interfacing and iron it on to the wrong side of one collar.

7. With right sides together, pin, tack and stitch collar pieces together on 2 short sides and the longest side. Neaten seam, turn through to right side and press. Close opening by tacking free edges together. Right sides together, pin and tack collar to neck edge (Diagram 6), matching centre back of collar to centre back of dress.

8. Cut a piece of interfacing to fit back neck facing and iron on to wrong side of fabric. Right sides together, pin, tack and stitch ends of facing to ends of front facing (Diagram 7). Press seams open.

9. Turn under 3mm [⅛ in] to wrong side all round front facings and back facing. Pin, tack and stitch in place (Diagram 7).

10. Matching shoulder seams with facing seams, and folding front facing over at centre fronts, pin, tack and stitch facings to neck edge through all thicknesses (Diagram 8). Clip seam and

neaten; turn through to right side and press. Carefully slip-stitch free ends of facings to wrong side of dress (Diagram 9, top).

11. Stitch 2 rows of gathering stitches round the crown of each sleeve inside the seam allowance. Pull up gathers until sleeves fit armholes. Right sides together, pin, tack and stitch each sleeve armhole opening, adjusting gathers evenly.

12. Right sides together, pin and stitch side and sleeve seams in one operation, leaving 5cm [2 in] open at lower edge of each sleeve. Press seams open. On wrong side, neatly hem seam turnings around openings. Press.

13. Cut a piece of interfacing to fit one cuff. Cut this in half lengthways. Iron each piece on to wrong side of each cuff piece.

14. Right sides together, fold each cuff in half lengthways; pin, tack and stitch across the two short ends. Turn through to

right side and press to flatten.

15. Gather lower edge of each sleeve to fit cuff. Right sides together, pin, tack and stitch sleeves to cuffs through one thickness only. Press seam up. Turn under 15mm [⅝ in] to wrong side on free edge of each cuff and slip-stitch in place on wrong side.

16. Make a buttonhole on inside edge of each cuff. Stitch a button to correspond on other side of cuff. Make 5 buttonholes where marked on right front. Stitch buttons to correspond on left front.

17. Turn up hem and slip-stitch in place on wrong side.

18. (Optional) To finish, working in blanket stitch, embroider around cuffs, collar, edge of yoke and down front facing.

All the diagrams you'll need to make the Two-colour Dress. Use the picture on page 65 as a guide if working the blanket stitching

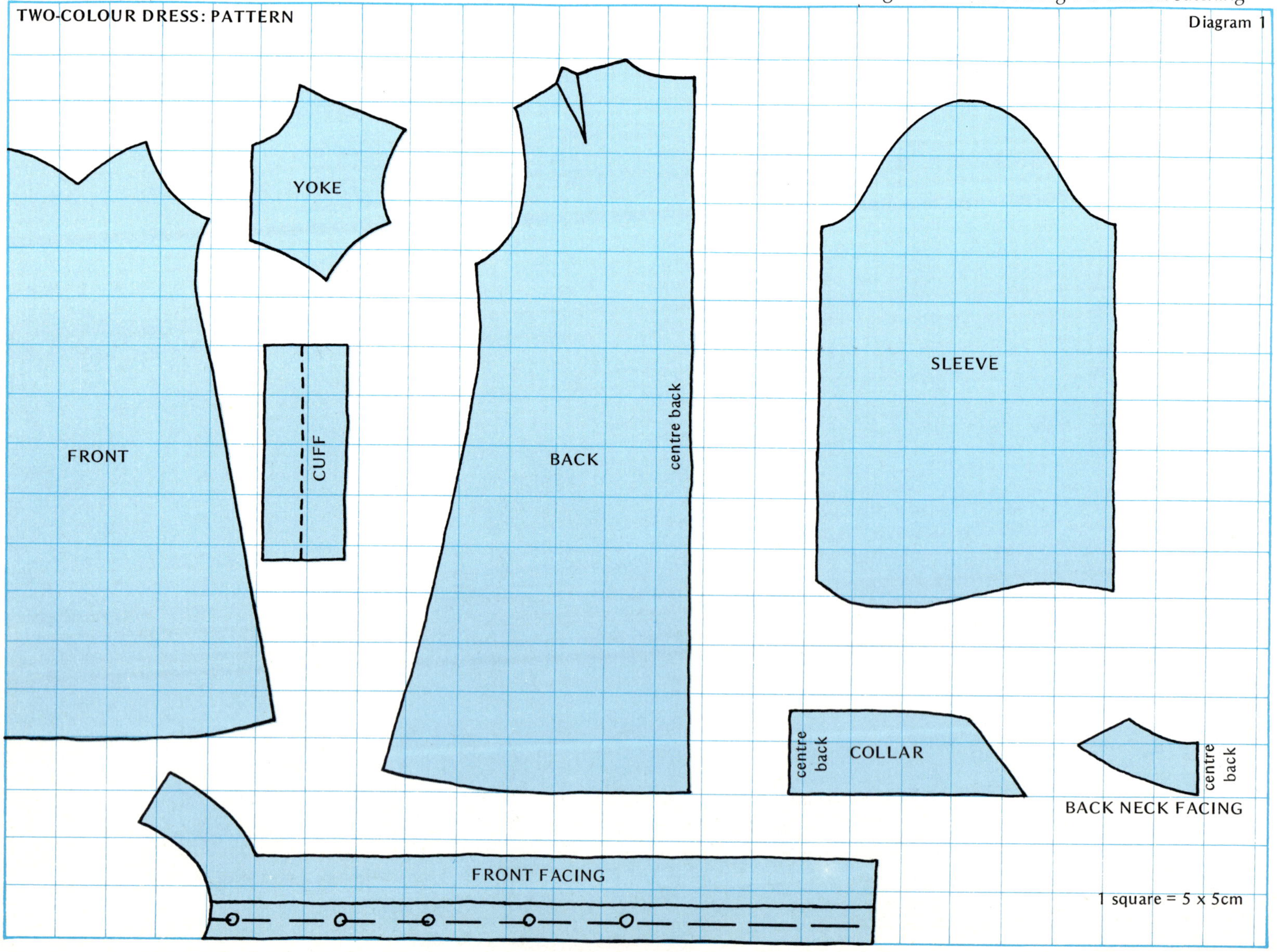

TWO-COLOUR DRESS: PATTERN

Diagram 1

YOKE

FRONT

CUFF

BACK

centre back

SLEEVE

centre back   COLLAR

centre back

BACK NECK FACING

FRONT FACING

1 square = 5 x 5cm

TWO-COLOUR DRESS:
MAIN CUTTING GUIDE
Diagram 2

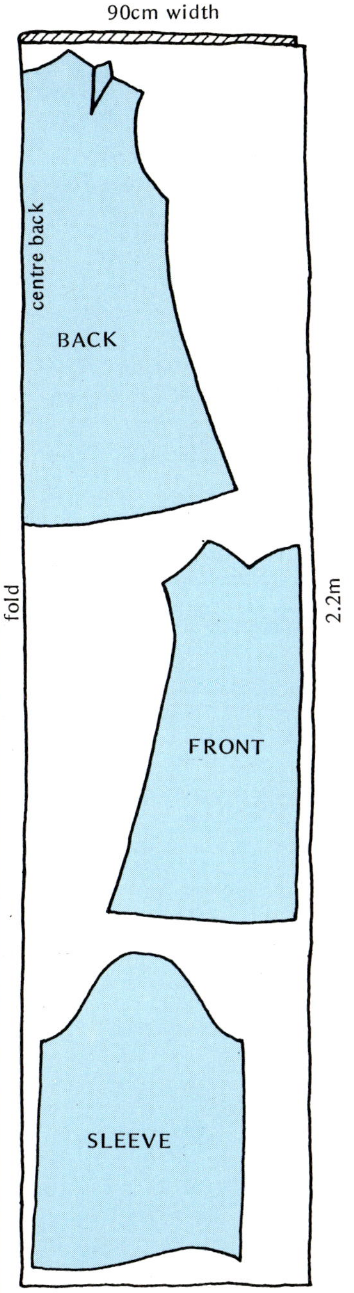

90cm width

centre back

fold

BACK

2.2m

FRONT

SLEEVE

Diagram 4

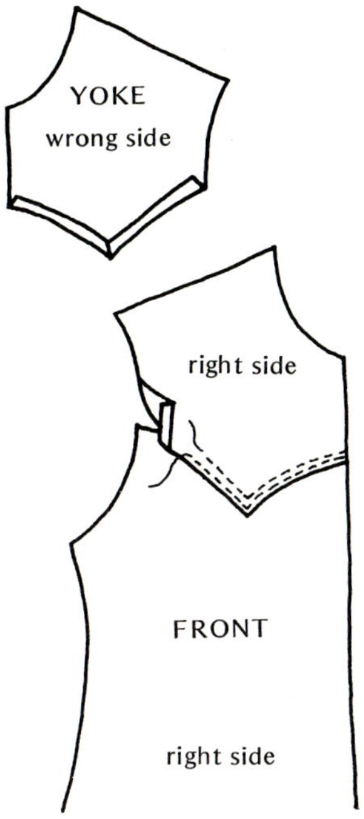

YOKE
wrong side

right side

FRONT
right side

FRONT
right side

Diagram 5

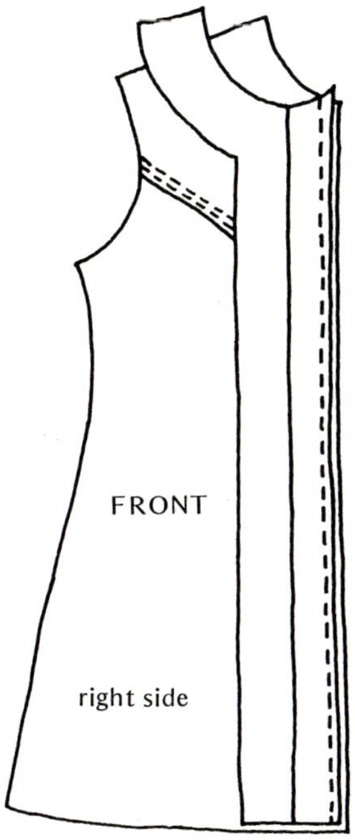

FRONT
right side

Diagram 6

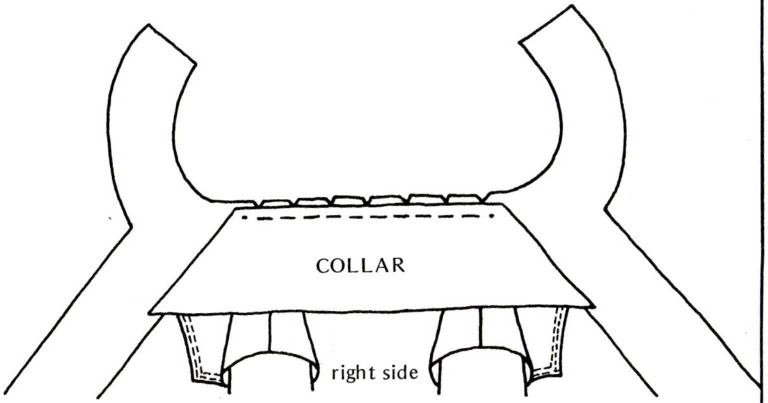

COLLAR

right side

Diagram 7

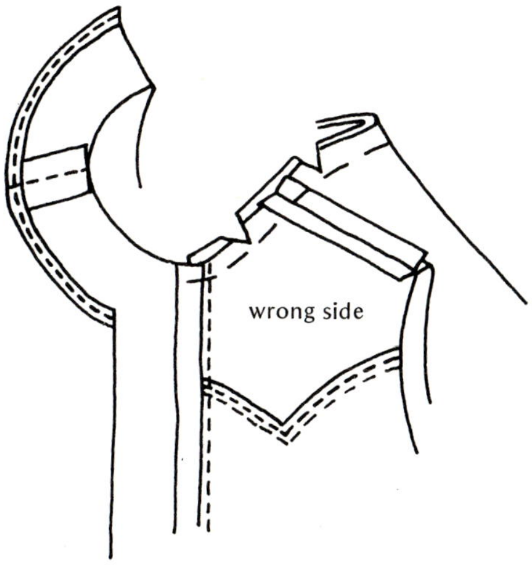

wrong side

Diagram 8

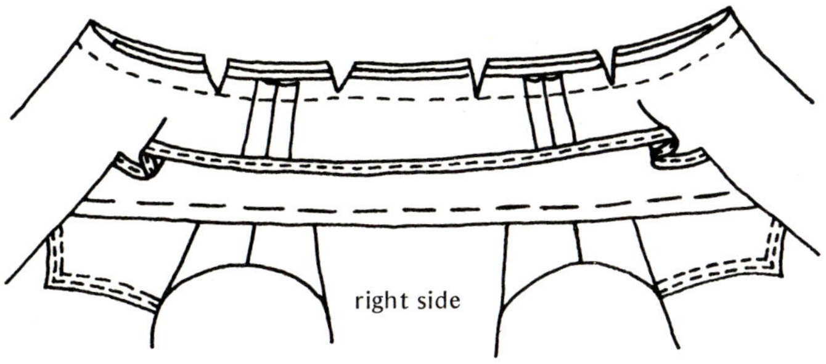

right side

Diagram 9

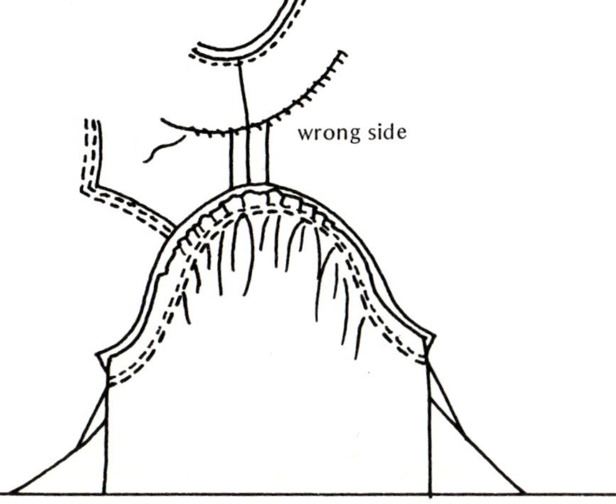

wrong side

TWO-COLOUR DRESS: CONTRAST CUTTING GUIDE   Diagram 3

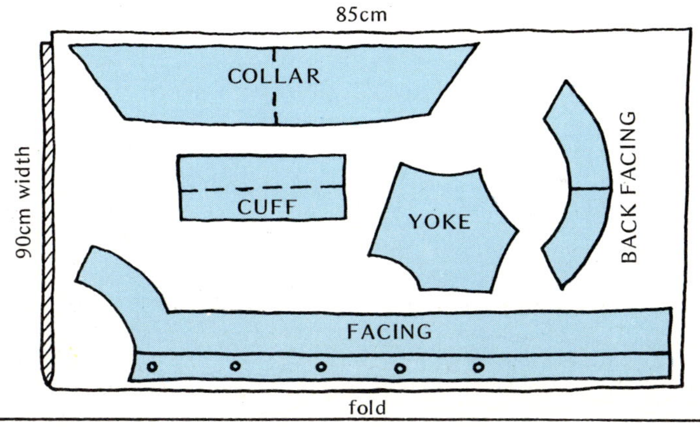

85cm

90cm width

COLLAR

CUFF

YOKE

BACK FACING

FACING

fold

Tartan suit

8 to 12 years

A smart twosome to make in cotton or wool plaid.

Materials 1m [39½ in] of 140cm [55 in] wide fabric (you may want to buy a little more to ensure pattern matching); 60cm [23½ in] of broad elasticated welt; 4 buttons for pocket flaps; matching machine twist; iron-on interfacing (optional).

Measurements To fit 76cm [30 in] chest and 65cm [25½ in] waist. For a larger or smaller size add or subtract 2cm [¾ in] at side seams and hems.

TO MAKE THE PATTERN

Rule squares of 5cm [2 in] on to a sheet of paper or use graph paper to that scale then reproduce the pattern exactly as shown in Diagram 1. The dotted lines indicate cutting lines to make patterns for facings.

TO CUT OUT

Cut fabric in half lengthways. Fold 1st piece in half lengthways, right sides together (matching design if possible) and place waistcoat front, back, front facing, 2 pocket flaps and back neck facing on straight grain (see Diagram 5A).
Fold 2nd piece as shown in Diagram 2B. Join front and back armhole facings at shoulders A, to cut out in one piece. Place front and back skirt pieces to folds and armhole facing and 2 pocket flaps on straight grain.
Mark all round each piece then cut out adding 15mm [⅝ in] seam turnings and 5cm [2 in] hems. Mark all notches and guide lines. Use pattern to cut out interfacing.

TO SEW THE SKIRT

1. To make pocket flaps stitch 2 layers together, right sides together at side and pointed edges (Diagram 3). Trim seam turnings and turn right side out. Top-stitch 6mm [¼ in] from seamed edges.
2. Tack top raw edges of 2 pocket flaps in position on left side of front.
3. Right sides together, stitch one side seam. Press seam.
4. Cut elastic to fit waist comfortably. On right side lap one edge of elastic over waist edge of skirt (Diagram 4) and pin and tack in position. Stitch elastic to skirt, stretching it to fit.
5. Right sides together stitch re-

TARTAN SUIT: PATTERN Diagram 1

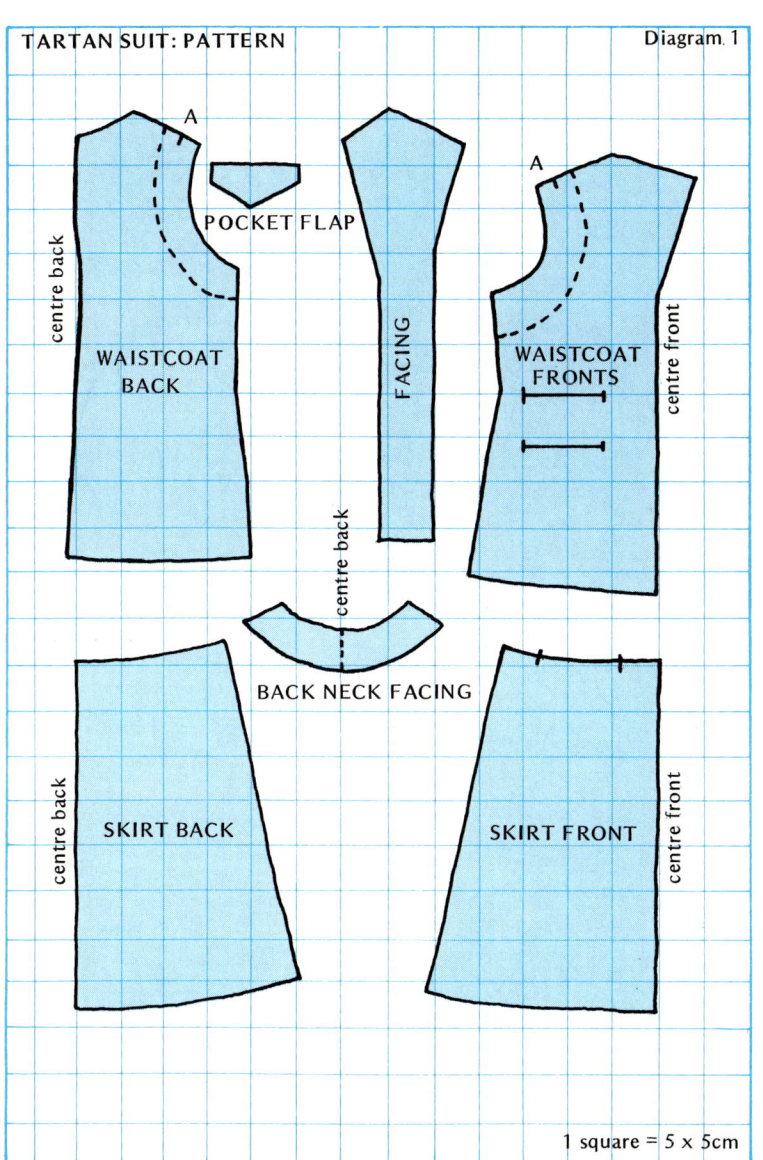

A

POCKET FLAP

centre back

WAISTCOAT BACK

FACING

centre back

A

WAISTCOAT FRONTS

centre front

BACK NECK FACING

centre back

SKIRT BACK

centre front

SKIRT FRONT

1 square = 5 x 5cm

TARTAN SUIT: CUTTING GUIDES Diagram 2A

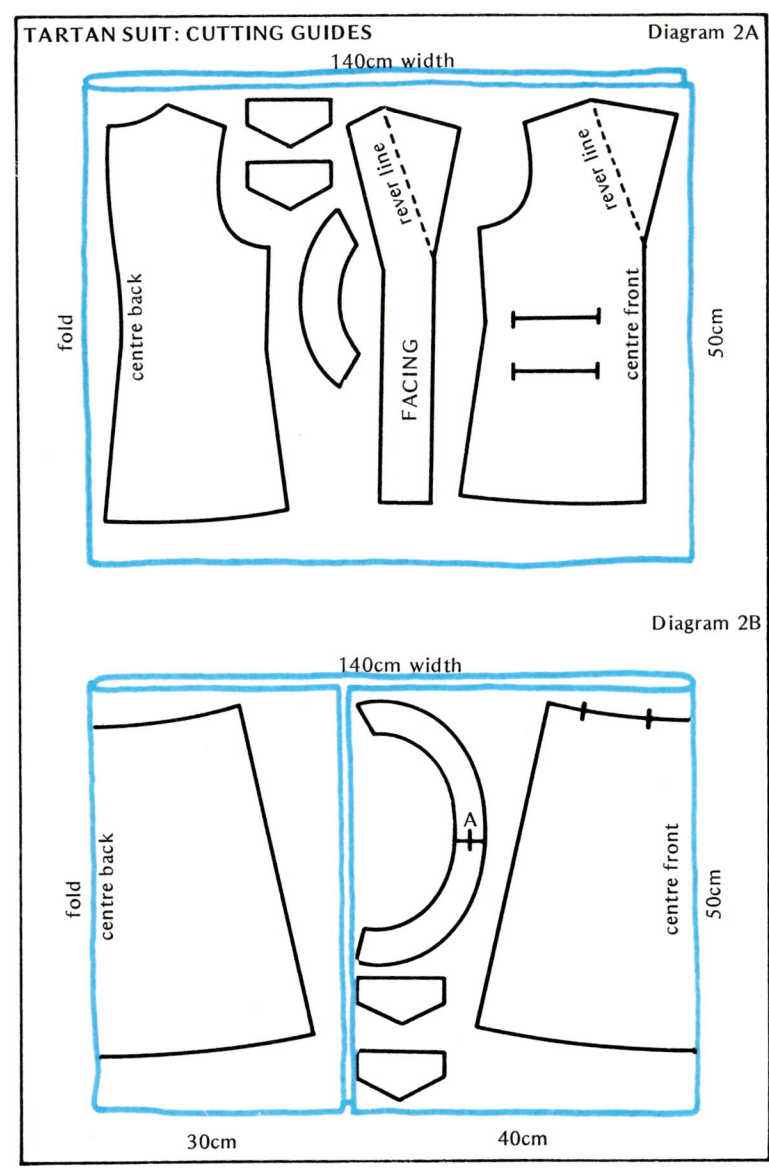

140cm width

fold

centre back

FACING

rever line

rever line

centre front

50cm

Diagram 2B

140cm width

fold

centre back

A

centre front

50cm

30cm

40cm

Left: the Tartan Suit which has fake pockets on the waistcoat and skirt, and an elasticated waist for ease of wearing. The making diagrams are on this page

maining side seam, continuing seam to join ends of elastic. Press seam open.

6. Turn up hem. Turn under raw edges and catch-stitch inner edge in place. Press. Sew buttons to flaps.

TO SEW THE WAISTCOAT

1. Stitch pocket flaps as step 1 of the skirt. Turn to right side and sew in position on right front as shown in Diagram 5, with two lines of stitching. Press flaps down.

2. Right sides together, stitch back seam. Press seam open. Iron interfacing to front, arm-hole and back neck facings (optional).

3. Right sides together, stitch fronts to back at shoulders and front facings to back neck facing

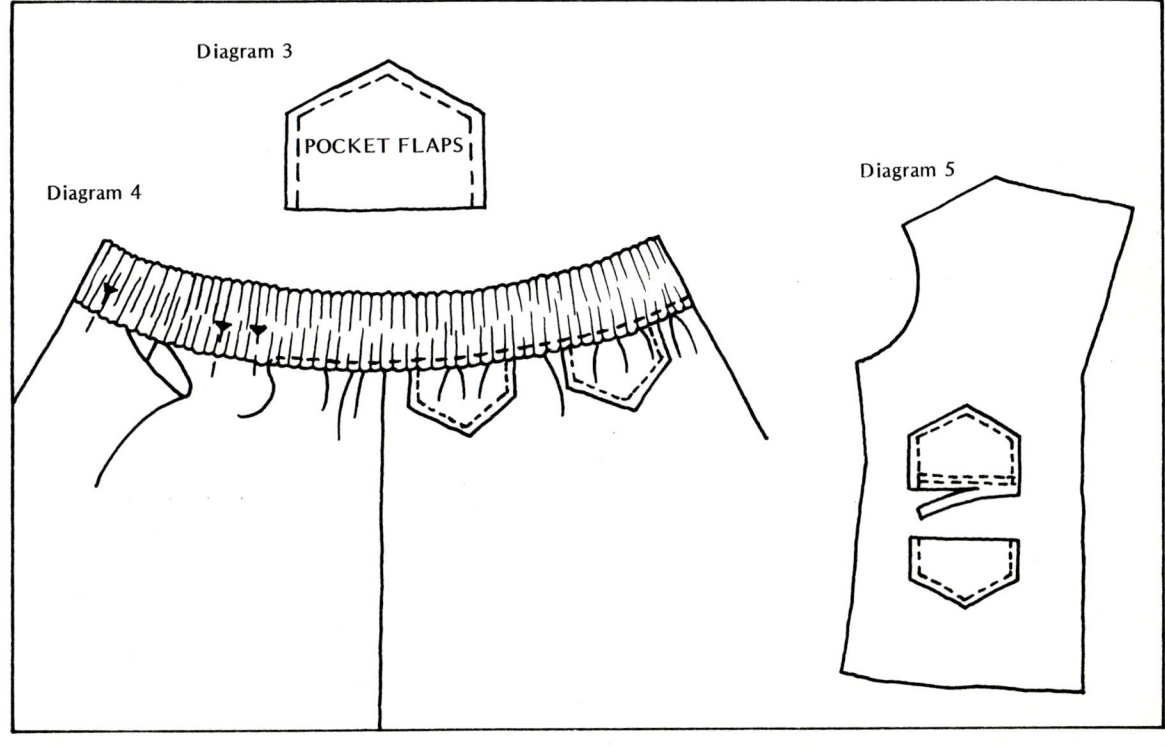

Diagram 3

POCKET FLAPS

Diagram 4

Diagram 5

Continued on next page

Tartan suit . . . continued

at shoulders. Cut away bulk of interfacing at seams and press seams open.

4. Right sides together, raw edges level and shoulder seams matching, stitch facings to waistcoat at neck and front edges (dotted lines on Diagram 6). Over-sew or pink inner raw edges of facings to neaten. Clip and trim turnings where necessary. Turn facings to wrong side. Press.

5. Right sides together and raw edges level, stitch armhole facings to armhole edges (Diagram 7). Clip around curves and over-sew or pink outer curve to neaten.

6. Right sides together, stitch side seams incorporating armhole facings (Diagram 8). Press seam turnings open. Press facings flat and catch-stitch in several places on wrong side.

7. Turn up hem. Turn under raw edges and catch-stitch inner edge in place. Press. Sew buttons to pocket flaps. Lightly press revers back so they stay open.

Below: the diagrams which will help you achieve a professional finish on the tartan waistcoat

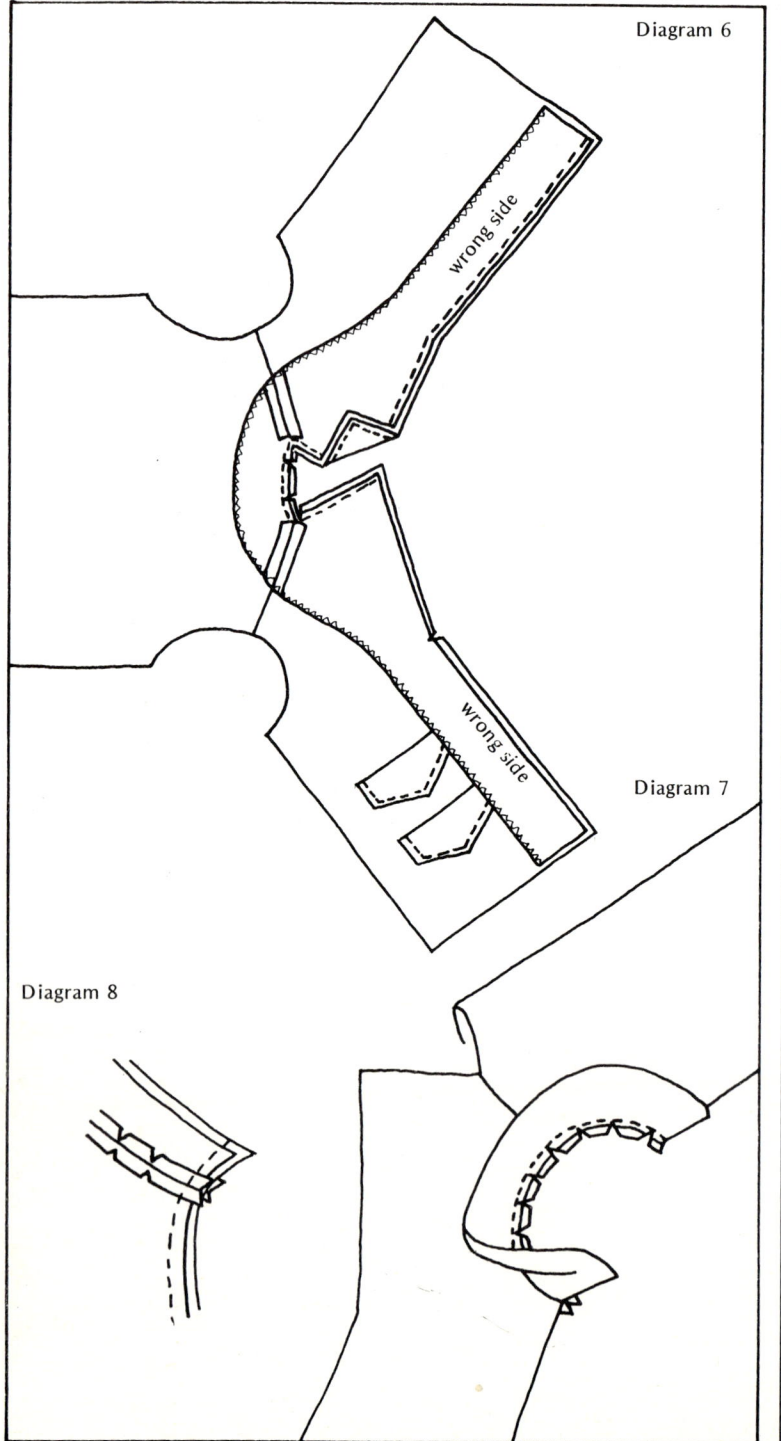

Diagram 6

Diagram 7

Diagram 8

Hooded battle jacket
Teenagers

These tops go by many names – anorak, blouson, windcheater – and they're popular for casual wear (see another version on our cover). It's such a relaxed style that one could be made for evening wear in softest satin or crushed velvet you could even add pretty decoration with embroidery, sequins or beads.

Materials 2m [79 in] of 140cm [55 in] wide fabric; 1.20m [47½ in] of 8cm [3 in] wide soft trimming elastic; 46cm [18 in] open-ended zip; 1m [39½ in] of fine cord; matching machine twist.

Measurements To fit 81cm [32 in] chest. For a larger size see *Note*.

Note All seams measure 15mm [⅝ in]. Square brackets contain imperial measurements. To make a larger size (86cm/34 in): add 2.5cm [1 in] to all sides of all pieces except the facing and front bands; adjust the length of front/back pieces, facing and sleeves. You should be able to cut the larger size from the same amount of fabric if you fold it widthways and rearrange the pattern pieces till they fit. You'll need to get more elastic so that the wrists and waist will be comfortably snug, not tight.

Continued on page 72

Right: the Hooded Battle Jackets Below: the pattern from which they are made. The rest of the diagrams are on pages 72 and 73

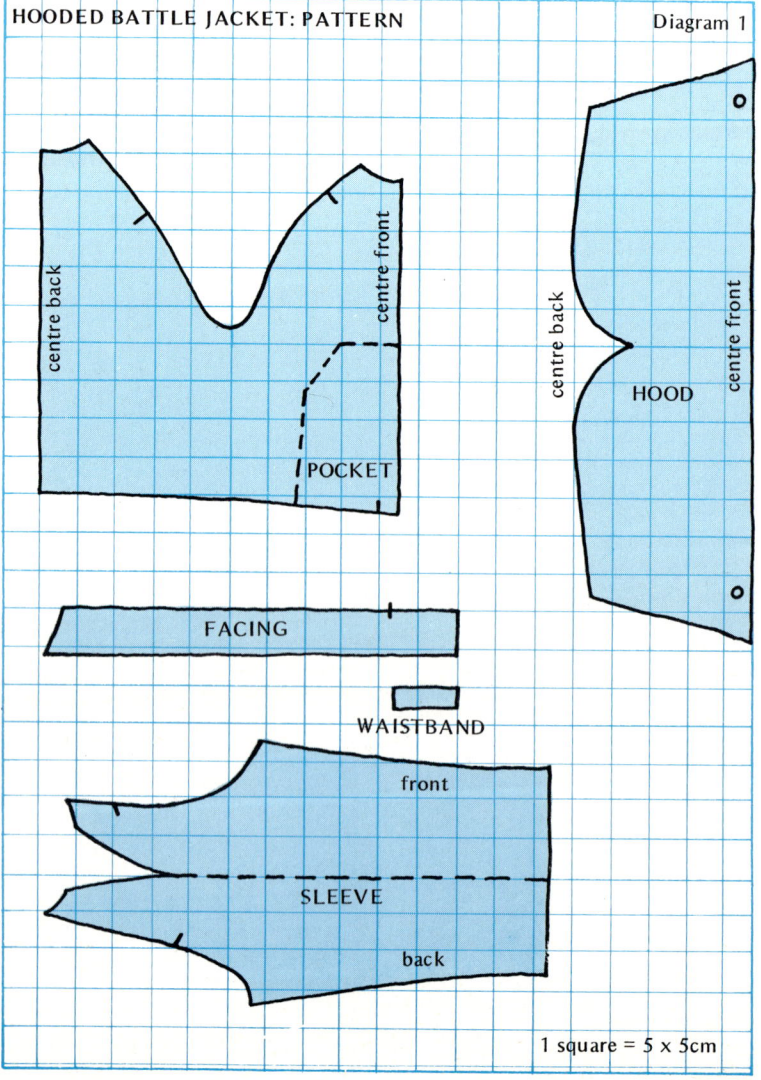

HOODED BATTLE JACKET: PATTERN Diagram 1

1 square = 5 x 5cm

TO SEW

1. Make patterns for front/back, hood, sleeve, facing and front band on squared paper (1 square = 5cm) following Diagram 1.

2. Fold fabric in half widthways and lay pattern pieces as shown (Diagram 2) placing body piece and hood piece on the fold. Before cutting the pockets, mark in a 4cm [1½ in] wide facing, shown as a dotted line in the diagram. When cutting pieces out, add an extra 15mm [⅝ in] all round each piece for seams.

3. Fold facing to wrong side on both pocket pieces and hem neatly in place. On right side, top stitch close to fold.

4. Turn under seam allowance along top and sloped edges of each pocket piece, pin and tack in place. With right side of body piece facing, lay each pocket on body fronts, wrong side down, lining up with lower edge and centre fronts (Diagram 3). Pin and tack pockets to body fronts then machine stitch across top and sloped edges, lining stitching up with top-stitching of faced edge.

5. Cut an 80cm [31½ in] length of elastic (or length required to fit waist snugly). Right sides together, pin, tack and stitch a front band to each short end of elastic. Right sides together, stitch band and facing to lower edge of body piece: mark centre of length of elastic with a pin. Right sides together, match this to centre back of body and also pin bands to centre fronts. Now pull the elastic out to fit the lower edge of body piece, pinning at 5cm [2 in] intervals. With elastic uppermost, begin to stitch to body piece, pulling the elastic out between the pins as you stitch (Diagram 4). Neaten seam and press down.

6. Right sides together, stitch centre seam at top of each sleeve piece. Press open.

7. Cut two 20cm [8 in] lengths of elastic. Right sides together, pin

HOODED BATTLE JACKET: CUTTING GUIDE — Diagram 2

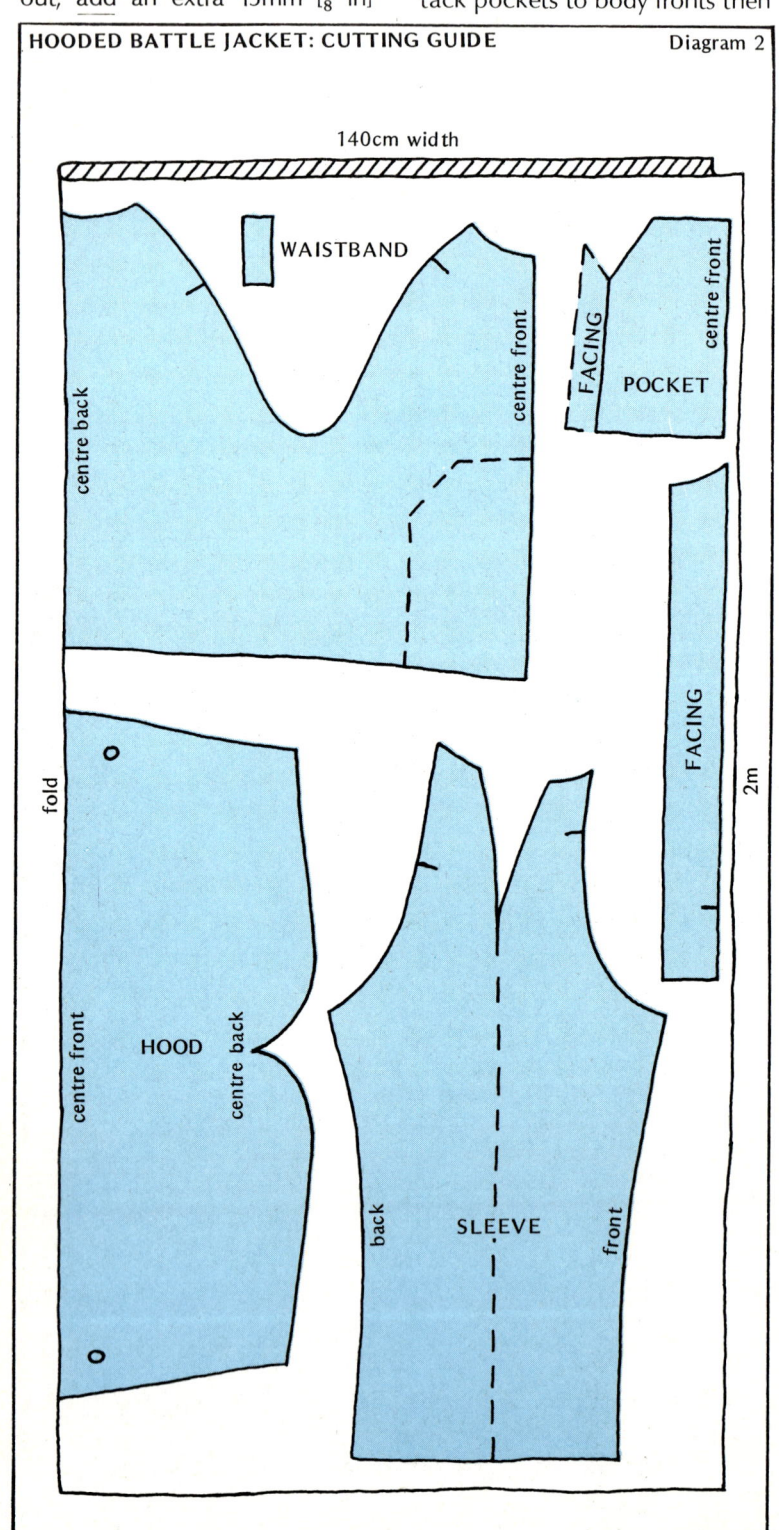

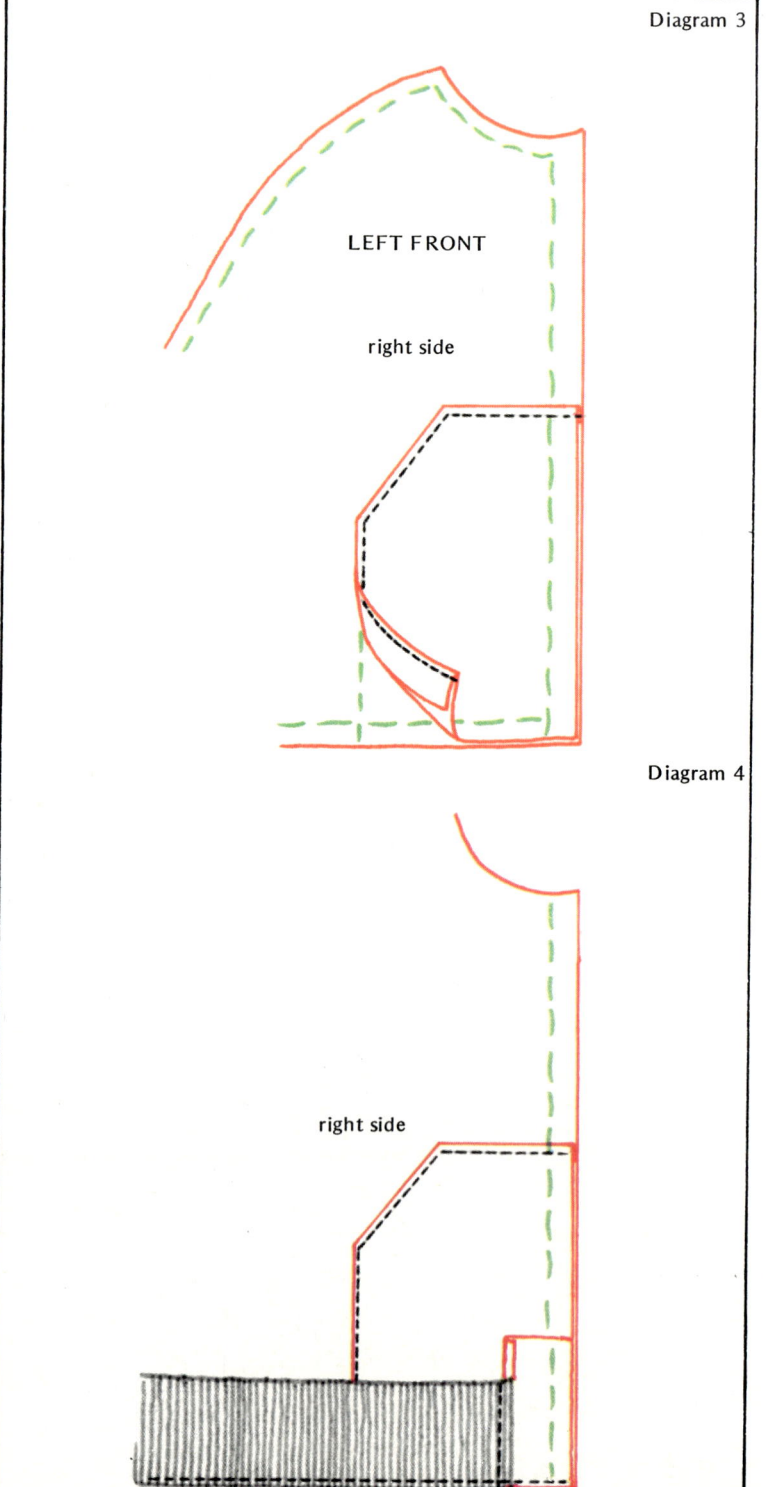

Diagram 3

Diagram 4

and stitch each piece to lower edge of each sleeve as for body piece.

8. Right sides together, pin, tack and stitch underarm seam in each sleeve piece, including elastic in seam. Neaten seam, press open, turn sleeves through to right side.

9. Matching notches, and with right sides together, pin, tack and stitch each sleeve into armhole openings. Trim and clip seams if necessary, then press open (Diagram 5).

10. Right sides together, pin, tack and stitch one front facing to each centre front. Fold facing back to wrong side of jacket on stitch line then turn under a small hem on outer edge, stitch then press. Turn in seam allowance on band and front facing at lower edge then pin, tack and top stitch to secure. Pin, tack and stitch zip in place. For an alternative method of inserting zip see boxed section.

11. Open hood piece out to a single piece of fabric. Make two eyelet holes where marked on one side of hood only.

12. With right sides together, fold fabric in half widthways. Pin, tack and stitch curved edges.

Right: the Hooded Battle Jacket made for warmer weather in a cheerfully-coloured showerproof fabric (also pictured on cover)

13. Fold hood so that the two seams are on top of one another at the centre and the eyelet holes are on the outside of the hood. Pin and tack round folded edge.

14. Top stitch close to folded edge, then sew a second line of top stitching the other side of the eyelet hole to make a casing.

15. With right sides together, match hood to neck edge, matching at centre back and fronts. Pin, tack and stitch hood to neck through bottom layer of fabric only taking in facing into stitching line. Neaten seam and press up. Fold free edge of hood up 15mm [⅝ in] to wrong side. Slip-stitch in position to cover the first line of stitching.

16. Thread length of cord through the casing and knot the ends to prevent it pulling through.

AN ALTERNATIVE METHOD OF INSERTING ZIP

With wrong side of zip to right side of facing, pin then stitch close to the edge (Diagram 6). Place wrong side of facing to wrong side of garment then pin, tack and stitch down front close to teeth (Diagram 7). Do the same with the second part of the zip on the other side. On wrong side turn under and stitch small hem on outer edge of facing, then press flat.

Diagram 5

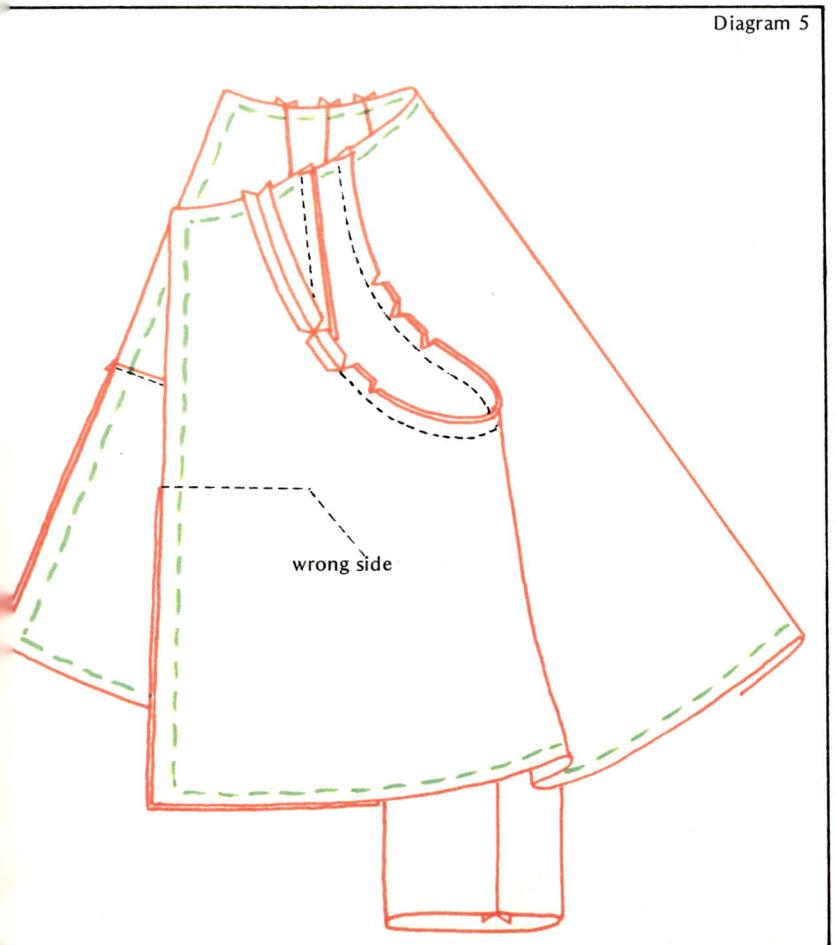

wrong side

Diagram 6

Diagram 7

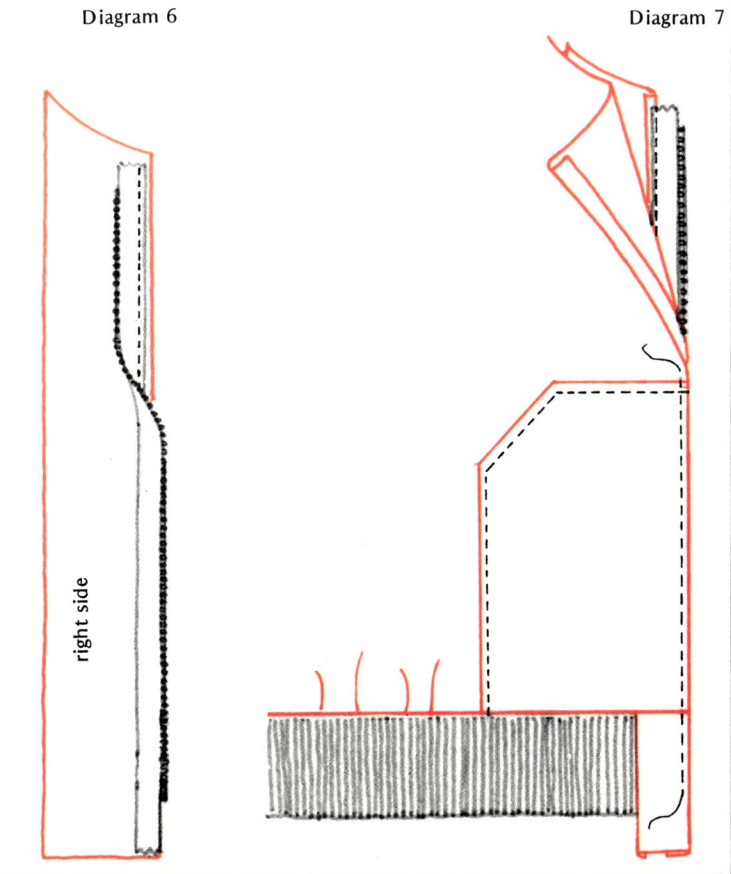

right side

Knitting

**Classic styles for children of all ages.
With the basic patterns you can choose the colours and decorative touches that
make one year's fashion different from another.**

Within this section you'll find a wide variety of garments to knit, clothes for children from newly-born to teenage. If you have a good understanding of knitting and are practised in the craft, they'll be no problem. If you're a beginner or still becoming skilled, tackle the ones that have been included with you in mind – they'll be described as simple, not so hard or perfect for a beginner. Then, when you have more confidence and want to knit the more complicated patterns, you'll find the instructions are clearly set out with very little occasion to refer back to something that's gone before.

Choosing your yarn

The type of yarn that would be most suited to the garment is given but you can make your own choice. All you have to remember is that if the garment is to be knitted successfully, you must get the tension right – the one you need is stated at the beginning of each set of instructions. If it proves difficult to achieve even when you change to larger or smaller sized needles, it could mean that you have chosen the one that won't substitute well – all yarns and wools have their own peculiarities.

Ply indicates the number of single spun threads twisted together to form a strand. As a thread can be spun to any thickness a reference to ply will not necessarily establish the thickness of the yarn. However, there is a broad classification system which applies to hand-knitted yarns

whether made from wool, man-made fibres or a mixture of both.
Baby yarns – 3 or 4 ply
Quicker knit yarns – lightweight 4 ply
Double knitting yarns – usually double the thickness of 4 ply yarns
Double-double knitting yarns – extra thick yarns
Chunky yarns – extra thick yarns
Crepe yarns – 4 ply and double knitting (can be called single and double crepe)

Because we have not recommended yarns from specific manufacturers, the amount required can only be considered a "near as possible" guide. Since metrication, yarns are produced in 20g, 25g and 50g balls so it will be up to you to buy the weight nearest. If you over-estimate, you can easily use up the extras on the superbly simple Patchwork Jacket (see

page 74) or the Red Indian Waist-coat (see page 194).

When buying always get the whole quantity needed or have it laid by at the shop for you to buy as you want it – this way you'll ensure that the yarn is from the same dye lot. If, however, this plan goes astray and you do find yourself short of a ball or two, then try to use the new yarn for ribbing at cuffs or neck. The rib tends to conceal any variation in colour.

Needle knowledge

You will notice a little imp(erial) creeping into the metric scheme of knitting needles. We give you the imperial alternative in every case so you can use your old needles if you want but you will see that the metric measurement for No 9, for example, is 3¾ rather than 3.75. This impish mixup has occurred because 3.75 won't fit on the needle head! Crochet hooks on the other hand have gone completely metric.

Before you begin a pattern, do check you have all the materials – if crochet is involved as well, a crochet hook will be included in the list. Crochet is often used to enhance a knitted garment, or to give a neat edge (to cardigan fronts and collars for example).

Age and sizing

Our age guide can only be a guide. With the best will in the world we cannot be more definite. Children come in all shapes and sizes at the same age so it's

very important to get your measurements right. The wearer should always have freedom of movement and a top that's a little bit bigger than the chest measurement will ensure comfort. And do remember that when you're taking a sleeve measurement, run the tape along the outside of the bent arm – a straight arm measurement will give you short length.

Go carefully through the instructions, underlining in pencil (so it can be rubbed out) the size you are making and noting the alterations. Usually the place to lengthen or shorten is given but if not, sleeves can be adjusted before beginning the top shaping; the body length can be altered before the armhole shaping commences. If you intend to lengthen buy extra yarn.

When measuring during knitting, keep the work flat and measure along the middle of it, not along the shaped edges (unless specifically asked to). Don't give the work a crafty pull to force it into shape – you'll only be disappointed by the end result.

Opening hints

Zips can be a problem especially if you're altering a measurement. Zips only come in certain lengths so buy the size above or below the given one and adjust your knitting only by the difference between them. If you try to put in a zip that's too long, the garment will buckle in an unsightly way; if it's too short you

HOW TO MAKE A TWISTED CORD

Cut three lengths of yarn each about three times the required length. Put the three strands together and hand one end to another person. Twist in opposite ways until it is so tightly twisted that it begins to wrinkle. Now allow it to double on itself, holding it in the middle to keep it taut – then releasing the middle. Smooth it out by running your hand along the length. Tie or bind the ends.

In all patterns, an asterisk * (sometimes there will be more than one) indicates that the next few stitches or rows will be repeated. Follow the instructions after the * once, then repeat from the * as many times as specified.

HOW TO MAKE A POMPON

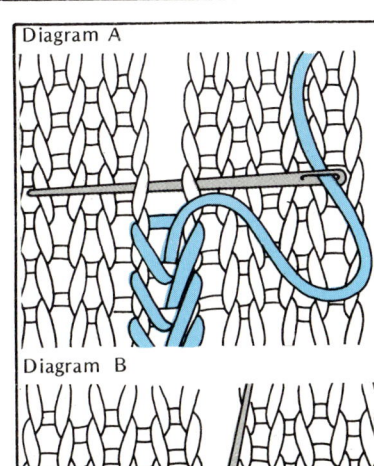

Use either one colour or two together. Cut two circles of card, each the diameter of the pompon size you want. Cut a hole in the centre of each approx $\frac{1}{3}$ of the circle. Now, using needle and yarn, keep winding through the centre to the outside of the circle using both the circles together.

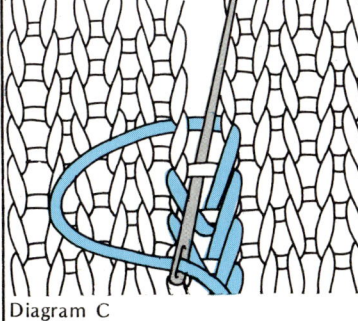

When the central hole is filled, carefully snip with scissors round the outer edge of the circle, until all the threads are cut. Do not remove the card circles yet. Tie and bind the threads between the two cards tightly. Now remove the card circles and fluff out the pompon.

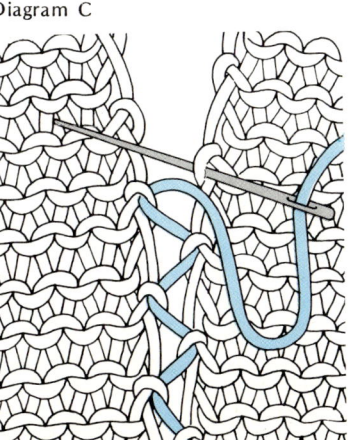

and the wearer will be irritated by the garment's shrunken look.

When putting in a front zip, it often helps to oversew the two fronts together with big stitches (use a contrasting yarn so you find the stitches again). Turn the garment to the wrong side and lay the zip along the centre join then pin and tack in place. When you've sewn it in, by machine or hand, remove the oversewing stitches and tacking.

Buttonholes are important too – make sure they are placed at equal distances apart otherwise the garment will look uneven.

With neckbands, do pick up the number of stitches given – no more, no less. The number has not been arrived at at random – only that number will achieve the right look and give the opening needed for the head to fit comfortably through.

Attention to details like these ensure that your knitting will have the professional, stylish result the designer intended.

Making up

Not everyone likes this stage – it seems to take so much time and after all the effort you've put into the knitting, it seems an unnecessary inconvenience (for those who really do hate seams, treat yourself to the garments made in the round or those made all in one piece – there are quite a few to choose from).

The sewing up is important and if you do it well, your handiwork will benefit. Don't rush it. Follow the instructions carefully, pressing each part and using the suggested stitch.

For seams, back-stitch is most commonly used. Place the pieces together with right sides facing and matching the rows and shaping (take extra care when a design or stripes are involved). Pin and tack together about 6mm [$\frac{1}{4}$ in] from the edge. Sewing is best done with a knitter's needle which is blunt ended and won't split the yarn. Using one strand of yarn, and working one stitch in from the edge, take each stitch back to the point of entry of the previous stitch. Do not pull too tightly, and darn in the ends.

Ribbing, bands and decorative shoulder seams should be made with a flat seam (often referred to as slip-stitch). Wrong side facing, lay the pieces flat, side by side on a table. You join them together by placing the needle in the matching "knobs" at the ends of rows, drawing the two pieces together. Again, be careful not to pull the stitch too tight.

Fancy knits

If you're not used to working from a chart, don't worry. You'll find that the alternatives are mostly described. With Fair Isle the instructions are written out line by line. If you prefer you can also knit the garment plain and add the design by the Swiss darning method – embroidery that's added after the knitting's done. All the necessary details are given with the patterns.

Diagram A

Diagram B

Diagram C

INVISIBLE SEAMING

Babies clothes and more tailored garments made in plain fine knitting can be treated to invisible seaming which requires patience but adds that little something extra to the final look. To do it, work from the right side. Fasten sewing thread securely to the lower edge of one side and bring needle through to right side. Hold the edges to be joined in the left hand with the first finger slightly separating them. Now bring the needle over to the second edge and pick up the thread that lies between the first and second stitches (see Diagram A). Bring the needle back to the first side via the linking thread and pick up the thread between the first and second stitches (see Diagram B). Keep on repeating those steps working your way up the edges as though lacing together the rungs of a ladder. It does take a while and you must be careful to pick up every thread on both sides between the stitches.

A slightly quicker way is to lace the "knobs" at the ends of rows together with an oversewing stitch so that when pressed the seam will lie flat (see Diagram C).

Children's Clothes

Sets for beginners

A collection of bonnets, mitts and bootees for 1st and 2nd stage babies.

Bonnet, mitts and bootees

Newborn baby

Materials 25g 4-ply knitting yarn in main colour (M); small quantity in contrast (C); pair 3¼mm [No 10] knitting needles; 3mm [No 11] crochet hook.

Tension 32 sts and 36 rows to 10cm [4 in] in rib slightly stretched.

Abbreviations k, knit; p, purl; st(s), stitch(es); cm, centimetre(s); in, inch(es); st-st, stocking stitch; alt, alternate; beg, beginning; cont, continue; dec, decrease; dc, double crochet; ch, chain; ss, slipstitch; sl, slip; psso, pass slip stitch over; tog, together; rep, repeat; rem, remain(ing); y fwd, yarn forward. Square brackets contain imperial measurements.

BONNET

CENTRE PIECE
With M, cast on 22 sts and work 20cm [8 in] k1, p1 rib. Cast off in rib. This piece forms the centre to fit from centre front of the head to centre back of the neck.

SIDE PIECES (make 2)
With M, cast on 69 sts. Cont in k1, p1 rib, dec in the centre to form a square thus: **1st row** (K1, p1) 16 times, sl 1, k1, psso, k the centre st, k2 tog, (p1, k1) 16 times. **2nd row** (P1, k1) 15 times, p1, p2 tog, p the centre st, p2 tog, p1 (k1, p1) to end. **3rd row** (K1, p1) 15 times, sl 1, k1, psso, k the centre st, k2 tog, (p1, k1) 15 times. **4th row** (P1, k1) 14 times, p1, p2 tog, p the centre st, p2 tog, p1, (k1, p1) 14 times. Cont in this way, keeping the centre st in st-st and dec 1 st at both sides of the centre st on every row to 3 sts. K3 tog. Fasten off.

CUFF
With M, cast on 80 sts. Work 3cm [1¼ in] k1, p1 rib. Now, with C, work 2 rows st-st. Cast off. With C, work 1 row dc along the 2 short ends and 1 long edge of cuff, do not turn, but work a row of shrimp stitch along previous row (shrimp stitch is dc worked from left to right). Fasten off.

TO MAKE UP
Sew the centre piece between the two side pieces as shown. With right side of work facing, using M, pick up and k86 sts along lower edge. Work 4 rows k1, p1 rib. **5th row** (make eyelets) Rib 6, (y fwd, k2 tog, rib 6) to end. Rib 3 rows more. Cast off in rib. Join the M edge of cuff to front edge of bonnet and fold back the crocheted C edge. Make a twisted cord (see page 75) and thread it through the holes to tie at front neck.

MITTENS

Materials 25g 4-ply knitting yarn; pair 2¾mm [No 12] knitting needles; small quantity of contrast 4-ply for stripes and cords.

Tension 32 sts and 40 rows to 10cm [4 in] in st-st.

TO MAKE
With M, cast on 36 sts. Cont in k2, p2 rib in stripes of 4 rows M, 4 rows C. Repeat last 8 rows once more, then first 4 rows, inc 1 st at both ends of last row . . . 38 sts. **Next row** Rib 3, (y fwd, k2 tog, rib 3) to end. Break C. Beg k row, work 22 rows st-st. **Shape Top 1st row** *K2 tog, k15, k2 tog*; rep from * to *. **2nd row** *P2 tog, p13, p2 tog*; rep from * to *. **3rd row** *K2 tog, k11, k2 tog*; rep from * to *. **4th row** *P2 tog, p9, p2 tog*; rep from * to *.
Cont dec 4 sts in this way on every row to 6 sts.
Break yarn and thread through rem 6 sts, draw up, secure and fasten off.

TO MAKE UP
With right sides together, back-stitch the seam. Turn to right side. With C, cut 3 lengths approx 3 times the wrist measurement plus ties. Make a twisted cord (see page 75) and thread through the holes at ends of rib. Press following instructions on ball band, omitting the rib.

BOOTEES

Materials 25g 4-ply knitting yarn; pair 2¾mm [No 12] knitting needles; small quantity of contrast yarn.

Tension 32 sts and 56 rows to 10cm [4 in] in g-st.

TO MAKE
With C, cast on 40 sts. K4 rows. Break C. With M, work 4 rows k2, p2 rib. Now work 23 rows g-st.
Next row *K2, p2; rep from * to end.
Next row Rib 3, *y fwd, k2 tog, rib 2; rep from * to last st, p1.
Next row *K2, p2; rep from * to end.
Shape Instep 1st row K26, turn.
2nd row K12, turn.
Cont on these 12 sts only. K22 rows more. Break yarn.
With right side of work facing, beg where the 14 sts were left and using the same needle, with C, pick up and k10 sts evenly along side of instep, k12 sts of instep, then pick up and k10 sts along other side of instep, join M to rem 14 sts and k to end.
Next row With M, k14, with C, k32, with a second ball of M, k14.
Rep last row 3 times more, taking care to twist the yarns when changing colour to avoid making a hole. Break C. With M, k12 rows.
Shape Sole Cont with M in st-st and dec thus: **1st row** K3, k2 tog, k20, sl 1, k1, psso, k6, k2 tog, k20, sl 1, k1, psso, k3. **2nd row and foll alt rows** P. **3rd row** K3, k2 tog, k18, sl 1, k1, psso, k6, k2 tog, k18, sl 1, k1, psso, k3. **5th row** As 3rd, working k16 between decreases. **7th row** As 5th, working k14 between decreases. Cast off rem sts.

TO MAKE UP
With right sides together, join the back and sole seam with backstitch. Turn to right side. Make a twisted cord (see page 75) and thread it through the holes at ankle. Tie into bow at front.

Left: a straightforward set that looks smart because of the contrasting white trim and the stripes on the mittens
Above right: the colour coordinates this threesome though each is knitted differently

Bonnet with brim, mitts and bootees
Newborn baby

Materials 25g 4-ply knitting yarn; a pair 3¼mm [No 10] knitting needles; 3mm [No 11] crochet hook.

Tension 32 sts and 36 rows to 10cm [4 in] in rib slightly stretched.

Abbreviations k, knit; p, purl; st(s), stitch(es); in, inch(es); cm, centimetre(s); st-st, stocking stitch; alt, alternate; beg, beginning; cont, continue; dec, decreas(e)ing; dc, double crochet; sl, slip; psso, pass slip stitch over; tog, together; rep, repeat; rem, remain(ing); y fwd, yarn forward. Square brackets contain imperial measurements.

BONNET
CENTRE PIECE
Cast on 22 sts and work 20cm [8 in] k1, p1 rib. Leave sts on a spare needle.

SIDE PIECES (make 2)
Cast on 69 sts. Cont in k1, p1 rib, dec in the centre form a square thus:
1st row (K1, p1) 16 times, sl 1, k1, psso, k the centre st, k2 tog, (p1, k1) 16 times.
2nd row (P1, k1) 15 times, p1, p2 tog, p the centre st, p2 tog, p1, (k1, p1) to end.
3rd row (K1, p1) 15 times, sl 1, k1, psso, k the centre st, k2 tog,

Continued on next page

Bonnet with brim . . . continued

(p1, k1) 15 times.

4th row (P1, k1) 14 times, p1, p2 tog, p the centre st, p2 tog, p1, (k1, p1) to end.

Cont in this way, keeping the centre st in st-st and dec 1 st on both sides of the centre st on every row to 3 sts. K3 tog. Fasten off yarn.

TO MAKE UP

Join the two side pieces to the centre piece with the spare needle to the centre forehead.

Brim With right side of work facing, pick up and k10 sts to the right of the spare needle, k across the sts on spare needle, pick up and k10 sts to the left of centre. *Work 10 rows k1, p1 rib, at the same time casting off 2 sts at the beg of every row. Cast off rem sts in rib.

Brim Facing Cast on 42 sts. Work 2 rows k1, p1 rib, then work from * to end of brim. Place this brim facing inside the bonnet brim matching the two shaped edges. With right side of bonnet facing you, work 1 row dc along the outer edge, working through both thicknesses. Sew the free edge of the facing to the inside of bonnet with slip-stitch seam.

Eyelet Border With right side of work facing, pick up and k86 sts around the neck edge of the bonnet. Work 4 rows k1, p1 rib.

5th row (eyelets) Rib 6, (y fwd, rib 2 tog, rib 6) to end. Now work 3 more rows k1, p1 rib. Cast off in rib. Make a twisted cord (see page 75) and thread through the eyelets and tie.

MITTENS

Materials 25g 4-ply knitting yarn; a pair 2¾mm [No 12] knitting needles.

Tension 32 sts and 48 rows to 10cm [4 in].

Abbreviations k, knit; p, purl; st(s), stitch(es); cm, centimetre(s); in, inch(es); alt, alternate; beg, beginning; cont, continue; g-st, garter stitch (every row k); st-st, stocking stitch; rep, repeat; rem, remain(ing); tog, together; sl, slip; psso, pass slip stitch over; y fwd, yarn forward.

TO MAKE

Cast on 38 sts. Work 24 rows k1, p1 rib.

Now cont in double moss st patt thus: **1st row** K2, *p2, k2; rep from * to end. **2nd row** P2, *k2, p2; rep from * to end. **3rd row** As 2nd. **4th row** As 1st.

These 4 rows form the patt. Rep

Above: prettily striped, this set would be suitable for a boy or a girl

the 4 rows 5 times more (24 rows patt worked).

Shape Top 1st row *K2 tog, patt 15, k2 tog*; rep from * to *. **2nd row** *P2 tog, patt 13, p2 tog*; rep from * to *. Cont in this way, dec 4 sts on every row until 6 sts remain.

Break yarn and thread through remaining 6 sts. Draw up and secure and fasten off.

TO MAKE UP

With right sides together, join the seams. Turn to right side.

BOOTEES

Materials 25g 4-ply knitting yarn in main colour; pair 2¾mm [No 12] knitting needles.

Tension 32 sts and 40 rows to 10cm [4 in] in st-st.

TO MAKE

Cast on 30 sts. **1st to 5th rows** K. **6th to 10th rows** Beg p row, work 5 rows st-st. **11th to 30th rows** Rep last 10 rows twice more. **31st row** (eyelets) K5, *y fwd, k2 tog, k3; rep from * to end. **32nd row** P.

Shape Instep 1st row K20, turn. **2nd row** P10, turn. Work 12 rows more in st-st on these centre 10 sts. Break yarn.

With right side of work facing, beg where the first 10 sts were left and using the same needle, join in yarn and pick up and k10 sts evenly along side of instep, k across the 10 instep sts, pick up and k10 sts along other side of instep, and finally, k the rem 10

sts . . . 50 sts. Work 5 rows g-st.

Shape Sole 1st row K2, k2 tog, k17, sl 1, k1, psso, k4, k2 tog, k17, sl 1, k1, psso, k2. **2nd row** K. **3rd row** K2, k2 tog, k15, sl 1, k1, psso, k4, k2 tog, k15, sl 1, k1, psso, k2. **4th row** K. **5th row** K2, k2 tog, k13, sl 1, k1, psso, k4, k2 tog, k13, sl 1, k1, psso, k4. **6th row** K. Cast off rem sts.

TO MAKE UP

With right sides together, join back and sole seams. Turn to right side. Make a twisted cord (see page 75) – thread through the eyelets at ankle and tie.

Bonnet and bootees

3 to 6 months

Materials 25g 4-ply knitting yarn in each of main colour (M) and contrast (C); pair 3¼mm [No 10] knitting needles.

Tension 32 sts and 56 rows to 10cm [4 in] in g-st.

Abbreviations k, knit; p, purl; st(s), stitch(es); cm, centimetre(s); in, inch(es); alt, alternate; beg, beginning; cont, continue; foll, following; dec, decrease; inc, increase; y fwd, yarn forward; tog, together; sl, slip; psso, pass slip stitch over; rep, repeat; rem, remain; g-st, garter stitch (every row k). Square brackets contain imperial measurements.

BONNET

TO MAKE

With C, cast on 92 sts. **1st to 4th rows** K. **5th and 6th rows** With M, k2 rows. These 6 rows form the patt. Cont in patt until 60 rows in all have been worked, thus ending after an M stripe.
Shape Back 1st row With M, cast off 36 sts, k20, cast off rem 36 sts. Fasten off. With wrong side of work facing, rejoin M to rem 20 sts and k to end. Cont on these sts in g-st in stripes of 2 rows C, 2 rows M, at the same time inc 1 st at both ends of every row to 36 sts.
Now dec 1 st at both ends of every foll 8th row to 26 sts. Cont without shaping until the back measures 12cm [4¾ in]. Leave these sts on a spare needle.

TO MAKE UP

Sew the cast-off edges to the row ends of the centre back. With right side of work facing, using C, pick up and k82 sts along the neck edge of the bonnet, including the sts on the spare needle. Cont with C only. K2 rows. **3rd row** (eyelets) K2, *y fwd, k2 tog, k2; rep from * to end. K3 rows more. Cast off.
Make a twisted cord (see page 75) and thread it through the eyelets and tie.

Right: diagrams and advice to help you master the art of knitting for babies

BOOTEES

Materials 25g 4-ply knitting yarn in each of main colour (M) and contrast (C); pair 2¾mm [No 12] knitting needles.

Tension 32 sts and 40 rows to 10cm [4 in] in st-st.

TO MAKE

With M, cast on 45 sts. Work 8 rows g-st.
Cont in patt thus: **1st to 6th rows** With M, beg k row, in st-st. **7th row** *K2 M, 4 C; rep from * to last 3 sts, 3 M. **8th row** P3 M, *4 C, 2 M; rep from * to end.
Rep these 8 rows twice more, then with M, work 6 rows st-st.
Next row (eyelets) K1, *y fwd, k2 tog, k2; rep from * to end. Beg p row, work 3 rows st-st.
Shape Instep 1st row With M, k30, turn. **2nd row** With M, p15, turn. Now work 26 more rows st-st on these centre 15 sts. Break yarn.
With right side of work facing, beg where the first 15 sts were left and using the same needle, join in C and pick up and k12 sts along side of instep, with C, k across the 15 instep sts, pick up and k12 sts along the other side of instep and finally k across the rem 15 sts ... 69 sts. With C, work 10 rows g-st.
Shape Sole Cont in st-st with C and dec thus: **1st row** K4, k2 tog, k23, sl 1, k1, psso, k7, k2 tog, k23, sl 1, k1, psso, k4. **2nd row and foll alt rows** P. **3rd row** K4, k2 tog, k21, sl 1, k1, psso, k7, k2 tog, k21, sl 1, k1, psso, k4. **5th row** K4, k2 tog, k19, sl 1, k1, psso, k7, k2 tog, k19, sl 1, k1, psso, k4. **6th row** P. Cast off.

TO MAKE UP

With right sides inside, join back and sole seam. Turn to right side. Make a twisted cord (see page 75) and thread it through the eyelets at ankle.

SPECIAL ADVICE

All of these bonnets, bootees and mittens are shaped in the classic way. The bonnets can be made with a broad band to fit over the head from side to side, then the centre sts are worked downwards towards the neck and the sides joined to the back in the making up (see Diagram 1). They can also be made by working a broad band to fit from front to back with two side pieces and these too are sewn together in the making up (see Diagram 2).
The mittens are very straightforward. They are simply a straight shape with eyelet holes at the wrist and shaped both in the centre and the outer edges. (See Diagram 3).
Classic style bootees always start at the leg. The ankle portion is worked ending with a row of eyelets. Now the instep is shaped – by working to and fro on the centre third of the total sts. The yarn is broken and rejoined to the right of the instep; using the first needle sts are picked up along the right-side row-ends of the instep, k across the instep sts, then sts are picked up and k along the other side of the instep and finally the rem sts are worked on to the needle. A small pocket has been formed which will become the instep for the toes. The depth of the foot is worked on all the sts. The sole is carefully shaped by dec 4 sts on every row (or, in some patterns, alt rows) until the sole forms a neat shape the width of the instep. The sts are cast off and then the sole and back seams are joined neatly (see Diagrams 4, 5, 6 and 7).

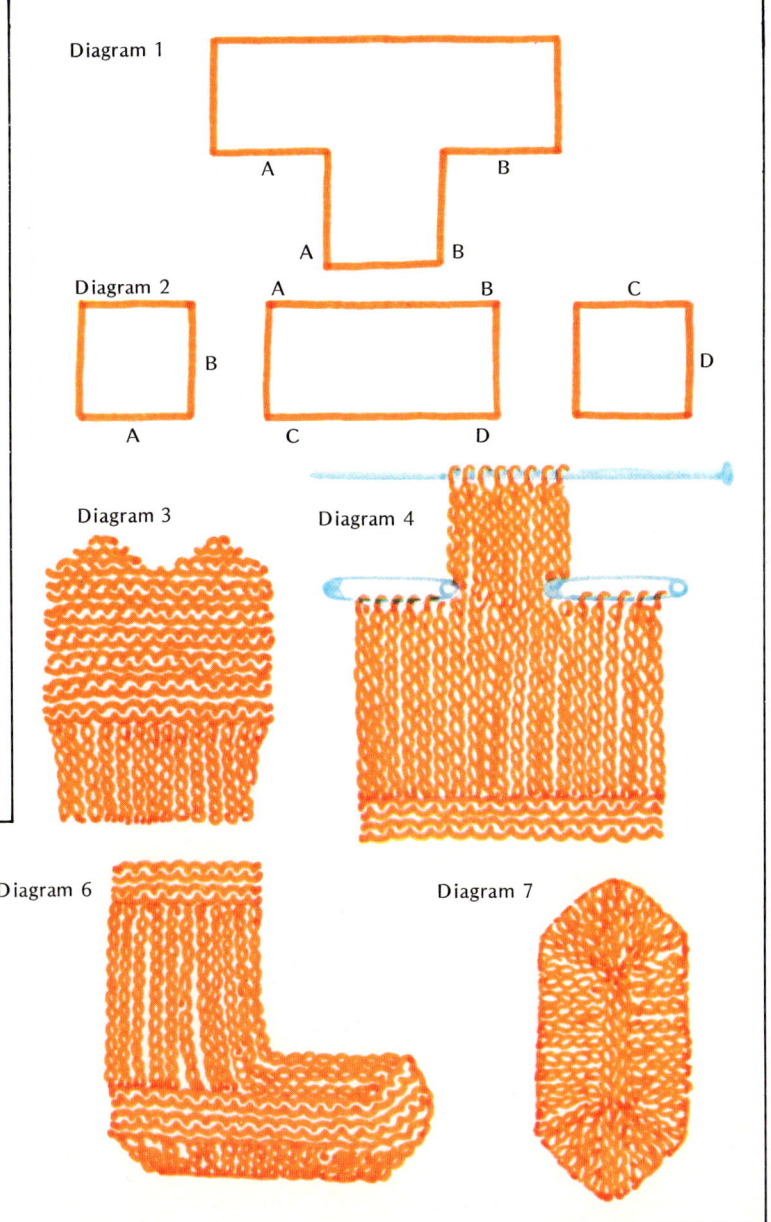

Yoked top

New to 6 months

This is a smock shape with a back opening, but you could easily reverse it and have the yoke at the back, the opening at the front with ribbon ties at the neck.

Materials 100g of 4-ply baby wool; pair 2¾mm [No 12] knitting needles; matching baby ribbon; crochet hook.

Measurements To fit a 41–46cm [16–18 in] chest.

Tension 34 sts and 45 rows measure 10cm [4 in].

Abbreviations k, knit; p, purl; st(s), stitch(es); patt, pattern; rep, repeat; beg, beginning; alt, alternate; cont, continue; foll, following; g-st, garter stitch; wl fwd, wool forward; wl bk, wool back; sl, slip; tog, together; ch, chain. Square brackets contain imperial measurements.

Special Note Turning is used to shorten the rows, so work thus

when instructions are given to turn : **Next row** K sts stated in row, wl to front, sl next st, wl bk, turn. **Next row** Sl first st purlwise, work to end.

TO MAKE
The jacket is worked sideways in one piece. Beg from the centre back cast on 70 sts and work in g-st for 10 rows. Cont in patt working thus:
1st row K54, turn (see special note above).
2nd row P to last 4 sts, k4.
3rd row K54, turn.
4th row As 2nd row.
5th row K64 sts, turn.
6th row K to end.
7th row K to end.
8th row K16, p to last 4 sts, k4.
9th row K50, turn.
10th row P to last 4 sts, k4.
11th and 12th rows As 5th and 6th rows.
13th and 14th rows As 7th and 8th rows.
Cont thus working 5 rows in stocking st, then work a k row, keeping g-st borders as given and repeating the 14 shortening rows throughout, until 60 rows of patt have been worked.
** **Next row** (lower edge) K38, and leave on spare needle, cast on 6 sts, k to end.
Keeping continuity of patt, g-st

yoke and shortening rows, cast on 6 sts at beg of next 5 right-side rows, then 8 sts on foll right-side rows. Cont thus:
1st row (neck edge) In patt to last 8 sts, turn (for shortening for cuff).
2nd row In patt.
3rd row In patt to last 8 sts, k8.
4th row In patt.
5th and 6th rows As 3rd and 4th rows.
Rep these 6 rows of shortening of wrist until 90 rows (from widest part of sleeve worked, ie, the first 6 sts cast on) thus ending at cuff edge. Now cast off 8 sts at beg of next row and 6 sts on foll 6 alt rows ** (sleeve completed).
Next row (neck edge) Patt to end, then patt across 38 sts left on spare needle and cont for Front and work 48 rows. Centre of Front has now been reached.
Cont in patt as before, for another 48 rows, then work from ** to ** (2nd sleeve completed).
Next row (neck edge) Patt to end, then patt across 38 sts left on spare needle. Cont in patt for 60 rows, then work 10 rows across all sts in g-st. Cast off.
Neckband With right side facing, pick up and k86 sts along neck edge and work in g-st for 2 rows.
Next row K1, *wl fwd, k2 tog. Rep from * to last st, k1. K3 rows and cast off.

TO MAKE UP
Press following ball band instructions. Sew up sleeve seams. Press seams. Work a row of ch sts along division of yoke (see picture). Thread ribbon through holes at neck edge leaving length at back for ties.

Cotton bibs

Smart, substantial bibs that will stand up to much wear and tear.

Materials For either bib you will require 1 ball of thick crochet cotton in white (M) and 1 ball in either pink or red (C); pair of 2¾mm [No 12] knitting needles; 2.5mm [No 12] crochet hook.

Abbreviations k, knit; st(s), stitch(es); mst, moss stitch; cont, continue; ch, chain; dc, double crochet; st-st, stocking stitch. Square brackets contain imperial measurements.

BROAD-STRIPED BIB
Using M and knitting needles, cast on 61 sts and work in mst for 10 rows. Cont in st-st on the 43

Below: the Yoked Top – so practical because it's easy to put on and take off

centre sts and in mst on the 9 sts on either side, working 10 rows C and 10 rows M alternately. When the 4th C stripe has been worked, cast off centre 21 sts and cont on each side separately, working 1 M stripe, 1 C and 1 M stripe. Cast off. Using crochet hook and M, work round all outer edges in dc, do not turn, but work backwards from left to right in dc. This makes a knotted edge and is known as shrimp st. Fasten off. Join M to corner edge at neckline, make 50 ch, turn and work 1 row of dc. Fasten off. Work another tie in the same way at corresponding corner.

NARROW-STRIPED BIB

Using M and knitting needles, cast on 61 sts and working in stripes of 2 rows M and 2 rows C, k4 rows, then work 9 rows in mst. Now cont in st-st on centre 45 sts, with 8 sts either side in mst until 20 M stripes have been completed.
Cast off centre 21 sts and work on each side separately until 8 more C stripes have been worked. Cast off.
Using M and crochet hook, work in dc round all outer edges, then work 1 row of shrimp st as given for Broad-striped bib. Make 2 ties as for Broad-striped bib.
Press bibs on wrong side with a warm iron over a damp cloth.

Cot cover

A very adaptable cover as it can be used for a cradle, cot and pram.

Materials 300g of very thick, loose-spun wool; pair 5½mm [No 5] knitting needles.

Measurements 52cm [20½ in] wide and 65cm [25½ in] long.

Tension 10 sts measures 10cm [4 in] over pattern.

Abbreviations k, knit; p, purl; st(s), stitch(es); rep, repeat; g-st, garter stitch; tog, together; patt, pattern; cont, continue; beg, beginning; cm, centimetre(s); in, inch(es). Square brackets contain imperial measurements.

TO MAKE

Cast on 54 sts and work in g-st for 6 rows. Work in the following patt:
1st row K3, p to last 3 sts, k3.

2nd row K3, *k1, then (k1, p1, k1) into next st. Rep from * to last 3 sts, k3.
3rd row K3, *k3, p1. Rep from * to last 3 sts, k3.
4th row K3, *k1, p3 tog. Rep from * to last 3 sts, k3.
5th row K3, p to last 3 sts, k3.
6th row K3, *(k1, p1, k1) in next st, k1. Rep from * to last 3 sts, k3.
7th row K3, *p1, k3. Rep from * to last 3 sts, k3.
8th row K3, *p3 tog, k1. Rep from * to last 3 sts, k3.
These 8 rows form the patt. Rep them until work measures about 63cm [25 in] from the beg ending after a 1st or 5th patt row, then work 6 rows of g-st across all sts. Cast off.
Press work as given on ball band, but pressing on wrong side so as not to flatten the design.

Above: quick to make gifts for a new baby – you'll find similar ones in the crochet section, on page 178
Right: warm and chunky Cot Cover made in thick wool

Children's Clothes

Helmet
3 to 6 months

This is worked in one with a crocheted strap. A head warmer for boy or girl.

Materials One 25g ball 3-ply baby yarn; a pair 2¾mm [No 12] knitting needles; 2·5mm [No 12] crochet hook; 1 button.

Tension 32 sts to 10cm [4 in] in g-st.

Abbreviations k, knit; p, purl; st(s), stitch(es); cm, centimetre(s); in, inch(es); inc, increase(e)ing; inc 1k, increase by picking up loop before next st and knitting into back of it; tog, together; ch, chain; dc, double crochet; cont, continue; rep, repeat; g-st, garter stitch. Square brackets contain imperial measurements.

MAIN PIECE
Cast on 161 sts. Cont in chevron shaped g-st thus: **1st row** K2, inc 1k, k30, (k1, p1, k1) all in next st, k30, k3 tog, k14, (k1, p1, k1) all in next st, k14, k3 tog, k30, (k1, p1, k1) all in next st, k30, inc 1k, k2 . . . 161 sts. **2nd row** K.
Rep these 2 rows 35 times more . . . 72 rows worked. Cast off.

STRAP
With crochet hook, make 42 ch.
1st row 1 dc in 7th ch from hook (to form a button loop), 1 dc in each ch to end, do not turn but cont working 1 dc in each of other side of base ch to end. Fasten off.

TO MAKE UP
Join back seam of helmet (AB to AB). By placing the two top highpoints to the point formed by the back seam and joining the resulting seams you will form the crown that you can see in the picture. Sew the strap to lower side point, and the button to the other side point.

Below: the finished helmet . . . after it has been knitted in one piece, it is cleverly joined to create a smooth crown

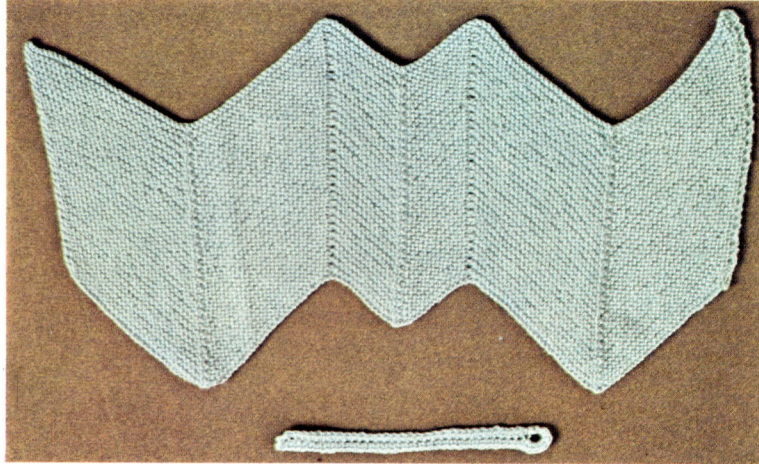

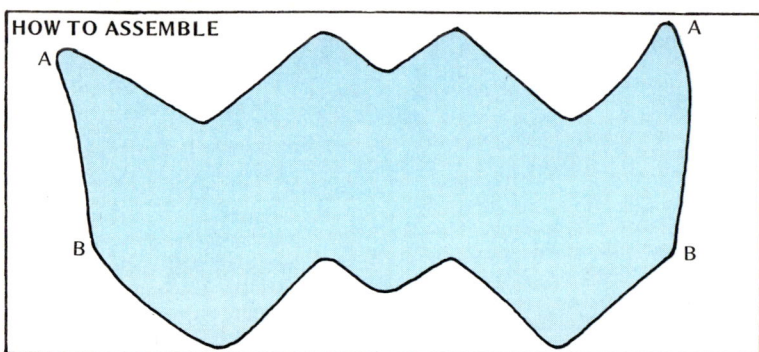

HOW TO ASSEMBLE

Sets for bigger babies

Illustrated on pages 84 and 85

Simple-to-knit coordinates to give the out-going baby something classy to wear.

White suit edged with green

3 to 6 months

Materials 200g 4-ply yarn used *double* in main colour (M); a small quantity of 4-ply in contrast (C) also used *double*; pair 3¾mm [No 9] knitting needles.

Measurements To fit 41cm [16 in] chest.

Tension 23 sts to 10cm [4 in] in moss stitch pattern.

Abbreviations k, knit; p, purl; st(s), stitch(es); cm, centimetre(s); in, inch(es); alt, alternate; beg, beginning; cont, continue; foll, following; dec, decreas(e)ing; inc, increas(e)ing; patt, pattern; y fwd, yarn forward; tog, together; rep, repeat; rem, remain(ing); inc 1k, increase by picking up the loop lying before the next st and knitting into the back of it; st-st, stocking stitch; sl, slip; psso, pass slip st over.

When working moss st patt remember that if you have an even number of sts, the rows will be 1st row *K1, p1* to end. 2nd row *P1, k1* to end. On an odd number of sts the rows are always the same k1, *p1, k1; rep from * to end.

PANTS

BACK AND FRONT (worked in one piece)
Beg at Back waist. With C, cast on 64 sts. Work 2 rows k1, p1 rib, then with M, work 2 rows rib. **5th row** (eyelets) With C, k1, *y fwd, k2 tog; rep from * to last st, k1. **6th row** With C, rib to end. With M, work 2 rows k1, p1 rib. With C, work 2 rows k1, p1 rib, inc 1 st at end of last row . . . 65 sts.
Dec row With M, rib 4, *k2 tog,

rib 3; rep from * to last st, rib 1 . . . 53 sts.
Now cont in moss st patt – every row k1, *p1, k1; rep from * to end. – inc 1 st at both ends of every 6th row to 61 sts. Mark both ends of the last row with a short length of bright thread. Cont without shaping in moss st patt until work measures 13cm [5 in] from the dec row. Mark this row with thread also.
Shape Legs and Crotch 1st row Cast off 7 sts, patt 23, inc 1k, k1, inc 1k, patt 30. **2nd row** Cast off 7 sts, patt 23, p3, patt 23. **3rd row** Cast off 3 sts, patt 20, inc 1k, k3, inc 1k, patt 23. **4th row** Cast off 3 sts, patt 20, p5, patt 20. **5th row** Cast off 3 sts, patt 17, inc 1k, k5, inc 1k, patt 20. **6th row** Cast off 3 sts, patt 17, p7, patt 17. **7th row** Cast off 3 sts, patt 14, inc 1k, k7, inc 1k, patt 17. **8th row** Cast off 3 sts, patt 14, p9, patt 14. **9th row** Cast off 3 sts, patt 11, inc 1k, k9, inc 1k, patt 14. **10th row** Cast off 3 sts, patt 11, p11, patt 11. **11th row** Cast off 3 sts, patt 8, inc 1k, k11, inc 1k, patt 11.
12th row Cast off 3 sts, patt 8, p13, patt 8. **13th row** K2 tog, patt 6, k13, patt 6, k2 tog. **14th row** Patt 7, p13, patt 7. **15th row** K2 tog, patt 5, k13, patt 5, k2 tog. **16th row** Patt 6, p13, patt 6. **17th row** K2 tog, patt 4, k13, patt 4, k2 tog. **18th row** Patt 5, p13, patt 5. **19th row** K2 tog, patt 3, k13, patt 3, k2 tog. **20th row** Patt 4, p13, patt 4. End of Back.
Cont on these sts for Front thus:
1st row Inc in 1st st, patt 3, k13, patt 3, inc in last st. **2nd row** Patt 5, p13, patt 5. **3rd row** Inc in 1st st, patt 4, k13, patt 4, inc in last st. **4th row** Patt 6, p13, patt 6. **5th row** Inc in 1st st, patt 5, k13, patt 5, inc in last st. **6th row** Patt 7, p13, patt 7. **7th row** Inc in 1st st, patt 6, k13, patt 6, inc in last st. **8th row** Patt 8, p13, patt 8. **9th row** Inc in 1st st, patt 7, k13, patt

7, inc in last st. **10th row** Patt 9, p13, patt 9. **11th row** Cast on 3 sts, patt 9, k2 tog, k9, k2 tog, patt to end.
12th row Cast on 3 sts, patt 9, p11, patt 12. **13th row** Cast on 3 sts, patt 12, k2 tog, k7, k2 tog, patt 12. **14th row** Cast on 3 sts, patt 12, p9, patt 15. **15th row** Cast on 5 sts, patt 15, k2 tog, k5, k2 tog, patt 15. **16th row** Cast on 5 sts, patt 15, p7, patt 20. **17th row** Cast on 5 sts, patt 20, k2 tog, k3, k2 tog, patt 20. **18th row** Cast on 5 sts, patt 20, p5, patt 25. **19th row** Cast on 5 sts, patt 25, k2 tog, k1, k2 tog, patt 25. **20th row** Cast on 5 sts, patt 25, p3, patt 30. **21st row** Patt 30, sl 1, k2 tog, psso, patt 30 . . . 61 sts.
Cont in moss st patt until this section is the same length as between the marker threads of the Back. Now dec 1 st at both ends of next row and every foll 6th row to 53 sts. Work 5 rows without shaping.
Inc row With M, patt 4, *inc in next st, patt 3; rep from * to last 5 sts, patt 5 . . . 64 sts. With C, work 2 rows k1, p1 rib. With M, work 2 rows rib. **5th row** (eyelets) With C, k1, *y fwd, k2 tog; rep from * to last st, k1. **6th row** With C rib to end. With M, work 2 rows rib. With M, work 2 rows rib. Cast off sts.

LEG BORDERS

With right side of work facing, using C, pick up and k 52 sts round leg edge. Work in k1, p1 rib in stripes of 2 rows C, 2 rows M, then 2 rows C. Cast off sts.

TO MAKE UP

With right sides together, join the side seams with a back-stitch seam. Turn to right side. With M, make a twisted cord (see page 75) and thread it through the eyelets at waist.

JACKET

BACK AND FRONT (worked together to armhole)
With C, cast on 146 sts and work in k1, p1 rib in stripes of *2 rows C, 2 rows M*; rep from * to * once more, then 2 rows C. Break C.
Dec row K2, *k2 tog, k2; rep from * to end . . . 110 sts.
Cont in moss st patt – **1st row** *K1, p1; rep from * to end. **2nd row** *P1, k1; rep from * to end – until work measures 3cm [1¼ in] from the rib border.
Make Belt Opening Next row Patt 78 sts (these are for the Right Front and the Back), turn. Cont on these sts only for 10 rows. Break yarn.
Rejoin the yarn to the rem 32 sts, patt to end. Work 10 rows patt on these sts only. **11th row** Patt 32 sts, then on to the same needle, patt the rem 78 sts . . . 110 sts. Cont in moss st patt until work measures 9cm [3½ in] from the rib border, ending after a wrong-side row.
Shape Neck Dec 1 st at both ends of next row and every foll 3rd row until work measures 11cm [4½ in] from the rib border.
Divide for Back and Fronts 1st row K2 tog, patt 28, k2 tog, turn and cont on these 30 sts only for Right Front. **2nd row** Patt to end. **3rd row** K2 tog, patt 26, k2 tog. **4th row** Patt to end. Cont in this way, dec 1 st at both ends of right-side rows until all sts are worked off.
With right side of work facing, rejoin yarn to rem sts. **1st row** K2 tog, patt 42, k2 tog, turn and cont on these 44 sts only for the Back. **2nd row** Patt to end. **3rd row** K2 tog, patt 40, k2 tog. **4th row** Patt to end. Cont in this way, dec 1 st at both ends of right-side rows until 14 sts rem. Cast off rem 14 sts.
With right side of work facing,
Continued on next page

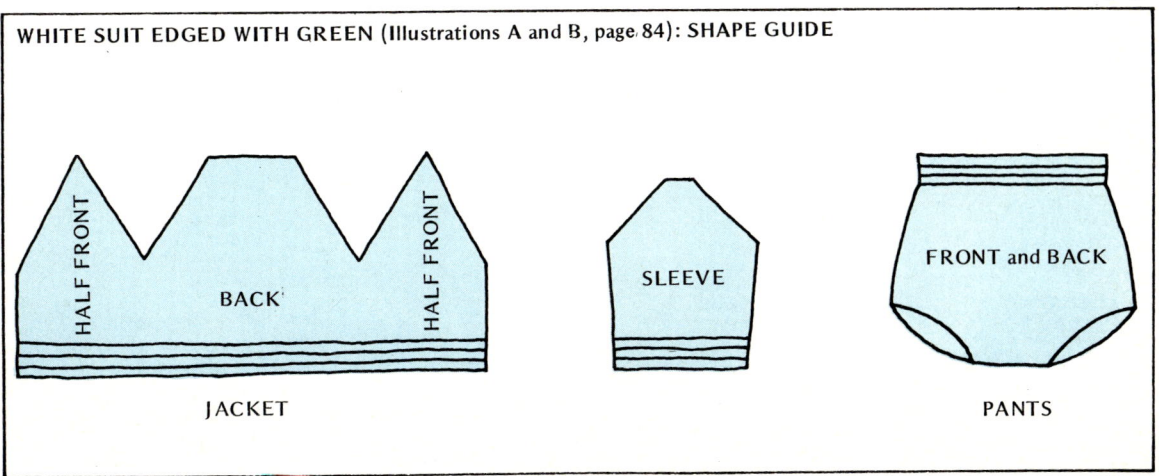

WHITE SUIT EDGED WITH GREEN (Illustrations A and B, page 84): SHAPE GUIDE

HALF FRONT — BACK — HALF FRONT

JACKET

SLEEVE

FRONT and BACK

PANTS

Sets for bigger babies . . . continued

rejoin yarn to rem sts for Left Front.

1st row K2 tog, k to last 2 sts, k2 tog. **2nd row** Patt to end. Rep 1st and 2nd rows until all sts are worked off.

SLEEVES

With C, cast on 40 sts and work 2 rows k1, p1 rib. Now work *2 rows rib in M, 2 rows rib in C* then rep from * to * once. Break C. **Dec row** *K2 tog, rib 3; rep from * to end . . . 32 sts.

Cont in moss st patt, inc 1 st at both ends of 3rd row foll and every foll 4th row to 40 sts. Cont without shaping until moss st patt measures 10cm [4 in] from the rib border.

Shape Raglan Top 1st row K2 tog, patt to last 2 sts, k2 tog. **2nd row** Patt to end. Rep last 2 rows until 4 sts rem, ending after a 2nd row. Cast off rem sts.

TO MAKE UP

Join the raglan shaping of the sleeve tops to the raglan shaping on the Back and Fronts thus: With right side of work facing, using yarn singly, first take up a

st from the right side, then a st from the left side and draw them together. Take another st, one row higher from the right side then another one row higher from the left side and draw these together, cont in this way drawing the two edges together to produce a flat seam – do not draw the yarn too tightly.

Front Band Cast on 6 sts with C. Work 2 rows C, then 2 rows M, twice, then 2 rows C once more all in k1, p1 rib. Break C. Cont in k1, p1 rib until the band, when slightly stretched will fit from cast-on edge of Right Front to top of border on the Left Front, join in C and work 5 stripes of rib to match the border rib. Cast off sts. Join the band to the front edges with a flat seam as for the raglan seams.

Belt (make 2) With M, cast on 7 sts. Work 22cm [8¾ in] moss st patt – every row, K1, *p1, k1; rep from * to end. Cast off. Sew the end of each piece to the Front edge, each one 3cm [1¼ in] from the top of the border of lower edge.

Green set with white borders
6 to 9 months

Materials 200g 4-ply knitting yarn used double (you can use 100g of double knitting used single) in Main colour (M); 25g in contrast colour (C); pairs of 3¾mm and 4mm [No 9 and No 8] knitting needles; sets of four double-pointed 3¾mm and 4mm [No 9 and No 8] needles; 5 buttons.

Measurements To fit 46cm [18 in] chest.

Tension 22 sts to 10cm [4 in] in either 4-ply used double or double knitting yarn on 4mm [No 8] needles in st-st.

Abbreviations k, knit; p, purl; st(s), stitch(es); cm, centimetre(s); in, inch(es); alt, alternate; beg, beginning; cont, continue; st-st, stocking stitch; rem, remain(ing); g-st, garter stitch (every row k); dec, decreas(e)ing; inc, increas(e)ing; inc 1k, increase by picking up loop before next st and knitting into back of it.

> The trousers, worked in two pieces, are a combination of stocking stitch, rib and moss stitch. The top is worked in the round to the armhole shaping – this avoids side seams and gives comfortable underarm gussets and an envelope neckline which is easy to put on and take off a baby.

TROUSERS
BACK

Beg at waist. With 3¾mm [No 9] needles and M, cast on 48 sts. Work 4cm [1½ in] k2, p2 rib. Change to 4mm [No 8] needles and beg k row, work 10cm [4 in]

Below and right: the mix and match set – white with green, green with white, and top and pants in garter stitch

st-st, ending after a p row, inc 1 st end of row.

Shape for Crotch 1st row Cast off 6 sts, k18, inc 1k, k1, inc 1k, k24. **2nd row** Cast off 6 sts, p to end. **3rd row** Cast off 4 sts, k14, inc 1k, k3, inc 1k, k18. **4th row** Cast off 4 sts, p to end. **5th row** Cast off 4 sts, k10, inc 1k, k5, inc 1k, k14. **6th row** Cast off 4 sts, p to end. **7th row** Cast off 4 sts, k6, inc 1k, k7, inc 1k, k10. **8th row** Cast off 4 sts, p to end. **9th row** Cast off 4 sts, k2, inc 1k, k9, inc 1k, k6. **10th row** Cast off 4 sts, p to end. **11th row** Cast off 2 sts inc 1k, k11, inc 1k, k2. **12th row** Cast off 2 sts, p to end . . . 13 sts. Work 6 rows g-st on these 13 sts. Cast off.

FRONT

With 4mm [No 8] needles and M, cast on 18 sts. Work 24 rows st-st for bib. **Next row** Cast on 15 sts, k across these sts, k the 18 sts. **Next row** Cast on 15 sts, p the 15 sts, p the rem 33 sts . . . 48 sts. Change to 3¾mm [No 9] needles and work 4cm [1½ in] k2, p2 rib, inc 1 st at end of last row . . . 49 sts.

Shape for Crotch 1st row Cast off 6 sts, k18, inc 1k, k1, inc 1k, k24. **2nd row** Cast off 6 sts, p to end. **3rd row** Cast off 4 sts, k14, inc 1k, k3, inc 1k, k18. **4th row** Cast off 4 sts, p to end. **5th row** Cast off 4 sts, k10, inc 1k, k5, inc 1k, k14. **6th row** Cast off 4 sts, p to end. **7th row** Cast off 4 sts, k6, inc 1k, k7, inc 1k, k10. **8th row** Cast off 4 sts, p to end. **9th row** Cast off 4 sts, k2, inc 1k, k9, inc 1k, k6. **10th row** Cast off 4 sts, p to end. **11th row** Cast off 2 sts, inc 1k, k11, inc 1k, k2. **12th row** Cast off 2 sts, p to end . . . 13 sts.

Work 2 rows g-st. **Next row** (buttonholes) K2, *cast off 2, k2*, rep from * to * once more, cast off 2, k1. **Next row** K1, *cast on 2, k2*, rep from * to * twice more. Work 2 rows more in g-st. Cast off.

LEG BORDERS

With right side of Back facing, using 3¾mm [No 9] needles and C, pick up and k24 sts round leg edge between crotch g-st border and side edge. Work 6 rows k2, p2 rib. Cast off sts. Beg at side seam, pick up and k24 sts along other leg edge to crotch. Work 6 rows k2, p2 rib. Cast off sts. Work borders in C along the two Front leg edges in the same way.

STRAPS

With 4mm [No 8] needles and C, cast on 6 sts. Work 24 rows moss st – **1st row** *K1, p1; rep from * to end. **2nd row** *P1, k1; rep from * to end. Rep last 2 rows for moss st pattern. Leave these sts on a spare needle. Make a second piece in the same way.

With the right side of the bib facing, slip the 6 sts of one strap on to a 4mm [No 8] needle, with this needle pick up and k the 18 sts of the bib, then moss st across the 6 sts of the other strap. Cont with C in moss st on all the sts for 8 rows.

Next row With C, moss st 6 sts, cast off the centre 18 sts, moss st 6 sts. Cont separately for each strap on each set of 6 sts. Work 24cm [9½ in] in moss st, working a buttonhole in the 3rd and 4th rows from the end. **3rd row** Pattern 2, cast off 2, pattern 2. **4th row** Pattern 2, cast on 2, pattern 2. Work 2 rows more.

Cast off. Work the other strap in the same way.

TO MAKE UP

Press following instructions on ball band. Join the side edges of the straps to the side edges of the bib, with neat oversewing. Sew the lower ends of the straps to the waist rib. With right sides together, back-stitch the side seams. Turn to right side. Sew 3 buttons on the g-st border of the crotch to correspond with the buttonholes. Sew the other 2 buttons on back waist rib to correspond with the buttonholes in the straps.

TOP

BACK AND FRONT

Worked in one piece in the round to armholes. With set of four double-pointed 3¾mm [No 9] needles and M, cast on 96 sts . . . 32 sts on each needle. Work 4 rounds k1, p1 rib. Change to set of 4mm [No 8] needles and cont in rounds of st-st for a further 15cm [6 in].

Divide for Back, Front and Underarms Place the sts on to separate

Continued on next page

Sets for bigger babies . . . continued

needles thus: slip 40 sts on to one needle for the Back; 8 sts on to one needle for one underarm; 40 sts on to one needle for the Front and 8 sts on to one needle for the other underarm.

On first set of 8 sts, work 8 rows st-st. Dec 1 st at both ends of next row. Work 8 rows more. Dec 1 st at both ends of next row. Work 1 row. Cast off rem 4 sts. Work the other underarm in the same way. On the 40 sts of the Back, cont in rows of st-st for a further 5cm [2 in] ending after a p row. **Next row** K10, turn and cont on these sts only. Dec 1 st at neck edge on every 3rd row following until all the sts are worked off.

With right side of work facing, slip the centre 20 sts on to a spare needle, k to end. On rem 10 sts, cont in st-st, dec 1 st at neck edge on 2nd row following then every following 3rd row until all sts are worked off.

On the 40 sts of the Front, cont in rows of st-st for a further 12·5mm [½ in] ending after a p row. **Next row** K12, turn and cont on these sts only. Dec 1 st at neck edge on every following 3rd row until all sts are worked off.

With right side of work facing, slip centre 16 sts on to a spare needle, k to end. On rem 12 sts, cont in st-st, dec 1 st at neck edge on 2nd row following and every following 3rd row until all the sts are worked off.

SLEEVES

With pair of 4mm [No 8] needles and M, cast on 32 sts. Cont in st-st, inc 1 st at both ends of every 5th row to 38 sts. Work 3 rows more.

Shape Top Cast off 2 sts at beg of next 14 rows. Cast off rem sts. Work a second sleeve in the same way.

TO MAKE UP

With the right side of the Back facing, using 3¾mm [No 9] needles

and C, beg at point on right shoulder, pick up and k24 sts down to back neck, k across the 20 sts from spare needle, pick up and k24 sts to the point at left shoulder . . . 68 sts. Work 4 rows k2, p2 rib. Cast off sts.

With the right side of the Front facing, using 3¾mm [No 9] needles and C, beg at point on left shoulder, pick up and k32 sts down neck edge to centre, k across the 16 sts from spare needle, pick up and k32 sts to right point. Work 4 rows k2, p2 rib. Cast off sts.

With the wrong sides of Back and Front together, overlap the back shoulder points over the front as shown in picture and tack along the shoulder edge. With the right sides of work together sew in the sleeve tops from armhole gusset to armhole gusset, using a back-stitch seam taking in both of the tacked together thicknesses at the shoulder. While work is still the wrong way out, back-stitch the seam along the gusset joining it at each side to the sleeve side. Turn the work to right side.

Using set of 3¾mm [No 9] needles and C, pick up and k40 sts round sleeve edge. Work 4 rounds k2, p2 rib. Cast off sts. Work the other border in the same way. Press following instructions on ball band.

Below: the simple shapes of the green set with white borders Opposite page: shape guide for the set knitted in garter stitch

Garter stitch set
3 to 6 months
Illustrated on page 85

Materials 200g 4-ply knitting yarn in main colour (M); 25g in contrast (C); pair 3¼mm [No 10] knitting needles; 9 buttons; 30cm [12 in] elastic, 2cm [¾ in] wide; set of four double-pointed needles.

Measurements To fit 41cm [16 in] chest.

Tension 28 sts to 10cm [4 in].

Abbreviations k, knit; p, purl; st(s), stitch(es); in, inch(es); cm, centimetre(s); g-st, garter stitch (every row k); beg, beginning; foll, following; cont, continue; tog, together; y fwd, yarn forward; sl, slip; psso, pass sl st over; dec, decreas(e)ing; inc, increas(e)ing; st-st, stocking stitch.

> This set has a minimum number of pieces – just one for the trousers and three for the jacket, including the sleeves. This means a minimum of seams too, just the sleeves and the sewing on of the front bands for the jacket and folding in the edges of the trousers to ensure a firm fit. Do not be put off by the use of 4 needles for the jacket yoke, they are used only to accommodate the larger number of sts, if you prefer you can place all the sts on to a long needle.

TROUSERS
TO MAKE

Beg at front waist. With M, cast on 42 sts. Beg k row, work 10 rows st-st. Now cont in g-st, inc 1 st at both ends of every 10th row to 54 sts. Cont in g-st without shaping until the g-st measures 10cm [4 in] ending after a wrong-side row.

Shape Legs Cont in g-st, casting off 3 sts at beg of next 6 rows . . . 36 sts. Dec 1 st at both ends of every foll 4th row until 26 sts remain. Work 8 rows g-st on these 26 sts for the crotch.

Shape back legs Cont on these 26 sts in g-st, inc 1 st at both ends of every row to 66 sts. Cast on 6 sts at beg of next 6 rows . . . 102 sts. Cont in g-st without shaping for 10cm [4 in]. Now work 16 rows k1, p1 rib. Cast off in rib.

TO MAKE UP

With M, pick up and k60 sts round one leg edge. Work 14 rows k1, p1 rib. Cast off in rib. Work round the other leg edge in the same way.

With right side of work facing, using M, pick up and k36 sts along the row-end edge of the 10cm [4 in] straight section of the Back. Work 8 rows k1, p1 rib. Cast off in rib. Work along the other side edge of the Back in the same way. Now work the buttonhole borders on the front thus: With right side of work facing, using M, pick up and k36 sts along the 10cm [4 in] row-ends between the st-st border and leg shaping. Work 34 rows k1, p1 rib. **4th row** (buttonholes) Rib 4, *cast off 2, rib 11; rep from * once more, cast off 2, rib 4. **5th row** Rib 4, *cast on 2, rib 11; rep from * once more, cast on 2, rib 4. Work 3 more rows k1, p1 rib. Cast off sts in rib. Work the other front edge in the same way. Fold the 14 row border of leg shaping in half to wrong side and sew to wrong side with slip-stitch. Fold the back waist rib in half to wrong side and slip-stitch. Trim the elastic to fit baby's waist (not too tightly) and insert the elastic through the folded back waist rib. Sew the elastic to the rib at both ends, then sew the ends of the rib. Fold the st-st edging at beg of front to wrong side, completely concealing it and slip-stitch this to wrong side.

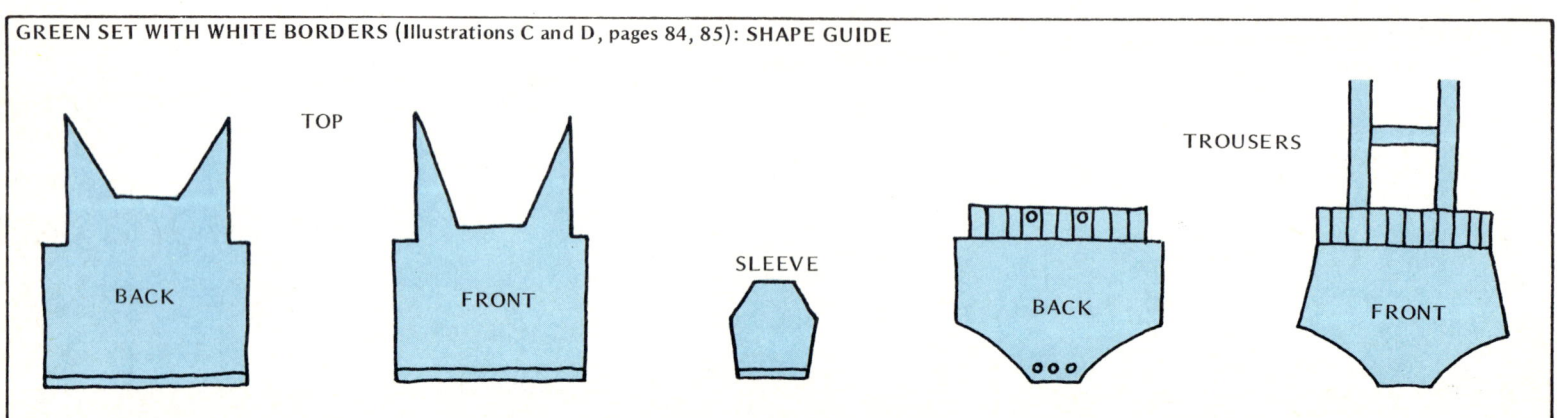

GREEN SET WITH WHITE BORDERS (Illustrations C and D, pages 84, 85): SHAPE GUIDE

TOP · BACK · FRONT · SLEEVE · TROUSERS · BACK · FRONT

Sew on the buttons, 3 on each side of back side borders to correspond with the buttonholes. Bring the Back to the Front to be buttoned as shown in picture.

JACKET

BACK AND FRONT

This is worked in one piece to armholes. Cast on 156 sts. Work 11cm [4½ in] g-st. Now divide the sts for back and fronts. On to one stitch holder place 38 sts for Right Front, on to 2nd stitch holder place 80 sts for Back and on to 3rd stitch holder place 38 sts for Left Front. Leave these sts aside for the time being.

SLEEVES

Beg at cuff edge, cast on 26 sts with M. Work 12 rows k1, p1 rib.
Next row Inc by knitting twice in each st to end . . . 52 sts. Work 11cm [4½ in] g-st and leave them aside for the time being. Work the second Sleeve the same way.
Raglan Shaping Prepare and place all the sts on to 3 of the set of double-pointed needles thus: Sl the 38 sts of the Right Front on to the 1st needle, place a loop of bright yarn next as a marker, then on to the same needle place the sts of one sleeve, place another marker loop; place the 80 sts of the Back next on to the 2nd needle, place another marker loop; place the 2nd sleeve sts on to the 3rd needle, place a 4th marker loop and finally on to the same needle place the 38 sts of the Left Front. It may help to use markers in different colours. Using the 4th needle, work to and fro – <u>not in rounds</u>.
1st row K to within 2 sts of the 1st marker, *k2 tog, sl the marker loop, sl 1, k1, psso*, k to within 2 sts of the 2nd marker, rep from * to *, k to within 2 sts of the 3rd marker, rep from * to *, k to within 2 sts of the 4th marker, rep from * to *, k to end.

2nd row K to end.
Rep the last 2 rows 9 times more . . . 180 sts.

YOKE

The marker loops may be removed now and if preferred all the sts placed on to one needle.
1st row K2, *k2 tog* rep from * to * 11 times more, k2, k6, rep from * to * 10 times, k6, k4, rep from * to * 26 times, k4, k6, rep from * to * 10 times, k6, k2, rep from * to * 12 times, k2 . . . 110 sts.
Cont in g-st without shaping in stripes of 2 rows C, 2 rows M until the 6th C stripe has been worked.
Next row (eyelets) With M, k1, *y fwd, k2 tog; rep from * to last st, k1. **Next row** With M, k to end. With C, k2 rows. With M, work 6 rows k1, p1 rib. Cast off.

LEFT FRONT BAND

With M, cast on 6 sts. Work in k1, p1 rib until the band, when slightly stretched, fits up Left Front edge from cast-on row to cast-off row. Cast off and sew to Left Front with an oversew seam.

RIGHT FRONT BAND

First mark the Left Front Band with pins to indicate buttons, the top one level with the centre of the k1, p1 rows round neck and the bottom one level with the 1st row of C in the Yoke. The other to be spaced equally between the two. Complete this band to match the first, working buttonholes to correspond with the pinned positions thus: **Buttonhole Row** Rib 2, y fwd, k2 tog, rib 2. When the band is the same length as the Left Front band, cast off the sts. Sew band to the Right Front edge.

TO MAKE UP

With right side inside, backstitch the sleeve seams. Turn to right side. Sew on the buttons at pinned positions. Make a twisted cord (see page 75) and thread through holes in the neck rib.

Bootees
3 to 6 months

Illustrated on page 84

Materials 25g 4-ply yarn; pair 3¼mm [No 10] knitting needles; 2 buttons.

Measurements To fit 2nd stage size.

Tension 28 sts to 10cm [4 in] in st-st.

TO MAKE

Cast on 40 sts. K2 rows.
Shape Instep 1st row K26, turn.
2nd row P12, turn. Work 16 rows more in st-st on these 12 sts. Break yarn.
With right side of work facing, beg where the first 14 sts were left and using the same needle, join in yarn and pick up and k11 sts along side of instep, k across the 12 sts, pick up and k11 sts along other side of instep and finally, k the rem 14 sts. Cont in g-st on the 62 sts for 14 rows.
Shape Sole 1st row K4, k2 tog, k20, sl 1, k1, psso, k6, k2 tog, k20, sl 1, k1, psso, k4. **2nd row** P to end.
3rd row K4, k2 tog, k18, sl 1, k1, psso, k6, k2 tog, k18, sl 1, k1, psso, k4. **4th row** P to end. **5th row** K4, k2 tog, k16, sl 1, k1, psso, k6, k2 tog, k16, sl 1, k1, psso, k4. **6th row** P to end. Cast off rem 50 sts.

STRAPS (make 2)

Cast on 38 sts. K4 rows. **Next row** K2, y fwd, k2 tog, k to end. K3 rows more. Cast off.

TO MAKE UP

With right side inside, join back and sole seam with back-stitch. Turn to right side. Sew approx 12·5mm [½ in] of centre of strap to back seam of bootee. Sew on button to correspond with the buttonhole.

GRAFTING – a good method for joining

Break off the yarn so that you have an end about four times as long as half the width of the work. Arrange the stitches equally on two needles so that, with the purl sides facing one another, both needle points are to your right, the nearest needle having the end of the yarn at its point. To do this, knit half the stitches and fold the work with the purl side on the inside – the fold will be on your right.
Begin at the right-hand side, * insert needle carrying yarn knitwise into the first stitch on the nearest needle. Draw yarn through stitch slipping the stitch off the needle.
Insert the needle carrying yarn purlwise into the second stitch on the nearest needle. Draw yarn through but leave the stitch on the needle. Take yarn under nearest needle and insert the needle carrying yarn purlwise into the first stitch on the back needle. Draw yarn through stitch and slip stitch off the needle.
Insert needle carrying yarn knitwise into second stitch on back needle. Draw yarn through but leave stitch on the needle. Bring needle carrying yarn forward to front needle and repeat from * to end. The two parts of the work will be joined with an invisible seam. Fasten off yarn neatly.

Diagram 1
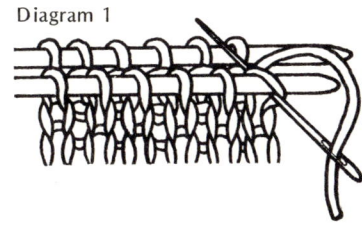

Diagram 2
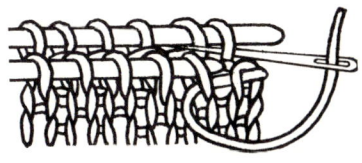

Diagram 3
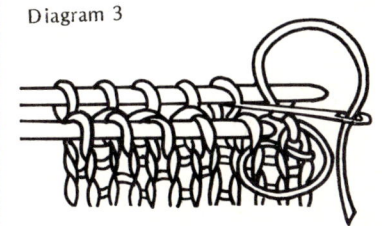

GARTER STITCH SET (Illustrations E and F, page 85): SHAPE GUIDE

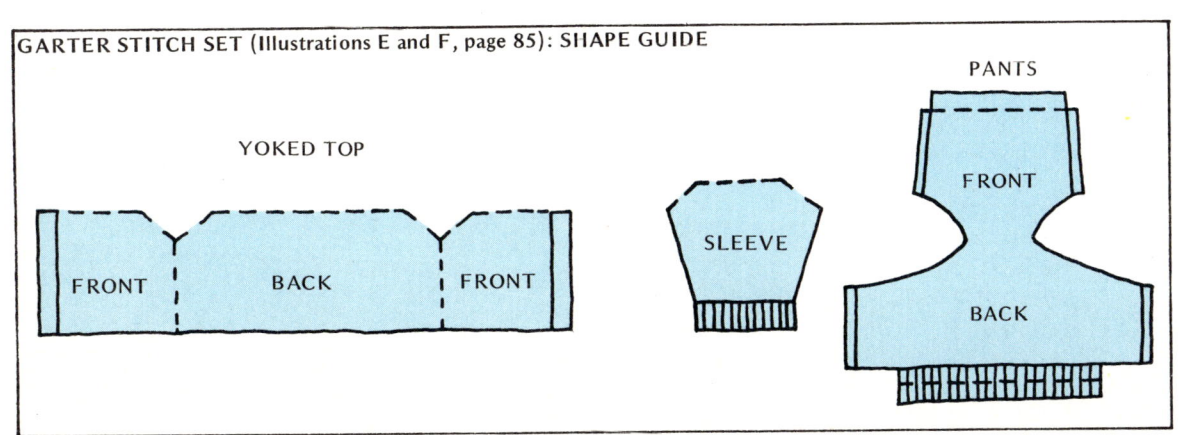

YOKED TOP — FRONT | BACK | FRONT

SLEEVE

PANTS — FRONT | BACK

Layette in smart tradition

3 to 9 months

The unusual pattern gives this layette a very special look. Before you start, read the special advice.

Materials Ten 25g balls 4-ply yarn in main colour (M); 2 balls in contrast (C); pair 3¼mm [No 10] needles; set of four double-pointed 3¼mm [No 10] needles; 5 buttons; 3mm [No 11] crochet hook.

Measurements To fit 46cm [18 in] chest.

Tension 28 sts and 36 rows to 10cm [4 in] in st-st.

Abbreviations k, knit; p, purl; st(s), stitch(es); cm, centimetre(s); in, inch(es); alt, alternate; beg, beginning; cont, continue; dec, decreas(e)ing; g-st, garter stitch; foll, following; inc, increas(e)ing; patt, pattern; st-st, stocking stitch; tbl, through back of loop; tog, together; y fwd, yarn forward; sl, slip; psso, pass slip st over; rnd, round(s); dc, double crochet. Square brackets contain imperial measurements.

Once you've mastered the pattern, this layette is very simple to make. Here's the 12-row pattern for easy reference:

1st to 4th rows Beg k row, in st-st.

5th row K2, (y fwd, k2 tog, k5) to last 4 sts, y fwd, k2 tog, k2.

6th to 10th rows Beg p row in st-st.

11th row K5, (y fwd, k2 tog, k5) to last 8 sts, y fwd, k2 tog, k6.

12th row P.

Take care with the patt when changing to set of 4 needles on the Playsuit, or knitting on 4 needles for the Bootees and Mittens — the 5th and 11th rounds are slightly different.

Right · an unusual pattern and combination of colours make this layette especially stunning

PULLOVER

BACK AND FRONT (alike)

With C and 3¼mm [No 10] needles cast on 69 sts. *1st row K2, (p1, k1) to last st, k1. 2nd row K1, (p1, k1) to end. Rep last 2 rows 4 times more. Break C and join in M.*
Cont in patt thus: **1st to 4th rows** Beg k row, in st-st. **5th row** K2, (y fwd, k2 tog, k5) to last 4 sts, y fwd, k2 tog, k2. **6th to 10th rows** Beg p row in st-st. **11th row** K5, (y fwd, k2 tog, k5) to last 8 sts, y fwd, k2 tog, k6. **12th row** P.
These 12 rows form the patt. Cont in patt until work measures 15cm [6 in] from cast-on edge, ending after a p row.

Shape Raglan Cast off 2 sts at beg of next 2 rows . . . 65 sts. **3rd row** K2, k2 tog, patt to last 4 sts, k2 tog, k2. **4th row** K2, p to last 2 sts, k2. ****Rep last 2 rows 9 times more . . . 45 sts. Leave rem sts on spare needle.

SLEEVES (make 2)

With C and 3¼mm [No 10] needles cast on 41 sts. Work in rib as Back from * to *. Now cont in patt as Back, inc 1 st at both ends of every 3rd row working the increased stitches in st-st to 49 sts. Cont straight until work measures 5cm [2 in] ending after a p row.

Shape Raglan Cast off 2 sts at beg of next 2 rows. Now rep 3rd and 4th shaping rows as Back raglan shaping to 25 sts. Leave sts on spare needle.

YOKE

With three of the set of double-pointed needles and M, k across 25 sts on one Sleeve, 45 sts of Back, 25 sts of second Sleeve then 45 sts of Front . . . 140 sts. Arrange 46 on each of 2 needles, and 48 sts on the third. Work using the 4th needle 16 rnds k1, p1 rib.
Change to C and cont thus: **1st rnd** K the k sts and sl the p sts with yarn at front of work. **2nd rnd** Sl the k sts with yarn at back of work and p the p sts. Rep last 2 rnds twice more. **Next rnd** As 1st

rnd, working y fwd, k2 tog at centre front to make eyelet. Work 3 rnds more. Cast off in rib.

TO MAKE UP

Press following instructions on ball band. With matching yarn join the raglan shapings with a flat seam. Using back-stitch join side and sleeve seams. Make a twisted cord (see page 75) with C and thread it through neck border, making a bow through eyelet at centre front.

JACKET

BACK

Work as Back of Pullover to **. Rep last 2 rows to 27 sts. Cast off.

LEFT FRONT

With C and 3¼mm [No 10] needles cast on 35 sts. Work in k1, p1 rib as Pullover Back from * to *, dec 1 st at end of last row . . . 34 sts. Now cont in patt as Back until Left Front matches Back to raglan shaping, ending after p row.

Shape Raglan Cast off 2 sts at beg of next row. Work 1 row straight. **Next row** K2, k2 tog, patt to end. **Next row** P to last 2 sts, k2. Rep last 2 rows to 22 sts, ending at Front edge.

Shape Neck Cont dec at raglan edge as before and at the same time shape neck edge by casting off 4 sts at beg of next wrong-side row then at same neck edge cast off 2 sts at beg of foll 2 wrong-side rows. Keeping raglan shaping dec as before, dec 1 st at neck edge on foll 5 wrong-side rows. Cast off rem 1 st.

RIGHT FRONT

Work as Left Front to beg of raglan shaping, but ending after a right-side row at the side edge.

Shape Raglan Cast off 2 sts at beg of next row. **Next row** Patt to last 4 sts, k2 tog, k2. **Next row** K2, p to end. Rep last 2 rows to 22 sts, ending after a wrong-side row at front edge.

Shape Neck Shape on right-side of work as given for Left Front to end.

SLEEVES (make 2)

With C and 3¼mm [No 10] needles cast on 39 sts. Work in rib as given for Back of Pullover for 5cm [2 in] inc 1 st at both ends of last row . . . 41 sts. Break C. Join in M. Cont in patt as Back, inc 1 st at both ends of 9th row foll and every foll 8th row to 47 sts. Work the increased sts in st-st. Cont straight until work measures 18cm [7 in] ending after a p row.

Shape Raglan Cast off 2 sts at beg

of next 2 rows . . . 43 sts. **3rd row** K2, k2 tog, patt to last 4 sts, k2 tog, k2. **4th row** K2, p to last 2 sts, k2. Now rep last 2 rows to 5 sts. Cast off.

TO MAKE UP

Press following instructions on ball band. Join raglan seams. With right side facing, using C, pick up and k67 sts along Left Front edge. Work 6 rows k1, p1 rib as welt. Cast off in rib (ie: k1, p1). Work Right Front border in the same way, making a buttonhole on the 3rd and 4th rows thus: **3rd row** Rib 3, cast off 2 sts, rib to end. In **4th row** cast on 2 sts over those cast off in previous row. Using matching yarn join side and sleeve seams with back-stitch on wrong side of work. With right side facing, using C, pick up and k81 sts round neck edge allowing 6 sts for each of the front borders, 27 sts across back neck, 7 sts for each sleeve top and 14 sts down each neck edge. Work 6 rows k1, p1 rib. Cast off in rib (ie: k1, p1). Sew on button.

PLAYSUIT

> This is all-in-one but as the top is knitted first, you could make a little vest and separate leggings. In this case work 12 rows of k1, p1 rib before starting the pattern on the legs (the rib can be doubled over and stitched down and elastic inserted for a waist, when the garment has been knitted).

TOP (Back and Front alike)

With M and 3¼mm [No 10] needles cast on 75 sts. Work 12 rows k1, p1 rib as given for Back of Pullover, inc 1 st at end of last row . . . 76 sts. Now cont in patt as Pullover until work measures 7cm [2¾ in].

Divide for Neck Next row K30, turn. Complete this side first. **1st row** Cast off 2 sts, patt to end. **2nd row** Cast off 6 sts, patt to end. **3rd to 7th rows** Cast off 2 sts at beg of row, patt to end. **8th row** K2 tog, patt to end. **9th row** Cast off 2 sts, p to end. **10th row** K2 tog, patt to end . . . 8 sts. Cont in patt for 7cm [2¾ in] for strap. Cast off. With right side facing, join M to rem sts at neck edge. Cast off centre 16 sts, patt to end. P1 row. Now work other side of neck: **1st row** Cast off 2 sts, patt to end. **2nd row** Cast off 6 sts, p to end. **3rd to 7th rows** Cast off 2 sts at beg of row, patt to end. **8th row**

P2 tog, p to end. **9th row** Cast off 2 sts, patt to end. **10th row** P2 tog, p to end. Cont in patt for 7cm [2¾ in] for strap. Cast off. Work a second piece in the same way for Front.

LEGGINGS

These are worked downwards from the rib of the top. *With M and 3¼mm [No 10] needles pick up and k76 sts carefully along the cast-on edge of the Top Back. Work 16cm [6¼ in] straight in basic layette patt, ending after a right-side row. **Next row** Patt 28, cast off centre 20 sts, patt 28.* Rep from * to * along cast-on edge of Top Front.

Sew the centre two sets of 20 sts together for gusset.

Place the rem 28 sts of right front leg together with the corresponding 28 rem sts of right back leg on to three of the set of double-pointed needles. With a strand of brightly coloured yarn make a loop through the 2 sts at the centre of the back of each leg.

Cont in rnds, dec thus: Work 4 rnds straight in pattern. *5th rnd Patt to within 3 sts of the marked sts, k2 tog, k2, k2 tog tbl, patt to end. **6th to 9th rnds** Work straight*. Rep from * to * 11 times more . . . 32 sts. Cont straight until leg measures 20cm [8 in] from gusset.

Divide for Heel Next rnd k the 16 back leg sts, turn. Slip the rem sts on to a safety-pin, cont on first set of sts only. Work 11 rows st-st. **Turn Heel 1st row** K10, k2 tog, turn. **2nd row** Sl 1, p4, p2 tog, turn. **3rd row** Sl 1, k5, k2 tog, turn. Cont in this way, taking in 1 more st before dec, until all sts are worked . . . 10 sts rem. K1 row. Return sts from pin on to a working needle.

Next rnd, 1st needle pick up and k6 sts down side of 12 rows of heel and k1 st from sts that were on pin. **2nd needle** K14 sts from the sts that were on the pin. **3rd needle** K1 rem st from pin, pick up and k6 sts up side of 12 rows of heel and 5 sts from 1st needle . . . 14 sts on 2nd needle and 12 sts on each of 1st and 3rd needles. **Shape foot, 1st needle** K to last 2 sts, k2 tog. **2nd needle** Patt to end. **3rd needle** Sl 1, k1, psso, k to end. **2nd rnd, 1st and 3rd needles** K. **2nd needle** Patt to end. Rep last 2 rnds to 32 sts. Cont straight in patt on the 14 sts and rem in st-st for 8cm [3 in] from beg of heel.

Shape Toe, 1st needle K to last 2 sts, k2 tog. **2nd needle** Sl 1, k1,

psso, k to last 2 sts, k2 tog. **3rd needle** Sl 1, k1, psso, k to end. **Next rnd** K to end. Rep last 2 rnds until 6 sts rem. Thread yarn through rem sts, draw up sts and secure.

Work the other leg the same.

TO MAKE UP

Press following instructions on ball band. With right side of Top facing, using C, pick up and k37 sts along armhole edge, to top of strap. Work 6 rows rib as Pullover. Cast off in rib. Work the other 3 armholes in the same way. With right side facing, using C, pick up and k71 sts round Front neck edge and work border as armhole. Work the Back neck border in the same way. With C, work 2 rows dc along each Back shoulder edge. Work the Front shoulder edges in the same way, working 2 ch in place of 1 dc (twice) on 2nd row for button loops. Sew on buttons to correspond. Join side seams using back-stitch.

BONNET

TO MAKE

With C and 3¼mm [No 10] needles cast on 83 sts. *1st row K2, (p1, k1) to last st, k1. 2nd row K1, (p1, k1) to end. Rep last 2 rows 4 times more. Break C and join in M. Cont in basic layette patt until work measures 12cm [4¾ in] from beg, ending after a p row.

Shape Back Next row Cast off 28 sts, patt 27, cast off rem 28 sts and break off yarn. Join M to rem centre 27 sts and cont on these sts only in k1, p1 rib, dec 1 st at both ends of 9th row foll and every foll 8th row to 19 sts. Cont straight until rib measures 10cm [4 in]. Cast off sts loosely in rib.

TO MAKE UP

Press following instructions on ball band. Join sides of rib section to cast-off edges as shown in picture. With M, cast on 60 sts for strap, then, with right side facing, on to same needle, pick up and k60 sts along lower edge of hat, then cast on 60 sts for second strap. On these 180 sts, work 6 rows g-st. Cast off loosely.

BOOTEES

TO MAKE

With set of four double-pointed needles and C, cast on 42 sts – 14 on each needle. Work 6 rnds k1, p1 rib. Break C. Join in M and work in rnds using basic pattern but making these changes: **5th rnd** (Y fwd, k2 tog, k5) to end. **11th rnd** K2 (y fwd, k2 tog, k5) to last 5 sts, y fwd k2 tog, k3. Cont until

Continued on next page

Layette ... continued

work measures 5cm [2 in] from beg.

Shape Instep 1st rnd Patt 14 of 1st needle, patt 13 of 2nd needle, turn, patt 12, turn. Leaving all other sts for the time being, cont on these 12 sts only for the instep, working 16 rows k1, p1 rib. Break yarn. Now, using M, join the yarn to the place where the 2nd needle 1 st has already been worked, pick up and k10 sts along the side of the instep, k across the 12 instep sts, pick up and k10 sts along other side of instep, then work in patt on the 14 sts of 1st needle, 1 rem st of 2nd needle and the 14 sts of the 3rd needle . . . 62 sts.

Sole Cont in g-st for the sole (ie: rnds of 1 rnd k, 1 rnd p). Work 2 rnds. **3rd rnd** Beg centre back – k2 tog, k22, k2 tog, k10, k2 tog, k22, k2 tog. **4th rnd** P. **5th rnd** K2 tog, k21, k2 tog, k8, k2 tog, k21, k2 tog. Cont dec on alt rnds in this way 4 times more.

TO MAKE UP

Join lower seam. Make a twisted cord (see page 75) with M and C and thread through eyelets at ankle. Make a pompon and attach to each end of cord.

MITTENS

TO MAKE

With set of four double-pointed needles and C, cast on 36 sts – 12 on each needle. Work 8 rnds k1, p1 rib. **Next rnd** (eyelets) (k1, y fwd, k2 tog) to end. Change to M. **Next rnd** (K twice in next st, k5) 6 times . . . 42 sts.

Cont in basic layette patt in rnds but making these changes: **5th rnd** (y fwd, k2 tog, k5) to end. **11th rnd** K2 (y fwd, k2 tog, k5) to last 5 sts, y fwd k2 tog, k3. Cont until work measures 10cm [4 in] from beg.

Shape Top 1st rnd (k1, k2 tog, k15, sl 1, k1, psso, k1) twice. **2nd rnd** (k1, k2 tog, k13, sl 1, k1, psso, k1) twice . . . 34 sts. Cont dec in this way on every rnd to 22 sts. Cast off.

TO MAKE UP

Press following instructions on ball band. Join cast-off sts. Make a twisted cord (see page 75) with M and thread it through eyelets at wrist. With M and C, make pompons (see page 75) and attach to cords.

Red and white set

3 to 9 months

Materials 3(4) 25g balls Double Knitting yarn in main colour (M); 2 balls in contrast (C); a pair $3\frac{3}{4}$mm and $3\frac{1}{4}$mm [No 9 and No 10] knitting needles; 2 press-studs; set of four double-pointed $3\frac{3}{4}$mm [No 9] needles.

Measurements To fit 41(46)cm [16(18) in] chest.

Tension 22 sts and 46 rows to 10cm [4 in] in g-st.

Abbreviations k, knit; p, purl; st(s), stitch(es); cm, centimetre(s); in, inch(es); alt, alternate; beg, beginning; cont, continue; dec, decreas(e)ing; inc, increas(e)ing; g-st, garter stitch; rep, repeat; rem, remain(ing); tog, together; y fwd, yarn forward.

Size Note Figures in brackets refer to larger size. One figure only refers to both sizes. Square brackets contain imperial measurements.

This simple-knit set makes use of the very first stitch we learn. The top is worked all in one with clever shaping as you can see in the diagram. The neat pants can be seamed as shown in the picture or fastened at the crotch if you prefer by working 2 rows dc on back edge and 2 rows on front. Work a 3rd row on the front thus: 2 dc, 2 ch, miss 1 dc, work to last 3 dc, 2 ch, miss 1 dc, work to end. Sew on buttons to correspond.

TOP – worked sideways

Beg at right back opening edge, with $3\frac{3}{4}$mm [No 9] needles and M, cast on 58(64) sts. K10 rows.

Shape for Skirt ***1st and 2nd rows** K36(39), turn, k to end. **3rd and 4th rows** K52(58), turn, k to end. **5th and 6th rows** K on all sts.*

Note that the skirt is worked over 36(39) sts, the yoke over 16(19) sts and the rem 6 sts for neck.

Rep from * to * throughout except on sleeves where instructions are given. Cont until work measures 14(15)cm [$5\frac{1}{2}$(6) in] from beg, ending after a 4th shaping row.

Make 1st sleeve (worked sideways) **K36(39) sts and leave these sts on a stitch holder. Cast on 40 (43) sts and on to same needle k to end of rem sts . . . 62(68) sts. K1 row. Cont working the turns at top for neck and yoke, at the same time turning for cuffs thus: **1st and 2nd rows** K to last 22(25) sts, turn, k to last 9 sts, turn. **3rd and 4th rows** K to last 6 sts, turn, k to end. **5th and 6th rows** K2 rows on all sts. Rep last 6 rows until sleeve measures 16(18)cm [$6\frac{1}{2}$(7) in] from the cast-on 40(43) sts, ending at cuff edge. **Next row** Cast off the 40(43) sleeve sts.

With right side facing sl the 36(39) sts from spare needle on to the working needles, k across rem 22(25) sts . . . 58(64) sts.**

Cont in g-st, turning as before sleeve until Front measures 22(24)cm [$8\frac{3}{4}$($9\frac{1}{4}$) in] ending after a 4th row.

Make 2nd sleeve Work as 1st sleeve from ** to **. Cont in g-st, turning as before until Left Back measures as Right to border. Now work 10 rows g-st without shaping. Cast off.

TO MAKE UP

Press following instructions on ball band but only very lightly. With right side facing, using C, pick up and k30(33) sts along cuff edge. K4 rows. Cast off. In the same way, pick up and k76 sts round neck edge. K4 rows. Cast off. Join sleeve seams. Sew on press-studs.

PANTS

BACK

With $3\frac{1}{4}$mm [No 10] needles and C, cast on 72 sts. Work 6 rows k1, p1 rib. **Next row** (eyelets) K1, *rib 2, k2 tog, y fwd; rep from * to last st, k1. Work 6 rows more in rib. Change to $3\frac{3}{4}$mm [No 9] needles and cont in g-st until work measures 15cm [6 in] from beg. **

Shape Leg Dec 1 st at both ends of next 4 rows then 1 st at both ends of alt rows to 16 sts. Cont straight until work measures 23cm [9 in] measured straight down centre. Cast off.

FRONT

Work as Back to **.

Shape Leg Cast off 5 sts at beg of next 4 rows; 3 sts at beg of next 2 rows; 2 sts at beg of next 2 rows. Now dec 1 st at both ends of next row and foll alt rows to 16 sts. Cont straight until Front matches Back. Cast off.

TO MAKE UP

Press following instructions on ball band but only very lightly. Join the crotch seam. With right side facing, using $3\frac{1}{4}$mm [No 10] needles and M, pick up and k84 sts round leg edge. K8 rows. Cast off. Join side seams. Fold leg borders in half to wrong side and slip-stitch. With M, make a cord (see page 75) to fit waist plus enough to tie, and thread through eyelets at waist.

BOOTEES

TO MAKE

With $3\frac{1}{4}$mm [No 10] needles and M, cast on 42(45) sts. Cont in g-st until work measures 5cm [2 in].

Next row (eyelets) *K1, y fwd, k2

tog; rep from * to end. K2 rows more. Change to 3¾mm [No 9] needles and C.
Next row (right side) K16(17) sts and leave these sts on a pin, k10, turn and leave rem 16(18) sts on a pin.
Cont in g-st on centre 10 sts for 21(23) rows. Leave these sts. With set of four needles, slip the sts from the first pin on to 1st needle, pick up and k10(12) sts along side of instep rows, k the 10 instep sts, pick up and k10(11) sts along second side of instep, k the sts from second pin.
Arrange these 62(68) sts on 3 needles and with the fourth work backwards and forwards, <u>not in rounds,</u> for 10 rows.

Next row K36(39), turn. **Next row** K9, k2 tog, turn. Rep last row taking up 1 st at each side of centre 10 sts until 20 sts rem. Cast off.

TO MAKE UP
Press very lightly. Sew back and sole seams. With C, make a twisted cord (see page 75) and thread through eyelets.

Below: cheerful and snug, this set is knitted in simple garter stitch and the top is worked in one piece – great if you don't like too many seams
Right: the diagram you'll need for the Red and White Set. Note the clever shaping of the Top

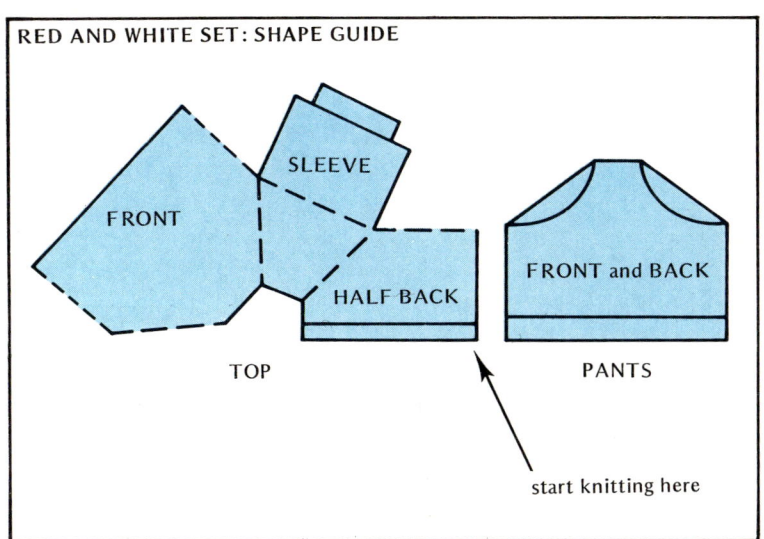

RED AND WHITE SET: SHAPE GUIDE

SLEEVE
FRONT
HALF BACK
TOP
FRONT and BACK
PANTS
start knitting here

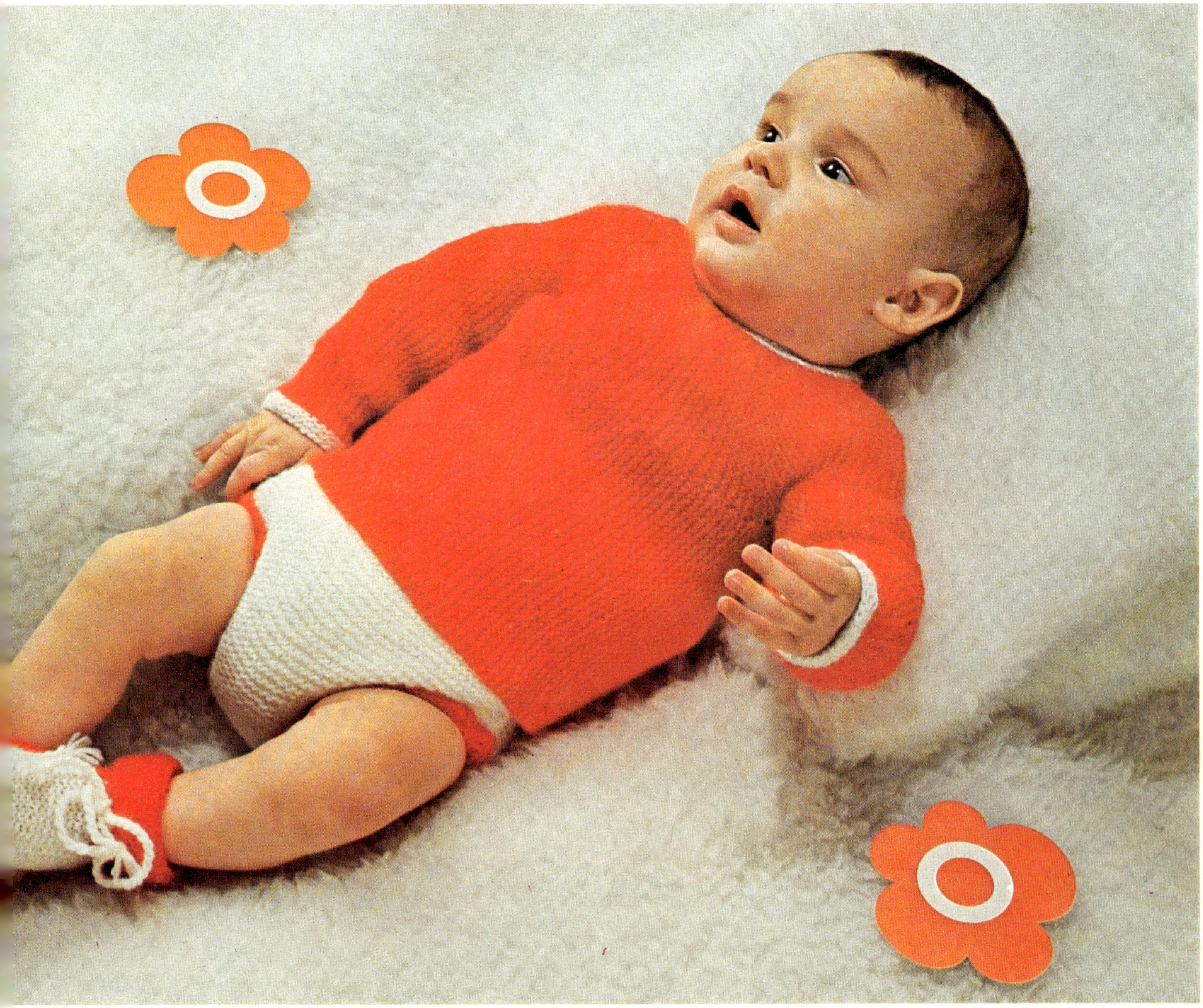

Carrying cape

3 to 12 months

In or out of the pushchair this cape is warm and good looking. Add a few more rows to the hood, change the colour and a two year old would love it as well.

Materials Five 50g balls yarn for Aran Knitting; a pair 4½mm [No 7] knitting needles.

Measurements Length 40cm [15¾ in] to beg of hood.

Tension 18 sts and 22 rows to 10cm [4 in] in st-st.

Abbreviations k, knit; p, purl; st(s), stitch(es); cm, centimetre(s); in, inch(es); cont, continue; beg, beginning; foll, following; st-st, stocking stitch; tog, together; inc, increase; rep, repeat. Square brackets contain imperial measurements.

> You knit this cape from the bottom up, shaping by decreasing as you go and the textured look is achieved by making the purl side the right side of stocking stitch. If you flat sew the hood seam, the cape could be worn either side – in this case do be careful about making joins with new yarn.

TO MAKE

Cast on 271 sts. K4 rows. Cont in reverse st-st (p side is right side) in panels, placing sts thus:
1st row K5 – border – k1, (p19, k1) 13 times, k5.
2nd row K5, p1, (k19, p1) 13 times, k5.
Rep last 2 rows twice more. Now shape panels thus:
7th row Dec: K5, k1, (p2 tog, p15, p2 tog, k1) 13 times, k5 . . . 245 sts.
8th row K5, p1, (k17, p1) 13 times, k5.
Work 4 rows straight with panels as set.
13th row Dec: K5, k1, (p2 tog, p13, p2 tog, k1) 13 times, k5 . . . 219 sts.
14th row K5, p1, (k15, p1) 13 times, k5.

Work 4 rows straight with panels as set.
19th row Dec: K5, k1, (p2 tog, p11, p2 tog, k1) 13 times, k5 . . . 193 sts.
20th row K5, p1, (k13, p1) 13 times, k5.
Work 6 rows straight with panels as set.
27th row Dec: K5, k1, (p2 tog, p9, p2 tog, k1) 13 times, k5 . . . 167 sts.
28th row K5, p1, (k11, p1) 13 times, k5.
Work 6 rows straight with panels as set.
35th row Dec: K5, k1, (p2 tog, p7, p2 tog, k1) 13 times, k5 . . . 141 sts.

CARRYING CAPE: SHAPE GUIDE

front

centre back

36th row K5, p1, (k9, p1) 13 times, k5.
Work 10 rows straight with panels as set.
47th row Dec: K5, k1, (p2 tog, p5, p2 tog, k1) 13 times, k5 . . . 115 sts.
48th row K5, p1, (k7, p1) 13 times, k5.
Work 10 rows straight with panels as now set.
59th row Dec: K5, k1, (p2 tog, p3, p2 tog, k1) 13 times, k5 . . . 89 sts.
60th row K5, p1, (k5, p1) 13 times, k5.
Work 14 rows straight with panels as now set.
75th row Dec: K5, k1, (p2 tog, p1, p2 tog, k1) 13 times, k5 . . . 63 sts.
76th row K5, p1, (k3, p1) 13 times, k5.
Work 8 rows straight with panels as now set. Cast off sts.

HOOD

Cast on 26 sts. **1st row** K5 – border – p to end. **2nd row** K. Cont in reverse st-st with border as set, inc 1 st at end of 5th row foll and every foll 8th rows to 31 sts. Cont straight until 42 rows have been worked.
Keeping border as set – **Next row** (right side) K. Beg k row, work 3 rows st-st. Rep last 4 rows once more. **Next row** (right side) K. Now work 42 rows as first side, dec at end of 5th row foll and every foll 8th row to 26 sts. Work 5 rows straight. Cast off. Join back seam using flat-stitch.

TO MAKE UP

Press according to instructions on ball band. Place Hood to neck edge of cape with right sides together, pin the back seam to centre of back of cape and using flat-stitch seam sew on the Hood, leaving a small gap in the seam each time you come to the k1 ridge of the cape, this will form a series of eyelet holes in which to insert the cord. Make a long twisted cord (see page 75) and after tying or binding the ends, insert it through the small gaps between the hood and cape seam.

Above: a very easy-to-wear wrap-up for a little girl. The unusual texture is achieved by making the purl side the right side, and by making a feature of the decreasings
Left: the diagram which will help you to shape the cape correctly

Short and sweet playsuit

6 to 12 months

A pretty little outfit for a child who's just beginning to be mobile.

Materials 4(5) 25g balls Double Knitting yarn in main colour (M); 1 ball in contrast (C); pairs of 3¾mm and 4mm [No 9 and No 8] knitting needles; 3·5mm [No 9] crochet hook; 2 buttons.

Measurements To fit 41(46)cm [16 (18) in] chest; length at side, 15 (17)cm [6(7) in].

Tension 24 sts and 32 rows to 10cm [4 in] in st-st.

Abbreviations k, knit; p, purl; st(s), stitch(es); cm, centimetre(s); in, inch(es); alt, alternate; beg, beginning; foll, following; dec, decreas(e)ing; rep, repeat; st-st, stocking stitch; sl, slip; psso, pass slip stitch over; tog, together; cont, continue; rem, remain(ing); y fwd, yarn forward; k1b, k into back of st; inc, increas(e)ing; ch, chain; dc, double crochet.

Size Note Figures in brackets refer to larger size. One figure only refers to both sizes.

> As this playsuit is worked in just two pieces, you can have a buttoned crotch if you prefer. Don't make a seam and, with right side facing, work 2 rows dc along back edge in place of seam. Mark this border to indicate 4 buttons. Work 2 rows dc on the front edge working buttonholes to correspond thus (work to marker, 2 ch, miss 2 dc) to end.

FRONT

Beg at lower edge of left leg. With 4mm [No 8] needles and M, cast on 23(24) sts. Work 6 rows st-st, inc 1 st at beg of 3rd and 5th rows. Leave these sts on a spare needle. Work a second piece for the right leg in the same way but inc at end of 3rd and 5th rows.
Join the legs with crotch thus:
1st row K25(26) of left leg, turn, cast on 13(15) sts for crotch, turn and k across 25(26) sts of right leg ... 63(67) sts. **2nd row** P. **3rd row** K25(26), sl 1, k1, psso, k9(11), k2 tog, k25(26). **4th row and foll alt rows** P. **5th row** K25(26), sl 1, k1, psso, k7(9), k2 tog, k to end. Cont in this way, dec 1 st at both sides of crotch until 3 sts rem.
Next row K25(26), sl 1, k2 tog, psso, k to end. Cont straight on rem 51(53) sts until side measures 15(17)cm [6(7) in] ending after p row.
Change to 3¾mm [No 9] needles and cont in twisted rib thus: **1st row** K1, *p1, k1b; rep from * to last 2 sts, p1, k1.
2nd row K2, *p1, k1b; rep from * to last st, k1.

Rep last 2 rows for 3cm [1¼ in]. Change to 4mm [No 8] needles and cont in st-st in stripes of 2 rows M, 2 rows C. Work 10 rows straight.
Shape Armholes Cast off 6(7) sts at beg of next 2 rows; 2 sts at beg of next 4 rows. Dec 1 st at both ends of next 3 rows. Now cont straight until the 6th C stripe has been worked.
Shape Neck **Next row** K5, turn and * cont on these sts in st-st in M for 9 rows. **Next row** K2, y fwd, k2 tog, k1. **Next row** P. **Next 2 rows** Dec 1 st at both ends. Fasten off.*
With right side facing, join M at neck edge to rem sts, cast off centre 15 sts, k to end. Work from * to * on rem sts for second strap.

BACK

Work as for Front, working in M throughout (ie, omitting stripes).
Shape Back Neck and Straps **Next row** K5, turn and cont on these sts in st-st in M for 46 rows. Cast off.
With right side facing, join M at neck edge to rem sts, cast off centre 15 sts, k to end. Work 46 rows st-st on rem 5 sts for second strap. Cast off.

TO MAKE UP

Press following instructions on ball band. Using back-stitch join inner leg and crotch seams, then join side seams.
Work a border round edges and straps in crochet thus: With right side facing, using C, (3 dc, 3 ch, dc in 1st of 3 ch) to end.
Sew on buttons.

Left: the Short and Sweet Playsuit that's both smart and practical Below: the shape guide for both the front and back of the suit

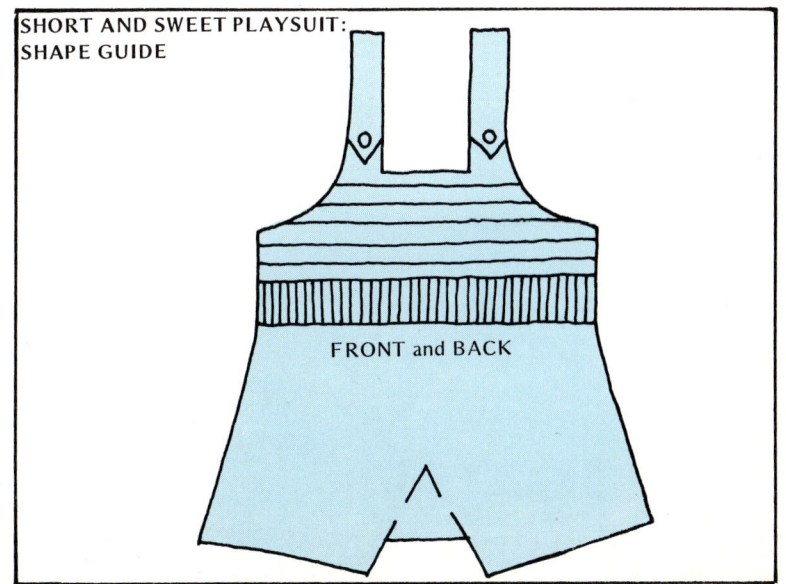

SHORT AND SWEET PLAYSUIT: SHAPE GUIDE

FRONT and BACK

Pramsuit

6 to 12 months

Just perfect for travelling or you could make a dressing gown for a toddler instead.

Materials Ten 25g balls Double Knitting yarn in White (W); four balls in Red (R); four balls in Green (G); four balls in Blue (B) and four balls in Yellow (Y); pair 3¾mm [No 9] knitting needles; 35cm [14 in] zip.

Tension 24 sts and 32 rows to 10cm [4 in] in st-st.

Abbreviations k, knit; p, purl; st(s), stitch(es); cm, centimetre(s); in, inch(es); alt, alternate; beg, beginning; cont, continue; foll, following; st-st, stocking stitch; rep, repeat, rem, remain(ing); sl, slip, y fwd, yarn forward; y bk, yarn back; tbl, through back of loop. Square brackets contain imperial measurements.

Note The pramsuit is worked in one piece, beg and ending at the shoulders. If you wish to make the garment as a dressing gown for a 1 year old, cast off at the half way mark. Cast on 104 sts and follow instructions for Front.

TO MAKE

Beg at **Back Right Shoulder** With W, cast on 32 sts. **1st row** With W, cast on 3 sts for neck, k to end. **2nd row** With W, p to end. **3rd and 4th rows** As 1st and 2nd. **5th row** With B, cast on 4 sts, k to end. **6th row** With B, p to end. **7th row** With B, cast on 10 sts, k to end. **8th row** With B, p to end . . . 52 sts. Leave sts on a spare needle. Now work the **Back Left shoulder**, reversing shaping thus: **1st row** With W, k to end. **2nd row** With W, cast on 3 sts, p to end. **3rd and 4th rows** As 1st and 2nd rows. **5th row** With B, k to end. **6th row** With B, cast on 4 sts, p to end. **7th row** With B, k to end. **8th row** With B, cast on 10 sts, p to end. **9th row** With B, k to end, then on to same needle, k across the 52 sts on spare needle . . . 104 sts. **10th row** With B, p to end. Cont in st-st on all sts in stripes of 8 rows W, 6 rows G, 8 rows W, 6 rows R, 8 rows W, 6 rows Y, 8 rows W, 6 rows B, until the second R stripe has been worked. With W, work the slip rib for the waist cord. **1st row** *K1, yarn forward, sl 1 purlwise, yarn back; rep from * to end. **2nd row** *P1, slip the k st, keeping the yarn towards you; rep from * to end. Rep last 2 rows 7 times more. Beg with 6 rows Y, cont in the striped st-st pattern until the 4th Y stripe has been worked. Work 8 rows W.

This is the halfway mark of the bag if you are making the gown. Now cont for the Front, but reversing the stripes thus: Beg 8 rows W, 6 rows Y, 8 rows W, 6 rows R, 8 rows W, 6 rows G, 8 rows W, 6 rows B. Cont in stripes until the 2nd R stripe has been worked. Work 8 rows W.

Divide for Front Opening 1st row With G, k52, turn. Cont on these sts only for Left Front. Cont in stripes until the 3rd Y stripe has been worked. With W, work 16 rows in slip rib as Back. **1st row** *K1, sl 1; rep from * to end. **2nd row** *Sl the k st, k the sl st; rep from * to end. Rep last 2 rows 7 times more.

Cont in stripes, beg 6 rows R, until the 3rd G stripe has been worked after the division.

Shape Neck 1st row With W, k to end. **2nd row** With W, cast off 6 sts, p to end. **3rd row** As 1st row. **4th row** Cast off 4 sts, p to end.

5th row As 1st row. **6th row** With W, cast off 3 sts, p to end. **7th row** With W, k to end. **8th row** With W, as 6th. **9th row** With B, k to end. **10th row** With B, cast off 2 sts, p to end. **11th row** With B, k to end. **12th row** With B, cast off 2 sts, p to end . . . 32 sts. Complete the B stripe then work 4 rows W. Cast off.

With right side of work facing, rejoin G to rem sts to complete Right Front. Cont without shaping as for the first side, and working the slip rib at waist, until the 3rd G stripe has been worked after the division.

Shape Neck 1st row With W, cast off 6 sts, k to end. **2nd row and foll alt rows** P to end. **3rd row** With W, cast off 4 sts, k to end. **5th row** With W, cast off 3 sts, k to end. **7th row** With W, cast off 3 sts, k to end. **9th row** With B, cast off 2 sts, k to end. **10th row** With B, p to end. **11th row** With B, cast off 2 sts, k to end. **12th row** With B, p to end. Complete the B stripe, then work 4 rows W. Cast off.

HOOD
Beg with the back. This begins in two pieces, joined on the 4th row. With R, cast on 10 sts. **1st row** K to end. **2nd row** Cast on 4 sts, p to end. **3rd row** K to end. **4th row** Cast on 6 sts, p to end. Do not break yarn but leave these sts on the needle for the time being.
With a spare pair of needles, with R, cast on 10 sts. **1st row** Cast on 4 sts, k to end. **2nd row** P to end. **3rd row** Cast on 6 sts, k to end. Break yarn. Now with the first needles, p across these sts of the second piece . . . 40 sts.
Cont in st-st in stripes of 8 rows W, 6 rows G, 8 rows W, 6 rows B, 8 rows W, 6 rows Y, 8 rows W, 6 rows R.
Now shape the top edge Beg with 8 rows W, then 6 rows G, then 4 rows W – at the same time dec 1 st at beg of next 4 rows; cast off 2 sts at beg of next 4 rows; cast off 3 sts at beg of next 2 rows; cast off 4 sts at beg of next 4 rows. Cast off rem 6 sts.
With W, cast on 130 sts for the Hood sides. Work 8 rows W, 6 rows G, 8 rows W, 6 rows B, 8 rows W, 12 rows Y, 8 rows W, 6 rows B, 8 rows W, 6 rows G, 8 rows W. Cast off.

SLEEVES
With W, cast on 58 sts. Work 16 rows slip rib. **1st row** *K1, sl 1; rep from * to end. **2nd row** *P the sl stitches and sl the k sts of the 1st row; rep from * to end. Rep last 2 rows 7 times more.
Now cont in st-st in stripes of 8 rows W, 6 rows B, 8 rows W, 6 rows Y, 8 rows W, 6 rows R, 8 rows W. Cast off. Work a second sleeve in the same way.

TO MAKE UP
With right sides together, back-stitch the shoulder seams. With right sides together fold the sleeve in half lengthways and place the centre fold to the shoulder seams. Back-stitch the cast-off edge of sleeve to side edge of Front and Back. Sew on the second sleeve in the same

way. With right sides inside, back-stitch the side and sleeve seams, matching the stripes. Fold the long piece of Hood sides in half with the broad Y stripe to the front. With right sides together sew one long edge to the rounded part of the Hood back. Fold the other over and hem-stitch to the wrong side of the work. Join the two sides made at the beg of the Hood back, to form a tiny tuck. Join the two pieces of the back neck in the same way. Placing the two tucks together and having right sides together, back-stitch the Hood to the neck edge. Using a 3·5mm [No 9] crochet hook and W, work row of dc round the front opening edge to neaten the edge. Sew in the zip. Make a long twisted cord (see page 75) and thread it through the slip-rib channel at waist.

(see page 75)

If you find that the zip fastener on the bag is a little too short for the opening, oversew the opening on the wrong side for a few sts at the lower edge. If the zip fastener is a little long for the opening, place the extra length on the wrong side below the division and only sew as far as the division – never try to sew a zip of the wrong size to the knitting by either trying to stretch the knitting to the size or gathering the knitting to the size. To prevent losing the mitts, make twisted cords as for the waist of the bag – each about 15cm [6 in] long – and attach one end to the mitt and the other to the wrist of the bag. Not one long cord through the sleeves – that could be dangerous with a small, never-still baby.

MITTS
You will need two more 25g balls to make these. Using 3¾mm [No 9] knitting needles, cast on 42 sts. Work 16 rows slip rib. **1st row** *K1, y fwd, sl 1 purlwise, y bk; rep from * to end. **2nd row** As the 1st row but k the sl sts and sl the k sts purlwise. Rep these 2 rows 7 times more.
Dec 6 sts evenly on the first row, work 8 rows st-st.
Shape for thumb 1st row K17, inc 1 by picking up loop between sts and knitting into back of it – called inc 1k – k2, inc 1k, k17. **2nd row** P. **3rd row** K17, inc 1k, k4,

inc 1k, k17. **4th row** P. **5th row** K17, inc 1k, k6, inc 1k, k17. **6th row and foll alt rows** P. **7th row** K17, inc 1k, k8, inc 1k, k17. **9th row** K17, inc 1k, k20, inc 1k, k17. **10th row** P.
Work Thumb 1st row K29, turn. **2nd row** P12, cast on 2 sts, turn. **3rd row** K14. **4th row** P14. Rep these 2 rows once more.
Next row K1, k2 tog, k to last 3 sts, k2 tog tbl, k1. **Next row** P to end. Rep these 2 rows once more. Thread rem sts on to double yarn, draw up and secure with knot on the inside.
Work Hand Return to sts rem on needle, with right side facing, rejoin yarn in front of sts on left-hand needle and k these 17 sts. **Next row** P17, cast on 2 sts, p across rem set of 17 sts . . . 36 sts. Cont in st-st on these sts until hand measures 10cm [4 in] from slip rib or required length to top

shaping, less 1cm [½ in] ending after a p row.
Shape Top 1st row *K1, k2 tog, k12, k2 tog tbl, k1*, rep from * to * once more. **2nd row** P to end. **3rd row** *K1, k2 tog, k10, k2 tog tbl, k1*, rep from * once more. Cont in this way, dec 4 sts on right-side rows until 8 sts rem. Thread yarn through rem sts, draw up and secure with knot on the inside. Work a second Mitt.

TO MAKE UP
Press st-st sections according to the instructions on the ball band. With right side inside, back-stitch round the hand seams. Back-stitch the thumb seams.

Opposite and below: the Pramsuit and diagram to show the shaping

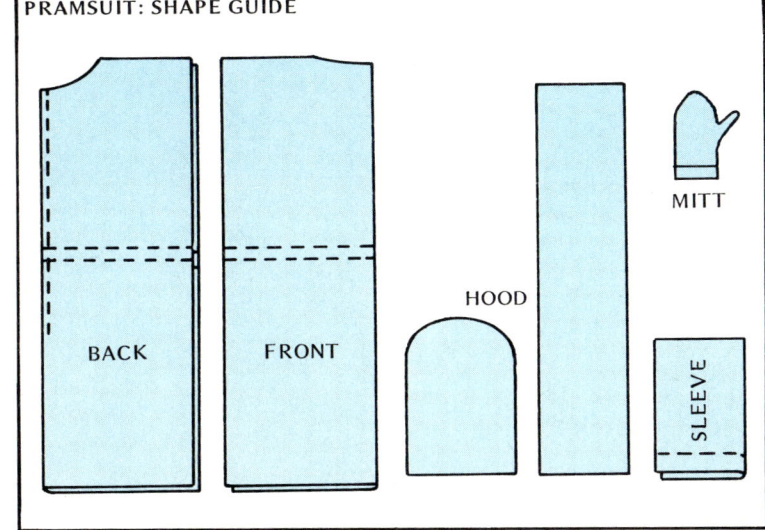

PRAMSUIT: SHAPE GUIDE

BACK   FRONT   HOOD   SLEEVE   MITT

Children's Clothes

Smart slipover

Toddler to teenager

This djellaba-style gown can be quickly popped on to even the wriggliest little body and there are no fastenings to contend with.

Materials Ten 25g balls Double Knitting Shetland type wool; pair 4mm [No 8] knitting needles.

Measurements To fit a 53–58cm [21–23 in] chest (see TIP for making larger sizes).

Tension 5 sts measure 2.5cm [1 in].

Abbreviations k, knit; p, purl; st(s), stitch(es); st-st, stocking stitch; rep, repeat; cont, continue; beg, beginning; g-st, garter stitch; cm, centimetre(s); in, inch(es). Square brackets contain imperial measurements.

You can make this slipover for any size, large or small. First cut out a paper pattern, following the shape in the diagram, making the sleeves and body the lengths you require. On all sizes add about 4cm [1½ in] in extra width to front and back to ensure comfort.
Measure lower edge: if using metric double the results; if using imperial multiply by 5. For example if an 86cm [34 in] bust is needed, the lower edge of front should measure about 47cm [18½ in], so 47 × 2 = 94 or 18½ × 5 = 92½. You would therefore cast on 94 or 92 stitches – you will always get a couple of stitches difference because a conversion to metric is not exact but they will make no difference to the finished garment.

MAIN PIECE

The garment is worked in one piece. Beg at lower edge of Front. Cast on 65 sts and work in g-st for 6 rows. Change to st-st and cont until work measures 34cm [13½ in] from beg ending after a p row. Now cast on 42 sts at beg of next 2 rows . . . 149 sts now on needle.

Next row K to end.
Next row K5, p to last 5 sts, k5. Rep last 2 rows 11 times more.
To work neckline Next row K to end. **Next row** K5, p46, k47, p46, k5. Rep last 2 rows once more.
Next row K. **Next row** K5, p52, cast off 35 sts, p52 – including st already on needle from casting off – k5. **Next row** K57, cast on 35 sts, k57.
Next row K5, p46, k47, p46, k5.
Next row K. Rep last 2 rows once more.
Next row K5, p to last 5 sts, k5.
Next row K. Rep last 2 rows 11 times more.
Now cast off 42 sts at beg of next 2 rows, then cont straight in st-st on remaining 65 sts for same number of rows as Front to g-st border. Work 5 rows in g-st. Cast off loosely.

Belt
Take 15 threads about 250cm (98 in) long, knot one end then divide into groups of 5. Work a plait, knotting the end.

TO MAKE UP
Press work on wrong side following ball band instructions. Join sides and sleeves with a flat seam leaving the g-st border at lower edge of sides free.

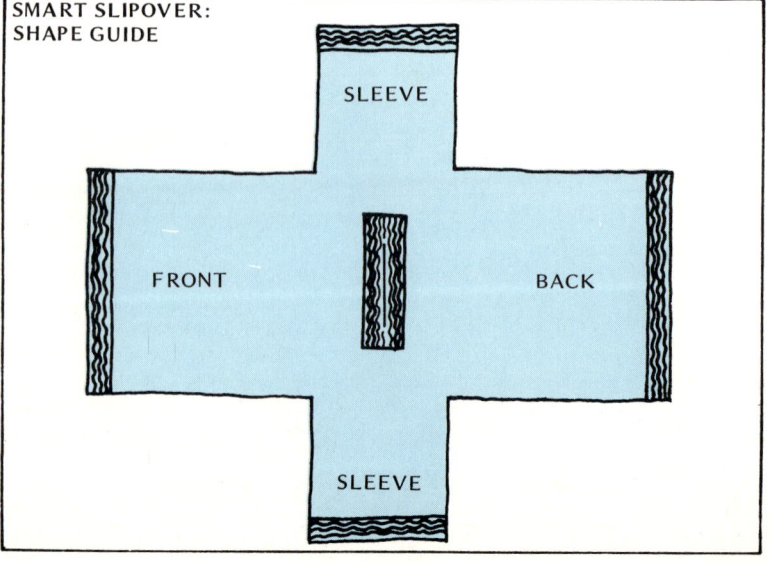

Above: just the thing to relax in. It's a simple garment and it can be made for any size with the special advice, left, and the shaping diagram, below

SMART SLIPOVER: SHAPE GUIDE

SLEEVE

FRONT   BACK

SLEEVE

Peruvian socks and hats

Toddler to teenager

Illustrated here and on pages 98 and 99

Brightly coloured socks and hats that will appeal to any age.

PERUVIAN SOCKS

Materials A total quantity of 50 (110:170)g Double Knitting yarn made up of at least 25(40:60)g in main colour (M) and rem in an assortment of 11 other colours; pair 3mm [No 11] knitting needles.

Measurements Length of foot: 1st size, 14cm [5½ in]; 2nd size, 19cm [7½ in]; 3rd size, 24cm [9½ in]. Leg length: adjustable.

Tension 24 sts and 32 rows to 10cm [4 in] in st-st.

Abbreviations k, knit; p, purl; st(s), stitch(es); cm, centimetre(s); in, inch(es); alt, alternate; beg, beginning; cont, continue; dec, decreas(e)ing; inc, increas(e)ing; inc 1k, increase by picking up loop between sts and knitting into back of it; rep, repeat; rem, remain(ing); st-st, stocking stitch; tog, together; sl, slip; psso, pass slip st over; y fwd, yarn forward; tbl, through back of loop.

Size Note Figures in brackets refer to larger sizes. One figure only refers to all sizes. Square brackets contain imperial measurements. The first size socks are given separately as they are worked in a different manner.

Special Note Carry yarns not in use loosely across the back of the work. Twist yarns when changing colour to avoid making a hole.

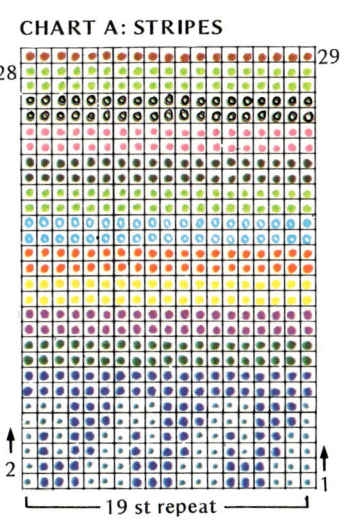

Left and below: the striped socks and the chart you'll need

Right and below: jacquard socks and chart

CHART B: JACQUARD

46   47

2   1

└─ 36 st repeat ─┘

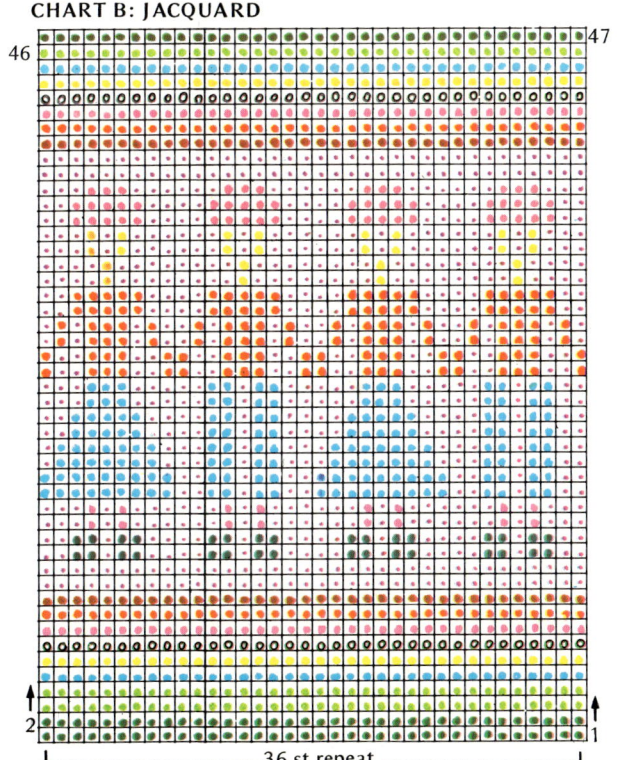

CHART A: STRIPES

28   29

2   1

└─ 19 st repeat ─┘

Notice that the smallest size of socks is worked from the foot upwards, the larger two sizes are worked from the leg down. When making the hats, mark the 11 colours with a letter – A, B, C etc and use one symbol from chart C for each colour.

THE FIRST SIZE

Beg at the underside of the foot. With M, cast on 51 sts. **1st row** K1, inc 1k, k24, inc 1k, k1, inc 1k, k24, inc 1k, k1. **2nd row** P to end.

3rd row K2, inc 1k, k24, inc 1k, k3, inc 1k, k24, inc 1k, k2. **4th row** P to end. **5th row** K3, inc 1k, k24, inc 1k, k5, inc 1k, k24, inc 1k, k3. **6th row** P to end. **7th row** K4, inc 1k, k24, inc 1k, k7, inc 1k, k24, inc 1k, k4 . . . 67 sts.
8th to 10th rows P to end.
Cont in st-st and work 4 rows.
Shape for Toe 1st row K38, turn.
2nd row Sl 1, p7, p2 tog, turn. **3rd row** Sl 1, k7, k2 tog, turn. **4th row** Sl 1, p7, p2 tog, turn. Rep last 2 rows 5 times more. **15th row** Sl 1, k to end . . . 54 sts. Work 5 rows in st-st without shaping.
Now work either the jacquard

pattern from chart B or the striped pattern (chart A) above. Work all 47 rows for the jacquard pattern and follow with 2 row stripes of colour to lengthen leg if required, ending after a p row.

Make Picot Edge With M, work 4 rows st-st. **5th row** *K2 tog, y fwd; rep from * to last 2 sts, k2. Beg p row, work 5 rows st-st. Cast off.

To work the striped pattern Cont in st-st working the 29 rows from chart A then reverse the stripes and work the chart downwards using the top row as the 1st row. If you wish to lengthen the leg add a few stripes at the top of the

chart but remember to include these when reversing the stripes to work down the chart.
When the stripes and wavy pattern are completed work 4 rows st-st with M. **5th row** Make Picot Edge. *K2 tog y fwd; rep from * to last 2 sts, k2. Beg p row work 5 rows st-st. Cast off.
Work another sock the same.

TO MAKE UP

Press on the wrong side of work according to the instructions on the ball band. With right side of work inside, back-stitch the back seam then cont down and join

Continued on next page

Peruvian socks . . . continued

the underfoot with a flat seam. Turn the top edge to wrong side at picot row and slip-stitch on the wrong side. Turn socks to right side and press seams.

THE 2nd AND 3rd SIZES
Charts are on page 97
Beg at top leg. With M, cast on 63(81) sts.

Beg k row, work 4 rows st-st. **5th row** Make Picot Edge: *K2 tog, y fwd; rep from * to last st, k1. Beg p row, work 5 rows st-st.

For the striped socks beg at 1st row of chart A and work to 29th row, then reverse the chart and work from 29th row down to the last striped row – 52 rows worked.

For the jacquard design socks work the 47 rows of the jacquard design (chart B).

Both designs Cont in st-st, in stripes or, if preferred in M only, dec 1 st at both ends of next right side row and every foll 8th row until 57(71) sts rem. Cont without shaping until work measures 31 (36)cm [12(14) in] from picot row or required length to heel, ending after a p row. Striped socks *only* should end with the last 6 rows of the chart, see picture below.

Divide for Instep and Heel Next row With M, K14(18) sts, sl these sts on a white thread for the heel, k29(35) sts, then slip rem 14(18) sts on a black thread for 2nd half of heel.

Instep Cont in stripes or M as preferred on centre 29(35) sts for 11(17)cm [4½(6½) in] ending after a wrong-side row and dec 1 st at centre of last row . . . 28(34) sts.

Shape Toe 1st row K2, k2 tog tbl, k to last 4 sts, k2 tog, k2. **2nd row** P to end. Rep last 2 rows until 8(10) sts rem. Leave these sts on a safety-pin for the time being.

Shape Heel With right side of work facing, join matching yarn at inner end of sts on black thread and k these sts, then on to same needle, k across the sts on the white thread . . . 28(36) sts. P1 row.

Turn Heel 1st row Sl 1, k26(34), turn. **2nd row** Sl 1, p25(33), turn. **3rd row** Sl 1, k24(32), turn. **4th row** Sl 1, p 23(31), turn.

Cont in this way, working 1 st less before turning on every row until the row 'Sl 1, p9(13), turn' has been worked. **Next row** Sl 1k, k9(13), inc 1k together with the next st, turn. **Next row** Sl 1, p10(14), pick up loop between sts and p it together with next st, turn.

Cont in this way, working 1 more st before working the loop and the next st together on every row until the row 'Sl 1, p26(34), p loop and last st together' has been worked . . . 28(36) sts.

Cont in st-st until the foot measures same length as instep to beg of toe, ending after a p row and dec 2 sts evenly on the larger size only.

Shape Toe 1st row K2, k2 tog tbl, k to last 2 sts, k2 tog, k2. **2nd row** P to end. Rep last 2 rows until 8(10) sts rem. Leave these sts on a safety-pin.

Work a second sock the same.

TO MAKE UP
Press on the wrong side of the work following instructions on the ball band. Place the two sets of sts rem on to two needles with the points facing in the same direction and the right sides of work together. Now with a third needle and M, cast off the two sets of sts together, inserting the third needle through a st on front and back needle together and working them together. When two loops are on the right-hand needle, slip the first loop over the second in the usual way. Repeat along the two sets of sts until all are worked off. With right side of work inside, back-stitch the back seam and then flat seam along the sides of the foot. Fold the top at the picot row and slip-stitch the hem on the wrong side. Turn to right side.

PERUVIAN HATS

Materials A total quantity of 50(75)g Double Knitting yarn made up of approx 25(35)g in main colour (M) and small balls of 11 other colours; pair 3mm [No 11] knitting needles; 3mm [No 11] crochet hook.

Measurements Small size 46cm [18 in] round head; large size 53cm [21 in] round head; 3rd size is baby's size, 42cm [16½ in]. Length to point – 1st hat 24(28)cm [9½(11) in]; 2nd hat 28(33)cm [11(13) in]; 3rd hat 20cm [8 in].

Tension 24 sts and 32 rows to 10cm [4 in] in st-st.

Abbreviations k, knit; p, purl; st(s), stitch(es); cm, centimetre(s); in, inch(es); alt, alternate; beg, beginning; cont, continue; dec, decrease(ing); inc, increase(ing); foll, following; rep, repeat; rem, remain(ing); st-st, stocking stitch; tog, together; sl, slip; psso, pass slip st over, g-st, garter stitch, (every row knit).

Size Note Figures in brackets refer to larger sizes. One figure only refers to all sizes. Square brackets contain imperial measurements.

Special Note Carry yarns not in use loosely across back of work. Twist yarns when changing colour to avoid making a hole.

THE SHORT HAT (for child and adult)
MAIN PART
With M, cast on 108(126) sts. Work 4 rows g-st. Beg k row, cont in st-st and work 4 rows. Now work the jacquard pattern from chart C, working 34 rows without shaping.

35th row *K7, k2 tog; rep from * to end . . . 96(112) sts. Cont on these sts until the chart is completed. Note On larger size only, inc 1 st at both ends of 37th row and dec these sts at ends of last row.

Now with M only, cont in st-st on 96(112) sts and work 4 rows.

Shape Top 1st row *K6, k2 tog; rep from * to end . . . 84(98) sts. Work 3(5) rows straight. **5th(7th) row** *K5, k2 tog; rep from * to end . . .72(84) sts. Work 3(5) rows straight. **9th(13th) row** *K4, k2 tog; rep from * to end . . . 60(70) sts. Work 3(5) rows straight. **13th(19th) row** *K3, k2 tog; rep from * to end . . . 48(56) sts. Work 1(3) rows straight. **15th(23rd) rows** *K2, k2 tog; rep from * to end. Work 1(3) rows straight. **17th(27th) row** *K1, k2 tog; rep from * to end . . . 24 (28) sts. Work 1(3) rows straight. **19th(31st row)** *K2 tog; rep from * to end . . . 12(14) sts. Work 1(3) rows. **21st(35th) rows** *K2 tog; rep from * to end . . . 6(7) sts. Thread yarn through rem sts, draw up and secure. Fasten off.

EAR FLAPS
With any colour other than M, cast on 7(9) sts. Cont in g-st working 10-row stripes of varying colours until 50 rows have been worked. Cast off.

Now with right side of this piece facing, pick up and k49 sts evenly along one edge. Mark the centre st. Work 8 rows of g-st in stripes of 2 rows of each of four colours, at the same time dec at the centre thus: **1st 2 rows** With chosen colour, k to within one st

---

Below: little feet all in a row show how stunning Peruvian knits look. You can choose either of the two designs for the socks – both are knitted from charts which are on page 97

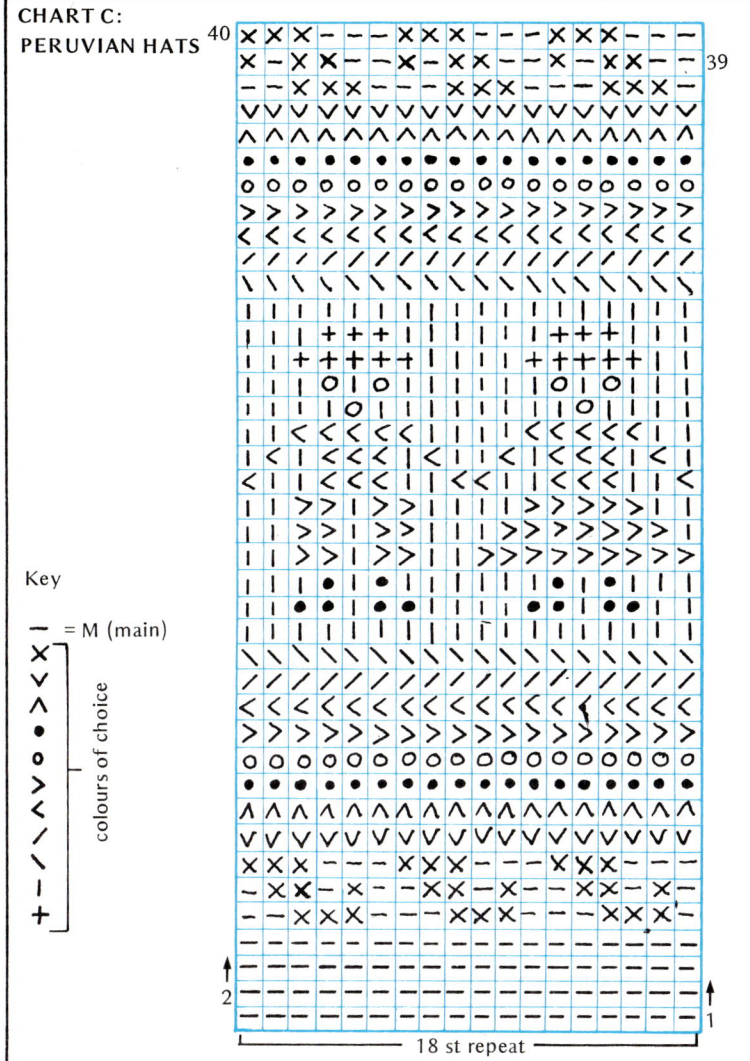

of the marked centre st, sl 1, k2 tog, psso, k to end. **2nd 2 rows** Using another colour, rep the first 2 rows. Cont in this way until the 8 rows are completed . . . 33 sts. Cast off.

With a flat seam, using matching yarn, fold the cast-off edges together and neatly seam these rem sts to form the flap shape as shown in picture. Work another flap in the same way.

TO MAKE UP
Press pieces carefully following instructions on the ball band. With right side inside, back-stitch the back seam of the hat. Sew on the ear flaps as shown in picture, with the hat edge just overlapping the edge of the flaps. With right side of work facing, and M, work 1 row dc round outer edge of the ear flaps.

Cut lengths of all the colours to twice the length of the required tassel. Fold the lengths in half over a long length of yarn. Hold the cut ends tightly in the hand while binding the folded ends near the fold with a piece of matching yarn. Let go of the ends. Trim these, then sew the tassel using the long length, to the top point of the hat.

THE LONG HAT (for child and adult)
MAIN PART
With M, cast on 108(126) sts. Work 4 rows g-st. Beg k row, cont in st-st and work 4 rows. Now work the jacquard pattern from chart C, working 34 rows without shaping.

35th row *K7, k2 tog; rep from * to end . . . 96(112) sts. Cont on these sts until the chart is completed. Note On larger size only, inc 1 st at both ends of 37th row and dec these 2 sts on last row. Now with M only, cont in st-st on 96(112) sts and work 4 rows.

Shape Top 1st row *K6, k2 tog; rep from * to end . . . 84(98) sts.

Above: the Long Hat and, below, the Short and Small versions with a close-up of the jacquard design worked from Chart C

Work 5(7) rows straight. **7th(9th) row** *K5, k2 tog; rep from * to end . . . 72(84) sts. Work 5(7) rows straight. **13th(17th) row** *K4, k2 tog; rep from * to end . . . 60(70) sts. Work 5(7) rows straight. **19th (25th) row** *K3, k2 tog; rep from * to end . . . 48(56) sts. Work 3(5) rows straight. **23rd(31st) row** *K2, k2 tog; rep from * to end. Work 3(5) rows straight. **27th(37th) row** *K1, k2 tog; rep from * to end. Work 3(5) rows straight. **31st**

(43rd) row *K2 tog; rep from * to end . . .12(14) sts. Work 3(5) rows straight. **35th(49th) row** *K2 tog; rep from * to end . . . 6(7) sts. Thread yarn through rem sts, draw up tightly and secure. Fasten off.

EAR FLAPS
Cast on 5(7) sts with any colour other than M. Cont in g-st. Work 30 rows in 6-row stripes of five different colours. Now work 4

rows in another colour and finally 2 rows in another colour – 36 rows worked. Complete the strip by working the same number of rows in reverse sequence, beg 2 rows in the last colour worked, then 4 rows in another colour and five stripes in the same colour as at the beg. Cast off.

Pick up and k70 sts evenly along one side of the strip using a light colour. K1 row. Change to M and k4 rows. Cast off.

Continued on next page

CHART C: PERUVIAN HATS

Key
— = M (main)

X, V, ∧, •, o, >, <, /, \, I, + = colours of choice

18 st repeat

Peruvian hats . . . continued

With right side of the strip facing, pick up and k71 sts evenly along the other side, using a dark colour. Mark the centre st. **1st row** With same colour k to within one st of the centre marked st, sl 1, k2 tog, psso, k to end. Cont in g-st, using 4 rows of each colour and dec as the 1st row, forming a semi-circle, until 7 sts rem. Cast off. Work another ear flap in the same way.

TO MAKE UP

Press pieces carefully following instructions on the ball band. With right side inside, back-stitch the back seam of the hat. Sew on the ear flaps, with the hat edge just overlapping the edge of the flaps (see picture).

For an alternative method of making the tassel – wind lengths of yarn round a narrow piece of wood or stout card. Using a sewing needle threaded with yarn, insert the needle between the card and the wound yarn and tie the wound yarn tightly. Snip the lengths in two along the opposite edge and remove from the card. Catch the loose ends together and tie tightly again into a bunch, near the top. Trim ends and sew tassel to top of hat.

Below: the Peruvian hat and socks worn with an oriental-style quilted jacket – you'll find instructions on page 27

THE SMALL HAT (Baby's size only)

With M, cast on 99 sts. Work 4 rows g-st. Beg k row, work 4 rows st-st. Now work the jacquard pattern from chart C, noting that you will have 11 figures only, and work 28 rows.

29th row *K7, k2 tog; rep from * to end in colour as indicated from the chart . . . 88 sts. Cont working from the chart for 7 rows more.

37th row Inc 1, k to last st, inc in last st . . . 90 sts. Work the last 3 rows from the chart dec 1 st at both ends of last row . . . 88 sts.

Shape Top Cont in st-st with M, dec on alt rows thus: **1st row** *K6, k2 tog; rep from * to end . . . 77 sts. P1 row. **3rd row** *K5, k2 tog; rep from * to end . . . 66 sts. P1 row. Cont dec in this way until 11 sts rem, ending after a p row.

Next row *K2 tog; rep from * to last st, k1 . . . 6 sts. P1 row. **Next row** *K2 tog; rep from * to end. Thread yarn through rem sts. Draw up tightly and secure. Fasten off.

EAR FLAPS

Cast on 7 sts. With 1st colour k12 rows, then work 10 rows g-st in each of 3 different colours and finally 12 rows in the 1st colour. Cast off. With right side of work facing, pick up and k 53 sts evenly along one side edge. Mark the centre st. **1st row** K to within one st of the centre marked st, sl 1, k2 tog, psso, k to end. Rep the last row 8 times more, working 2 rows of different colours 4 times. Cast off. Fold the cast off edges together in half and neatly flat seam together to form a semi-circle. Flatten out again and with right side facing and using crochet hook work 1 row dc. Fasten off. Work another ear flap in the same way.

TO MAKE UP

Press pieces carefully following instructions on the ball band. With right side inside, back-stitch the back seam of the hat. Sew on the ear flaps as shown in the picture, with the hat edge just overlapping the edge of the flaps. Using various colours, make a tassel in either of the two ways given for the larger hats.

Dungarees with turn-ups

1 to 2 years

Almost his first long 'uns and very smart they look too – there's even a little pocket for secret storage.

Materials Ten 25g balls Double Knitting yarn in main colour (M); two balls in contrast colour (C); a pair 3¾mm [No 9] knitting needles; 3·5mm [No 9] crochet hook; 2 buttons.

Measurements Chest 56cm [22 in]; leg seam 33cm [13 in] to beg of crotch shaping – not including turn-ups.

Tension 26 sts and 34 rows to 10cm [4 in] on 3¾mm [No 9] needles.

Abbreviations k, knit; p, purl; st(s), stitch(es); cm, centimetre(s); in, inch(es); alt, alternate; beg, beginning; cont, continue; foll, following; dec, decreas(e)ing; st-st, stocking stitch; rep, repeat; rem, remain(ing); tog, together; dc, double crochet; g-st, garter stitch. Square brackets contain imperial measurements.

> The front and back legs of these well-shaped trousers are worked separately and joined in to one piece at the crotch thus doing away with the need for a centre front and back seam. Make sure that you end each leg piece on the side of the work specified in the pattern or your joining will not be correct.

BACK

Beg at **Left Back Leg** With 3¾mm [No 9] needles and M, cast on 46 sts. Beg k row, cont in st-st for 20cm [8 in] ending after a p row. **Next row** Inc in 1st st, k to end. Beg p row, work 5 rows st-st. Rep last 6 rows 6 times more . . . 53 sts. Cont in st-st without shaping until work measures 33cm [13 in] ending after a p row.

Shape for Crotch 1st row Cast off 5 sts, k to end. **2nd row and foll alt rows** P to end. **3rd row** Cast off 3 sts, k to end. **5th row** Cast off 2 sts, k to end. **7th row** K2 tog, k to end. **8th row** P to end. **9th to 12th rows** Rep 7th and 8th rows twice more . . . 40 sts. Leave these

Above: smart knitted Dungarees

40 sts on a spare needle for the time being, breaking off yarn.

Now work the **Right Back Leg** With 3¾mm [No 9] needles and M, cast on 46 sts. Beg k row, cont in st-st for 20cm [8 in] ending after a p row. **Next row** K to last st, inc in last st. Beg p row, work 5 rows st-st. Rep last 6 rows 6 times more . . . 53 sts.

Cont in st-st until work measures 33cm [13 in] ending after a k row. **Shape for Crotch 1st row** Cast off 5 sts, p to end. **2nd row and foll alt rows** K to end. **3rd row** Cast off 3 sts, p to end. **5th row** Cast off 2 sts p to end. **7th row** P2 tog, p to end. **8th row** K to end. **9th to 12th rows** Rep 7th and 8th rows twice more . . . 40 sts. You will have ended after a k row – on to this same needle, k across the 40 sts of the spare needle.

Beg p row, cont in st-st without shaping on these 80 sts until work measures 40cm [15¾ in]

from beg, ending after a p row.
Shape Sides Dec 1 st at both ends of next row and foll k rows to 66 sts.

Cont in st-st without shaping until work measures 58cm [23 in] from beg, ending after a p row. Work 4 rows g-st (every row k).
5th row (make buttonholes) K26, cast off 4 sts, k6, cast off 4 sts, k26.
6th row K26, cast on 4 sts, k6, cast on 4 sts, k26. K4 more rows g-st. Cast off sts loosely.

FRONT

Beg with **Right Leg** With 3¾mm [No 9] needles and M, cast on 40 sts. Beg k row cont in st-st for 20cm [8 in] ending after a p row.
Next row Inc in 1st st, k to end. Beg p row, work 5 rows st-st. Rep last 6 rows to 47 sts. Cont in st-st without shaping until work measures 33cm [13 in] ending after a p row.
Shape for Crotch 1st row Cast off 4 sts, k to end. **2nd row and foll alt rows** P to end. **3rd row** Cast off 3 sts, k to end. **5th row** Cast off 2 sts, k to end. **7th row** K2 tog, k to end. **8th row** P to end. **9th row to 12th rows** Rep 7th and 8th rows twice more ... 35 sts. Leave these sts on a spare needle for the time being.
Now work the **Left Leg** With 3¾mm [No 9] needles and M, cast on 40 sts. Beg k row, cont in st-st for 20cm [8 in] ending after a p row. **Next row** K to last st, inc in last st. Beg p row, work 5 rows st-st. Rep last 6 rows to 47 sts. Cont in st-st without shaping until work measures 33cm [13 in] ending after a k row.
Shape for Crotch 1st row Cast off 4 sts, p to end. **2nd row and foll alt rows** k to end. **3rd row** Cast off 3 sts, p to end. **5th row** Cast off 2 sts, p to end. **7th row** P2 tog, p to end. **8th row** K to end. **9th row to 12th rows** Rep 7th and 8th rows twice more ... 35 sts. You will have ended after a k row — on to this same needle, k across 35 sts from the spare needle. Cont in st-st without shaping on these 70 sts until work measures 40cm [15¾ in] ending after a p row.
Shape Sides Dec 1 st at both ends of next row and every foll 6th row until 58 sts rem. Cont in st-st without shaping until work measures 56cm [22 in] ending after a p row.
Now cont in st-st with g-st borders thus: **1st row** K to end. **2nd row** K18, p22, k18. Rep last 2 rows 5 times more. **13th row** Cast off 10 sts, k38, cast off last 10 sts. Break yarn. With wrong side facing, rejoin yarn to rem sts.

14th row K8, p22, k8. **15th row** K to end. Rep last 2 rows 6 times more, then the 14th row once.

STRAPS

With right side of work facing, **1st row** K8, turn. Cont in g-st on these 8 sts only until the strap is 28cm [11 in] from beg. Cast off. With right side of work facing, rejoin yarn to rem sts, cast off centre 22 sts, k8 to end. Cont on these 8 sts in g-st for second strap until strap is 28cm [11 in] long. Cast off.

TURN-UPS (make 2)

With 3¾mm [No 9] needles and C, cast on 80 sts. Work 28 rows in g-st. Cast off.

POCKET

With 3¾mm [No 9] needles and C, cast on 7 sts. K2 rows. **3rd row** Cast on 4 sts, k to end. **4th row** Cast on 4 sts, k to end. **5th and 6th rows** Cast on 2 sts, k to end. **7th and 8th rows** As 5th and 6th ... 23 sts. K3 rows without shaping. Now inc 1 st at both ends of next row and every foll 4th row to 31 sts. Work 28 rows in g-st without shaping. Cast off.

TO MAKE UP

With C, work 2 rows dc round pocket edge. With right side inside, back-stitch the inner leg seams. Using hem-stitch sew the curved edge of the pocket to the front, having the straight top opening to beg of bib as shown in the picture. Oversew the narrow ends of the turn-ups to form a circle of each. With wrong side of turn-up to right side of leg, sew a turn-up to each trouser leg, matching the turn-up seam to the inner leg seam. Fold the turn-ups to the right side of work. With right side facing, work 2 rows dc round edge of each turn-up. Sew a button to the end of each strap.

Bib and brace

1 to 3 years

Illustrated on cover and next page

Her first bib and brace, and pretty enough for a special party.

Materials 12(13:14) 25g balls Double Knitting yarn; 3¾mm [No 9] knitting needles; 2 buttons; scraps of yellow, black, green, blue, white and brown for embroidery; elastic for back waist.

Measurements To fit 46(51:56)cm [18(20:22) in] chest; 55(58:61)cm [21½(23:25) in] leg length.

Tension 24 sts and 32 rows to 10cm [4 in].

Abbreviations k, knit; p, purl; st(s), stitch(es); cm, centimetre(s); in, inch(es); alt, alternate; beg, beginning; cont, continue; dec, decreas(e)ing; inc, increas(e)ing; patt, pattern; foll, following; y fwd, yarn forward; tog, together; st-st, stocking stitch; g-st, garter stitch; rep, repeat; rem, remain(ing).

Size Note Figures in brackets refer to larger sizes. One figure only refers to all sizes. Square brackets contain imperial measurements.

> As each leg is worked separately to waist, you can ensure a good fit by joining back and front seams first. Try the garment on the child, wrong-side out, and adjust the leg seams: tack first then back-stitch. The seams can then be let out later if needed.

LEFT LEG

Beg at lower edge. Cast on 75 (79:83) sts. K4 rows. Beg k row, cont in st-st until work measures 5cm [2 in] from beg, ending after a p row.
Now cont in lace patt thus: **1st row** K1, *y fwd, k2 tog; rep from * to end. **2nd row and foll alt rows** P. **3rd row** K. **5th row** K2, *y fwd, k2 tog; rep from * to last st, k1. **6th row** P.
Rep last 6 rows until work measures 9cm [3½ in] from beg, ending after a p row.
Cont in st-st until work measures 28(30:32)cm [11(12:12¾ in] from beg, ending after a p row.
Inc 1 st at both ends of next row

and every foll 6th row to 83(87:91) sts. Cont straight until work measures 36(38:40)cm [14(15:15¾) in] from beg, ending after a p row.*
Shape Gusset 1st row Cast off 2 sts, k to end. **2nd row** Cast off 3 sts, p to end. **3rd row** K2 tog, k to end. **4th row** Cast off 2 sts, p to end. **5th and 6th rows** As 3rd and 4th. Cont straight until work measures 55(58:61)cm [21½ (23:25) in] ending after a p row. K4 rows.
Divide for Bib and Straps Next row K35, and slip these sts on to a spare needle, cast off centre 13(17:21) sts, k to end. Leave these rem 24 sts also on a spare needle.

RIGHT LEG

Work as Left Leg to *.
Shape Gusset 1st row Cast off 3 sts, k to end. **2nd row** Cast off 2 sts, p to end. **3rd row** Cast off 2 sts, k to end. **4th row** P2 tog, p to end. **5th and 6th rows** As 3rd and 4th. Cont straight in st-st until work measures 55(58:61)cm [21½ (23:25) in] from beg, ending after a p row. K4 rows.
Divide for Bib and Straps Next row K24 and slip these sts on to a spare needle, cast off centre 13(17:21) sts, k to end, slip these last 35 sts also on to a spare needle.

BIB

With wrong side facing, p across both sets of 24 + 24 sts from spare needles on to one needle. Cont on these 48 sts thus: **1st row** K. **2nd row** K5, p38, k5. Rep last 2 rows until Bib measures 8cm [3 in] from beg, ending after a wrong-side row. Now rep the 6 lace patt rows as given for Left Leg on the centre 38 sts only omitting k1 at beg of 1st rows and working k1 in place of k2 at beg of 5th rows. Cont in lace patt until Bib measures 11cm [4½ in] ending after a p row. Work 4 rows st-st with g-st borders as 1st and 2nd rows of Bib. **Next row** K15, cast off centre 18 sts, k15.

STRAPS

On each set of 15 sts work thus: **Next row** K5, p5, k5. **Next row** (right side) K. Rep last 2 rows until strap measures 38cm [15 in]. **Next row** K6, cast off 3, k6. On foll row cast on 3 sts over those cast off in previous row. Work 3 rows g-st. Cast off.

TO MAKE UP

Join leg and back and front seams. With right side facing, k across on

Continued on next page

Bib and brace . . . continued

to one needle both sets of 35 + 35 sts from the spare needles at centre back. Work 8 rows st-st. Cast off. Fold this piece in half to wrong side and slip-stitch. Insert back waist elastic and secure at ends. Sew buttons on the inside of the back waist hem to correspond with buttonholes. Press according to instructions on ball band.

To work the Swiss Embroidery

Begin at the bottom of the Bib, right-hand corner. Leaving an end at the back, bring the needle out to the front through the centre of the stitch below the one to be covered, then in and out again behind the stitch in the row

above, back into the same hole at the bottom and out through the centre of the next st to the left.

Cover each stitch in the first row like this and at the end of the row slip the needle upwards into the centre of the last stitch covered instead of taking it along to the left. Now turn the work upside down so that you are still working from right to left.

Cover all the parts in one colour at a time before going on to the next part of the design. Use the picture to help you place your design. Work a few "lazy daisy" flowers in colours round the leg: this is a circle of chain stitches.

(Bring the yarn out through the centre of a stitch, and hold down with the thumb. Insert the needle again where it came out and bring out in centre of stitch approx 2 rows or sts further along, holding the yarn under the needle point with the left thumb each time, secure the "petal" with a short stitch.) Make little green stalks and, with black, work 4 cross stitches below each flower.

___

Below · the Bib and Brace with its attractive embroidery which is worked on by the Swiss method after the garment has been knitted

Pinafore dress

1 to 3 years

A pretty, simple popover that will have a double life over sweaters and trousers in winter. The shape's neat and there's a cleverly concealed opening on the left shoulder.

Materials 5(6:7) 25g balls Double Knitting yarn; pairs of 3¼mm and 3¾ mm [No 10 and No 9] knitting needles; 3mm [No 11] crochet hook; 4 buttons; 4 press studs.

Measurements To fit 46(51:56)cm [18(20:22) in] chest; length, 39 (43:46)cm [15½(17:18) in].

Tension 26 sts and 34 rows to 10cm [4 in] in st-st.

Abbreviations k, knit; p, purl; st(s), stitch(es); cm, centimetre(s); in, inch(es); alt, alternate; beg, beginning; cont, continue; dec, decreas(e)ing; foll, following; g-st, garter stitch (every row k); inc 1k, increase by picking up the loop between the sts and knitting into the back of it; rem, remain(ing); rep, repeat; st-st, stocking stitch; dc, double crochet.

Size Note Figures in brackets refer to larger sizes. One figure only refers to all sizes. Square brackets contain imperial measurements.

BACK

With 3¼mm [No 10] needles, cast on 96(102:108) sts. Beg k row, work 9 rows st-st. **Next row** K for hemline. Change to 3¾mm [No 9] needles and beg k row cont in st-st until work measures 6cm [2½ in] from hemline, ending after a p row.

Dec 1 st at both ends of next row and every foll 6th row to 76(82:88) sts. Cont straight until work measures 27cm [10½ in] from hemline, ending after a p row.

Shape Armholes Cast off 4(5:6) sts at beg of next 2 rows. Cast off 2 sts at beg of next 6 rows. Dec 1 st at both ends of next row and foll alt row . . . 52(56:60) sts. ** Cont straight until work measures 38(42:45)cm [15(16½:17½) in] from hemline, ending after a p row.

Divide for Neck Next row K19 (21:23), turn. Complete this side

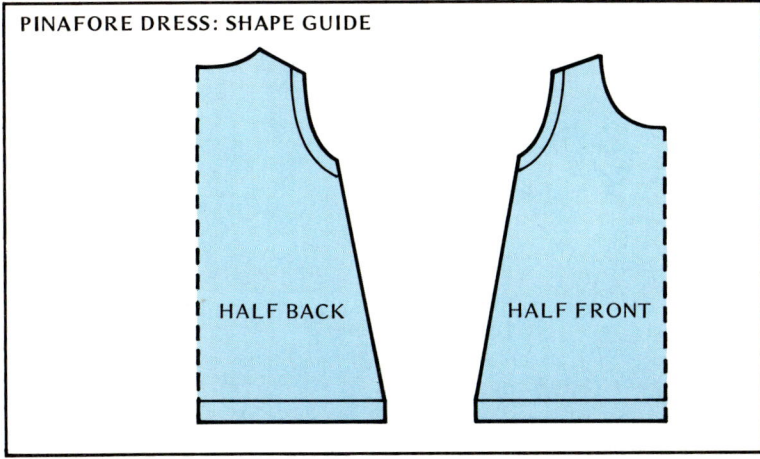

PINAFORE DRESS: SHAPE GUIDE

HALF BACK

HALF FRONT

first. **Next row** Cast off 5(6:7) sts, p to end. Cont shaping neck and, at the same time, shape shoulder thus: **Next row** Cast off 5(6:7) sts, k to end. **Next row** Cast off 4 sts, p to end. Cast off rem 5 sts. With right side facing, join yarn at neck edge to rem sts. Cast off centre 14 sts, k to end. P1 row. **Next row** Cast off 5(6:7) sts, k to end. **Next**

turn. Complete this side first. **Next row** Cast off 3(4:5) sts, p to end. **Next row** K. Now cast off 2 sts at beg of next 4 wrong-side rows. Cont straight until work matches Back to shoulder, ending after a wrong-side row.
Shape Shoulder Cast off 5(6:7) sts at beg of next row. P1 row. Cast off rem 5 sts. With right side facing, join yarn at neck edge to rem sts. Cast off centre 10 sts, k to end. Complete this side to match the first side thus: P1 row. **Next row** Cast off 3(4:5) sts, k to end. P1 row. Now cast off 2 sts at beg of foll 4 right-side rows. Cont straight until work matches Back to shoulder, ending after a right-side row.
Shape Shoulder Cast off 5(6:7) sts at beg of next row. K1 row. Cast off rem sts.

STRAPS (make 2)
With 3¼mm [No 10] needles cast on 8 sts. Work 7cm [2¾ in] g-st. Dec 1 st at both ends of next row and foll alt rows to 2 sts. Work 1 row. Cast off.

HALF-BELT
With 3¼mm [No 10] needles cast on 30 sts. Cont in g-st, shaping thus: **1st row** K. **2nd row** K1, inc 1k, k to last st, inc 1k, k1. Rep last 2 rows 3 times more. Now dec thus: K1 row. **Next row** K1, k2 tog, k to last 3 sts, k2 tog, k1. Rep last 2 rows to 30 sts. Cast off.

TO MAKE UP
Press following instructions on ball band. Join right shoulder seam. With right side facing, using 3¼mm [No 10] needles, pick up and k82(84:86) sts along neck edge. K4 rows. Cast off. With crochet hook work 3 rows dc along shoulder edges of Left Front and Back. With right side facing, using 3¼mm [No 10] needles, pick up and k70(72:74) sts along right armhole edge. K4 rows. Cast off. K4 rows on front and back of left armhole in the same way on 36(37:38) sts only for each side. Join side seams. Fold hem at ridge to wrong side and slip-stitch in position. Sew press studs on dc at left shoulder. Sew straight end of strap to back of each shoulder. Sew the shaped end of the right strap to shoulder with a button as shown. On the shaped end of the left strap sew a button but underneath sew a press stud. Sew half-belt at back with a button at each end.

FRONT
Work as Back to **. Cont straight until work measures 32(33:34)cm [12½(13:13½) in] ending after a p row.
Shape Neck Next row K21(23:25),

Jacket with hood
1 to 5 years
Illustrated on next page

Handy for all seasons, this will suit a boy or a girl (don't forget to place the buttonloop fastenings on the right front rather than the left for her).

Materials 10(12:14) 25g balls Aran weight knitting yarn; pairs of 3¾mm and 4mm [No 9 and No 8] knitting needles; 3·5mm [No 9] crochet hook; 8 buttons.

Measurements To fit 51(56:61)cm [20(22:24) in] chest; length, 34 (36:38)cm [13½(14¼:15) in]; sleeve seam, 18(20:23)cm, [7(8:9) in].

Tension 21 sts to 10cm [4 in] in st-st.

Abbreviations k, knit; p, purl; st(s), stitch(es); cm, centimetre(s); in, inch(es); rep, repeat; alt, alternate; beg, beginning; cont, continue; dec, decreas(e)ing; foll, following; inc, increas(e)ing; patt, pattern; st-st, stocking stitch; tog, together; sl, slip; psso, pass sl st over; ch, chain; dc, double crochet.

Size Note Figures in brackets refer to larger sizes. One figure only refers to all sizes. Square brackets contain imperial measurements.

BACK
With 4mm [No 8] needles, cast on 77(83:87) sts. Cont in patt thus:
1st row K1, *p1, k1*, rep from * to * to end. **2nd row** P1, *k1, p1*, rep from * to * to end. **3rd row** As 2nd. **4th row** As 1st. These 4 rows form the patt.
Cont in patt, dec 1 st at both ends of 17th row foll and every foll 18th row to 71(77:81) sts. Cont straight until work measures 23 (24:25)cm [9(9½:10) in].
Shape Armholes Cast off 4 sts at beg of next 2 rows; 2 sts at beg of foll 2 rows. Dec 1 st at both ends of next 1(2:3) rows . . . 57(61:63) sts. Cont straight until work measures 34(36:38)cm [13½ (14¼:15) in] from beg.
Shape Shoulders Cast off 6 sts at beg of next 4 rows; 6(7:8) sts at beg of foll 2 rows. Cast off rem 21(23:23) sts.

Continued on next page

Jacket with hood . . . continued

LEFT FRONT

With 4mm [No 8] needles, cast on 47(49:53) sts. Work 20 rows in patt as Back.* **Next row** K2 tog, patt to end. Work 7 rows straight.

Divide for Pocket Next row Patt 17(19:23), cast off 4 sts, patt 25. Cont in patt on these 25 sts only for 24 rows more. Leave these sts on a spare needle, do not break yarn.

With wrong side facing, join another ball to rem 17(19:23) sts. Work 24 rows in patt on these sts, dec 1 st at side edge on 10th row foll only. Break yarn.

Return to needle holding 25 sts, with wrong side facing, patt to end, turn, cast on 4 sts, turn, then on to same needle, work across rem 16(18:22) sts . . . 45(47:51) sts. Dec 1 st at side edge on 3rd row foll only. Cont straight until Left

Front matches Back to armhole, ending after wrong-side row.

Shape Armhole 1st row Cast off 4 sts, patt to end. **2nd row and foll alt rows** In patt. **3rd row** Cast off 2 sts, patt to end. **5th row** K2 tog, patt to end. **2nd and 3rd sizes only** Dec 1 st at armhole edge 1(2) times more . . . 37(38·41) sts.

Cont straight until work is 5 rows less than Back to shoulder, thus ending at front (neck) edge.

Shape Neck 1st row Cast off 9(9:11) sts, patt to end. **2nd row** In patt. **3rd row** Cast off 3 sts, patt to end. **4th row** In patt. **5th row** As 3rd.

Shape Shoulder Beg shoulder edge – **1st row** Cast off 6 sts, patt to end. **2nd row** Cast off 2 sts, patt to end. Rep 1st and 2nd rows once more. Cast off rem 6(7:8) sts.

RIGHT FRONT

Work as Left Front to *. Dec 1 st at end of next row. Work 8 rows straight, thus ending at side edge.

Divide for Pocket Work as given for Left Front, noting that you will have the wrong side of the work facing you, with the 25 sts at the front edge. After completing pocket opening, continue in patt, dec 1 st at side edge on 3rd row foll only, then without shaping until work matches Back to armhole, ending armhole edge.

Shape Armhole With wrong side of work facing: **1st row** Cast off 4 sts, patt to end. **2nd row and foll alt rows** In patt. **3rd row** Cast off 2 sts, patt to end. **5th row** K2 tog, patt to end. **2nd and 3rd sizes only** Dec 1 st at armhole edges 1(2) times more . . . 37(38:41) sts.

Cont straight until work is 5 rows less than Back to shoulder, thus ending at front (neck) edge.

Shape Neck 1st row Cast off 9(9:11) sts, patt to end. **2nd row** In patt. **3rd row** Cast off 3 sts, patt to end. **4th row** In patt. **5th row** As 3rd.

Shape Shoulder Beg shoulder edge – **1st row** Cast off 6 sts, patt to end. **2nd row** Cast off 2 sts, patt to end. Rep last 2 rows once more. Cast off rem 6(7:8) sts.

SLEEVES

With 4mm [No 8] needles, cast on 45(47:49) sts. Cont in patt as Back inc 1 st at both ends of 9th row and every foll 12th row to 53(55:57) sts. Cont straight until work measures 18(20:23)cm [7 (8:9) in] ending after a wrong-side row.

Shape Top Cast off 2 sts at beg of next 20 rows. Cast off rem 13 (15:17) sts.

HOOD

With 4mm [No 8] needles, cast on 25 sts. Work 16cm [6½ in] in patt as Back. **Next row** Patt 18 sts, sl 1, k1, psso, work 1 st, turn. **Next row** Sl 1, patt 12, p2 tog, work 1 st, turn. **Next row** Sl 1, patt 13, sl 1, k1, psso, work 1 st, turn.

Cont in this way, taking in 1 more st before dec until all sts are worked. Now, on same needle, pick up and k30 sts along one side of the 16cm [6½ in] worked, turn, work to end and pick up and k30 sts along other side.

Work a further 9cm [3½ in] on these sts, at the same time inc 1 st at both ends of 5th row foll and every foll 8th row until 6 sts have been increased altogether. Cast off loosely.

POCKETS (make 2)

With 3¾mm [No 9] needles, cast on 22 sts. Work 11cm [4½ in] in st-st. Cast off.

TO MAKE UP

Press following instructions on ball band.

Borders With 3¾mm [No 9] needles, pick up and k15 sts along front edge of pocket opening. **1st row** P, inc 1 st at both ends. Beg k row, work 7 rows st-st. Cast off. Work in the same way along other pocket opening edge. Fold each border in half and slip-stitch on wrong side. Sew down ends neatly to the cast-off 4 sts at each end.

Pockets On the wrong side of one Front place a pocket lining with the right side of the lining to the wrong side of the coat and having the cast-off edge to the side of

opening nearest to the side seam. Oversew the cast-off edge to the wrong side of the opening and slip-stitch the rem three sides to the wrong side of the coat, thus leaving a gap behind the side of the opening nearest to the front edge. Work the other lining in the same way.

Seams and Sleeves Join shoulder seams, with right sides together, using back-stitch. Place the sleeve top to the armhole edge, right sides together, pinning the ends in place and the top against the shoulder seams. Back-stitch in place the sleeve top to the armhole. Keeping right sides together, back-stitch the side seams then the sleeve seams. Turn to right side.

Hood With right sides together pin the cast on edge of hood to back of coat neck edge and the side edges to neck edges. Back-stitch in place.

With right side facing, along left front edge, work 1 row dc. Work a second row dc, working 3-ch loops in place of 2 dc for buttonholes, thus (2 dc, 3 ch, miss 2 dc) 6 times, ending 2 dc, fasten off. Work 2 rows dc along right front edge.

Work the 2 crochet rows along the st-st border of pockets, working 1 3-ch loop in centre for 1 buttonhole on front border. Sew 1 button on each of the pocket borders nearest the side seams to correspond with the loop on the border nearest the front edge. Sew on 6 buttons to front.

Left and below: the Hooded Jacket and the diagram which will help you get the shape right

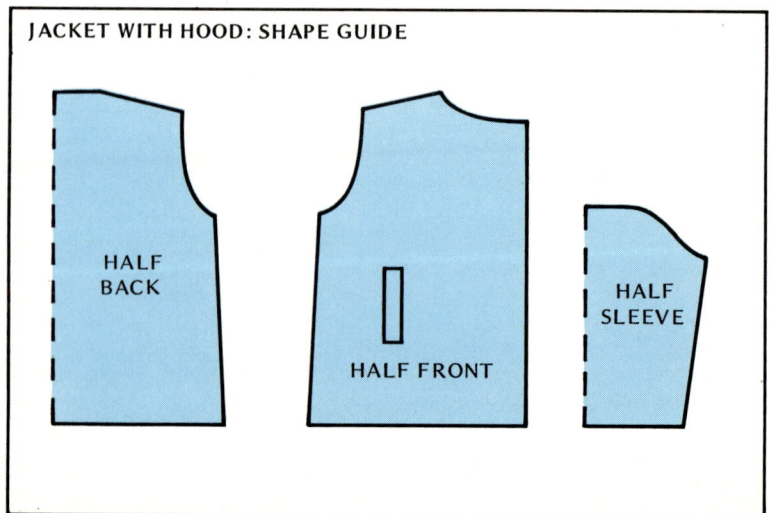

JACKET WITH HOOD: SHAPE GUIDE

HALF BACK

HALF FRONT

HALF SLEEVE

Little people set

18 months to 2 years

This design looks just like cut-out paper dolls and is used to great effect on a set for a baby. The measurements are generous so you could change the colours for a toddler up to 2 years. The pattern is given in full but if you prefer to work from a chart, see page 106.

Cover

Materials 100g Double Knitting in each of Yellow (Y); White (W); 50g in each of Orange (O) and Rust (R); pair 5mm [No 6] knitting needles.

Measurements 72cm [28 in] by 84cm [33 in].

Tension 14 sts and 18 rows to 10cm [4 in] in st-st.

Abbreviations k, knit; p, purl; st(s), stitch(es); cm, centimetre(s); in, inch(es); alt, alternate; beg, beginning; cont, continue; st-st, stocking stitch; rep, repeat; rem, remain(ing); patt, pattern.

> To make this into an even warmer cover line the back with a piece of flannelette or soft blanket, perhaps with a layer of quilting wadding between. To keep the colour pattern lying smooth carry the yarn not in use LOOSELY across the back of the work.

TO MAKE

With Y, cast on 90 sts. **1st row** *K1, p1; rep from * to end. **2nd row** *P1, k1; rep from * to end. Rep last 2 rows 4 times more, to form moss st border. Beg k row, work 18 rows st-st. Break Y. With W, work 2 rows st-st.
Now work the colour patt with W and R thus: **1st row** *K2 W, 2 R, 1 W, 2 R, 2 W; rep from * to end. **2nd row** *P3 W, 1 R, 1 W, 1 R, 3 W; rep from * to end. **3rd row** *K3 W, 1 R, 1 W, 1 R, 3 W; rep from * to end. **4th row** As 2nd row. **5th row** *K1 W, 7 R, 1 W; rep from * to end. **6th row** *P2 W, 5 R, 2 W; rep

Continued on next page

Above: a co-ordinating collection for toddlers. The instructions continue on pages 106–108

Little people set . . . continued

from * to end. **7th row** *K2 W, 5 R, 2 W; rep from * to end. **8th row** *P1 R, 2 W, 3 R, 2 W, 1 R; rep from * to end. **9th row** *K1 W, 1 R, 1 W, 3 R, 1 W, 1 R, 1 W; rep from * to end. **10th row** As 6th row. **11th row** *K3 W, 3 R, 3 W; rep from * to end. **12th row** *P3 W, 3 R, 3 W; rep from * to end. **13th row** As 7th row. **14th row** As 12th row. End of colour patt. Break R. With W, work 2 rows st-st. Break W.
With O, work 18 rows st-st. Break O. With W, work 2 rows st-st. Now, reading Y for R, rep the 14 rows of colour patt with W and Y. When the 14 rows have been worked, break Y. With W, work 2 rows st-st. Break W. With R, work 18 rows st-st. Break R. With W, work 2 rows st-st.
Now, reading O for R, rep the 14 rows of colour patt with W and O. When the 14 rows have been worked, break O. With W, work 2 rows st-st. Break W. With Y, work 18 rows st-st. Now, with Y, work 10 rows moss st. Cast off.

SIDE BORDERS (make 2)

With Y, cast on 8 sts. Rep the two moss st rows until the border fits along the side edges of the cover. Cast off. With the right sides of the border and cover together, neatly oversew the borders to the side edges. Press the st-st and colour patt sections following instructions on the ball band. Press the seams, but avoid pressing the moss st flat.

Jacket

Materials 75g 4-ply knitting yarn in white (W); 25g in each of yellow (Y); orange (O) and rust (R); pair 3¾mm [No 9] knitting needles; 3·5mm [No 9] crochet hook; 4 small buttons.

Measurements To fit 56cm [22 in] chest.

Tension 24 sts and 32 rows to 10cm [4 in] on 3¾mm [No 9] needles.

Special Note This garment may be closed at front or back. The instructions give the opening at the back, but the garment may be reversed in wear.

> Use a separate small ball of colour to work each figure, this removes the need to carry long strands of yarn across the back of the work. Twist the yarns on the wrong side when changing colour to avoid making a hole. Use the charts in place of reading the rows if you prefer, but make sure that you allow for the extra sts at the front edge of the work.

FRONT

With W, cast on 70 sts. **1st row** *K1, p1; rep from * to end. **2nd row** *P1, k1; rep from * to end. These 2 rows form the moss st. Work 6 rows more in moss st. Beg k row, work 2 rows st-st. Now work the colour patt thus:
1st row K3 W, *2 W, 2 R, 1 W, 2 R, 4 W, 2 Y, 1 W, 2 Y, 4 W, 2 O, 1 W, 2 O, 2 W; rep from * once more, 2 W, 2 R, 1 W, 2 R, 6 W.
2nd row P7 W, 1 R, 1 W, 1 R, 3 W, *3 W, 1 O, 1 W, 1 O, 6 W, 1 Y, 1 W, 1 Y, 6 W, 1 R, 1 W, 1 R, 3 W; rep from * once more, 3 W.
3rd row K in colours as purled in 2nd row.
4th row As 2nd row.
5th row K3 W, *1 W, 7 R, 2 W, 7 Y, 2 W, 7 O, 1 W; rep from * once more, 1 W, 7 R, 5 W.
6th row P4 W, 2 W, 5 R, 2 W, *2 W,

5 O, 4 W, 5 Y, 4 W, 5 R, 2 W; rep from * once more, 3 W.
7th row K in colours as purled in 6th row.
8th row P4 W, 1 R, 2 W, 3 R, 2 W, 1 R, *1 O, 2 W, 3 O, 2 W, 1 O, 1 Y, 2 W, 3 Y, 2 W, 1 Y, 1 R, 2 W, 3 R, 2 W, 1 R; rep from * once more, 3 W.
9th row K3 W, *1 W, 1 R, 1 W, 3 W, 1 W, 1 R, 2 W, 1 Y, 1 W, 3 Y, 1 W, 1 Y, 2 W, 1 O, 1 W, 3 O, 1 W, 1 O, 1 W; rep from * once more, 1 W, 1 R, 1 W, 3 R, 1 W, 1 R, 5 W.
10th row As 6th row.
11th row K3 W, *3 W, 3 R, 3 W, 3 Y, 6 W, 3 O, 3 W; rep from * once more, 3 W, 3 R, 7 W.
12th row P in colours as knitted in 11th row.
13th row As 7th row.
14th row As 12th row. Break R, Y and O.
With W, cont in st-st until work measures 18cm [7 in] ending after p row.
Shape for Sleeves Cast on 35 sts at beg of next 2 rows . . . 140 sts. Cont in st-st without shaping for 5cm [2 in] ending after a p row.
Next row K55, moss st 30, k55.
Next row P55, moss st 30, p55. Rep last 2 rows twice more.
Shape Neck 1st row K55, moss st 5, cast off 20 sts, moss st 5 sts, k55. Cont on last set of sts only.
2nd row P55, moss st 5. **3rd row** Moss st 5, k55. Rep last 2 rows until work measures 3cm [1¼ in] from beg of neck shaping, ending after wrong-side row. Leave sts on a spare needle for the time being. With right side of work facing, rejoin W to rem sts. **2nd row** Moss st 5, p55. **3rd row** K55, moss st 5. Rep last 2 rows until work measures 3cm [1¼ in] from beg of neck shaping, ending after a wrong-side row. Leave sts on a spare needle for the time being.

LEFT BACK

With W, cast on 35 sts. **1st row** K1, *p1, k1; rep from * to end. This row forms the moss st. Rep 1st row 7 times more. **9th row** Moss st 5, k to end. **10th row** P to last 5 sts, moss st 5.
Now work the colour patt, with moss st 5 at beg of k rows.
1st row Moss st 5, k3 W, 2 W, 2 R, 1 W, 2 R, 4 W, 2 Y, 1 W, 2 Y, 4 W, 2 O, 1 W, 2 O, 2 W.
2nd row P3 W, 1 O, 1 W, 1 O, 6 W, 1 Y, 1 W, 1 Y, 6 W, 1 R, 1 W, 1 R, 6 W, moss st 5.
3rd row Moss st 5, k in colours as purled in 2nd row.
4th row As 2nd row.
5th row Moss st 5, k4 W, 7 R, 2 W, 7 Y, 2 W, 7 O, 1 W.
6th row P2 W, 5 O, 4 W, 5 Y, 4 W, 5 R, 5 W, moss st 5.
7th row Moss st 5, k in colours as purled in 6th row.
8th row P1 O, 2 W, 3 O, 2 W, 1 O, 1 Y, 2 W, 3 Y, 2 W, 1 Y, 1 R, 2 W, 3 R, 2 W, 1 R, 3 W, moss st 5.
9th row Moss st 5, k4 W, 1 R, 1 W, 3 R, 1 W, 1 R, 2 W, 1 Y, 1 W, 3 Y, 1 W, 1 Y, 2 W, 1 O, 1 W, 3 O, 1 W, 1 O, 1 W.
10th row As 6th row.
11th row Moss st 5, k6 W, 3 R, 6 W, 3 Y, 6 W, 3 O, 3 W.
12th row P in colours knitted on 11th row, ending moss st 5.
13th row As 7th row.
14th row As 12th row. Break R, Y and O.
With W, cont in st-st with moss st 5 border until work measures 18cm [7 in] ending after a k row.
Shape for Sleeve Next row Cast on 35 sts, p to last 5 sts, moss st 5. Cont on 70 sts in st-st with moss st border for 5cm [2 in] ending after a p row. **Next row** Moss st 15, k to end. **Next row** P to last 15 sts, moss st 15. Rep last 2 rows twice more.
Shape Neck Next row Cast off 10 sts, moss st 5, k to end. Keeping 5 sts in moss st and rem in st-st, cont until work measures 3cm [1¼ in] from beg of neck shaping, ending after a p row. Leave these sts on a spare needle but before setting aside, mark the moss st back band with four pins to represent buttons: place the top pin in the neck border and the other three spaced at 4cm [1½ in] intervals below.

RIGHT BACK

With W, cast on 35 sts. **1st row** K1, *p1, k1; rep from * to end. Rep 1st row 7 times more. **9th row** K to last 5 sts, moss st 5. **10th row** Moss st 5, p to end.
Rep the last 2 rows including colour patt below until work

For those who find working from a chart simpler than following the row pattern, use the chart, working the k row from right to left and the purl rows from left to right

LITTLE PEOPLE SET: JACQUARD CHART

14

13

2

1

orange   yellow   rust

measures 18cm [7 in] <u>at the same time</u> working buttonholes to correspond with the marked positions on Left Back thus: **1st row** (right side) K to last 5 sts, moss st 2, y fwd, k2 tog, moss st 1. This one row will form a small buttonhole.

Work the patt in reverse thus:
1st row K2 W, 2 R, 1 W, 2 R, 4 W, 2 Y, 1 W, 2 Y, 4 W, 2 O, 1 W, 2 O, 5 W, moss st 5.
2nd row Moss st 5, p6 W, 1 O, 1 W, 1 O, 6 W, 1 Y, 1 W, 1 Y, 6 W, 1 R, 1 W, 1 R, 3 W.
3rd row K in colours as purled on 2nd row, ending moss st 5.
4th row As 2nd row.
5th row K1 W, 7 R, 2 W, 7 Y, 2 W, 7 O, 4 W, moss st 5.
6th row Moss st 5, p5 W, 5 O, 4 W, 5 Y, 4 W, 5 R, 2 W.
7th row K in colours as purled on 6th row, ending moss st 5.
8th row Moss st 5, p3 W, 1 O, 2 W, 3 O, 2 W, 1 O, 1 Y, 1 W, 2 Y, 3 Y, 2 W, 1 Y, 1 R, 2 W, 3 R, 2 W, 1 W.
9th row K1 W, 1 R, 1 W, 3 R, 1 W, 1 R, 2 W, 1 Y, 1 W, 3 Y, 1 W, 1 Y, 2 W, 1 O, 1 W, 3 O, 1 W, 1 O, 4 W, moss st 5.
10th row As 6th row.
11th row K3 W, 3 R, 6 W, 3 Y, 6 W, 3 O, 6 W, moss st 5.
12th row P in colours as knitted in 11th row.
13th row As 7th row.
14th row As 12th row. Break R, Y and O.

Work until Right Back matches Left Back to sleeve (18cm [7 in]) ending after a p row.
Shape for Sleeve Next row Cast on 35 sts, k to last 5 sts, moss st 5. Cont in st-st with moss st 5 border at front edge for 5cm [2 in] ending after a k row. **Next row** Moss st 15, p to end. **Next row** K55, moss st 15. Rep last 2 rows twice more.
Shape Neck Next row Cast off 10 sts, moss st 5, p to end. Keeping 5 sts in moss st and rem in st-st cont until work measures 3cm [1¼ in] from beg of neck shaping, ending after a p row. Leave these sts on a spare needle for now.

TO MAKE UP

To join the shoulder seams, place the two left shoulder sets of sts together, right sides together and with needle points towards the right, then with a third needle, cast off the two sets of sts together, ie, *inserting the point of the right-hand needle into the first st from the front needle together with the first st from the back needle, then likewise with the second two sts, slip the first st on right-hand needle over the second st; rep from * until all sts are worked off. Cast off the sts of the right shoulder in the same way.

With right side of work facing, pick up and k with W, 41 sts evenly along Sleeve edge, for cuff. **1st row** K1, *p1, k1; rep from * to end. Rep 1st row 5 times more. Cast off. Work the other cuff in the same way.

With right side of work facing, using 3·5mm [No 9] crochet hook and W, work 1 row dc all round neck edge, 1 ch, turn. **Picot row** 1 dc in 1st dc, *3ch, ss in 1st of 3 ch, miss 1 dc, 1 dc in next dc; rep from * to end.

Press work following instructions on ball band. Sew on buttons.

Trousers

Materials 75g 4-ply knitting yarn; pair 4mm [No 8] knitting needles; 2 buttons; 15cm [6 in] elastic 6mm [¼ in] wide.

Measurements 56cm [22 in] round at widest part; length to waist 20cm [8 in].

Tension 18 sts and 24 rows to 10cm [4 in] yarn used double.

Abbreviations k, knit; p, purl; st(s), stitch(es); cm, centimetre(s); in, inch(es); alt, alternate; beg, beginning; cont, continue; dec, decreas(e)ing; inc, increas(e)ing; sl, slip; psso, pass slip stitch over, rep, repeat; rem, remain(ing); st-st, stocking stitch; tog, together.

Special Note Yarn is used double throughout for the trousers.

BACK RIGHT LEG

With 4mm [No 8] needles, cast on 26 sts. Cont in moss st and inc at inner leg thus: **1st row** *K1, p1; rep from * to end. **2nd row** Inc in 1st st, k1, *p1, k1; rep from * to end. **3rd row** *K1, p1; rep from * to last st, k1. **4th row** Inc in 1st st, *p1, k1; rep from * to end. **5th and 6th rows** As 1st and 2nd rows.
Now cont in st-st with moss st border at outer edge inc at inner leg as before thus: **7th row** K1, p1, k1, k to end. **8th row** Inc in 1st st, p to last 3 sts, k1, p1, k1. **9th to 14th rows** Rep last 2 rows 3 times more . . . 33 sts. Leave these sts on a spare needle for the time being.

BACK LEFT LEG

With 4mm [No 8] needles, cast on 26 sts. Cont in moss st and inc at inner leg thus: **1st row** *K1, p1; rep from * to end. **2nd row**

*P1, k1; rep from * to last 2 sts, p1, inc in last st. **3rd row** P1, *k1, p1; rep from * to end. **4th row** *P1, k1; rep from * to last st, inc in last st. **5th and 6th rows** As 1st and 2nd rows.
Now cont in st-st with moss st border at outer edge, inc at inner leg as before thus: **7th row** Inc in 1st st, k to last 3 sts, moss st 3. **8th row** Moss st 3, p to end. **9th to 14th rows** Rep last 2 rows 3 times more . . . 33 sts, break yarn.
Take up the Back Right Leg sts on the spare needle, moss st 3, k to end, turn, cast on 15 sts, turn and k across the sts of Back Left Leg, ending with moss st 3 . . . 81 sts. **Next row** Moss st 3, p to last 3 sts, moss st 3.
Shape for Crotch 1st row Moss st 3, k28, sl 1, k2 tog, psso, k13, k3 tog, k28, moss st 3. **2nd row and foll alt rows** Moss st 3, p to last 3 sts, moss st 3. **3rd row** Moss st 3, k27, sl 1, k2 tog, psso, k11, k3 tog, k27, moss st 3. **5th row** Moss st 3, k26, sl 1, k2 tog, psso, k9, k3 tog, k26, moss st 3 . . . 69 sts.
Cont dec 4 sts on every right-side row in this way until 57 sts rem. **Next row** Moss st 3, k22, sl 1, k1, psso, k1, k2 tog, k22, moss st 3 . . . 53 sts.
Cont without shaping in st-st with 3 sts in moss st at outer edges until work measures 17cm [6¾ in] from beg, ending after a p row.
Now work the waist rib with 3 sts in moss st as before at outer edges: **1st row** Moss st 3, *k1, p1; rep from * to last 4 sts, k1, moss st 3. **2nd row** Moss st 3, *p1, k1; rep from * to last 4 sts, p1, moss st 3. Rep last 2 rows once more.
5th row Moss st 3, *k1, yarn for-

ward, sl 1, yarn back; rep from * to last 4 sts; k1, moss st 3. **6th row** Moss st 3, p1, *p1, keeping yarn towards you, sl 1 purlwise; rep from * to last 3 sts, moss st 3. Rep last 2 rows 3 times more, forming a slot for the back waist elastic. Cast off.

FRONT LEFT LEG

With 4mm [No 8] needles, cast on 26 sts. Cont in moss st and inc at inner leg thus: **1st row** *K1, p1; rep from * to end. **2nd row** Inc in 1st st, k1, *p1, k1; rep from * to end. **3rd row** *K1, p1; rep from * to last st, k1. **4th row** Inc in 1st st, *p1, k1; rep from * to end. **5th and 6th rows** As 1st and 2nd rows.
Now cont in st-st with moss st border at outer edge, inc at inner leg as before thus: **7th row** K1, p1, k1, k to end. **8th row** Inc in 1st st, p to last 3 sts, moss st 3. **9th to 14th rows** Rep last 2 rows 3 times more . . . 33 sts. Leave these sts on spare needle for now.

FRONT RIGHT LEG

With 4mm [No 8] needles, cast on 26 sts. Cont in moss st, inc at inner leg thus: **1st row** *K1, p1; rep from * to end. **2nd row** *P1, k1; rep from * to last 2 sts, p1, inc in last st. **3rd row** P1, *k1, p1; rep from * to end. **4th row** *P1, k1; rep from * to last st, inc in last st. **5th and 6th rows** As 1st and 2nd rows.
Now cont in st-st with moss st borders at outer edge, inc at inner leg as before thus: **7th row** Inc in 1st st, k to last 3 sts, moss st 3. **8th row** P Moss st 3, p to end. **9th to 14th rows** Rep last 2 rows 3

Continued on next page

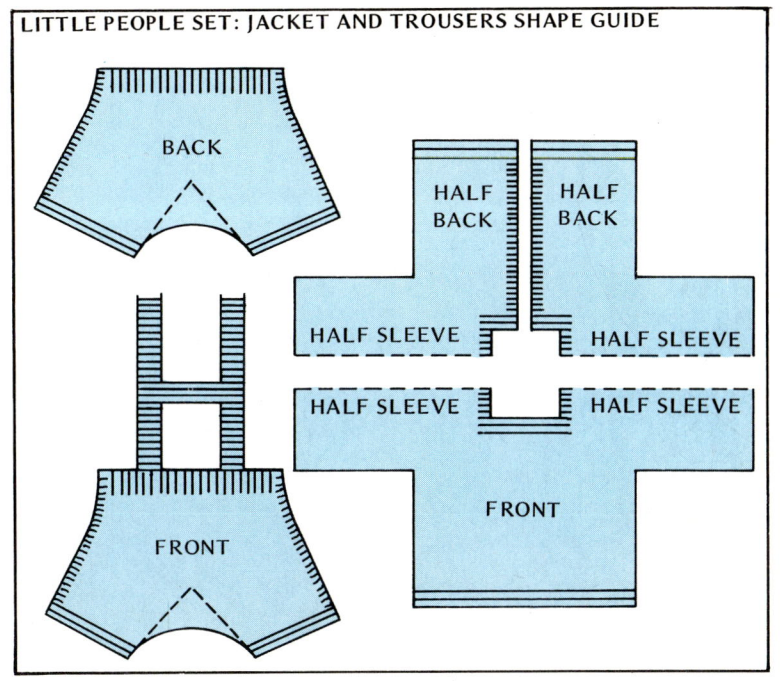

LITTLE PEOPLE SET: JACKET AND TROUSERS SHAPE GUIDE

BACK

HALF BACK · HALF BACK

HALF SLEEVE · HALF SLEEVE

HALF SLEEVE · HALF SLEEVE

FRONT

FRONT

Little people set . . . continued

times more . . . 33 sts, break yarn. Take up the Front Left Leg sts on the spare needle, moss st 3, k to end, turn, cast on 15 sts, turn and k across the sts of Front Right Leg to last 3 sts, moss st 3 . . . 81 sts. **Next row** Moss st 3, p to last 3 sts, moss st 3.

Shape for Crotch 1st row Moss st 3, k28, sl 1, k2 tog, psso, k13, k3 tog, k28, moss st 3. **2nd row and foll alt rows** Moss st 3, p to last 3 sts, moss st 3. **3rd row** Moss st 3, k27, sl 1, k2 tog, psso, k11, k3 tog, k27, moss st 3. **5th row** Moss st 3, k26, sl 1, k2 tog, psso, k9, k3 tog, k26, moss st 3.

Cont dec 4 sts on every right-side row in this way until 57 sts rem. **Next row** Moss st 3, k22, sl 1, k1, psso, k1, k2 tog, k22, moss st 3 . . . 53 sts.

Cont without shaping in st-st with 3 sts in moss st at outer edges until work measures 17cm [6¾ in] ending after a wrong-side row.

Work the waist rib with 3 sts in moss st at edges thus: **1st row** Moss st 3, *k1, p1; rep from * to last 4 sts, k1, moss st 3. **2nd row** Moss st 3, *p1, k1; rep from * to last 4 sts, p1, moss st 3. Rep last 2 rows 3 times more.

9th row Cast off 14 sts, moss st 6, k13, moss st 6, cast off last 14 sts. Break yarn. With wrong side of work facing, rejoin yarn to rem 25 sts. Cont on these 25 sts with 13 sts in st-st at centre and 6 sts in moss st at each end until the bib measures 9cm [3½ in] ending after a wrong-side row. Now work 8 rows in moss st across all 25 sts.

Next row Moss st 8, turn. Cont on these 6 sts for first strap. Work 26cm [10½ in] in moss st. **Next row** Moss st 2, cast off 2, moss st 2. **Next row** Moss st 2, cast on 2, moss st 2. Moss st 2 rows more. Cast off.

With right side of work facing, rejoin yarn to rem sts, cast off centre 13 sts, moss st to end. Work 26cm [10½ in] moss st on these 6 sts. **Next row** Moss st 2, cast off 2, moss st 2. **Next row** Moss st 2, cast on 2, moss st 2. Moss st 2 rows more. Cast off.

TO MAKE UP
With right sides of work together, back-stitch the side seams and inner leg and crotch seams. Insert the elastic through back rib. Sew buttons on back rib. Cross straps over at back and button.

Skirt

Materials 100g 4-ply yarn in main colour (M); a small quantity in each of 1st, 2nd and 3rd contrasts (A, B and C); pair 4mm [No 8] knitting needles; 2 buttons, 2 press studs; elastic 15mm [⅝ in] wide to fit back waist.

Measurements To fit 56cm [22 in] chest.

Tension 21 sts and 28 rows to 10cm [4 in] with yarn used double.

Abbreviations k, knit; p, purl; st(s), stitch(es); cm, centimetre(s); in, inch(es); alt, alternate; beg, beginning; cont, continue; foll, following; patt, pattern; rep, repeat; rem, remain(ing); y fwd, yarn forward; yb, yarn back; st-st, stocking stitch.

Special Note Yarn is used double throughout.

TO MAKE
The skirt folds over at front and is made in one piece. With M, cast on 161 sts. Work 5 rows moss st patt thus: **Every row** K1, (p1, k1) to end.

Now cont in st-st with moss borders thus: **1st row** K1, p1, k1, p1, k1, k to last 5 sts, k1, p1, k1, p1, k1. **2nd row** K1, p1, k1, p1, k1, p to last 5 sts, k1, p1, k1, p1, k1.

Now work the colour patt. You will need a small ball (yarn doubled) for each new colour change. Twist the yarns when changing colour to avoid making a hole.

1st row Moss st 5 M, k5 M, *k2 M, 2 A, 1 M, 2 A, 4 M, 2 B, 1 M, 2 B, 4 M, 2 C, 1 M, 2 C, 2 M; rep from * 4 times more, k2 M, 2 A, 1 M, 2 A, 4 M, moss st 5 M.
2nd row Moss st 5 M, p5 M, 1 A, 1 M, 1 A, 3 M, *3 M, 1 C, 1 M, 1 C, 6 M, 1 B, 1 M, 1 B, 6 M, 1 A, 1 M, 1 A, 3 M; rep from * 4 times more, 5 M, moss st 5 M.
3rd row Moss st 5 M, k5 M, *3 M, 1 A, 1 M, 1 A, 6 M, 1 B, 1 M, 1 B, 6 M, 1 C, 1 M, 1 C, 3 M; rep from * 4 times more, 3 M, 1 A, 1 M, 1 A, 5 M, moss st 5 M.
4th row Moss st 5 M, patt as 2nd row, moss st 5 M.
5th row Moss st 5 M, k5 M, *1 M, 7 A, 2 M, 7 B, 2 M, 7 C, 1 M; rep from * 4 times more, 1 M, 7 A, 3 M, moss st 5 M.
6th row Moss st 5 M, p4 M, 5 A, 2 M, *2 M, 5 C, 4 M, 5 B, 4 M, 5 A, 2 M; rep from * 4 times more, 5 M, moss st 5 M.
7th row Moss st 5 M, k5 M, *2 M, 5 A, 4 M, 5 B, 4 M, 5 C, 2 M; rep

from * 4 times more, 2 M, 5 A, 4 M, moss st 5 M.
8th row Moss st 5 M, p2 M, 1 A, 2 M, 3 A, 2 M, 1 A, *1 C, 2 M, 3 C, 2 M, 1 C, 1 B, 2 M, 3 B, 2 M, 1 B, 1 A, 2 M, 3 A, 2 M, 1 A; rep from * 4 times more, 5 M, moss st 5 M.
9th row Moss st 5 M, k5 M, *1 M, 1 A, 1 M, 3 A, 1 M, 1 A, 2 M, 1 B, 1 M, 3 B, 1 M, 1 B, 2 M, 1 C, 1 M, 3 C, 1 M, 1 C, 1 M; rep from * 4 times more, 1 M, 1 A, 1 M, 3 A, 1 M, 1 A, 3 M, moss st 5 M.
10th row As 6th row.
11th row Moss st 5 M, k5 M, *3 M, 3 A, 6 M, 3 B, 6 M, 3 C, 3 M; rep from * 4 times more, 3 M, 3 A, 5 M, moss st 5 M. **12th row** Moss st 5 M, p5 M, 3 A, 3 M, *3 M, 3 C, 6 M, 3 B, 6 M, 3 A, 3 M; rep from * 4 times more, 5 M, moss st 5 M.
13th row As 7th row.
14th row As 12th row.

End of colour patt. Break A, B and C. Cont in M only as before in st-st with moss st borders over 5 end sts until work measures 20cm [8 in] ending after a p row. Work in slip rib for waist thus:
1st row Moss st 5, * k1, y fwd, sl 1 purlwise, yb; rep from * to last 6 sts, k1, moss st 5. **2nd row** Moss st 5, *y fwd, sl 1 purlwise, yb, k1; rep from * to last 6 sts, y fwd, sl 1 purlwise, yb, moss st 5. Rep last 2 rows 4 times more. Cast off the sts.

TO MAKE UP
Press the st-st and colour patt following instructions on the ball band. Sew the two buttons at waist to the right overfold as shown in the picture. On the reverse side of the buttons sew half of the press studs and the corresponding half to the underlay. Using a safety-pin insert the elastic into the waist slip rib, beg and ending at the press studs on front, having the elastic around the back only. Sew down the ends of the elastic.

Sporty sets

18 months to 2 years

A useful warm suit that can be made in three different ways – either a plain suit for speed; a plain suit with one or other of the designs worked with embroidery that looks like Fair Isle. Or, for the more ambitious, a simple Fair Isle to be worked from a chart on to a straight piece of stocking stitch.

Materials Six 25g balls 4-ply knitting yarn in main colour (M); a small quantity of yellow and blue for the sun design; a small quantity of white, red and green for the boat design; pairs of 3mm and 3¼mm [No 11 and No 10] knitting needles; 50cm [18 in] elastic 2·5cm [1 in] wide.

Measurements Chest size 56cm [22 in].

Tension 28 sts and 36 rows to 10cm [4 in] on 3¼mm [No 10] needles.

Abbreviations k, knit; p, purl; st(s), stitch(es); cm, centimetre(s); in, inch(es); alt, alternate; beg, beginning; cont, continue; dec, decreas(e)ing; inc, increas(e)ing; st-st, stocking stitch; tog, together; rem, remain(ing); rep, repeat; foll, following. Square brackets contain imperial measurements.

Special Note The Top is given in main colour only. The motif can then be worked on the front with embroidery or left plain. The embroidery instructions are given in the making up. If you prefer to work the motif in with the knitting, follow the colour chart and place the pattern on the front as given in the making up instructions (to work Fair Isle).

TROUSERS
LEFT LEG
Beg at lower edge. With 3mm [No 11] needles and M, cast on 76 sts. Work 3cm [1¼ in] k2, p2 rib. Change to 3¼mm [No 10] needles. Cont in st-st, inc 1 st at both ends of 3rd row foll and every foll 4th row to 82 sts. Cont in st-st without shaping until work measures 10cm [4 in] ending after a p row.

Shape for Crotch 1st row Cast off 4 sts (back edge), k to end. **2nd row** Cast off 2 sts, p to end. **3rd row** Cast off 2 sts, k to end. **4th row** P2 tog, p to end. **5th row** K2 tog, k to end. **6th row** P2 tog, p to end. **7th row** K2 tog, k to end. **8th row** P2 tog, p to end. **9th row** K2 tog, k to end. **10th row** P2 tog, p to end. **11th row** K to end. **12th row** P2 tog, p to end. **13th row** K2 tog, k to end. **14th row** P to end. **15th row** K to end. **16th row** P2 tog, p to end. **17th row** K2 tog, k to end. **18th row** P to end. **19th row** K to end. **20th row** P2 tog, p to end. **21st row** K2 tog, k to end . . . 61 sts.
Cont in st-st without shaping until work measures 22cm [8¾ in] ending after a p row. Cast off.

RIGHT LEG
With 3mm [No 11] needles and M, cast on 76 sts. Work 3cm [1¼ in] k2, p2 rib. Change to 3¼mm [No 10] needles. Cont in st-st, inc 1 st at both ends of 3rd row foll and every foll 4th row to 82 sts. Cont without shaping until work measures 10cm [4 in] ending after a p row.
Shape for Crotch 1st row Cast off 2 sts, (front edge), k to end. **2nd row** Cast off 4 sts, p to end. **3rd row** K2 tog, k to end. **4th row** Cast off 2 sts, p to end. **5th row** K2 tog, k to end. **6th row** P2 tog, p to end. **7th row** K2 tog, k to end. **8th row** P2 tog, p to end. **9th row** K2 tog, k to end. **10th row** P2 tog, p to end. **11th row** K2 tog, k to end. **12th row** P to end. **13th row** K to end. **14th row** P2 tog, p to end. **15th row** K2 tog, k to end. **16th row** P to end. **17th row** K to end. **18th row** P2 tog, p to end. **19th row** K2 tog, k to end. **20th row** P to end. **21st row** K to end. **22nd row** P2 tog, p to end . . . 61 sts.
Cont in st-st without shaping until work measures 22cm [8¾ in] from beg of crotch shaping, ending after a p row. Cast off.

TO MAKE UP
With right sides together sew the centre back seam from cast-off edges to beg of crotch shaping, using a back-stitch seam, then cont joining the centre front seam in the same way. Now with right side still inside, join the two inner leg seams with back-stitch. Fold at waist 2·5cm [1 in] to wrong side and slip-stitch to wrong side, leaving a small opening in which to insert the waist elastic. Using a safety-pin at one end, insert the elastic through the channel, catch both ends and sew into a circle. Slip-stitch the rem section

Continued on next page

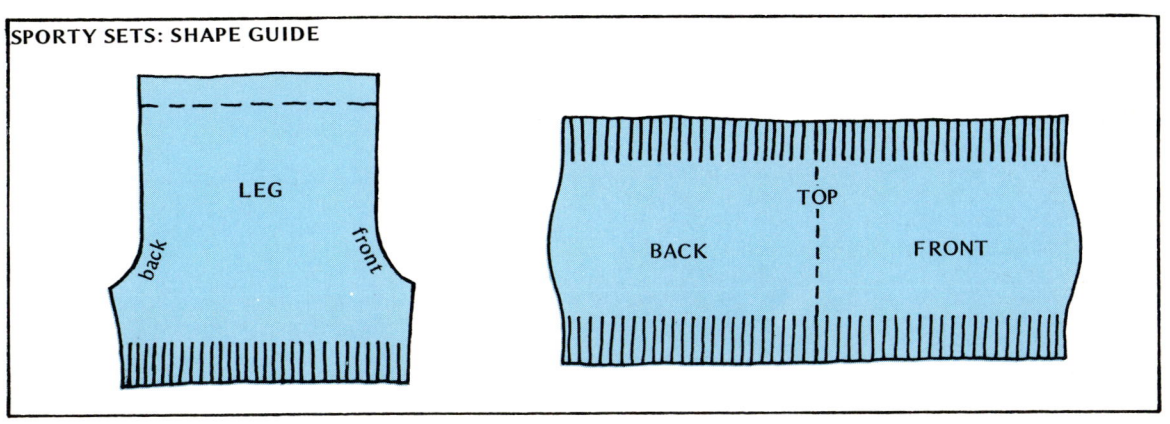

SPORTY SETS: SHAPE GUIDE

LEG

back   front

TOP

BACK   FRONT

Sporty sets . . . continued

of the opening. Press according to the instructions on ball band, omitting ribbed borders.

TOP

FRONT AND BACK

These are worked in one piece, the seam coming under one arm. With 3mm [No 11] needles and M, cast on 152 sts. Work 5cm [2 in] k2, p2 rib. Change to 3¼mm [No 10] needles and cont in st-st for 46 rows. Change to 3mm [No 11] needles and work 5cm [2 in] k2, p2 rib. Cast off loosely in rib.

SHOULDER STRAPS

These are worked sideways. With 3mm [No 11] needles and M, cast on 68 sts. Work 6cm [2½ in] k2, p2 rib. Cast off sts in rib. Make the second strap in the same way.

TO MAKE UP

If you have knitted the top plain and wish to embroider one of the motifs, this should be worked now – see instructions below for working the Swiss Embroidery.
Boat Motif With right side of work facing, count 17 sts from the side edge and work the 1st green st in the 18th. The side seam will be on the left underarm when the garment is completed.
Sun Motif With right side of work facing, count only 1 st from the side edge (this 1 st to be used for

the seam) and work the 1st blue st in the 2nd. The side seam will be on the left underarm when the garment is completed.
With the right side of the work inside, back-stitch the side seam, just within one stitch from the side edge, to avoid taking in the motif edge. Sew on the narrow ends of the shoulder straps, concealing the ends behind the top of the rib.

How to work motifs in Fair Isle
Boat Join in the appropriate colour in the same stitch as that given for the start of the Swiss Embroidery. Cont working from the chart, working the odd rows k from right to left and the even rows p from left to right and the rem of the row, plain colour. When the motif is completed,

cont until 46 rows have been worked in st-st.
Sun Follow the instructions as for the boat motif but you'll see that the chart is different. You will k from right to left for half the pattern then reverse and work from left to right.
On the p rows work in the same way. In this manner you will make both halves of the design exactly the same.
Press work, omitting rib.

Left: the sun motif which can be worked on to the Sporty Set by Swiss Embroidery or knitted into the set by Fair Isle. The suit with the boat motif can be seen in colour on page 109

SWISS EMBROIDERY

To work the embroidery, begin at the bottom right hand corner of the chosen motif at the stitch given (see To Make Up, above).
1. Leave an end at the back and bring needle out to the front through centre of stitch below one to be covered, then in and out again behind the stitch in the row above. Now go back into the same hole at the bottom and out through centre of next stitch to the left.
2. Cover each stitch in the first row like this and at the end of the row slip the needle upwards into the centre of the last stitch covered instead of taking it along to the left.
3. Now turn the work upside down so you are still working from right to left. Cover all the parts in one colour first then fill in with any others.

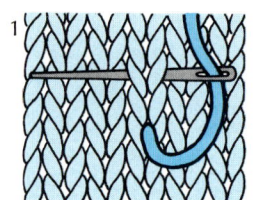

BOAT MOTIF: FAIR ISLE CHART

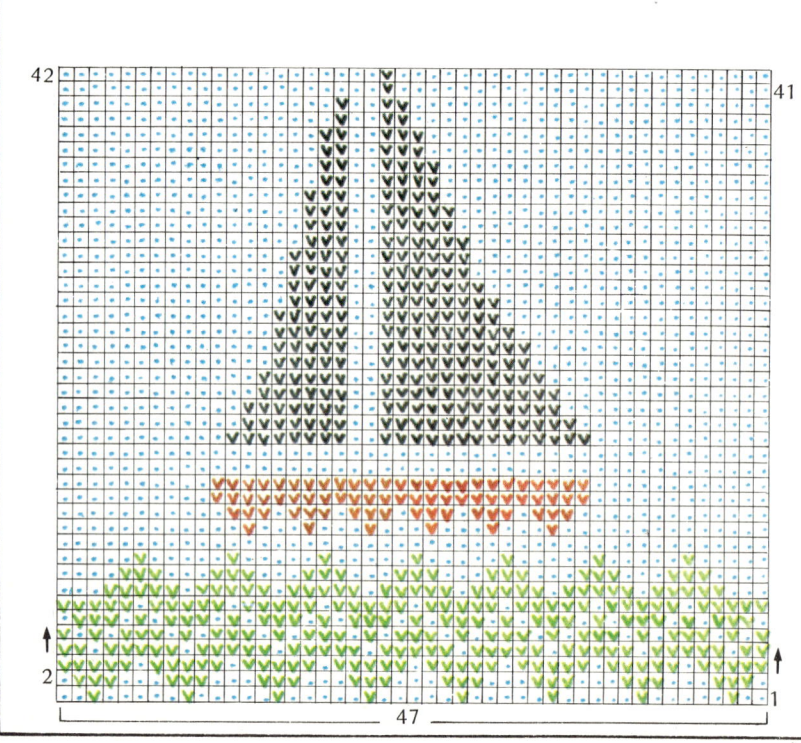

SUN MOTIF: FAIR ISLE CHART

Key X = yellow
     V = blue

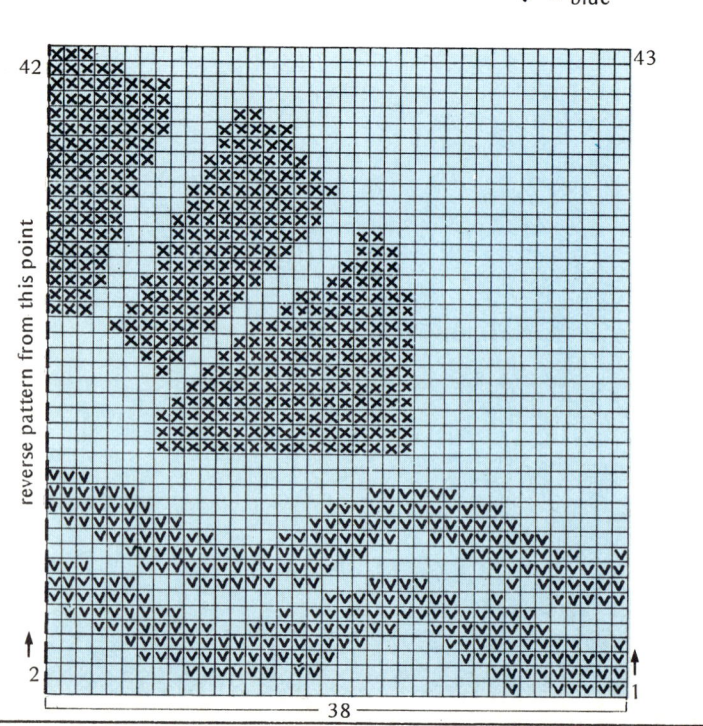

Buster suit

18 months to 3 years

Just right for the toughest playtime – an all-in-one suit that's the same front and back. Easy to knit, and very easy to wear over a sweater or a shirt.

Materials Four 25g balls Double Knitting yarn in light colour (L); four balls in dark colour (D); pair 3¾mm [No 9] knitting needles.

Measurements Actual size round chest, 40cm [15¾ in] unstretched.

Tension 40 sts and 34 rows to 10cm [4 in] in rib unstretched.

Abbreviations k, knit; p, purl; st(s), stitch(es); cm, centimetre(s); in, inch(es); alt, alternate; beg, beginning; cont, continue; dec, decreas(e)ing; foll, following; st-st, stocking stitch; tog, together; rem, remain(ing); rep, repeat. Square brackets contain imperial measurements.

> The knit 2, purl 2 rib gives a nice elasticity to this suit and at full stretch it should fit a size up to 10cm [4 in] larger than the actual size given.

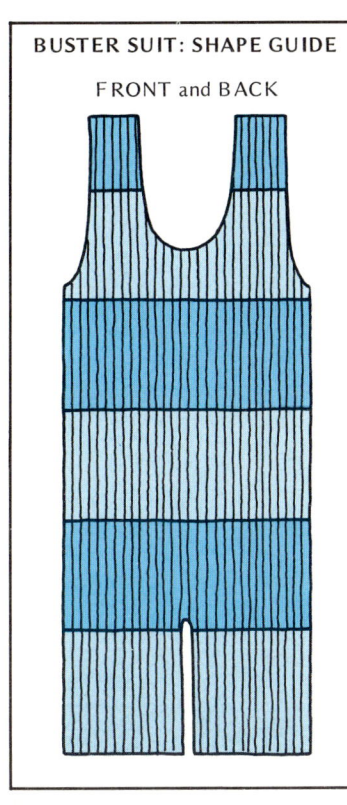

BUSTER SUIT: SHAPE GUIDE

FRONT and BACK

FRONT
Beg at lower edge of left leg. With L, cast on 40 sts. Work 10cm [4 in] k2, p2 rib. Change to D and work 12.5mm [½ in] k2, p2 rib. Break yarn. Leave these sts on a spare needle for now.
Beg at lower edge of right leg, with L, cast on 40 sts. Work 10cm [4 in] k2, p2 rib. Change to D and work 12.5mm [½ in] k2, p2 rib.
Next row (Join two leg pieces) Rib to end, then on to same needle, rib across the sts of left leg on spare needle . . . 80 sts.
Cont in k2, p2 rib until the D stripe measures 10cm [4 in] from the change of colour. Change to L and work another 9cm [3½ in] in rib. Change to D and work another 9cm [3½ in] in rib. Change to L and cont in rib for a further 12.5mm [½ in].
Shape Armholes Cast off 2 sts at beg of next 4 rows. Dec 1 st at both ends of next row and foll 3 alt rows . . . 64 sts.
Divide for Neck Shaping 1st row

Rib 26, turn and work on these sts only to complete first side.
2nd row Cast off 4 sts, rib to end. **3rd row** Rib to end. **4th row** Cast off 2 sts, rib to end. **5th row** Rib to end. **6th row** K2 tog, rib to end. Rep last 2 rows 3 times more . . . 16 sts. Cont in rib without shaping until this stripe is 9cm [3½ in] from change of colour. Cast off the sts loosely in rib.
With right side of work facing, join yarn at neck edge. Cast off centre 12 sts, rib to end and complete to match first side, reversing shaping.

BACK
Work another piece the same.

BORDERS
With L, cast on 120 sts for the neck border. Work 3cm [1¼ in] st-st. Cast off. With L, cast on 72 sts for one armhole border. Work 3cm [1¼ in] st-st. Cast off. Work a second armhole border in the same way.

TO MAKE UP
Join the front and back side seams with back-stitch, matching the stripes and using matching yarn for sewing. Back-stitch the inner leg seams in the same way. With right sides together back-stitch the shoulder seams. With the right side of work facing, place the neck border to the neck edge, have the two ends of the border to the centre back neck and the right side of the border to the right side of the garment. Pin the border first to ease the rib to fit the border evenly. Back-stitch, just one stitch in from the edges all round. Remove any pins or tacking. Fold the border in half to the wrong side. Slip-stitch to the wrong side and neatly oversew the centre back join. If preferred the border may be neatly oversewn to front and back. Sew the armhole borders on in the same way, with the join at the under arm.

Children's Clothes

Dress with flowers

18 months to 3 years

A simple dress with side shapings that could just as easily be worn over favourite trousers.

Materials 8(9) 25g balls Double Knitting yarn in main colour (M); 1 ball in contrast colour (C); pairs of 3mm and 3¾mm [No 11 and No 9] knitting needles; 3mm [No 11] crochet hook; 4 buttons.

Measurements Actual size 51 (56)cm [20(22) in] round chest; length 38·5(41)cm [15(16) in].

Tension 24 sts and 32 rows to 10cm [4 in] in st-st.

Abbreviations k, knit; p, purl; st(s), stitch(es); cm, centimetre(s); in, inch(es); alt, alternate; beg, beginning; cont, continue; dec, decreas(e)ing; inc, increas(e)ing; g-st, garter stitch (every row K); st-st, stocking stitch; rep, repeat; rem, remain(ing); tog, together; ch, chain; dc, double crochet; tr, treble; rnd, round; foll, following.

Size Note Figures in brackets refer to larger size. One figure only refers to both sizes. Square brackets contain imperial measurements.

BACK

With 3¾mm [No 9] needles and M, cast on 90(96) sts. Work 10 rows g-st. Beg k row, cont in st-st dec 1 st at both ends of next row and every foll 12th row to 78(84) sts. Cont without shaping in st-st until work measures 27(28)cm 10½(11) in] ending after a p row.
Shape Armholes Cast off 3(4) sts at beg of next 2 rows; 2 sts at beg of next 2 rows. Dec 1 st at both ends of next row and foll 1(2) alt rows . . . 64(66) sts. Cont in st-st without shaping until work measures 38·5(41)cm [15(16) in] ending after a p row.

Shape Shoulders and Neck 1st row Cast off 5 sts, k22, turn. Leave rem sts for the time being and complete this side first. **2nd row** Cast off 3 sts, p to end. **3rd row** Cast off 5 sts, k to end. **4th row** Cast off 3 sts, p to end. **5th row** Cast off 5 sts, k to end. **6th row** P to end. **7th row** Cast off rem 6 sts.

With right side of work facing, slip the centre 10(12) sts on to a stitch holder to be used later in neck band; rejoin M to rem sts, k to end.
Complete this side to match the first side, reversing shapings thus:

1st row Cast off 5 sts, p to end. **2nd row** (right side) Cast off 3 sts, k to end. **3rd row** Cast off 5 sts, p to end. **4th row** Cast off 3 sts, k to end. **5th row** Cast off 5 sts, p to end. **6th row** K to end. **7th row** Cast off rem 6 sts.

FRONT

With 3¾mm [No 9] needles and M, cast on 90(96) sts. Work 10 rows g-st. Beg k row, cont in st-st, dec 1 st at both ends of next row and every foll 12th row to 78(84) sts. Cont without shaping in st-st until work measures 27(28)cm 10½(11) in] ending after p row.
Shape Armholes Cast off 3(4) sts at beg of next 2 rows; 2 sts at beg of next 2 rows. Dec 1 st at both ends of next row and foll 1(2) alt rows . . . 64(66) sts. Cont in st-st without shaping until work measures 33·5(35)cm [13(13¾) in] ending after p row.
Shape Neck 1st row K28 sts, turn. Leave rem sts on a spare needle for the time being and complete this side first. **2nd row** Cast off 2 sts, p to end. **3rd row** K to end. **4th to 7th rows** Rep last 2 rows twice more. **8th row** P2 tog, p to end . . . 21 sts.
Cont in st-st without shaping until work matches Back to shoulder, ending after a p row.
Shape Shoulder Cast off 5 sts at beg of next 3 right-side rows. Work 1 row. Cast off rem 6 sts.
With right side of work facing, slip the centre 8(10) sts on to a stitch holder to be used later in neckband; rejoin M to rem sts, k to end.
Complete this side to match the other side reversing shapings thus: **1st row** P to end. **2nd row** (right side) Cast off 2 sts, k to end. **3rd row** P to end. **4th to 7th rows** Rep last 2 rows twice more. **8th row** K2 tog, k to end . . . 21 sts. Cont in st-st without shaping until work matches Back to shoulder, ending after a k row.
Shape Shoulder Cast off 5 sts at beg of next 3 wrong-side rows. Work 1 row. Cast off rem 6 sts.

SLEEVES

With 3mm [No 11] needles and M, cast on 50(56) sts. Work 8 rows g-st. Change to 3¾mm [No 9] needles and inc 4 sts evenly on 1st row, cont in st-st without shaping until work measures 5cm [2 in] ending after a p row.
Shape Top Cast off 2(3) sts at beg of next 4 rows . . . 46(48) sts. Dec 1 st at both ends of next row and foll alt rows to 28(30) sts. P1 row. Cast off 2 sts at beg of next 8(10) rows. Cast off rem 12(10) sts.

TO MAKE UP

With right sides together, backstitch the left shoulder seam. With right side of work facing, using 3mm [No 11] needles and M, pick up and k90(94) sts evenly all round neck edge. Work 6 rows

g-st. Cast off. Press pieces following instructions on ball band. With right sides together, join side seams. With right sides inside, join the sleeve seams, using back-stitch seams. With right sides together, place the sleeve top in the armhole, with side seam to sleeve seam. Tack the sleeves in place, then back-stitch neatly and remove tackings. The right shoulder cast-off edges must be placed edge to edge while sewing in the right sleeve to allow for the crochet opening border.

With right side of work facing, using crochet hook and M, work 1 row dc round right shoulder opening on both front and back, thus ending at back neck, 1 ch, turn. On the 2nd row of dc, work 4 buttonloops, thus: dc along to front edge, 2 dc, *2 ch, miss 2 dc, dc in each of next 3 dc; rep from * until 4 loops have been made, dc to end, 1 ch, turn. **3rd row** Dc in each dc to end, working 2 dc in each 2 ch loop. Fasten off yarn.

FLOWERS (make 8)

With crochet hook and C, make 5 ch, join into a circle with a slip stitch. **1st rnd** 10 dc in circle, join with a slip stitch. **2nd rnd** *2 dc in 1st dc, 1 dc in next dc; rep from * to end, join with slip stitch . . . 15 dc. **3rd rnd** *3 ch, miss 2 dc, dc in next dc; rep from * to end . . . 5 loops. **4th rnd** *1 dc, 3 tr, 1 dc in next 3 ch loop; rep from * to end. **5th rnd** 1 dc in each st to end, join to 1st dc with slip stitch. Fasten off.

Sew the motifs to the dress as shown in picture. With right side facing, using crochet hook and C, work a neat ch down from flower to g-st border to form a stem. Sew on buttons to right shoulder.

> **If you don't like the idea of crocheting the flowers, why not knit the dress in different coloured stripes? Eight rows will give you 2·5cm [1 in] stripes.**

Left: a sweet little dress with flowers that are crocheted and sewn on to the finished garment Right: a very smart dress that is not what it seems – the pattern's simple and the cherries are embroidered on to the finished dress. A helpful shape guide and embroidery chart are overleaf

Dress with cherries

18 months to 4 years

This pretty dress has the look of pin tucks and Fair Isle but it's simple to knit and the cherries are embroidered on later.

Materials 6(7:8) 25g balls Double Knitting yarn in main colour (M); 1 ball in each of red (R) and green (G); pairs of 3mm and 3¾mm [No 11 and No 9] knitting needles; 3mm [No 11] crochet hook.

Measurements To fit a 51 (56:61)cm [20(22:24) in] chest; length, 38(41:45)cm [15(16:17½) in]; sleeve seam, 15mm [⅝ in].

Tension 26 sts and 34 rows to 10cm [4 in] in st-st.

Abbreviations k, knit; p, purl; st(s), stitches; cm, centimetre(s); in, inch(es); alt, alternate; beg, beginning; cont, continue; foll, following; patt, pattern; rem, remain(ing); rep, repeat; st-st, stocking stitch; tog, together; dc, double crochet; ch, chain; rnd, round; ss, slip stitch.

Size Note Figures in brackets refer to larger sizes. One figure only refers to all sizes. Square brackets contain imperial measurements.

BACK

With 3¾mm [No 9] needles and M, cast on 123(127:132) sts. Beg k row, cont in st-st until work measures 16(18:20)cm [6¼(7:8) in] ending after a p row.
Shape Flare 1st row K to last 14 sts, turn. **2nd row** P to last 14 sts, turn. **3rd row** K to last 27(28:29) sts, turn. **4th row** P to last 27(28:29) sts, turn. **5th row** K to last 40 (42:44) sts, turn. **6th row** P to last 40(42:44) sts, turn. Now cont in st-st on all sts until work measures 20(22:24)cm [8(9:9½) in] ending after a k row.
Next row P5(7:8), (p2 tog, p1) to

Continued on next page

Dress with cherries . . . continued

last 4(6:7) sts, p to end . . . 85 (89:93) sts. Change to 3mm [No 11] needles and cont in rib thus: **1st row** K2, *p1, k1, rep from * to last st, k1. **2nd row** K1, *p1, k1, rep from * to end. Rep last 2 rows until work measures 27(30:33)cm [11(12:13) in] ending after a wrong-side row.

Shape Armholes Cast off 10 (11:12) sts at beg of next 2 rows . . . 65(67:69) sts.**

Cont straight in rib until armholes measure 11(14:18)cm [4¼(5½:7) in] ending after wrong-side row.

Shape Neck and Shoulders Cast off 2(3:4) sts at beg of next 2 rows. **Next row** Cast off 4 sts, rib 21 sts, turn. Cont on these sts only. **Next row** Cast off 7 sts, rib to end. **Next row** Cast off 4 sts, rib to end. **Next row** Cast off 6 sts, rib to end. Cast off rem 4 sts.

With right side facing, join M at neck edge to rem sts. Cast off centre 11 sts, rib to end. Now complete this side to match the first side thus: **Next row** Cast off 4 sts, rib to end. **Next row** Cast off 7 sts, rib to end. **Next row** Cast off 4 sts, rib to end. **Next row** Cast off 6 sts, rib to end. Cast off rem 4 sts.

FRONT

Work as Back to ** . . . 65(67:69) sts. Cont straight until work measures 31(35:40)cm [12(14:15¾) in] ending after a wrong-side row.

Shape Neck Next row Rib 29 (30:31) sts, turn. Cont on these sts only. **Next row** Cast off 4 sts, rib to end. **Next row and foll alt rows, beg side edge** Rib to end. **Next row** Cast off 3 sts, rib to end. **Next row** Cast off 2 sts, rib to end. **Next row** Beg side edge, rib to end. Rep last 2 rows 3 times more. Cont straight until armhole matches Back to shoulder, ending after wrong-side row.

Shape Shoulder Cast off 2(3:4) sts at beg of next row. Work 1 row. Now cast off 4 sts at beg of next row and foll 2 alt rows.

With right side facing, join M to rem sts at neck edge. Cast off centre 7 sts, rib to end. Complete this side to match the first side thus: Rib 1 row straight. **Next row** Cast off 4 sts, rib to end. **Next row and foll alt rows** In rib. **Next row** Cast off 3 sts, rib to end. **Next row** Cast off 2 sts, rib to end. **Next row** In rib. Rep last 2 rows 3 times more. Cont straight until armhole matches Back to shoulder, ending side edge. Now shape second shoulder as first.

SLEEVES (make 2)

With 3¾mm [No 9] needles and M, cast on 96(100:106) sts. Work 15mm [⅝ in] st-st, ending after a p row.

Shape Flare 1st row K to last 3 sts, turn. **2nd row** P to last 3 sts, turn. **3rd row** K to last 6 sts, turn. **4th row** P to last 6 sts, turn. **5th row** K to last 9 sts, turn. **6th row** P to last 9 sts, turn. Cont in this way, working 3 less sts before each turn until the **15th row** K to last 24 sts, turn, has been worked. **16th row** P to end. K1 row. Cast off.

TO MAKE UP

Press following instructions on ball band but avoid rib. Join shoulder and side seams. Join sleeve seam and sew sleeves to armholes, easing in gathers at top – use the picture as a guide.

Neck Border With right side facing, using crochet hook and G work 1 rnd dc round neck edge and join with ss. **Picot rnd** 1 dc in each of next 4 dc, (3 ch, work 1 dc in same place as last dc worked, 1 dc in each of next 4 dc) to end, omitting last 4 dc at end.

Work a border in the same way round the sleeves and lower edge.

Cherries These are added to the finished skirt by the Swiss Embroidery method (see page 110). Allow 18 sts for each motif with 6 sts between each motif. It is advisable to find the centre stitch and work outwards. Beg at the bottom right-hand corner of the motif and leaving an end at the back, bring the needle out to the front through the centre of the stitch below the one to be covered, then in and out again behind the stitch in the row above, back into the same hole at the bottom and out through the centre of the next stitch to the left. Cover each stitch required in the first row like this and at the end of the row slip the needle upwards into the centre of the last stitch covered instead of taking it along to the left. Now turn the work upside down so that you are still working from right to left. Cover in one colour first then fill in the second.

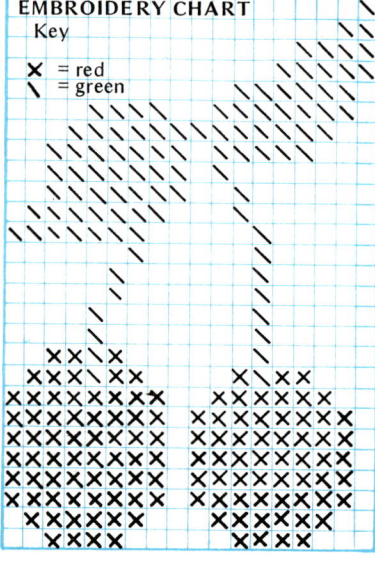

EMBROIDERY CHART

Key

X = red
\ = green

Party dress
2 to 4 years

Also illustrated on the cover

A pinafore-style dress that's open at the back to show off pretty petticoats. On page 4 you'll find instructions for sewing this dress for smaller sizes.

Materials 140(160:180)g 4-ply nylon yarn in colour of choice; 50cm [20 in] of broderie anglaise, 3cm [1¼ in] wide; 50cm [20 in] of ribbon for the insertion; 153cm [60 in] of satin ribbon, 2cm [¾ in] wide; pair 2¾mm [No 12] knitting needles; 2·5mm [No 12] crochet hook.

Measurements To fit a 56(60: 63·5)cm [22(23½:25) in] chest.

Tension 32 sts and 44 rows measure 10cm [4 in].

Abbreviations k, knit; p, purl; st(s), stitch(es); st-st, stocking stitch; g-st, garter stitch; patt, pattern; rep, repeat; sl, slip; tog, together; psso, pass slip stitch over; alt, alternate; rem, remain(ing); beg, beginning; dec, decrease; dc, double crochet; M1, make 1; foll, following; cm, centimetre(s); in, inch(es). Square brackets contain imperial measurements.

Lace Pattern shown in Turquoise overleaf:
1st row K1, *yarn round needle twice, (k2 tog) twice. Rep from * to last st, yarn round needle twice, k1.
2nd row P, working into each made st.
3rd row *(K2 tog) twice, yarn round needle twice. Rep from * to last 4 sts, (k2 tog) twice.
4th row As 2nd row.
These 4 rows form the patt. (Note that in 1st row 2 sts have been increased. These sts are decreased in 3rd row. Always count sts after a 4th patt row.)
Lace Pattern shown in Orange overleaf:
1st row *K1, p1, M1, sl 1, k2 tog, psso, M1, p1. Rep from * to end.
2nd and alt row *K1, p3, k1, p1. Rep from * to end.
3rd and 5th row *K1, p1, k3, p1. Rep from * to end.
6th row As 2nd row.
These 6 rows form the patt.

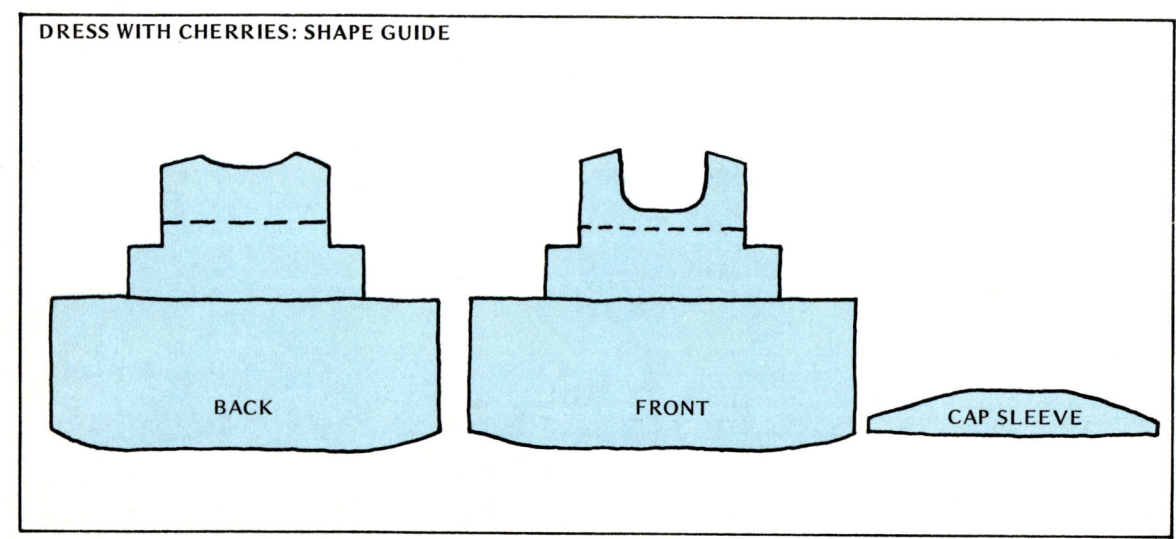

DRESS WITH CHERRIES: SHAPE GUIDE

BACK

FRONT

CAP SLEEVE

Continued on page 116

Party dress . . . continued

SKIRT

Cast on 230(242:254) sts and work in st-st for 6 rows.

Next row (Picot edge) K1, *k2 tog, M1. Rep from * to last st, k1. Now beg with a p row cont in st-st, but keeping 4 sts each end in g-st until work measures 35(38:43)cm [13¾(15:17) in] or length required, from picot edge. Cast off.

BODICE

Cast on 186(198:210) sts and work 4 rows in g-st, then work in either of the open-work patts for 4 rows. Now keeping continuity of patt work thus:

Next row Patt 116(125:134) sts, turn and leave rem 70(73:76) sts on a spare needle.

Next row Patt to end. Work straight for 6(8:8) rows, then cast off 36 sts at beg of next row.

Next row Patt to end.

Now dec 1 st at beg of next row and foll 3 alt rows.

Next row Patt to end.

Next row Cast off 30(33:36) sts, patt to end.

Work on rem 46(52:58) sts casting off 2 sts at beg of next 10(10:12) rows. Cast off rem sts.

Go back to the 70(73:76) sts left on spare needle, rejoin yarn at opening edge and patt to end. Work in patt for 8(10:10) rows. Cast off 36 sts at beg of next row, then dec 1 st at beg of next 4 alt rows.

Next row Patt to end. Cast off rem 30(33:36) sts.

TO MAKE UP

Press work following ball band instructions. Turn up lower edge of skirt at picot edge and slip-stitch neatly on wrong side. Using matching yarn work 2 rows of running sts along top of skirt drawing the skirt in to about 45cm [17½ in] or width required. Fasten off firmly.

Sew bodice to skirt leaving the shaped edges of back bodice straps free. Sew the edges together at top of opening leaving 3cm [1¼ in] free for slot. Work a row of shrimp st – ie, working dc from left to right, working all round outer edges.

Thread insertion ribbon through broderie anglaise, cut straps in two equal parts and sew to bodice at back and front (see picture). Cut satin ribbon in two parts and stitch to each end of back bodice straps. Fasten as shown in drawings.

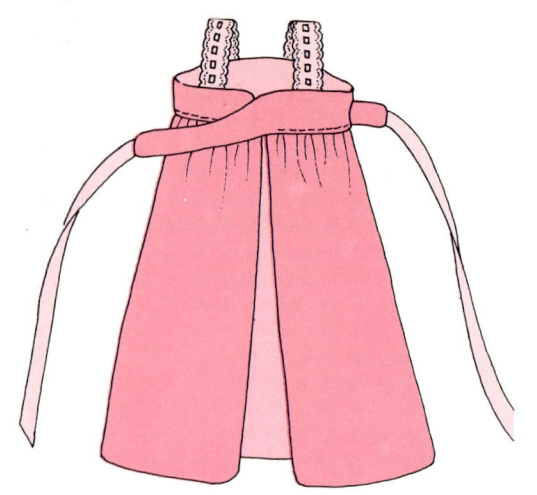

Above: front and back views of the Party Dress showing how simply the ribbon ties are brought to the front for tieing

Below: close-ups of the two different lace patterns which can be knitted for the bodice – or the skirt if you prefer

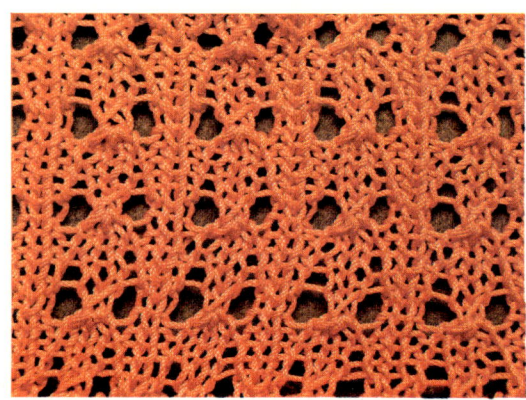

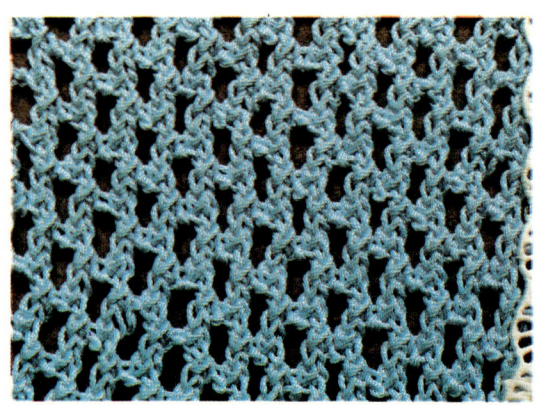

Lacy dress

2 to 4 years

A stylish dress to make a hit with any young miss.

Materials 4(5:6) 25g balls 4-ply knitting yarn in Light colour (L); 2(3:4) balls in Dark colour (D); pair 3mm [No 11] knitting needles; 3mm [No 11] crochet hook; 6 buttons.

Measurements Actual size round chest 62(67:72)cm [24½(26½:28½) in]; length 36(38:40)cm [14(15: 15¾) in].

Tension 32 sts to 10cm [4 in] in patt.

Abbreviations k, knit; p, purl; st(s), stitch(es); cm, centimetre(s); in, inch(es); alt, alternate; beg, beginning; cont, continue; dec, decreas(e)ing; inc, increas(e)ing; foll, following; rep, repeat; rem, remain(ing); tog, together; y fwd, yarn forward; g-st, garter stitch; st-st, stocking stitch; sl, slip; psso, pass slip st over; tbl, through back of loop; dc, double crochet; patt, pattern.

Size Note Figures in brackets refer to larger sizes. One figure only refers to all sizes. Square brackets contain imperial measurements.

Take care with the pattern when working the decreases at the side edge, remember that if you work a y fwd in the pattern there must be a work 2 tog to compensate.

BACK

With D, cast on 123(131:139) sts. Work 6 rows g-st.
Cont in lacy patt thus: **1st row** With L, k2(6:2), *y fwd, k5, k2 tog tbl, k2 tog, k5, y fwd, k1; rep from * to last 1(5:2) sts, k1(5:2). **2nd row** With L, p to end. **3rd to 8th rows** As 1st and 2nd.
With D, work 6 rows g-st. Now cont in lacy patt, working 1st 8 rows in L followed by 2 rows only g-st in D, at the same time dec 1 st at both ends of next row and every foll 6th row until 99(107:115) sts rem.
Cont in lacy patt without shaping until work measures 26(27:28)cm [10¼(10½:11) in] ending after a p row.
Shape Armholes Cast off 4(5:6) sts at beg of next 2 rows . . . 91(97:103) sts.

Divide for Back Opening and cont armhole shaping **1st row** Cast off 2(3:4) sts, patt 43(45:48) turn. Leave rem sts for the time being and complete this side first. **2nd row** Cast on 4 sts for the button band and keep these 4 sts in g-st on every row, k4, p to end. **3rd row** K2 tog, patt to last 4 sts, k4. **4th row** As 2nd. Rep last 2 rows 2(4:6) times more . . . 44(44:45) sts.
Cont in patt until the 13th D stripe has been worked. Now, with L cont in st-st, omitting the y fwd sts on each row . . . 38(38:39) sts until armhole measures 10(11:12) cm [4(4½:4¾) in] ending after a p row.

Above: the Lacy Dress and, below, a close-up of the wavy design

Continued on next page

Lacy dress . . . continued

Shape Shoulder and Neck 1st row
Cast off 10 sts, k to end. **2nd row**
Cast off 9 sts, p to end. **3rd row**
Cast off 10 sts, k to end. **4th row**
Cast off rem 9(9:10) sts.
With right side of work facing, rejoin matching yarn to rem sts, at neck edge. **1st row** K3, for buttonhole band, patt to end. Mark the button band on the left side with pins to represent buttons: the 1st should be 2 rows above the beg of the back opening, the other five spaced evenly with the top one just below beg of neck shaping.
Second side Work to match the first reversing the shapings and working buttonholes in the g-st band thus: **1st row** Cast off 2(3:4) sts, patt to last 3 sts, k3. **2nd row** K3, y fwd, k1, patt to last 2 sts, k2 tog. **3rd row** Patt to last 3 sts, k3. **4th row** K3, patt to last 2 sts, k2 tog. Rep last 2 rows until 44(44:45) sts rem. Cont to work buttonholes when necessary, <u>at the same time</u> cont in patt until the 13th D stripe has been worked. Cont in st-st with L only, omitting the y fwd sts and keeping the g-st border . . . 41(41:42) sts until armhole measures 10(11:12)cm [4(4½:4¾) in] ending after a k row.
Shape Shoulder and Neck 1st row Cast off 9(9:10) sts, p to end.
2nd row Cast off 9 sts, k to end.
3rd row Cast off 9 sts, p to end.
4th row Cast off 4 sts, k to end.
5th row Cast off rem sts.

FRONT
With D, cast on 123(131:139) sts. Work 6 rows g-st.
Cont in lacy patt thus: **1st row**
With L, k2(6:2), *y fwd, k5, k2 tog tbl, k2 tog, k5, y fwd, k1; rep from * to last 1(5:2), k1(5:2). **2nd row** P to end. **3rd to 8th rows** As 1st and 2nd.
With D, work 6 rows g-st. Now cont in lacy patt, working 1st 8 rows in L followed by *2 rows only* g-st in D, <u>at the same time</u> dec 1 st at both ends of next row and every foll 6th row until 99(107:115) sts rem. Cont in lacy patt without shaping until work measures 26 (27:28)cm [10¼(10½:11) in] ending after a p row.
Shape Armholes Cast off 4(5:6) sts at beg of next 2 rows; 2(3:4) sts at beg of next 2 rows . . . 87(91:95) sts. Dec 1 st at both ends of next 3(5:7) right-side rows . . . 81(81:81) sts. Cont in patt without shaping until the 13th D stripe has been worked. Cont in st-st with L only, omitting the y fwd sts . . . 71 sts rem. Work 2 rows.

Shape Neck 1st row K30, turn. Leave rem sts on a spare needle for the time being and complete this side first. **2nd row** Cast off 3 sts, p to end. **3rd row** K to end. **4th row** Cast off 2 sts, p to end. **5th row** K to end. **6th and 7th rows** As 4th and 5th rows. **8th row** P2 tog, p to end. **9th row** K to end. **10th to 13th rows** Rep last 2 rows twice more . . . 20 sts. Cont in st-st without shaping until armhole matches Back to shoulder ending after a p row.
Shape Shoulder Cast off 10 sts at beg of next and foll alt row. With right side of work facing, rejoin L to rem sts, cast off centre 11 sts, k to end. Shape this side to match the first side reversing shapings thus: **1st row** P to end. **2nd row** Cast off 3 sts, k to end. **3rd row** P to end. **4th row** Cast off 2 sts, k to end. **5th row** P to end. **6th and 7th rows** As 4th and 5th rows. **8th row** K2 tog, k to end. **9th row** P to end. **10th to 13th rows** Rep last 2 rows twice more . . . 20 sts. Cont in st-st without shaping until work matches Back to shoulder, ending after a k row.
Shape Shoulder Cast off 10 sts at beg of next and foll alt row.

SLEEVES
With D, cast on 50(54:58) sts. Work 6 rows g-st. With L, inc 8 sts evenly on the 1st row, cont in st-st for 4 rows. Now inc 1 st at both ends of next row and every foll 4th row to 66(70:74) sts. Cont in st-st without shaping until sleeve measures 6cm [2½ in] ending after a p row.
Shape Top Cast off 4(5:6) sts at beg of next 2 rows; 2(3:4) sts at beg of next 2 rows; 2 sts at beg of next 2 rows. Dec 1 st at both ends of next row and foll alt rows to 34(36:38) sts. Cast off 2 sts at beg of next 4 rows; 4 sts at beg of next 2 rows. Cast off rem sts.

TO MAKE UP
Press on the wrong side following instructions on the ball band. With right sides together, back-stitch the shoulder seams. With right side of work facing, using D, pick up and k124 sts evenly round neck edge. Work 6 rows g-st. Cast off. With right sides together, flat-stitch the side edges. With right sides inside, back-stitch the sleeve seams. With right sides facing, set the sleeve top in place, sleeve seam to side seam. Back-stitch neatly in place. Turn to right side. With right side of work facing, work 1 row dc with D round the opening edge. Fasten off. Sew on buttons.

Coat and hat in cable pattern
2 to 5 years

A smart, and warm, twosome that will stand up to a lot of active play out of doors.

Materials 17(18:19) 25g balls Double Knitting yarn; pairs of 3¾mm and 4mm [No 9 and No 8] knitting needles; set of four double-pointed 4mm [No 8] needles; cable needle; 9 buttons (8 for coat, 1 for hat).

Measurements To fit 51(56:61)cm [20(22:24) in] chest; length, 43 (44:47)cm [17(17½:18½) in]; sleeve seam, 23(25:28)cm [9(10:11) in]. Hat to fit average head.

Tension 20 sts and 28 rows to 10cm [4 in] in st-st.

Abbreviations k, knit; p, purl; st(s), stitch(es); cm, centimetre(s); in, inch(es); alt, alternate; beg, beginning; cont, continue; dec, decrease(ing); foll, following; g-st, garter stitch (every row k); inc 1k, increase by picking up loop lying between the sts and knitting into back of it; rem, remain(ing); rep, repeat; st-st, stocking stitch; patt, pattern; tog, together; tbl, through back of loop; sl, slip; psso, pass slip stitch over; rnd, round; y fwd, yarn forward; c2f or b, cable 2 front or back.

Size Note Figures in brackets refer to larger sizes. One figure only refers to all sizes. Square brackets contain imperial measurements.

> **When knitting a cable pattern, a gadget that keeps account of the rows worked is invaluable. Or keep a booklet and pencil in your knitting bag so you can note down which row of the pattern you were on when you put your work down.**

COAT
BACK
With 3¾mm [No 9] needles, cast on 80(86:92) sts. K8 rows. Change to 4mm [No 8] needles. **Next row** K38(41:44) sts, *inc 1k, k2*; rep

from * to * twice more, inc 1k, k to end . . . 84(90:96) sts. P1 row.
Now cont in st-st with cable panel, placing patt thus: **1st row** K36(39:42), p2, k8, p2, k36(39:42). **2nd row** P the k sts and k the p sts of previous row. **3rd and 4th rows** As 1st and 2nd. **5th row** K36(39:42), p2, sl next 2 sts on cable needle and hold at front of work, k next 2 sts from main needle then the 2 sts from cable needle – called c2f, sl the next 2 sts on cable needle and hold at back of work, k the next 2 sts from main needle then k the 2 sts on cable needle – called c2b, p2, k36(39:42). **6th row** As 2nd. These 6 rows form the patt.
Cont in patt and, <u>at the same time</u>, dec 1 st at both ends of 3rd row foll and every foll 14th row to 78(84:90) sts. Cont straight in patt until work measures 26cm [10¼ in] from beg, ending after a wrong-side row.
Shape Raglan *Cast off 3 sts at beg of next 2 rows, then 2 sts at beg of foll 6 rows . . . 60(66:72) sts. **9th row** K3, k2 tog, work to last 5 sts, k2 tog tbl, k3. **10th row** K3, work to last 3 sts, k3.* Rep last 2 rows to 22(24:26) sts, ending after a wrong-side row. Cast off.

LEFT FRONT
With 3¾mm [No 9] needles, cast on 50(53:56) sts. K8 rows. **Next row** K17(20:23), *inc 1k, k2*; rep from * to * twice more, inc 1k, k to end . . . 54(57:60) sts. **Next row** K6, p9, k5, p5, k2, p8, k2, p to end. Change to 4mm [No 8] needles and cont in panels of st-st, cable patt and g-st placing sts thus: **1st row** K17(20:23), p2, k8, p2, k25. **2nd row** K6 (border), p9, k5, p5, k2, p8, k2, p17(20:23). **3rd and 4th rows** As 1st and 2nd. **5th row** K17(20:23), p2, c2f, c2b, p2, k25. **6th row** As 2nd.
Keeping cable and g-st panels as set, cont in patt, dec 1 st at beg of 3rd row foll and every foll 14th row to 51(54:57) sts.
Cont straight until Front matches Back to raglan shaping, ending after a wrong-side row.
Shape Raglan Cast off 3 sts at beg of next row, then 2 sts at beg of foll 3 alt rows . . . 42(45:48) sts. P1 row. **Next row** K3, k2 tog, patt to end. **Next row** Patt to last 3 sts, k3. Rep last 2 rows to 27 sts, ending at neck edge.
Shape Neck Keeping dec at side edge as before, cast off at neck edge, 9 sts once, then 2 sts twice. Work 1 row. Cont dec at side edge and, <u>at the same time</u>, dec 1 st at neck edge on foll wrong-side rows until 3 sts rem. Cast off.

CABLE COAT: SHAPE GUIDE

HALF BACK

RIGHT FRONT

HALF SLEEVE

RIGHT FRONT

First mark the g-st panels on Left Front with pins to indicate buttons. Place the first pair 15cm [6 in] from cast-on edge, the 3rd pair just below neck shaping and the centre pair spaced equally between the other two.

Now work the Right Front to match the Left placing the cable panel and g-st panels thus: **Inc row** K27, *inc 1k, k2*; rep from * to * twice more, inc 1k, k17(20:23). Place next row: P17(20:23), k2, p8, k2, p5, k5, p9, k6. The **5th row** will read: k25, p2, c2f, c2b, p2, k17(20:23). The dec will be at the ends of the 3rd row foll and every foll 14th row to 51(54:57) sts. Work buttonholes at pinned positions thus: With right side facing, k3, cast off 2 sts, k11, cast off 2 sts, work to end. In foll row cast on 2 sts over those cast off in previous row.

When Right Front matches Back to raglan shaping, end after right-side row. Cast off 3 sts at beg of next row and 2 sts at beg of foll 3 alt rows. **Next row** Patt to last 5 sts, k2 tog tbl, k3. **Next row** K3, patt to end. Rep last 2 rows to 27 sts, ending after a wrong-side row.

Shape Neck Beg at neck edge, work as given for Left Front.

SLEEVES

With 3¾mm [No 9] needles cast on 47(47:49) sts. Work 6cm [2½ in] g-st. Change to 4mm [No 8] needles. Cont in st-st inc 1 st at both ends of 5th row foll and every foll 4th row to 59(63:67) sts. Cont straight until sleeve measures 23(25:28)cm [9(10:11) in] ending after a p row.

Shape Raglan Work as given for Back from * to *. Now rep the last 2 rows to 3 sts, ending after a p row. Cast off.

COLLAR

With 3¾mm [No 9] needles, cast on 56 sts. **1st row** K. **2nd row** K6, p to last 6 sts, k6. Rep last 2 rows once more. **Next row** K20, *inc 1k, k3*; rep from * to * 4 times more, inc 1k, k to end. Change to 4mm [No 8] needles and cont in st-st with g-st borders until work measures 6cm [2½ in] ending after wrong-side row. K3 rows. Cast off.

HALF BELT

With 3¾mm [No 9] needles, cast on 20 sts. Cont in g-st, shaping thus: **1st row** K. **2nd row** K1, inc 1k, k to last st, inc 1k, k1. Rep these 2 rows 3 times more. Now dec thus: k1 row. **Next row** K1, k2 tog,

k to last 3 sts, k2 tog, k1. Rep last 2 rows to 20 sts. Cast off.

HAT

With set of 4 needles, cast on 16 sts (5 sts on each of 2 needles, and 6 sts on 3rd needle). **1st rnd** K1, p2, *k2, p2*, rep from * to * twice more, k1. **2nd rnd** K3, *inc 1k, k2, inc 1k, k2*, rep from * to * twice more, k1. **3rd rnd** K1, p4 – to obtain g-st – *k2, p4*, rep from * to * twice more, k1. **4th rnd** K1, k4, *inc 1k, k2, inc 1k, k4*, rep from * to * twice more, k1. **5th rnd** K1, p6, *k2, p6*, rep from * to * twice more, k1. **6th rnd** K1, k6, *inc 1k, k2, inc 1k, k6*, rep from * to * twice more, k1. **7th rnd** K1, p8, *k2, p8*, rep from * to * twice more, k1. Cont in panels as set for a further 10cm [4 in]. **Next rnd** K5, p12 – g-st – k18, p34 – g-st, k13. **Next rnd** K. Rep last 2 rnds twice more. **Next rnd** K9, cast off 4 sts purlwise (centre back), k26, cast off 26 sts purlwise (centre front), k rem sts.

Break yarn and cont on each set of 26 sts separately for ear flaps: Working in g-st and st-st as set, dec 1 st at each end within the 4 g-st borders on next 7 right-side rows . . . 12 sts. **Next row** K4, sl 2, k2 tog, psso, k4. **Next row** K. **Next row** K3, sl 1, k2 tog, psso, k3. **Next row** K. **Next row** K2, sl 1, k2 tog, psso, k2. ***Cast off. Work the right ear flap to *** Cont in g-st on rem 5 sts for a further 7cm [2¾ in]. **Next row** K2, y fwd, k2 tog, k1. Work 3 rows more. Cast off.

TO MAKE UP

Coat Press according to the instructions on ball band. Join front and back raglan shaping to shaping on sleeves by oversewing. Join side and sleeve seams with back-stitch. Sew half-belt at back with 2 buttons. Sew on collar. Sew buttons at pinned positions on Left Front.

Hat Draw together sts at crown and secure. Make a large pompon (see page 75) and sew to crown. Sew on button to left flap to match buttonhole.

Above: cables add even more smartness to this double-breasted style coat that can be worn over skirts and trousers. The diagram gives you an idea of the shape of the different parts of the coat

Two-colour dress

3 to 5 years

Just the sort of standby every girl needs in her wardrobe. The shape's good and the dress will stand up to lots of wear and tear.

Materials 5(6:7) 25g balls 4-ply yarn in red (R); 4(5:6) balls in blue (B); pairs of 3mm and 2¾mm [No 11 and No 12] knitting needles; 2·5mm [No 12] crochet hook; 13cm [5 in] zip.

Measurements To fit 3(4:5) year old; actual size 51(56:61)cm [20 (22:24) in] round chest; length, 51(52:53)cm [20(20½:21) in].

Tension 28 sts to 10cm [4 in] in st-st.

Abbreviations k, knit; p, purl; st(s), stitch(es); cm, centimetre(s); in, inch(es); alt, alternate; beg, beginning; cont, continue; dec, decreas(e)ing; inc, increas(e)ing; rep, repeat; rem, remain(ing); tog, together; tbl, through back loop; sl, slip; psso, pass slip st over; st-st, stocking stitch; foll, following; dc, double crochet.

Size Note Figures in brackets refer to larger sizes. One figure only refers to all sizes. Square brackets contain imperial measurements.

> Take care with the neat skirt shaping – the last decreasing row is different.

BACK

With 3mm [No 11] needles and B, cast on 122(128:134) sts. **1st row** *K1, p1; rep from * to end. **2nd row** *P1, k1; rep from * to end. These 2 rows form the moss stitch pattern. Cont in moss st until work measures 5cm [2 in]. Change to R and st-st. Work 2 rows straight. **Next row** K1, k2 tog, k36(38:40), sl 1, k2 tog, psso, k38(40:42), k3 tog tbl, k36(38:40), sl 1, k1, psso, k1 . . . 116(122:128) sts.
Beg p row, work 4cm [1½ in] in st-st without shaping. **Next row** K1, k2 tog, k33(35:37), sl 1, k2 tog, psso, k38(40:42), k3 tog tbl, k33(35:37), sl 1, k1, psso, k1 . . . 110(116:122) sts. Beg p row, work 4cm [1½ in] in st-st without shaping.

Cont dec in this way on next row and every 4cm [1½ in] dec 6 sts on the dec rows but keeping the centre panel the same until 86 (92:98) sts rem.
Beg p row, work 4cm [1½ in] st-st.
Next row K1, k3 tog tbl, k17(19:21), sl 1, k2 tog, psso, k38(40:42), k3 tog tbl, k17(19:21), sl 1, k2 tog, psso, k1 . . . 78(84:90) sts.
Change to B and cont in moss st, inc 1 st at both ends of every 6th row to 82(88:94) sts. Cont in moss st without shaping until work measures 36cm [14 in] ending after a wrong-side row.
Shape Armholes Cast off 3(4:5) sts at beg of next 2 rows; 2(3:4) sts at beg of next 2 rows; 2 sts at beg of next row and every foll 6th row to 58(60:62) sts. Cont in st-st without shaping until work measures 20(20:21)cm [8 (8:8½) in] ending after a wrong-side row.
Change to B and cont in moss st until work measures 27(28:29)cm [10½(11:11½) in] ending after a wrong-side row.
Shape Top Cast off 3 sts at beg of next 2 rows; 2 sts at beg of next 2 rows. Dec 1 st at both ends of next row and every foll alt row to 20(22:24) sts. Cast off 3(4:5) sts at beg of next 2 rows. Cast off rem 14 sts. Work another sleeve the same.

TO MAKE UP

Press pieces according to the instructions on the ball band. With right sides together back-stitch the shoulder seams, then the side seams, using matching yarns. With right side inside, back-stitch the sleeve seam, using flat seam for the rib and matching the yarns. Set the sleeve top in place with right sides together. Back-stitch the sleeve tops into the armholes. With right side of work facing, using 2¾mm [No 12] needles and R, pick up and k108 sts evenly round the neck edge. Work 2cm [¾ in] k2, p2 rib. Cast off in rib.
With right side of Back facing, using crochet hook and B, work 1 row dc evenly round back opening edge. Fasten off. Sew in zip neatly and press.

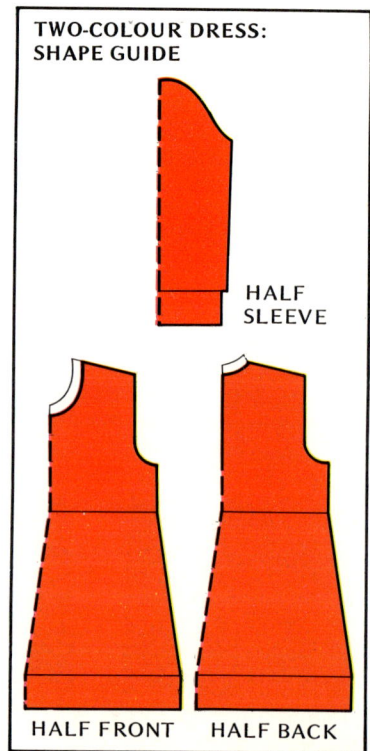

TWO-COLOUR DRESS: SHAPE GUIDE

HALF SLEEVE

HALF FRONT   HALF BACK

at both ends of next row and every 4cm [1½ in] dec 6 sts on the dec rows but keeping the centre panel the same until 86 (92:98) sts rem.
Beg p row, work 4cm [1½ in] st-st, ending after a p row. Cont dec in this way on next row and every 4cm [1½ in] dec 6 sts on the dec rows but keeping the centre panel the same until 86(92:98) sts rem.
Beg p row, work 4cm [1½ in] st-st.
Next row K1, k3 tog tbl, k17(19:21), sl 1, k2 tog, psso, k38(40:42), k3 tog tbl, k17(19:21), sl 1, k2 tog, psso, k1 . . . 78(84:90) sts.
Change to B and cont in moss st, inc 1 st at both ends of every 6th row to 82(88:94) sts. Cont in moss st without shaping until work measures 36cm [14 in] ending after a wrong-side row.
Shape Armholes Cast off 3(4:5) sts at beg of next 2 rows; 2(3:4) sts at beg of next 2 rows; 2 sts at beg of next 2 rows. Dec 1 st at both ends of next row . . . 66 (68:70) sts. Cont in moss st without shaping until work measures 43(44:45)cm [17(17½:17¾) in] from beg, ending after a wrong-side row.
Shape Neck 1st row Patt 27(28:29) sts, turn. Leave rem sts on a spare needle and complete this side first. **2nd row** Cast off 3 sts, moss st to end. **3rd row and foll alt rows** Moss st to end. **4th row** Cast off 2 sts, moss st to end. **6th row** K2 tog, moss st to end . . . 21(22:23) sts. Cont in moss st without shaping until Front matches Back to shoulder ending after a wrong-side row.
Shape Shoulder Cast off 7 sts at beg of next and foll alt rows. Work 1 row. Cast off rem 7(8:9) sts.
With right side of work facing, rejoin B to rem sts, cast off the centre 12 sts, moss st to end. Complete this side to match the first reversing shapings, thus: **1st row and foll alt rows** Moss st to end. **2nd row** Cast off 3 sts, moss st to end. **4th row** Cast off 2 sts, moss st to end. **6th row** K2 tog, moss st to end . . . 21(22:23) sts.
Cont in moss st without shaping until Front matches Back to shoulder ending after a right-side row.
Shape Shoulder Cast off 7 sts at beg of next and foll alt rows. Work 1 row. Cast off rem sts.

SLEEVES

With 2¾mm [No 12] needles and B, cast on 40 sts. Work 5cm [2 in] k1, p1 rib. Change to 3mm [No 11] needles and R. Inc 10 sts evenly on 1st row, cont in st-st until work measures 9·5cm [3¾ in] ending after a p row. Inc 1 st at

Next row K1, k2 tog, k33(35:37), sl 1, k2 tog, psso, k38(40:42), k3 tog tbl, k33(35:37), sl 1, k1, psso, k1 . . . 110(116:122) sts.
Beg p row work 4cm [1½ in] in st-st, ending after a p row. Cont dec in this way on next row and every 4cm [1½ in] dec 6 sts on the dec rows but keeping the centre panel the same until 86(92:98) sts rem.
Beg p row, work 4cm [1½ in] st-st.
Next row K1, k3 tog tbl, k17(19:21), sl 1, k2 tog, psso, k38(40:42), k3 tog tbl, k17(19:21), sl 1, k2 tog, psso, k1 . . . 78(84:90) sts.
Change to B and cont in moss st, inc 1 st at both ends of every 6th row to 82(88:94) sts. Cont in moss st without shaping until work measures 36cm [14 in] ending after a wrong-side row.
Shape Armholes Cast off 3(4:5) sts at beg of next 2 rows; 2(3:4) sts at beg of next 2 rows. Dec 1 st at both ends of next row . . . 66(68:70) sts. Cont in moss st without shaping until work measures 38(39:40)cm [15(15¼:15¾) in] ending after a wrong-side row.
Divide for Back Opening 1st row Moss st 33(34:35) sts, turn. Leave rem sts on a spare needle for the time being and complete this side first. Cont in moss st without shaping until work measures 51 (52:53)cm [20(20½:21) in] from beg, ending after a wrong-side row.
Shape Shoulder and Neck 1st row Cast off 7 sts, patt to end. **2nd row** Cast off 6 sts, patt to end. **3rd row** Cast off 7 sts, patt to end. **4th row** Cast off 6 sts, patt to end. **5th row** Cast off rem 7(8:9) sts.
With right side of work facing, rejoin B to rem sts, patt to end. Complete this side to match the first side, reversing shapings thus: work in moss st patt without shaping until work measures 51 (52:53)cm [20(20½:21) in] ending after a right-side row.
Shape Shoulder and Neck 1st row Cast off 7 sts, patt to end. **2nd row** Cast off 6 sts, patt to end. **3rd row** Cast off 7 sts, patt to end. **4th row** Cast off 6 sts, patt to end. **5th row** Cast off rem 7(8:9) sts.

FRONT

With 3mm [No 11] needles and B, cast on 122(128:134) sts.
1st row *K1, p1; rep from * to end. **2nd row** *P1, k1; rep from * to end. Cont in moss st pattern until work measures 5cm [2 in].
Change to R and st-st. Work 2 rows straight. **Next row** K1, k2 tog, k36(38:40), sl 1, k2 tog, psso, k38(40:42), k3 tog tbl, k36 (38:40), sl 1, k1, psso, k1 . . . 116(122:128) sts.
Beg p row cont in st-st for 4cm [1½ in] without shaping, ending after a p row. **Next row** K1, k2 tog, k33(35:37), sl 1, k2 tog, psso,

Warm playsuit

3 to 5 years

The shapes are easy and the knitting is basic stocking stitch – very useful garments for a beginner to get started on.

Materials Nine 25g balls 4-ply yarn in main colour (M) for Trousers; four balls M and seven balls contrast (C) for Top; pair 3mm [No 11] knitting needles; 60cm [⅔ yd] elastic, 2cm [¾ in] wide.

Measurements Chest 61cm [24 in]; length of top, 38cm [15 in]; sleeve seam 30cm [12 in]; length of trousers, 59cm [23 in].

Tension 30 sts and 38 rows to 10cm [4 in].

Abbreviations k, knit; p, purl; st(s), stitch(es); cm, centimetre(s); in, inch(es); alt, alternate; beg, beginning; cont, continue; dec, decreas(e)ing; foll, following; rem, remain(ing); rep, repeat; st-st, stocking stitch; tog, together.

Square brackets contain imperial measurements.

TROUSERS

TO MAKE

Beg at lower edge of leg. Cast on 102 sts. Beg k row, cont in st-st until work measures 6cm [2½ in] ending after a p row. Dec 1 st at both ends of next row and every foll 18th row to 96 sts. Cont in st-st without shaping until work measures 41cm [16 in] ending after a p row.

Shape for Crotch 1st row Cast off 3 sts, k to end. **2nd row** Cast off 3 sts, p to end. **3rd row** K2 tog, k to last 2 sts, k2 tog. **4th row** P to end. **5th to 8th rows** Rep 3rd and 4th rows twice more. Cont in st-st without shaping until work measures 24cm [9½ in] from beg of crotch shaping, ending after a p row. Cast off. Work a second piece in the same way.

TO MAKE UP

Press following instructions on ball band. With right side inside, back-stitch each inside leg seam from lower edge to crotch. With right side of work inside, back-stitch the centre front seam through to the back and up to the waist. Fold 3cm [1¼ in] at lower edge of each leg to wrong side and slip-stitch this hem to wrong side. At the waist fold a similar 3cm [1¼ in] hem and slip-stitch, leaving a small opening for the elastic. Using a safety-pin, insert the elastic through the channel of the waist hem, draw both ends through and sew into a circle. Smooth out the elastic in the hem, then sew up opening.

TOP

BACK

With C, cast on 96 sts. Beg k row, cont in st-st until work measures 40cm [15¾ in] ending after a p row.

Shape Neck 1st row K39, turn and cont on these sts only for first side of neck only. **2nd row** Cast off 4 sts, p to end. **3rd row** K to end. **4th row** Cast off 3 sts, p to end. **5th row** K to end. **6th row** Cast off 2 sts, p to end. Cast off rem 30 sts. With right side of work facing, rejoin yarn to rem sts, cast off centre 18 sts, k39 sts to end. Complete to match first side, reversing the shaping thus: **1st row** P to end. **2nd row** Cast off 4 sts, k to end. **3rd row** P to end. **4th row** Cast off 3 sts, k to end. **5th row** P to end. **6th row** Cast off 2 sts. Cast off rem 30 sts.

FRONT

With C, cast on 96 sts. Beg k row, cont in st-st until work measures 34cm [13½ in] ending after a p row.

Shape Neck 1st row K41, turn and cont on these sts only for first side of neck only. **2nd row** Cast off 3 sts, p to end. **3rd row** K to end. **4th row** Cast off 2 sts, k to end. **5th row** K to end. **6th row** Cast off 2 sts, p to end. **7th row** K to end. **8th row** P2 tog, p to end. **9th to 14th rows** Rep 7th and 8th rows 3 times more. Cont in st-st without shaping until work matches Back to shoulder, ending after a p row. Cast off.

With right side of work facing, rejoin C to rem sts. Cast off centre 14 sts, k to end. Complete this side to match the first side, reversing shaping thus: **1st row** P to end. **2nd row** Cast off 3 sts, k to end. **3rd row** P to end. **4th row** Cast off 2 sts, k to end. **5th row** P to end. **6th row** Cast off 2 sts, k to end. **7th row** P to end. **8th row** K2 tog, k to end. **9th to 14th rows** Rep last 2 rows 3 times more . . . 30 sts.

Cont in st-st without shaping until work matches Back to shoulder, ending after a k row. Cast off.

SLEEVES

With M, cast on 56 sts. Beg k row, work 8cm [3 in] st-st, ending after a p row. Change to C and beg k row, cont in st-st, inc 1 st at both ends of 5th row foll and every foll 6th row to 82 sts. Cont in st-st without shaping until sleeve measures 30cm [12 in] from beg, ending after a p row. Cast off. Work another sleeve the same.

HOOD

With M, cast on 120 sts. Beg k row, cont in st-st without shaping for 30cm [12 in] ending after a p row. To join the top seam graft the sts tog thus: Break off the yarn leaving an end about four times as long as half the width of the knitting. Arrange the sts equally on two needles so that, with the purl sides facing one another, both needle points are to your right, the nearest needle having the end of the yarn at its point. To do this, it will be necessary to k half the sts and fold the work in half with the p side on the inside, with the needles in the correct position, the fold is to your right.

Beg at the right-hand side: *Insert needle carrying yarn knitwise into the first st on the front needle, draw yarn through the st,

---

slipping the st off the needle. Insert the needle purlwise into the second st on the front needle, draw yarn through but leave the st on the knitting needle. Take yarn under front knitting needle and insert the yarn needle purlwise into the first st on the back knitting needle, draw yarn through st and slip off the needle. Insert yarn needle knitwise into second st on back knitting needle, draw yarn through and leave st on the knitting needle. Bring yarn forward and rep from * to end. The sts are all joined forming an invisible seam. Fasten off yarn neatly.

Hood border With C, cast on 150 sts. Beg k row, work 5cm [2 in] st-st. Cast off. With right sides together, back-stitch one long edge of the border to the front edge of the hood. Fold the border in half and slip-stitch the other long edge on the wrong side of the hood, concealing the back-stitch seam.

POCKET

With M, cast on 48 sts. Beg k row cont in st-st until work measures 9cm [3½ in] ending after a p row. **Shape Top** Cast off 9 sts at beg of next 2 rows . . . 30 sts. Dec 1 st at both ends of next row and foll alt

WARM PLAYSUIT: SHAPE GUIDE

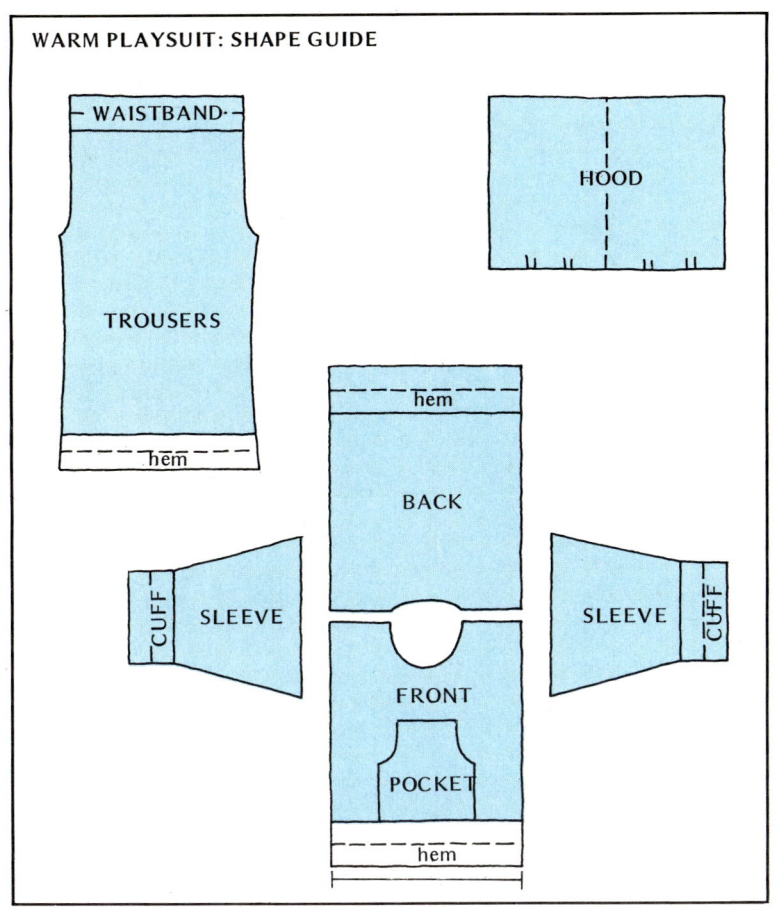

rows to 24 sts. Cont in st-st without shaping until pocket measures 16cm [6¼ in] ending after a p row. Cast off.

TO MAKE UP
Press the pieces following instructions on ball band.
Seams With right sides facing, back-stitch the shoulder seams. Now back-stitch the side seams, leaving an opening of 14cm [5¾ in] free at top for armholes – total armhole 28cm [11½ in] all round. With right side of work inside, back-stitch the sleeve seams. With right sides together, pin the cast-off edge of the sleeves to the armhole opening, with the sleeve seam to the underarm seam. Back-stitch the sleeves in place. Remove the pins.
Hood With right sides together pin the centre of the cast-on edge of the hood to the centre back neck edge and pin the border to the centre front neck, crossing one over the other. Pin and tack the remaining edge of hood to neck edge, pleating in the fullness of the hood to the neck edge – DO NOT stretch the neck to fit the hood. Back-stitch the hood firmly, stitching the pleats twice to secure and stitching through the double thickness of the hood

border to the neck at centre front. Remove all pins and tackings. Fold a 4cm [1½ in] hem at lower edge and cuffs to wrong side and slip-stitch on the wrong side.
Pocket *At 4cm [1½ in] from the lower edge sew on the pocket – measure and pin the centre of the pocket to the measured centre of the front. Pin the pocket in place along the lower edge. Neatly hem-stitch along the lower edge with matching yarn. Hem the straight side edges. Finally hem across the top straight edge. Remove pins.
*If desired a neat border may be worked round the pocket before sewing on – using a 3mm [No 11] crochet hook and matching yarn, with right side of pocket facing, work 1 row dc all round outer edge. Fasten off.

Opposite page: trousers and a snugly practical top make a perfect playsuit when the weather is cold and windy Above: the diagram shows just how simple the pieces are. Shaping is kept to a minimum to achieve the comfortable and casual look

Decorated overalls

4 and 7 years

Tortoises get a splendid airing on these overalls. If you can't work from a chart, then add the motifs later by the Swiss Embroidery method – see the instructions overleaf.

Materials 9(10) 25g balls Double Knitting yarn in main colour (M); 1 ball in contrast colour (C); pair 3¾mm [No 9] knitting needles; 2 buttons.

Measurements 50(55)cm [20(22) in] waist; 72(78)cm [28¼(30¾) in] length to waist.

Tension 24 sts and 32 rows to 10cm [4 in] in st-st.

Abbreviations k, knit; p, purl; st(s), stitch(es); cm, centimetre(s); in, inch(es); alt, alternate; beg, beginning; cont, continue; st-st, stocking stitch; tog, together; dec, decreas(e)ing; inc, increas(e)ing; rep, repeat; rem, remain(ing).

Size Note Figure in brackets refers to larger size. One figure only refers to both sizes. Square brackets contain imperial measurements.

These trousers are made in two pieces, beginning at the lower edge of each leg. When making up, the front waist to crotch seam is made first then the centre back seam. The inside leg seams are made last. If you prefer to work the tortoise design in Fair Isle knitting, follow the chart on the next page in the usual way over the centre 35 sts of each leg, knitting the odd rows from right to left and purling the even rows from left to right.

RIGHT LEG
Beg at lower edge. Cast on 92(96) sts. Beg k row work 30 rows st-st.
Dec row K2 tog, k to last 2 sts, k2 tog. Beg p row, work 29 rows st-st. Rep last 30 rows twice more . . . 86(90) sts.
Beg p row, cont in st-st without shaping until work measures 55 (60)cm [21¾(23¾)] ending after a p row.
Shape for Crotch 1st row Cast off

Continued on next page

Decorated overalls . . . continued

3 sts (this is the centre front edge), k to end. **2nd row** Cast off 4 sts (this is the centre back edge), p to end. **3rd row** Cast off 2 sts, k to end. **4th row** Cast off 3 sts, p to end. **5th row** Cast off 2 sts, k to end. **6th row** Cast off 2 sts, p to end. **7th row** K2 tog, k to end. **8th row** Cast off 2 sts, p to end. **9th row** K2 tog, k to end. **10th row** P2 tog, p to end. **11th row** K2 tog, k to end. **12th row** P2 tog, p to end. **13th row** K2 tog, k to end. **14th row** P2 tog, p to end . . . 61(65) sts. You will notice that the centre back shaping is deeper than the front to allow for the seat. Cont in st-st without shaping until work measures 17(18)cm [6½(7) in] from beg of crotch shaping, ending after a p row. Leave sts on a spare needle for the time being.

LEFT LEG
Cast on 92(96) sts. Beg k row, work 30 rows st-st. **Dec row** K2 tog, k to last 2 sts, k2 tog. Beg p row work 29 rows st-st. Rep last 30 rows twice more . . . 86(90) sts. Beg p row, cont in st-st until work measures 55(60)cm [21¾ (23½) in] ending after a p row.
Shape for Crotch 1st row Cast off 4 sts (this is the centre back edge), k to end. **2nd row** Cast off 3 sts (this is the centre front edge), p to end. **3rd row** Cast off 3 sts, k to end. **4th row** Cast off 2 sts, p to end. **5th row** Cast off 2 sts, k to end. **6th row** Cast off 2 sts, p to end. **7th row** Cast off 2 sts, k to end. **8th row** P2 tog, p to end. **9th row** K2 tog, k to end. **10th row** P2 tog, p to end. **11th row** K2 tog, k to end. **12th row** P2 tog, p to end. **13th row** K2 tog, k to end. **14th row** P to end. **15th row** K2 tog, k to end . . . 61(65) sts. Beg p row, cont in st-st until work measures 17(18)cm [6½(7) in] from beg of crotch shaping, ending after a p row. Leave sts on spare needle for the time being.

WAISTBAND AND BIB
With right sides together, back-stitch the centre front seam. Place all the 122(130) sts on to one needle. Cont in k2, p2 rib thus:
1st row K2, *p2, k2; rep from * to end. **2nd row** P2, *k2, p2; rep from * to end. Rep last 2 rows until the rib waistband measures 7cm [2¾ in] ending after a wrong-side row.
Next row Cast off 44(48) sts, rib 34 sts, cast off rem 44(48) sts. Break yarn. With wrong side of work facing, rejoin the yarn to the centre 34 sts and cont in k2, p2 rib for bib for a further 15cm [6 in]. Cast off loosely.

STRAPS (make 2)
Cast on 14 sts. **1st row** K2, *p2, k2; rep from * to end. **2nd row** P2, *k2, p2; rep from * to end. Rep last 2 rows until strap measures 35cm [13¾ in].
Next row (buttonhole) Rib 5, cast off 4, rib 5. **Next row** Rib 5, cast on 4, rib 5. Cont in rib for a further 2cm [¾ in]. Cast off.

TO MAKE UP
Using the chart, right, work the tortoise design on each leg covering centre 35 sts and using Swiss Embroidery thus: Begin at the bottom right-hand corner of the design and leaving an end at the back, bring the needle out to the front through the centre of the stitch below the one to be covered, then in and out again behind the stitch in the row above, back into the same hole at the bottom and out through the centre of the next st to the left. Cover each stitch in the first row like this and at the end of the row slip the needle upwards into the centre of the last st covered instead of taking it along to the left. Now turn the work upside down so that you are still working from right to left.
Seams With the right side of work inside, back-stitch the inside leg to crotch. With the right side inside, back stitch the inside leg seams. Fold a 5cm [2 in] hem to wrong side at the bottom edge of each leg and slip stitch to the wrong side. Turn the trousers to the right side.
Straps Sew the straps to the back waistband and sew the buttons on to the corners of the bib at the front. Cross the straps at the back and fasten to the buttons of the bib.
Press garment according to instructions on ball band.

Right: at the top is the chart which will guide you in adding the tortoises to the overalls either by the Swiss Embroidery method (see instructions in TO MAKE UP) or by knitting it in as you go. The design covers 35 stitches of each leg — the odd rows are knitted from right to left and the even rows are purled from left to right Below: the chart is the shape guide which will help you when knitting the overalls

TORTOISE MOTIF: PATTERN

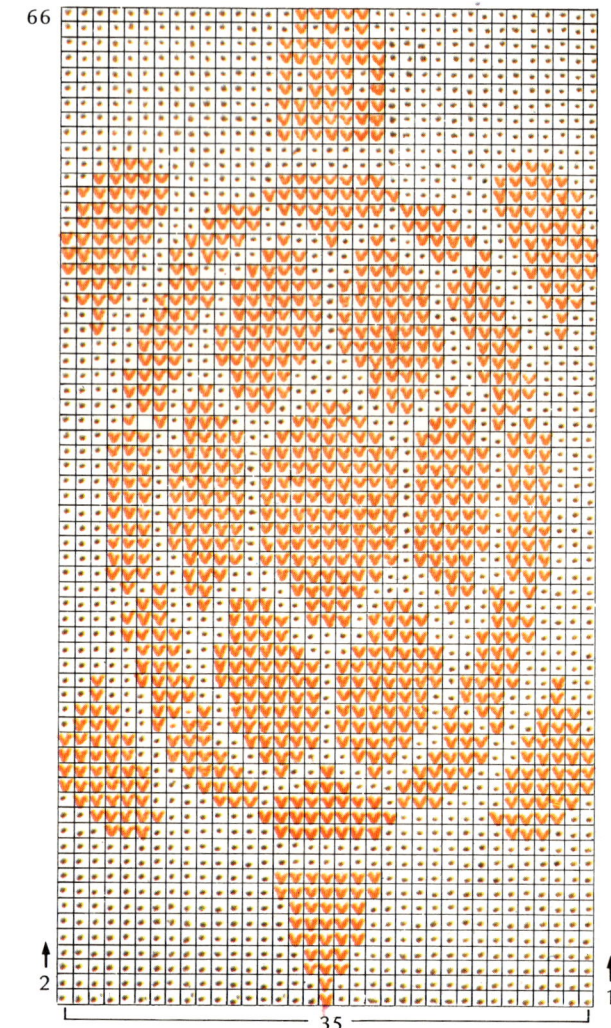

66   65

2   1

35

DECORATED OVERALLS: SHAPE GUIDE

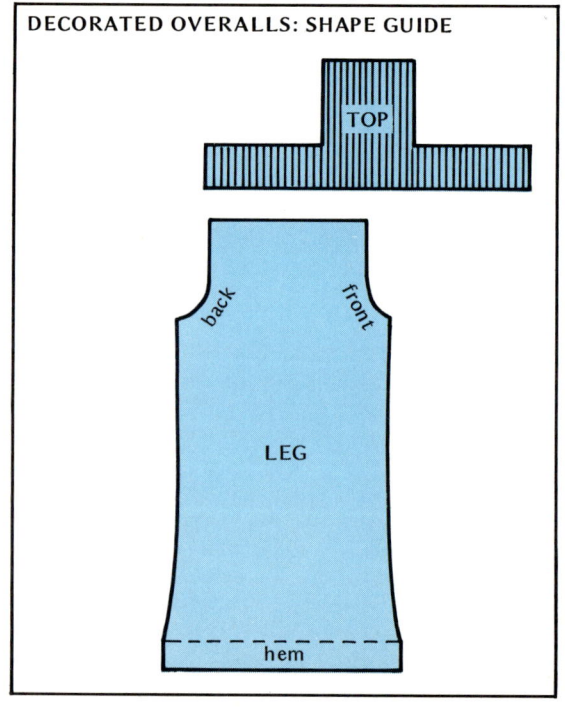

TOP

back   front

LEG

hem

Classy cape

In turquoise

4 to 6 years

Fun to wear and good to look at, this cape and the red one on page 127 bridge that time when girls grow so fast it's not worth spending money on an overcoat.

Materials 10(12) 25g balls Double Knitting yarn; pair 3¾mm [No 9] knitting needles; 4 buttons.

Measurements Length 53(58)cm [21(23) in] to neck at centre back.

Tension 24 sts and 32 rows to 10cm [4 in] in st-st.

Abbreviations k, knit; p, purl; sts, stitch(es); cm, centimetre(s); in, inch(es); alt, alternate; beg, beginning; cont, continue; dec, decreas(e)ing; inc, increas(e)ing; foll, following; g-st, garter stitch; psso, pass slip st over; rem, remain(ing); rep, repeat; sl, slip; st-st, stocking stitch; tog, together.

Size Note Figures in brackets refer to larger size. One figure only refers to both sizes. Square brackets contain imperial measurements.

BACK

Cast on 24(36) sts. Beg k row, cont in st-st, casting on 3 sts at beg of next 12 rows; 2 sts at beg of next 8 rows; 1 st at beg of next 20 rows; 3 sts at beg of next 2 rows and 4 sts at beg of next 6 rows . . . 126(138) sts. Work 6 rows st-st without shaping.
Shape Sides Dec row K 2, sl 1, k 1, psso, k to last 4 sts, k 2 tog, k 2. Beg p row, work 5 rows st-st. Rep last 6 rows to 120(130) sts. Work 3 rows straight.
Work the dec row as before on next row and every foll 4th row to 98(108) sts. P 1 row. Dec as before on next row and every foll alt row to 62 sts, ending after a p row. Now dec 1 st at both ends of every row to 50 sts. Cast off 2 sts at beg of every row to 36 sts.
Shape Neck 1st row Cast off 2 sts, k until there are 10 sts on needle after cast-off, turn. **1st row** P 2 tog, p to end. **2nd row** Cast off 2 sts, k to last 2 sts, k 2 tog. **3rd row** As 1st row. **4th row** Cast off 2, k 3. **5th row** P 3. Cast off rem 3 sts.

With right side of work facing, join yarn to rem sts at neck edge, cast off centre 12 sts, k to end.
Shape second side of Neck 1st row Cast off 2 sts, p to end. **2nd row** K 2 tog, k to end. **3rd row** Cast off 2 sts, p to last 2 sts, p 2 tog. **4th row** As 2nd. **5th row** Cast off 2 sts, p 3. **6th row** K 3. Cast off rem 3 sts.

LEFT FRONT

Cast on 12(18) sts. Beg k row, cont in st-st, casting on sts at beg of right-side rows thus: 3 sts, 6 times; 2 sts, 4 times; 1 st, 10 times;

3 sts once and 4 sts, 3 times, ending after a k row . . . 63(69) sts. Beg p row, work 7 rows st-st without shaping.
Shape Side Dec row K 2, sl 1, k 1, psso, k to end. Beg p row, work 5 rows st-st. Rep last 6 rows to 60(65) sts. Work 3 rows straight.
Work the dec row as before on next row and every foll 4th row to 49(54) sts. P 1 row. Dec as before on next row and every foll alt row to 30 sts, thus ending at Front edge.
Shape Neck and cont side shaping: **1st row** Cast off 5 sts, p to

last 2 sts, p 2 tog. **2nd row** K 2 tog, k to end. **3rd row** Cast off 2 sts, p to last 2 sts, p 2 tog. **4th row** As 2nd row. **5th row** P 2 tog, p to last 2 sts, p 2 tog. **6th row** Cast off 2 sts, k to end. **7th row** P 2 tog, p to end. Rep last 2 rows twice more. **12th row** Cast off 2 sts, k to end. **13th row** P to end. Rep last 2 rows to 2 sts. Cast off rem 2 sts.

RIGHT FRONT

Cast on 12(18) sts. Beg k row, cont in st-st, casting on sts at beg of wrong-side rows thus: 3 sts, 6 times; 2 sts, 4 times; 1 st, 10 times;

Continued on next page

Turquoise cape . . . continued

3 sts once and 4 sts, 3 times, ending after a p row . . . 63(69) sts. Beg k row, work 6 rows st-st without shaping.

Shape Side Dec row K to last 4 sts, k 2 tog, k 2. Beg p row, work 5 rows st-st. Rep last 6 rows to 60(65) sts. Work 3 rows straight. Work the dec row as before on next row and every foll 4th row to 49(54) sts. P 1 row. Dec as before on next row and every foll alt row to 30 sts, thus ending after a k row. **Next row** P 2 tog, p to end.

Shape Neck and cont side shaping: **1st row** Cast off 5 sts, k to last 2 sts, k 2 tog. **2nd row** P 2 tog, p to end. **3rd row** Cast off 2 sts, k to last 2 sts, k 2 tog. **4th row** P 2 tog, p to end. **5th row** K 2 tog, k to end. **6th row** Cast off 2 sts, p to end. Rep last 2 rows twice more. **11th row** K 2 tog, k to end. **12th row** Cast off 2 sts, p to end. Keeping neck edge straight, cont to cast off 2 sts at beg of p rows until all sts are worked off.

Special Tip A neat way to cast off the hood in one piece and avoid sewing a seam – K to the centre 2 sts, k 1 st and k the 2nd st tog with the foll st, *turn, p 1, p 2 tog, turn, k 1, k 2 tog; rep from * until only 2 sts rem. Cast off these 2 sts in the normal way. In this way you are working only on the 2 central stitches of which the last is always worked with the following stitch. Except · in this case always slip the first stitch after turning in the middle of a row to avoid leaving a hole.

HOOD

Cast on 34 sts for Right side of hood. Cont in st-st, shaping thus: **1st row** K 3 sts, turn. **2nd row and foll alt rows** Sl 1, p to end. **3rd row** K 6, turn. **5th row** K 9, turn. **7th row** K 12, turn. **9th row** K 16, turn. **11th row** K 20, turn. **13th row** K 24, turn. **14th row** Sl 1, p to end.

Shape Darts and Back Edge 1st to 4th rows Beg k row, in st-st. **5th row** K 12, pick up loop between sts and k into back of it (called inc 1 k), k 12, inc 1 k, k to last st, inc in last st . . . 37 sts. Beg p row, work 3 rows st-st. **9th row** K 12, inc 1 k, k 14, inc 1 k, k to last st, inc in last st . . . 40 sts. **10th to 12th rows** In st-st. **13th row** K 12, inc 1 k, k 16, inc 1 k, k to last st, inc in last st . . . 43 sts. **14th to 16th**

rows In st-st. **17th row** K to last st, inc in last st . . . 44 sts. **18th to 20th rows** In st-st. **21st and 22nd rows** As 17th and 18th rows . . . 45 sts. **23rd row** K 12, inc 1 k, k 18, inc 1 k, k to end . . . 47 sts.

24th to 26th rows In st-st. **27th row** K 12, inc 1 k, k 20, inc 1 k, k to last st, inc in last st . . . 50 sts. **28th to 30th rows** In st-st. **31st row** K 12, inc 1 k, k 22, inc 1 k, k to end . . . 52 sts. **32nd row** P to end. **33rd row** K to last st, inc in last st . . . 53 sts. **34th row** P to end. **35th row** K 12, inc 1 k, k 24, inc 1 k, k to end . . . 55 sts. **36th to 38th rows** In st-st. **39th row** K to last st, inc in last st . . . 56 sts. **40th to 44th rows** In st-st. **45th row** K 12, inc 1 k, k 26, inc 1 k, k to last st, inc in last st . . . 59 sts. Now inc 1 st at end of every 6th row foll to 64 sts. Work 5 rows straight. Cast off.

Left side of hood Cast on 34 sts. Cont in st-st, shaping thus: **1st row** K to last 3 sts, turn. **2nd row and foll alt rows** Sl 1, p to end. **3rd row** K to last 6 sts, turn. Cont in this way, working 3 less sts before turning, until the (7th) row: k to last 12 sts, turn, has been worked. **Next row** Sl 1, p to end. **Next row** K to last 16 sts, turn. **Next row** Sl 1, p to end. Cont in this way, working 4 less sts before turning, until the (13th) row: k to last 24 sts, turn, has been worked. **Next row** Sl 1, p to end.

Shape Darts and Back Edge 1st to 4th rows Beg k row, in st-st. **5th row** Inc in 1st st, k to last 24 sts, inc 1 k, k 12, inc 1 k, k 12 . . . 37 sts. Beg p row, work 3 rows straight. **9th row** Inc in 1st st, k to last 26 sts, inc 1 k, k 14, inc 1 k, k 12 . . . 40 sts. **10th to 12th rows** In st-st. **13th row** Inc in 1st st, k to last 28 sts, inc 1 k, k 16, inc 1 k, k 12 . . . 43 sts. Work 3 rows straight. **17th row** Inc in 1st st, k to end . . . 44 sts. Work 3 rows straight. **21st row** As 17th row . . . 45 sts. Work 1 row. **23rd row** K to last 30 sts, inc 1 k, k 18, inc 1 k, k 12 . . . 47 sts. Work 3 rows straight. **27th row** Inc in 1st st, k to last 32 sts, inc 1 k, k 20, inc 1 k, k 12 . . . 50 sts. Work 3 rows straight. **31st row** K to last 34 sts, inc 1 k, k 22, inc 1 k, k 12 . . . 52 sts. P 1 row. **33rd row** Inc in 1st st, k to end. P 1 row. **35th row** K to last 36 sts, inc 1 k, k 24, inc 1 k, k 12 . . . 55 sts. Work 3 rows straight. **39th row** Inc in 1st st, k to end . . . 56 sts. Work 5 rows straight. **45th row** Inc in 1st st, k to last 38 sts, inc 1 k, k 26, inc 1 k, k 12 . . . 59 sts. Work 5 rows straight. Now inc at beg of next row and every foll 6th row

to 64 sts. Work 5 rows straight. Cast off.

BORDERS

With right side of work facing, pick up and k 130(142) sts evenly along lower edge of Back. Work 6 rows g-st. Cast off. With right side of work facing, pick up and k 65(71) sts evenly along lower edge of Left Front. Work 6 rows g-st. Cast off. Work the lower edge of the Right Front in the same way.

With right side of work facing, pick up and k 120(140) sts evenly along Left Front edge. Work 10 rows k 2, p 2 rib. Cast off in rib. Mark the border with pins to represent buttons: the top one just below the beginning of the neck shaping and the other 3 spaced at 5cm [2 in] intervals below.

Work the right border to match the left, working buttonholes to correspond with the pinned positions thus: **5th row** *Rib to next pin, cast off 4 sts; rep from * 3 times more, rib to end. **6th row** In rib, casting on 4 sts over those cast off in the previous row. On the wrong side join the top hood seam with a flat stitch. With right side of work facing, pick up and k 98 sts evenly along the straight front edge of the hood. Work 7 rows k 2, p 2 rib. Cast off in rib.

TO MAKE UP

Press following instructions on the ball band. With right sides facing, back-stitch the side shaping seams to neck edge. With right side inside, join the back-shaped edge of the hood. Turn to right side and tack the neck-edge of the hood to the shaped neck-edge of the cape, having the right sides of the work together. Back-stitch neatly and remove tackings. Sew on buttons. Make a large tassel by winding yarn round a piece of cardboard. Run the thread through one edge and tie tightly. Snip at the other edge. Now tie again at the folded edge, about 2.5cm [1 in] from the fold. Trim ends. Sew the tassel to the point of the hood.

Opposite page: the unusual shaping at the bottom of the red cape makes it perfect to wear over tights, trousers, long or short skirts. This cape and the turquoise one on page 125 provide warmth and style

Classy cape
In red
4 to 6 years

Materials 10(12) 25g balls Double Knitting yarn; pair 3¾mm [No 9] knitting needles; 4 buttons.

Measurements Length 39(44)cm [15½(17½) in] to neck at centre back.

Tension 24 sts and 32 rows to 10cm [4 in] in st-st.

Abbreviations k, knit; p, purl; st(s), stitch(es); cm, centimetre(s); in, inch(es); alt, alternate; beg, beginning; cont, continue; dec, decreas(e)ing; inc, increas(e)ing; patt, pattern; rep, repeat; rem, remain(ing); tog, together; st-st, stocking stitch; foll, following; sl, slip; psso, pass sl st over.

Size Note Figures in brackets refer to larger size. One figure only refers to both sizes. Square brackets contain imperial measurements.

BACK

Cast on 120(126) sts. Work 6 rows k 1, p 1 rib.

Shape Lower Curve 1st row K 70 (73), turn. **2nd row** Sl 1, p 19(22), turn. **3rd row** Sl 1, k 21(24), turn. **4th row** Sl 1, p 23(26), turn. **5th row** Sl 1, k 25(28), turn. **6th row** Sl 1, p 27(30), turn. Cont in this way, taking in 2 more sts on every row before turning until the **28th row** Sl 1, p 71(74), turn, has been worked.

29th row Sl 1, k 75(78), turn. **30th row** Sl 1, p 79(82), turn. **31st row** Sl 1, k 83(86), turn. **32nd row** Sl 1, p 87(90), turn. **33rd row** Sl 1, k 91(94), turn. **34th row** Sl 1, p 95 (98), turn. **35th row** Sl 1, k 101(104), turn. **36th row** Sl 1, p 107(110), turn and k to end. **Next row** P to end.

Shape Sides Dec row K 1, k 2 tog, k to last 3 sts, sl 1, k 1, psso, k 1 . . . 118(124) sts. Beg p row work 3 rows st-st. Rep last 4 rows 13 times more . . . 92(98) sts. Now dec in the same way on next row and foll alt rows 10(13) times . . . 72 sts. Leave these sts on a spare needle to be joined later to the two fronts for the yoke.

LEFT FRONT

Cast on 76(79) sts. Work 5 rows k 1, p 1 rib.

Shape Lower Curve 1st row Rib

10, p 10(13), turn. **2nd row** Sl 1, k 9(12), rib 10. **3rd row** Rib 10, p 12 (15), turn. **4th row** Sl 1, k 11(14), rib 10. Cont in this way, taking in 2 more sts on p rows before turning until the row: Sl 1, k 35 (38), rib 10, has been worked.
Next row Rib 10, p 40(43), turn.
Next row Sl 1, k 39(42), rib 10.
Next row Rib 10, p 44(47), turn.
Next row Sl 1, k 43(46), rib 10.
Next row Rib 10, p 48(51), turn.
Next row Sl 1, k 47(50), rib 10.
Next row Rib 10, p 58(61), turn.
Next row Sl 1, k 57(60), rib 10.
Next row Rib 10, p to end . . . 76(79) sts.
Shape Side Dec row K 1, k 2 tog, k to last 10 sts, rib 10. **Next row** Rib 10, p to end. Keeping 10 sts in rib at front edge for front border, work in st-st, dec 1 st at side edge on 3rd row foll and every foll 4th row until 62(65) sts rem, ending after a 4th row.
Now dec at side edge as before, at beg of next row and foll alt rows until 52 sts rem, ending after a wrong-side row. Leave these sts on a spare needle to be joined later to the back for the yoke. Mark the front border with pins to represent buttons, the lowest one to be on the 20th row from the beg of the straight part of the work, the following two each to be 20 rows above the other. Place the pins to the centre of the border.

RIGHT FRONT
Cast on 76(79) sts. Work 6 rows k 1, p 1 rib.
Shape Lower Curve 1st row Rib 10, k 10(13), turn. **2nd row** Sl 1, p 9(12), rib 10. **3rd row** Rib 10, k 12(15), turn. **4th row** Sl 1, p 11(14), rib 10. Cont in this way, keeping 10 sts in rib for front border and rem in st-st, taking in 2 more sts before each turn until the row: Sl 1, p 35(38), rib 10, has been worked.
Now cont in the same way, taking in 4 sts before the turns, 3 times, then 10 sts once, thus ending after a wrong-side row.
Shape Side Keep 10 sts in rib for front border and work buttonholes in the border to correspond with the pins on left front thus:
1st row (right side) Rib 3, cast off 4, rib until there are 3 sts on right-hand needle, work to end. **2nd row** Work to last 10 sts, rib 3, cast on 4 sts, rib 3. At the same time **Dec row** Rib 10, k to last 3 sts, sl 1, k 1, psso, k 1. Beg p row, work 3 rows st-st. Keeping rib and buttonholes correct, dec at side edge on next row and foll 4th rows until 62(65) sts rem,

ending after a 4th row. Now dec at side edge as before on next row and foll alt rows until 52 sts rem, ending after a wrong-side row.
Join Front and Back Next row On to one needle, rib 10 of Right Front, cont in rib to end, rib across sts of Back then rib across sts of Left Front, ending with the 10 sts of front border . . . 176 sts.
Next row Rib 52, mark the next st and work it, rib 70 sts, mark the next st and work it, rib 52. Keep the 2 marked sts as k on the right side of the work and dec thus: **1st row** Rib to within 2 sts of the marked st, k 2 tog, k the marked st, k 2 tog, rib to within 2 sts of the 2nd marked st, k 2 tog, k the marked st, k 2 tog, rib to end.
Next row Rib to end. Rep last 2 rows 7 times more . . . 144 sts. Don't forget to work the 4th buttonhole, just below the neck edge.
Shape Neck and cont shoulder shaping: **1st row** Cast off 5 sts, rib to within 2 sts of the marked st, k 3 tog, k the marked st, k 3 tog, rib to within 3 sts of the 2nd marked st, k 3 tog, k the marked

st, k 3 tog, rib to end.
Next row Cast off 5 sts, rib to end.
Next row Rib to within 3 sts of the marked st, k 3 tog, k 1, k 3 tog, rib to within 3 sts of the 2nd marked st, k 3 tog, k 1, k 3 tog, rib to last 5 sts, turn. **Next row** Sl 1, rib to last 5 sts, turn. **Next row** Sl 1, rib to within 3 sts of the marked st, k 3 tog, k 1, k 3 tog, rib to within 3 sts of the 2nd marked st, k 3 tog, k 1, k 3 tog, rib to last 6 sts, turn. **Next row** Sl 1, rib to last 6 sts, turn. Cont in this way, dec 2 sts both sides of the 2 marked sts on right-side rows

Continued on next page

Red cape . . . continued

and working 1 st less before turning on every row until 38 sts rem.

Work 10 rows k 1, p 1 rib without shaping on these sts. Now pick up and k 10 sts down the side of these 10 rows, pick up and k 11 sts along the shaped edge to the cast-off 5 sts and pick up and k 5 sts along this edge, turn, rib to end then pick up and k 10 sts along side of 10 rows worked straight, pick up and k 11 sts down shaped edge to 5 cast-off sts and k 5 sts along this edge . . . 88 sts. Work 12 rows k 1, p 1 rib.

Shape Hood Cont in st-st with 10 sts in rib at both ends and shape thus: **1st row** Rib 10, k 11, mark next 3 sts, k 19, k and mark next 2 sts, k 19, k and mark next 3 sts, k 11, rib 10. * **2nd row** Rib 10, p to last 10 sts, rib 10. **3rd row** Rib 10, k to centre 2 marked sts, pick up loop between sts and k into back of the loop – called inc 1 k – k the 2 marked sts, inc 1 k, k to last 10 sts, rib 10. **4th row** As 2nd row. **5th row** Rib 10, k to first set of 3 marked sts, inc 1 k, k 3 marked sts, inc 1 k, k to the centre 2 marked sts, inc 1 k, k the 2 marked sts, inc 1 k, k to the second set of 3 marked sts, inc 1 k, k 3, inc 1 k, k to last 10 sts, rib 10. * Rep last 4 rows from * to * 5 times more.

This concludes the *side* hood increasing. Inc at back as before on foll 6 right-side rows on both sides of the centre 2 marked sts only. After the last inc row, work 3 rows straight. Now inc at both sides of the centre 2 marked sts on next row and foll 4th rows 9 times, working 3 rows straight after last increase row. Cast off.

TO MAKE UP
Press pieces, avoiding ribbed sections and following instructions on ball band. Join side seams to yoke. Join top of hood seam. Sew on buttons. Make a pompon by winding yarn round cardboard to required thickness. Run thread through one edge and tie very tightly. Snip the other edge and shake the pompon vigorously. Sew the pompon to the point of the hood as shown in photograph on previous page. If you prefer to add a tassel, see instructions in the TO MAKE UP section of the turquoise cape on page 126.

Striped jacket

4 to 8 years

Sure to be a hit whether knitted in school or best sporting colours.

Materials 4(5:6) 25g balls Double Knitting yarn in each of three colours, A, B and C; pairs of 3mm and 3¾mm [No 11 and No 9] knitting needles; open-ended zip fastener 41cm [16 in].

Measurements To fit 61(66:71)cm [24(26:28) in] chest; length, 54cm [21½ in].

Tension 27 sts to 10cm [4 in] in k5, p3 rib.

Abbreviations k, knit; p, purl; st(s), stitch(es); cm, centimetre(s); in, inch(es); alt, alternate; beg, beginning; cont, continue; dec, decreas(e)ing; inc, increas(e)ing; rep, repeat; rem, remain(ing); tog, together; foll, following; patt, pattern.

Size Note Figures in brackets refer to larger sizes. One figure only refers to all sizes. Square brackets contain imperial measurements.

> Make sure that the fronts are of a length suitable for zips on the market, especially if you're adjusting the length where indicated in the instructions. Never try and fit in a zip that's too long for the opening and always pin or tack the zip in position before sewing it in.

BACK
With 3mm [No 11] needles and A, cast on 82(90:98) sts.
1st row With A, *K2, p2; rep from * to last 2 sts, k2.
2nd row With A, P2, *k2, p2 to end.
3rd to 6th rows Rep 1st and 2nd rows twice more.
7th to 12th rows With B, as 1st to 6th rows.
13th to 18th rows With C, as 1st to 6th rows, inc 3 sts evenly on last row . . . 85(93:101) sts.
Change to 3¾mm [No 9] needles. Cont in rib patt with stripes thus:
1st row With A, (right side) K5, *p3, k5; rep from * to end.
2nd row With A, P5, *k3, p5; rep from * to end.
3rd to 6th rows Rep 1st and 2nd rows twice.
7th to 12th rows With B, as 1st to 6th rows.
13th to 18th rows With C, as 1st to 6th rows.
These 18 rows form the striped rib pattern. Cont in rib pattern until work measures 26cm [10¼ in] (adjust length here if liked) ending after a wrong-side row.
Shape Armholes Cast off 4(5:6) sts at beg of next 2 rows; 3 sts at beg of next 2 rows; 2 sts at beg of next 2 rows . . . 67(73:79) sts. Cont in rib patt until armholes measure 18cm [7 in] ending after a wrong-side row.
Shape Shoulders 1st row Cast off 7 sts, work 23(24:25) turn and complete this side first. **2nd row** Cast off 5 sts, rib 18(19:20). **3rd row** Cast off 7 sts rib 11(12:13). **4th row** Cast off 4(5:6) sts, rib 7. **5th row** Cast off rem 7 sts.
With right side of work facing, rejoin matching yarn to rem sts at neck edge. Cast off centre 7(11:15) sts, k to end. Complete this side to match first side thus:
1st row Cast off 7 sts, rib to end.
2nd row Cast off 5 sts, rib to end.

3rd row As 1st. **4th row** Cast off 4(5:6) rib to end. Cast off rem sts.

LEFT FRONT
With 3mm [No 11] needles and A, cast on 48(52:56) sts. Cont in striped k2, p2 rib thus:
1st row With A, *K2, p2; rep from * to end.
2nd row With A, *P2, k2; rep from * to end.
3rd to 6th rows Rep 1st and 2nd rows twice.
7th to 12th rows With B, as 1st to 6th rows.
13th to 18th rows With C, as 1st to 6th rows, inc 1 st at both ends of last row . . . 50(54:58) sts.
Change to 3¾mm [No 9] needles and work striped rib pattern thus:
1st row With A (right side) *K5, p3; rep from * to last 2(6:2) sts, k2(6:2).
2nd row With A, p2(6:2), *k3, p5; rep from * to end.
3rd to 6th rows Rep 1st and 2nd rows twice.
7th to 12th rows With B, as 1st to 6th rows.
13th to 18th rows With C, as 1st to 6th rows.
Note that you will have different sts at the front edge.
Cont in striped rib pattern until work measures 26cm [10¼ in], (adjust length here if liked) ending after a wrong-side row.
Shape Armhole 1st row Cast off 4(5:6) sts, rib to end. **2nd row and foll alt rows** Rib to end. **3rd row** Cast off 3 sts, rib to end. **5th row** Cast off 2 sts, rib to end. Now cont in rib until work measures 36cm [14 in] ending after a right-side row.
Shape Neck 1st row Cast off 9(10:11) sts, rib to end. **2nd row and foll alt rows** Rib to end. **3rd row** Cast off 2, rib to end. **5th row** As 3rd. **7th row** As 3rd. **9th row** K2 tog, rib to end. Rep last 2 rows until 21(21:21) sts rem. Cont in rib pattern without shaping until armhole measures 18cm [7 in] ending after a wrong-side row.
Shape Shoulder Cast off 7 sts at beg of next row and foll 2 alt rows.

RIGHT FRONT
With 3mm [No 11] needles and A, cast on 48(52:56) sts. Work in striped k2, p2 rib thus:
1st row With A, *K2, p2; rep from * to end.

Continued on page 130

Right: always a favourite – the simple zip-up top. The textured effect is created by a knit 5, purl 3 rib
Left: shape guide for the jacket

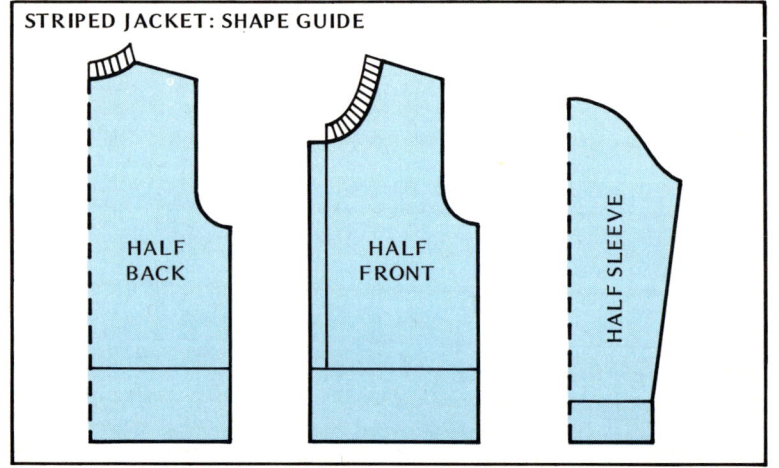

STRIPED JACKET: SHAPE GUIDE

HALF BACK

HALF FRONT

HALF SLEEVE

Striped jacket . . . continued

2nd row With A, *P2, k2; rep from * to end.

3rd to 6th rows Rep 1st and 2nd rows twice.

7th to 12th rows With B, as 1st to 6th rows.

13th to 18th rows With C, as 1st to 6th rows, inc 1 st at both ends of last row . . . 50(54:58) sts. Change to 3¾mm [No 9] needles and work striped rib pattern thus:

1st row With A, (right side), K2(6:2), *p3, k5; rep from * to end.

2nd row With A, *K5, p3; rep from * to last 2(6:2) sts, k2(6:2).

3rd to 6th rows Rep 1st and 2nd rows twice.

7th to 12th rows With B, as 1st to 6th rows.

13th to 18th rows With C, as 1st to 6th rows.

Note that you will have different stitches at the front edge.

Cont in striped rib pattern until work measures 26cm [10¼ in], (adjust length here if liked) ending after a right-side row.

Shape Armhole 1st row Cast off 4(5:6) sts, rib to end. **2nd row and foll alt rows** Rib to end. **3rd row** Cast off 3 sts, rib to end. **5th row** Cast off 2 sts, rib to end. Now cont in striped rib pattern until work measures 36cm [14 in] ending after a wrong-side row.

Shape Neck 1st row Cast off 9(10:11) sts, rib to end. **2nd row and foll alt rows** Rib to end. **3rd row** Cast off 2 sts, rib to end. **5th and 7th rows** As 3rd row. **9th row** K2 tog, rib to end. Rep last 2 rows until 21 sts rem. Cont in rib pattern until armhole measures 18cm [7 in] ending after a right-side row.

Shape Shoulder Cast off 7 sts at beg of next row and foll 2 alt rows.

SLEEVES

With 3mm [No 11] needles and A, cast on 46(50:54) sts. Work 5cm [2 in] k2, p2 rib thus: **1st row** K2, *p2, k2; rep from * to end. **2nd row** P2, *k2, p2; rep from * to end. Inc 3(1:1) st on last row . . . 49(51:55) sts. Change to 3¾mm [No 9] needles.

Inc 1 st at both ends of every 6th row to 73(75:77) sts, cont in the rib pattern and placing the first two rows thus: **1st row** With A, (right side), P1(3:7), *k5, p3; rep from * to end. **2nd row** *K3, p5; rep from * to last 1(3:7) sts, k1(3:7). When the increasing is completed cont in striped rib without shaping until the sleeve measures 28(31:33)cm [11(12:13) in], (adjust length here if liked) ending after a wrong-side row.

Shape Top Cast off 4 sts at beg of next 2 rows; 3 sts at beg of next

2 rows. **5th and 6th rows** Cast off 2 sts, rib to end. **7th and 8th rows** K2 tog, rib to end. Rep 5th to 8th rows 3 times more. **21st and 22nd rows** Cast off 2 sts, rib to end. **23rd to 26th rows** Rep 21st and 22nd rows twice more. **27th and 28th rows** Cast off 3 sts, rib to end. **29th and 30th rows** Cast off 2 sts, rib to end Cast off rem 13(15:17) sts.

Work a second sleeve the same.

TO MAKE UP

Do not press. Lay the pieces flat under a damp cloth overnight. This smooths out the knitting without pressing the pattern flat. With right sides together, back-stitch the shoulder seams. With right sides together and matching the stripes, back-stitch the side seams. With right side inside, matching the stripes, back-stitch the sleeve seams. Pin the under-arm seam to the sleeve seam and the sleeve top to the shoulder seam, with right sides together, back-stitch the sleeve top in place. Remove pins. At the front edge, fold back 3 sts to the wrong side down the straight edge. Slip-stitch this 3 st facing to the wrong side to form a firm surface on which to sew the zip fastener. Do not sew in the zip yet.

Neckband With right side of work facing, using 3mm [No 11] needles and A, pick up and k90 sts evenly round neck edge. **1st row** P2, *k2, p2; rep from * to end. **2nd row** K2, *p2, k2; rep from * to end. Rep last 2 rows until rib measures 10cm [4 in]. Cast off loosely. Fold half of the neckband to the wrong side and slip-stitch in place. Sew in the zip.

Twinset

4 to 8 years

A cheerful twosome for a wintry day, and as the jumper's short-sleeved it will have a second life when the weather's not so cold.

Materials 7(8:10) 25g balls 4-ply knitting yarn; pair 3mm [No 11] knitting needles; set of four 3mm [No 11] double-pointed needles; 10 buttons.

Measurements Actual size of jumper 58(64:69)cm [23(25:27) in] all round, length 28(29:31)cm [11(11½:12) in]; of cardigan 61 (66:71)cm [24(26:28) in] all round, length 29(31:33)cm [11½(12:13) in]. Sleeve seam of short sleeved jumper, 9(9:10)cm [3½(3½:4) in]; of cardigan 25(28:31)cm [10(11:12) in].

Tension 30 sts and 38 rows to 10cm [4 in] in st-st.

Abbreviations k, knit; p, purl; st(s), stitch(es); cm, centimetre(s); in, inch(es); alt, alternate; beg, beginning; cont, continue; dec, decreas(e)ing; foll, following; inc, increas(e)ing; st-st, stocking stitch; tog, together; rep, repeat; rem, remain(ing); y fwd, yarn forward.

Size Note Figures in brackets refer to larger sizes. One figure only refers to all sizes. Square brackets contain imperial measurements.

> Make sure that you stop after a k (or right-side) row before starting the open work pattern – the first row is a k row on the wrong side which forms the ridge.

JUMPER

BACK

Cast on 86(94:102) sts using 3mm [No 11] needles. **1st row** K2, *p2, k2; rep from * to end. **2nd row** P2, *k2, p2; rep from * to end. Rep last 2 rows until rib measures 8·5cm [3 in]. Cont in st-st until work measures 13(14:15)cm [5 (5½:6) in] ending after a k row. Now work the open work pattern thus: **1st row** (wrong side) K to end. **2nd row** K to end. **3rd row** P to end. **4th row** *K1, y fwd, k2 tog; rep from * to last 2(1:3) sts, k2(1:3). **5th row** P to end. **6th row**

K to end. **7th row** K to end.

Beg k row cont in st-st until work measures 15(16:18)cm [6(6½:7) in] from beg, ending after a p row.

Shape Armholes Cast off 4(5:6) sts at beg of next 2 rows; 2(3:4) sts at beg of next 2 rows; 2 sts at beg of next 2 rows. Dec 1 st at both ends of next row . . . 68 (72:76) sts. Beg p row, cont in st-st without shaping until armholes measure 13cm [5 in] ending after a p row.

Shape Shoulders and Neck 1st row Cast off ¡5 sts, k23(24:25), turn. Complete this side first. **2nd row** Cast off 5 sts, p18(19:20). **3rd row** Cast off 5 sts, k13(14:15). **4th row** Cast off 5 sts, p8(9:10). **5th row** Cast off 5 sts, k3(4:5). **6th row** P3(4:5). **7th row** Cast off rem 3(4:5) sts.

With right side of work facing, rejoin yarn at neck edge to rem sts, cast off centre 12(14:16) sts, k to end.

Beg wrong side facing, complete this side to match first side thus:

1st row Cast off 5 sts, p23(24:25). **2nd row** Cast off 5 sts, k18(19:20). **3rd row** Cast off 5 sts, p13(14:15). **4th row** Cast off 5 sts, k8(9:10). **5th row** Cast off 5 sts, p3(4:5). **6th row** K3(4:5). **7th row** Cast off rem 3(4:5) sts.

FRONT

Cast on 86(94:102) sts. **1st row** K2, *p2, k2; rep from * to end. **2nd row** P2, *k2, p2; rep from * to end. Rep last 2 rows until rib measures 8·5cm [3 in]. Cont in st-st until work measures 13 (14:15)cm [5(5½:6) in] ending after a k row.

Now work the open work pattern thus: **1st row** (wrong side) K to end. **2nd row** K to end.

3rd row P to end. **4th row** *K1, y fwd, k2 tog; rep from * to last 2(1:3) sts, k2(1:3). **5th row** P to end. **6th row** K to end. **7th row** K to end.

Beg k row, cont in st-st until work measures 15(16:18)cm [6(6½:7) in] from beg ending after a p row.

Shape Armholes Cast off 4(5:6) sts at beg of next 2 rows; 2(3:4) sts at beg of next 2 rows; 2 sts at beg of next 2 rows, Dec 1 st at both ends of next row . . . 68 (72:76) sts. Beg p row, cont in st-st until armholes measure 8(9:10)cm [3(3½:4) in] ending after a p row.

Shape Neck 1st row K22(24:26) sts, turn and complete this side first. **2nd row** Cast off 3 sts, p to end. **3rd row** K19(21:23) sts. **4th row** Cast off 1(2:3) sts, p18(19:20). Cont in st-st on rem 18(19:20) sts until armhole measures 14cm

[5½ in] ending after a p row.
Shape Shoulder Cast off 5 sts at beg of next row and foll 2 alt rows. Work 1 row. Cast off rem sts.

With right side of work facing, rejoin yarn to rem sts at neck edge, cast off centre 24 sts, k to end. **2nd row** P22(24:26) sts. **3rd row** Cast off 3 sts, k to end. **4th row** P19(21:23) sts. **5th row** Cast off 1(2:3) sts, k18(19:20). **6th row** K18(19:20). Cont in st-st on these 18(19:20) sts until armhole measures 13cm [5 in] ending after a k row.
Shape Shoulder Cast off 5 sts at beg of next row and foll 2 alt rows. Work 1 row. Cast off rem sts.

SLEEVES
Cast on 56(60:64) sts. **1st row** *K2, p2; rep from * to end. **2nd row** *K2, p2; rep from * to end. Rep last 2 rows until rib measures 5·5cm [2¼ in]. Cont in st-st without shaping until work measures 9 (9:10)cm [3½(3½:4) in] ending after a p row.
Shape Top Cast off 4 sts at beg of next 2 rows; 3 sts at beg of next 2 rows. Dec 1 st at both ends of next row and every foll 4th row until 12(14:16) sts rem, ending after a p row. Dec 1st at both ends of next row. P1 row. Cast off rem 10(12:14) sts.
Work another sleeve the same.

TO MAKE UP
Press pieces following instructions on ball band. With right sides together, join shoulder and side seams. With right side inside, join sleeve seams. Join all st-st seams with back-stitch, joining the ribbed edges with a flat seam. Place the underarm seam of sleeves to side seams of jumper with right sides facing. Back-stitch the sleeves in place. With right side of work facing, pick up and k108 sts round the neck edge. Work 2cm [¾ in] k2, p2 rib. Cast off the sts loosely in rib. Press seams lightly (don't flatten).

CARDIGAN
BACK
Cast on 96(100:104) sts using 3mm [No 11] needles. **1st row** *K2, p2; rep from * to end. **2nd row** *K2, p2; rep from * to end. Rep these 2 rows until rib measures 8cm [3 in]. Cont in st-st

Continued on next page

Right: a very stylish twinset for a little girl or young lady. The open work pattern makes an amazing difference to the look

Twinset . . . continued

until work measures 14(15:17)cm [5½(6:6½) in] ending after a k row. Now work the open-work pattern: **1st row** (wrong side) K to end. **2nd row** K to end. **3rd row** P to end. **4th row** *K1, y fwd, k2 tog; rep from * to last 3(1:2) sts, k3(1:2). **5th row** P to end. **6th row** K to end. **7th row** K to end. Cont in st-st without shaping until work measures 15(16:18)cm [6(6½:7) in] from beg ending after a p row.

Shape Armholes Cast off 4(5:6) sts at beg of next 2 rows; 3 sts at beg of next 2 rows; 2 sts at beg of next 2 rows. Dec 1 st at both ends of next row . . . 76(78:80) sts. Cont in st-st without shaping until armholes measure 14(16:18) cm [5½(6¼:7) in] ending after a p row.

Shape Shoulders and Neck 1st row Cast off 5 sts, k23(24:25), turn. Complete this side first. **2nd row** Cast off 5 sts, p18(19:20). **3rd row** Cast off 5 sts, k13(14:15). **4th row** Cast off 5 sts, p8(9:10). **5th row** Cast off 5 sts, k3(4:5). **6th row** P3(4:5). **7th row** Cast off 3(4:5) sts.

With right side of work facing, rejoin yarn at neck edge to rem sts, cast off centre 20 sts, k to end. With wrong side facing, complete to match first side thus: **1st row** Cast off 5 sts, p23(24:25). **2nd row** Cast off 5 sts, k18(19:20). **3rd row** Cast off 5 sts, k13(14:15). **4th row** Cast off 5 sts, k8(9:10). **5th row** Cast off 5 sts, p3(4:5). **6th row** K3(4:5) sts. **7th row** Cast off rem 3(4:5) sts.

LEFT FRONT
Cast on 44(48:52) sts. **1st row** *K2, p2; rep from * to end. Rep this row for k2, p2 rib until rib measures 8cm [3 in], dec 1 st at end of last row . . . 43(47:51) sts. Cont in st-st until work measures 14(15:17)cm [5½(6:6½) in] ending

after a k row.
Now work the open work pattern thus: **1st row** (wrong side) K to end. **2nd row** K to end. **3rd row** P to end. **4th row** *K1, y fwd, k2 tog; rep from * to last 1(2:3) sts, k1(2:3). **5th row** P to end. **6th row** K to end. **7th row** K to end. Cont in st-st until Front matches Back to armhole ending after a p row.

Shape Armhole Cast off 4(5:6) sts at beg of next row; 3 sts at beg of foll alt row; 2 sts at beg of foll alt row. Dec 1 st at beg of next right-side row . . . 33(36:39) sts. Cont in st-st without shaping until work measures 27(28:29)cm [10½(11:11½) in] ending after a k row.

Shape Neck 1st row Cast off 6(8:10) sts, p to end. **2nd and foll alt rows** K to end. **3rd row** Cast off 3 sts, p to end. **5th row** Cast off 2 sts, p to end. **6th row** K to end. Rep last 2 rows twice more . . . 18(19:20) sts. Cont in st-st without shaping until armhole matches Back to shoulder, ending after a p row.

Shape Shoulder Cast off 5 sts at beg of next row and foll 2 alt rows. Work 1 row. Cast off rem sts.

RIGHT FRONT
Cast on 44(48:52) sts. **1st row** *K2, p2; rep from * to end. Rep this row for k2, p2 rib until rib measures 8cm [3 in], dec 1 st at end of last row . . . 43(47:51) sts. Cont in st-st until work measures 14(15:17)cm [5½(6:6½) in] ending after a k row.
Now work the open work pattern thus: **1st row** (wrong side) K to end. **2nd row** K to end. **3rd row** P to end. **4th row** *K1, y fwd, k2 tog; rep from * to last 1(2:3) sts, k1(2:3). **5th row** P to end. **6th row** K to end. **7th row** K to end. Cont in st-st until Front matches Back to armhole, ending after a k row.

Shape Armhole Cast off 4(5:6)

sts at beg of next row; 3 sts at beg of foll alt row; 2 sts at beg of foll alt row. Dec 1 st at end of next right-side row . . . 33(36:39) sts. Cont in st-st without shaping until work measures 27(28:29)cm [10½(11:11½) in] ending after a p row.

Shape Neck 1st row Cast off 6(8:10) sts, k to end. **2nd row and foll alt rows** P to end. **3rd row** Cast off 3 sts, k to end. **5th row** Cast off 2 sts, k to end. **6th row** P to end. Rep last 2 rows twice more . . . 18(19:20) sts. Cont in st-st without shaping until armhole matches Back to shoulder, ending after a right-side row.

Shape Shoulder Cast off 5 sts at beg of next row and foll 2 alt rows. Work 1 row. Cast off rem sts.

SLEEVES
Cast on 46(50:54) sts. **1st row** K2, *p2, k2; rep from * to end. **2nd row** P2, *k2, p2; rep from * to end. Rep last 2 rows until rib measures 5·5cm [2¼ in]. Cont in st-st, inc 1 st at both ends of 5th row foll and every foll 6th(8th:8th) row to 62(66:70) sts. Cont in st-st without shaping until work measures 25 (28:31)cm [10(11:12) in] ending after a p row.

Shape Top Cast off 4 sts at beg of next 2 rows; 3 sts at beg of next 2 rows. **Next row** K2 tog, k to last 2 sts, k2 tog. **Next row** P to end. Rep last 2 rows 13 times more. Cast off 2 sts at beg of next 6 rows. Cast off rem 8(12:16) sts.
Work another sleeve the same.

TO MAKE UP
With right side of work together, back-stitch the shoulder seams and then the side seams. With right side inside, back-stitch the sleeve seams. With right sides together, place the sleeve top in the armhole with the side seam to the sleeve seam. Back-stitch

the sleeve in place.
With right side of work facing, using set of 3mm [No 11] double-pointed needles, pick up and k290(302:314) sts evenly up right front, round neck edge and down left front. **1st row** K2, *p2, k2; rep from * to end. **2nd row** P2, *k2, p2; rep from * to end.
Rep these 2 rows, inc 2 sts at neck corner on every right-side row. After the first 2 rows mark the left front edge with pins for button positions – the top one level with beg of neck shaping, the lowest one 2 rows from cast-on edge and the other eight spaced equally between.
Work the buttonholes on the 4th row, beg at right front thus: rib to first marked position, y fwd, k2 tog, *rib to next marked position, y fwd, k2 tog; rep from * until all the buttonholes have been worked then rib to end. Cont in rib until 8 rows have been worked. Cast off in rib. Press work following instructions on ball band. Sew on buttons.

Below: the shape guides that will help you when knitting the jumper and cardigan which make up the Twinset. If you wish to lengthen the garments make sure you do it by the same amount on both before you begin the open work pattern

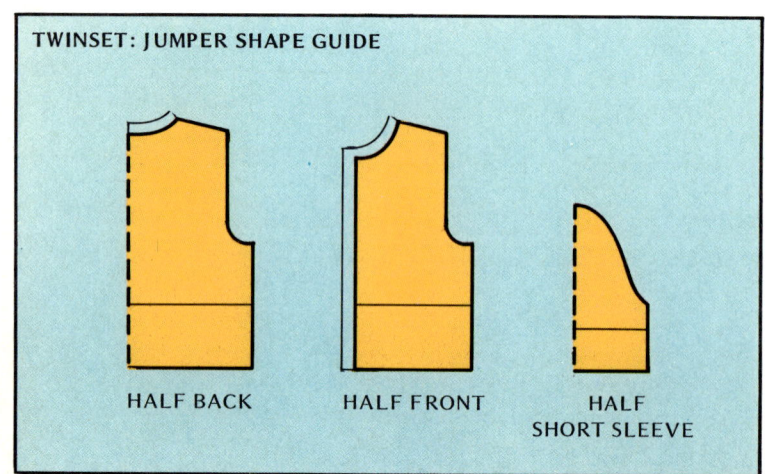

TWINSET: JUMPER SHAPE GUIDE

HALF BACK HALF FRONT HALF SHORT SLEEVE

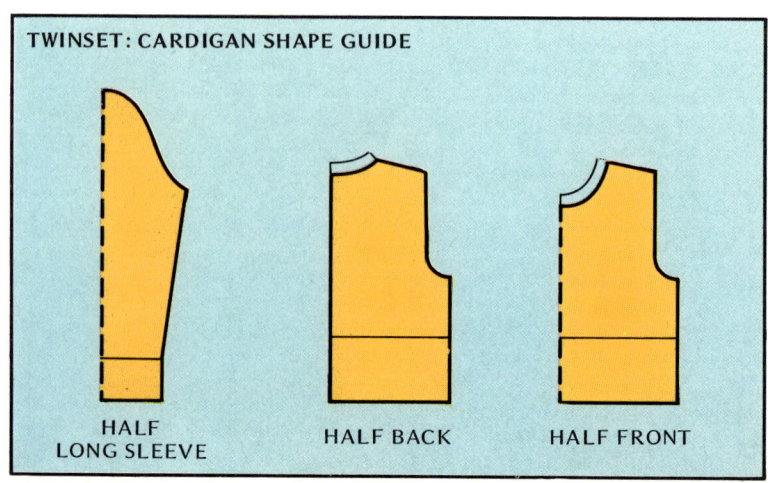

TWINSET: CARDIGAN SHAPE GUIDE

HALF LONG SLEEVE HALF BACK HALF FRONT

Knitting

Yoked jacket

4 to 8 years

This would look equally good on a girl – but remember to put the buttonholes on the right, and the buttons on the left.

Materials 350(400:450)g of Double Double Wool; pair 5mm [No 6] and 6mm [No 4] knitting needles; cable needle; 3 buttons.

Measurements To fit a 61(66:71)cm [24(26:28) in] chest.

Tension 15 sts and 22 rows measure 10cm [4 in].

Abbreviations k, knit; p, purl; st(s), stitch(es); cont, continue; g-st, garter stitch; patt, pattern; sl, slip; cm, centimetre(s); in, inch(es); tog, together; rep, repeat; beg, beginning; rem, remain(ing); inc, increase; wl fwd, wool forward.

Size Note Figures in brackets refer to larger sizes. One figure only refers to all sizes. Square brackets contain imperial measurements.

BACK

Using 6mm [No 4] needles cast on 56(60:64) sts and work in g-st for 8 rows. Work thus:
1st row K10(12:14), p1, k4, p1, k24, p1, k4, p1, k10(12:14).
2nd row K11(13:15), p4, k26, p4, k11(13:15).
3rd row As 1st row.
4th row As 2nd row.
5th row K10(12:14), p1, sl next 2 sts on cable needle and leave at front of work, k next 2 sts, then k the 2 sts from cable needle (called cable 4), p1, k24, p1, cable 4, p1, k10(12:14).
6th row As 2nd row.
These 6 rows form the patt. Cont until 54(60:66) rows have been worked. (Work more rows if longer length required.)
Shape Armholes Cast off 3 sts at beg of next 2 rows. Leave work for the present.

RIGHT FRONT

Using 6mm [No 4] needles cast on 28(30:32) sts and work in g-st for 8 rows. Cont thus:
1st row K12, p1, k4, p1, k10(12:14).
Continued on next page

Left: chunky cables, garter stitch and an attractive rib on the yoke add up to a very smart look

Yoked jacket . . . continued

2nd row K11(13:15), p4, k13.

3rd and 4th rows As 1st and 2nd rows.

5th row K12, p1, cable 4, p1, k10(12:14).

6th row As 2nd row.

Rep these 6 rows 8(9:10) times more, then 1st row once more. (If more rows were worked in Back, then work to match ending after a right-side row.)

Shape Armhole Next row Cast off 3 sts, patt to end. Leave sts for the present.

LEFT FRONT

Using 6mm [No 4] needles cast on 28(30:32) sts and work in g-st for 8 rows. Cont thus:

1st row K10(12:14), p1, k4, p1, k12.

2nd row K13, p4, k11(13:15).

3rd and 4th rows As 1st and 2nd rows.

5th row K10(12:14), p1, cable 4, p1, k12.

6th row As 2nd row.

Rep these 6 rows until same depth as Back to armholes.

Shape Armhole Cast off 3 sts, patt to end. **Next row** Patt to armhole edge. Leave for the present.

SLEEVES

Using 5mm [No 6] needles cast on 30 sts for each size and work in k1, p1 rib for 9 rows. **Next row** K3 (0:0) then (k1, inc in next st, k1) 8(10:10) then k3 for 1st size only . . . 38(40:40) sts.

Change to 6mm [No 4] needles and work thus:

1st row K16(17:17), p1, k4, p1, k16(17:17).

2nd row K17(18:18), p4, k17(18:18).

3rd and 4th rows As 1st and 2nd rows.

5th row K16(17:17), p1, cable 4, p1, k16(17:17).

6th row As 2nd row.

Cont in patt as set inc 1 st each end of following 10th row for 3rd size only and for all sizes, rep the 6 rows 7(8:9) times – or length required.

Shape Top Cast off 3 sts at beg of next 2 rows. Leave sts for the present.

YOKE

Using 6mm [No 4] needles, right side facing, k across sts in order thus:

Right Front K4 (for border) then across rem 21(23:25) sts work, (k2 tog, k1) 7(7:8) times, k2 tog for 2nd size and k1 for 3rd size . . . 18(19:21) sts for Right Front.

1st sleeve Across 32(34:36) sts work, k0(2:4), then (k2 tog, k2) 8 times . . . 24(26:28) sts for Sleeve.

Back Across 50(54:58) sts work, k6(5:1) then (k2 tog, k1) 13(15:19) times, k5(4:0) . . . 37(39:39) sts for Back.

2nd sleeve As 1st sleeve.

Left Front (K2 tog, k1) 7(7:8) times, k2 tog for 2nd size and k1 for 3rd size, k4 . . . 21(23:25) sts.

There are now 121(129:137) sts.

Next row (wrong side) K4, p1, *k3, p1, rep from * to last 4 sts, k4. Keeping 4 sts each end in g-st cont in rib as set but work a buttonhole in next row at beg of row for girl and end of row for boy thus (worked in border) k2, wl fwd, k2 tog. Cont straight until 8 rows of rib have been worked.

Next row (wrong side) K4, p1, *k2 tog, k1, p1, rep from * to last 4 sts, k4.

Cont in new rib of k2, p1 on wrong side for 1(3:5) rows, then in next row work another buttonhole as before. Work straight for 2 rows.

Next row K4, p1, *k2 tog, p1, rep from * to last 4 sts, k4.

Keeping continuity of g-st border, work rem sts in k1, p1 rib for 5(7:9) rows.

Next row K1(9:1) then (k2 tog, k6(4:4) 8(10:12) times.

Work in g-st across all sts for 7 rows, working another buttonhole in line with previous one on 2nd row. Cast off.

POCKETS (make 2)

Using 6mm [No 4] needles cast on 10(12:14) sts and work thus:

Next row K2(3:4), p1, k4, p1, k2(3:4).

Cont in patt cabling on 5th and every 6th row until 17(19:19) rows have been worked. Cast off.

TO MAKE UP

Press work following ball band instructions. Sew up side and sleeve seams. Sew on pockets with slip-stitch matching cables as shown in picture. Sew on buttons opposite buttonholes.

Thick-knit jacket

4 to 10 years

A snuggle-into jacket that can be worn with trousers or a skirt.

Materials 15(17:19:21) 50g balls high-bulk triple knitting yarn; pair 6mm [No 4] knitting needles; 3 buttons or toggles.

Measurements To fit 61(66:71:76) cm [24(26:28:30) in] chest; length, 39(41:47:53)cm [15½(16:18½:21) in]; sleeve seam, 34(38:41:43)cm [13½(15:16:17) in].

Tension 11 sts and 22 rows to 10cm [4 in] in g-st.

Abbreviations k, knit; p, purl; st(s), stitch(es); in, inch(es); cm, centimetre(s); alt, alternate; beg, beginning; cont, continue; g-st, garter stitch (every row k); patt, pattern; rep, repeat; rem, remain(ing); foll, following.

Size Note Figures in brackets refer to larger sizes. One figure only refers to all sizes. Square brackets contain imperial measurements.

Except for the hood and pockets this garment is worked in one piece and you begin knitting at the lower edge of the Back. The stitches for the Sleeves are cast on to the needle which holds the Back sts and the Sleeves are worked in one with the Back until the neck is shaped. Once the neck division is made, the work carries on with the Left Sleeve and Front until that section is cast off. The sts that have been left aside are then worked on for the Right Sleeve and Front.

MAIN PART

This is worked all in one piece, beg at Back. Cast on 38(42:46:48) sts. Cont in g-st until work measures 25(27:33:36)cm [10 (10½:13:14) in].

Now cont in patt thus: **1st row** (right side) K to end. **2nd row** K1 (3:5:1), *p1, k4; rep from * to last 2(4:6:2) sts, p1, k1(3:5:1).

These 2 rows form the patt. Rep them once more.

Shape for Sleeves On to same needle holding Back sts, cast on 37(41:45:47) sts at beg of next 2 rows . . . 112(124:136:142) sts. Cont in patt thus: **1st row** (right side) K to end. **2nd row** K3(4:5:3), *p1, k4; rep from * to last 4(5:6:4) sts, p1, k3(4:5:3). Cont without shaping in patt until work measures 37(39:45:51)cm [41½(15½:17½:20) in] from beg, measured from cast-on edge of Back, ending after a wrong-side row.

Shape Neck 1st row Patt 50(55: 60:62) sts, cast off centre 12 (14:16:18) sts, patt 50(55:60:62) sts to end. The work here divides: place the first set of 50(55:60:62) sts worked before the centre cast off in the previous row on to a stitch holder for the time being, these will be used later for the Right Sleeve and Front. Cont on the last set of 50(55:60:62) sts for the Left Sleeve and Front thus: Cont in patt until 2·5cm [1 in] has been worked from the division – place a safety-pin or a coloured loop at neck edge to indicate the shoulder line or halfway mark. Cont in patt for a further 2·5cm [1 in] ending at neck edge.

Next row Cast on 8(9:11:13) sts for Front, patt to end. Cont in patt for 3 rows more, thus ending at Front edge. Place a safety-pin, 3 sts in from front edge to indicate top button position. Now cont in patt until the sleeve rows are the same as the Back Sleeve rows, counted between the cast-on sleeve sts and the halfway marker, ending after a right-side row.

Next row Cast off 37(41:45:47) sts, patt to end. Cont in patt on rem 21(23:26:28) sts for 4 rows more. Mark the last row for the 2nd button position with a safety-pin. Now cont in g-st until the Front matches the Back from the cast-on edge to the halfway marker at shoulder. Cast off.

With wrong side of work facing, rejoin yarn to sts on holder placing them on to 6mm [No 4] needle. Work 2·5cm [1 in] in patt, ending at neck edge. Place a safety-pin or coloured loop at this edge to indicate the shoulder line or halfway mark. Cont in patt for a further 2·5cm [1 in] ending at front edge. **Next row** Cast on 8(9:11:13) sts, patt to end.

Cont in patt on 58(64:71:75) sts working a buttonhole to correspond with the top pin thus (do not work these rows like this if using toggles): **1st row** Patt 2, cast off 3, patt to end. **2nd row** Patt to last 5 sts, cast on 3, patt 2. Now cont in patt until the sleeve

rows are the same as the Back Sleeve rows, counted between the cast-on sleeve sts and the halfway marker, ending after a wrong-side row.

Next row Cast off 37(41:45:47) sts, patt to end. Cont in patt on rem 21(23:26:28) sts for Front, working a buttonhole to correspond with 2nd pin in the same way as the first buttonhole. Now cont in g-st, working a 3rd buttonhole equidistant from the other two in the same way as the first buttonhole. When this Front matches the Back to the cast-on edge, cast off the sts.

HOOD

Cast on 19(23:23:24) sts. Cont in g-st, inc 1 st at <u>end</u> of 12th row then every full 6th row to 23 (27:27:28) sts. Work 6 rows straight. Dec 1 st at shaped edge on next and every foll 6th row to 19(23:23:24) sts. Work 11 rows straight. Cast off.

POCKETS (make 2)

Cast on 14 sts. Cont in patt thus:
1st row (right side) K to end. **2nd row** K4, *p1, k4; rep from * to end. Rep last 2 rows until work measures 11(13:13:15)cm [4½(5:5:6) in]. Cast off.

TO MAKE UP

With right sides together, join side and sleeve seams with back-stitch. It is advisable to tack the sleeve seams before back-stitching to decide the finished sleeve length. Having marked the cuff allowance, remember to back-stitch this allowance with the seam on the right side of the work so that it will not show when the cuff is turned back.

Fold the hood in half, the shaped edge together forming the back edge. Neatly oversew the hood back seam to make a flat join on the inside. Pin the hood seam to the centre of back neck with right sides together, pin the corners of the straight edges to the corners of the neck, within the sts cast on at neck for the front – see picture. Now, with right sides together, back-stitch the edge of the hood to the neck edge of the coat.

Sew on the pockets to the fronts as shown in the picture, using either a neat over-sew stitching or running stitches within 1 st from the edge. You will find the pockets easy to place if you line them up with the straight g-st rows.

Sew the buttons on to the left front edge at the pinned positions to correspond with the buttonholes, or sew on toggles if used. Turn back the cuffs.

Above: two versions of the Thick-knit Jacket, with buttons or toggles to close the front
Right: the shape guide to the all-in-one jacket, and the hood

Knitted in Paton's Husky, colour Tundra

THICK-KNIT JACKET: SHAPE GUIDE

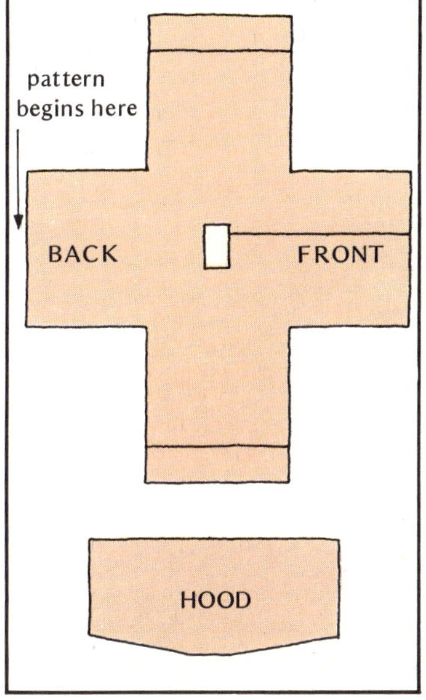

pattern begins here

BACK   FRONT

HOOD

Quilted waistcoats

4 years and teenager

Superbly-styled waistcoats that are warm and comfortable to wear . . . and simple to make.

Materials 8(16) 25g balls 4-ply knitting yarn (*see note below*); pair 3¼mm [No 10] knitting needles; 2(3) toggles; 50cm(1m) [½(1) yard] terylene wadding, 90cm [35½ in] wide.

Note If you prefer a fabric lining, halve these amounts. Fabric lining: 40cm [16 in] by 90cm [35½ in] wide; 60cm [24 in] by 110cm [43 in] wide.

Measurements To fit 61cm [24 in] chest and 84cm [33in] bust – loosely.

Tension 28 sts and 36 rows to 10cm [4 in] in st-st.

Abbreviations k, knit; p, purl; st(s), stitch(es); cm, centimetre(s); in, inch(es); alt, alternate; beg, beginning; cont, continue; dec, decreas(e)ing; rep, repeat; rem, remain(ing); st-st, stocking stitch.

Size Note Figures in brackets refer to the larger size. One figure only refers to both sizes. Square brackets contain imperial measurements.

> **Two waistcoats must be made so that you can sandwich a layer of wadding in between. Both can be knitted, or the inside one can be made of a brightly contrasting fabric. The shape will be the same as the knitted waistcoat but 15mm [⅝ in] must be allowed all round for turnings.**

TO MAKE

BACK AND FRONTS (worked in one piece to armholes)
Cast on 196(280) sts. Beg k row, cont in st-st until work measures 22(32)cm [8½(12½) in] ending after a purl row.
Divide for Armholes 1st row K42(63) turn. Cont on these sts only for the Right Front. **2nd row** P. **3rd row** K to last 2 sts, k2 tog. Rep last 2 rows until 35(56) sts rem, ending after a p row. Cont without shaping until work mea-

sures 30(40)cm [12(16) in] ending after a p row.
Shape Neck Dec 1 st at beg of next row and foll alt rows until 22(36) sts rem. Cont in st-st without shaping until work measures 39(51)cm [15½(20) in] ending after a k row.
Shape Shoulder Cast off 5(9) sts at beg of next 3 wrong side rows. K1 row. Cast off rem 7(9) sts.
With right side of work facing, rejoin yarn to rem sts, cast off 14 sts for underarm, k84(126) sts for Back, turn. Cont on these 84(126) sts only. **1st row** P to end. **2nd row**

K2 tog, k to last 2 sts, k2 tog. Rep last 2 rows until 70(112) sts rem, ending after a purl row. Cont in st-st without shaping until work measures 39(51)cm [15½(20) in] ending after a p row.
Shape Shoulders Cast off 5(9) sts at beg of next 6 rows; 7(9) sts at beg of foll 2 rows. Cast off rem 26(40) sts.
With right side of work facing, rejoin yarn to rem sts, cast off 14 sts for underarm, k42(63) sts to end. Cont on these 42(63) sts for Left Front. **1st row** P to end. **2nd row** K2 tog, k to end. Rep last 2

rows until 35(56) sts rem, ending after a p row. Cont without shaping until work measures 30(40)cm [12(16) in] ending after a k row.

Shape Neck Dec 1 st at beg of next row and foll alt rows until 22(36) sts rem. Cont in st-st without shaping until work measures 39(51)cm [15½(20) in] ending after a p row.
Shape Shoulder Cast off 5(9) sts at beg of next 3 right-side rows. P1 row. Cast off rem 7(9) sts.

THE LINING

Either knit another waistcoat in the same way or make a fabric lining following the shaping guide, adding 15mm [⅝ in] all round.

TO MAKE UP

Press both waistcoats. Using the lining, tack to the piece of wadding, adjusting carefully to obtain a good shape. Cut round the outer edge of the wadding and remove the tacking. Make a sandwich of the wadding, laying it between the two waistcoat pieces, the wrong sides of the knitting to the wadding. Tack the three thicknesses together. Now carefully cut away a 12·5mm [½ in] margin of wadding all round. Turn in the edges of both waistcoats to cover wadding and neatly oversew. Sew the armhole edges in the same way but not the shoulders.

Keeping the three thicknesses in place with the tacking, while it is still flat begin the quilting . . . see Diagram 1. Starting at the bottom corner of the Right Front, with the help of a ruler, mark with pins the diagonal lines from corner to corner to produce the diamond shapes. Make them approx 18 sts wide and start within 3 sts of the corner, ending in the same way. Now remove the pins and substitute with tacking (Diagram 2). Quilt by hand with back-stitch using matching embroidery silk or, if your machine is suitable, machine quilt it (Diagrams 3 and 4).

Finally, either machine stitch or back-stitch a border round the outside edge and the armhole edge, approx 12·5mm (½ in) from the edge. Join the shoulder seams on both the right and the wrong sides by turning in the edges neatly and oversewing together, concealing the wadding.

Sew on the toggle fastenings as shown in the picture, on the larger waistcoat there are three, sew at 13, 26, 38cm [5, 10, 15 in] from the bottom; on the child's there are only two, sew at 15 and 29cm [6 and 11½ in] from the bottom of the waistcoat.

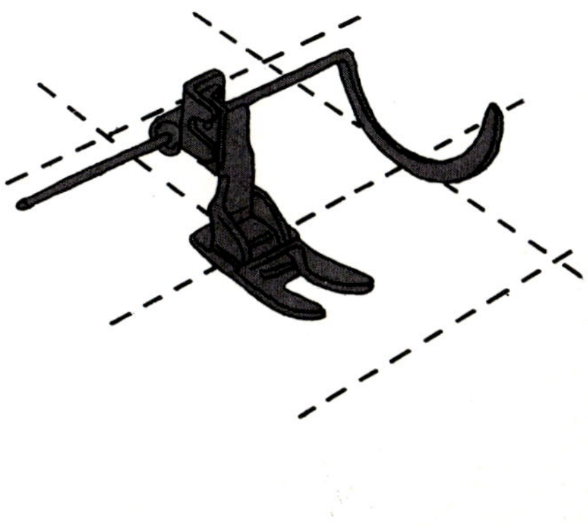

Right, top: the shape guide for the large and small quilted waistcoats. If you prefer a fabric lining make a pattern using the diagram as a guide and add 15mm [⅝ in] all round for turnings

Right, bottom: how to quilt the waistcoats by hand or machine. You can also see the waistcoat without toggles worn with the velvet culottes on page 36

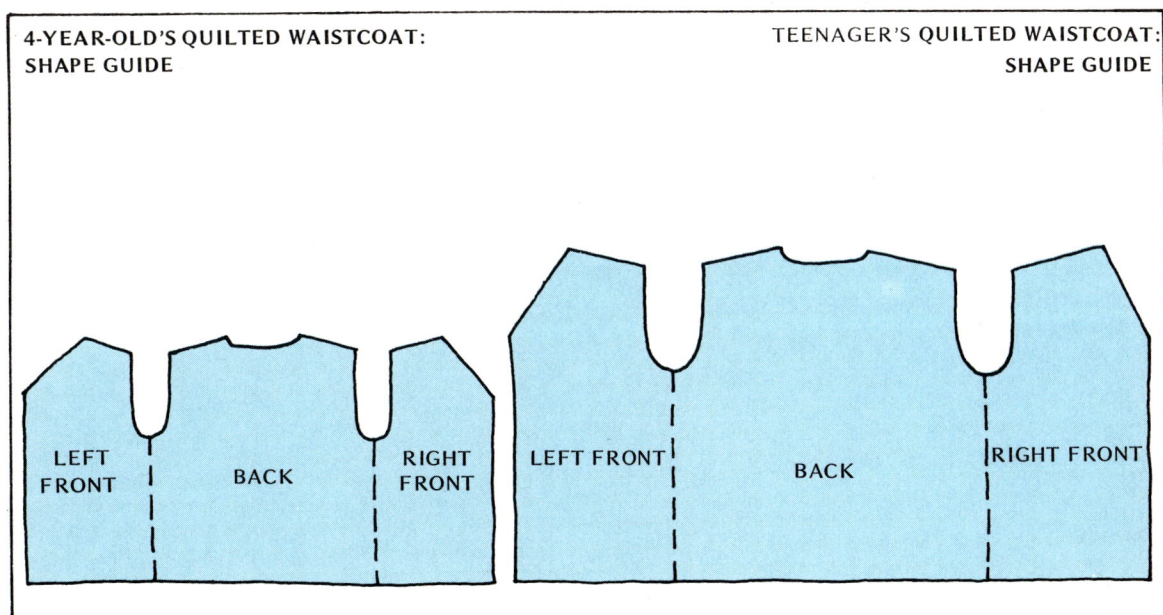

4-YEAR-OLD'S QUILTED WAISTCOAT: SHAPE GUIDE

LEFT FRONT — BACK — RIGHT FRONT

TEENAGER'S QUILTED WAISTCOAT: SHAPE GUIDE

LEFT FRONT — BACK — RIGHT FRONT

HOW TO QUILT THE WAISTCOATS
Diagram 1

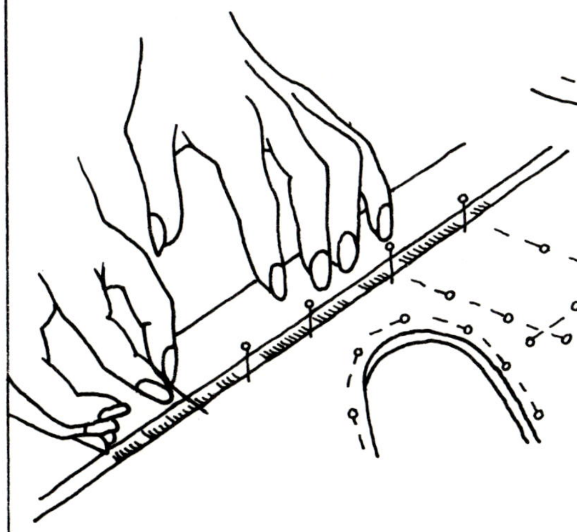

Diagram 2

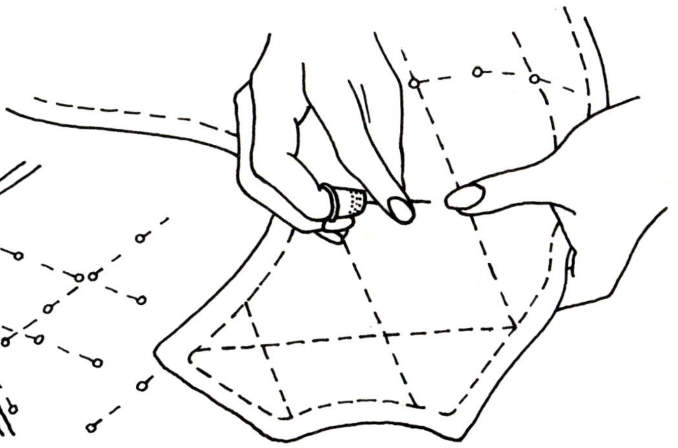

Diagram 3

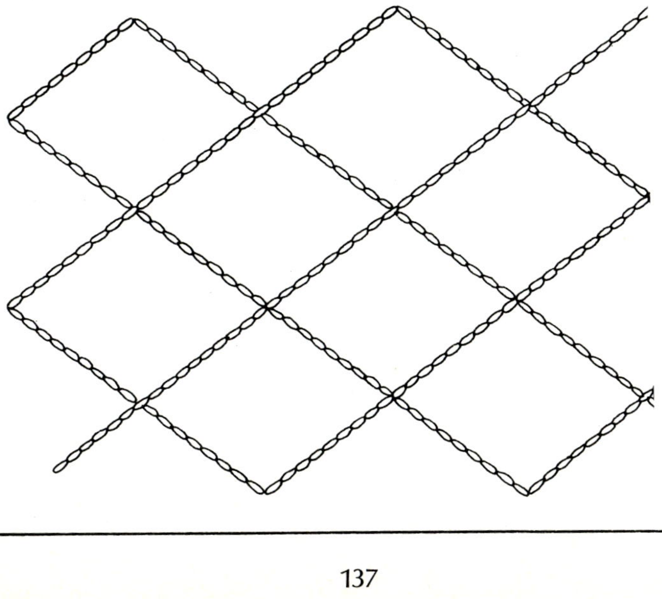

Diagram 4

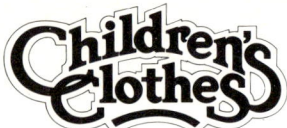

Jacquard coat

4 years and teenage

Always popular and good looking, this jacquard coat can be made to fit six sizes. And if you find it difficult to work from a chart, there are special instructions for creating the pattern on the opposite page.

Materials 5(6:7:8:10:12) 25g balls Double Knitting yarn in main colour (M); 4(4:4:5:6:6) balls in each of blue (B), green (G) and black (BL); 1(1:1:2:2:2) balls in each of yellow (Y), red (R) and orange (O); pair each $3\frac{1}{4}$mm and $3\frac{3}{4}$mm [No 10 and No 9] knitting needles.

Measurements To fit 61(66:71:76:81:86)cm [24(26:28:30:32:34) in] chest/bust; actual size 68(73:80:85:89:93)cm [$26\frac{3}{4}$($28\frac{3}{4}$:$31\frac{1}{2}$:33:35:$36\frac{1}{2}$) in]; length, 44(49:52:56:59:63)cm [$17\frac{1}{2}$($19\frac{1}{4}$:$20\frac{1}{2}$:22:$23\frac{1}{4}$:$24\frac{3}{4}$) in]; sleeve seam 31(33:36:38:41:43)cm [12(13:14:15:16:17) in].

Tension 25 sts and 33 rows to 10cm [4 in] in pattern.

Abbreviations k, knit; p, purl; st(s), stitch(es); cm, centimetre(s); in, inch(es); alt, alternate; beg, beginning; cont, continue; foll, following; inc, increase; st-st, stocking stitch; patt, pattern; dec, decrease; rep, repeat.

Size Note Figures in brackets refer to larger sizes. One figure only refers to all sizes. Square brackets contain imperial measurements.

BACK

With $3\frac{1}{4}$mm [No 10] needles and M, cast on 73(81:89:97:105:113) sts. Beg k row, work 9 rows st-st.
10th row K for hemline.
Change to $3\frac{3}{4}$mm [No 9] needles and cont in patt from chart or from patt instructions – see tip this page – until work measures 33(36:38:41:41:43)cm [13(14:15:16:16:17) in] from hemline, ending after wrong-side row.
Mark both ends of this last row as beg of armholes.
Cont in patt until armholes measure 11(13:14:15:18:20)cm [$4\frac{1}{2}$(5:$5\frac{1}{2}$:6:7:8) in] from markers, ending after wrong-side row.
Shape Shoulders Cast off 24(26:28:30:32:34) sts, patt across next 25(29:33:37:41:45) sts, cast off remaining 24(26:28:30:32:34) sts. With wrong side facing, rejoin yarn and cast off centre 25(29:33:37:41:45) sts for neck.

RIGHT FRONT

With $3\frac{1}{4}$mm [No 10] needles and M, cast on 37(41:45:49:53:57) sts. Beg k row, work 9 rows st-st.
10th row K for hemline. Change to $3\frac{3}{4}$mm [No 9] needles and cont in patt from chart or special instructions until work measures 26(27:30:32:32:34)cm [$10\frac{1}{4}$($10\frac{1}{2}$:$11\frac{3}{4}$:$12\frac{1}{2}$:$12\frac{1}{2}$:$13\frac{1}{2}$) in] from hemline, ending after a wrong-side row.**
Shape Neck Dec 1 st at beg of next row and at same edge (neck edge) on every foll 3rd row until work measures 33(36:38:41:41:43)cm [13(14:15:16:16:17) in] from hemline, ending after a wrong-side row.
Mark side edge of last row as beg of armhole.
Keeping armhole edge straight, cont in patt dec at neck edge as before until 24(26:28:30:32:34) sts remain. Cont straight until armhole matches Back to shoulder, ending after wrong-side row. Cast off.

LEFT FRONT

Work as Right Front to **.
Shape Neck Dec 1 st at end of next row and at same edge (neck edge) on next row and every foll 3rd row until work measures 33(36:38:41:41:43)cm [13(14:15:16:16:17) in] from hemline, ending after a wrong-side row.
Mark side edge of last row as beg of armhole.

Below: the chart for the Jacquard Coat at left, and a guide to the shape of the various pieces

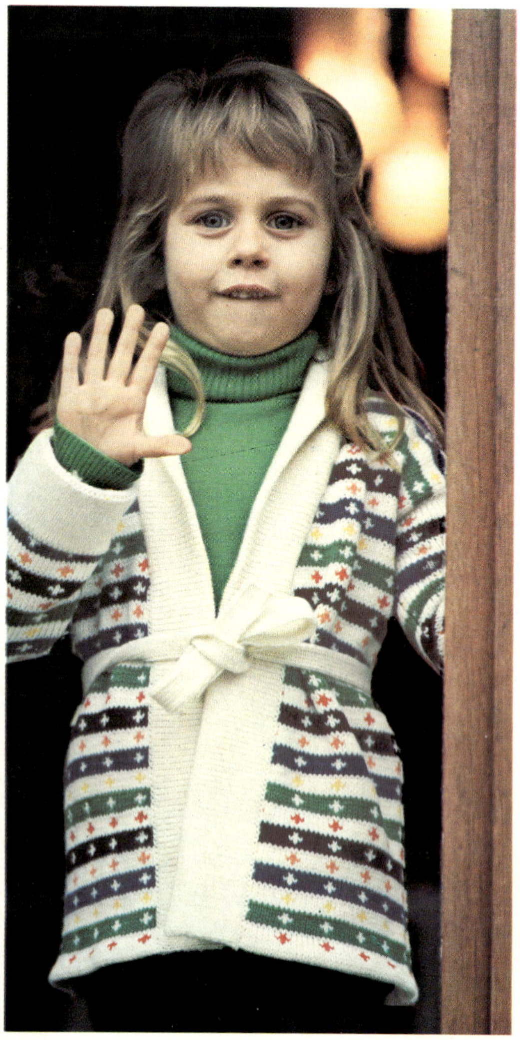

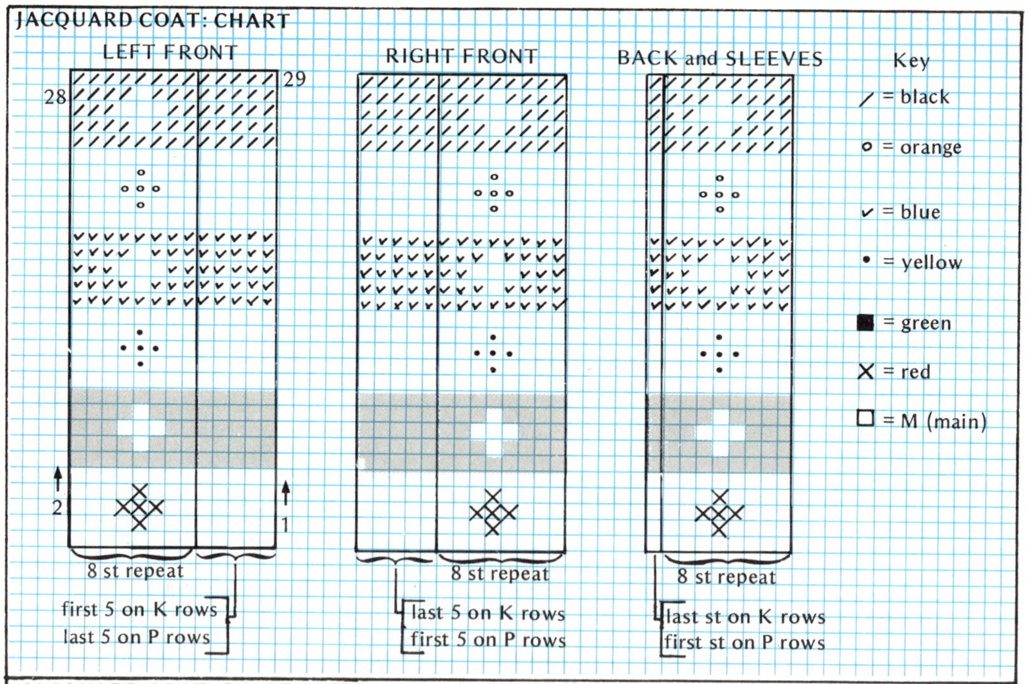
JACQUARD COAT: CHART
LEFT FRONT
RIGHT FRONT
BACK and SLEEVES
Key
/ = black
o = orange
✓ = blue
• = yellow
■ = green
X = red
□ = M (main)
28
29
2
1
8 st repeat
first 5 on K rows
last 5 on P rows
last 5 on K rows
first 5 on P rows
last st on K rows
first st on P rows

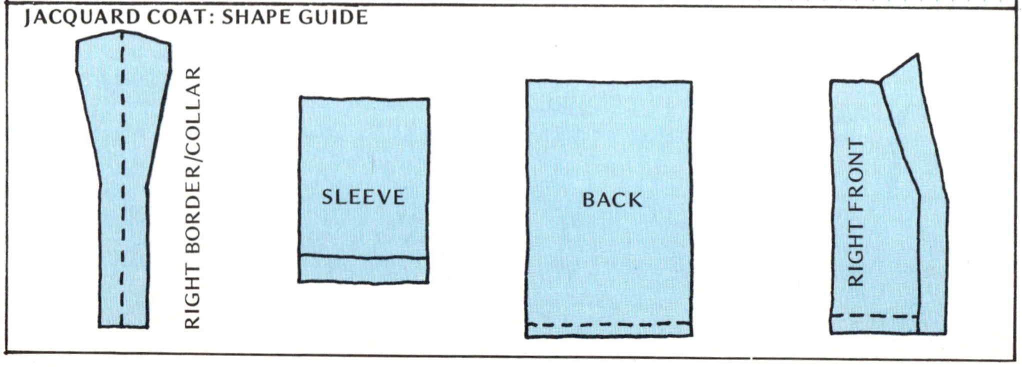
JACQUARD COAT: SHAPE GUIDE
RIGHT BORDER/COLLAR
SLEEVE
BACK
RIGHT FRONT

Keeping armhole edge straight, cont in patt dec as before at neck edge until 24(26:28:30:32:34) sts remain. Cont straight until armhole matches Back to shoulder, ending after a wrong-side row. Cast off.

SLEEVES (make 2)

With 3¼mm [No 10] needles and M, cast on 57(65:73:81:89:97) sts. Beg k row cont in st-st for 5cm [2 in] ending after a k row. **Next row** K for hemline.
Change to 3¾mm [No 9] needles and cont in st-st for 5cm [2 in] ending after a p row. Now cont in patt as Back until work measures 31(33:36:38:41:43)cm [12(13:14:15:16:17) in] ending after a wrong-side row. Cast off.

FRONT BORDERS AND COLLAR (make 2)

With 3¼mm [No 10] needles and M, cast on 17(19:21:23:25:27) sts. Cont in k1, p1 rib, inc thus: **1st row** K1, *p1, k1, rep from * to end. **2nd row** P1, *k1, p1, rep from * to end. **3rd row** Cast on 7 sts, rib to last st, inc in last st. **4th row** Rib to end. **5th row** As 3rd. **6th row** As 4th. **7th to 16th rows** Rep last 2 rows 5 times more. **17th row** Cast on 53(65:75:81:87:93) sts, rib to end.
Cont straight until border measures 5cm [2 in] from the cast-on 53(65:75:81:87:93) sts. Half collar now completed.
Work second half thus: Work 5cm [2 in] rib. **1st row** Cast off 53(65:75:81:87:93) sts, rib to end. **2nd row** Rib to end. **3rd row** Cast off 7 sts, rib to last 2 sts, k2 tog. **4th row** Rib to end. Repeat last 2 rows until 17(19:21:23:25:27) sts remain. Work 2 rows in rib. Cast off in rib.

TO MAKE UP

Press pieces following instructions on ball band.
Join shoulder seams. Join sleeve seams and side seams to markers. Sew in sleeves. Fold the hem at lower edge on ridge to wrong side and slip stitch. Fold the facing at cuff to wrong side and slip stitch in the same way.
With right sides together, sew shaped edge of border and collar to front edge and half back neck, with the straight row ends to lower edge and shaped row ends to centre back neck. Fold collar and border in half concealing the first seam and neatly slip stitch on the inside. When both pieces are sewn on, join the collar at back neck with a flat seam. Join the front border halves together at

lower edge with neat oversewing. With 3¼mm [No 10] needles and M, cast on 13 sts for the belt. Work 100cm [39½ in] in k1, p1 rib. Cast off in rib.

KNITTING WITHOUT A CHART

This jacket is worked in very simple shapes. The Back and Sleeves are in straight pieces, the two Fronts have a slope for the neck shaping. If you have trouble working from a chart, follow the patt thus:

BACK AND SLEEVE PATTERN INSTRUCTIONS

1st row With M, k. **2nd row** P1 M, (3 M, 1 R, 4 M) to end. **3rd row** K(3 M, 3 R, 2 M) to last st, 1 M. **4th row** As 2nd. **5th row** As 1st. **6th row** With G, p to end. **7th row** K(4 G, 1 M, 3 G) to last st, 1 G. **8th row** P1 G (2 G, 3 M, 3 G) to end. **9th row** As 7th. **10th row** As 6th. **11th row** As 1st. **12th row** P1 M, (3 M, 1 Y, 4 M) to end. **13th row** K(3 M, 3 Y, 2 M) to last st, 1 M. **14th row** As 12th. **15th row** As 11th. **16th row** With B, p to end. **17th row** K(4 B, 1 M, 3 B) to last st, 1 B. **18th row** P1 B, (2 B, 3 M, 3 B) to end. **19th row** As 17th. **20th row** As 16th. **21st row to 25th rows** As 1st to 5th, working O in place of R. **26th row to 30th rows** As 6th to 10th, working BL in place of G. These 30 rows form the patt for Back and Sleeves.

PATT FOR THE RIGHT FRONT
(1st, 3rd and 5th sizes only)

1st row With M, k to end. **2nd row** P5 M, (3 M, 1 R, 4 M) to end. **3rd row** K(3 M, 3 R, 2 M) to last 5 sts, 5 M. **4th row** As 2nd. **5th row** As 1st. **6th row** With G, p to end. **7th row** K(4 G, 1 M, 3 G) to last 5 sts, 5 M. **8th row** P5 G, (2 G, 3 M, 3 G) to end. **9th row** As 7th. **10th row** As 6th. **11th row** As 1st. **12th row** P5 M, (3 M, 1 Y, 4 M) to end. **13th row** K(3 M, 3 Y, 2 M) to last 5 sts, 5 M. **14th row** As 12th. **15th row** As 11th. **16th row** With B, p to end. **17th row** K(4 B, 1 M, 3 B) to last 5 sts, 5 B. **18th row** P5 B, (2 B, 3 M, 3 B) to end. **19th row** As 17th. **20th row** As 16th. **21st row to 25th rows** As 1st to 5th, working O in place of R. **26th to 30th rows** As 6th to 10th, working BL in place of G. These 30 rows form the patt.
For the Left Front, reverse the order, placing the 5 extra sts on these sizes at beg of right side rows. Thus the 2nd row reads: P(4 M, 1 R, 3 M) to last 5 sts, 5 M. **3rd row** K5 M, (2 M, 3 R, 3 M). For the 2nd, 4th and 6th sizes foll the patt instructions as for Back.

Ridged jackets

4 years to teenage

Attractive but unusual jackets that look both casual and smart at the same time.

Materials 18(20:22:24:26:28) 25g balls Double Knitting yarn; pair 3¾mm [No 9] knitting needles; 3mm [No 11] crochet hook, elastic for wrists.

Measurements To fit 61(66:71:76:81:86)cm [24(26:28:30:32:34) in] chest/bust, actual size, approx 8cm [3 in] larger; length, 43(49:54:59:61:65)cm [17(19¼:21¼:23¼:24:25½) in] at centre back; sleeve seam, 27(30:30:33:36:38:42)cm [10½(12:12:13:14:15:16½) in].

Tension 25 sts and 33 rows to 10cm [4 in] in pattern.

Continued on next page

Below: the Ridged Jackets which can be knitted in six sizes. The guide to the shapes is overleaf with knitting instructions

Ridged jackets . . . continued

Abbreviations k, knit; p, purl; st(s), stitch(es); cm, centimetre(s); in, inch(es); alt, alternate; beg, beginning; cont, continue; dec, decrease; inc, increase; st-st, stocking stitch; patt, pattern; rep, repeat; rem, remain(ing); tog, together.

Size Note Figures in brackets refer to larger sizes. One figure only refers to all sizes. Square brackets contain imperial measurements.

> This unusual pattern is easy to work but might need a little practice: cast on 27 sts and rep the 20 rows of pattern at least 3 times before you start to knit the jacket. You should note that the shaping is never made during the forming of a tuck, therefore the sts before and after a tuck will always be the same.

BACK
Cast on 90(96:102:108:114:120) sts. Beg k row, work 10 rows st-st.
11th row Make a hem by knitting the next st together with the corresponding st in the cast-on edge across the row to the end (thus folding work in half).
12th row P to end.
Now cont in patt thus: **1st to 8th rows** Beg k row, in st-st.
9th row Cut a length of brightly contrasting yarn longer than the width of the work. K the row, carrying the length of contrasting yarn at the back of the work and wrapping the working yarn back and forth round it – this holds the yarn in place to mark the row, without knitting it in.
10th to 18th rows Beg p row, in st-st.
19th row Make the ridge (or tuck) thus: Insert the point of the

right-hand needle through the back of the loop of the 1st st on the 9th (marked) row and lift this loop on to the right-hand needle; k the 9th row loop tog with the 1st st and slip both loops off left-hand needle tog. Now lift the next loop and k tog with next st all across the row.
20th row P to end. These 20 rows form the patt.
Cont in patt until 9(10:11:12:13: 14) tucks have been formed, ending after a 20th patt row. <u>Do</u> <u>not</u> count the hem at lower edge as a tuck.
Shape Raglan ****1st row** K to end.
2nd row P2 tog, p to last 2 sts, p2 tog. **3rd to 8th rows** Rep 1st and 2nd rows 3 times more. **9th to 19th rows** Without shaping work as 9th to 19th patt rows. **20th row** As 2nd . . . 80(86:92:98: 104:110) sts.
Rep last 20 rows until 34(36:38: 40:42:44) sts rem, ending after wrong-side row. Cast off.

LEFT FRONT
Cast on 45(48:51:54:57:60) sts and work as Back to ******.
Shape Raglan 1st row K to end.
2nd row P to last 2 sts, p2 tog.
3rd to 8th rows Rep 1st and 2nd rows 3 times more. **9th to 19th rows** Without shaping work as 9th to 19th patt rows. **20th row** As 2nd. Rep these 20 rows 3(3:3: 4:4:5) times more. *******
Shape Neck 1st row K to end.
2nd row Cast off 9(8:7:11:10:14), p to last 2 sts, p2 tog. **3rd row** K to end. **4th row** P2 tog, p to last 2 sts, p2 tog. **5th to 8th rows** Rep 3rd and 4th rows twice. **9th to 19th rows** Without shaping as 9th to 19th rows of patt. **20th row** As 4th. **21st and 22nd rows** As 3rd and 4th.
Rep from 3rd to 22nd rows until all sts are worked off.

RIGHT FRONT
Work as Left Front to *******, dec at beg of p rows instead of at end.
Shape Neck 1st row Cast off 9(8:7:11:10:14) sts, k to end. **2nd row** P2 tog, p to last 2 sts, p2 tog. **3rd row** K to end. **4th row** As 2nd. **5th to 8th rows** Rep 3rd and 4th rows twice. **9th to 19th rows** Without shaping as 9th to 19th rows of patt. **20th row** As 4th. **21st and 22nd rows** As 3rd and 4th.
Rep last 20 rows until all sts are worked off.

SLEEVES (make 2)
Cast on 60(66:72:78:84:90) sts. Work the hem and first ridge (tuck) 20 rows of patt as Back.
Now rep the 20-patt rows 7(8:8: 9:10:11:12) times more, ending after a 20th row.
Shape Raglan Work as given for Back until 4(6:8:10:12:14) sts rem, ending after a wrong-side row, completing the tuck where necessary. Cast off.
Neck Border (*first 3 sizes*) Cast on 10 sts and work 110 cm [43¼ in] in st-st. Cast off.
Neck Border (*last 3 sizes*) Cast on 15 sts and work 200cm [78 in] in st-st. Cast off.

TO MAKE UP
With right sides together join the raglan seams of Back and Fronts to raglan shaping on Sleeves. Make a back-stitch seam, catching in the ends of the tucks into the seam. Turn to right side. Join the side and sleeve seams in the same way, leaving the hem of sleeve free.
Press following instructions on ball band.
Fold the neck border in half lengthways with the wrong side inside. Place the centre to the centre back neck and tack to neck edge with right side of border to right side of neck. Sew this seam, then fold over the border and with flat seam, sew to inside of neck, concealing the first seam. With fine oversewing, join the two extensions of border as neck ties.
Insert elastic to fit wrists through the cuff hem and join into a circle. Neatly join the hem ends. With right side facing, work 1 row double crochet along each front edge, without catching in the ends of the tucks. The tucks and hems at front edge may be neatly oversewn if desired.

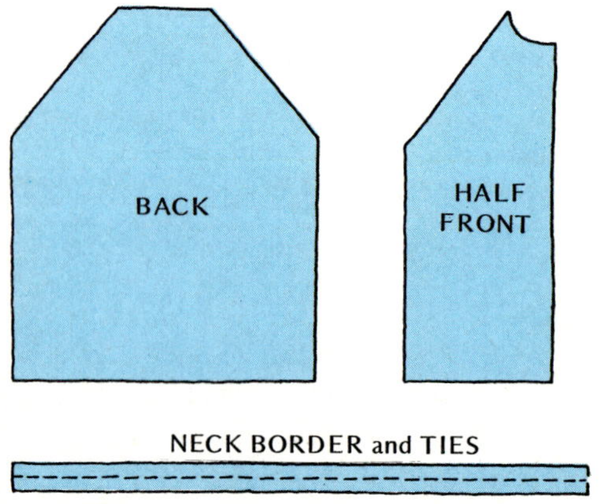

Anchor sweaters
4 years to teenager

Traditional Guernsey "fisherman's" sweaters in sizes for all the family from the smallest to the largest. There are no armholes in the usual way but the sleeves and neckband are joined in with a gusset for comfort. The shoulders are cast off in a special way to give the characteristic ridge.

Materials 12(13:14:15:16) 25g balls Double Knitting yarn; pairs of 3mm, 3¼mm and 3¾mm [No 11, 10 and No 9] knitting needles; set of four double-pointed 3mm [No 11] needles.

Measurements To fit 61(66:71:76: 81)cm [24(26:28:30:32) in] chest/bust; sleeve seam, 29(33:37: 41:43)cm [11½(13:14½:16:17) in]; length, 37(39:42:46:51)cm [14½ (15½:16½:18:20) in] adjustable.

Tension 26 sts and 34 rows in st-st to 10cm square [4 in].

Abbreviations k, knit; p, purl; st(s), stitch(es); cm, centimetre(s); in, inch(es); alt, alternate; beg, beginning; cont, continue; st-st, stocking stitch; inc, increase; dec, decrease; rem, remain(ing); foll, following; rep, repeat.

Size Note Figures in brackets refer to larger sizes. Where only one figure is given, this refers to all sizes. Square brackets contain imperial measurements.

BACK
With 3mm [No 11] needles, cast on 86(94:98:106:114) sts. Work 5cm [2 in] k2, p2 rib thus: **1st row** K2, *p2, k2; rep from * to end. **2nd row** P2, *k2, p2; rep from * to end.
Change to 3¾mm [No 9] needles. Beg k row, cont in st-st until work measures 35(37:40:44:49)cm [13¾ (14½:15¾:17½:19¼) in] from beg,

---

Above right: a family affair – Anchor Sweaters to knit for child or adult. Instructions for the three larger sizes are on page 142. Each row of the design is given but there is a chart on page 143 for the anchor motif

---

RIDGED JACKETS: SHAPE GUIDE

BACK

HALF FRONT

SLEEVE

NECK BORDER and TIES

1st row K42(46:48:52:56), p2, k42(46:48:52:56).

2nd row P42(46:48:52:56), p2, p42(46:48:52:56).

3rd row K41(45:47:51:55), p4, k41(45:47:51:55).

4th row P41(45:47:51:55), p4, p to end.

5th row K40(44:46:50:54), p1, k1, p2, k1, p1, k to end.

6th row P40(44:46:50:54), p1, k4, p1, p to end.

7th row K39(43:45:49:53), p1, k1, p4, k1, p1, k to end.

8th row P39(43:45:49:53), p1, k6, p1, p to end.

9th row K38(42:44:48:52), p1, k1, p6, k1, p1, k to end.

10th row P38(42:44:48:52), p1, k8, p1, p to end.

11th row K37(41:43:47:51), p1, k1, p3, k2, p3, k1, p1, k to end.

12th row P37(41:43:47:51), p1, k4, p2, k4, p1, p to end.

13th row K36(40:42:46:50), p1, k1, p3, k4, p3, k1, p1, k to end.

14th row P36(40:42:46:50), p1, k4, p4, k4, p1, p to end.

15th row K35(39:41:45:49), p1, k1, p5, k2, p5, k1, p1, k to end.

16th row P35(39:41:45:49), p1, k6, p2, k6, p1, p to end.

17th row K34(38:40:44:48), p1, k1, p3, k8, p3, k1, p1, k to end.

18th row P34(38:40:44:48), p1, k4, p8, k4, p1, p to end.

19th row K33(37:39:43:47), p1, k1, p2, k12, p2, k1, p1, k to end.

20th row P33(37:39:43:47), p1, k3, p12, k3, p1, p to end.

21st row K32(36:38:42:46), p1, k1, p2, k2, p4, k2, p4, k2, p2, k1, p1, k to end.

22nd row P32(36:38:42:46), p1, k3, p2, k4, p2, k4, p2, k3, p1, p to end.

23rd row K31(35:37:41:45), p1, k1, p2, k2, p5, k2, p5, k2, p2, k1, p1, k to end.

24th row P31(35:37:41:45), p1, k3, p2, k5, p2, k5, p2, k3, p1, p to end.

25th row K30(34:36:40:44), p1, k1, p3, k2, p5, k2, p5, k2, p3, k1, p1, k to end.

26th row P30(34:36:40:44), p1, k4, p2, k5, p2, k5, p2, k4, p1, p to end.

27th row K29(33:35:39:43), p1, k1, p4, k3, p4, k2, p4, k3, p4, k1, p1, k to end.

28th row P29(33:35:39:43), p1, k5, p3, k4, p2, k4, p3, k5, p1, p to end.

29th row K29(33:35:39:43), p1, k1, p4, k1, p6, k2, p6, k1, p4, k1, p1, k to end.

30th row P29(33:35:39:43), p1, k5, p1, k6, p2, k6, p1, k5, p1, p to end.

31st row K29(33:35:39:43), p1, k1, p11, k2, p11, k1, p1, k to end.

Continued on next page

---

ending after a p row. Allow more or less here if different length is required.

Shape Neck 1st row K30(32:33: 36:38) sts, turn and cont on this set of sts only.

2nd row Cast off 3 sts (neck edge), p to end. **3rd row** K. **4th row** Cast off 3 sts, p to end. **5th row** K. **6th row** Cast off 2(2:1:2:4) sts, p to end. Leave rem 22(24:26: 28:28) sts on a spare needle. These will be cast off later for shoulder in a special way.

With right side of work facing, join yarn to rem sts at neck edge.

Slip the centre 26(30:32:34:38) sts on to a spare needle to be used later in the neckband, k to end. Cont on the last set of 30(32:33:36:38) sts for other side of neck shaping. **1st row** P. **2nd row** Cast off 3 sts, k to end. **3rd row** P. **4th row** Cast off 3 sts, k to end. **5th row** P. **6th row** Cast off 2(2:1:2:4) sts, k to end. Leave rem 22(24:26:28:28) sts on a spare needle to be cast off later for shoulder in a special way.

FRONT

With 3mm [No 11] needles cast on

86(94:98:106:114) sts. Work 5cm [2 in] k2, p2 rib thus: **1st row** K2, *p2, k2; rep from * to end. **2nd row** P2, *k2, p2; rep from * to end. Change to 3¾mm [No 9] needles. Cont in st-st until work measures 19(21:24:28:33)cm [7½(8¼:9½:11: 13) in] from beg, ending after a p row. Adjust length here if necessary, noting that the work at this stage must be 16cm [6¼ in] less than Back before the neck shaping begins.

Now work the Anchor Design: centre 28 sts for motif, rem sts in st-st:

Anchor sweaters . . . continued

32nd row P29(33:35:39:43), p1, k12, p2, k12, p1, p to end.

33rd to 36th rows Rep last 2 rows twice more.

37th row K29(33:35:39:43), p1, k1, p10, k4, p10, k1, p1, k to end.

38th row P29(33:35:39:43), p1, k11, p4, k11, p1, p to end.

39th row K29(33:35:39:43), p1, k1, p9, k6, p9, k1, p1, k to end.

40th row P29(33:35:39:43), p1, k10, p6, k10, p1, p to end.

41st row K29(33:35:39:43), *p1, k1*, rep from * to * 4 times more, p1, k6, p1, **k1, p1**, rep from ** to ** 4 times more, k to end.

42nd row P29(33:35:39:43), p1, *p1, k1*, rep from * to * 4 times more, k1, p6, **k1, p1**, rep from ** to ** 4 times more, p1, p to end.

43rd row K29(33:35:39:43), p1, k1, p11, k2, p11, k1, p1, k to end.

44th row P29(33:35:39:43), p1, k12, p2, k12, p1, p to end.

45th to 48th rows Rep last 2 rows twice more.

49th row K29(33:35:39:43), p1, k1, p6, k12, p6, k1, p1, k to end.

50th row P29(33:35:39:43), p1, k6, p14, k6, p1, p to end.

51st row K29(33:35:39:43), p1, k1, p4, k16, p4, k1, p1, k to end.

52nd row P29(33:35:39:43), p1, k4, k18, k4, p1, p to end.

53rd row K29(33:35:39:43), p1, k1, p2, k20, p2, k1, p1, k to end.

54th row P29(33:35:39:43), p1, k1, p2, k22, p2, k1, p1, p to end.

55th row K29(33:35:39:43), p1, k1, p24, k1, p1, k to end.

56th row P29(33:35:39:43), p1, k28, p1, k29(33:35:39:43) to end. End of Anchor pattern. Work should match Back to beginning of neck shaping.

Shape Neck 1st row K30(32:33:36:38) sts, turn and cont on these sts only. **2nd row** Cast off 4 sts, p to end. **3rd row** K26(28:29:32:34). **4th row** Cast off 2 sts, p to end. **5th row** K to end. **6th row** Cast off 2(2:1:2:4) sts, p to end. Leave rem 22(24:26:28:28) sts on a spare needle to be cast off later in a special way.

With right side of work facing, slip centre 26(30:32:34:38) sts on to a spare needle to be used later in neckband, join yarn to rem 30(32:33:36:38) sts and k to end. Complete this side to match the first side thus: **1st row** P to end. **2nd row** Cast off 4 sts, k to end. **3rd row** P26(28:29:32:34). **4th row** Cast off 2 sts, k to end. **5th row** P to end. **6th row** Cast off 2(2:1:2:4) sts, k to end. Leave rem 22(24:26:28:28) sts on a spare needle to be cast off later in a special way.

Cast-off Shoulders This is the traditional way of casting off the shoulder sts on "Fisherman's" sweaters and forms the characteristic ridge: With the wrong sides of Back and Front together, slip 22(24:26:28:28) sts purlwise (ie, inserting the needle as if you were going to purl the st) from both Back and Front needles on to a 3rd needle, taking 1 st from the Back, then 1 st from the Front alternately . . . 44(48:52:56:56) sts now on the 3rd needle; turn the work round to place the 3rd needle in the left hand and work across these sts – P2 tog to end . . . 22(24:26:28:28) sts. Turn the work again and cast off these sts in the normal way. Cast off the sts from the other two needles in the same way.

If you prefer, you can cast off the sts in the usual way and make a back-stitch seam, this time with the right sides of the work together.

SLEEVES

With 3¼mm [No 10] needles, cast on 44(48:48:52:52) sts. Cont in k2, p2 rib for 5cm [2 in]. Change to 3¾mm [No 9] needles. Cont in st-st, inc 1 st at both ends of 5th row foll and every foll 6th row to 62(66:78:82:92) sts. Cont in st-st without shaping until sleeve measures 29(33:37:41:43)cm [11½(13: 14½:16:17) in] ending after a p row. Cast off. Work another sleeve in the same way.

UNDERARM GUSSETS (make 2)

With 3¾mm [No 9] needles, cast on 1 st. **1st row** (K1, p1, k1) all into the one st . . . 3 sts now on the needle for all sizes. **2nd row** P3. **3rd row** Inc in 1st st, k1, inc in last st. **4th row** P5. **5th row** Inc in first st, k to last st, inc in last st. **6th row** P to end. Rep last 2 rows to 13(15:17:19:21) sts, ending after a p row. Now cont in st-st, dec 1 st at both ends of every k row until 1 st remains. Fasten off.

NECKBAND

With right side of work facing, beg by working a gusset at each side of neck: Join yarn at inner edge of the left shoulder cast-off edge. Pick up and k 1 st from Back neck shaping, 1 st from Front neck shaping; turn and p these 2 sts, turn.

2nd two rows Pick up and k 1 st from Back neck shaping, k2, pick up and k 1 st from Front neck shaping, turn, p4, turn.

Cont in st-st in this way, picking up 1 st more on Back and Front neck shapings on every right-side row to 18 sts – 9 sts each from Back and Front. Leave sts on a spare needle for the time being. Work the other gusset in the same way, but taking 1 st from the Front, then 1 st from the Back, to 18 sts. Leave these sts on a spare needle.

Note Pick up and k the sts evenly, the final row being in line with the centre front and back neck sts which are on spare needles. Now with set of four double-pointed needles, arrange all the sts at neck on to three needles . . . 88(96:100:104:112) sts. Using the 4th needle, work 10 rounds k2, p2 rib. Cast off.

TO MAKE UP

Press following instructions on ball band.

With right side inside, join the Sleeve seams, leaving enough opening at the cast-off top edge to allow for the insertion of one of the points of the diamond shaped gusset. Use a back-stitch seam and sew in the point of the gusset, right sides together. The opening left at the Sleeve seam now attaches to the halfway point of the gusset. The second half of the gusset will be inserted in the top of the side seam.

With right sides together, tack the side seams – it is traditional to begin immediately above the rib at lower edge. You must leave an opening of 11(13:15:16:18)cm [4½(5:6:6½:7) in] at the top to shoulder seam to allow for the armhole. Before sewing these tacked edges, take the Sleeves, also right side inside, and place the gusset to the top of the tacked side seam. Open the tacking a little at the underarm edge to insert the free edges of the gusset. First back-stitch the remaining half of the diamond shape into the top of your side seam, one edge to the Front and one edge to the Back – to do this the gusset will be folded in half, the one half into the side seam and the other half in the top of the Sleeve. When the gussets are in place, back-stitch the side seams down the remaining seam below the gusset to the top of the rib at lower edge. Fasten off securely to prevent the seam opening at this edge.

With right sides facing, pin the remaining Sleeve cast-off edge in place in the armhole opening and back-stitch in place. Sew in both sleeves in this way.

Anchor sweaters

Teenage to adult

Illustrated on page 141

Materials 18(19:21) 25g balls Double Knitting yarn; pairs of 3mm, 3¼mm and 3¾mm [No 11, No 10 and No 9] knitting needles; set of four double-pointed 3mm [No 11] knitting needles.

Measurements To fit 86(91:97)cm [34(36:38) in] chest; sleeve seam 43(43:46)cm [17(17:18) in]; length, 58(61:66)cm [23(24:26) in] (adjustable).

Tension 26 sts and 34 rows in st-st to 10cm [4 in] square.

Abbreviations k, knit; p, purl; st(s), stitch(es); cm, centimetre(s); in, inch(es); alt, alternate; beg, beginning; cont, continue; st-st, stocking stitch; inc, increas(e)ing; dec, decreas(e)ing; rep, repeat; rem, remain(ing); foll, following.

Size Note Figures in brackets refer to larger sizes. Where only one figure is given, this refers to all sizes. Square brackets contain imperial measurements.

BACK

With 3mm [No 11] needles, cast on 122(126:134) sts. Work 5cm [2 in] k2, p2 rib thus: **1st row** K2, *p2, k2; rep from * to end. **2nd row** P2, *k2, p2; rep from * to end, inc 1 st at end of *last* row only . . . 123(127:135) sts. Change to 3¾mm [No 9] needles. Beg k row, cont in st-st until work measures 56 (59:64)cm [22(23¼:25) in] from beg, ending after a p row. Allow more or less here if required.

Shape Neck 1st row K42(44:48) sts, turn and cont on this set of sts only. **2nd row** Cast off 3 sts (neck edge) p to end. **3rd row** K to end. **4th row** Cast off 3 sts, p to end. **5th row** K to end. **6th row** Cast off 4(4:6) sts, p to end. Leave rem 32(34:36) sts on a spare needle to be cast off later for shoulder in a special way.

With right side of work facing, join yarn on rem sts at neck edge. Slip the centre 39 sts on to a spare needle to be used later in the neckband, k to end. Cont on last set of 42(44:48) sts for other side of neck shaping. **1st row** P to end. **2nd row** Cast off 3 sts, k to end. **3rd row** P to end. **4th row** Cast off 3 sts, k to end. **5th row** P to end. **6th row** Cast off 4(4:6)

k to end. Leave rem 32(34:36) sts on a spare needle to be cast off later for shoulder in a special way.

FRONT

With 3mm [No 11] needles cast on 122(126:134) sts. Work 5cm [2 in] k2, p2 rib thus: **1st row** K2, *p2, k2; rep from * to end. **2nd row** P2, *k2, p2; rep from * to end, inc 1 st at end of *last* row only ... 123 (127:135) sts. Change to 3¾mm [No 9] needles. Beg k row, cont in st-st until work measures 36 (39:44)cm [14(15½:17½) in] ending after a p row. Adjust length here if necessary, noting that work at this stage must be 20cm [8 in] less than Back before the neck shaping begins.

Now work the Anchor Design; Centre 39 sts for motif, rem sts in st-st: **1st row** K to end. **2nd row** P42(44:48), p19, k1, p19, p to end. **3rd row** K to end. **4th row** P42(44:48), p18, k3, p18, p to end. **5th row** K42(44:48), k19, p1, k19, k to end. **6th row** P42(44:48), p17, k2, p1, k2, p17, p to end. **7th row** K to end. **8th row** P42(44:48), p16, k1, p1, k3, p1, k1, p16, p to end. **9th row** K42(44:48), k17, p5, k17, k to end. **10th row** P42(44:48), p15, k1, p1, k5, p1, k1, p15, p to end. **11th row** K42(44:48), k16, p7, k16, k to end. **12th row** P42(44:48), p14, k1, p1, k7, p1, k1, p14, p to end. **13th row** K42(44:48), k15, p4, k1, p4, k15, k to end. **14th row** P42(44:48), p13, k1, p1, k4, p1, k4, p1, k1, p13, p to end. **15th row** K42(44:48), k14, p4, k3, p4, k14, k to end. **16th row** P42(44:48), p12, k1, p1, k4, p3, k4, p1, k1, p12, p to end. **17th row** K42(44:48), k13, p4, k5, p4, k13, k to end. **18th row** P42(44:48), p11, k1, p1, k4, p5, k4, p1, k1, p11, p to end. **19th row** K42(44:48), k12, p4, k7, p4, k12, k to end. **20th row** P42(44:48), p10, k1, p1, k4, p7, k4, p1, k1, p10, p to end. **21st row** K42(44:48), k11, p6, k5, p6, k11, k to end. **22nd row** P42(44:48), p9, k1, p1, k6, p5, k6, p1, k1, p9, p to end. **23rd row** K42(44:48), k10, p8, k3, p8, k10, p to end. **24th row** P42(44:48), p8, k1, p1, k8, p3, k8, p1, k1, p8, p to end. **25th row** K42(44:48), k9, p9, k3, p9, k9, k to end. **26th row** P42(44:48), p7, k1, p1, k5, p11, k5, p1, k1, p7, p to end. **27th row** K42(44:48), k8, p6, k11, p6, k8, k to end. **28th row** P42(44:48), p6, k1, p1, k4, p14, k4, p1, k1, p6, p to end. **29th row** K42(44:48), k7, p5, k15, p5, k7, k to end. **30th row** P42(44:48), p5, k1, p1, k4, p3, k2, p7, k2, p3, k4, p1, k1, p5, p to end. **31st row** K42(44:48), k6, p5, k3, p2, k7, p2, k3, p5, k6, k to

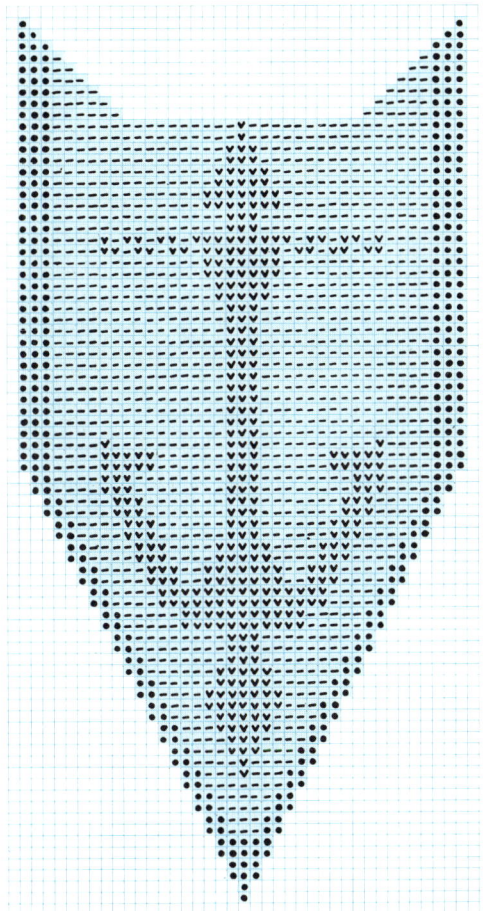

ANCHOR MOTIF: PATTERN

Above: the anchor design shown in chart form – the larger sizes are worked across the centre 39 stitches, the smaller sizes across 28 stitches Below: a close-up of the anchor design. You'll find the shape guide overleaf

end. **32nd row** P42(44:48), p4, k1, p1, k4, p3, k4, p5, k4, p3, k4, p1, k1, p4, p to end. **33rd row** K42(44:48), k5, p5, k3, p4, k5, p4, k3, p5, k5, k to end. **34th row** P42(44:48), p3, k1, p1, k4, p3, k6, p3, k6, p3, k4, p1, k1, p3, p to end. **35th row** K42(44:48), k4, p5, k3, p6, k3, p6, k3, p5, k4, k to end. **36th row** P42(44:48), p2, k1, p1, k4, p3, k7, p3, k7, p3, k4, p1, k1, p2, p to end. **37th row** K42(44:48), k3, p5, k3, p7, k3, p7, k3, p5, k3, k to end. **38th row** P42(44:48), p1, k1, p1, k4, p3, k8, p3, k8, p3, k4, p1, k1, p1, p to end. **39th row** K42(44:48), k2, p5, k3, p8, k3, p8, k3, p5, k2, k to end. **40th row** P42(44:48), k1, p1, k5, p5, k6, p3, k6, p5, k5, p1, k1, p to end. **41st row** K42(44:48), k1, p1, k1, p4, k5, p6, k3, p6, k5, p4, k1, p1, k1, k to end. **42nd row** P42(44:48), k1, p1, k5, p1, k10, p3, k10, p1, k5, p1, k1, p to end. **43rd row** K42(44:48), k1, p1, k1, p15, k3, p15, k1, p1, k1, k to end. **44th row** P42(44:48), k1, p1, k16, p3, k16, p1, k1, p to end. **45th to 54th rows** Rep last 2 rows 5 times more. **55th row** K42(44:48), k1, p1, k1, p14, k5, p14, k1, p1, k1, k to end. **56th row** P42(44:48), k1, p1, k15, p5, k15, p1, k1, p to end. **57th row** K42(44:48), k1, p1, k1, p13, k7, p13, k1, p1, k1, k to end. **58th row** P42(44:48), k1, p1, k14, p7, k14, p1, k1, p to end. **59th row** K42(44:48), k1, p1, k1, p4, k2, p1, k2, p1, k2, p1, k7, p1, k2, p1, k2, p1, k2, p4, k1, p1, k1, k to end. **60th row** P42(44:48), k1, p1, k5, p1, k1, p2, k1, p2, k1, p9, k1, p2, k1, p2, k1, p1, k5, p1, k1, p to end.

61st and 62nd rows As 43rd and 44th rows.

63rd and 64th rows As 57th and 58th rows.

65th and 66th rows As 55th and 56th rows.

67th and 68th rows As 43rd and 44th rows. **69th row** K42(44:48), k1, p1, k1, p16, k1, p16, k1, p1, k1, k to end. **70th row** P42(44:48), k1, p1, k17, p1, k17, p1, k1, p to end. End of Anchor pattern. Work should match Back to beg of neck shaping.

Shape Neck 1st row K42(44:48) sts, turn and cont on this set of sts only. **2nd row** Cast off 4 sts, p to end. **3rd row** K to end. **4th row** As 2nd row. **5th row** As 3rd. **6th row** Cast off 2(2:4) sts, p to end. Leave rem sts on a spare needle to be cast off later for shoulder. With right side of work facing, join yarn to rem sts at neck edge. Slip centre 39 sts on to a spare needle to be used later in the neckband, k to end. Cont on last set of sts for other side of neck

Continued on next page

shaping: **1st row** P to end. **2nd row** Cast off 4 sts, k to end. **3rd and 4th rows** Rep last 2 rows. **5th row** As 1st row. **6th row** Cast off 2(2:4) sts, k to end. Leave rem sts on a spare needle to be cast off later.

Cast-off Shoulders This is the traditional way of casting off the shoulder sts on "Fisherman's" sweaters and forms the characteristic ridge: With wrong sides of Back and Front together, slip the 42(44:48) shoulder sts purlwise (ie, inserting the needle as if you were going to purl the st) from both Back and Front needles on to a 3rd needle, taking 1 st from the Back, then 1 st from the Front alternately . . . 84(88:96) sts now on 3rd needle; turn the work round to place the 3rd needle in the left hand and work across these sts: p2 tog to end . . . 42(44:48) sts. Turn the work again and cast off these sts in the normal way.

If you prefer you can cast off the sts in the usual way and make a back-stitch seam, this time with the right sides together.

SLEEVES

With 3¼mm [No 10] needles cast on 56(60:64) sts. Work 5cm [2 in] k2, p2 rib. Change to 3¾mm [No 9] needles. Cont in st-st, inc 1 st at both ends of 5th row foll and every foll 6th row to 92(96:100) sts. Cont in st-st without shaping until sleeve measures 43(43:46) cm [17(17:18) in] ending after a p row. Cast off. Work another sleeve in the same way.

UNDERARM GUSSETS (make 2)

With 3¾mm [No 9] needles, cast on 1 st. **1st row** (K1, p1, k1) all into the one st . . . 3 sts now on the needle for all sizes. **2nd row** P3. **3rd row** Inc in 1st st, k1, inc in last st. **4th row** P5. **5th row** Inc in 1st st, k to last st, inc in last st. **6th row** P to end. Rep last 2 rows to

29(31:33) sts, ending after a p row. Now cont in st-st, dec 1 st at both ends of every k row until 1 st remains. Fasten off.

NECKBAND

With right side of work facing, beg by working a gusset at each side of neck: Join yarn at inner edge of the left shoulder cast-off edge. Pick up and k 1 st from Back neck shaping, 1 st from Front neck shaping; turn and p these 2 sts, turn. **2nd two rows** Pick up and k 1 st from Back neck shaping, k2, pick up and k 1 st from Front neck shaping, turn, p4, turn. Cont in st-st in this way, picking up 1 st more on Back and Front neck shapings on every right-side row to 18 sts — 9 sts each from Back and Front. Leave sts on a spare needle. Work the other gusset in the same way, taking 1 st from the Front, then 1 st from the Back to 18 sts and leave these sts on a spare needle.

Note Pick up and k the sts evenly, the final row being in line with the centre front and back neck sts which are on spare needles. Now with set of four double-pointed needles, arrange all the sts at neck on to three needles . . . 120(124:132) sts. Using the 4th needle, work 10 rounds k2, p2, rib. Cast off.

TO MAKE UP

Press following instructions on ball band.

With right side inside, join Sleeve seams, leaving enough opening at the cast-off top edge to allow for the insertion of one of the points of the diamond shaped gusset. Use a back-stitch seam and sew in the point of the gusset, right sides together. The opening left at the Sleeve seam now attaches to the halfway point of the gusset. The second half of the gusset will be inserted in the top

of the side seam.

With right sides together, tack the side seams — it is traditional to begin immediately above the rib at lower edge. You must leave an opening of 19(20:22)cm [7½(8:8½) in] at the top to shoulder seam to allow for the armhole. Before sewing these tacked edges, take the Sleeves, also right side inside, and place the gusset to the top of the tacked seams. Open the tacking a little at the underarm edge to insert the free edges of the gusset. First back-stitch the remaining half of the diamond shape into the top of your side seam, one edge to the Front and one edge to the Back — to do this the gusset will be folded in half, the one half into the side seam and the other half in the top of the Sleeve. When the gussets are in place, back-stitch the side seams down the remaining seam below the gusset to the top of the rib at lower edge. Fasten off securely to prevent the seam opening at this edge.

With right side facing, pin the remaining Sleeve cast-off edge in place in the armhole opening and back-stitch in place. Sew both sleeves in this way. Remove pins and tackings.

Below: the shape guide for the Anchor Sweaters
Right: attractive shaping on the skirt and sleeves makes this a dress for best. It is knitted on long and short circular needles

Sunday best dress

5 to 8 years

Good looking and easy to wear, this dress has a nicely flared skirt and attractive shaping.

Materials 13(14) 25g balls 4-ply yarn in turquoise (C1); 2(2) in Ecru (C2) and 1(1) in dark blue (C3); pair 3¾mm [No 9] knitting needles; 3¾mm [No 9] long and short circular needles; medium size crochet hook; 15cm [6 in] zip.

Measurements To fit a 64(69)cm [25(27) in] chest.

Tension 26 sts 10cm [4 in].

Abbreviations k, knit; p, purl; st(s), stitch(es); st-st, stocking stitch; rep, repeat; sl, slip; psso, pass slip st over; cont, continue; rem, remain(ing); dec, decrease; tog, together; cm, centimetre(s); in, inch(es); beg, beginning; rnd, round.

Size Note Figures in brackets refer to larger size. One figure only refers to both sizes. Square brackets contain imperial measurements.

BACK AND FRONT

Using long circular needle and C2, cast on 370(390) sts and k in rnds for 2cm [¾ in].

Next rnd P for hemline.

Work in rnds — all k, for 2cm [¾ in]. Break off C2. Join on C1.

Next rnd *K2 tog, k33(35), sl 1, k1, psso. Rep from * to end of rnd . . . 20 sts decreased.

Rep this dec rnd 6(4) times more at 3cm [1¼ in] intervals, allowing 2 sts less between decs each time, then 3(5) times at 5cm [2 in] intervals . . . 170(190) sts. Cont straight until work measures 41(46)cm [16(18) in] from hemline (or length required).

Change to 3¾mm [No 9] knitting needles and work Back and Front separately in rows of st-st. **Next row** K85(95) for Back, turn and leave rem sts on spare needle.

Shape Armholes At beg of every row cast off 3 sts twice, 2 sts twice and 1 st 2(4) times . . . 73(81) sts. Work straight until Back measures 44(50)cm [17½(19¾) in] from beg, ending after a p row.

Divide for Opening Next row K36(40), cast off next st, k to end.

Continued on page 146

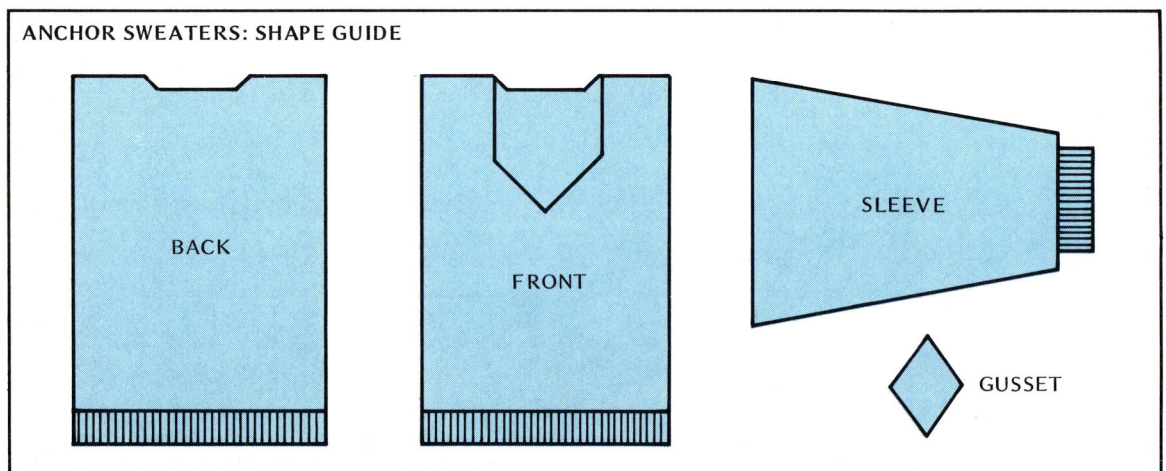

ANCHOR SWEATERS: SHAPE GUIDE

BACK

FRONT

SLEEVE

GUSSET

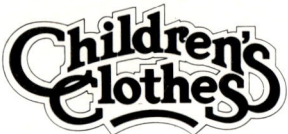

Sunday best dress . . . continued

Cont on last 36(40) sts until armhole measures 14·5(15)cm [$5\frac{3}{4}$(6) in] from beg, ending at armhole edge.
Shape Shoulder Cast off 5(6) sts on next row and next 3 alt rows. Leave rem 16 sts on safety-pin. Go back to other sts, and work in the same way, shaping shoulder after a p row.
Return to Front sts and work as for Back until armhole measures 9·5(10)cm [$3\frac{3}{4}$(4) in] ending after a p row . . . 73(81) sts.
Shape Neck Next row K30(34), turn and leave other sts on spare needle. Now work on the 30(34) sts, casting off at beg of p rows, 4 sts once, 2 sts twice, and 1 st twice. Work straight until Front measures as Back to shoulder ending after a p row, then shape shoulder as for Back.
Go back to other sts, slip centre 13 sts on to safety-pin, rejoin yarn at neck edge and at beg of k rows, cast off 4 sts once, 2 sts twice and 1 st twice. Cont as for other side shaping shoulder after a p row.

SLEEVES
Using C1, and $3\frac{3}{4}$mm [No 9] needles cast on 64(72) sts and work in st-st for 3 rows.
Shape Top At beg of every row cast off 2 sts 20(24) times, 3 sts twice and 4 sts twice. Cast off.

TO MAKE UP
Press work on wrong side following ball band instructions. Using back-stitch join shoulders. Sew in sleeves, sewing the 3 rows at lower edge to armhole shaping, but leave free the 2 sets of 3 sts and 2 sts cast off at armhole edge. Using C2 and short circular needle and with right side facing, pick up and k72 sts along cast on edge of sleeve, and 10 sts along armhole edge. K in rnds for 2cm [$\frac{3}{4}$ in] then p next rnd for hemline. K in rnds for 2cm [$\frac{3}{4}$ in]. Cast off loosely.
Neckband Holding work right side towards you and using short circular needle and C2, beg at left back opening. K across the 16sts, pick up and k17(19) sts to Front Neck, k13 sts across centre, pick up and k17(19) sts to shoulder, then k across the 16 sts of Right Back. Work neckband as sleeve-band. Turn all hems to wrong side at p ridge and catch-stitch neatly. Using crochet hook work in dc along both Back Neck opening edges. Sew in zip. Using C3, embroider flowers in lazy-daisy stitch. Press hems.

Winter warmers

5 to 8 years

An attractive set that's easy to knit and has an unusual border.

Materials 10(12:14) 25g balls Double Knitting yarn; in red (R); 6(8:10) balls in white (W); 1(2:3) balls in blue (B); pair 5mm [No 6] knitting needles; set of four double-pointed needles size 5mm [No 6]; 5mm [No 6] crochet hook; 5 buttons; leather elbow patches (optional).

Measurements Actual size 61 (65:71)cm [24(26:28) in] around chest; Jacket length, 34(36:38)cm [13(14:15) in].

Tension 19 sts to 10cm [4 in] in st-st with yarn used double.

Abbreviations k, knit; p, purl; st(s), stitches; cm, centimetre(s); in, inch(es); alt, alternate; beg, beginning; cont, continue; dec, decreas(e)ing; inc, increas(e)ing; inc 1 k, increase by picking up loop lying between the sts and knitting into back of it; foll, following; rep, repeat; rem, remain(ing); sl, slip; tog, together; st-st, stocking stitch; rnd, round; dc, double crochet.

Size Note Figures in brackets refer to larger sizes. One figure only refers to all sizes. Square brackets contain imperial measurements.

JACKET

BACK
With R, used double, cast on 69(75:81) sts.
Work in fancy rib thus: **1st row** P1, *k2, p1; rep from * to last 2 sts, k1, p1. **2nd row** K1, p1, *k1, p2; rep from * to last st, k1. **3rd row** P1, *k2, p1 wrapping the yarn twice round the needle; rep from * to last 2 sts, p1, k1. **4th row** K1, p1, *sl the next st making a long loop on to right-hand needle, p2, sl the long loop over the p2; rep from * to last st, k1. **5th row** P1, *k2, inc 1 k; rep from * to last 2 sts, k1, p1. Rep 2nd to 5th rows for the fancy rib.
Cont until rib measures 6cm [$2\frac{1}{2}$ in]. Now, using 1 strand of R and 1 strand of W together, cont in st-st for 16 rows, then with 1 strand in each of B and W together work 2 rows st-st, at the same time dec 6(7:8) sts evenly along the 1st row. Rep the 18 stripe rows until work measures 24(25:26)cm [$9\frac{1}{2}$(10:$10\frac{1}{4}$) in] from beg, ending after a p row.
Shape Armholes Cast off 3(3:4) sts at beg of next 2 rows; 2 sts at beg of next 2 rows. Dec 1 st at both ends of next and foll 1(2:2) alt rows . . . 49(52:55) sts. Cont in patt without shaping until work measures 34(36:38)cm [13(14:15) in] ending after a p row.
Shape Shoulders Cast off 7 sts at beg of next 4 rows. Cast off rem 21(24:27) sts.

LEFT FRONT
With R used double, cast on 31(34:37) sts. Work in fancy rib as Back until rib measures 6cm [$2\frac{1}{2}$ in]. Now dec 3(4:5) sts evenly along 1st row, work the 18 row st-st (mixing colours) as Back until work matches Back to armhole, ending after a p row . . . 28(30:32) sts.
Shape Armhole Cast off 3(3:4) sts at beg of next row. Work 1 row. Cast off 2 sts at beg of next row. Work 1 row. Dec 1 st at beg of next 5 right-side rows . . . 18 (20:21) sts.
Keeping colour mix and stripes as before cont without shaping until work measures 28(30:32)cm [11($11\frac{3}{4}$:$12\frac{1}{2}$) in] from beg, ending after a right-side row.
Shape Neck Cast off 3 sts at beg of next row. Dec. 1 st at beg of foll 1(3:4) alt rows . . . 14 sts.
Cont in striped st-st until work matches Back to shoulder, ending after a wrong-side row.
Shape Shoulder Cast off 7sts at beg of next and foll alt rows.

RIGHT FRONT
With R used double, cast on 31(34:37) sts. Work in fancy rib as Back until rib measures 6cm [$2\frac{1}{2}$in]. Now dec 3(4:5) sts evenly along 1st row, work the 18 row st-st (mixing colours) as Back until work matches Back to armhole, ending after a k row . . . 28(30:32) sts.
Shape Armhole Cast off 3(3:4) sts at beg of next row. Work 1 row. Cast off 2 sts at beg of next row. Work 1 row. Dec 1 st at beg of next 5 wrong-side rows . . . 18 (20:21) sts.
Keeping colour mix and stripes as before cont without shaping until work measures 28(30:32)cm [11($11\frac{3}{4}$:$12\frac{1}{2}$) in] from beg, ending after a wrong-side row.
Shape Neck Cast off 3 sts at beg of next row. Dec 1 st at beg of foll 1(3:4) alt rows . . . 14 sts.
Cont in striped st-st until work matches Back to shoulder ending after a right-side row.
Shape Shoulder Cast off 7 sts at beg of next and foll alt rows.

SLEEVES
With R double, cast on 31(35:35) sts. Work 6cm [$2\frac{1}{2}$ in] in fancy rib. Now cont in 18 row striped st-st as Back, inc 1 st at both ends of 7th row and every foll 8th rows to 41(43:47) sts. Cont without shaping until sleeve measures 24 (25:27)cm [$9\frac{1}{2}$(10:$10\frac{1}{2}$) in] ending after a p row.
Shape Top Dec 1 st at both ends of next row and foll alt rows to 21(23:25) sts, ending after a p row. Dec 1 st at both ends of every row to 9(11:13) sts. Cast off rem sts.
Work another sleeve the same.

Continued on page 148

Right: a set for winter with a random-knit look achieved by using two different colour yarns together which also gives extra thickness and warmth
Below: the shape guide to help you when knitting the jacket

WINTER WARMERS: JACKET SHAPE GUIDE

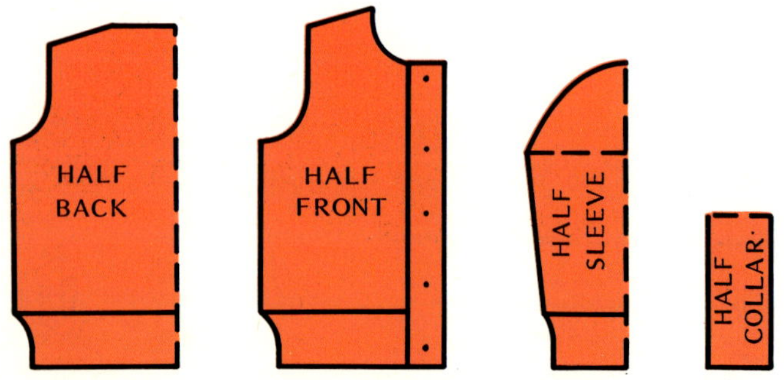
HALF BACK
HALF FRONT
HALF SLEEVE
HALF COLLAR

Children's Clothes

Winter warmers . . . continued

LEFT FRONT BAND

With R used double, cast on 81(84:90) sts. Work 3cm [1¼ in] fancy rib. Cast off. Mark this front band with pins to represent buttons, the 1st and 5th pin 2 sts from the top and lower edges and the other three pins spaced evenly between. The pins should be approx 12·5mm [½ in] from the front edge.

RIGHT FRONT BAND

With R used double, cast on 81(84:90) sts. Work 12·5mm [½ in] fancy rib. On next 2 rows work buttonholes. **1st row** * Rib to pinned position, cast off 2 sts; rep from * until all buttonholes have been worked, rib to end. **2nd row** Cast on 2 sts over those cast off in the 1st row. Cont in fancy rib until the Right Band matches the Left. Cast off.

COLLAR

With R used double; cast on 84(84:90) sts. Work 7cm [2¾ in] fancy rib. Cast off.

TO MAKE UP

With right sides together, back-stitch the shoulder seams. Press all pieces, following instructions on the ball band. With right side of work facing, sew on the front bands with a flat seam. With right sides together, back-stitch the side seams, matching stripes. With right sides inside, back-stitch the sleeve seams. Set the sleeve tops in the armholes, right sides together and back-stitch neatly in place. Sew on the collar with a flat seam. If using them, back-stitch the elbow patches on to each of the elbows. Sew on the buttons. With R used single, work 1 row dc round lower edge of rib and up front edges and round collar edge to give neat finish.

HELMET

TWO-NEEDLE METHOD
Work the two straps on two needles as given in the Four-needle Method, but arrange the front and back sts in a different order thus: With R used double, cast on 6 sts for half back, k across first strap, cast on 20 sts for front, work across second strap, cast on 6 sts for half back. 1st row K to end. 2nd row K6, p14, k20, p14, k6. Rep last 2 rows twice more. Now cont as for the four needle helmet but working back and forth. On the crown shaping, work the dec rows on every row in st-st.

FOUR-NEEDLE METHOD

Beg with 1st strap. With R and W used together, cast on 2 sts. Working in the 18 row stripes in st-st, work 8 rows without shaping. Now inc 1 st at both ends of next row and every foll 8th row to 14 sts. Cont on 14 sts until work measures 40cm [15¾ in] ending after a p row.
Leave this strap on a spare needle. Work another strap in the same way. Leave this strap on a spare needle.
Now, using set of four 5mm [No 6]

needles, cast on 20 sts for the front, work across 14 sts of one strap, cast on 12 sts for the back and work across 14sts of the other strap . . . 60 sts. Cont in rnds, having the two sets of 14 sts in st-st and the front 20 sts and the back 12 sts in g-st for 6 rows thus:
1st rnd K to end. **2nd rnd** P20, k14, p12, k14. Rep the last 2 rnds twice more.
Now cont in st-st on all sts (every rnd k) for 18 rows. Work 2 rnds st-st with B and W together. Work 8 rnds with R and W together.
Shape Top Cont with R used double only. **1st rnd** *K10, k2 tog; rep from * to end. **2nd rnd** *K9, k2 tog; rep from * to end. **3rd rnd** K8, k2 tog; rep from * to end. Cont dec in this way on every rnd to 10 sts. Thread yarn through these rem sts, draw up tightly and secure. Fasten off.

TO MAKE UP

With right side of work facing, using crochet hook and R double, work 1 row dc all round edge of straps. Press following instructions on the ball band.

Above: the mittens with the fancy rib at the cuff. Like the helmet, you can knit the mittens by two or four needle methods (see complete set page 147)

MITTENS

TWO-NEEDLE METHOD
Cast on and work the fancy rib as for the four-needle method. Dec 3 sts on the 1st row of 6 rows st-st. Place the thumb shaping thus: 1st row K13, inc 1 k, k1, inc 1 k, k 3. 2nd row P to end. Working back and forth cont as for four needle mittens.

TO MAKE UP
Press as for four needle mittens. With right sides inside, back-stitch the side and thumb seams of the mittens. Turn to right side.

FOUR-NEEDLE METHOD

With 5mm [No 6] needles and R used double, cast on 30 sts. Work 5cm [2 in] fancy rib. Now place sts on set of 5mm [No 6] needles, dec 3 sts . . . 9 sts on each of three needles. Change to R and W together and work 6 rnds st-st.
Shape for Thumb 1st rnd Inc 1 k, k1, inc 1 k, k to end. **2nd rnd and foll alt rnds** K to end. **3rd rnd** Inc 1 k, k3, inc 1 k, k to end. **5th rnd** Inc 1 k, k5, inc 1 k, k to end. **7th rnd** Inc 1 k, k7, inc 1 k, k to end. **9th rnd** Inc 1 k, k9, inc 1 k, k to end. **10th rnd** K to end. **11th rnd** Sl first 11 sts on to a safety-pin. Cont on rem 26 sts for 6(8:10) rnds, inc 2 sts on last rnd . . . 28 sts.
Shape Top With R used double, **1st rnd** *K2 tog, k5; rep from * to end. **2nd rnd** K2 tog, k4; rep from * to end. **3rd rnd** *K2 tog, k2; rep from * to end. **4th rnd** K2 tog, k1; rep from * to end. **5th rnd** K2 tog; rep from * to end. Thread yarn through rem sts, draw up tightly and secure. Fasten off. With right side of work facing, sl the 11 sts of the thumb on to needles and with R and W together, work 6(8:10) rnds st-st. **Next rnd** K1, *k2 tog; rep from * to end . . . 6 sts. **Next rnd** K2 tog; rep from * to end . . . 3 sts. Thread yarn through these sts, draw up tightly and secure. Fasten off.
Work another mitten in the same way.

TO MAKE UP

Press following instructions on the ball band.

Patchwork jacket

For any age

You can use up a lot of leftover yarns in making this attractive jacket but all must be the same weight. If you use two together make sure you knit to the correct tension.

Size Note The instructions are given for squares measuring a basic 8cm [3 in]. This gives a finished size of 61cm [24 in] all round chest. To make the larger sizes see instructions overleaf.
The jacket back and fronts are made from 28 whole squares and 12 part squares. The sleeves are knitted in one piece in stripes. The part-squares are labelled to help you when assembling the jacket (see diagram below).

Tension 26 sts and 34 rows to 10cm [4 in] square in st-st.

Materials Remnants of Double Knitting yarn in various colours; 3¾mm [No 9] knitting needles; 3mm [No 11] crochet hook; 5 press-studs.

Measurements To fit 56(61:66: 71:76:81)cm [22(24:26:28:30:32) in] chest/bust; length, adjustable.

Abbreviations k, knit; p, purl; st(s), stitch(es); cm, centimetre(s); in, inch(es); st-st, stocking stitch; inc, increas(e)ing; dec, de-creas(e)ing; beg, beginning; cont, continue; alt, alternate; foll, fol-lowing; dc, double crochet; ss, slip stitch; rnd, round.

> Label each patch as you make it so that you know exactly where it is to go when you're putting the jacket together later.

Continued on next page

Left: the clever jacket that looks superb even though it is made in leftover yarns

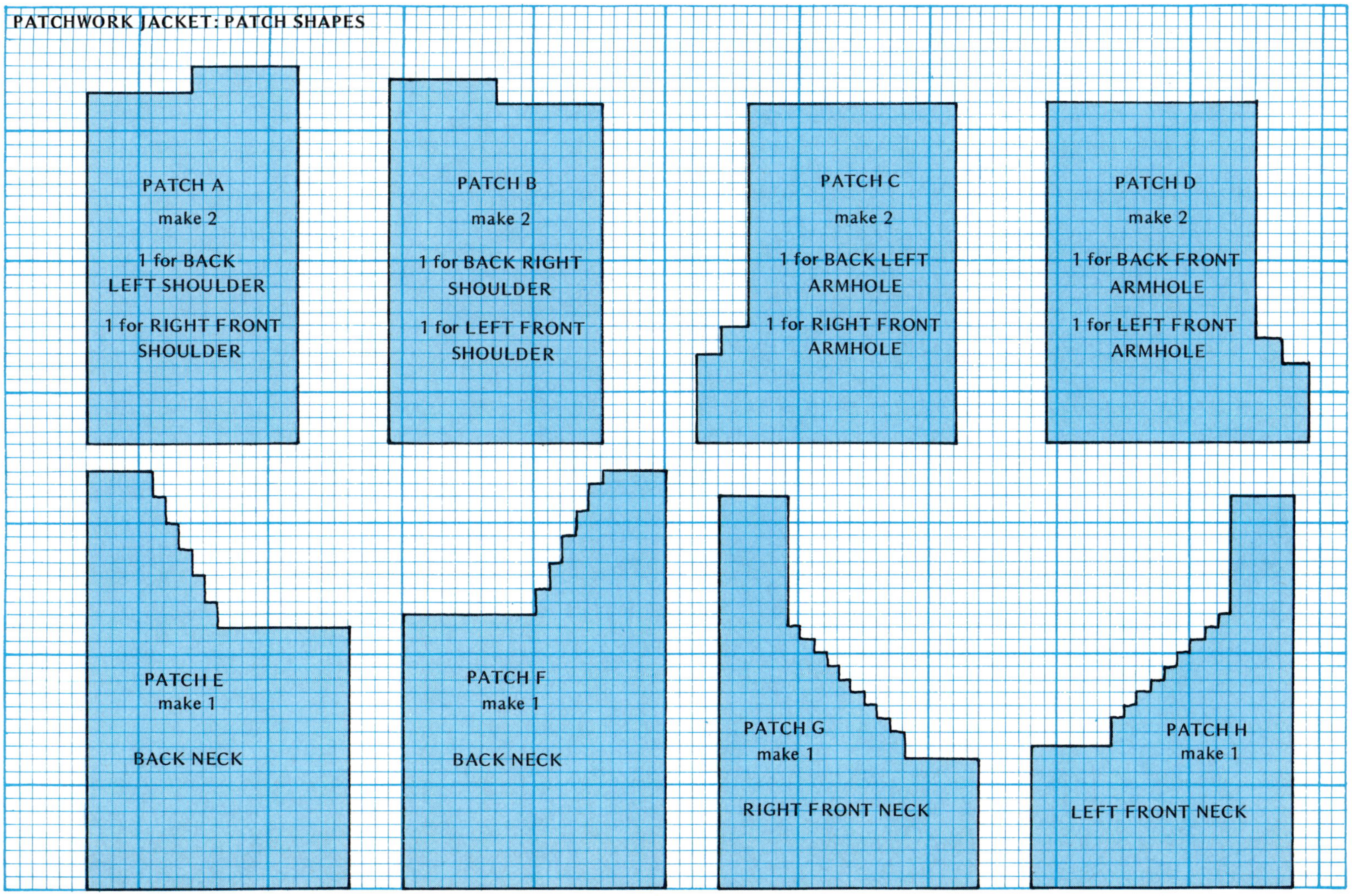

PATCHWORK JACKET: PATCH SHAPES

PATCH A
make 2

1 for BACK LEFT SHOULDER

1 for RIGHT FRONT SHOULDER

PATCH B
make 2

1 for BACK RIGHT SHOULDER

1 for LEFT FRONT SHOULDER

PATCH C
make 2

1 for BACK LEFT ARMHOLE

1 for RIGHT FRONT ARMHOLE

PATCH D
make 2

1 for BACK FRONT ARMHOLE

1 for LEFT FRONT ARMHOLE

PATCH E
make 1

BACK NECK

PATCH F
make 1

BACK NECK

PATCH G
make 1

RIGHT FRONT NECK

PATCH H
make 1

LEFT FRONT NECK

Patchwork jacket . . . continued

Whole Squares (28) Cast on 20 sts. Work 26 rows st-st. Cast off.
Patch A (make 2) Cast on 16 sts. Work 27 rows st-st. *Cast off 8 sts at beg of next row and foll alt row.*
Patch B (make 2) Cast on 16 sts. Work 26 rows. Work as patch A from * to *.
Patch C (make 2) Cast on 20 sts. Work 7 rows st-st. *Cast off 2 sts at beg of next row and foll alt row. Cont straight on rem sts until 26 rows have been worked. Cast off.*
Patch D (make 2) Cast on 20 sts. Work 6 rows st-st. Work as patch C from * to *.
Patch E (make 1) Cast on 20 sts. Work 20 rows st-st. *Cast off 10 sts at beg of next row. Work 1 row. Dec 1 st at beg of next row and foll alt rows to 5 sts. Work 1 row. Cast off.*
Patch F (make 1) Cast on 20 sts. Work 21 rows st-st. Work as patch E from * to *.
Patch G (make 1) Cast on 20 sts. Work 10 rows st-st. Cast off 6 sts at beg of next row. Work 1 row. *Dec 1 st at neck edge on next 9 rows. Cont straight until 30 rows have been worked. Cast off.*
Patch H (make 1) Cast on 20 sts. Work 11 rows st-st. Cast off 6sts at beg of next row. Work 1 row. Now work from * to * as patch G.

SLEEVES
Cast on 40 sts. Work 4cm [1½ in] k1, p1 rib. Cont in st-st, changing colour every 26 rows and inc 1 st at both ends of 7th row foll and every foll 6th row to 60 sts. Cont straight until sleeve measures 28cm [11 in] or required length, ending after a p row.
Shape Top Dec 1 st at both ends of every k row to 6 sts. Cast off.

TO MAKE UP
Press following instructions on ball band. Using back-stitch sew the patches together as shown in diagram. Using back-stitch sew side and sleeve seams, then sew in sleeves. Work the border thus: work 7 rnds dc in 2 rows colour stripes, with the 7th in contrasting colour. Work 3 dc in st at each corner on every rnd. Sew on the press-studs, the top one on the neck border, the 5th one 6cm [2½ in] from the lower edge and the other 3 spaced equally between them.

TO MAKE LARGER SQUARES FOR LARGER SIZES
Add 5cm [2 in] to the actual chest/bust size and divide by 2 to obtain the finished measurement across back: eg, 76cm [30 in] + 5cm [2 in] = 81cm [32 in] for finished size, 40cm [16 in] across back.
Divide the across back measurements by 4 and this will give you the size to make your squares. In the example given above – 40cm [16 in] divided by 4 = 10cm [4 in] squares. Thus, working to the correct tension, the foll number of sts should be cast on:
2nd size 21 sts and work 28 rows.
3rd size 23 sts and work 30 rows.
4th size 25 sts and work 32 rows.
5th size 27 sts and work 34 rows.
6th size 29 sts and work 38 rows. The total length will be approx. 3¼cm [1¼ in] longer between sizes.
When working the shaped patches, cast off 1 st more at underarm on each size and the rem extra sts over the shoulder shaping.
To make larger sleeves Cast on 2 extra sts for each size and increase as given 10 times. Cont on these sts adding 2·5cm [1 in] for each size. The number of sts to be cast off at end of top shaping will be: 6(6:8:8:10:10) sts.

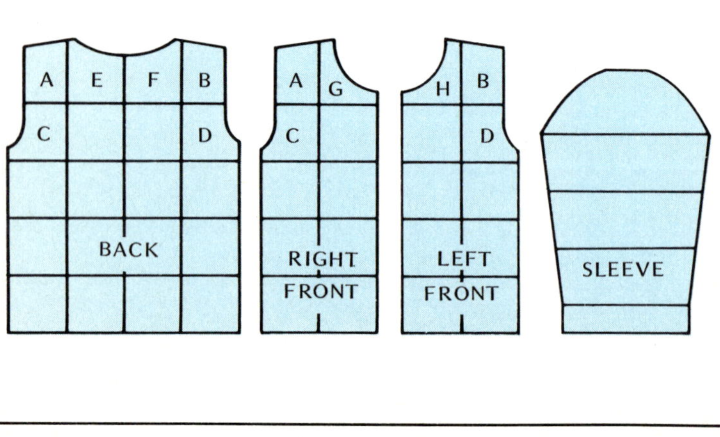

Smart set

5 to 12 years
Polka dots never really go out of favour and they look spot-on worn with a matching skirt or trousers.

Materials Polka-dot Two Piece 375(400:425)g of 4-ply wool in yellow (M), 70(80:80)g in claret (C); **Square Neck Jumper** 200 (225:250)g in claret (M), 70 (80:80)g in yellow (C); **For both** pair of 3¾mm [No 9] knitting needles. Circular 3¾mm [No 9] needle; elastic for waistband.

Measurements To fit a 63–66 (68–71:73–76)cm [25–26(27–28: 29–30) in] chest.

Tension 26 sts measure 10cm [4 in].

Abbreviations k, knit; p, purl; st(s), stitch(es); st-st, stocking stitch; rep, repeat; cont, continue; inc, increase; beg, beginning; patt, pattern; alt, alternate; foll, following; cm, centimetre(s); in, inch(es); rnd, round.

Size Note Figures in brackets refer to larger sizes. One figure only refers to all sizes. Square brackets contain imperial measurements.

THE PATTERN – formed in 12 rows
1st to 4th rows In M in st-st.
5th row K, *6 M, 2 C. Rep from * ending 6 M.
6th row As 5th row but p.
7th to 10th rows In M in st-st.
11th row K, *2 M, 2 C, 4 M. Rep from * to last 6 sts: 2 M, 2 C, 2 M.
12th row As 11th row but p.

TWO PIECE JUMPER

BACK
Using 3¾mm [No 9] needles and C, cast on 78(86:94) sts and work in k2, p2 rib for 5·5cm [2¼ in]. Now work in the 12-row patt, at the same time, inc 1 st every 8th (8th:10th) row until there are 88(96:104) sts. Work straight to 21(21·5:25)cm [8(8½:10) in] from beg, or length required.
Shape Armholes Cast off at beg of rows, 3(4:5) sts twice, 3 sts twice, 2 sts 4 times . . . 68(74:80) sts. Work straight until armhole measures 15(16:16·5)cm [6(6¼:6½) in] from beg.
Shape Neck and Shoulders Next row Cast off 6 sts, patt 22(24:26) sts, including st already on needle

from casting off, turn and leave other sts on spare needle.
Now cast off 4 sts at beg of next and foll alt row at neck edge, but at the same time cast off 6 sts at beg of next armhole edge row, 4(6:6) sts on foll alt row and 4(4:6) sts on next alt row.
Go back to main sts, cast off centre 12(14:16) sts, patt to end.
Next row Cast off 6, patt to end. Now rep from ** to ** of other side.

FRONT
Work as for Back until Front measures 31(33:37)cm [12¼ (13:14½) in] . . . 68(74:80) sts.
Shape Neck Next row Patt 28 (30:32) sts, turn and leave rem sts on spare needle. Now cast off 3 sts at beg of next row, 2 sts on next alt row and 1 st on next 3 alt rows. Cont straight until work measures as Back to shoulders ending at armhole edge.
Shape Shoulder Cast off 6 sts at beg of next 2 armhole edge rows, 4(6:6) sts on next alt row and 4(4:6) sts on next alt row. Go back to main sts, cast off centre 12(14:16) sts, patt to end. **Next row** Patt to neck edge. Now cont to shape neck and shoulders as for other side.

SLEEVES
Using 3¾mm [No 9] needles and C, cast on 38(38:42) sts and work in k2, p2 rib for 4 cm [1½ in]. **Next row** *K7(7:4), inc in next st. Rep from * 3(3:7) times more, k6(6:2) . . . 42(42:50) sts.
Cont in patt inc 1 st every 8th (6th:10th) row until there are 58(64:70) sts. Cont in patt without inc until sleeve measures 35 (37:39·5)cm [13¾(14½:15½) in] ending after a p row.
Shape Top At beg of every row cast off 3(3:4) sts twice, 2 sts 2(2:4) times, 1 st 18(24:24) times, 2 sts 4 times, 3 sts twice. Cast off rem 16 sts.

TWO PIECE SKIRT
Using circular needle and M, cast on 168(174:180) sts and k in rnds for 2cm [¾ in]. **Next rnd** P (for hem ridge). Cont in k rnds to 7(8:10)cm [3(3¼:4) in].
Next rnd *K13(14:15), pick up loop before next st and k it, k next st and mark this st with coloured yarn, pick up loop before next st and k, then k14. Rep from * 5 times more . . . 180(186:192) sts.
Continued on page 152

Right: prettily polka-dotted, there are round and square-necked jumpers to choose from

---

PATCHWORK JACKET: ASSEMBLY GUIDE

Smart set . . . continued

Work straight until skirt measures 9(10:13)cm [3½(4:5) in] from hem-line, then in next rnd inc as before each side of marked st. Rep this inc at 2cm [¾ in] intervals until 13 inc rnds, in all, have been worked. After last inc rnd work straight for 2(2:6) rnds, then work 2cm [¾ in] in garter st; ie, 1 rnd k, 1 rnd p. Cast off.

TO MAKE UP

Press on wrong side following ball band instructions. **Jumper** Using back-stitch join right shoulder, then with right side of front facing and using C, beg at left shoulder and pick up and k18 sts down side of neck, 12(14:16) sts from front neck, 18 sts to shoulder, 11 sts to centre back, 12(14:16) sts across back and 11 sts to shoulder. Now work in k2, p2 rib for 6 rows. Cast off in the rib. Join left shoulder and neckband. Sew in sleeves, then sew up sleeve and side seams.

Skirt Fold hem at waist to wrong side and stitch down neatly. Cut elastic to fit waistline and insert through hem.

SQUARE NECK JUMPER

BACK

Using C and 3¾mm [No 9] needles cast on 86(94:102) sts and work in k2, p2 rib for 5cm [2 in]. Now work in the 12-row patt until Back measures 28(30·5:33)cm [11(12:13) in] or length required.

Shape Armholes Cast off at beg of row, 2(3:4) sts twice, 3 sts twice and 2 sts 4 times . . . 68(74: 80) sts. Work straight until arm-hole measures 15(16:16·5)cm [6 (6¼:6½) in] from beg.

Shape Shoulders Now at beg of every row cast off 5 sts twice, 6 sts twice, 4(6:6) sts twice and 4(4:6) sts twice. Cast off rem sts.

FRONT

Work as for Back until Front measures 38·5(42:44·5)cm [15¼ (16½:17½) in].

Shape Neck Next row Patt 19 (21:23) sts, turn and leave rem sts on spare needle.

Now work straight on first sts until work measures as Back to shoulder ending at armhole edge.

Shape Shoulder Cast off 5 sts at beg of next armhole edge row, 6 sts on next alt row, 4(6:6) sts on next alt row and 4(4:6) sts on next

alt row. Go back to other sts, cast off centre 30(32:34) sts and work to end. Now work as for other side.

SLEEVES

Using 3¾mm [No 9] needles and C, cast on 38(38:42) sts and work in k2, p2 rib for 6cm [2½ in]. Now work as for Sleeves of Two-Piece.

NECKBAND

Join right shoulder. Now using C, pick up and k13 sts to front edge, mark corner, 30(32:34) sts to next corner, mark corner, 13 sts to shoulder, and 30(32:34) sts across back neck. Now work in k2, p2 rib for 6 rows, dec 1 st each side of marked st on every alt row. Cast off in the rib.

TO MAKE UP

Press as for Two-Piece. Join left shoulder and neckband. Sew in sleeves, then sew up sleeve and side seams.

Striped tunics

5, 9 and 16 years

As cool as ice-cream and just right for casual wear.

Materials 2(4) 25g balls 4-ply knitting yarn in each of four different colours, A, B, C and D; pair 2¾mm [No 12] knitting needles.

Measurements Actual size 70 (100)cm [28(39½) in] all round; length 43(75)cm [17(29½) in]; sleeve length 36(45)cm [14(17¾) in].

Tension 32 sts and 40 rows to 10cm [4 in] in st-st.

Abbreviations k, knit; p, purl; st(s), stitch(es); cm, centimetre(s); in, inch(es); alt, alternate; beg, beginning; cont, continue; dec, decrease(e)ing; inc, increas(e)ing; foll, following; rep, repeat; rem, remain(ing); st-st, stocking stitch.

Size Note Figure in brackets refers to large size. One figure only refers to both sizes. Square brackets contain imperial measurements.

To work this design faster, use the yarn doubled. You will need needles sized 4mm [No 8] in place of the 2¾mm [No 12] needles. First cast on 21 sts and work 27 rows. This should give you a 10cm [4 in] square. Change either needles or number of sts and rows until you have a 10cm [4 in] square. From this square you will be able to work out just how many sts and rows you will need to 2·5cm [1 in]. Multiply this by the number of cm or inches you require your finished garment to be.
If knitting for a 5 year old, follow the 1st size but adjust the length of the sleeves. For all ages keep an eye on the row tension as the finished length of the garment is dependent upon this.

FRONT AND BACK (both pieces worked alike)
With A, cast on 112(160) sts. Beg k row, work 13(15) rows st-st. **Next row** (wrong side) K to end to form hemline.
Now cont in striped st-st pattern.

SMART SET: SQUARE NECK JUMPER SHAPE GUIDE

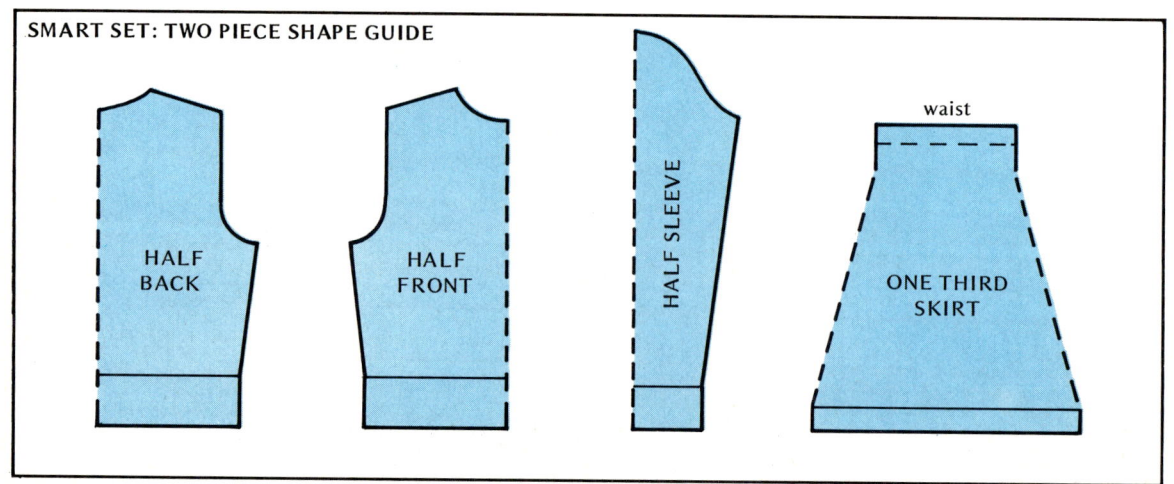

Left: the shape guide for the square-neck jumper
Below: a guide to the shapes of the skirt and jumper of the two-piece suit. The garments can be seen in colour on page 151

SMART SET: TWO PIECE SHAPE GUIDE

Beg k row, work 18(26) rows st-st in each of A, B, C and D. Rep the four stripes until 9(11) stripes have been worked from the hemline. With B(D), work 8(12) rows st-st. **Shape Neck Next row** K26(45), cast off centre 60(70) sts, k26(45). Leave these rem sets of sts on a spare pair of needles.

SLEEVES

With A, cast on 77(115) sts. Beg k row work 13(15) rows st-st. **Next row** (wrong side) K to end to form hemline. Now cont in striped st-st pattern. Beg k row, work 18(26) rows st-st in each of A, B, C and D. Rep the four stripes until 8(7) stripes have been worked from the hemline. Note that the smaller has more stripes as these are narrower and more are required for the correct length. Cast off. Work second sleeve the same.

TO MAKE UP

The sts at shoulder may be cast off together, with right sides together or grafted. To graft the sts, place the front and back sts of one shoulder together with the right sides outside and the needles pointing towards the right. Beg at right-hand side — *Insert the sewing needle knitwise into the first st on the front needle draw yarn through the st, slipping the st off the knitting needle. Insert the sewing needle purlwise into the second st on the front needle, draw yarn through but leave the st on the knitting needle. Take yarn under front knitting needle and insert the sewing needle purlwise into the first st on the back knitting needle, draw yarn through st and slip off the needle. Insert sewing needle knitwise into second st on back knitting needle, draw yarn through and leave the st on the knitting needle. Bring yarn forward and rep from * to end. The sts are all joined forming an invisible seam. Fasten off yarn neatly. Graft other shoulder in the same way.

Matching the stripes and having right sides together, back-stitch the side seams leaving 12(18)cm [4¾(7) in] free at top for armholes. With right side inside, back-stitch the sleeve seams, matching the stripes. With right sides together set in the cast off edge of sleeves and back-stitch neatly to armholes. Fold hems at ridges to wrong side and slip stitch. Fold back about three rows at neck edges to wrong side and slip-stitch neatly in position.

Press according to instructions on ball band.

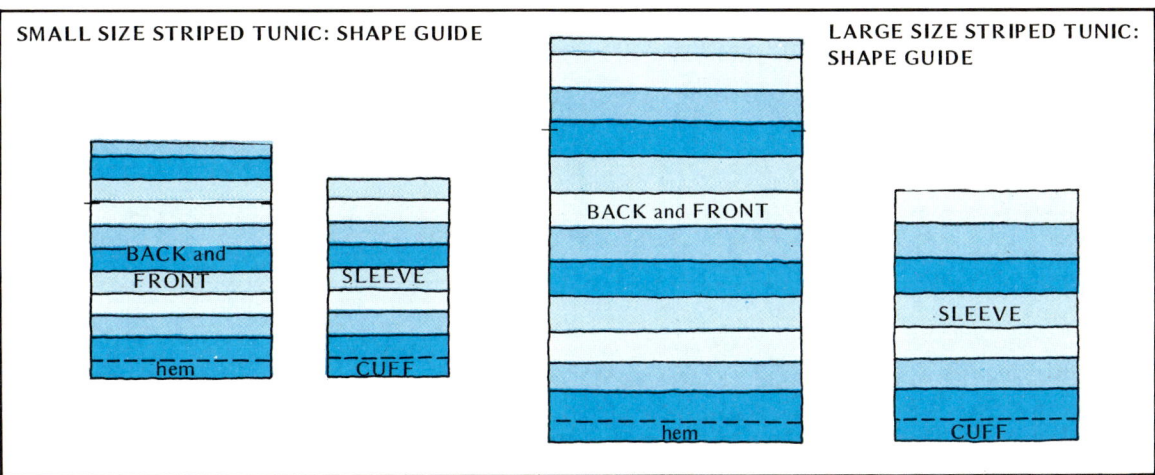

Above: the cool-and-casual striped tunics to fit 3 sizes   Below: the guides to the shapes of the tunics

SMALL SIZE STRIPED TUNIC: SHAPE GUIDE

LARGE SIZE STRIPED TUNIC: SHAPE GUIDE

BACK and FRONT

SLEEVE

CUFF

hem

BACK and FRONT

SLEEVE

CUFF

hem

Reindeer jacquard set

6 to 8 years

Different shades of red lightened with beige puts this set in the expensive looking class. Perfectly simple for someone a little more advanced in knitting.

Materials 5(6) 25g balls Double Knitting yarn in red (A); 4(5) balls in each of beige (B) and orange (C); 3(3) balls in maroon (D) and rose (E); pairs of 3¾mm and 4mm [No 9 and No 8] knitting needles; sets of four double-pointed needles sizes 3¾mm and 4mm [No 9 and No 8].

Measurements To fit 66(71)cm [26(28) in] chest; length approx 41(43)cm [16(17) in]; sleeve length 31(33)cm [12(13) in]; hat and mittens average size.

Tension 22 sts to 10cm [4 in].

Abbreviations k, knit; p, purl; st(s), stitch(es); cm, centimetre(s); in, inch(es); alt, alternate; beg, beginning; cont, continue; dec, decreas(e)ing; foll, following; inc, increas(e)ing; inc 1k, increase by picking up loop between sts and knitting into back of it; rep, repeat; rem, remain(ing); st-st, stocking stitch; sl, slip; psso, pass slip stitch over; tog, together; rnd(s), round(s).

Size Note Figures in brackets refer to larger size. One figure only refers to both sizes. Square brackets contain imperial measurements.

Special Note Carry yarns not in use loosely across back. Twist yarns when changing colour to avoid making a hole.

This set is worked mostly in the round, saving time on seams. If you prefer you can work the reindeer motif after the garment is knitted. In this case, apart from the colour patterns, work the garment in st-st and work the motif in Swiss Embroidery: Note first that you have 76 sts for each Back and Front and that the motif will cover 34 sts at its widest part. Tack a shape to cover 34 sts across and the 31 rows depth on the Front and Back. Begin at the first st to be covered at the bottom right hand corner of the motif and leaving an end at the back, bring the needle out to the front through the centre of the st below the one to be covered, then in and out again behind the st in the row above, back into the same hole at the bottom and out through the middle of the next st along on the left. Work over each st in the first row in this way and at the end of the row slip the needle upwards into the middle of the last st covered instead of taking it along to the left as before. Now turn the work upside down and work from right to left along this row.

SWEATER

THE BODY

Worked in one piece to armhole shaping.

With set of four 3¾mm [No 9] needles and C, cast on 140(150) sts having 47 sts on each of two needles and 46 sts on third (50 on each needle). Work 4cm [1½ in] k1, p1 rib, inc 10 sts evenly on last rnd . . . 150(160) sts. Change to set of four 4mm [No 8] needles. Using B, D and E, work the 21 rnds of diamond colour pattern from the chart below, on the left.

With A, and inc 2(4) sts evenly on the first rnd, work 6 rnds of st-st . . . 152 (164) sts. Now, using B on A, work the reindeer motif on the Front and Back from the chart below, on the right. The widest number of sts will be 34, therefore your first six rnds will read thus:

1st rnd *K31(37) A, 2 B, 5 A, 2 B, 3 A, 2 B, 7 A, 2 B, 22(28) A *, rep from * to * for front.

2nd rnd *K31(37) A, 2 B, 5 A, 2 B, 3 A, 3 B, 6 A, 2 B, 22(28) A*, rep from * to * for front.

3rd rnd *K32(38) A, 2 B, 5 A, 2 B, 3 A, 1B, 8 A, 2 B, 21(27) A*, rep from * to * for front.

4th to 6th rnds *K32(38) A, 1B, 6 A, 1 B, 4 A, 1 B, 8 A, 1 B, 22(28) A*, rep from * to * for front.

Beg 7th rnd cont from the chart. When the reindeer motif has been completed break B and cont in A only until work measures 29(31)cm [11½(12) in].

Cont in pattern thus: **1st rnd** *K1 D, 1 E; rep from * to end. **2nd rnd** *K1 E, 1 D; rep from * to end. **3rd and 4th rnds** As 1st and 2nd.

Divide for Back and Front here.

BACK

1st row With E, cast off 2 sts, k74(80) sts, turn. Cont in rows on these sts only for the Back.

2nd row With E, cast off 2 sts, p to end. **3rd to 6th rows** With E, in st-st casting off 2 sts at beg of every row . . . 64(70) sts.

7th row K2 tog E, *k1 D, 1 E; rep from * to last 2 sts, k2 tog D.

8th row *P1 E, 1 D; rep from * to end.

9th and 10th rows As 7th and 8th rows . . . 60(66) sts. Leave these sts on a spare needle for now.

FRONT

1st row With E, cast off 2 sts, k74(80), turn. Cont on these sts for the Front.

2nd row With E, cast off 2 sts, p to end. **3rd to 6th rows** With E, in st-st casting off 2 sts at beg of every row . . . 64(70) sts.

7th row K2 tog E, *k1 D, 1 E; rep from * to last 2 sts, k2 tog D.

8th row *P1 E, 1 D; rep from * to end.

9th and 10th rows As 7th and 8th rows . . . 60(66) sts. Leave these sts on a spare needle for the time being – with the Back and Sleeve sts they will form the yoke.

SLEEVES

With set of four 3¾mm [No 9] needles and C, cast on 36(42) sts having 12(14) sts on each needle. Work 4cm [1½ in] k1, p1 rib. Change to set of four 4mm [No 8] needles and A and inc 10(14) sts evenly in first rnd, work 4 rnds st-st . . . 46(56) sts.

Next rnd (inc rnd) K1, inc 1k, k to last st, inc 1k. Work 5 rnds without shaping. Rep last 6 rnds once more . . . 50(60) sts.

Work 11 rnds of the diamond colour pattern from the chart, without shaping.

Now cont in st-st with A, inc rnd on next rnd and every foll 6th rnd to 54(62) sts. Cont in st-st without shaping until work measures 31(33)cm [12(13) in].

Shape Top Work back and forth after the 4th rnd as on Back and Front thus: **1st rnd** *K1 D, 1 E; rep from * to end. **2nd rnd** *K1 E, 1 D; rep from * to end. **3rd and 4th rnds** As 1st and 2nd.

Divide here for top shaping **1st row** With E, cast off 2 sts, k52, turn. **2nd row** With E, cast off 2 sts, p50. **3rd to 6th rows** With E, in st-st, casting off 2 sts at beg of every row. **7th row** K2 tog E, *k1 D, 1 E; rep from * to last 2 sts, k2 tog D. **8th row** *P1 E, 1 D; rep from * to end. **9th and 10th rows** As 7th and 8th rows . . . 38(46) sts.

Leave these sts on a spare needle for the time being and work a second sleeve in the same way.

Continued on page 156

Right: the Reindeer Jacquard Set Left: the charts you will need – though you can embroider the reindeer motif on later if you like

DIAMOND PATTERN
Key
● = maroon
✖ = rose
□ = beige

REINDEER MOTIF
Key
✖ = beige
□ = red

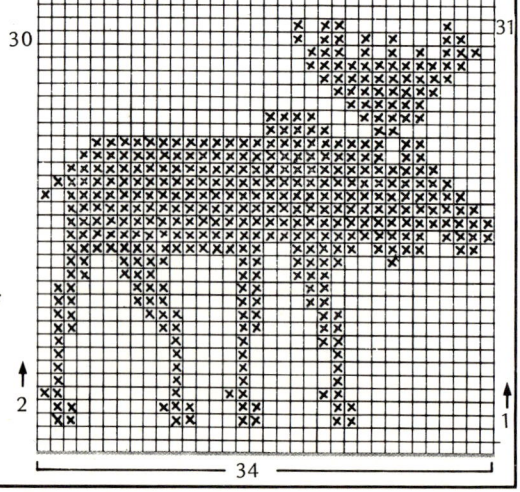

└─ 10 st repeat ─┘

└─ 34 ─┘

YOKE

On to set of 4mm [No 8] needles, take up in this order, 60(66) sts of the Front, 38(46) sts of the Sleeve, 60(66) sts of the Back then 38(46) sts of the second Sleeve, <u>at the same time</u> arranging the sts 65(74) on each of two needles and 66(76) on the third. With C, work 10 rnds k1, p1 rib.

11th rnd *Rib 11 sl 1, k2 tog, psso; rep from * to end . . . 168(196) sts. Rib 8 rnds without shaping.

20th rnd *Rib 9, sl 1, k2 tog, psso; rep from * to end . . . 140(168) sts. Rib 8 rnds without shaping.

29th rnd *Rib 7, sl 1, k2 tog, psso; rep from * to end.
Work 8 rnds without shaping.

38th rnd *Rib 6, sl 1, k2 tog, psso; rep from * to end . . . 84(112) sts.
Change to set of four 3¾mm [No 9] needles and cont in k1, p1 rib without shaping for further 10cm [4 in]. Cast off loosely in rib.

TO MAKE UP

Press work lightly on the wrong side following instructions on the ball band. With the right side inside, back-stitch the armhole shaping seams. Turn to right side.

HAT

TO MAKE

With set of four 3¾mm [No 9] needles and C, cast on 90(100) sts having 30(33 on two, 34 on 3rd) sts on each needle. Work 3·5cm [1¼ in] k1, p1 rib.
Change to 4mm [No 8] needles and cont in pattern thus: **1st rnd** *K1 D, 1 E; rep from * to end. **2nd rnd** *K1 E, 1 D; rep from * to end.
3rd and 4th rnds As 1st and 2nd rnds. **5th to 10th rnds** With E, in st-st. **11th to 14th rnds** As 1st to 4th rnds.
Now cont in st-st working the 21 rnds of diamond colour pattern from the chart. When these rnds are completed, cont in st-st with C until work measures 18cm [7 in], dec 1 st both ends of last row on 2nd size only.
Shape Crown *K2 tog; rep from * to end . . . 45(49) sts. **2nd rnd** K1, *k2 tog; rep from * to end . . . 23(25) sts. **3rd rnd** As 2nd rnd . . . 12(13) sts. Break yarn leaving a long end. Thread end through rem sts, draw up and secure, leaving the end to sew on a pompon (see page 75 for how to make one).

MITTENS

TO MAKE

With set of four 3¾mm [No 9] needles and C, cast on 40 sts having 13 sts on each of two needles and 14 sts on the third.

Work 5cm [2 in] k1, p1 rib.
Change to set of four 4mm [No 8] needles: **1st rnd** *K1 D, 1 E; rep from * to end. **2nd rnd** *K1 E, 1 D; rep from * to end. **3rd and 4th rnds** As 1st and 2nd rnds.

Divide for Thumb 1st rnd With E, k19, inc 1k, k2, inc 1k, k19. **2nd rnd** With E, k to end. **3rd rnd** With E, k19, inc 1k, k4, inc 1k, k19. **4th rnd** With E, k to end. **5th rnd** With E, k19, inc 1k, k6, inc 1k, k19. **6th rnd** With E, k to end. **7th rnd** *K1 D, 1 E* 9 times, 1 D, with E inc 1k, k8, inc 1k, rep from * to * 9 times, 1 D. **8th rnd** *K1 E, 1 D* 9 times, 1 E, with E, k10, rep from * to * 9 times, 1 E. **9th rnd** *K1 D, 1 E* 9 times, 1 D, place next 10 sts on a safety-pin, rep from * to * 9 times, 1 D. **10th rnd** *K1 E, 1 D* 9 times, 1 E, turn, cast on 2 sts, turn, rep from * to * 9 times, 1 E . . . 40 sts.
Now work the 11 rnds of diamond pattern from the chart. Break B, D and E. With C, cont in st-st until work measures 17(18)cm [6½(7) in].

Shape Top 1st rnd With C, *K1, sl 1, k1, psso, k14, k2 tog, k1*, rep from * to * once more. **2nd rnd** With C, *K1, sl 1, k1, psso, k12, k2 tog, k1*, rep from * to * once more.
Cont dec 4 sts on every rnd in this way until 8 sts rem. Cast off.
Thumb With set of four 4mm [No 8] needles and C, take up the 10 sts of the thumb. **1st rnd** Inc in 1st st, k to last st, inc in last st . . . 12 sts. Cont in rnds of st-st for 3(4)cm [1¼(1½) in].
Next rnd *K2 tog; rep from * to end . . . 6 sts.
Thread yarn through the sts, draw up and secure. Press following instructions on ball band. With right side inside and with palm flat, back-stitch across the top sts. Turn to right side. Work another mitten the same.

Random smartness

6 to 10 years

It's the yarn that gives this dress its smartness — the pattern itself is simple: stocking stitch with garter stitch borders.

Materials 160(180:200)g Double Knitting yarn in teal random (Main); 40(40:50)g Double Knitting yarn in teal (Contrast); pair 3mm [No 11] knitting needles; circular 3mm [No 11] or set 3mm [No 11] double-pointed knitting needles.

Measurements To fit a 66 (71:76)cm [26(28:30) in] chest.

Tension 24 sts measure 10cm [4 in] over st-st.

Abbreviations k, knit; p, purl; st(s), stitch(es); st-st, stocking stitch; cm, centimetre(s); in, inch(es); dec, decrease; tog, together; beg, beginning; rem, remain(ing); sl, slip; psso, pass slip stitch over; rep, repeat; inc, increase; alt, alternate; cont, continue; M, main; C, contrast; g-st, garter stitch; rnd, round.

Size Note Figures in brackets refer to larger sizes. One figure only refers to all sizes. Square brackets contain imperial measurements.

BACK

Using M, cast on 158(164:170) sts and work 8 rows in g-st, then cont in st-st until work measures 4cm [1½ in] from beg, ending after a p row.
Next row *K2, k2 tog, k46(48:50) sl 1, k1, psso*, rep from * to *

twice more, k2. Dec thus every 8th(8th:10th) row allowing 2 sts less in sts between decs each time, until 74(80:86) sts rem. Cont straight until work measures 37 (41:45)cm [14½(16:17½) in] or length required to waist.
Next row *K14(15:16), inc in next st. Rep from * 3 times more, then k14(16:18) . . . 78(84:90) sts. Now inc 1 st at each end of every 6th(8th:10th) row until there are 88(94:100) sts, then cont straight until work measures 51(56:61)cm [20(22:24) in] or length required to armholes.
Shape Armholes Cast off at beg of every row, 3 sts twice, 2 sts 4 times and 1 st 6 times . . . 68 (74:80) sts. Work straight until armhole measures 15(16:17)cm [6(6¼:6¾) in] ending after a p row.
Shape Shoulders Cast off 4(5:5) sts at beg of next 4 rows. **Next row** Cast off 4(4:5) sts, k7(7:8) sts — including st already on needle from casting off, turn and leave other sts on spare needle.
Next row Cast off 3, p to end. Cast off rem 4(4:5) sts.
Go back to other sts, rejoin wool at centre, cast off 30(32:34) sts, k to end. **Next row** Cast off 4(4:5) sts, p to end. **Next row** Cast off 3, k to end. Cast off rem 4(4:5) sts.

FRONT

Work as for Back until armhole measures 7cm [2¾ in] ending after a p row.
Shape Neck Next row K19(21:23) sts, turn and leave other sts on spare needle. Cont on Left Front sts, dec 1 st at neck edge on every 8th(10th:10th) row 3 times. Work until armhole measures as Back to shoulder, ending at armhole edge.
Shape Shoulder Cast off 4(5:5) sts on next 2 armhole edge rows and 4(4:5) sts on next 2 armhole edge rows.
Go back to sts left on spare

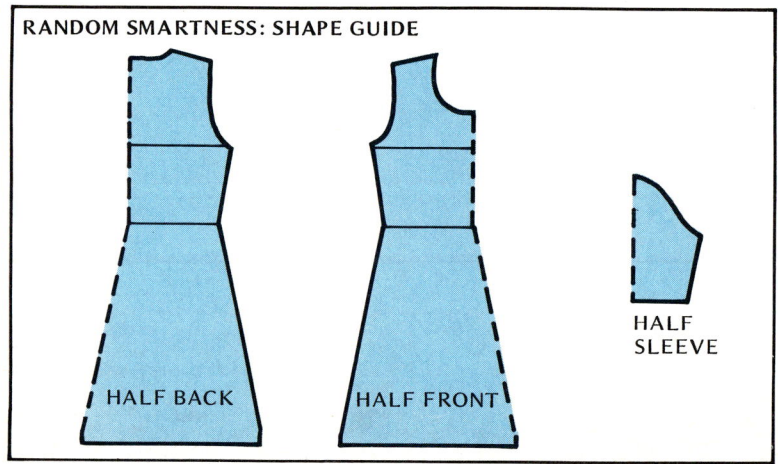

RANDOM SMARTNESS: SHAPE GUIDE

HALF BACK · HALF FRONT · HALF SLEEVE

needle, slip centre 30(32:34) sts on to stitchholder, rejoin yarn to rem sts and k to end. Now work Right Front exactly as Left Front.

SLEEVES

Using C, cast on 44(46:50) sts and work 8 rows in g-st. **Next row** *K8(8:9) sts, inc in next st. Rep from * 3 times more, k8 (10:10). Work straight in st-st on the 48(50:54) sts to 4cm [1½ in], then inc 1 st at each end of next row and every 5th(5th:7th) row until there are 56(60:64) sts. Work straight to 10(12:13)cm [4 (4¾:5) in].
Shape Top Cast off 3 sts at beg of next 2 rows, then dec 1 st at beg of next 28(32:36) rows. Now cast off 2 sts at beg of next 4 rows. Cast off rem 14 sts.

BELT

Using C, cast on 18 sts and work in st-st for 107(120:150)cm [42 (47:59) in]. Cast off.

TO MAKE UP

Press work following instructions on ball band. Using back-stitch join shoulders. Now using the circular needle or set of 4 double-pointed needles beg at left shoulder and pick up and k22 (24:28) sts down to front; 30 (32:34) sts across Front; 22(24:28) sts to shoulder; 4 sts to centre back neck: 30(32:34) sts across Back and 4 sts to left shoulder. Next mark the 4 corners with coloured thread. Now working in rnds of 1 rnd p and one rnd k, dec at corners on every alt rnd by sl 1, k1, psso, k2 tog on each front corner and k2 tog at marked thread on the 2 back corners. When 8 rows have been worked, cast off.
Sew in sleeves, then sew up sleeve and side seams. Fold belt length-ways, right sides facing, sew along one short edge, then long edge, turn to right side, press, then sew up open short end.

*Right: simple-to-make dress that uses random yarn to achieve the flecked, tweedy look without any problems. When choosing the contrast yarn, pick the predominant colour of the random mixture
Left: shape guide for the dress*

Set for the cold

6 to 10 years

A set for all knitters who hate the sewing up at the end! The sweater is worked in the round to the armholes where it divides, and the sleeves, hat and mittens are all worked in the round.

Materials 16(17:18) 25g balls Double Knitting yarn in Blue (B); 3(4:4) balls in each of Cream (C) and Red (R); sets of four double-pointed needles sizes 3¾mm [No 9], 4½mm [No 7] and 4mm [No 8].

Measurements Actual size, 66 (71:76)cm [26(28:30) in] round chest; length 43(44:45)cm [17 (17½:17¾) in]. Hat and mittens to fit average sizes.

Tension 22 sts to 10cm [4 in] in main patt on 4mm [No 8] needles.

Abbreviations k, knit; p, purl; st(s), stitch(es); cm, centimetre(s); in, inch(es); alt, alternate; beg, beginning; cont, continue; dec, decrease(e)ing; inc, increas(e)ing; foll, following; rep, repeat; rem, remain(ing); tog, together; sl, slip; psso, pass slip stitch over; inc 1 k, increase 1 by picking up the loop between sts and knitting into back of it; patt, pattern; st-st, stocking stitch; rnd, round.

Size Note Figures in brackets refer to larger sizes. One figure only refers to all sizes. Square brackets contain imperial measurements.

Special Note Carry yarns not in use loosely across back of work. Twist yarns when changing colour in order to avoid making a hole.

SWEATER

THE BODY

With set of 3¾mm [No 9] needles and B, cast on 144(156:168) sts having 48(52:56) sts on each needle. Work 5cm [2 in] k1, p1 rib.

Change to set of 4mm [No 8] needles and cont in main patt thus: **1st rnd** With B, k to end. **2nd rnd** K3 B, *1 C, 5 B; rep from * to last 3 sts, 1 C, 2 B. **3rd to 6th**

Left: sweater, hat and mittens that make up the Set For The Cold

rnds With B, k to end. **7th rnd** *K1 C, 5 B; rep from * to end. **8th to 11th rnds** With B, k to end.

2nd to 11th rnds form the main patt. Cont in main patt until work measures 21(22:23)cm [8¼(8½:9) in] ending after an 11th patt rnd. Change to 4½mm [No 7] needles and work the colour patt from Chart No 1. The 1st row of the patt will be as 1st row of the main patt. In this way the points of the Chart patt will form between the main patt as shown in the picture. Cont from the Chart until work measures 27(28:29)cm [10½ (11:11½) in]. Now divide for Back and Front.

BACK

Shape Armholes Work across the first 72(78:84) sts of the next rnd thus: **1st row** Cast off 4 sts, patt 68(74:80), turn. Cont to work back and forth on these sts only. **2nd row** Cast off 4 sts, patt 64(70:76) sts, purling the Chart patt. **3rd row and 4th rows** Cast off 3 sts, patt to end . . . 58(64:70) sts. **5th and 6th rows** Cast off 2 sts, patt to end . . . 54(60:66) sts.

Dec 1 st at both ends of foll right-side rows until 50(56:62) sts rem. End of armhole shaping.

Cont in patt from the Chart until armholes measure 16cm [6½ in] ending after a wrong-side row.

Shape Shoulders 1st row Cast off 6 sts, patt 15 (17:19), turn. Complete this side first. **2nd row** Cast off 4 sts, patt 11(13:15). **3rd row** Cast off 6 sts, patt 5(7:9). **4th row** Cast off 3 sts, patt 2(4:6). **5th row** Cast off rem 2(4:6) sts. With right side facing, rejoin yarn to rem sts at neck edge, cast off centre 8(10:12) sts, patt to end. Complete this side to match first side, reversing shapings thus: **1st row** Cast off 6 sts, patt 15(17:19) **2nd row** Cast off 4 sts, patt 11(13:15). **3rd row** Cast off 6 sts, patt 5(7:9). **4th row** Cast off 3 sts, patt 2(4:6). **5th row** Cast off rem 2(4:6) sts.

FRONT

Shape Armholes Work across the rem 72(78:84) sts thus: **1st row** Cast off 4 sts, patt 68(74:80). Work back and forth. **2nd row** Cast off 4 sts, patt 64(70:76), purling from the Chart patt. **3rd and 4th rows** Cast off 3 sts, patt to end . . . 58 (64:70) sts. **5th and 6th rows** Cast off 2 sts, patt to end . . . 54(60:66) sts.

Dec 1 st at both ends of foll right-side rows until 50(56:62) sts rem. End of armhole shaping.

Cont in patt from the Chart until

work matches Back to shoulder less 10 rows, ending after a wrong-side row.

Shape Neck 1st row Patt 22 (24:26), turn. Complete this side first. **2nd row** Cast off 3 sts, patt to end. **3rd row and foll alt rows** Patt to end. **4th row** Cast off 2 sts, patt to end. **6th row** Cast off 2 sts, patt to end. **8th row** K2 tog, patt to end. Work 2 rows without shaping.

Shape Shoulders Cast off 6 sts at beg of next row and foll alt row. Work 1 row. Cast off rem sts. With right side of work facing, rejoin yarn to rem sts at neck edge. Cast off centre 6(8:10) sts, patt to end. **2nd row and foll alt rows** Patt to end. **3rd row** Cast off 3 sts, patt to end. **5th row** Cast off 2 sts, patt to end. **7th row** As 5th row. **9th row** K2 tog, patt to end. Work 2 rows without shaping, thus ending after a right-side row.

Shape Shoulder Cast off 6 sts at beg of next row and foll alt row. Work 1 row. Cast off rem sts.

SLEEVES

With set of 3¾mm [No 9] needles and B, cast on 36(36:42) sts having 12(12:14) sts on each needle. Work 5cm [2 in] k1, p1 rib. Change to set of 4½mm [No 7] needles and work the 14 rnds of patt from Chart No 2.

Now change to set of 4mm [No 8] needles and cont in main patt: **1st rnd** With B, k to end. **2nd rnd** K3 B, *1 C, 5 B; rep from * to last 3 sts, 1 C, 2 B. **3rd to 6th rnds** With B, k to end. **7th rnd** *K1 C, 5 B; rep from * to end. **8th to 11th rnds** With B, k to end.

Rep 2nd to 11th rnds for main patt, at the same time, inc thus: **12th rnd** K1 B, inc 1k, as 2nd rnd to last st, inc 1k, k1 B. Patt 5 rnds straight.

Cont in this way, inc 2 sts every 4th(4th:6th) rnd to 52(54:56) sts. This neat inc either side of 2 sts forms the underarm shaping.

Now cont without shaping until sleeve measures 36(37:39)cm [14

Continued on next page

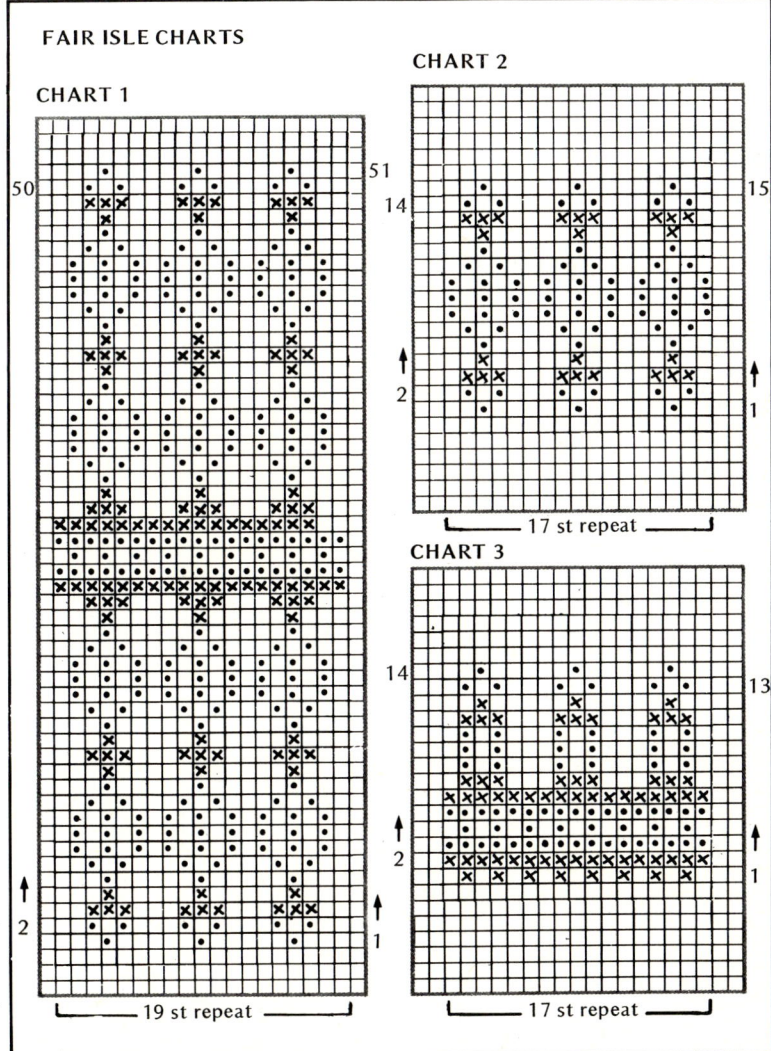

FAIR ISLE CHARTS

CHART 1

CHART 2

CHART 3

19 st repeat

17 st repeat

17 st repeat

Above: the three charts that you will need to knit the Set For The Cold – Chart 1 is used for the sweater; Chart 2 for the sleeves and mittens; Chart 3 for the hat. The contrasting flecks are knitted in as you go

Children's Clothes

Set for the cold ... continued

(14½ : 15½) in] ending at underarm.
Shape Top 1st row Cast off 3 sts, patt to end of rnd, turn. Cont back and forth. **2nd row** Cast off 3 sts, patt to end, purling the patt. **3rd and 4th rows** Cast off 2 sts, patt to end. **7th row** K2 tog, patt to last 2 sts, k2 tog. **8th row** Patt to end. Rep 7th and 8th rows 7(8:9) times more. **27th to 30th rows** Cast off 2 sts, patt to end. **31st and 32nd rows** Cast off 3 sts, patt to end. Cast off rem 12 sts.

TO MAKE UP
Press pieces lightly following instructions on ball band. With right side inside, back-stitch the shoulder seams. Placing underarms of sleeves to side edges and the cast-off 12 sts to shoulder seams, with right sides together, back-stitch the sleeve tops to the armholes.

Neckband With right side of work facing, using set of 3¾mm [No 9] needles and B, pick up and k70 (74:78) sts round neck edge. Work 7cm [2¾ in] k1, p1 rib. Cast off loosely in rib. Fold the neckband in half to wrong side and slip-stitch in place.

HAT
TO MAKE
With set of 3¾mm [No 9] needles and B, cast on 90(96:102) sts having 30(32:34) sts on each needle. Work 3cm [1¼ in] k1, p1 rib.

Change to set of 4½mm [No 7] needles and work the 14 rnds of patt from Chart No 3.

Change to 4mm [No 8] needles and cont in rnds of main patt: **1st rnd** With B, k to end. **2nd rnd** K3 B, *1 C, 5 B; rep from * to last 3 sts, 1 C, 2 B. **3rd to 6th rnds** With B k to end. **7th rnd** *K1 C, 5 B; rep from * to end. **8th to 11th rnds** With B k to end.

Rep 2nd to 11th rnds for the main patt until work measures 20cm [8 in].

Shape Crown 1st rnd * With B, k2 tog; rep from * to end ... 45(48:51) sts. **2nd rnd** With B, k to end. **3rd rnd** *With B, k2 tog; rep from * to last 3(2:3) sts, k3(2:3) tog ... 22(24:25) sts. **4th rnd** As 2nd rnd. **5th rnd** With B, *K2 tog; rep from * to last 2(2:3) sts, k2(2:3) tog ... 11(12:12) sts. **6th rnd** As 2nd. Thread yarn through rem sts, draw up and secure. Sew in the end neatly. Make a pompon (see page 75) and sew on.

MITTENS
TO MAKE
With set of 3¾mm [No 9] needles and B, cast on 36 sts having 12 sts on each needle. Work 6cm [2½ in] k1, p1 rib, inc 1 st at end of last rnd.

Change to 4½mm [No 7] needles and on these 37 sts cont in main patt as hat at the same time, shaping for thumb thus: **1st rnd** With B, k to end. **2nd rnd** *K5 B, 1 C* rep from * to * twice more, inc 1k, k1, inc 1k, rep from * to * 3 times. **3rd rnd** With B, k to end. **4th rnd** With B, k18, inc 1k, k3, inc 1k, k18. **5th rnd** With B, k to end.

6th rnd With B, k18, inc 1k, k5, inc 1k, k18. **7th rnd** K3 B, *1 C, 5 B* rep from * to * once more, 1 C, k12 B, * 1 C, 5 B * rep from * to * once more, 1 C, 2 B ... 43 sts. **8th rnd** With B, k18, inc 1k, k7, inc 1k, k18. **9th rnd** With B, k to end. **10th rnd** As 9th.

Change to 4½mm [No 7] needles and cont in patt from Chart No 2, dividing for the thumb and palm on the next 2 rnds thus: **Next rnd** Patt 17, slip next 11 sts on to safety-pin, patt 17. **Next rnd** Patt 17, turn, cast on 2 sts, patt 17 ... 36 sts.

Cont in rnds on 36 sts until the 15 rnds of patt have been worked. Change to set of 4mm [No 8] needles. Cont in main patt: **1st rnd** With B, k to end. **2nd rnd** K3 B, *1 C, 5 B; rep from * to last 3 sts, 1 C, 2 B. **3rd to 6th rnds** With B, k to end. **7th rnd** K *1 C, 5 B; rep from * to end. **8th to 11th rnds** With B, k to end.

Rep 2nd to 11th rnds until work measures 17(18:19)cm [6½(7:7½) in].

Shape Top Cont with B only. **1st rnd** *K2 tog, k14, sl 1, k1, psso*, rep from * to * once more. **2nd rnd** *K2 tog, k12, sl 1, k1, psso*, rep from * to * once more. Cont dec 4 sts in this way on every rnd until 16 sts rem. Cast off.

Thumb With right side of work facing, join B to the 11 sts. **1st row** Inc in 1st st, k to last st, inc in last st ... 13 sts. Cont in st-st in B for 2(2:3)cm [1(1:1¼) in] ending after a p row.

Shape Top 1st row K1, *k2 tog; rep from * to end. **2nd row** As 1st. Thread yarn through rem sts, draw up and secure. Sew thumb seam. With right side inside, join top seam. Turn to right side. Work another mitten the same.

Sporty pullover

6 to 12 years

A superbly designed top with an attractive geometric look ... but do keep your eye on the instructions. There's a knit row before the pattern begins.

Materials 8(9:10) 25g balls Double Knitting yarn in Dark colour (D) and 6(7:8) balls in Light colour (L); pairs of 4mm and 4½mm [No 8 and No 7] knitting needles; set of 4mm [No 8] double-pointed knitting needles.

Measurements To fit 66(75:85)cm [26(29½:33½) in] chest; 46(51:56)cm [18(20:22) in] length; 37(39:43)cm [14½(15½:17) in] sleeve length.

Tension 20 sts to 10cm [4 in] in pattern.

Abbreviations k, knit; p, purl; st(s), stitch(es); cm, centimetre(s); in, inch(es); alt, alternate; beg, beginning; cont, continue; dec, decreas(e)ing; inc, increas(e)ing; patt, pattern; rep, repeat; rem, remain(ing); tog, together; st-st, stocking stitch; foll, following.

Size Note Figures in brackets refer to larger sizes. One figure only refers to all sizes. Square brackets contain imperial measurements.

BACK
With pair 4mm [No 8] needles and D, cast on 76(80:84) sts. Work 5cm [2 in] k1, p1 rib.
Change to 4½mm [No 7] needles and cont in patt thus: K1 row on the wrong side with D to form the first ridge. **1st row** (right side) With L, k to end. **2nd row** With L, k to end. **3rd row** With L, k to end. **4th row** With L, p to end. **5th row** * K1 D, 1 L; rep from * to end. **6th row** * P1 L, 1 D; rep from * to end. **7th row** With L, k to end. **8th row** With L, p to end. **9th row** With L, k to end. **10th row** With L, k to end. **11th to 20th rows** As 1st to 10th working D in place of L.
These 20 rows form the patt. Cont in patt until work measures 29(33:37)cm [11½(13:14½) in] ending after a wrong-side row.
Shape Armholes Cast off 4 sts at beg of next 2 rows; 2 sts at beg

of next 2 rows. Dec 1 st at both ends of next 3 right-side rows ... 58(62:66) sts. Cont in patt without shaping until armholes measure 17(18:19)cm [6½(7:7½) in] ending after a wrong-side row.
Shape Shoulders and Neck 1st row Cast off 5 sts, patt 19(21:23), turn. Complete this side first. **2nd row** Cast off 5(6:7) sts, patt 14(15:16). **3rd row** Cast off 5 sts, patt 9(10:11). **4th row** Cast off 4 sts, patt 5(6:7). **5th row** Cast off 5(6:7) sts.
With right side of work facing, rejoin matching yarn to rem sts at neck edge, cast off centre 10 sts, patt to end. Complete this side to match first side thus: **1st row** Cast off 5 sts, patt 19(21:23). **2nd row** Cast off 5(6:7) sts, patt to end. **3rd row** Cast off 5 sts, patt to end. **4th row** Cast off 4 sts, patt 5(6:7). **5th row** Cast off rem sts.

FRONT
With pair 4mm [No 8] needles and D, cast on 76(80:84) sts. Work 5cm [2 in] k1, p1 rib.
Change to 4½mm [No 7] needles and cont in patt thus: K1 row on the wrong side to form the first ridge. **1st to 3rd rows** With L, k to end. **4th row** With L, p to end. **5th row** * K1 D, 1 L; rep from * to end. **6th row** * P1 L, 1 D; rep from * to end. **7th row** With L, k to end. **8th row** With L, p to end. **9th row** With L, k to end. **10th row** With L, k to end. **11th to 20th rows** As 1st to 10th rows working D in place of L.
These 20 rows form the patt. Cont in patt until work measures 29(33:37)cm [11½(13:14½) in], ending after the same wrong-side patt row as on Back.
Shape Armholes Cast off 4 sts at beg of next 2 rows; 2 sts at beg of next 2 rows. Dec 1 st at both ends of next 3 right-side rows ... 58(62:66) sts. Cont in patt without shaping until work measures 39 (40:41)cm [15½(15¾:16) in] from beg, ending after wrong-side row.
Shape Neck 1st row Patt 15(16:17) sts, turn. Complete this side first. Cont in patt until armhole measures 17(18:19)cm [6½(7:7½) in] ending after a wrong-side row.
Shape Shoulder Cast off 5sts at beg of next row and foll alt row. Work 1 row. Cast off rem 5(6:7) sts. With right side of work facing, rejoin matching yarn to rem sts at neck edge, cast off centre 28(30:32) sts, patt to end. Cont

Continued on page 162

Right: the Sporty Pullover looks good on a boy and just as good on a girl ... see cover and overleaf

Sporty pullover . . . continued

in patt on these 15(16:17) sts until armhole measures 17(18:19)cm [6½(7:7½) in] ending after a right-side row.

Shape Shoulder Cast off 5 sts at beg of next row and foll alt row. Work 1 row. Cast off rem sts.

SLEEVES

With pair 4mm [No 8] needles and D, cast on 34(36:38) sts. Work 5cm [2 in] k1, p1 rib, inc 11 sts evenly on last row . . . 45(47:49) sts.

Change to 4½mm [No 7] needles and cont in patt thus: K1 row with D to form first ridge. **1st to**

3rd rows With L, k3 rows. **4th row** With L, p to end. **5th row** * K1 D, 1 L; rep from * to last st, 1 D. **6th row** * P1 D, 1 L; rep from * to last st, 1 D. **7th row** With L, k to end. **8th row** With L, p to end. **9th row** With L, k to end. **10th row** With L, k to end. **11th to 20th rows** As 1st to 10th rows working D in place of L, at the same time, inc 1 st at both ends of the 3rd row and every foll 6th row to 57(59:61) sts. Cont in patt until work measures 37(39:43)cm [14½(15½:17) in] ending after the same patt row as on Back and Front.

Shape Top Cast off 2 sts at beg of next 4 rows. Dec 1 st at both ends of next row and foll alt rows to 31(33:35) sts, ending after wrong-side row. Dec 1 st at both ends of next row and every foll 4th row to 27 sts. Cast off 2 sts at beg of next 2 rows; 3 sts at beg of next 2 rows. Cast off rem 17 sts.
Work another sleeve the same.

TO MAKE UP

Press pieces very lightly on the wrong side following instructions on the ball band. With right sides together, join the shoulder and side seams, using a back-stitch seam and taking care to match the colour pattern. With right side inside, back-stitch the sleeve seams. With right sides together, place the sleeve tops to the arm-holes and tack in place underarm seams to sleeve seams. Sew in the sleeves and remove tackings.
With right side of work facing, using set of four double-pointed 4mm [No 8] needles, and D, pick up and k120 sts evenly round neck edge. Work 5 rounds k1, p1 rib, dec 2 sts in the front neck corners on right-side rows. Cast off rem sts loosely in rib.

Left: the hard-wearing pullover
Below: the shapes to guide you

SPORTY PULLOVER: SHAPE GUIDE

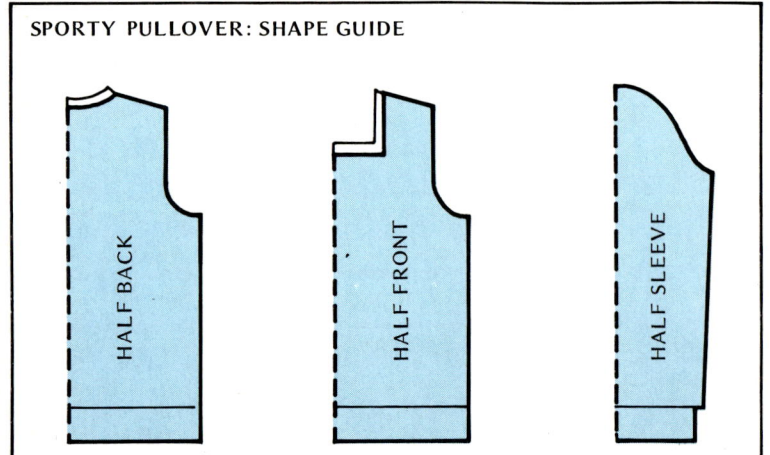

HALF BACK

HALF FRONT

HALF SLEEVE

Shortie bomber jacket

7 to 11 years

Choose a cheerful colour combination for this attractive zip-fronted jacket that fits snugly on the midriff.

Materials 180(200:250)g of Double Knitting yarn in cream (M); 70(70:90)g in blue (C1); 60 (60:80)g in orange (C2) and 60 (60:80)g in green (C3); pair 3mm [No 11] and 3¾mm [No 9] knitting needles; 3mm [No 11] crochet hook; 30(30:35)cm [12(12:14) in] open-ended zip.

Measurements To fit a 66 (71:76)cm [26(28:30) in] chest.

Tension 18 sts measure 10cm [4 in].

Abbreviations k, knit; p, purl; st(s), stitch(es); patt, pattern; cont, continue; rep, repeat; beg, beginning; dc, double crochet; alt, alternate; inc, increase; rem, remain(ing); foll, following; dec, decrease; cm, centimetre(s); in, inch(es).

Size Note Figures in brackets refer to larger sizes. One figure only refers to all sizes. Square brackets contain imperial measurements.

> If you like you can use 6 colours working 4 rows of each instead of 8 on the body, and 3 rows instead of 6 on the cuffs. Do remember to watch the zip length if you want to alter the length to the armholes — they go up in 5cm [2 in] so you have to add a multiple of this to achieve a neat finish.

FISHERMAN'S RIB

1st row K1, * k into st below next st on needle slipping st above off needle at the same time (known as k1b) k1. Rep from * to end.
2nd row K1b, * k1, k1b. Rep from * to end.
Rep these 2 rows for patt. Note that rib does not appear to form until about 5cm [2 in] of patt has been completed.

BACK

Using M and 3mm [No 11] needles cast on 64(68:72) sts and work in k1, p1 rib for 8cm [3¼ in], inc 1 st at end of last row . . . 65(69:73) sts. Change to 3¾mm [No 9] needles and work in Fisherman's Rib for 8 rows C1, 8 rows C2 and 8 rows C3. Cont in this sequence of stripes until the 3rd(3rd:4th) C3 stripe has been worked.

Shape Armholes Cast off 3 sts at beg of next 2 rows, 2 sts at beg of next 2 rows then dec 1 st at beg of next 4 rows . . . 51(55:59) sts. Cont straight until the 5th (5th:6th) C1 stripe has been worked. Break off colours, join on M and cont straight until work measures 35·5(37:42)cm [14(14½: 16½) in].

Shape Neck and Shoulders Cast off 3(4:5) sts at beg of next 2 rows. **Next row** Cast off 4 sts, patt 14(15:16) sts – including st already on needle from casting off, turn. ****Next row** (neck edge) Cast off 4, patt to end. **Next row** Cast off 4, patt to end. **Next row** Cast off 3, patt to end. Cast off rem 3(4:5) sts.**
Go back to other sts, cast off centre 9 sts, patt to end. **Next row** Cast off 4 sts, patt 14(15:16) sts. Now work from ** to ** of other side.

RIGHT FRONT

Using M and 3mm [No 11] needles cast on 32(34:36) sts and work in k1, p1 rib for 8cm [3¼ in], inc 1 st at beg of last row . . . 33(35:37) sts. Change to 3¾mm [No 9] needles and work in stripe sequence as Back and Fisherman's Rib until the 3rd(3rd:4th) C3 stripe has been completed.

Shape Armhole Next row Patt to end. **Next row** Cast off 3 sts, patt to front edge. Now cast off 2 sts at beg of next armhole edge row, then dec 1 st on next 2 alt armhole edge rows . . . 26(28:30) sts rem.
** Keeping continuity of patt, cont straight until the 5th(5th:6th) C1 stripe has been completed. Break off colours, join on M and cont in patt until work measures 30·5(30·5:35·5)cm [12(12:14) in] ending at front edge.

Shape Neck Now cast off 3 sts at beg of next row, 2 sts on next alt row and 1 st on foll alt row, then

Continued on page 164

Right: a short jacket with a lot of style — just right when the weather's cool, not cold. The shape guide is on page 164

Shortie bomber jacket . . . continued

1 st at neck edge on every 4th row until 14(16:18) sts rem. Cont straight until work measures as Back to shoulder ending at armhole edge.

Shape Shoulder Cast off 3(4:5) sts at beg of next row, 4 sts on next 2 armhole edge rows and 3(4:5) sts on foll alt row.

LEFT FRONT

Using M and 3mm [No 11] needles cast on 32(34:36) sts and work in k1, p1 rib for 8cm [3¼ in], inc 1 st at end of last row . . . 33(35:37) sts. Now work as for Right Front until 3rd(3rd:4th) C3 stripe has been completed.

Shape Armhole Keeping continuity of stripes cast off 3 sts at beg of next row, 2 sts at beg of next alt row and 1 st on next 2 alt armhole edge rows. Now cont as for Right Front from ** to end.

SLEEVES

Using C1 and 3mm [No 11] needles cast on 34(36:38) sts and work in k1, p1 rib in stripe patt of 6 rows C1, 6 rows C2, 6 rows C3 and 6 rows C1, inc 1 st at end of last row. Break off colours, join on M, change to 3¾mm [No 9] needles and work in Fisherman's Rib for 5cm [2 in], then inc 1 st each end of next row and at 5cm [2 in] intervals until there are 45(47:51) sts.

Cont straight until sleeve measures 33(35·5:39)cm [13(14:15½ in] – or length required.

Shape Top (all sizes) At beg of rows cast off 3 sts twice, 2 sts twice, 1 st 2(4:6) times then (2 sts twice, 1 st twice) 4 times, 2 sts twice. Cast off rem 5(5:7) sts.

NECKBAND

Join shoulders. Now using 3mm [No 11] needles and M yarn and with right side of work facing, begin at Right Front neck edge and pick up and k63(67:67) sts all round neck edge. P one row then work in Fisherman's Rib for 4 rows. Now work in colour stripes of 8 rows C1, 8 rows C2 and 8 rows C3, but at same time turning at ends of rows thus: * Leave 3 sts unworked at end of next 2 rows, 3 sts more at end of next 2 rows, 4 sts more at end of next 2 rows, then work over all sts for 4 rows. Rep from * once more. Cast off in the patt.

TO MAKE UP

Sew in sleeves, then sew up sleeve and side seams. Turn collar to inside and stitch down loosely. Using crochet hook and M yarn, work 2 rows of dc along each front edge. Fasten off. Sew in zip.

Below: the shape guide for the Shortie Bomber Jacket

SHORTIE BOMBER JACKET: SHAPE GUIDE

HALF BACK   HALF FRONT   HALF SLEEVE

Stripes with style

8 to 12 years

A simple pattern that can be made up in school, or football, colours.

Materials 125(150)g of 4-ply wool in light blue (C1) and white (C2); 100(100)g of 4-ply wool in dark blue (C3); pair 2¾mm [No 12] and 3mm [No 11] knitting needles.

Measurements To fit a 68–71 (76–79)cm [27–28(30–31) in] chest.

Tension 33 sts and 36 rows measure about 10cm [4 in].

Abbreviations k, knit; p, purl; st(s), stitch(es); st-st, stocking stitch; rep, repeat; sl, slip; psso, pass slip st over; tog, together; tbl, through back of loop; beg, beginning; patt, pattern; cont, continue; dec, decrease; rem, remain(ing); inc, increase; cm, centimetre(s); in, inch(es).

Size Note Figures in brackets refer to larger size. One figure only refers to both sizes. Square brackets contain imperial measurements.

STRIPE PATTERN

This is worked in st-st thus: *4cm [1½ in] C2, 4cm [1½ in] C1. Rep from * twice more, then 4cm [1½ in] C2, 5cm [2 in] C3, then (4cm [1½ in] C2 and 4cm [1½ in] C1) to completion.

BACK

Using 2¾mm [No 12] needles and C3, cast on 114(122) sts and work in k2, p2 rib for 4cm [1½ in]. Change to 3mm [No 11] needles and C2 and inc in next row in every 11th(12th) st to end . . . 124(132) sts. Cont in st-st in stripe patt as given until work measures 34(35)cm [13½(13¾) in] from beg ending after a p row.

Shape Armholes Next row K1, sl 1, k1, psso, k to last 3 sts, k2 tog, k1. **Next row** K1, p2 tog, p to last 3 sts, p2 tog tbl, k1. Rep last 2 rows until 78(82) sts rem, then dec on right side rows only to 38(40) sts. Cast off.

FRONT

Work as for Back to armhole.

Shape Armhole and Divide for Neck Next row K1, sl 1, k1, psso, k59(63) sts, turn and leave rem sts on spare needle. **Now dec 1 st at front edge on next and every 3rd row until 18(19) sts have been dec at this edge, but at the same time dec 1 st at armhole edge to match back on next 22(24) rows, then on every alternate row until 1 st remains. Fasten off**.

Go back to other sts, rejoin yarn at centre front, k to last 3 sts, k2 tog, k1. Now work to match other side from ** to **.

SLEEVES

Using C3 and 2¾mm [No 12] needles, cast on 58(62) sts and work in k2, p2 rib for 6cm [2½ in]. Change to C2 and 3mm [No 11] needles and in next row inc in every 5th(6th) st, 10 times . . . 68(72) sts. Cont in stripe patt until same row as Back to armhole has been worked.

Shape Top Rep the first 2 rows of Back armhole shaping until 54(56) sts rem, then dec on every alternate row to 14 sts. Cast off.

NECKBAND

Sew in sleeves using back-stitch. Now with right side facing, and using 2¾mm [No 12] needles and C3, pick up and k62(66) sts along sleeve top and down left side of neck, 1 st from centre, 62(66) sts up right side of neck and along sleeve top, and 36(40) sts from back neck. **Next row** Work in k2, p2 rib to within 2 sts of centre st, k2 tog, p1, k2 tog tbl, rib to end. **Next row** Rib to within 2 sts of centre st, p2 tog tbl, k1, p2 tog, rib to end.

TO MAKE UP

Press on wrong side following ball band instructions and avoiding the ribbing. Join neckband seam then sew up sleeve and side seams.

Right: the perennial favourite – a v-necked sweater that can be knitted in any colours you like

164

Roll-neck sweaters

9 (or 10) and 16 years

This is a very popular shape and an easy pattern.

Materials 12(16) 25g balls Double Knitting yarn; pairs of 3mm and 3¾mm [No 11 and No 9] knitting needles.

Measurements Actual size 70 (86)cm [28(34) in] round chest; length 45(48)cm [17¾(19) in]; sleeve length, 37(47)cm [14½(18½) in].

Tension 23 sts and 38 rows to 10cm [4 in] in ridged st-st.

Abbreviations k, knit; p, purl; st(s), stitch(es); cm, centimetre(s); in, inch(es); alt, alternate; beg, beginning; cont, continue; dec, decreas(e)ing; inc, increas(e)ing; patt, pattern; rep, repeat; rem, remain(ing); foll, following, tog, together.

Size Note Figure in brackets refers to larger size. One figure only refers to both sizes. Square brackets contain imperial measurements.

> A row counter on the end of the needle will be useful so you can remember which row you're on. It looks as if it's all stocking stitch with an occasional purl row but in fact it's all purl with an occasional knit row!

BACK

With 3mm [No 11] needles, cast on 80(100) sts. Work 6cm [2½ in] k1, p1 rib. Change to 3¾mm [No 9] needles.
Change to patt: **1st row** P to end. **2nd row** P to end. **3rd row** K to end. **4th row** As 2nd. These 4 rows form the ridged st-st patt. Cont in patt until work measures 45 (48)cm [17¾(19) in] ending after a wrong-side row.
Shape Shoulders Cast off 6(8) sts at beg of next 4 rows; 6(7) sts at beg of foll 4 rows. Cast off rem 32(40) sts.

FRONT

With 3mm [No 11] needles, cast on 80(100) sts. Work 6cm [2½ in] k1, p1 rib. Change to 3¾mm [No 9] needles.

Change to patt: **1st row** P to end. **2nd row** P to end. **3rd row** K to end. **4th row** As 2nd. These 4 rows form the ridged st-st patt. Cont in patt until the Front matches Back to shoulder, <u>less 12 rows</u>.
Shape Neck 1st row Work 35(45) sts, turn. Leave rem sts on a spare needle and cont on first set of sts thus: **2nd row** Cast off 3(4) sts, p to end. **3rd row** Work to end. **4th row** As 2nd. **5th row** As 3rd. **6th row** Cast off 2(2), p to end.

7th row Work to end. **8th and 9th rows** As 6th and 7th. **10th row** Cast off 1(3), p to end. Work 2 rows straight.
Shape Shoulder Cast off 6(8) sts at beg of next row and foll alt row; 6(7) sts at beg of foll 2 alt rows.
With right side of work facing, rejoin yarn to rem sts at neck edge. Cast off centre 10(10) sts, work to end. Complete this side to match the first side thus: **1st**

row P to end. **2nd row** Cast off 3(4) sts, work to end. **3rd row** P to end. **4th row** As 2nd. **5th row** P to end. **6th row** Cast off 2(2), work to end. **7th row** P to end. **8th and 9th rows** As 6th and 7th rows. **10th row** Cast off 1(3) sts, work to end. Work 2 rows straight, thus ending after a right-side row.
Shape Shoulder Cast off 6(8) sts at beg of next row and foll alt row; 6(7) sts at beg of foll 2 alt rows.

SLEEVES

With 3mm [No 11] needles, cast on 42(46) sts. Work 6(7)cm [2½(2¾) in] k1, p1 rib. Change to 3¾mm [No 9] needles.

Cont in patt: **1st row** P to end. **2nd row** P to end. **3rd row** K to end. **4th row** As 2nd. These 4 rows form the patt.

Cont in patt inc 1 st at both ends of 3rd row foll and every foll 8th row to 60(70) sts. Cont in patt without shaping until work measures 37(47)cm [14½(18½) in] ending after a wrong-side row. Cast off the sts loosely. Work a second sleeve in the same way.

COLLAR

With 3¾mm [No 9] needles, cast on 60(70) sts. Cont in the 4 rows ridged patt as Back until work measures 35(40)cm [13¾(15¾) in] ending after a wrong-side row. Cast off.

TO MAKE UP

Press very lightly according to the instructions on the ball band, taking care not to flatten the ridges.

Seams With right sides together join the shoulder seams, using back-stitch. Leaving 13(15)cm [5(6) in] free at top, back-stitch the side seams, matching the ridges. With right side inside, matching the ridges, back-stitch the sleeve seams. Tack the sleeve cast-off edge into the armhole left at top

of side seam, with the sleeve and underarm seam together. With right sides together, back-stitch the sleeve in place. Remove tackings.

Collar With right sides together, back-stitch the narrow ends of the collar. Place the collar seam to centre back of neck edge. With right side of collar to right side of neck edge, tack the collar in place round neck edge. Carefully back-stitch this seam then remove tacking. Fold collar to inside and slip-stitch to inside, concealing back-stitch. Roll collar to outside as shown in the picture opposite.

Left: the Roll-neck Sweaters which are always popular for outdoor play – the pattern looks unusual but is very easy Below: the shapes to guide you

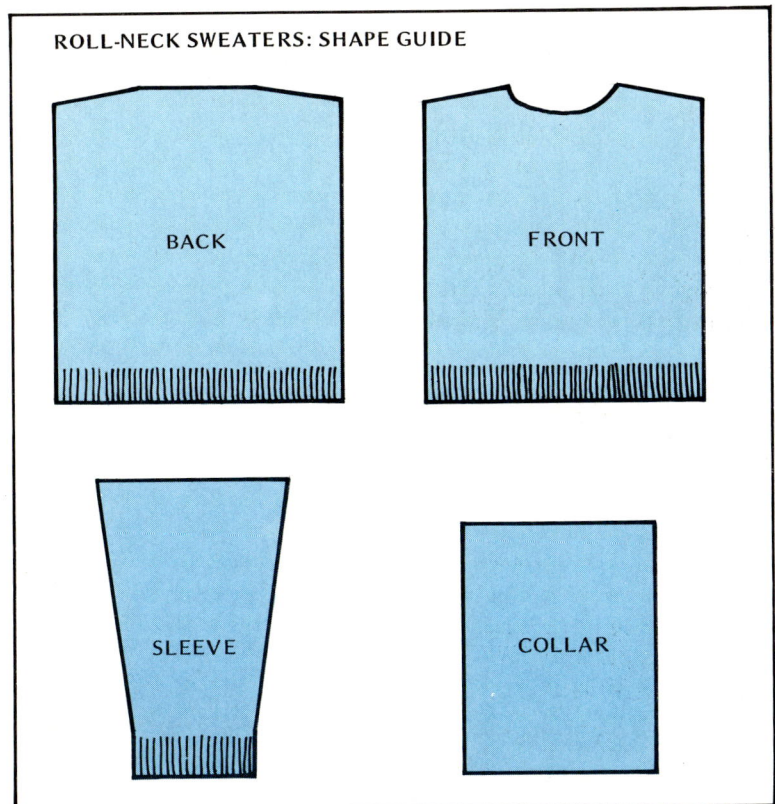

ROLL-NECK SWEATERS: SHAPE GUIDE

BACK

FRONT

SLEEVE

COLLAR

Sailor-style sweaters

9 and 16 years

Illustrated overleaf

All the nice girls . . . love sailor-style sweaters! The attractive stripes rate these ones way above the ordinary.

Materials 4(12) 25g balls 4-ply knitting yarn in Dark colour (D); 8(8) balls in Light colour (L); pair 3¼mm [No 10] knitting needles.

Measurements Actual size 70 (88)cm [28(34½) in] all round; length, 48(56)cm [19(22) in]; sleeve length, 34(47)cm [13½(18½) in].

Tension 28 sts and 36 rows to 10cm [4 in].

Abbreviations k, knit; p, purl; st(s), stitch(es); cm, centimetre(s); in, inch(es); alt, alternate; beg, beginning; cont, continue; dec, decreas(e)ing; inc, increas(e)ing; rep, repeat; rem, remain(ing); tog, together; st-st, stocking stitch; foll, following.

Size Note Figure in brackets refers to larger size. One figure only refers to both sizes. Square brackets contain imperial measurements.

> Although this is a simple design and quite suitable for the novice knitter, it would be spoiled if the stocking stitch is not worked evenly. If you find that yours is becoming ridged it usually means that you knit or purl a little loosely. Try a size tighter needle for either one until you eliminate the ridges entirely.

BACK

With D(L), cast on 100(124) sts. Beg p row, cont in reversed st-st (p side is right side) until work measures 8(12)cm [3(4¾) in] ending after a k row.

Now cont in striped patt in reversed st-st thus: *Work 4 rows L(D); 4 rows D(L)* Rep from * to * 4 times more. Five stripes have now been worked in each colour. With L(D), cont in reversed st-st until work measures 37(46)cm [14½(18) in] ending after a k row.

Now cont in striped patt in

reversed st-st reversing colours thus: **Work 4 rows D(L); 4 rows L(D)**. Rep from ** to ** 4 times more. Five stripes have now been worked in each colour. With D(L), cont in reversed st-st until work measures 52(62)cm [20½(24½) in] ending after a k row.

Shape Neck Next row P26(31), turn, k to end. **Next row** Cast off 26(31). With right side facing, rejoin matching yarn to neck edge of rem sts, cast off centre 48(62) sts, p26(31) sts to end. K1 row. Cast off rem sts.

FRONT

With D(L), cast on 100(124) sts. Beg p row, cont in reversed st-st (p side is right side) until work measures 8(12)cm [3(4¾) in] ending after a k row.

Now cont in striped patt in reversed st-st thus: *Work 4 rows L(D); 4 rows D(L)*. Rep from * to * 4 times more. Five stripes have now been worked in each colour. With L(D), cont in reversed st-st until work measures 35(45)cm [13¾(17¾) in] ending after a k row.

Divide for Neck Opening and Collar Shaping 1st row P50(62), turn. Leave rem sts on a spare needle and cont on 1st set of sts thus: Inc 1 st at centre edge (neck edge) on next row and foll 3rd rows 1(11) times more, then inc at the same edge on foll alt rows to 74(92) sts. At the same time, when work measures 37(46) cm [14½(18) in] work the ten rows of stripes to match the Back and then cont in D(L). When all the inc rows have been worked, cont for a few rows if necessary until Front matches Back to shoulder – 52(62)cm [20½(24½) in] ending after a p row.

Next row Cast off 48(61) sts, k to end. **Next row** Cast off rem 26(31) sts.

With right side of work facing, join matching yarn to rem sts at centre front. Inc 1 st at centre edge on next row and at same edge on foll 3rd rows 1(11) times more, then inc at same edge on foll alt rows to 74(92) sts, at the same time working in stripes to match the first side worked and then cont in D(L). When all the inc rows have been worked cont if necessary for a few rows until the Front matches Back to shoulder 52(62)cm [20½(24½) in] ending after a k row.

Next row Cast off 48(61) p to end. **Next row** Cast off 26(31) sts.

SLEEVES (make 2)

With D(L), cast on 62(80) sts. Cont in reversed st-st for 8(12) cm

Continued on next page

Sailor-style sweaters . . . continued
[3(4¾) in]. Cont in reversed st-st in stripes of 4 rows L(D); 4 rows D(L) until 5 stripes in each colour have been worked.

Cont in reversed st-st in L(D), inc 1 st at both ends of every foll 5th(30th) row to 82(88) sts. Cont in reversed st-st until work measures 38(53)cm [15(21) in] ending after a k row. Cast off.

COLLAR

With D(L), cast on 96(124) sts. Work 20(28)cm [8(11) in] st-st, ending after a k row. Cast off.

TO MAKE UP

Press following instructions on ball band. With p sides together, join shoulder seams with back-stitch. With p sides together and matching stripes, back-stitch the side seams, leaving 15(16)cm [6 (6¼) in] free at top for armhole. With p side inside, matching stripes, back-stitch the sleeve seams.

With sleeve seam to underarm seam, tack the cast-off edge of sleeve to armhole, with p sides together. Back-stitch the sleeve in place and remove tackings. Fold the hems at lower edges and cuffs to wrong side and slip stitch allowing 6cm [2½ in] hem on adult size and 4cm [1½ in] on child's size. Fold the inc edge of lapel to wrong side and slip-stitch in place as shown in picture. With p side inside back-stitch the narrow ends of the collar. Turn collar to right side. With right side of one open edge of collar to right side of neck edge, pin the collar in place – beg at centre back and place pin at each end, taking in both layers of the lapels, then pinning the remainder. Back-stitch neatly along this edge. Remove the pins. Now fold collar over to inside of neck and neatly hem-stitch concealing the back-stitch seam. Take special care with this last seam as it will show when the lapels are laid open. Press the collar.

SAILOR-STYLE SWEATERS: SHAPE GUIDE

FRONT and BACK

WAIST

SLEEVE

CUFF

COLLAR

Above left: these attractive sweaters with their sailor-style collars would be perfect for spring or autumn if knitted in a silky cotton yarn. In winter they can be worn over another sweater for added warmth
Left: the shape guide which also indicates where the stripes come

Chess bed cover

Bright squares knitted separately are joined together to make this attractive spread. See below if you prefer to make a lightweight version.

Materials Fifty 50g balls Double Double or chunky weight yarn in each of 2 contrasting colours (A and B); a pair 7½mm [No 1] knitting needles; 7mm [No 2] crochet hook.

Measurements 125cm [49½ in] square, not including borders.

Tension Each square measures 25cm [10 in] in patt, with yarn used triple.

Abbreviations k, knit; p, purl; st(s), stitch(es); cm, centimetre(s); in, inch(es); tog, together; patt, pattern; cont, continue; rep, repeat; y fwd, yarn forward; dc, double crochet; tr, treble; ch, chain. Square brackets contain imperial measurements.

Because this is knitted in thick yarn used triple the cover is superbly heavy. If you would prefer to make a smaller, lightweight version it is quite simple: First, choose your yarn and decide whether you want it in triple thickness – perhaps plain double knitting will suit your purpose. Use a suitable size of needle for your choice, say 3¾mm [No 9] for double knitting or for 2 strands of 4 ply used together. Cast on the stitches as given and cont in the patt until the length of work is the same as the width, thus forming a square. Multiply the length of the side of the square by 5 and this will give you some idea of the size you will finish up with.

TO MAKE

Blackberry Stitch squares (red in picture): Using 3 strands tog throughout, cast on 32 sts. **1st row** (right side) P. **2nd row** *P3 tog, (k1, p1, k1) all in next st; rep from * to end. **3rd row** P. **4th row** *(k1, p1, k1) all in next st, p3 tog; rep from * to end.
These 4 rows form the patt. Cont

in patt until square measures 25cm [10 in]. Cast off.

Quilt Stitch squares (white in picture): Using 3 strands together throughout, cast on 30 sts. **1st row** (right side) P1, (k1, p2) to end, ending last rep, p1. **2nd to 4th rows** K the p sts and p the k sts. **3rd row** As 1st. **5th row** P1, k1, p2, (y fwd to make a st, k1, p2, k1, pass the made st over the last 4 sts worked, p2) to last 2 sts, k1, p1. **6th row** As 2nd. **7th to 10th rows** As 1st to 4th rows. **11th row** P1, (y fwd to make a st, k1, p2, k1, pass the made st over the last 4 sts

worked, p2) to end, ending last rep, p1. **12th row** As 6th.
These 12 rows form the patt. Cont in patt until square measures 25cm [10 in]. Cast off.
With colour A, make 18 squares in Quilt stitch. With B, work 17 squares in Blackberry stitch.

TO MAKE UP

Place the squares into a chess patt as shown and oversew tog using only one strand of yarn. With A, work 1 row dc along each strip of squares, then with B work a similar row of dc

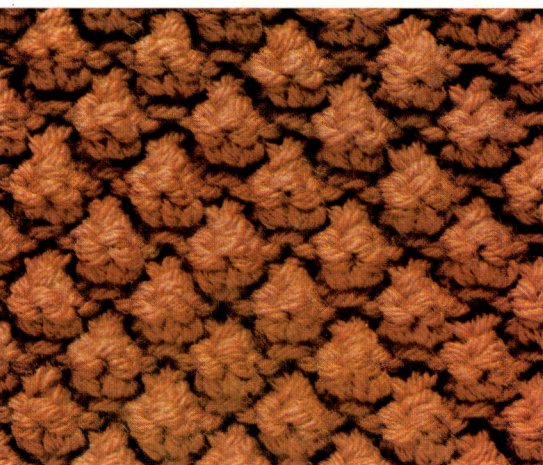

Above: a bright and cheerful cover that's knitted in squares and can be done at your leisure. The red square shows Blackberry Stitch in detail; the white square is Quilt Stitch

along strips in the opposite direction to cover uneven edges of squares.
Border With B, work 1 row dc all round outer edge, working 3 dc in each córner, join with a slip-stitch. **2nd row** (2 tr in next dc, 1 ch, miss 1 dc) all round, join with a slip-stitch. Fasten off.

Sporty outfit
Teenage to adult

The random-dyed yarn gives the look of fabric – used to good effect in this sporty suit.

Materials Eighteen 25g balls Double Knitting yarn in random-dyed or multi-coloured yarn (M) for the Trousers; 10 balls in contrast (A) and 6 balls in M for the Hooded Sweater; pairs of 3mm and 3¾mm [No 11 and No 9] knitting needles; elastic for waist 3cm [1¼ in] wide; 15cm [6 in] zip.

Measurements To fit 81–86cm [32–34 in] bust; actual size of top 88cm [35 in]; length of top, 55cm [21½ in] at centre back; sleeve seam 35cm [14 in]; length of trousers 72cm [28½ in].

Tension 26 sts and 34 rows to 10cm [4 in] in st-st on 3¾mm [No 9] needles.

Abbreviations k, knit; p, purl; st(s), stitch(es); cm, centimetre(s); in, inch(es); alt, alternate; beg, beginning; cont, continue; dec, decreas(e)ing; inc, increas(e)ing; inc 1k, increase by picking up the loop between the sts and knitting into the back of it; st-st, stocking stitch; tog, together; tbl, through back of loop; rem, remain(ing); rep, repeat; foll, following. Square brackets contain imperial measurements.

> Write name of each trouser section on a scrap of paper and safety-pin the label to each part as it is made — it will help when placing the pieces for making up and it could also prevent the possibility of making too many pieces of the same shape. The same tip will help on the sleeves — in this case put the labels up high near the neck edge so that the sleeves are correctly placed between the back and front raglan shapings.

TROUSERS
FRONT LEFT LEG

With 3¾mm [No 9] needles, and M, cast on 100 sts. Beg k row, cont in st-st, dec 1 st at both ends of 7th row foll and every foll 8th row until 80 sts rem, ending after a k row.

Shape for Crotch 1st row Cast off 6 sts, p to end. **2nd row** K to end. **3rd row** Cast off 3 sts, p to end. **4th row** K to end. **5th row** Cast off 2 sts, p to end. **6th row** K to end. **7th row** Cast off 2 sts, p to end. **8th row** K2 tog, k to end. **9th row** P2 tog, p to end. **10th row** K to end. **11th row to 14th rows** Rep 9th and 10th rows twice. **15th row** P2 tog, p to end. **16th row** K2 tog, k to end. **17th row** P2 tog, p to end . . . 60 sts.
Beg k row, cont in st-st without shaping until work measures 75cm [29½ in]. Cast off. Work another piece in exactly the same way to form the Back Right Leg.

FRONT RIGHT LEG

With 3¾mm [No 9] needles, and M, cast on 100 sts. Beg k row, cont in st-st, dec 1 st at both ends of 7th row foll and every foll 8th row until 80 sts rem, ending after a p row.

Shape for Crotch 1st row Cast off 6 sts, k to end. **2nd row** P to end. **3rd row** Cast off 3 sts, k to end. **4th row** P to end. **5th row** Cast off 2 sts, k to end. **6th row** P to end. **7th row** Cast off 2 sts, k to end. **8th row** P2 tog, p to end. **9th row** K2 tog, k to end. **10th row** P to end. **11th to 14th rows** Rep last 2 rows twice more. **15th row** K2 tog, k to last 2 sts, k2 tog. **16th row** P to end. **17th row** K2 tog, k to end . . . 60 sts.
Beg p row, cont in st-st without shaping until work measures 75cm [29½ in]. Cast off. Work another piece in exactly the same way to form the Back Left Leg.

TO MAKE UP

With right sides together, back-stitch along the side seams. Now back-stitch along the inner leg seams. Back-stitch the back seam and then the front leaving 20cm [8 in] open to waist. Fold 2½cm [1 in] to wrong side at lower edge of each leg and slip-stitch all round. At waist fold 5cm [2 in] to wrong side and slip-stitch, leaving ends open. Press according to instructions on ball band. Insert the elastic through the waist channel and secure ends. Sew in the zip.

HOODED SWEATER
BACK

With 3mm [No 11] needles and A, cast on 116 sts. Work 5cm [2 in] k1, p1 rib. Change to 3¾mm [No 9] needles and cont in st-st until work measures 35cm [14 in] ending after a p row.
Shape Raglan 1st row Cast off 6 sts, k to end. **2nd row** Cast off 6 sts, p to end . . . 104 sts. **3rd row**

FRONT

With 3mm [No 11] needles, cast on 116 sts. Work 5cm [2 in] k1, p1 rib. Change to 3¾mm [No 9] needles and cont in st-st until work measures 35cm [14 in] ending after a p row.
Shape Raglan 1st row Cast off 6 sts, k to end. **2nd row** Cast off 6 sts, p to end. **3rd row** K3, k2 tog, k to last 5 sts, k2 tog tbl, k3. **4th row** P to end. Rep 3rd and 4th rows until 72 sts rem, ending after a p row.
Divide for Neck Opening 1st row K3, k2 tog, k31, turn. Leave rem sts on a spare needle and cont on first set of sts only thus: **2nd row** P to end. **3rd row** K3, k2 tog, k to end. **4th row** P to end. Rep last 2 rows until 18 sts rem, ending after a p row. Cast off.
With right side of work facing, rejoin yarn to rem 36 sts. **1st row** K31, k2 tog tbl, k3. **2nd row** P to end. **3rd row** K to last 5 sts, k2 tog tbl, k3. **4th row** P to end. Rep last 2 rows until 18 sts rem, ending after a p row. Cast off.

LEFT SLEEVE

With 3mm [No 11] needles and A, cast on 52 sts. Work 5cm [2 in] k1, p1 rib. Change to 3¾mm [No 9] needles and M. **Inc row** K4, *inc 1k, k4; rep from * to end . . . 64 sts. Beg p row, cont in st-st inc 1 st at both ends of 4th row foll and every foll 6th row to 94 sts, ending after a p row.
Shape Raglan 1st row Cast off 6 sts, k to end. **2nd row** Cast off 6 sts, p to end. **3rd row** K3, k2 tog, k to last 5 sts, k2 tog tbl, k3. **4th row** P to end. Rep 3rd and 4th rows until 14 sts rem, ending after a 4th row.
Shape Neck Edge 1st row K3, k2 tog, k9. **2nd row** Cast off 4 sts, p9. **3rd row** K3, k2 tog, k4. **4th row** Cast off 4 sts, p4. Cast off rem 4 sts.

RIGHT SLEEVE

With 3mm [No 11] needles and A, cast on 52 sts. Work 5cm [2 in] k1, p1 rib. Change to 3¾mm [No 9] needles and M. **Inc row** K4, *inc 1k, k4; rep from * to end . . . 64 sts. Beg p row, cont in st-st inc 1 st at both ends of 4th row foll and every foll 6th row to 94 sts, ending after a p row.
Shape Raglan 1st row Cast off 6 sts, k to end. **2nd row** Cast off 6 sts, p to end. **3rd row** K3, k2 tog, k to last 5 sts, k2 tog tbl, k3. **4th**

row P to end. Rep last 2 rows until 14 sts rem, ending after a 4th row.
Shape Neck Edge 1st row Cast off 4 sts, k to last 5 sts, k2 tog tbl, k3. **2nd row** P to end. **3rd row** Cast off 4 sts, k2 tog tbl, k3. **4th row** P4. Cast off rem 4 sts.

POCKET

With 3¾mm [No 9] needles and A, cast on 65 sts. Beg k row, cont in st-st until work measures 10cm [4 in] ending after a p row.

Above: the Sporty Outfit with culotte-style trousers

Shape Opening 1st row Cast off 8 sts, k to end. **2nd row** Cast off 8 sts, p to end. **3rd row** K2, k2 tog, k to last 4 sts, k2 tog tbl, k2. **4th row** P to end. Rep 3rd and 4th rows 6 times more . . . 35 sts. Cont in st-st without shaping until work measures 21cm [8¼ in] ending after a p row. Cast off.

HOOD

With 3¾mm [No 9] needles and M, cast on 126 sts. Cont in st-st until work measures 32cm [12¼ in] ending after a p row. Break off the yarn leaving a long end about four times as long as the width of half the knitting. Use this end with a knitters sewing needle (blunt ended, large eyed) to graft the top seam of the hood together. Knit half of the sts and fold the work in half with the purl side on the inside, the fold to your right and the two needle points pointing towards the right. Beg at the right-hand side – *insert needle carrying yarn knitwise into the first st on the front needle, draw the yarn through the st, slipping the st off the knitting needle. Insert the sewing needle purlwise into the second st on the front needle, draw yarn through but leave the st on the knitting needle. Take yarn under front knitting needle and insert the sewing needle purlwise into the first st on the back knitting needle, draw yarn through st and slip the st off the knitting needle. Insert sewing needle knitwise into second st on back knitting needle, draw yarn through and leave st on the knitting needle. Bring yarn forward and rep from * to end. The sts are all joined forming an invisible seam. Fasten off yarn neatly.

TO MAKE UP

Press following instructions on ball band.
Seams Join raglan shaping of front and back to shaping on sleeve tops, leaving the neck shaping free at front edge of sleeve tops. Join these seams with right side of work facing, just 1 st from the edge to form a neat finish. With right side inside, back-stitch the side and sleeve seams, using matching yarn for cuffs.
Hood Pin the centre of the cast-on edge of hood to the centre back neck, with right sides together. Pin the front edges to the corners of the front neck. Pin and tack to remaining edge of hood, easing any fullness to the neck

edge – DO NOT stretch the neck edge to fit the hood. Back-stitch the hood in place firmly. Remove all pins and tacking.
Pocket *Tack the pocket in place just above the ribbed border on centre front. Neatly hem-stitch along the lower edge then hem the straight sides. Finally hem across the straight top. Remove tackings.
*If desired a neat border may be worked round the pocket opening and the front of hood and neck edges: use a 3mm [No 11] crochet hook and matching yarn, with right side of work facing, work 1 row dc all round these edges. Fasten off.

Scarf and socks

All ages

Classic socks that are knitted in the good old fashioned way. You can adjust the foot length after the instep has been shaped.

Materials Eight 25g balls Double Knitting yarn in random-dyed or multi-coloured yarn (M) for the Scarf; six 25g balls in contrast (C) 4-ply yarn for the Socks; pair 3¾mm [No 9] knitting needles; a set of four double-pointed 3mm [No 11] knitting needles; 3mm [No 11] crochet hook for fringeing.

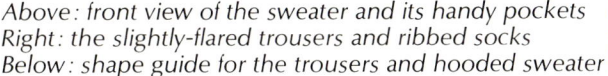

Above: front view of the sweater and its handy pockets
Right: the slightly-flared trousers and ribbed socks
Below: shape guide for the trousers and hooded sweater

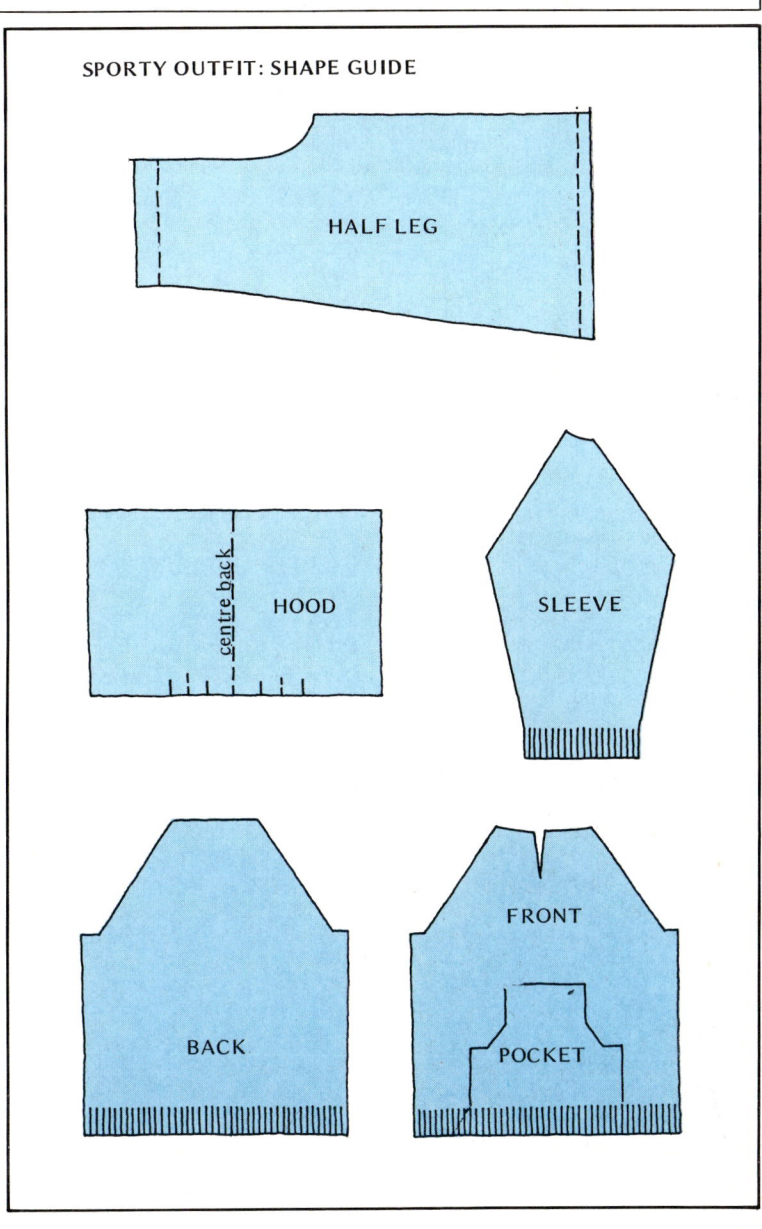

SPORTY OUTFIT: SHAPE GUIDE

HALF LEG

HOOD

centre back

SLEEVE

BACK

FRONT

POCKET

Continued on next page

Sporty outfit . . . continued

Measurements Scarf – 30cm [12 in] wide, 115cm [46 in] long, excluding fringe. Socks – to fit 23cm [9 in] adjustable.

Tension 26 sts and 34 rows to 10cm [4 in] in st-st on 3¾mm [No 9] needles. 34 sts to 10cm [4 in] over rib pattern for socks on 3mm [No 11] needles.

Abbreviations k, knit; p, purl; st(s), stitch(es); cm, centimetre(s); in, inch(es); alt, alternate; beg, beginning; cont, continue; dec, decreas(e)ing; inc, increas(e)ing; foll, following; rep, repeat; rem, remain(ing); rnd, round; sl, slip; tog, together; psso, pass slip st over; tbl, through back of loop; st-st, stocking stitch. Square brackets contain imperial measurements.

SCARF
TO MAKE

With 3¾mm [No 9] needles and M, cast on 80 sts. Beg k row, work 115cm [46 in] k2, p2 rib. Cast off sts in rib. Cut rem yarn into 37cm [14¼ in] lengths and using 3 strands together fringe the narrow ends of the scarf thus: fold the three strands in half. With the crochet hook, draw the loop end through the edge of the knitting then draw the ends through the loop and pull tight. Rep this all across the end. To make the fringe even, it is advisable to place the first two loops at either end and a third in the centre and work between. Press the fringe to straighten the ends but only lightly.

Above: back view of the hooded sweater and scarf

SOCKS
TO MAKE

With set of four 3mm [No 11] double-pointed knitting needles and C, cast on 60 sts – 20 sts on each of three needles, working with the 4th needle. Work 4 rnds k1, p1 rib.

Now change to the wide rib pattern. **1st rnd** *K4, p2; rep from * to end. Rep this rnd until work measures 36cm [14 in] from beg.
Divide for Heel Next rnd K15, sl the 15 sts from the 3rd needle on to end of these sts . . . 30 sts. Divide the rem sts on to two needles and leave for the instep.
Heel Working in rows, not rnds, work 6cm [2¼ in] in st-st, beg and ending with a p row.
Turn Heel 1st row K18, sl 1, k1, psso, turn. **2nd row** P7, p2 tog, turn. **3rd row** K8, sl 1, k1, psso, turn. **4th row** P9, p2 tog, turn. Cont in this way until all sts are worked on to one needle again . . . 18 sts.
Sl all the instep sts on to one needle. **Next rnd** K9, using the spare needle k the rem 9 sts from the heel, then pick up and k18 sts from the side of the heel rows; using 2nd needle, rib across the 30 instep sts; using 3rd needle pick up and k18 sts from the other side of heel rows, then k9 heel sts . . . 84 sts.
Shape Instep 1st rnd – 1st needle K; **2nd needle** Rib to end; **3rd needle** K. **2nd rnd – 1st needle** K to last 3 sts, k2 tog, k1; **2nd needle** Rib to end; **3rd needle** K1, k2 tog tbl, k to end. Rep last 2 rnds until 60 sts rem. With 2nd needle in rib and rem needles in st-st, cont without shaping until foot measures 17cm [66 in] from heel – adjust foot length here if required allowing approx 6cm [2¼ in] for toe shaping.
Shape Toe Cont in st-st throughout: **1st rnd – 1st needle** K to last 3 sts, k2 tog, k1; **2nd needle** K1, k2 tog tbl, k to last 3 sts, k2 tog, k1; **3rd needle** K1, k2 tog tbl, k to end. **2nd rnd – All needles** K to end. Rep last 2 rnds until 24 sts rem. K the sts from the first needle on to the sts of the third needle. Cast off the two sets of sts together. If you prefer, thread the yarn through the rem sts then break it and secure the end.
Work a second sock the same. Press if you wish but only very lightly or you will flatten the rib.

Yoked cardigan
Teenager to adult

An essential for every wardrobe and easily knitted even by a beginner. You knit the separate pieces then combine them all on one needle to make the yoke.

Materials 825(850:900)g of Shetland-type Double Knitting wool; pair 6mm [No 4] knitting needles. 1 button (optional).

Measurements To fit bust sizes 86(91:96)cm [34(36:38) in].

Tension 14 sts and 24 rows measure 10cm [4 in].

Abbreviations k, knit; p, purl; st(s), stitch(es); g-st, garter stitch; inc, increase; dec, decrease; cont, continue; rep, repeat; rem, remain(ing); cm, centimetre(s); in, inch(es); beg, beginning; tog, together.

Size Note Figures in brackets refer to larger sizes. One figure only refers to all sizes. Square brackets contain imperial measurements.

BACK

Cast on 64(68:72) sts and work in g-st for 24 rows. Now cast on 22 sts at beg of next 2 rows for Pocket, then cont in g-st for 24 rows. Cast off 22 sts at beg of next 2 rows, then cont on rem 64 (68:72) sts until work measures 54cm [21 in] or length required.
Shape Armholes Cast off 6 sts at beg of next 2 rows, and leave rem sts on spare needle.

LEFT FRONT

Cast on 40(42:44) sts and work in g-st for 54cm [21 in] or length required.
Shape Armhole Cast off 6 sts at beg of next row, k to end. **Next row** K to end. Leave sts on spare needle.

RIGHT FRONT

Work as for Left Front to armhole.
Next row K to side edge. **Next row** Cast off 6 sts, k to front edge. Leave for the present.

SLEEVES

Cast on 36 sts for each size and work in k1, p1 rib for 18 rows.
Next row 1st size only *K2, inc in next st. Rep from * to end. 2nd and 3rd sizes only K2, *k1, inc in next st. Rep from * to last 2 sts, k2. There are now 48(52:52) sts. Cont straight until work measures 33cm [13 in] or length required, from ribbed cuff.
Shape Top Cast off 6 sts at beg of next 2 rows and leave rem sts on spare needle.

YOKE

With right side of work facing, k across sts thus:
Right Front sts K across sts, but for 1st size only inc in 7th st from each end . . . 36(36:38) sts.
1st sleeve K, *inc* 1 st at end of row for 1st size and *dec* 1 st at end of row for 2nd and 3rd size . . . 37(39:39) sts.
Back K, dec 1 st at end of row . . . 51(55:59) sts.
2nd sleeve As 1st sleeve.
Left Front As Right Front. There are now 197(205:213) sts.
Next row (wrong side) K6 sts (border), p1, *k3, k1. Rep from * to last 6 sts, k6 (border). **Next row** K7, *p3, k1. Rep from * to last 6 sts, k6. Rep these 2 rows twice more.
Next row K6, p1, *k2 tog, k1, p1, k3, p1. Rep from * to last 6 sts, k6 . . . 174(181:188) sts.
Next row K7, *p3, k1, p2, k1. Rep from * to last 6 sts, k6.
Next row K6, p1, *k2, p1, k3, p1. Rep. from * to last 6 sts, k6.
Next row K7, *p3, k1, p2, k1. Rep from * to last 6 sts, k6.
Next row K6, p1, *k2, p1, k2 tog, k1, p1. Rep from * to last 6 sts, k6. . . . 151(157:163) sts.
Next row K7, *p2, k1. Rep from * to last 6 sts, k6.
Cont in new rib with g-st borders for 2 more rows.
Next row K6, p1, *k2 tog, p1. Rep from * to last 6 sts, k6 . . . 105 (109:113) sts. Keeping continuity of g-st border work rem sts in k1, p1 rib for 12 rows.
Next row K9 (k2 tog) to last 10 sts, k10 . . . 62(64:66) sts.
Cont in g-st across all sts for 9 rows but if the jacket is to be fastened at neck, work a button-hole in right front border on the 5th row, by k2, cast off 3, work to end. In next row cast on 3 sts in place of those cast off. After the 9th row cast off all sts loosely.

TO MAKE UP

Press work following ball band instructions. Sew up sleeve and side seams leaving the pocket space free. Place the 22 pocket sts inside the open seam, pin in position, then catch neatly down on wrong side of front. Sew on button if required.

Crochet

The beauty of crochet is that it is based on a
few simple stitches from which all patterns are made. Because it is quick to do,
you can rely on it when time is short.

To make the garments in this section successfully, you must be sure that you obtain the necessary tension – this is very important if you are to achieve the correct measurements. Always work at 10cm [4 in] square as this is the only way to be certain (the squares can always be used up – the patchwork top in the knitting section is one way!). If you don't get the right number of stitches, try again with a larger or smaller hook size.

Yarns to choose

All types of yarn are suitable for crochet but (like knitting) you must buy sufficient to complete the garment because there could be a slight difference in the next dye lot. If the best laid plans don't work out and you run short, use the extra you've bought for edgings or collar, pockets or even a hood – you must be crafty in making it appear as deliberate shading. To get a good finish, it's even worth unravelling what you've already done if it will help you spread the shade evenly.

If you are adjusting the pattern to make the garment bigger or smaller, do remember to buy more or less of the yarn needed.

When joining yarn always make the join – never a knot – at the end of a row, even if it means wasting quite a bit. It can be used later when making up the work.

Watch carefully in a pattern to see where a new colour is joined in – it can differ.

Tips for success

A row counter eliminates the tedium of trying to remember where you're at.

If you're working straight, work into the first and last stitch of every row. Work the edge stitches evenly and firmly so your eventual seam-making will be perfect.

If there are buttonholes in the garment, buy buttons slightly larger in size than the holes worked.

If something you've made drops (it could be because you've hung the garment up rather than folding it and keeping it in a drawer) or if fashion has declared a shorter hemline, run a piece of contrast yarn through the row immediately below where you want the new line to be. With scissors cut through every stitch which joins this one to the row above, then take away all loose bits. Finish off neatly. With some patterns it works better if you measure the length required, and at the end of a row cut the thread which connects the rows. With the thread pull the stitches undone along the row and finish off neatly.

When working in stripes, "steps" will be avoided if the last loop of the last stitch of the row is worked in the new colour.

Making up

Never ever stretch the edges to make them fit or the garment will look lopsided. This is especially important when a zip is being put in.

You can make an invisible seam by joining together both sides with a row of slip stitches or double crochet on the wrong side. This sort of seam is quickly and neatly undone later (if necessary) without the risk of cutting through a wrong thread. This is a good idea especially if a garment is too big.

When sewing up garments made in thick yarn, divide it into strands. You'll have a neater seam.

As in all making, you mustn't rush the making up. The whole look of the garment depends on the neat finish. And do follow the pressing instructions on the ball band.

Size and shape

All through the book we stress that the age guide might not always apply perfectly to the child you have in mind. As there are clear diagrams showing the shape with each garment, mark on this (in pencil) the measurements you need so that you'll remember where what you want differs from what the pattern says.

Don't let the finished garment lose its shape by the wrong washing method – squeeze out as much moisture as possible between two towels, ease it into the correct shape then dry it flat.

DOUBLE CROCHET

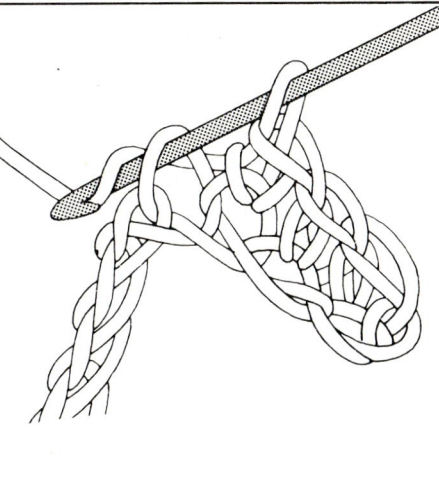

Insert the hook into the second chain from the end. Pass the yarn round the hook, anticlockwise, and catch in the hook's curve. Draw the yarn and the hook through the work to make a loop on the hook – now you should have two loops on the hook.

Pass the yarn round the hook again then draw the hook and yarn through the two loops on the hook so that you have just one loop on the hook.

Turning chains

For double crochet work one extra chain stitch at the end of a row. For treble crochet work three extra chains at the end of a row.

TREBLE CROCHET

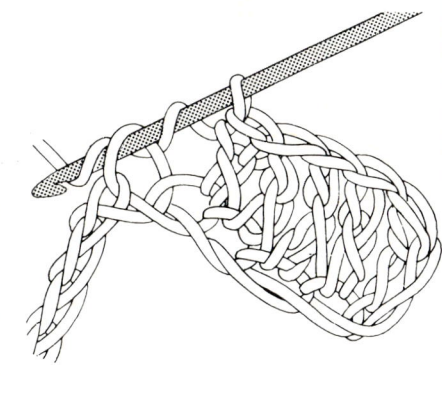

Pass yarn round the hook, miss two chain and work into the third chain.

Pass the yarn round the hook again and pull a loop through so you have three loops on the hook. Pass the yarn round the hook again. Pull hook and the yarn through the remaining two loops left on the hook – you should now only have one loop left on the hook. This completes one treble.

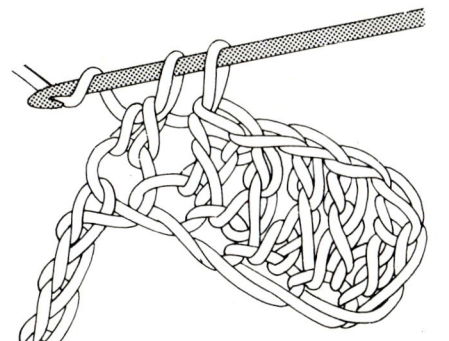

Romantic cover

Pretty way of cheering up a plain spread – you crochet the hearts and arrange them on the fabric. A nice idea for a child's duvet cover.

The cover

Materials 2 rectangles of cotton fabric 50cm × 60cm [20 in × 24 in]; 4m [4½ yd] of 8cm-wide [3 in] white broderie anglaise; 4m [4½ yd] of 4cm-wide [1½ in] red broderie anglaise; matching machine twist, filling (optional).

TO SEW

1. On one rectangle of fabric, right side facing, find centre and mark with a pin. From centre, mark in a lattice of nine squares, each side measuring 12cm [4¾ in].

2. Embroider the squares on to fabric in chain stitch, using some of the 4-ply wool used for the heart motifs.

3. Make the crocheted hearts (see right) and stitch each one to the centre of a square with stab stitches arranging the different sizes as liked.

4. Right sides together, sew the two short ends of the wide broderie anglaise together to form a band. Do the same with narrow broderie anglaise. Holding the two pieces together (smaller band on top), stitch bands together with a line of running stitches, 15mm [⅝ in] in from edge. Draw up gathers until band fits round outside of embroidered rectangle.

5. Right sides together, pin and tack band to rectangle, adjusting gathers evenly. Right sides together, pin, tack and machine plain rectangle to embroidered one, sandwiching bands between,

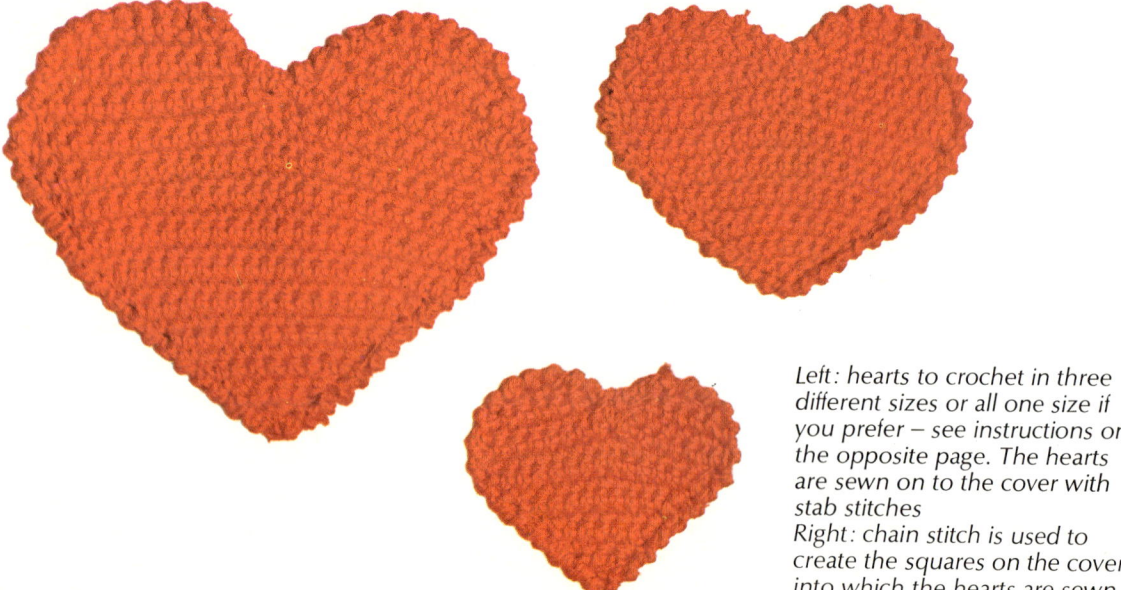

Left: hearts to crochet in three different sizes or all one size if you prefer – see instructions on the opposite page. The hearts are sewn on to the cover with stab stitches

Right: chain stitch is used to create the squares on the cover into which the hearts are sewn

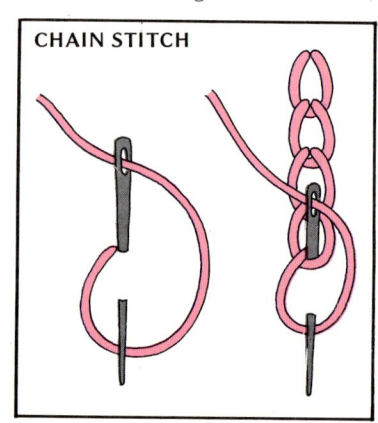

CHAIN STITCH

leaving a 30cm [12 in] opening along one side for filling (optional).
6. Turn cover through to right side and press. Insert filling and machine or hand sew over the chain stitch squares to keep it in place. Close opening.

The hearts

Materials 50g of 4-ply yarn; 3mm [No 11] crochet hook.

Abbreviations ch, chain; dc, double crochet; ss, slip stitch; dec, decrease; rep, repeat; st(s), stitch(es). Square brackets contain imperial measurements.

LARGE MOTIFS (3 required)
Make 3 ch and work in dc for 1 row (2 dc). **Next row** 2 dc into each dc (4 dc). **Next row** 2 dc in 1st st, dc to last st, 2 dc in st (6 dc).
Rep last row until there are 26 sts. Work 5 rows of dc on dc.
Shape Top 1st row 13 dc turn. **2nd row** Dec 1, then in dc to last st, turn. **3rd row** As 2nd row. **4th row** Ss along 2 dc, dc to last 3 dc turn. **5th row** Dec 1, dc to last st, turn. **6th row** 2 dc. Fasten off.
Rejoin yarn to centre and work 13 dc to end.
Now rep 2nd–6th rows of other side but do not turn or fasten off. Work in crab st (ie, dc worked from left to right) all round outer edges. Fasten off.

MEDIUM MOTIF (3 required)
Make 3 ch and work as for Large Motif until there are 22 dc, then work 3 rows of dc on dc.
Shape Top 1st row 11 dc, turn. **2nd row** Dec 1, in dc to last st, turn. **3rd row** As 2nd row. **4th row** Ss along 2 dc, 2 dc, turn. **5th row** 2 dc and fasten off.
Rejoin yarn at centre of work, 11 dc to end.
Now rep from 2nd to 5th rows of other side, do not fasten off or turn but work in crab st all round outer edge. Fasten off.

SMALL MOTIF (3 required)
Make 3 ch and work as for large motif until there are 18 dc. Work 1 row in dc.
Shape Top 1st row 9 dc, turn. **2nd and 3rd rows** Dec 1 st, dc to last st, turn. **4th row** Dec 1 st, dc to last 2 sts, turn. **5th row** 2 dc and fasten off.
Rejoin yarn to centre and work 9 dc to end.
Now rep 2nd–5th rows of other side, do not fasten off or turn but work in crab st all round outer edge. Fasten off.

Cover up

A clever wrap to keep the baby warm in your arms or in the cot. Later when the baby changes from cot to bed, just add more squares.

Materials 2 balls white (M), 1 ball pink (C1), 4 balls pale green (C2) of baby Double Knitting yarn; 3mm [No 11] crochet hook.

Tension Each square measures 10cm [4 in].

Abbreviations ch, chain; dc, double crochet; tr, treble; dtr, double treble; rep, repeat; st, stitch; ss, slip stitch; grs, groups; lp, loop; cm, centimetre(s); in, inch(es); beg, beginning; rnd, round. Square brackets contain imperial measurements.

THE SQUARE
Using M, make 6 ch and join into a ring with ss.
1st rnd 4 ch (first 2 ch to count as 1st tr), then * 1 tr 2 ch. Rep from * 6 times, ss in 2nd of 4 ch at beg of round. Fasten off.
2nd rnd Join on C1 to centre of a ch lp and with 2 ch as 1st tr of round, work 4 tr, 1 ch in each 2-ch lp of previous round, join with ss to top of 2 ch. Fasten off (8 grs of trs).
3rd rnd Join M to centre of a ch lp, and with 2 ch as 1st tr of round, work 3 ch, 1 ch, 3 tr, 1 ch into each ch lp of previous round, join with ss to top of 2 ch. Fasten off.
4th rnd Join C2 to centre of a ch lp and with 2 ch as 1st tr, work * 2 tr, 2 ch, 2 tr (corner worked), 2 ch, 1 dc in centre of next gr, 2 ch, 1 dc in ch lp between grs, 2 ch, 1 dc in centre of next gr, 2 ch. Rep from * 3 times, join with ss to top of 2 ch.
5th rnd In C2 work 2 ch, * 1 tr

between the 1st and 2nd tr of gr at corner, 4 tr into 2-ch lp, 1 tr between next 2 tr of gr, 3 tr in each of next 4 2-ch lps. Rep from * all round but omitting 1 tr in last 2-ch lp and join with ss to top of 2 ch. Fasten off. One square is now completed. Work 63 more squares in the same way.

TO MAKE UP
Join squares together with a flat seam, with 8 squares down and 8 squares across. Using C2, edge outer edges with 1 round of shells consisting of 9 dtr with 1 dc between shells, placing a shell over joining seams, 2 shells on each outer square and a shell in each of the 4 corners – see the photograph for reference. Lastly, work 1 round of dc, working 1 dc into each st. Fasten off. Sew in all ends neatly on wrong side taking the wool up the side of a st of same colour. Press very lightly following ball band instructions.

Children's Clothes

Cotton bibs

Make them in crochet cotton and you can boil them so they come up crisp and smart every time.

Round

Materials (to make 2 bibs) 3 balls of thick crochet cotton in Rust or Orange (M); 1 ball of thick crochet cotton in White (C); 1·5mm [No 15] crochet hook.

Abbreviations Ch, chain; dc, double crochet; ss, slip stitch; picot = 3 ch, 1 dc into 1st ch worked; rep, repeat; dec, decrease; tr, treble; st, stitch; rnd, round; lp, loop.

Please note Square brackets contain imperial measurements.

TO MAKE
Make 17 ch using M. **1st row** 1 tr in 4th ch from hook, then 1 tr in each ch to end (15 tr).
2nd–4th rows 3 ch (as 1st tr) 1 tr into base of 3 ch, in tr to centre tr, 2 tr, in tr to last 2 tr, 2 tr in each of 2 tr (30 tr).
5th–9th rows In tr, but working 2 tr in first and last tr (40 tr).
10th row In tr.
11th row In tr but working 2 tr in 1st and last tr (42 tr).
12th row In tr.
13th–18th rows Ss along 1st tr, in tr to last tr, turn (2 trs dec).
19th row Ss along 1st tr, 1 tr over next 4 tr, turn.
20th row Dec 1 st each end (2 tr remain). Fasten off.
Go back to main part, leave next 20 tr, rejoin yarn, ss along 1 tr, 4 tr. **Next row** Dec. 1 tr each end. Fasten off.
Using M join yarn to top left corner and work 2 rnds of dc round outer edge. **3rd row** * 1 dc, 1 ch, 1 picot, 1 ch, miss 1 dc. Rep from * and join with ss. Now work in rows thus:
1st row Ss to top of 1st picot, * 1 tr on picot, 2 ch. Rep from * to top right corner, turn and leave neck edge free.
2nd row 3 ch, * then 1 tr in 2-ch lp, 3 ch. Rep from * ending 1 tr in end st.
3rd row * 3 dc in 3-ch lp, 1 dc on dc. Rep from * to end.
4th row Dec on dc.
Note if making rust bib work in rnds, but if making orange bib cont in rows as before (see picture for reference).

5th rnd or row Join on C, * 1 dc, 1 ch, 1 picot, 1 ch, miss 2 dc. Rep from * ending a rnd with ss and a row with dc into end st.
6th rnd or row * Ss to top of picot, 1 tr on picot, 3 ch. Rep from *, ending by joining with ss for rnd or 1 tr into end st for row.
Next rnd (either bib) * 1 dc in ch loop, 1 ch, 1 picot, 1 ch. Rep from * all rnd, ss to 1st dc. Fasten off.

TIES (make 2)
Using C make 50 ch and work 1 row of dc. Fasten off. Sew on ties – one to each corner.

Shell-shaped

Materials 1 ball of thick crochet cotton in Rust or Orange (M); 1 ball of thick crochet cotton in White (C) – enough to edge 3 bibs; 1·5mm [No 15] crochet hook.

Abbreviations ch, chain; dc, double crochet; rep, repeat; ss, slip stitch; htr, half treble; tr, treble; dtr, double treble; rnd, round; lp, loop; cont, continue; inc, increase.

Please note Square brackets contain imperial measurements.

TO MAKE
In M make 5 ch and join into a ring with a ss. Now with 3 ch as 1st tr, work 16 tr into ring, join with a ss. Work in rows thus:
Next row 2 tr on 1st tr (1 tr on each of next 2 tr, 2 tr on next tr) 5 times, turn.
Next row 1 dc on each tr to end, turn.
Next row 2 tr on 1st dc (1 tr on each of next 3 dc, 2 tr on next dc) 5 times, turn.
Next row 1 dc on each tr to end, turn.
Cont in this way working 1 more tr between each inc on every alternate row until 24 rows have been worked, or until size required. Refer to either diagram or picture for shape.
Now work 2 rows of dc all around outer edge of bib.
Join on C and work 1 rnd of dc on dc.

For Orange Bib
Next rnd Work in dc around neckline, but work thus over other edge, * 1 dc, 5 ch, 3 tr working each tr into base of 5 ch, miss next dc. Rep from * all around, join with a ss and fasten off.

Above: shell-shaped and round bibs which can be any colour you like from the wide range of crochet cottons available
Right: a diagram of the shape of the shell bibs – handy to refer to as you work

For Rust Bib
Next rnd: * 1 dc, 1 ch, miss 1 dc. Rep from * all round, join with a ss.
Next rnd Work in dc round neckline, working dc on dc and 1 dc into ch lp, then work thus over other edges, * In next ch lp, work 1 htr, 1 tr, 1 dtr, 1 tr, 1 htr, then 1 dc in next ch lp. Rep from * all round, join with a ss and fasten off.
For the ties on each bib, join on C to corner of neckline, make 50 ch, then work 1 row of dc into ch. Fasten off.

SHELL-SHAPED BIBS: SHAPE GUIDE

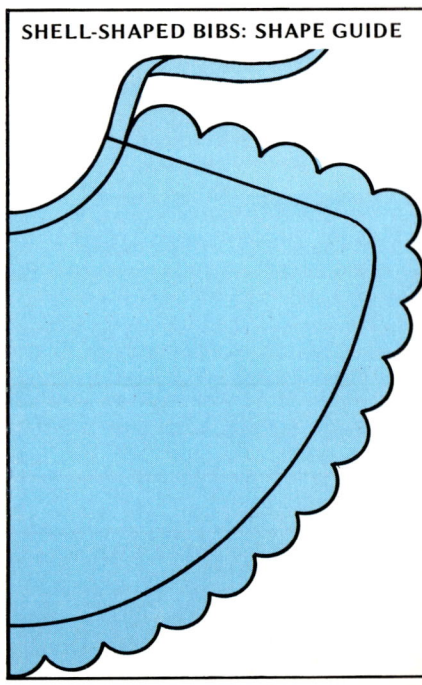

Christening robe and bonnet

3 to 6 months

A dress and bonnet with a future – after the special day it can be kept as an heirloom.

Materials 360g of silk cotton or 2 ply yarn; 2mm [No 14] crochet hook; 5 small buttons; fabric for lining (optional).

Tension 28 sts and 16 rows measure 10cm [4 in].

Abbreviations ch, chain; st(s), stitch(es); dc double crochet; tr, treble; ss, slip-stitch; cm, centimetre(s); in, inch(es); cont, continue; inc, increase; dec, decrease; rep, repeat; patt, pattern; rem, remain(ing); beg, beginning; alt, alternate; bobble: work 5 trs into next st, take hook from st, insert in top of 1st tr, then through top of 5th st, yarn over and draw through the 2 sts, 1 ch; rnd, round; sp, space. Square brackets contain imperial measurements.

Robe

Make 280 ch and join into a circle with a ss, then work in rnds of tr, joining each rnd with a ss, until work measures 10cm [4 in] from beg.
Next rnd * 1 tr, 1 ch, miss 1 tr. Rep from * all rnd, join with a ss. Now work from chart (8 sts and 6 rnds or rows forming 1 rep of patt) until work measures 58cm [23 in].
Next row Patt over 140 sts, turn and keeping continuity of patt work over these sts in rows for the Front until work measures 63cm [25 in] from beg.
Next row 5 tr, (miss 1 st, 1 tr) to last 5 sts, 5 tr . . . 75 sts.
Next row * 1 tr, miss 1 st, 1 ch. Rep from * to last st, 1 tr in st. Fasten off.
Leave 12 sts each end, rejoin cotton and cont in tr on centre 51 sts (working tr into ch sp of 1st row) until work measures 71cm [28 in].
Shape Neck Next row Patt 20, turn and work on these sts, dec 2 sts at neck edge on next 3 rows. Work straight for a few rows until work measures 73cm [28¾ in] ending at shoulder edge. At

armhole edge dec 4 sts once and 5 sts twice. Fasten off.
Go back to other sts, leave centre 11 sts, rejoin yarn and patt 20. Now dec 2 sts at neck edge on next 3 rows, then work straight until neck is same depth as other side ending at shoulder edge. Dec at shoulder edge 4 sts once and 5 sts twice. Fasten off.
Return to Back sts. **Next row** Patt 70 sts, turn. ** Keeping continuity of patt work to 63cm [25 in] ending at opening edge.
Next row 2 tr, then (miss next st, 1 tr) to last 2 sts, 2 tr . . . 37 sts. Fasten off.
Leave 12 sts unworked, rejoin yarn and work in tr on these 25 sts until work measures as Front to shoulders, ending at armhole edge. Dec 4 sts at beg of next row and 5 sts on next 2 alt rows . . . 11 sts rem. Fasten off.
Go back to other 70 sts and cont as for other side from **.

SLEEVES (make 2)

Make 62 ch. **1st row** 1 tr into 6th ch from hook, then * 1 ch, miss 1 ch, 1 tr in next ch. Rep from * to end . . . 59 sts.
Now work in patt in rows but have 2 extra tr at beg and 3 tr at end of every right-side row, therefore the 29th st (centre st) is a bobble st, and work straight to 16cm [6¼ in].
Shape Top Dec at each end of all rows, 3 sts twice, 2 sts 8 times and 3 sts 6 times. Fasten off.
Edging Go back to foundation row, rejoin yarn and work 1 row of tr into each st, then in next row work edging thus: 3 ch, * 2 tr, 1 ch 2 tr into next st, miss 2 tr. Rep from * to end working 2 tr, 1 ch 2 tr into last st. Fasten off.

HALF COLLAR (make 2)

Make 29 ch and working 1st tr into 3rd ch from hook, work 1 tr into rem ch to end. Work 1 row of tr on tr, then inc 1 tr each end of next 3 rows. Work 4 rows straight then dec 1 st each end of

Continued on next page

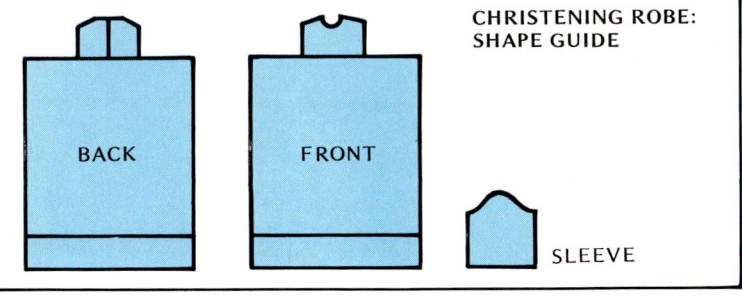

CHRISTENING ROBE: SHAPE GUIDE

BACK

FRONT

SLEEVE

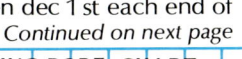
CHRISTENING ROBE: CHART

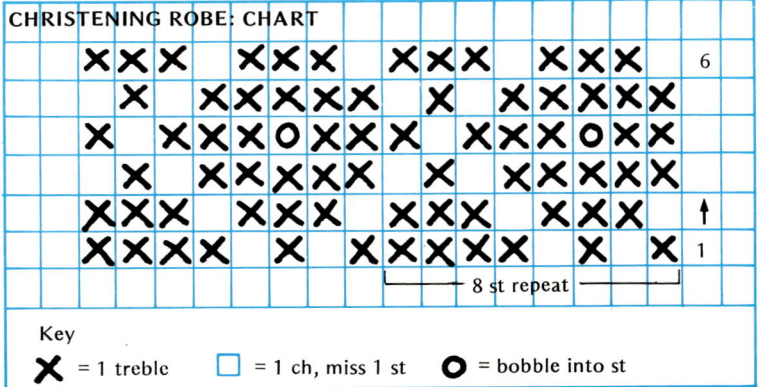

8 st repeat

6

1

Key

✗ = 1 treble ☐ = 1 ch, miss 1 st ⬤ = bobble into st

Above: the simple shapes which will help you when making the Christening Robe
Left: the chart from which you work the lattice-and-bobble pattern. It is an 8-stitch repeat worked over six rows

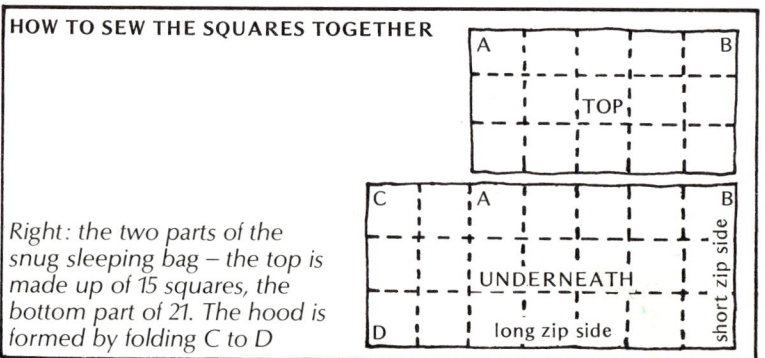

Christening robe . . . continued

next 2 rows. Fasten off. Now around sides and outer edge of collar work 1 tr on tr, then edging row as at lower edge of Sleeves. Fasten off.

TO MAKE UP

Join shoulders with a flat seam on wrong side. Now on right side work along armhole edge thus: * 1 tr 1 ch miss st or sp (equal to 1st). Rep from * to end, then work 1 row of dc in each st and ch sp. Fasten off.

Sew in sleeves, then sew up sleeve seam using a flat seam on wrong side for both. Down left side of Back opening, work 3 rows in tr. Fasten off. On right side of opening work 1 row of tr, then in next row of tr work 5 buttonholes, placing them at equal intervals and work 1 ch, miss 1 tr for each buttonhole. In next row work edging as for lower edge of Sleeves. Fasten off. Sew down underwrap at lower edge. Sew on half collars. Work 1 row of edging as for Sleeves along lower edge of robe. Sew on buttons. Line the pattern part, if required, but ending at yoke.

Bonnet

Make 6 ch and join into a ring with a ss.

1st rnd 15 trs into ring, join with a ss. (Join all rnds with a ss and beg all round with 3 ch as the 1st tr.)

2nd rnd (1 tr, 1 ch) all rnd . . . 30 sts.

3rd rnd In tr, inc in every 5th st (36 trs).

4th rnd (1 tr, 1 ch) all rnd . . . 72 sts.

5th rnd In tr.

6th rnd * 1 tr, 1 ch, miss 1 tr, 1 tr, 1 ch. Rep from * all rnd . . . 96 sts.

7th rnd In tr.

8th rnd * 1 tr, 1 ch, miss 1 tr. Rep from * all rnd.

Next row Work in tr over first 76 sts, turn leaving other 20 sts for the present and inc 1 st each end of every 4th row 3 times. Work 2 rows straight. Fasten off. Go back to the 20 sts, rejoin yarn at side edge of shaped part and work 23 tr down side, 20 tr across the 20 sts, and 23 tr along 2nd edge.

Next row Work filet crochet of (1 tr 1 ch miss 1 st) to last st, 1 tr.

Next row 1 tr on each st. Fasten off. Along front of bonnet work 1 row of filet crochet as before, 1 row of tr, then 1 row of edging patt (see Sleeves of Robe). Fasten off. Make a twisted cord (see page 75) of required length, or use ch st, and thread it through the last but one row at neck edge.

Sleeping bag

3 to 9 months

Perfect for travelling – and sleeping. A removable plastic lining round the bottom half will make sure your work is respected!

Materials 6 balls dark green (M), 3 balls lighter green (C1) and 3 balls pink (C2) in Double Double knitting yarn; 5mm [No 6] crochet hook; one 40cm [16 in] zip and an open-ended zip 66cm [26 in]; fabric for lining.

Tension Each square measures just over 13cm [5 in].

Abbreviations ch, chain; dc, double crochet; tr, treble; rep, repeat; ss, slip stitch; cm, centimetre(s); in, inch(es); rnd, round; gr, group. Square brackets contain imperial measurements.

THE SQUARE

Using C1 make 6 ch and join into a ring with a ss.

1st rnd With 3 ch as 1st tr, work 16 tr into ring, join with a ss to top of 3 ch.

2nd rnd In M and with 3 ch as 1st tr, *work 4 tr in next tr (corner), 1 tr in each of next 3 tr. Rep from * 3 times more, join with a ss to top of 3 ch.

3rd rnd With C2 and 3 ch as 1st tr work *1 tr on 1st tr of corner gr, 4 tr on 2nd tr, and 1 tr on each of 3rd and 4th tr of gr, then 1 tr on each of the 3 single tr. Rep from * all round, join with ss to top of 3 ch.

4th rnd With M work corner as for 3rd round, working 1 tr on each of the following 6 single tr instead of 3.

5th rnd With M work in dc on each tr, working 4 dc in each of the 4 corners – 16 dc each side of corner 4 dc. Fasten off. (One square completed.)

Work 17 more squares in the same way.

Now work 18 more squares but changing the colours thus: 1st round C2, 2nd round M, 3rd round C1, 4th and 5th rounds, M.

TO MAKE UP

Joining the squares with a flat stitch and alternating colours make two rectangles – one of 15 squares and one of 21 squares. Sew up side AB with a flat stitch. Open out to make L-shape then sew in warm lining. Now sew in open-ended zip along remaining long side, and shorter zip along lower edge. Fold top edge so C meets D and join with a flat stitch to form hood.

HOW TO SEW THE SQUARES TOGETHER

Right: the two parts of the snug sleeping bag – the top is made up of 15 squares, the bottom part of 21. The hood is formed by folding C to D

Hooded jacket

Very easy to make as there are no armhole or sleeve top shapings to worry about.

Materials Four 25g balls of 3 ply wool in red (M) and one 25g ball in dark blue (C); 3mm [No 11] crochet hook.

Measurements To fit a 46 (51)cm [18 (20) in] chest.

Tension 23 sts and 18 rows measure 10cm [4 in].

Abbreviations ch, chain; dc, double crochet; htr, half treble; st(s), stitch(es); beg, beginning; rep, repeat; rem, remain(ing); cont, continue; cm, centimetre(s); in, inch(es); patt, pattern; dec, decrease.

Size Note Figures in brackets refer to larger size. One figure only refers to both sizes. Square brackets contain imperial measurements.

BACK AND FRONT
Worked in one to armholes. Beg at lower edge and using M, make 111 (123) ch, turn and work 1 htr into 3rd ch from hook, then in htr to end . . . 110 (122) sts.
Work in htr to 10 (12)cm [4 (4¾) in] from beg. Join on C and work 1 row then work 1 row in M. Work in patt thus:
** **1st row** In M. 2 ch, 1 htr, * 2 ch, miss 2 htr, 1 htr on each of next 2 htr. Rep from * to end.
2nd row In C. 1 ch, 1 dc in next htr, * 2 htr inserting the crochet hook over ch and into the htrs of 2 rows below, 1 dc on each of next 2 htr. Rep from * to end.
3rd row In C. 2 ch, 1 htr, * 2 ch, miss 2 htr, 2 htr. Rep from * to end.
4th row In M. As 2nd row. **
Work 1 row in htr in M, then 1 row in C. Break off C. Cont straight in M in htr until work measures 14 (16)cm [5½ (6) in] from beg.
Divide for Armholes Leave 28 (31) htr each end on next row and cont on the 54 (60) centre sts for BACK to 25 (27)cm [10 (10½) in] from beg. Work 1 row C, 1 row M, then fasten off.

RIGHT FRONT
Work on the first 28 (31) sts and cont straight to 20 (22) cm

[8 (8½) in] from beg.
*** **Shape Neck** Dec (by slip-stitching along sts to be decreased) on every neck edge row, 4 sts once, 3 sts once, 2 sts once and 1 st 3 (4) times. Work on the rem 16 (18) sts to 25 (27)cm [10 (10½) in] then work 1 row C, 1 row M. Fasten off.

LEFT FRONT
Go back to rem sts, and work in htr to front edge. Now work from *** of Right Front.

SLEEVES
Using M, make 51 (55) ch and work 1 row as foundation row . . . 50 (54) sts. Now work 1 row C, 1 row M then work from ** to ** as Back for two-colour patt. Break off C and cont in M until sleeve measures 18 (19.5)cm [7 (7¾) in] from beg. Work 1 row C, 1 row M, 1 row C, then work 1 row of dc in M. Fasten off.

HOOD
Using M make 91 ch and work foundation row and on the 90 sts work in htr with 1 row C, 1 row M,

*Above: the Hooded Jacket which is worked in one to armholes
Right: the Jacket's shape guide*

then from ** to ** as Back for two-colour patt. Break off C. Cont in M to 19cm [7½ in].
Shape Back Dec each end of row 6 sts 4 times, and 7 sts once . . . 28 sts rem. Now cont dec 1 st each end of every 4th row 5 times. Cont on rem 18 sts to 36cm [14 in]. Fasten off.

TO MAKE UP
Press according to ball band instructions. Using back-stitch for sewing up, join shoulder seams, then sew up sleeves. Sew in sleeves to armholes. Along each front edge work: 1 row in M in dc, then 1 row of htr in C, then 1 row in M. Fasten off. Sew the shaped edges of hood to the side edges of back panel. Turn back the two-colour border and sew the foundation row neatly to neck edge. Make 2 twisted cords (see page 75) about 36cm [14 in] long and sew them to each side at neck edge.

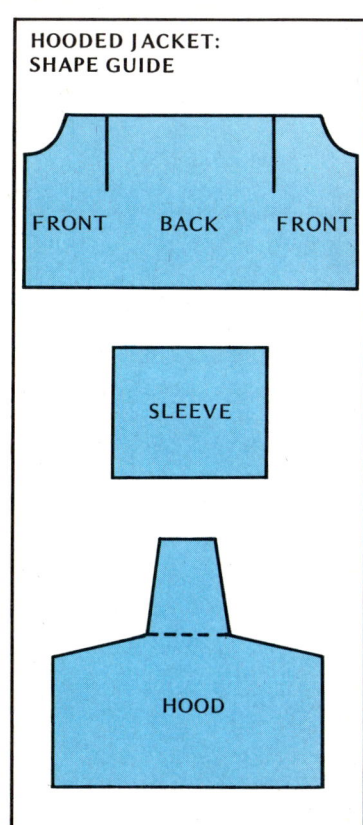

HOODED JACKET: SHAPE GUIDE

FRONT BACK FRONT

SLEEVE

HOOD

Overalls and jumper

9 months to 2 years

Good rough-and-tumble clothes for boy or girl.

Jumper

Materials 4(6) 25g balls of 4-ply wool; pair of 2mm [No 14] and 2¾mm [No 12] knitting needles; 15cm [6 in] zip fastener.

Measurements To fit 51(56)cm [20(22) in] chest.

Tension 33 sts and 46 rows measure 10cm [4 in] in k1, p1 rib.

Abbreviations k, knit; p, purl; st(s), stitch(es); cont, continue; rem, remain(ing); beg, beginning; alt, alternate; inc, increase; cm, centimetre(s); in, inch(es).

Size Note Figures in brackets refer to larger size. One figure only refers to both sizes. Square brackets · contain imperial measurements.

BACK

Using 2mm [No 14] needles cast on 93(99) sts and work in k1, p1 rib for 3cm [1¼ in] beg alt rows p1. Change to 2¾mm [No 12] needles and cont in k1, p1 rib until work measures 13.5(16.5)cm [5¼(6½) in] from beg.

Divide for Back Opening Next row Rib 47(50) sts, turn and leave other sts on spare needle. * Work straight to 16(18)cm [6¼(7) in] from beg ending at side edge.

Shape Armhole Cast off at beg of next row and alt rows, 4 sts once, 3 sts once, 2 sts once and 1 st 4 times . . . 34(37) sts rem. Cont straight until work measures 24.5 (27.5)cm [9½(10¾) in] ending at armhole edge.

Shape Shoulder Cast off at beg of next and alt rows, 3(4) sts once, 4(4) sts 4 times. Cast off rem 15(17) sts. Go back to sts on spare needle, cast on 1 st at opening edge and work on the 47(50) sts from * to match other side.

FRONT

Work as for Back to opening, then cont straight to 16(18)cm [6¼(7) in].

Shape Armholes Cast off at beg of every row, 4 sts twice, 3 sts twice, 2 sts twice and 1 st 8 times . . . 67(73) sts. Cont straight until work measures 23(25.5)cm [9(10) in] from beg.

Shape Neck Rib 28(30) sts, turn and leave rem sts on spare needle. Now cast off at neck edge on next and alt rows, 3(3) sts once, 2(3) sts once, 2(2) sts once and 1(1) st twice. Cont straight to 25.5(28.5)cm [10(11¼) in] from beg ending at armhole edge.

Shape Shoulder Work as for Back shoulder shaping. Go back to main sts, cast off centre 11(13) sts, rib to end. Now work from ** of neck shaping.

SLEEVES

Using 2¾mm [No 12] needles cast on 47(53) sts and work in k1, p1 rib, inc 1 st each end of every 7th (9th) row until there are 67(73) sts. Work straight until Sleeve measures 18(22)cm [7(8¼) in] from beg.

Shape Top Cast off at beg of every row, 3(3) sts twice, 2 sts 6(10) times, 1 st 20(18) times, 2(2) sts twice and 3(3) sts twice. Cast off rem 19 sts.

NECKBAND

Using 2mm [No 14] needles cast on 73(77) sts and work in k1, p1 rib for 2cm [¾ in]. Cast off in the rib (loosely – remember the baby's head!).

TO MAKE UP

Using back-stitch join side, shoulder and sleeve seams then sew in sleeves. Sew on neckband with cast-on edge to neck edge. Sew in zip.

Overalls

Materials 8(10) 25g balls of 4-ply yarn in green (M) and a small quantity of the same yarn in orange (C1), dark orange (C2), blue (C3) and black (C4); 2.5mm [No 12] crochet hook; pair of 2¾mm [No 12] knitting needles; 2 buttons.

Measurements To fit 51(56)cm [20(22) in] chest.

Tension 26 sts and 31 rows measure 10cm [4 in].

Abbreviations ch, chain; dc, double crochet; tr, treble; st(s) stitches; dec, decrease; cont, continue; inc, increase; beg, beginning; cm, centimetre(s); in, inch(es); rem, remain(ing); foll, following.

Size Note Figures in brackets refer to larger size. One figure only refers to both sizes. Square brackets contain imperial measurements.

BACK

Make 78 ch with M. Break thread. Rejoin yarn to centre 26 sts and work in tr over these sts. Break yarn. Rejoin yarn to centre 52 (44) sts and work in tr over these stitches. Break yarn. For larger size work in tr over centre 62 sts. Now work in tr – for both sizes – across all sts and cont in tr until work measures 13.5(14.5)cm [5¼ (5¾) in].

Divide for Legs Next row 1 tr on

38 sts, 2 tr in next st, turn and leave other sts for 2nd leg. Now inc 1 st at opening edge on 3rd row then 1(2) sts on next 2 rows. For 2nd size only inc 4 tr at opening edge on next row (by making 6 ch, turn, work 1 tr into 4th ch from beg, 1 tr in next 2 ch – 4 tr made) . . . 43(49) tr.

**Work 5(6) rows straight then dec 1 st each end of next row and foll 5th(6th) then foll 4th(6th) row. Work straight until Back measures 26.5(30.5)cm [10½(12) in] from beg, then inc 1 st each end of every 6th(7th) row 3 times ** . . . 43(49) sts. Cont straight until work measures 39.5(47)cm [15½(18½) in] from beg. Fasten off. Go back to other leg, 2 tr in 1st st, in tr to end. Now work as for other leg.

FRONT

Make 78 ch with M, then turn with 3 ch and work in tr on the first 13(8) sts. Break yarn. Rejoin to 24th(17th) st and work to beg of row. Break yarn. For 2nd size only work over the first 26 sts.

Break off yarn. Work the same shaping at end of ch, then cont across the 78 sts in tr. Work straight in tr to 12(12.5)cm [4¾(5) in] from beg.

Divide for Legs Next row In tr over 38 sts, 2 tr in next tr, turn and leave other sts. For 1st size inc 1 st at opening edge on 3rd row. For 2nd size inc at opening edge on every row, 1 st once, 2 sts once and 4 sts once . . . 41(47) sts. Now work from ** to ** of Back . . . 41(47) sts. Work straight to 38(45)cm [15(17¾) in] from beg. Fasten off. Go back to other leg, 2 tr in 1st tr, in tr to end; then work as for 1st leg.

BIB

Using M make 37 ch and work 1 dc into 2nd ch from hook, then in dc to end. **Next row** (wrong side) Work in colours thus: 5 sts C1, 8 sts in C2 (for the door) and 23 sts in C1. Work straight to 3cm [1¼ in] from beg ending after a wrong-side row. **Next row** 5 sts C1, 13 sts C3 (for window), 5 sts C1, 8 sts C2 (for door) and 5 sts

C1. Work thus for 3cm [1¼ in], then cont in C1 only to 9cm [3½ in] ending after a right-side row.

Next row 1 M, 35 C2. Cont in dc, work 1 more st in M in each row until there are 8 M sts. Fasten off C2 sts and cont these 8 sts in M ** until strap measures 30(34)cm [11¾(13¼) in] then make a buttonhole by working 2 dc, miss 3 dc, 3 ch, 2 dc. In next row work 3 dc into 3 ch loop. Cont until strap measures 32(36)cm [12½(14) in] from beg. Fasten off.

Go back to other side of Bib and work 12 rows in C2 (for chimney) then cont in M working as for first strap from **.

POCKET

Make 20 ch using C2 and work in dc for 8cm [3¼ in]. Fasten off.

WAIST BORDER (make 2)

Using M and 2¾mm knitting needles cast on 84 sts and work in k1, p1 rib for 3cm [1¼ in]. Cast off in rib.

TO MAKE UP

Following instructions on ball band, press work on wrong side avoiding ribbing. Using C4, embroider in ch st the cross of the window, the door surrounds, the roof surrounds, then top of chimney (see photo). Join leg and side seams using back-stitch. Sew the waist border on neatly, cast-on edge to foundation ch row. Sew Bib in position as shown in photo. Sew on pocket, back-stitching just inside the 3 edges, then sew on 2 buttons to back of waist rib.

Opposite page: the bright and cheerful jumper and overalls that are perfect for playtime – the jumper is knitted and the overalls crocheted
Below: the shape guides that will help you when making the outfit

OVERALLS: SHAPE GUIDE

BACK

FRONT

BIB

JUMPER: SHAPE GUIDE

BACK

FRONT

SLEEVE

Children's Clothes

Dressing gown

1 to 4 years

Just right for after-bath or breakfast wear.

Materials 10(11:12) 20g balls of 4 ply synthetic yarn in Green (M); one 20g ball in Orange (C) for each size; 3mm [No 11] crochet hook; 3 buttons.

Measurements To fit a 51(56:61)cm [20(22:24) in] chest.

Tension 10 tr measures 5cm [2 in].

Abbreviations ch, chain; st(s), stitch(es); dc, double crochet; tr, treble; inc, increase; cont, continue; beg, beginning; rep, repeat; patt, pattern; dec, decrease; cm, centimetre(s), in, inch(es).

Size Note Figures in brackets refer to larger sizes. One figure only refers to all sizes. Square brackets contain imperial measurements.

> You can easily turn this gown into a sleeping bag which could then become a dressing gown when the baby grows. Just work more rows of treble straight in skirt to required length and fasten off. Stitch lower edges together and when needed just undo the stitching. Remember to allow extra wool for lengthening and to add a few extra double crochet for front borders.

BACK

Beg at yoke and work to lower edge. Using M, make 62(66:70) ch.
1st row Work 1 tr into 3rd ch from hook, then 1 tr into each st to end. Cont in tr inc 1 tr each end of every 3rd row until 12 tr each end have been added. Work straight to 34(40:45)cm [13½(15¾: 17¾) in] or length required. Fasten off.
Go back to foundation row, rejoin M to other side of ch then work a row of dc, inc 8 sts across row by working 2 dc into every 7th(8th:8th) st . . . 69(73:77) sts.
Next row 4 ch, * miss 1 dc 1 tr on next dc, 1 ch. Rep from * omitting last 1 ch on last rep. Now work in filet patt of tr on tr with 1 ch between, but at the

same time shape armhole thus: Dec by slip-stitching along at beg of rows and turning at end of rows, at each end dec 4 sts once and 2 sts 3 times . . . 49(53:57) sts. Cont straight in patt until yoke measures 10(11:12)cm [4(4½:4¾) in] from beg.
Shape Shoulders At each end of row dec 6(7:8) sts once, 4(5:5) sts once and 4(4:4) sts once. Fasten off.

RIGHT FRONT

Using M make 32(35:38) ch and work in tr as for Back, inc 1 tr at beg of 3rd row and at this edge

on every 3rd row until 12 tr have been added. Work until same length as Back to lower edge. Fasten off.
Rejoin M to foundation ch and inc 4(3:2) sts by working a row in dc and inc in every 7th(9th:16th) ch to end . . . 35(37:39) sts.
Cont in filet patt as for Back for 1 row, then shape armhole at side edge by dec 4 sts once and 2 sts 4 times . . . 23(25:27) sts.
Work straight until Front yoke measures 9(10:11)cm [3½(4:4¾) in] from beg ending at neck edge.
Shape Neck At neck edge dec 4(4:6) sts once and 2 sts 2 times,

then cont straight at this edge, but at the same time when work measures as Back to shoulder, ending at armhole edge, dec at armhole edge, 6(7:8) sts once and 4(5:5) sts once. Work Back to armhole edge and fasten off.

LEFT FRONT

Work as given for Right Front, but for skirt inc at end of 3rd row and at this edge on every 3rd row until 12 tr have been added.

SLEEVES (make 2)

Using M, make 30(34:38) ch and work in tr as for Back, inc 1

Crocheted in Lister's Tricel Nylon 4 ply crepe in Green and Orange

DRESSING GOWN: SHAPE GUIDE

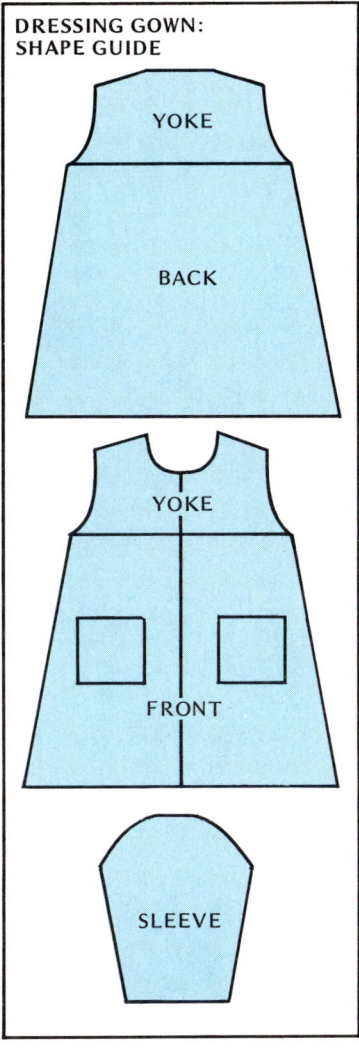

YOKE

BACK

YOKE

FRONT

SLEEVE

Opposite page and left: the dressing gown made for two sizes. The instructions tell you where to make the sleeves, back and fronts longer
Above: a guide to the simple shape of the dressing gown

Bolero and skirt

18 months to 3 years

Illustrated overleaf

Although the pattern is not difficult, you'll need experience to crochet this duo – the shapings are not for the amateur.

Materials 2(2:3) 25g balls of 4 ply in each of Ecru (C1) and Red (C2); 4(4:4) 25g balls of 4 ply in Brown (C3); 2½mm [No 12] crochet hook; pair of 2mm [No 14] knitting needles; 2 buttons; waist elastic.

Measurements To fit a 53(56:58.5) cm [21(22:23) in] chest.

Tension 20 sts measures 10cm [4 in]. One pattern consists of a 3 tr gr and 1 dc (4 sts).

Abbreviations ch, chain; dc, double crochet; tr, treble; dec, decrease; inc, increase; st(s), stitch(es); rep, repeat; cont, continue; patt, pattern; alt, alternate; beg, beginning; cm, centimetre(s); in, inch(es); rem, remain(ing); ss, slip stitch; gr, group; rnd, round; foll, following; k, knit; p, purl.

Size Note Figures in brackets refer to larger sizes. One figure only refers to all sizes. Square brackets contain imperial measurements.

THE 3-COLOUR PATTERN
Work foundation ch row as given in instructions.
1st row Turn with 3 ch, miss 1 ch, * 1 dc into next st, miss 1 ch, 3 tr into next st, miss 1 ch. Rep from * to last 3 ch, 1 dc in next st, miss 1 ch, 1 tr into end ch.
2nd row 2 ch, * 3 tr into top of dc, 1 dc in 2nd tr of 3 tr gr. Rep from * ending with last dc in end st.
3rd row 3 ch, * 1 dc in 2nd tr of 3 tr gr, 3 tr in dc. Rep from * ending 1 dc in tr gr, 1 tr on end st. Rep 2nd and 3rd rows.

THE STRIPE SEQUENCE
* 1 row each of C1, C3 and C2. Rep from * to completion.

SKIRT
BACK
Using C1 make 72(76:80) ch and work in the 3-colour patt for 3

Continued on next page

---

tr each end of every 3rd row 6 times. Cont straight until work measures 18(22:28)cm [7(8¾:11) in] or length required.
Shape Top Dec by slip-stitching along at beg of rows and turning at end of rows, at each end dec 3 sts once, 2 sts once, 1 st 4(6:8) times, 2 sts once and 3 sts once. Fasten off.

COLLAR
Using M make 58(58:60) ch and work 1 row in tr. **Next row** 3 ch, then 3(3:4) tr, * 2 tr in next tr, 3 tr. Rep from * ending 4(4:5) tr instead of 3 tr on last rep. Work 1 row of tr on tr.
Next row 3 ch, 3(3:4) tr, * 2 tr in next tr, 4 tr. Rep from * ending 5(5:6) tr instead of 4 tr on last rep. Work 2 rows of tr on tr and fasten off.

POCKETS (make 2)
Using M make 26(26:28) ch. **Next row** 1 tr in 4th ch from hook, * 1 ch, miss 1 ch, 1 tr in next ch. Rep from * to end.
Next row Turn with 4 ch, then * 1 tr on next tr, 1 ch. Rep from * ending 1 tr on top of turning ch. Rep last row 9(9:10) times more. Fasten off.

BUTTON BORDER
Using M make 90(96:102) ch and work dc for 6 rows. Fasten off.

BUTTONHOLE BORDER
Work as for button border, but make 3 buttonholes of 3 ch, missing 3 dc in 3rd row and work 3 dc into ch loop on 4th row, 1st one 25(31:37.5)cm [10(12¼:14¾) in] from lower edge and 2 more at 6(7:7)cm [2½(2¾:2¾) in] intervals.

TO MAKE UP
Press following instructions on ball band. Now using C and using 4 threads together at a time, weave 'under and over' trs to end of 1st row and in following row alternate the weave. Cont thus weaving yokes and pockets, being careful to keep work flat.
Using a flat seam join shoulders, then sew in sleeves. Sew up sleeve and side seams. Sew on borders with buttonhole border to Right Front for girl or Left Front for boy. Sew on collar beg and ending in centre of border. Pin pockets in position (see picture), then using back-stitch sew down. Sew on buttons to correspond with buttonholes.

Bolero and skirt . . . continued

rows, then dec 1 st each end of every 4th row until 56(60:64) sts rem, remembering that each patt consists of 4 sts, so when dec a st over a 3 tr gr, it will be 2 tr, and on the next dec, it will 1 tr instead of 2 tr.

When 56(60:64) sts rem, there will be 13(14:15) 3 tr gr in row. Work straight until Back measures 16(17:19)cm [6¼(6¾:7½) in] from beg, or length required. Fasten off.

FRONT

Work exactly as for Back.

WAISTBANDS (make 2)

Using C3 and knitting needles, cast on 88(92:96) sts and work in k1, p1 rib for 4cm [1½ in]. Cast off in the rib.

STRAPS (make 2)

Using C1, make 72(76:80) ch and work in dc along edge, 2 dc in corner and work along other side of foundation ch to end, 2 dc in 2nd corner. Change to C2 and work dc on dc to first corner, 3 ch, miss 3 dc, then in dc to 2nd corner, 2 dc on centre dc. Change to C3 and work in dc working 3 dc into ch loop, and 2 dc in centre dc on 2nd corner. Fasten off.

TO MAKE UP

Press according to ball band instructions. Using back-stitch throughout, sew waistbands to top of skirt, then sew up side and waistband seams. Turn waistband over to wrong side over a length of elastic and sew down neatly. Now using C3 work 2 rows of dc all around lower edges of skirt. Sew on the straps to back waistband and sew on 2 buttons to front waistband. Press seams.

BOLERO

This is worked in one piece. Make 96(100:104) ch and work in the 3-colour patt for 2 rows, then keeping continuity of patt inc each end of every row (1 st twice, then 2 sts once) 3 times – 9 inc rows, working extra sts in tr until 4 sts have been added each end, then working over these 4 sts as foundation row. One complete patt added for every 4 sts increased. Cont thus until there are 120(124:128) sts. There will be 30(31:32) 3 tr grs. Cont straight for a few rows until work measures 7(8:9)cm [2¾(3¼: 3½) in].

Divide for Back and Fronts Leave 30(31:32) sts each end and work on centre 60(62:64) sts.

Shape Back Armholes Dec 4 sts

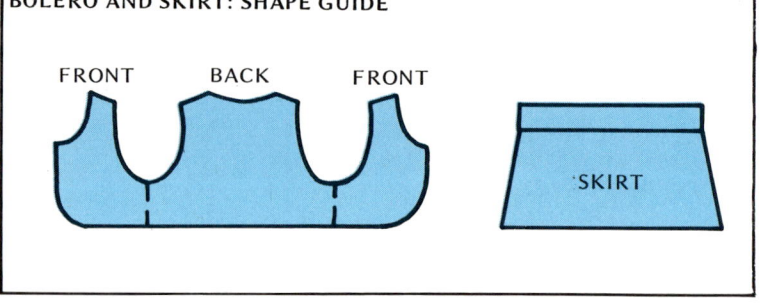

Above: the skirt and bolero – the smart pattern gives the outfit the look of fabric
Right: the shape guide which you will need to follow with care as shaping is very important in both garments

(ie, 3 tr gr and 1 dc) at each end of next row and foll 2 alt rows (3 complete patts decreased each end and 36(38:40) sts rem). Cont straight on these sts to 20.3(22: 24)cm [8(8¾:9½) in] from beg.

Shape Neck and Shoulders Patt 14(15:16) sts, turn and leave rem sts. **Next row** Ss along 6 sts, turn then patt to armhole edge. Now dec 4 sts on next armhole edge row. **Next row** Work to armhole edge. Fasten off.

Go back to rem Back sts, leave centre 8 sts unworked, rejoin

yarn and ss along 6 sts, work to end. Now shape shoulder as for other side. Rejoin yarn to Right Front sts, work to armhole, turn. Now dec 4 sts at beg of next 3 armhole edge rows . . . 18(19:20) sts rem**.

Cont straight until work measures 13.5(15:17)cm [5¼(6:6¾) in] ending at front edge.

Shape Neck Dec 4 sts at beg of next and foll alt row and 2 sts on next alt row . . . 8(9:10) sts rem. Work straight until Front measures as Back to shoulder ending at

BOLERO AND SKIRT: SHAPE GUIDE

armhole edge. Shape shoulder as given for Back.

Rejoin yarn to rem Left Front sts at armhole, ss along first 4 sts, then dec 4 sts at beg of next 2 armhole edge rows. Now work as for Right Front from **.

TO MAKE UP

Press according to ball band instructions. Using back-stitch, join shoulder seams. Using C3 work 2 rows of dc all around outer edges. Fasten off. Press seams.

Sunshine suits

18 months to 3 years

Pretty little playsuits that can be worn with or without a T-shirt or sweater underneath.

Orange playsuit

Take care to choose a soft-textured yarn for this playsuit. Try and achieve the tension with a soft Double Knitting used double (in which case you'll need twice the amount).

Materials 150g of thick Double Knitting yarn in a soft texture; 4mm [No 8] crochet hook; 6 buttons.

Measurements To fit a 51–56cm [20–22 in] chest.

Tension 12 sts to 10cm [4 in].

Abbreviations ch, chain; st(s), stitch(es); dc, double crochet; inc, increase; beg, beginning; dec, decrease; rem, remain(ing); cm, centimetre(s); in, inch(es); ss, slip stitch; rep, repeat; patt, pattern. Square brackets contain imperial measurements.

THE STITCH
Foundation row In dc working 1st dc into 2nd ch from hook.
2nd row: 2 ch, * hook in next st, yarn over and through, hook in next st, yarn over and through, then yarn over and through 2 sts on hook, yarn over and through last 2 sts. Rep from * ending 1 dc into last dc.
3rd row 2 ch as 1st dc, then 2 dc into each st to end. Rep 2nd and 3rd rows throughout.

FRONT
Make 19 ch and work foundation row – 18 dc, then continue in st as given inc 1 st each end of next 11 rows – remembering to work odd st in dc then when 2 sts are increased work these in pattern. Now inc 2 sts each end of next 4 rows. Work straight for 23cm [9 in] keeping odd st at end in dc.

Shape Armholes Next row Ss along to 5th st, then in patt to last 4 sts, turn. Now dec 1 st each end of next 2 rows. Work straight to 40cm [15¾ in].
Shape for Strap Next row Patt 15, turn and leave other sts for the present.
Now dec 1 st at neck edge on next 3 rows. Cont straight until strap measures 6cm [2½ in]. Fasten off.
Go back to other sts, leave centre 13 sts, rejoin yarn and work to end. Dec 1 st at neck edge on next 3 rows, then work until strap measures 6cm [2½ in]. Fasten off.

BACK
Work exactly as for Front but work on strap sts until strap measures 8cm (3 in).

TO MAKE UP
Press work following ball band instructions. Join crotch and side seams. Work 1 row of dc round legs, then 1 row of crab stitch – (ie, dc worked from left to right) forming a rolled edge. Fasten off. Sew on buttons using holes in pattern for buttonholes.

Yellow playsuit

Materials 150g of Double Double knitting yarn; 3mm [No 11] crochet hook, 6 buttons.

Measurements To fit a 51–56cm [20–22 in] chest.

Tension 12 sts to 10cm [4 in].

Abbreviations ch, chain; st(s), stitch(es); dc, double crochet; tr, treble; inc, increase; beg, beginning; dec, decrease; rem, remain(ing); cm, centimetre(s); in, inch(es); ss, slip stitch. Square brackets contain imperial measurements.

FRONT
Make 17 ch and work 1 tr into 3rd ch from the hook (15 tr), then work 1 tr into each ch to end. Now work in tr for 6 rows, inc 1 tr at end of every row, then inc 1 tr each end of next 7 rows (35 tr). Work straight for 23cm [9 in].

Shape Armholes Next row Ss along to 4th tr, tr to last 3 tr, turn. **Next row** Dec 1st each end of row (27 tr).
Shape for Straps Next row 11 tr, turn and leave other part for the present. Now dec 1 st at neck edge on next 2 rows. Work 8 rows in tr on these 9 tr. Fasten off. Go back to other part, miss centre 5 sts, rejoin yarn to rem sts, tr to end. Now dec 1 st at neck edge on next 2 rows, then work 8 rows in tr. Fasten off.

BACK
Make 14 ch and work foundation row as for Front then work 4 rows of tr on tr (12 tr). Now inc 1 st at end of next 4 row, then each end of next 10 rows. Work straight for 23cm [9 in] on these 36 tr.
Shape Armholes Next row Ss along to 3rd tr, tr to last 2 tr, turn. **Next 2 rows** Dec 1 st at each end (28 tr). **Next row** 11 tr, turn and leave other part for the present.
Cont on these 11 tr, dec 1 st at neck edge on next 2 rows. Work straight for 12 rows. Fasten off.
Go back to other part, leave centre 6 sts, rejoin yarn and tr to end. Now dec 1 st at neck edge on next 2 rows, then work 12 rows in tr. Fasten off.

TO MAKE UP
Press the work, following ball band instructions. Join sides and crotch neatly. Work 1 row of dc round outer edges of leg, then 1 row of crab stitch (ie, dc worked from left to right) giving a rolled edge. Sew on buttons using space in pattern for buttonholes.

Left and above: two playsuits for toddlers to wear indoors or out

Party dress

2 to 4 years

A very smart little dress and simple to make though you need to take care when shaping the skirt. The butterfly motif is worked from a chart.

Materials 4 (5) 25g balls 4-ply yarn in turquoise (T); 1 (1) ball in each of green (G) and pink (P) and yellow (Y); 3mm [No 11] crochet hook; 6 buttons; shirring elastic.

Measurements To fit 53 (58)cm [21 (23) in] chest; length, 46 (48)cm [18 (19) in].

Tension 24 tr to 10cm [4 in].

Abbreviations sts, stitch(es); cm, centimetre(s); in, inch(es); ch, chain; dc, double crochet; tr, treble; ss, slip stitch; tc, turning ch; tog, together; 0, no sts; dec, decreas(e)ing thus: leaving last loop of each tr on hook, work tr in each of next 2 sts, yoh and draw through all loops; yoh, yarn over hook; rep, repeat; rem, remain(ing).

Size Note Figures in brackets refer to larger size. One figure only refers to both sizes. Square brackets contain imperial measurements.

Special Note Unless otherwise stated the 3 ch at beg of each row stands as the first tr and the first tr should therefore be missed. The last tr on each row should be worked in the tc of the previous row.

BACK

With Y make 147 (151) ch.
Foundation row 1 tr in 3rd ch from hook, 1 tr in each ch to end, turn . . . 146 (150) sts. Change to T.
1st row 3 ch, miss 1st tr, 1 tr in each tr to end, turn. Rep last row 3 times more.
5th row Dec thus: 3 ch, miss 1st tr, 1 tr in each of next 5 (7) tr, dec over next 2 tr, *1 tr in each of next 6 tr, dec over next 2 tr, 1 tr in each of next 15 tr, dec over next 2 tr; rep from * 4 times more, 1 tr in each of next 6 tr, dec over next 2 tr, 1 tr in each of next 5 (7) tr, turn . . . 134 (138) sts.
6th row 1 tr in each tr to end, turn.
7th and 8th rows As 6th.
9th row Dec thus: 3 ch, miss 1st tr, 1 tr in each of next 4 (6) tr, dec

over next 2 tr, *1 tr in each of next 6 tr, dec over next 2 tr, 1 tr in each of next 13 tr, dec over next 2 tr; rep from * 4 times more, 1 tr in each of next 6 tr, dec over next 2 tr, 1 tr in each of next 4 (6) tr, turn . . . 122 (126) sts.
10th to 12th rows As 6th.
13th row Dec thus: 3 ch, miss 1st tr, 1 tr in each of next 3 (5) tr, dec over next 2 tr, *1 tr in each of next 6 tr, dec over next 2 tr, 1 tr in each of next 11 tr, dec over next 2 tr; rep from * 4 times more; 1 tr in each of next 6 tr, dec over next 2 tr, 1 tr in each of next 3 (5) tr, turn . . . 110 (114) sts.
14th and 16th rows As 6th.
Cont dec 12 sts in this way on next row and every foll 4th row until the **25th row** 1 tr in each of 1 (3) tr, dec over next 2 tr, *1 tr in each of next 6 tr, dec over next 2 tr, 1 tr in each of next 5 tr, dec over next 2 tr; rep from * 4 times more, 1 tr in each of next 6 tr, dec over next 2 tr, 1 tr in last tr on 2nd size only, turn . . . 74 (78) sts.
Cont in tr without shaping in centre for 1 row only. Now dec 1 tr at each end of next row and every foll alt row to 66 (70) sts. Cont without shaping until work measures 34 cm [13½ in].

Divide for Back Opening 1st row 1 tr in each of next 33 (35) sts, turn. Cont on these sts only. Cont in tr without shaping until work measures 36 (37)cm [14 (14½) in] ending at side edge.
Shape Armhole Next row Ss over first 2 sts, 3 ch, 1 tr in each tr to end, turn. Cont in tr on 31 (33) sts until armhole measures 10 (11)cm [4 (4½) in] ending at armhole edge.

Shape Shoulder and Neck Ss over 7 tr, tr to last 6 sts, turn.
2nd row Ss over 6 sts, tr to last 5 (7). Fasten off.
With right side of work facing, join T to rem sts at opening edge and work to end. Cont on these 33 (35) sts without shaping until work measures 36(37)cm [14(14½) in] ending at side edge.
Shape Armhole: Next row Ss over first 2 sts, 3 ch, 1 tr in each tr to end, turn. Cont in tr on 31 (33) sts until armhole measures 10 (11) [4 (4½) in] ending at armhole edge.
Shape Shoulder and Neck Ss over 7 tr, tr to last 6 sts, turn. **2nd row** Ss over 6 sts, tr to last 5 (7) sts. Fasten off.

FRONT

With Y make 147 (151) ch.
Foundation row 1 tr in 3rd ch from hook, 1 tr in each ch to end, turn . . . 146 (150) tr. Change to T.
1st row 1 tr in each tr to end, turn. Rep last row 3 times more.
5th row Dec thus: 1 tr in each of next 6 (8) tr, dec over next 2 tr, *1 tr in each of next 6 tr, dec over next 2 tr, 1 tr in each of next 15 tr, dec over next 2 tr; rep from * 4 times more, 1 tr in each of next 6 tr, dec over next 2 tr, 1 tr in each tr to end, turn . . . 134 (138) sts. Work 3 rows without shaping.
9th row Dec thus: 1 tr in each of next 5 (7) tr, dec over next 2 tr, *1 tr in each of next 6 tr, dec over next 2 tr, 1 tr in each of next 11 tr, dec over next 2 tr; rep from * 4 times more, 1 tr in each of next 6 tr, dec over next 2 tr, 1 tr in each tr to end, turn . . . 122 (126) sts.
10th to 12th rows As 6th row.
Cont dec 12 sts in this way on next row and every foll 4th row to

74 (78) sts. Work 1 row straight. Now dec 1 st at each end of next row and every foll alt row to 66 (70) sts.
Cont without shaping until work measures 28cm [11 in] ending after a wrong-side row.
Now cont in tr, working the butterfly motif from the chart. Use small balls of G where necessary and carry the Y loosely across the back, working over the loose strands in the following row. Use a separate ball of T for each side of the motif, twist the yarns when changing colour to avoid making a hole. Place the motif 1st row thus; With T 1 tr in each of next 31 (33) sts, with Y 1 tr in each of next 3 sts, with T 1 tr in each next 33 (34) sts. Cont from the chart as set until work measures 36 (37) cm [14 (14½) in] ending after a wrong-side row.
Shape Armholes Keeping motif correct, ss over first 2 sts, tr in each tr to last 2 sts, turn . . . 62 (66) sts. Keeping armhole edges straight cont working motif, then cont in T only until armholes measure 6 (7)cm [2½ (2¾) in] ending after wrong-side row.
Shape Neck 1st row 1 tr in each of next 26 (28) sts, turn. **2nd row** Ss over first 3 tr, 1 tr in each st to end, turn. **3rd row** 1 tr in each of 23 (25) sts, turn. **4th row** Ss over first 4 (4) tr, 1 tr in each st to end . . . 19 (21) sts. Cont in tr without shaping until armhole measures 10 (11)cm [4 (4½) in] ending at armhole edge.
Shape Shoulder 1st row Ss over 7 tr, 1 tr in each st to end, turn.
2nd row Tr to last 5 tr, turn. Fasten off.
With wrong side of work facing, beg at side edge, work the other

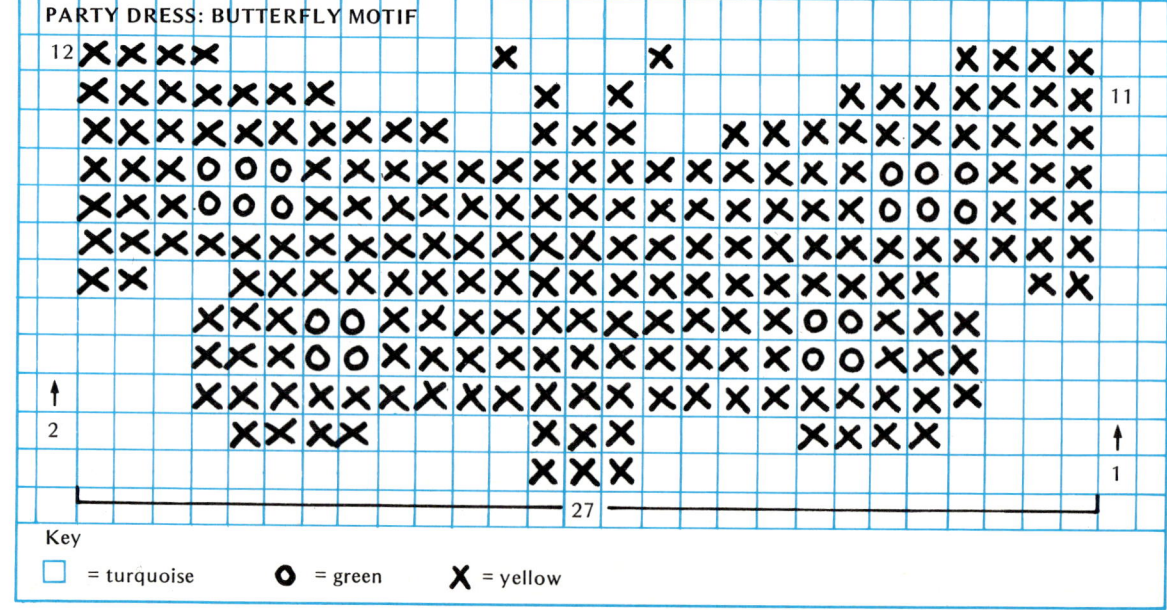

PARTY DRESS: BUTTERFLY MOTIF

Key

□ = turquoise   O = green   X = yellow

188

side of neck and shoulder in the same way.

SLEEVES

With P, make 77 ch. **Foundation row 1** tr in 3rd ch from hook, 1 tr in each ch to end, turn . . . 76 sts. **1st row** 1 tr in each tr to end, turn. Rep the last row 3 times more. Change to G.

Shape Top 1st row Ss over first 2 sts, 1 tr in each tr to last 2 sts, turn. Rep last row 3 times more . . . 50 sts. Change to Y and rep last row until 24 sts rem. Fasten off.

Work a second sleeve the same.

TO MAKE UP

Press lightly following instructions on the ball band. With right sides of work together, back-stitch the shoulder seams, sloping the seam across the 'stepped' shoulder line. With right sides together, join the side and sleeve seams with a neat over-sewing seam. With right sides together place the sleeve top to the armhole, easing in the fullness. Back-stitch the sleeve in place, sloping across the 'stepped' shaping.

Neck Border With right side of work facing, using T, work 1 row dc evenly round neck edge. **2nd row** With Y, *1 dc, 2 ch, miss 2 dc; rep from * all round ending 1 dc in last dc.

3rd row With Y, 2 ch, 6 tr in 1st 2-ch loop, turning work, make a tr between last tr worked and the top of the first 2 ch, turn, dc in next 2-ch loop, * 7 tr in next 2-ch loop, turn and make tr between last tr worked and first of these 7 tr, turn, dc in next 2-ch loop; rep from * all round. Fasten off.

With right side of work facing, using T, work 2 rows dc along both sides of back opening. Work 3rd row making buttonhole loops on right side opening thus: 2 dc, 3 ch, miss 2 dc; rep from * until the 6 loops have been made, cont in dc to end. Fasten off. Sew buttons on left side of opening to correspond with the loops. Sew a few rows of shirring elastic in the first row of sleeve to give the puffed effect.

Left: the chart from which you work the butterfly motif
Right: the Party Dress with its pretty butterfly and colourful puffed sleeves. There are special instructions for the neck border in the making up section

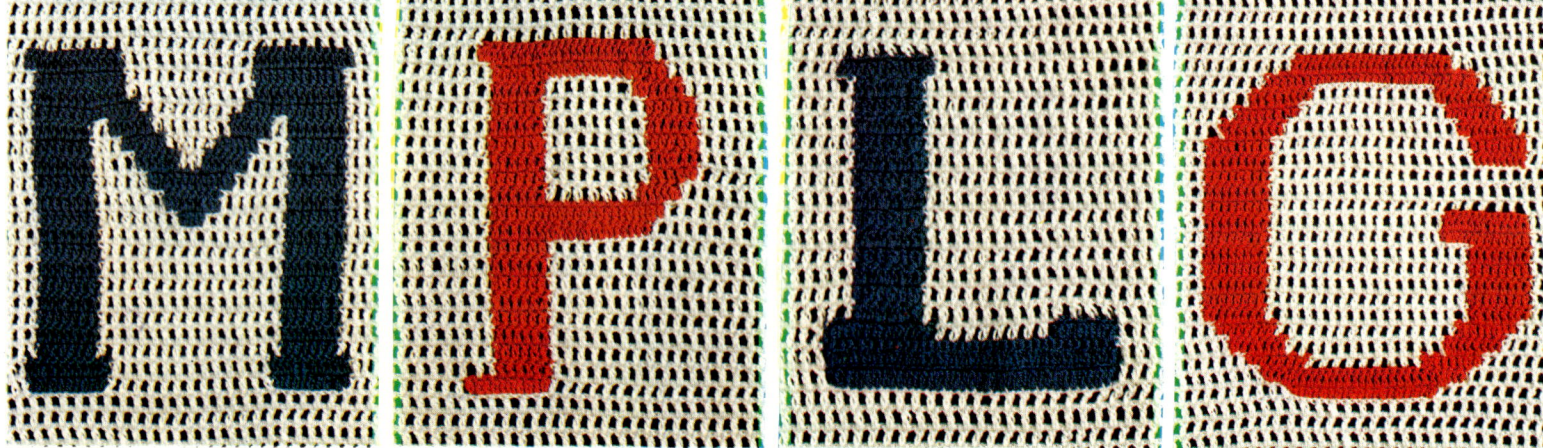

Family favourites

3 to 11 years

Easily laundered and practical, these tops can also be quickly identified by the particular initial.

Materials 200g of No 3 cotton; oddment of coloured cotton for initial; 2mm [No 14] crochet hook; 6 buttons.

Measurements To fit a 58 (63:68: 73)cm [23 (25:27:29) in] chest.

Tension 7 tr = (1 tr 1 ch) 3 times, 1 tr – measures 5cm [2 in].

Abbreviations ch, chain; dc, double crochet; tr, treble; st(s), stitch(es); rep, repeat; patt, pattern; cont, continue; cm, centimetre(s); in, inch(es). Square brackets contain imperial measurements.

BACK
Make 90 (98:106:114) ch and work in dc for 7 rows . . . 89 (97:105:113) dc.
Next row 4 ch, miss next dc, * 1 tr in next dc, miss 1 dc, 1 ch. Rep from * to last dc, 1 tr into dc.
Next row 4 ch, then * 1 tr on next tr, 1 ch. Rep from * ending 1 tr on 3rd of 4 ch.
Rep last row 27(31:33:35) times more.
Shape for Cap Sleeves Make 12(14:14:14) ch, turn, 4 ch, miss next ch, * 1 tr in next ch, miss 1 ch, 1 ch. Rep from * across ch, then in patt across main sts to end, make 12(14:14:14) ch, turn.
Next row Work across ch as for other side, then work in patt across all sts.
Work straight for 11(12:13:15) rows.
Shape Shoulders Slip-stitch along 4 squares, patt to last 4 squares, turn. Break thread. Leave 6 (6:7:7) squares, rejoin yarn and work to last 6(6:7:7) squares, turn. Slip-stitch along 4 squares patt to last 4 squares, turn. Fasten off.

FRONT
First work out the design you require on squared paper using the Back spaces as a guide for centralizing the initial. Work as for Back, but using the coloured yarn for the initial pattern.

TO MAKE UP
Borders Work 7 rows of dc along Back neck edge. Fasten off. On each shoulder at Back, use pins to mark positions for 3 buttonholes. Work 3 rows of dc along Front neck edge, then in next row work in dc to position of first pin, miss 3(3:4:4) dc, make 3(3:4:4) ch, then in dc to next position. Cont thus to end of row. Work 3 more rows of dc, working 3(3:4:4) dc into buttonhole ch spaces on next row. Fasten off. Lay Front border over Back border, then work 7 rows of dc along each Sleeve edge working through double thickness at shoulders. Join side seams with back-stitch. Press. Sew on 3 buttons on Back shoulders to correspond with buttonholes.

On a filet net base you can reproduce whatever design you like. Choose your initial or design and sketch it on to squared paper. Then cross the squares which are to be worked in a different colour yarn. In these tops, the initials are on the front only, so be guided by the spaces on the back of the work. When changing the colour yarn in the middle of a row, draw the new colour through the last 2 loops of the last tr st to be worked in the old colour and continue in the new colour, with 1 tr into space, 1 tr on next tr – to required number. In the next row work in pattern in old colour as before, working 1 tr on each tr in new colour for initial.
You can either use separate balls of old colour each side of the coloured initial or you can carry the unused yarn loosely behind.

Opposite: filet-net tops that are good for play because they're cool and wash well. The initials are worked out on graph paper

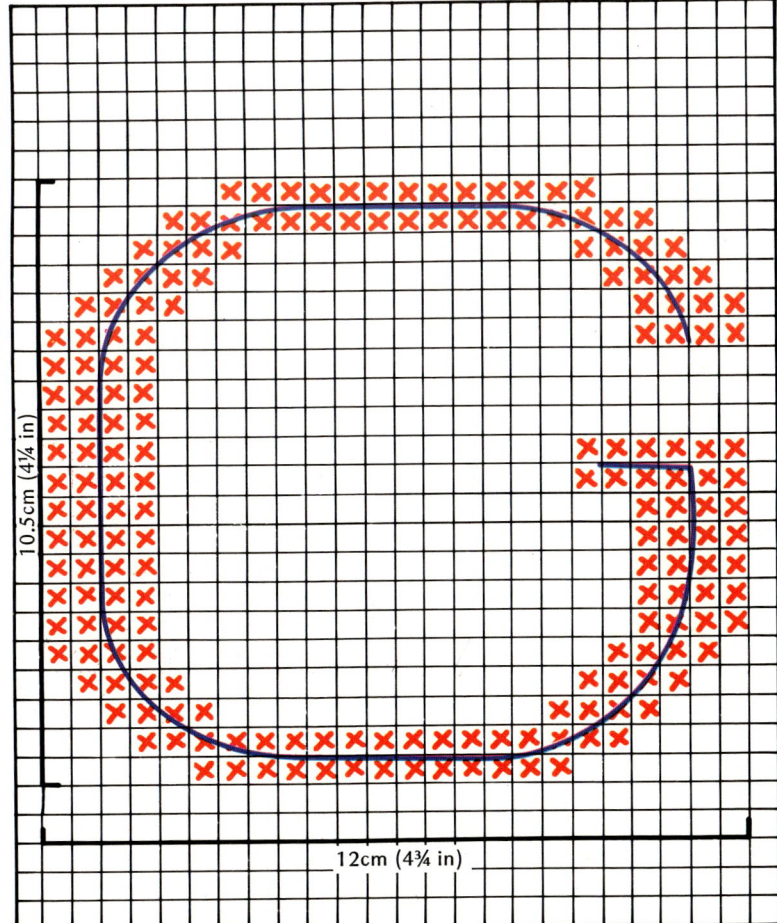

Below: two initials placed on squared paper so you can see how the thick and thin shaping is achieved. Each initial is 10·5cm deep, 12cm wide

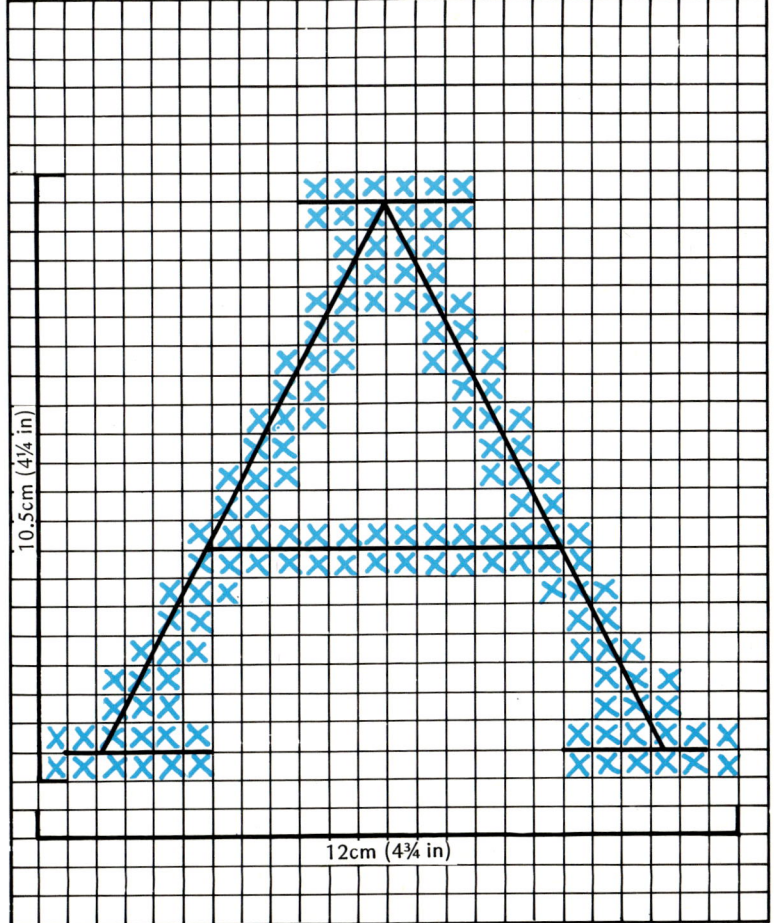

10·5cm (4¾ in)

12cm (4¾ in)

Coat and muff

4 to 6 years

Prettily-styled as well as warm, this coat and muff combines knitting and crochet.

Materials 21(22) 25g balls Double Knitting yarn in Main colour (M); two balls in Contrast (C); a small quantity main colour in 4-ply yarn; pairs of 3mm and $3\frac{3}{4}$mm [No 11 and No 9] knitting needles; 3.5mm [No 9] crochet hook; 4 buttons; shirring elastic; elastic 2cm [$\frac{3}{4}$ in] wide for waist; 4 buttons.

Measurements To fit 61(66)cm [24(26) in] chest, length 46(48)cm [18(19) in].

Tension 22 sts to 10cm [4 in] in st-st; 20 sts in loop st patt.

Abbreviations k, knit; p, purl; st(s), stitch(es); cm, centimetre(s); in, inch(es); alt, alternate; beg, beginning; cont, continue; dec, decreas(e)ing; inc, increas(e)ing; rep, repeat; rem, remain(ing); st-st, stocking stitch; tog, together; ss, slip stitch; ch, chain; dc, double crochet; tr, treble; dec in crochet – insert hook in next st and draw loop through, insert hook in next st, draw loop through yarn over hook and draw through all loops – dec made; yrh, yarn round hook; patt, pattern.

Size Note Figures in brackets refer to large size. One figure only refers to both sizes. Square brackets contain imperial measurements.

The loop stitch pattern is in crochet and is created on the back of the work. You can make the collar in the same colour as the rest and leave out the pockets if you wish – in which case don't leave an opening when you sew the side seams.

COAT

BACK

With $3\frac{3}{4}$mm [No 9] needles and M, cast on 114(120) sts. Cont in st-st dec 1 st at both ends of 15th row and every foll 16th row to 106(112) sts. Cont in st-st without shaping until work measures 27 (28)cm [$10\frac{1}{2}$(11) in] (adjust length here if liked) ending after a p row. Cast off.

With right side of work facing, using crochet hook and M, work 64(68) dc evenly across the cast-off edge. Cont in loop stitch pattern thus:

Loop row (wrong side) 1 ch, insert hook in first st, *wind yarn round middle finger of left hand, yrh draw through a loop, yrh draw through two loops, draw the wound loop off the finger, insert hook into next st*; rep from * to end. **2nd row** 1 ch, 1 dc in each st to end.

These 2 rows form the loop stitch pattern. Cont in pattern until work measures 4cm [$1\frac{1}{2}$ in] from beg of crochet. Inc 1 st at both ends of next row only, then cont in loop stitch pattern without shaping until work measures 35 (36)cm [$13\frac{3}{4}$(14) in] ending after a wrong-side row.

Shape Armholes 1st row Ss over first 4(5) sts, dc to last 4(5) sts, turn. **2nd row** Ss over first 2 sts, patt to last 2 sts, turn. **3rd row** Dec over first 2 sts, dc to last 2 sts, dec over last 2 sts. **4th row** Patt to end. **5th row** As 3rd row . . . 50 (52) sts. End of armhole shaping. Cont in loop pattern without shaping until armholes measure 11(12)cm [$4\frac{1}{4}$($4\frac{3}{4}$) in] ending after a wrong-side row.

Shape shoulders and neck 1st row Ss over first 5 sts, dc to last 5 sts, turn. **2nd row** Patt to end. **3rd row** Ss over first 5 sts, dc 6, turn. **4th row** Patt 6 sts. Fasten off. With right side of work facing, miss centre 18(20) sts, dc 6 sts, turn, patt 6. Fasten off.

LEFT FRONT

With $3\frac{3}{4}$mm [No 9] needles and M, cast on 67(70) sts. Cont in st-st dec 1 st at beg of 15th row foll and every foll 16th row to 63(66) sts. Cont in st-st without shaping until work measures 27(28)cm [$10\frac{1}{2}$(11) in] (adjust length here if liked), ending after a p row. Cast off.

With right side facing, using crochet hook and M, work 38(40) dc evenly across cast-off edge. Work in loop stitch patt with 7 sts in dc for button band thus: **1st row** (wrong side) Dc 7 sts, loop stitch to end. **2nd row** Dc to end.

Cont in this way until work measures 4cm [$1\frac{1}{2}$ in] from beg of crochet ending after a wrong-side row. Inc 1 st at beg of next row only, then cont in loop stitch pattern with 7 dc for button band until work matches Back to armhole, ending after a wrong-side row.

Shape Armhole 1st row Ss over first 5(6) sts, dc to end. **2nd row** Dc 7, patt to last 3 sts, turn. **3rd row** Ss over first 2 sts, dc to end. **4th row** Dc 7 sts, patt to last 2 sts, dec over 2 sts. Cont in patt with 7 dc at front edge until work measures 43(44)cm [17($17\frac{1}{4}$) in] from beg ending after a right-side row.

Shape Neck 1st row Ss over first 8 sts, patt to end. **2nd row** Patt to last 2 sts, turn. **3rd row** Dec over first 2 sts, patt to end. **4th row** Patt to last 2 sts, dec. **5th row** As 3rd row . . . 15(16) sts.

Cont in patt without shaping until work measures 46(48)cm [18(19) in] from beg, ending after wrong-side row.

Shape Shoulder Ss over first 5 sts, patt 10(11). **2nd row** Patt 6 sts. Fasten off.

RIGHT FRONT

With $3\frac{3}{4}$mm [No 9] needles and M, cast on 67(70) sts. Cont in st-st, dec 1 st at end of 15th row foll and every foll 16th row to 63 (66) sts. Cont in st-st without shaping until work measures 27 (28)cm [$10\frac{1}{2}$[11] in] (adjust length here if liked) ending after a p row. Cast off.

With right side of work facing, using crochet hook and M, work 38(40) dc evenly across cast-off edge.

Cont in loop stitch pattern on all sts but working buttonholes thus: First mark the button band on the Left Front with pins to represent buttons, the top one just below the beg of neck shaping, the lowest one 2cm [$\frac{3}{4}$ in] above beg of crochet the other two spaced equally between. On the rows corresponding with the pinned positions work right-side rows. Dc 3, 3 ch, miss 3 dc, dc to end. The foll row, patt to last 6 sts, 1 loop stitch in each of 3 ch, patt to end.

Cont in loop pattern with buttonholes and inc 1 st only at end of 4cm [$1\frac{1}{2}$ in] at end of right-side row. When work matches Back to armhole shaping cont on right side thus:

Shape Armhole 1st row Patt to last 5(6) sts, turn. **2nd row** Ss over first 3 sts, patt to end. **3rd row** Patt to last 2 sts, turn. **4th** row Dec over first 2 sts, patt to end. Cont in patt without shaping until work measures 43(44)cm [17($17\frac{1}{4}$) in] from beg, ending after a wrong-side row.

Shape Neck 1st row Ss over first 8 sts, patt to end. **2nd row** Patt to last 2 sts, turn. **3rd row** Dec over first 2 sts, patt to end. **4th row** Patt to last 2 sts, dec over 2 sts. **5th row** As 3rd row . . . 15(16) sts.

Cont in patt without shaping until work measures 46(48)cm [18(19) in], from beg, ending after right-side row.

Shape Shoulder Ss over first 5 sts, patt 10(11). **2nd row** Patt 6 sts. Fasten off.

SLEEVES

With $3\frac{3}{4}$mm [No 9] needles and M, cast on 48(52) sts. Cont in st-st inc 1 st at both ends of 7th row foll and every foll 6th row to 64 (68) sts. Cont in st-st without shaping until work measures 25 (26)cm [10($10\frac{1}{4}$) in] (adjust length here if liked) ending after a p row.

Shape Top Cast off 4 sts at beg of next 2 rows; 2 sts at beg of next 6 rows. Dec 1 st at both ends of next row and foll 7 alt rows. Cast off 2 sts at beg of next 2 rows; 3 sts at beg of next 2 rows; 4 sts at beg of next 2 rows. Cast off rem 10(14) sts.

Work another sleeve the same.

POCKETS (make 2)

With 3mm [No 11] needles and 4-ply yarn, cast on 54 sts. Work 16cm [$6\frac{1}{4}$ in] st-st without shaping. Cast off.

Fold the pocket in half with k side inside. Oversew the two halves together joining the folded cast-off edge then the folded cast-on edge.

COLLAR

With $3\frac{3}{4}$mm [No 9] needles and C, cast on 89 sts. Cont in st-st inc 1 st at both ends of every 4th row to 97 sts. Work 8 rows straight. Now dec 1 st at both ends of next row and every 4th row to 89 sts. Work 3 rows straight. Cast off.

TO MAKE UP

Press pieces following instructions on ball band, avoiding the looped pattern sections. With right sides of work together, join the shoulder seams, with back-stitch. Now join the side seams, also with back-stitch, leaving opening for the pocket on each side, approx 11cm [$4\frac{1}{2}$ in] below the armhole shaping. With right side inside, back-stitch the sleeve seam. With right sides together, tack in the sleeve top to the armhole shaping, then back-stitch neatly round the sleeve top. Remove tackings. Turn work to right side.

With right side facing, work 1 row dc all round pocket opening then work 3 more rows on the back edge. Fasten off. Sew in the pockets. Fold the collar in half lengthways, with right side inside. Oversew the short edges. Turn the collar to right side. With right sides together, pin the collar edge to the neck edge, then back-stitch along the edge. Remove pins. Fold other edge of collar over and hem-stitch to inner edge of neck, concealing the back-stitch seam. Work 1 row dc along front edges of coat. Work 1 row dc along lower edge, then 1 row tr. Fasten off. Sew on buttons. Sew elastic inside back waist.

MUFF

TO MAKE

With crochet hook and M, make 33 ch. Work the loop stitch pattern for 33cm [13 in] then fold the work in two with the loop side inside. Work 1 row across working dc into the 1st and last rows at the same time to work a join. Fasten off. Turn work to right side. Work 1 row tr round one edge. **Next row** *Work 1 tr round stem of next tr, inserting hook round the back of the stem, work 1 tr round next st, inserting hook round the front of the st; rep from * to end. Work another row in the same way. Fasten off. Work the other edge of the muff in the same way.

Sew shirring elastic round the muff edges to keep the crochet tr "rib" elasticated. Make a twisted cord (see page 75) and sew the ends inside the muff (see finished look in picture).

Right: the coat with its loopy bodice and the muff which picks up the same pattern. There's no need to make the collar in a contrasting colour and the pockets are also optional

Red Indian waistcoat

8 to 10 years

A chance to use up leftover wool . . . an effective and attractive design.

Materials Eight 25g balls Double Knitting yarn in Ecru (C1); 1 ball Double Knitting yarn in Orange (C2); Remnants of Double Knitting yarn in Turquoise (C3) and Green (C4); 3·5mm [No 9] and 4mm [No 8] crochet hooks.

Measurements To fit a 68–71cm [27–28 in] chest.

Tension 17 sts and 11 rows measure about 10cm [4 in] over tr using the 3½mm [No 9] hook.

Abbreviations Ch, chain; dc, double crochet; tr, treble; rep, repeat; beg, beginning; inc, increase(ing); cont, continue; in, inch(es); cm, centimetre(s); ss, slip stitch; st(s), stitch(es); dec, decrease. Square brackets contain imperial measurements.

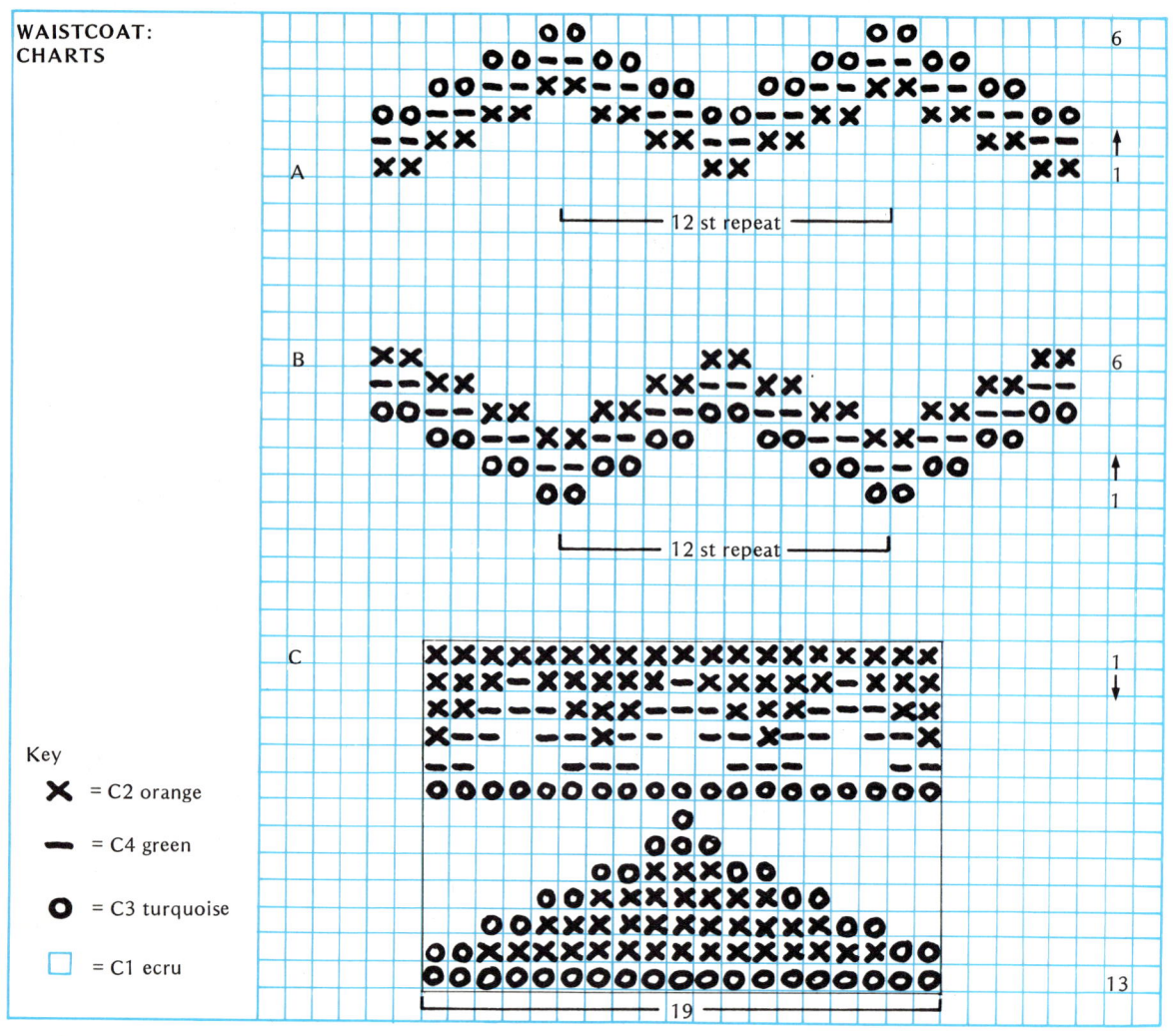

WAISTCOAT: CHARTS

Key
✖ = C2 orange
— = C4 green
⊙ = C3 turquoise
▫ = C1 ecru

> When changing colours in a row, draw the new colour through the last treble in the old colour . . . and continue in the new colour.

BACK
Beg at armholes. Using the 3·5mm [No 9] hook and C1 make 50 ch.
1st row 1 tr into 3rd ch from hook, then 1 tr into each ch to end. (48 tr).
Cont in tr inc at each end of each row, 1 st once, 2 sts once and 5 sts once (inc by making ch as needed, turn and work in tr on ch sts). There are now 64 tr. Leave work for the present.

LEFT FRONT
Using C1 and the 3·5mm [No 9] hook make 26 ch and work a tr row (24 tr). Now shape for armhole by inc 1 tr at end of next (2nd row), 2 sts at beg of 3rd row and 5 sts at end of 4th row (32 tr). Leave for the present.

RIGHT FRONT
Work as for Left Front, but inc 1 tr at beg of 2nd row, 2 sts at end of 3rd row and 5 sts at beg of 4th row (32 tr). Now work in tr across sts, then across back 64 tr and finally across Left Front 24 sts (128 sts).
Work 4 rows in tr across all sts, then follow chart A, placing sts thus: **Next row** Work 3rd–12th sts once, 1st–12th sts 9 times, then 1st–10th sts once.
Cont to follow chart until the 6 rows are completed then cont in C1 until work measures 14cm [5½ in] from beg. Mark with coloured thread the 33rd and 96th st and inc in tr either side of marked sts by working 2 tr into tr (4 incs made in row). Rep this inc row on every 6th row 3 times more (144 tr), then work straight to 34cm [13½ in] from beg. Fasten off.
Go back to the 48 Back sts and work in tr stripes of 1 row C2, 1 row C4 and 1 row C3, then work 2 rows C1.
Now follow chart B placing sts thus: **Next row** Rep 7th–12th sts once, 1st–12th sts 3 times then 1st–6th sts once. Work straight in C1 to 47cm [18½ in] from the beg.
Shape Neck and Shoulders Next row Ss along 6 sts, in tr over 14 tr, turn. **Next row** Ss along 7 sts, tr to end. **Next row** In tr. Fasten off.

Go back to other sts, leave centre 8 sts unworked, rejoin yarn and work in tr to end. **Next row** Ss along 6 sts, tr to end. **Next row** In tr. Fasten off.
Rejoin yarn to Right Front sts. * Using C2 work in stripes as for Back, then work 2 rows in C1. Now follow chart B working 1st row thus: 7th–12th sts once, 1st–12th sts once and 1st–6th sts once. Cont to follow chart but at the same time dec 1 tr on next 11 rows at neck edge, then cont straight in C1 to 47cm [18½ in] ending at armhole edge.
Shape Shoulder Next row Ss along 6 sts, tr to end. **Next row** In tr. Fasten off.
Rejoin yarn to Left Front and follow Right Front from *.

POCKETS (make 2)
Using C2 and the 3·5mm [No 9] hook, make 21 ch and work in tr to end (19 tr). Now work from chart C↓ beg at 2nd row and working to 13th row. Fasten off.
↓Please note that this chart is read downwards.

TO MAKE UP
Press according to ball band instructions. Join shoulders. Now using the 4mm [No 8] hook and C2 used double, join at lower edge of right front and work along lower edge thus * 1 dc into edge, miss tr, 1 tr up 1 row from edge, miss tr. Rep from * all along lower edges, 2 dc at corners, and up row ends work a dc into one row, and 1 tr up 2 tr on next row end. Cont thus working edges as given until round is completed, join with a ss. Now work 1 dc into each st all round. Fasten off. Work armholes borders to match. Sew on pockets.
Using three threads alternately in C2, C3 and C4 and about 10cm [4 in] long make a knotted fringe into the 1st row of 3 colour stripe working in every alternate tr on Back and Fronts alike. For the ties, using C2 double work 44 ch and fasten off. Work another tie and then sew to neck edge. Press seams.

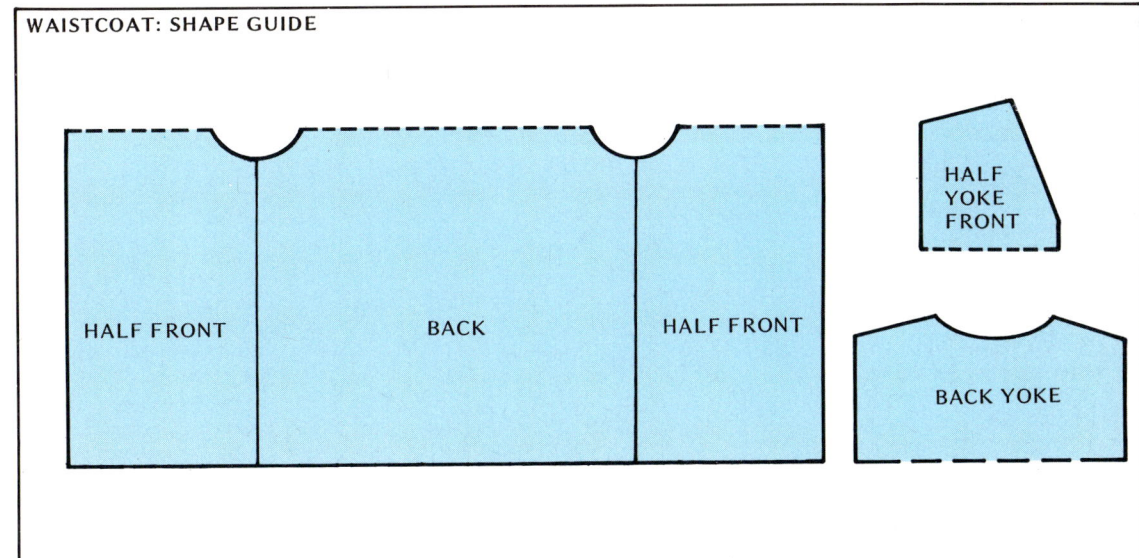

WAISTCOAT: SHAPE GUIDE

HALF FRONT   BACK   HALF FRONT

HALF YOKE FRONT

BACK YOKE

Above: the Red Indian Waistcoat with its fancy colours and fringeing – a great way of using up odds and ends of yarn but do make sure it's all the same weight
Right: a guide to the shape
Opposite page: the three charts which will give you the different patterns

Fashion Extras

**These are the little things that mean a lot,
especially to the pre-teens and teenagers – the little things that make
one year's fashion different from the next.**

Crazes are funny things – at the time you can't imagine how you ever lived without the particular one, yet when it's gone it's something to laugh at when you look back through a photograph album. The way fashion's going through, repeats are the order we've become used to, with slight changes that make it right for the time. The square dance skirts of the 50's with the layers of petticoats became the flower-scattered "paisley" flounced skirts of the 70's with less bulky but equally attractive petticoats beneath, but proudly *showing* and not hidden away as they were 20 years before.

In most fashion, the sign of the times is likely to be (apart from the materials, both type and colour) the extras – the decorations, what's worn with what. And here craft stands successive generations in good stead.

Here you'll find ideas that you can use as they are, or alter according to your wants. There are clothes to be made in suede or leather; a simple taste of card weaving; embroidery motifs; smocking stitches to go back to time and time again for all ages. As well, there are a few designs and instructions for batik and tie dyeing. And in other sections you'll find fashionable quilting, Aztec-style knitting, Swiss "darning" – favourites in some way or another for many a year.

This last section is a round-up of crafty ways to be prepared when the rustic or anything allied swings into our lives. The extra pleasure that comes from the "doing" is being able to provide what's needed at the right time. If you've learnt how to crochet, knit, embroider, do macrame, weave and smock, you'll be able to make the belts, bags, tops, hats or whatever that "everybody's wearing". And when you're making clothes for the growing child, in his or her eyes that can be important.

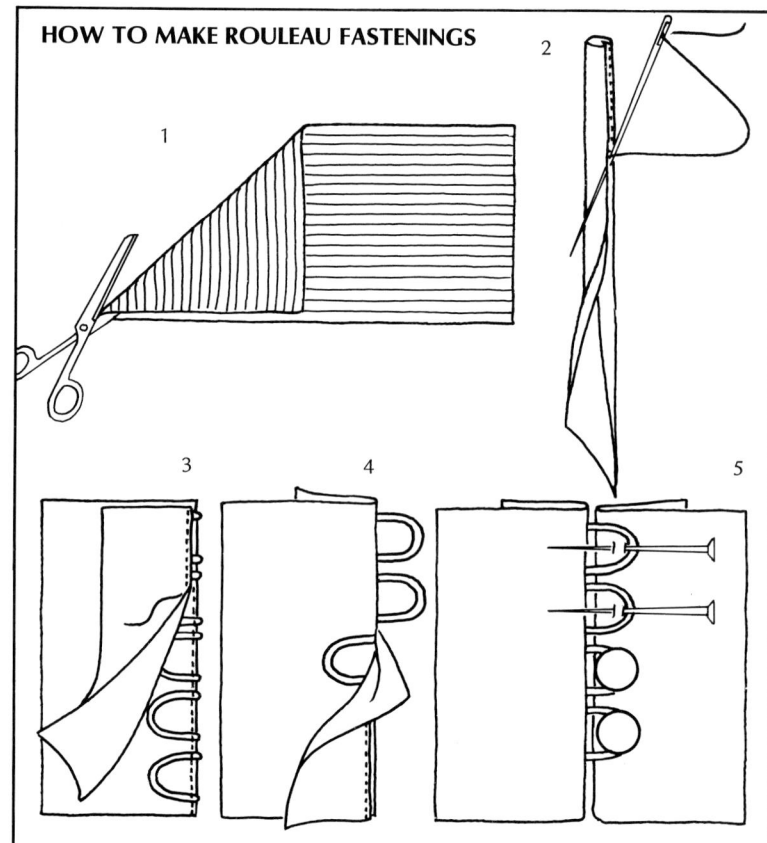

HOW TO MAKE ROULEAU FASTENINGS

1. Cut a strip of fabric on the bias.
2. Fold edges in to make a narrow tube and by hand sew tiny stitches to close gap.
3. On the right side of the garment place the rouleau loops where you want them and stitch in place by machine. Lay facing on top then stitch again covering first line of stitching.
4. Fold facing over to wrong side of garment and press well.
5. Place other side of opening under rouleau loops and hold in position with pins. Remove them only as each button is sewn on – this is important if you are to keep the opening even.

Folk-style tops

9 months to 2 years

Lighter than air cheese-cloth is practical for hot summer days. You can either over-sew the finished edges with a contrasting thread or decorate with embroidery.

Materials 90cm square [1 sq yd] of light cotton fabric; matching machine twist; 2 small buttons; 2 skeins of stranded embroidery thread.

Measurements to fit 56cm [22 in] chest; 33cm [13 in] length (adjustable).

Note all seams measure 15mm [⅝ in]. Square brackets contain imperial measurements.

TO CUT OUT

1. Make pattern on squared paper (1 square = 5cm) following Diagram 1. For 2 year old size add 2cm [¾ in] all round. Lay out pattern pieces on flat fabric and cut out, allowing 15mm [⅝ in] all round each piece for seams.
2. Cut down opening marked in a solid line at centre front. Cut two front facings from scraps of fabric (cut on the bias), following dotted line at centre front.

TO SEW

1. Right sides together, pin, tack and stitch side fronts to front. Right sides together, stitch side backs to back. Press seams open.
2. Right sides together, pin, tack and stitch shoulder seams. Press open.
3. Right sides together, pin, tack and stitch top edge of sleeves to shirt at shoulders, between side fronts and side backs. Press seams open.
4. Right sides together, pin, tack and stitch side seams, leaving a 10cm [4 in] side slit if liked. Press open.
5. Right sides together, pin, tack and stitch sleeve seams, leaving 5cm [2 in] gap at underarm.
6. Right sides together, pin, tack and stitch in underarm gussets, pivoting at corners. Press seams open. Turn shirt through to right side.
7. To make front opening: right sides together, pin, tack and stitch

one front facing to each side of front opening, taking stitching down to centre of 'v' at bottom of opening. Press seams towards opening. Turn in 3mm [⅛ in] on free edge of right-hand facing to wrong side. Fold facing down to 1st line of stitching and catch-stitch in place on wrong side. Fold in seam allowance on 'v' and tack in place on shirt.
8. Make left-hand facing in same way, overlapping on top of right-hand facing. Top-stitch facings together on to shirt along sides of 'v', close to edges.
9. Stitch two buttonholes to right-hand facing, one 2cm [¾ in] down from top edge, the second 5cm [2 in] down from the 1st. Stitch buttons to correspond on left-hand facing.
10. Turn up 2cm [¾ in] wrong side of sleeve edges and lower edges of front and back and slip-stitch in place.
11. To neaten neck opening, hand roll a hem to wrong side and catch-stitch in place.
12. To work embroidery, use either bought transfers or copy the pattern from Diagram 2, enlarging it and transferring on to the shirt. To stitch embroidery, use stem and satin stitch or for a delicate effect, use shadow stitch, working in two strands of embroidery thread throughout.

Above and right: pretty embroidered tops and their shape guide
Below: the pattern for either embroidery or easy fabric paints

Diagram 2

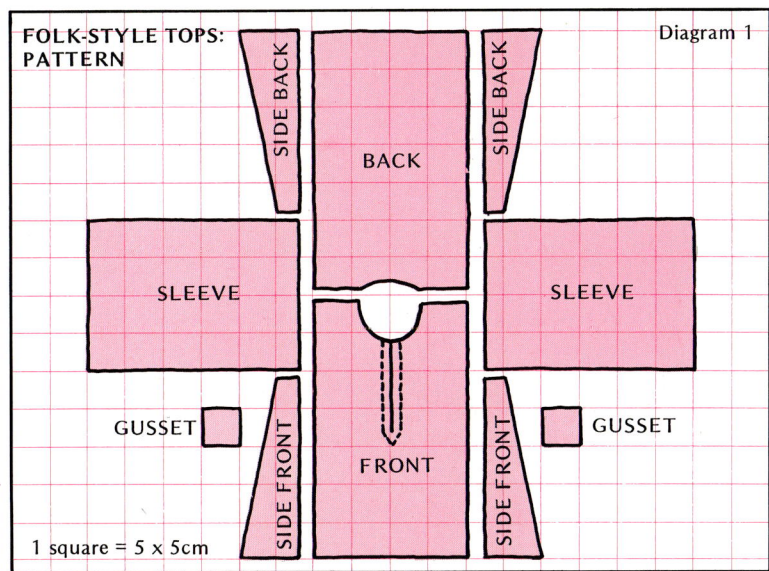

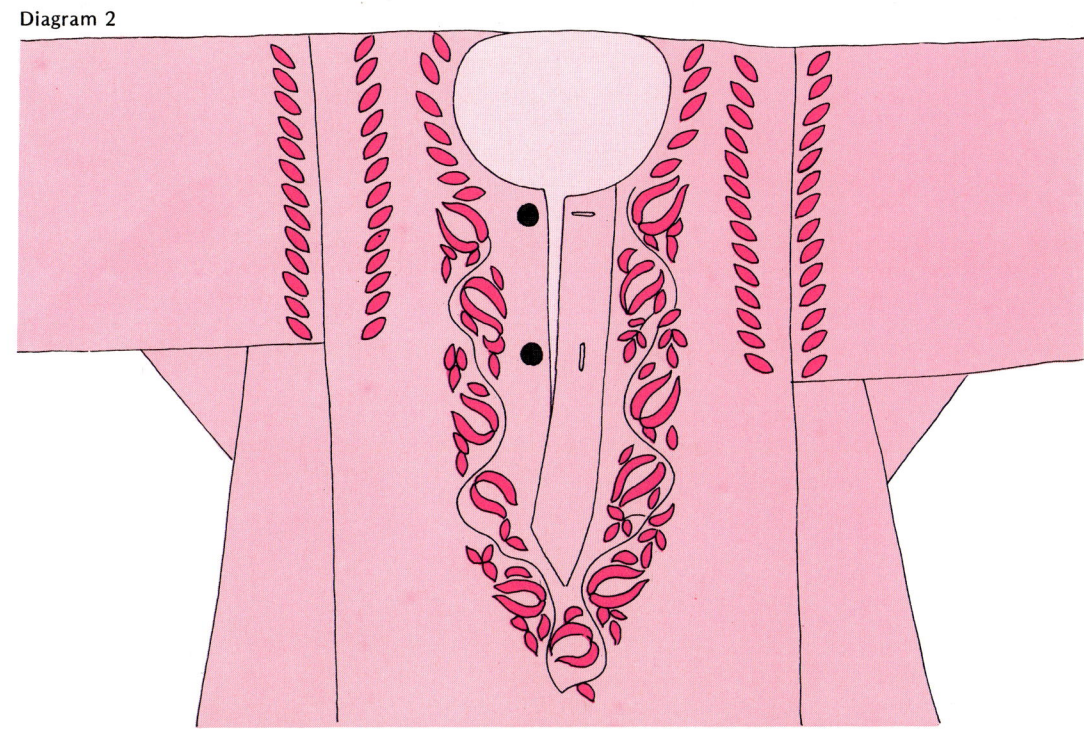

Children's Clothes

Peasant-style embroidery

Toddler to teenage

A simple cross-stitch design is used to enhance bedlinen and blouses you've made yourself but you could use it on jeans, sweaters, T-shirts – anything, in fact, that needs cheering up.

Sheet and pillowcase

Materials For the sheet: 100cm × 80cm]39½ in × 31½ in] piece of cotton fabric. For the pillow-case: 80cm × 40cm [31½ in × 15¾ in] piece of cotton fabric. For both: 2 skeins each of red and green stranded embroidery thread (or colour as liked); matching machine twist.

TO MAKE THE SHEET

1. Measure down 7.5cm [3 in] along one short side of fabric. On this mark carefully pull out four threads across width of fabric. On top edge, turn under 3mm [⅛ in] to wrong side. Then turn down fabric to just above line of pulled threads. Hem neatly in place by hand or use machine blind stitch.
2. Measure in 15mm [⅝ in] from edges on other 3 sides. Take out two threads from each length as for top edge. Fold down hems and stitch as for top edge.
3. Trace off the large actual size embroidery motif (Diagram 1, bottom) on to tissue paper. Lay the design on to sheet where you want to embroider it, and with a sheet of dressmaker's carbon paper between tissue and fabric, carefully trace the design through.
4. Work embroidery in cross stitch, using three strands of embroidery thread throughout.

TO MAKE THE PILLOWCASE

1. Cut fabric so you have a rectangle measuring 50cm × 40cm [19¾ in × 15¾ in]. Measure in 7.5cm [3 in] from each edge. Take out four strands of thread as for sheet, but be careful not to take out complete strands – the pulled threads should form a rectangle 7.5cm [3 in] smaller than the fabric. On all sides of outer

rectangle machine a 3mm [⅛ in] hem.
2. To make mitred corners for case as shown in Diagram 2 (bottom), on wrong side fold each corner across diagonally (pulled threads will lie on top of each other) measure 3.75cm [1½ in] up from pulled threads. Stitch seam at an angle of 45 deg, then trim off excess fabric at angle. Make 3 other corners in same way. Press mitred seams open then fold overlap over so right side of hemmed edge meets pulled threads. Hem in place by hand or use machine blind stitch.
3. Using the smaller, actual-size embroidery design (Diagram 1, top) trace off and transfer as for Sheet (step 3) – one design in each corner. Work in cross stitch using three strands of embroidery thread throughout.
4. To make backing for the pillow-

case, cut remaining fabric to a rectangle the size of the area within the thread marks, adding 3cm [1¼ in] to one short side and 6mm [¼ in] to other three sides.
5. Turn the 3cm [1¼ in] overlap on one short side to wrong side and machine in place (see Diagram 2).
6. Turn other three sides in 6mm [¼ in] to wrong side. Wrong sides together, pin and tack to front, just inside the pulled thread rectangle. Leaving one side open stitch backing to case with small hemming stitches or blind stitch in place by machine. Press.

Blouses

Materials 60cm × 80cm [23½ in × 31½ in] cotton fabric; matching and contrast machine twist; spool of shirring elastic; 1 skein each of red and green stranded em-

broidery threads (or colours as liked); 50cm [19¾ in] 3mm [⅛ in] wide elastic. For larger sizes see *Note*.

Measurements To fit toddler up to 3 years. For larger sizes see *Note*.

Note As the pattern pieces for this simple blouse are almost identical, it's easy to make larger sizes. All you have to do is alter the raglan length (measure from collar bone to underarm), the neck and chest width (add 10cm [4 in] to chest measurement to allow for loose fit) and the length (adjust sleeve, front and back from the end of the raglan measurement). The neck width is the same as the top of the sleeve – this will all be drawn in with elastic. Using squared paper, cut out your pattern pieces.

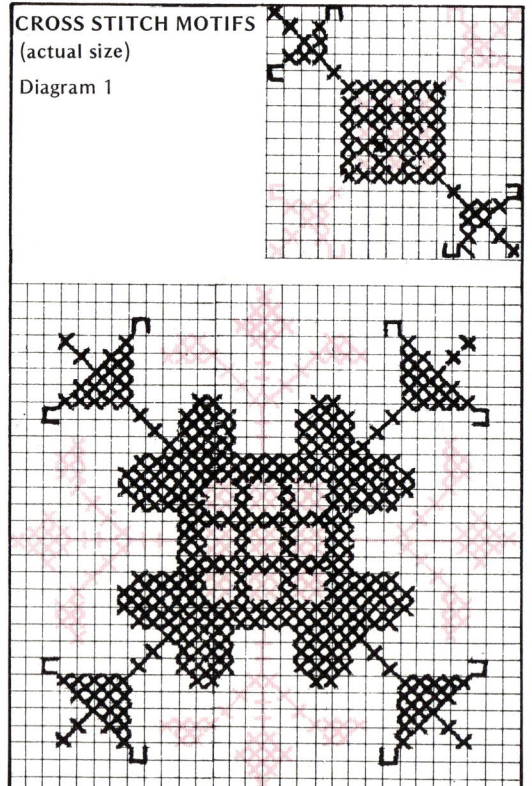

CROSS STITCH MOTIFS (actual size)
Diagram 1

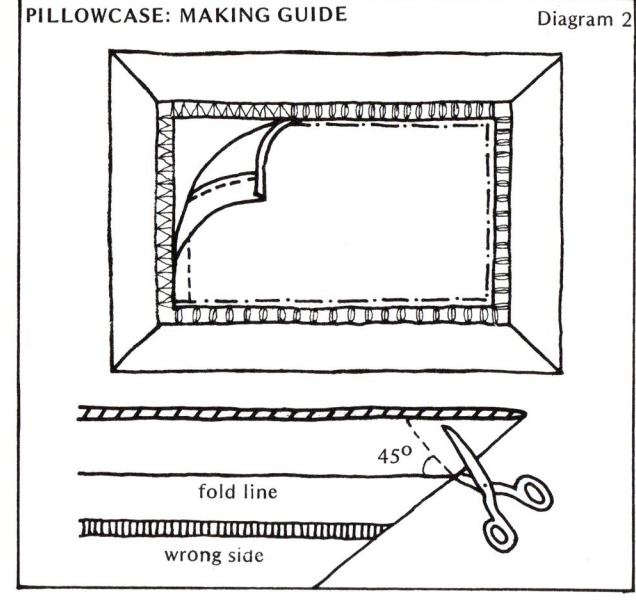

PILLOWCASE: MAKING GUIDE Diagram 2

45°
fold line
wrong side

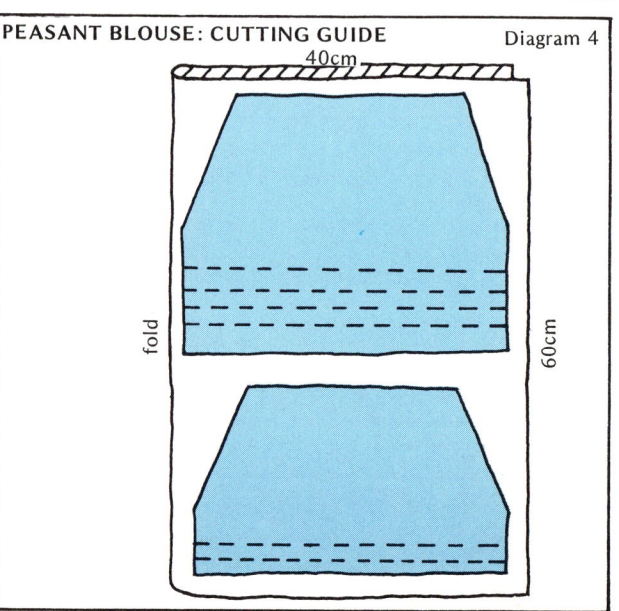

PEASANT BLOUSE: CUTTING GUIDE Diagram 4
40cm
fold
60cm

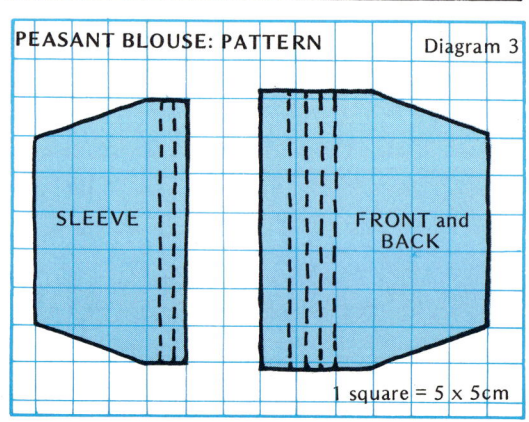

PEASANT BLOUSE: PATTERN Diagram 3
SLEEVE
FRONT and BACK
1 square = 5 x 5cm

To work out how much material you'll need, use large sheets of brown paper or newspaper (Sellotaped together if necessary) with the left side 90cm [35½ in], 114cm [45 in] or 140cm [55 in] — these are the most probable widths of fabric you'll be using. Place the pattern pieces 4 times on this paper (allowing 15mm [⅝ in] all round for seams and remembering that the fabric will have to be cut on the straight grain). The fabric you'll need will be 90cm [35½ in] 114cm [45 in] or 140cm [55 in] by the measurement from left to right which the pattern pieces cover.

TO MAKE

1. Make patterns from squared paper following Diagram 3 (1 square = 5cm). Cut two body pieces and two sleeves following layout in Diagram 4, <u>adding an extra 15mm [⅝ in] all round each piece</u> for seams.

2. Using colours as liked embroider three large motifs across front of blouse transferring and embroidering as for Sheet (step 3).

3. With right sides together, pin, tack and stitch front to back at one side seam only.

4. Place shirring elastic on to machine bobbin. Machine twist on top, and with a long stitch and loose tension, stitch first row of shirring 7.5cm [3 in] up from bottom edge. Sew a further 3 rows above first, 2cm [¾ in] apart or as liked. Stitch 2 rows of shirring round bottom of each sleeve in same way, first row 6cm [2¼ in] from edge, rows 6mm [¼ in] apart.

5. Right sides together and raw edges level, machine other side seam, then underarm seam of each sleeve. Press seams open (not over shirring) and turn sleeves through to right side.

6. To insert sleeves, with right sides together, pin, tack and machine sleeves to blouse, matching top edges and underarm seams. Press seams open.

7. Turn 2cm [¾ in] hem to wrong side at bottom of blouse and each sleeve so that edge of hem is just below first row of shirring, machine in place. Alternatively make a small rolled hem at bottom of blouse and each sleeve.

8. Turn down 6mm [¼ in] hem all round neck opening for elastic casing. Pin, tack and machine in place close to inside edge, leaving a small gap. Insert elastic through gap, secure ends then close opening. Press.

Top: the clever peasant blouses which are made from very simple shapes and can be enlarged to fit an adult
The tiny touch of embroidery transforms plain white sheets and pillowcase – whether made or bought
Inset: an embroidery frame is used to hold the fabric taut while the motif is being worked

Woven waistcoat

2 to 3 years

This pretty waistcoat with its rustic look can be made in leftover yarns by a technique that is very like darning. Using a thick piece of card as a loom, the warp (up and down threads) is wound on to the card over serrations cut into the top and bottom edges; the weft (cross threads) is made by weaving the yarn over and under the warp threads using a blunt ended rug, or long raffia, needle.

Materials

For the weaving card 24cm × 35cm [9½ in × 13¾ in] hard compact card at least the thickness of a 10p or 20 cent piece; steel ruler; pencil; sharp Stanley knife to cut card.

For the waistcoat Stretchy 4-ply yarn, 100g blue and 100g yellow (or what ever colours you fancy); 2 weaving needles; darning needle.

Measurements Finished waistcoat should measure approx 23.5cm [9¼ in] across, 34cm [13½ in] from shoulder to hem, 9cm [3½ in] across each shoulder, 29cm × 7cm [11½ in × 3 in] neck opening. To make a larger or smaller waistcoat, change the size of the card but keep the same proportions.

Note Square brackets contain imperial measurements.

To keep the weaving smooth and even the secret is not to pull the weft too tight, otherwise the work will look "waisted", and to gently push each weft row firmly into the previous row with your finger tips. To work in a new length of weft thread, weave it into the middle of the row, beginning where the last length ended. Stitch the loose ends into the back of the work when you've finished the whole piece.

Diagram 1

Diagram 2

Diagram 3

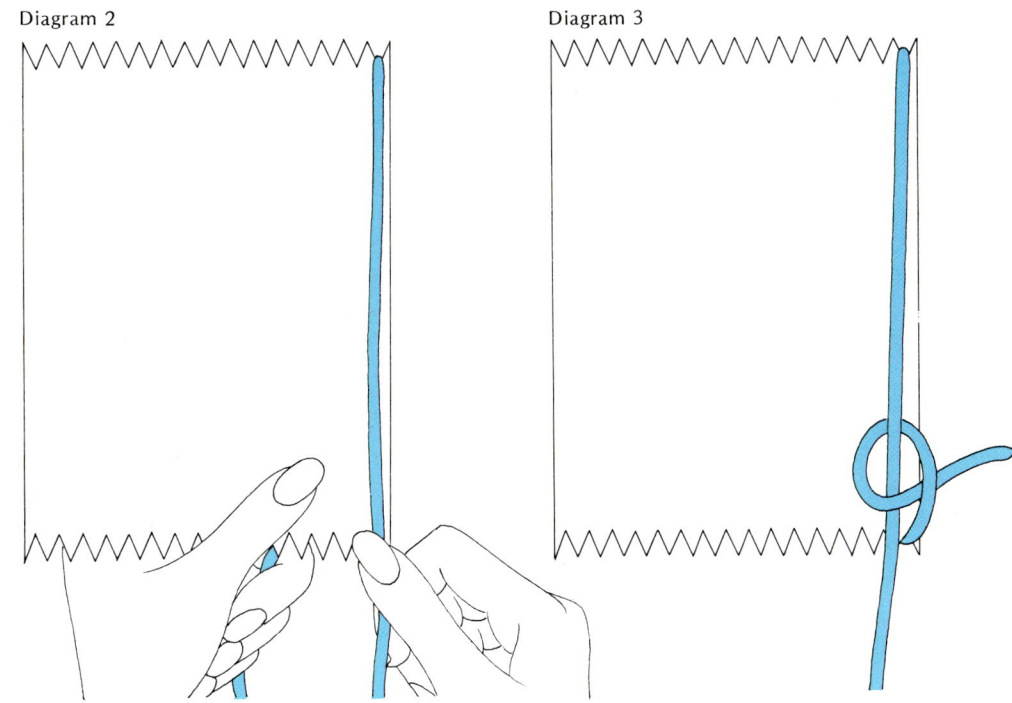

TO MAKE THE WEAVING CARD

Diagram 1 Using the Stanley knife and steel ruler, cut zig zag serrations 3mm [⅛ in] wide and 8mm [⅓ in] deep along the shorter, 24cm [9½ in] sides. You should have 48 "teeth" each side.

FRONT

Diagram 2 To wind on the warp (up and down threads) hold 20cm [8 in] at the tail end of the yarn and the card in your left hand. Take yarn up behind the card, over the top between the first and second tooth on the right and down to the bottom of the card.

Diagram 3 Bring the tail end of yarn in your left hand to the front and make a simple knot as shown.

Diagram 4 Tighten and lower the first knot and make a second as shown. Keep the end to one side so it will undo easily when you have finished weaving.

Diagram 5 Bring the second knot to the bottom, tighten it by tugging on the loop.

Diagram 6 Take yarn round behind the second tooth, bring it to the front, up to the top of the card, over between the second and third teeth and down to the bottom row of teeth.

Diagram 4

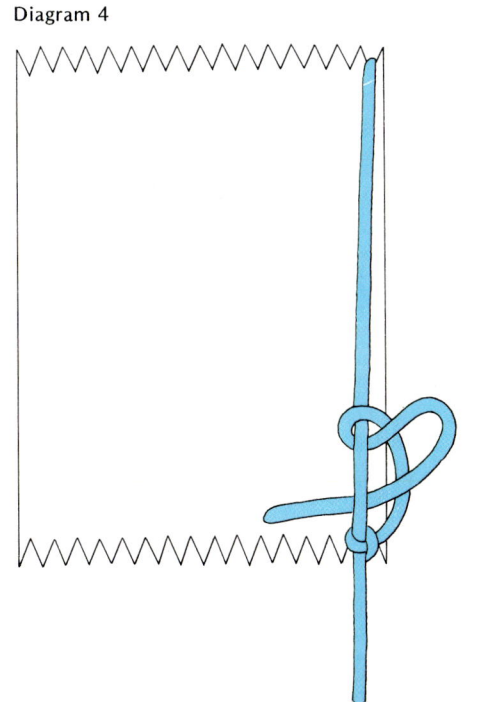

Diagram 5

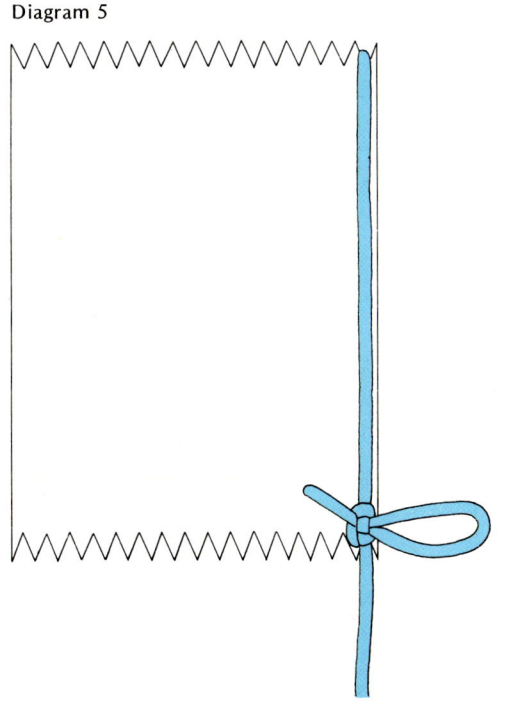

Diagram 6

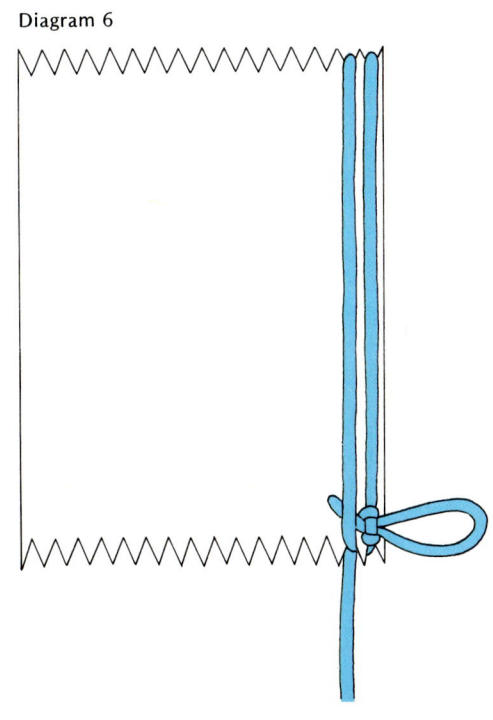

Continued on next page

Woven waistcoat . . . continued

Diagram 7

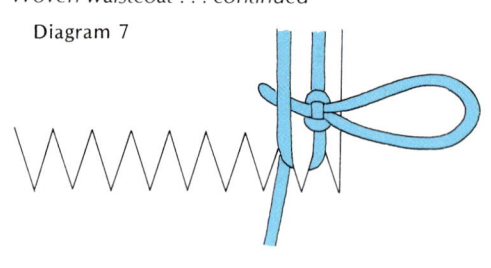

Diagram 8

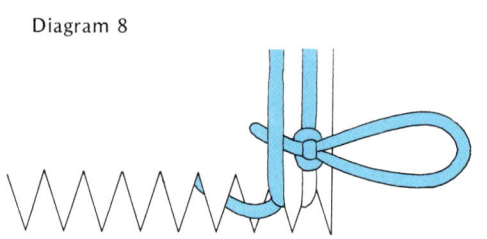

Diagram 9

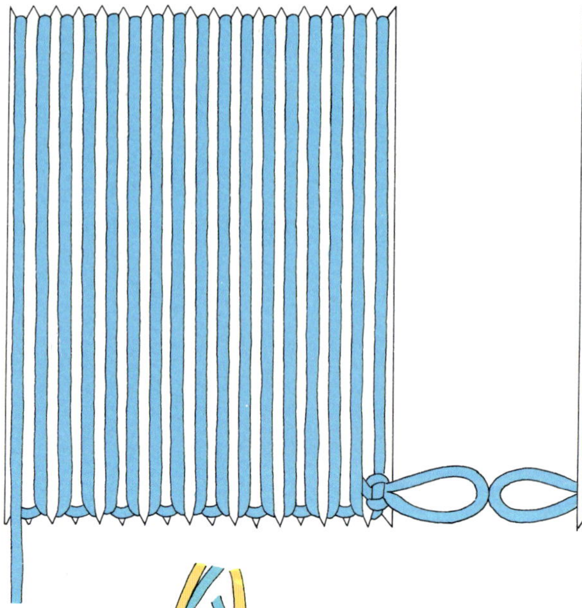

Diagram 10

Diagram 11

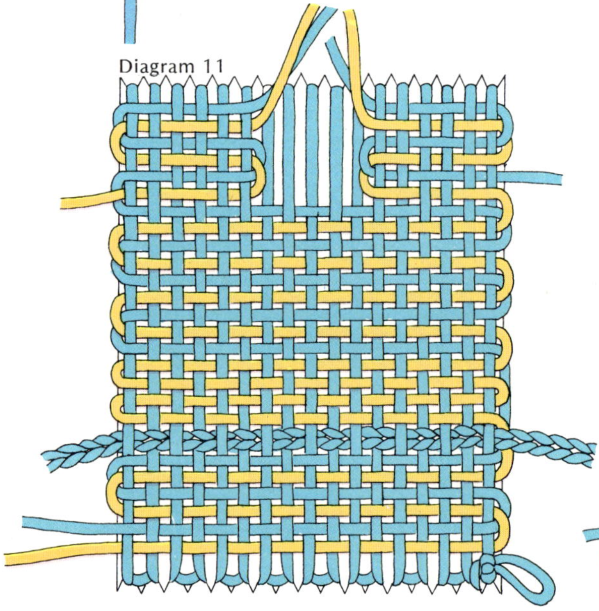

Diagram 12

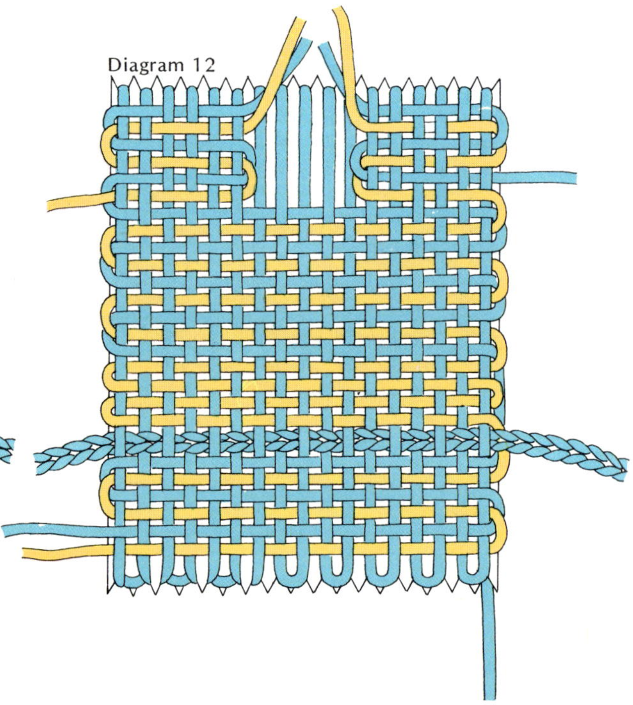

Diagrams 7 and 8 Bring yarn round the front of the third tooth and to the back of the card. Continue, taking wool up the back of the card, over the top in between the third and fourth teeth and down in front to the bottom edge. Take it round the back of the fourth tooth, up again in front of the card, over the top between the fourth and fifth teeth and to the bottom, taking it round the front of the fifth tooth. Continue in the same way till the card is covered.

Diagram 9 To tie in the end of the warp take yarn under the last bottom left hand notch, turn the card round, cut yarn leaving 20cm [8 in] tail.

Diagram 10 Secure the yarn making the same double knot as at the beginning (Diagrams 3, 4 and 5 on previous page).
You should have 47 warp threads on both sides of the card.

> **To work with 2 colours you must take care to see the colours cross each other at the edges as shown in Diagrams 11 and 12. If you find working with 2 colours confusing, then work with 1. You can always finish off round the edges with a second colour to give the waistcoat more interest.**

To make the weft (cross threads) Thread up weaving needles, one with blue, the other with yellow.

Diagrams 11 and 12 As you weave alternate the colours taking care

that the colours cross each other at the edges. Try out some of the variations shown here.

To make the ties When you have covered 13cm [5 in] of the card with weaving (measured from the tips of the teeth) make two 60cm [23½ in] long plaits of yarn, one for the back and one for the front. Weave the tie into the work just as you would any other weft thread, but taking care to leave equal lengths loose at both ends.

The neck opening Continue weaving till you have covered 20cm [8 in] of card, measured from the tips of the teeth. Then, leaving the 15 centre warp threads bare, weave one side of each shoulder piece at a time, cover-

ing the 16 outer warp threads. To make the chequer and fat stripe effects, go over and under 2 warp threads at a time, in alternate rows of colour.

BACK
When you reach the top of the card, turn it over and weave on the other side. Start at the bottom, weaving this side exactly as you did the front, keeping the pattern the same.

Diagram 12 (finishing off) To take weaving off the card, undo the knots at the beginning and end of the warp. Gently pull the warp threads over the bottom teeth, and almost as if by magic the two sides will separate and you should have one long piece of weaving.

To make the neckline Cut through the middle of the unwoven warp threads. Knot firmly together, close to the weave, back and front (see picture detail) in bunches of 2,3,2,3,2 and 3 threads respectively. Trim ends.

TO MAKE UP
If liked, strengthen side and bottom edges by over-sewing in blanket stitch. With a darning needle sew plaits in place so they won't pull through the weaving. Stitch any loose ends neatly into the back of the work. Press lightly on the wrong side with a damp cloth.

Waistcoat and skirt

From 3 years

Thonging threaded through holes gives an interesting look to this waistcoat and shirt made in soft suede or leather. To give them a proper "Indian style" finish you could snip the outer edges with sharp scissors.

Materials Suitably sized pieces of soft suede or leather; 5m [6 yds] matching thonging; Copydex adhesive; a hole puncher; chalk; a popper fastener kit for the skirt; newspaper and light cardboard for the patterns.

Measurements Waistcoat: to fit chest 58/61cm [23/24 in] Skirt: to fit waist 58cm [23 in]. The measurements given are for children but for larger sizes you could take the basic measurements directly from another skirt or waistcoat.

Choose your suede well. If you buy a bundle of pieces go through and pick out the largest ones. If they're not big enough to cut out the various pattern parts, you'll have to join them together with glue. Do take care not to get the adhesive on the hide. Spread it sparingly on the areas that are to be joined and leave for 10–15 minutes before pressing them together. The glue must be perfectly dry before any holes are punched.

TO MAKE PATTERNS

Following the measurements given on the next page or using an old garment as a pattern cut out the shapes in newspaper. Pin the pieces together and try on. Make any necessary adjustments then cut each pattern piece out in card.

TO CUT OUT

Place each card template on a piece of leather and chalk all round. Remove card and cut out on chalk lines.

Continued on next page

Suede clothes . . . continued

TO MAKE THE SKIRT

The skirt is made from just one piece joined to a waistband and seamed at the centre front. As the skirt is worn more on the hips than the waist, you could easily create the same shape for a larger size – the only problem is getting soft suede or leather in large pieces. You could always glue several pieces together in patchwork fashion, then cut out the shape adding in your own measurements but keeping the corner angles the same.

1. Overlap and glue waistband to top edge of skirt so that band extends 2cm [¾ in] either end.

2. When the glue is dry, punch holes along the seam at 6mm [¼ in] intervals.

3. Overlap and glue edges of skirt at centre front leaving an opening from the waist edge long enough to allow the skirt to be taken on and off.

4. Punch holes from hem to waist at 6mm [¼ in] intervals. Fasten the waistband with the popper fastener (following instructions given on kit).

5. Thread thonging through holes around waistband and at centre front starting and ending each seam with a knot.

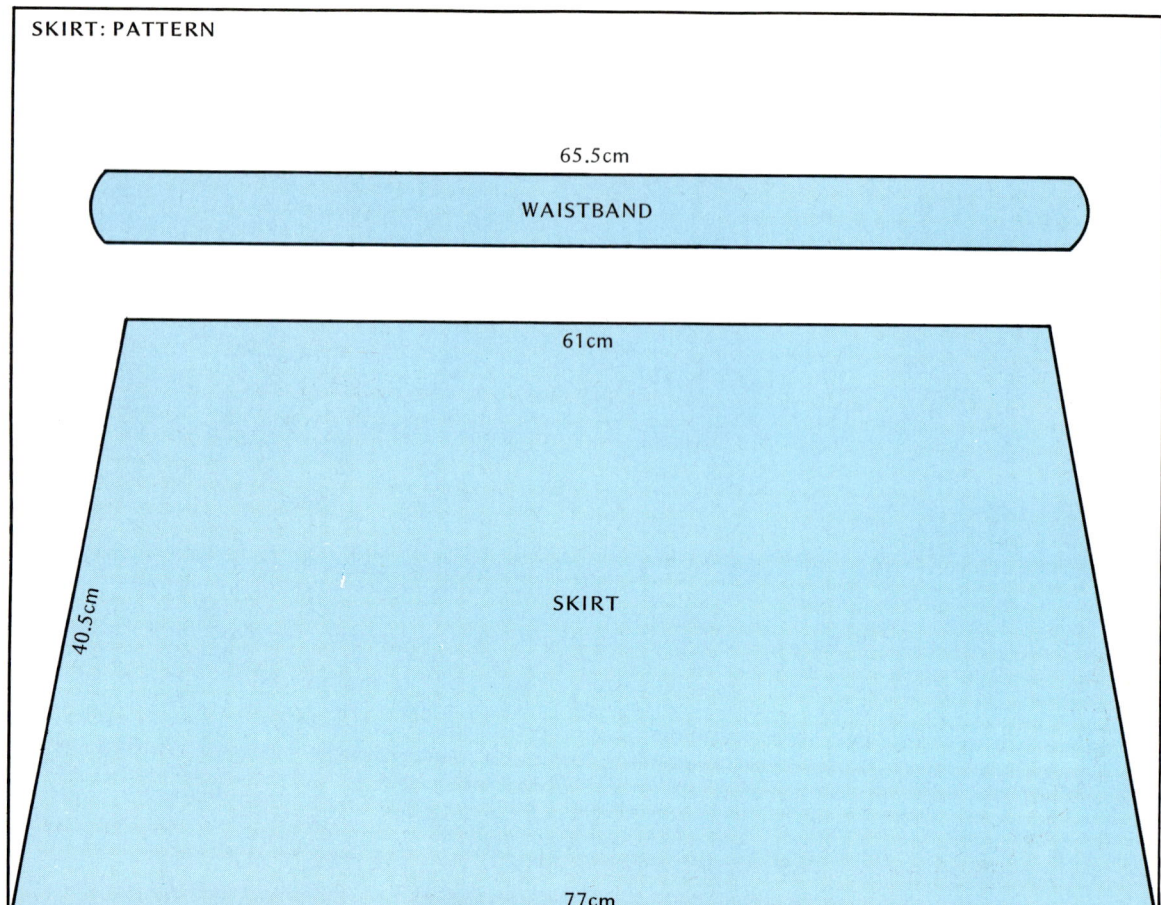

SKIRT: PATTERN

65.5cm

WAISTBAND

61cm

40.5cm

SKIRT

77cm

1

2

3

4

TO MAKE UP THE WAISTCOAT

1. Lightly overlap and glue the sides together.
2. Leave until the glue is dry, then punch holes at 6mm [$\frac{1}{4}$ in] intervals along both side seams.
3. Join the shoulders in the same way, punching holes along the seams when the glue is dry.
4. Thread thonging through the holes starting and finishing each seam with a knot.
5. Punch four holes in each front through which lengths of thonging can be knotted to close the waistcoat.

Right: the waistcoat, made from the pattern below. The pictures show the stages of making

WAISTCOAT: PATTERN

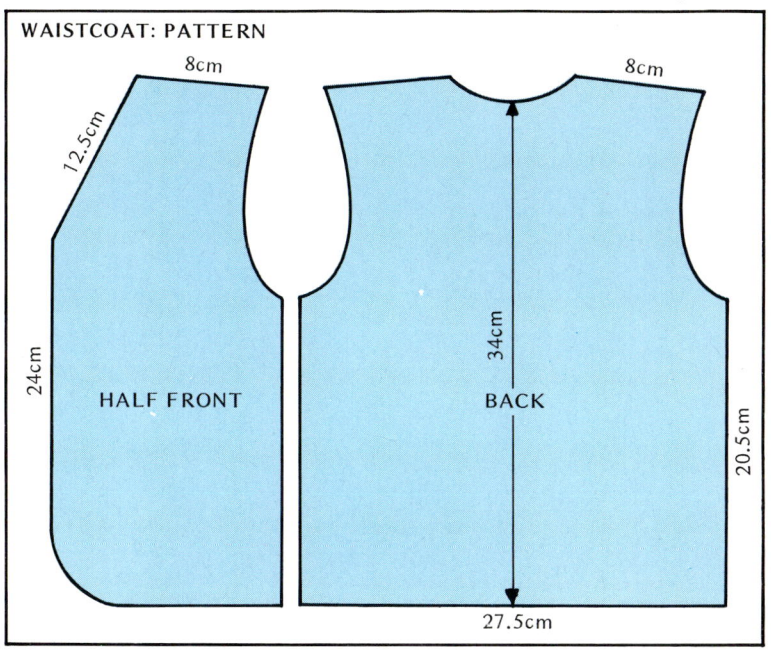

HALF FRONT — 8cm, 12.5cm, 24cm

BACK — 8cm, 34cm, 20.5cm, 27.5cm

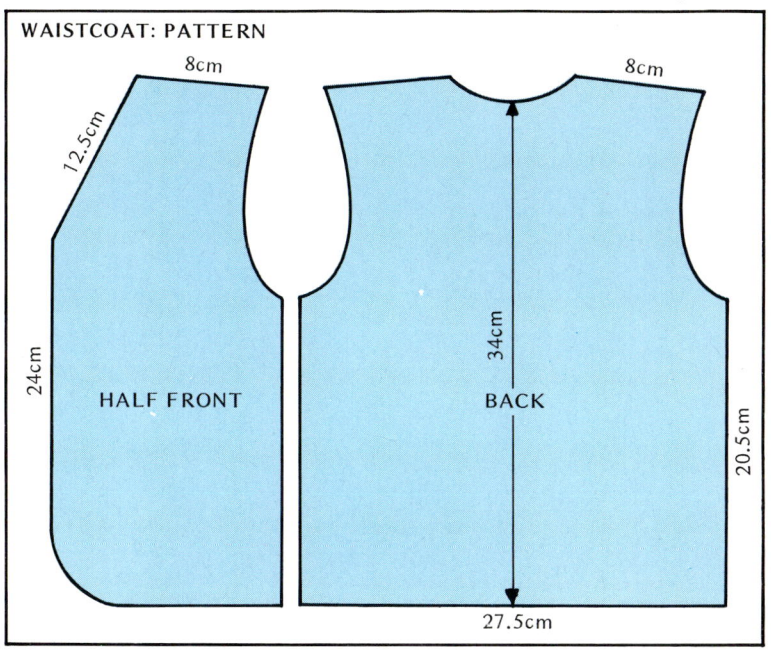

1

2

3

4

Sporty top

8 to 10 years

Knitting adds a fashion look to this corduroy top – a smart and hardwearing combination.

Materials 70cm [27½ in] corduroy fabric, 90cm [35½ in] wide; eight 25g balls Double Knitting yarn; pair 3¾mm [No 9] knitting needles; matching machine twist; squared paper for pattern.

Measurements To fit 76cm [30 in] chest.

Tension for Knitting 42 sts to 10cm [4 in] over unstretched rib.

Abbreviations k, knit; p, purl; st(s), stitch(es); cm, centimetre(s); in, inch(es); alt, alternate; beg, beginning; cont, continue; dec, decreas(e)ing; foll, following; rem, remain(ing); rep, repeat.

Adding knitted cuffs, collar and welts will also give new life to a favourite top that's just a bit too small. If you want to make the collar into a polo, knit it to the depth you want before you begin the decreasings

---

TO SEW

1. Make a pattern from the diagram below (top part), noting that each square represents 5cm [2 in].

2. Using the cutting guide (Diagram 2) cut out the pieces in the fabric – cutting the two sleeves together and folding the remaining portion sides to middle, then placing the centre front and the centre back to the two resulting folds as shown. In this way the grain of the fabric will run correctly. Seams of 15mm [⅝in] are allowed.

3. With right sides together, machine stitch the front to back along side seams.

4. Take one sleeve, fold in half, right side inside. Machine stitch the sleeve seam. Work the other sleeve in the same way. With right sides together pin sleeves into armholes, placing the side and sleeve seams together and easing in any slack material towards the top.

5. Tack in the sleeves, then machine stitch in position. Clip the seam allowance round armhole (taking care not to cut through seam), remove tackings. Press seams open. Turn to right side. Turn in the raw edges of lower edge and cuffs and tack to wrong side. Leave work aside.

TO KNIT

WELTS (make 2)
Cast on 130 sts. Work 10cm [4 in] k2, p2 rib. Cast off sts loosely.

CUFFS (make 2)
Cast on 68 sts. Work 10cm [4 in] k2, p2 rib. Cast off sts loosely.

COLLAR

Cast on 124 sts. Work 3cm [1¼ in] k2, p2 rib (or length required).

Next row Cast off 36 sts, rib 52, cast off rem 36 sts. Fasten off yarn. Rejoin yarn to rem sts. Cont in rib, dec 1 st at both ends of every foll alt row until 2 sts rem. K2 tog. Fasten off.

TO MAKE UP

Before joining the knitted pieces it is advisable to try on the fabric part for fit; adjust if necessary at seams.

Take up the knitted collar and join the narrow ends of the two cast off ends and oversew together, this seam forming centre back. With right sides together pin to top at four major points, centre back, centre front "V", and shoulder seams. Ease the knitting so that it fits evenly between these points. Tack 10mm [¼ in] from the edge. Machine stitch round the edge with a very loose stitch or, if preferred, oversew neatly by hand.

Check that the sleeves are the correct length allowing for the knitted cuffs. Run a line of gathers round the cuff end of the sleeve, approx 6mm [¼ in] from the folded back edge; draw the gathers up to fit the size of the folded cuff piece. Join the cuff edges with a flat seam. Tack the cast-off edge of the cuff just inside the edge of the sleeve end, easing the sts to fit the fabric. Either machine stitch very loosely or over-sew by hand. Work the second cuff in the same way.

Fold cuffs to right side.

With a flat seam, join the side edges of the welts. Run a line of gathers round the lower edge approx 6mm [¼ in] from the folded back edge; draw up the gathers to fit the size of the joined welts. Tack the welt to the lower edge, with the fold just over the edge of the welt. Either machine stitch round loosely or oversew by hand. Remove any tackings and press top.

Above: back view of the top
Opposite page: the top made in corduroy with knitted trim
Below left: the patterns for both the sewing and knitting
Below: how the fabric has to be folded so the grain on all pieces runs the same way

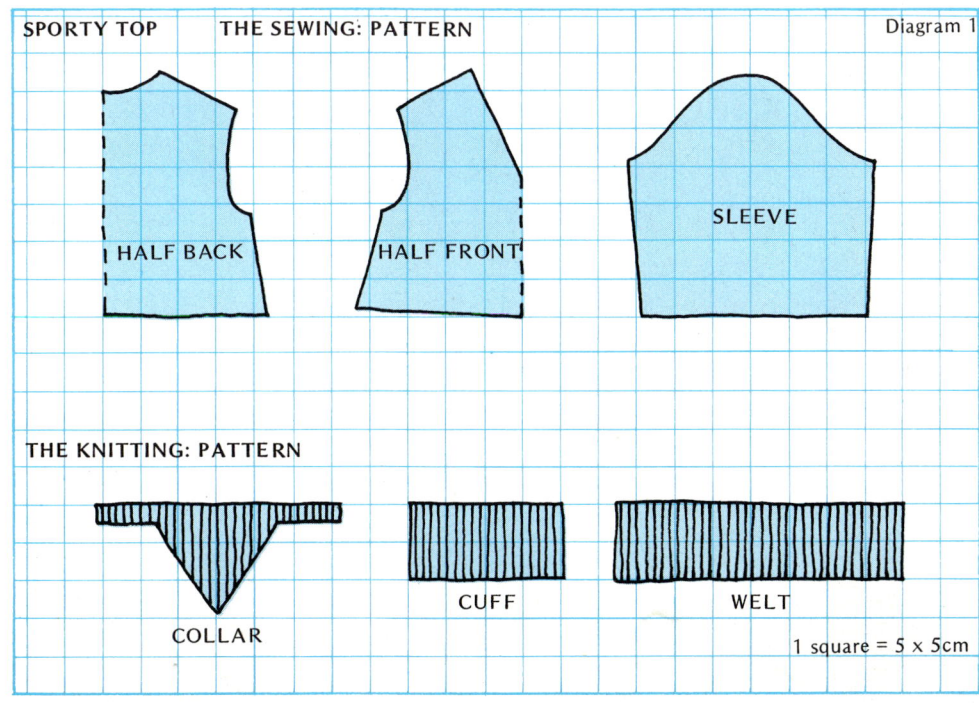

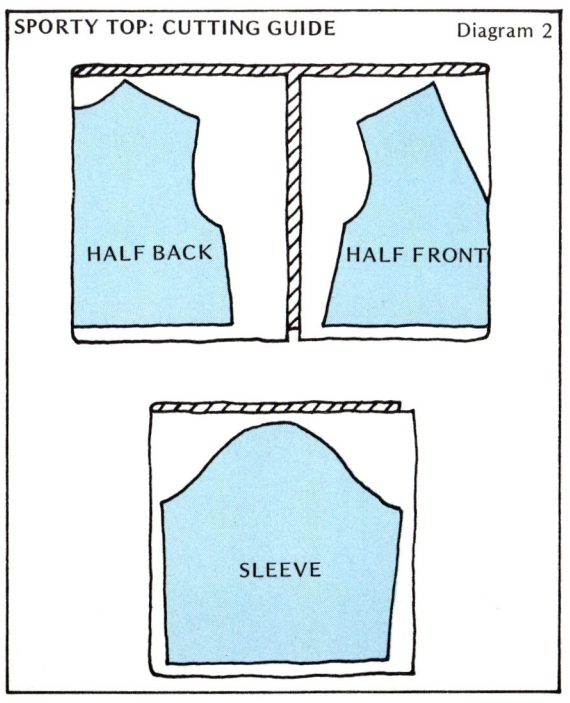

Macrame belts

Two very attractive macramé belts made from white string and parcel twine – both easy enough for a beginner in this popular (and often fashionable) craft to make.

Rustic belt

Materials Approx 48m natural parcel twine; knotting board; pin or tack for holding work; crochet hook (medium size).

TO MAKE
Cut 12 lengths of string each about 4m in length. About 50cm [20 in] from one end, join the strands together with an overhand knot. This knot will be untied at the finish. Pin the strands to the knotting board by the overhand knot to facilitate work. Smooth the strands out as flat as possible. Take the first strand to the right and use as leader cord to work 1 row horizontal cording. *Divide the strands into two sets of 6 strands each. On the left-hand set, work 2 rows diagonal cording from left to right, then on the right-hand set, work 2 rows diagonal cording from right to left to correspond.

Using the central 4 strands only, work a flat knot. Now divide the strands into two sets again and work 2 rows of diagonal cording in reverse – the left-hand set from right to left and the right-hand set from left to right. With the first strand to the left as leader, work 1 row horizontal cording. Divide the strands into three sets of 4 strands each. On each of the two outer sets, work 11 flat knots; on the centre set work 10 flat knots. Cross the two outer chains over the central chain as shown in picture. Using the first strand to the left after the cross-over as leader, anchor the crossed chains in place by working 1 row horizontal cording.*

Repeat from * to * until belt is slightly shorter than waist measurement, ending with a row of horizontal cording before three chains. DO NOT work the three chains.

**Divide the strands into 3 sets of 4 strands each. Work 2 flat knots on each set. Now divide the strands into two sets of 6 strands each. Work 1 flat knot on each set but using the two outer strands round the central four strands instead of two. Finally, join all strands with 1 flat knot. Wrap 1 strand several times round the other strands to prevent the work from untying, then thread this strand through the wound strands with a crochet hook to

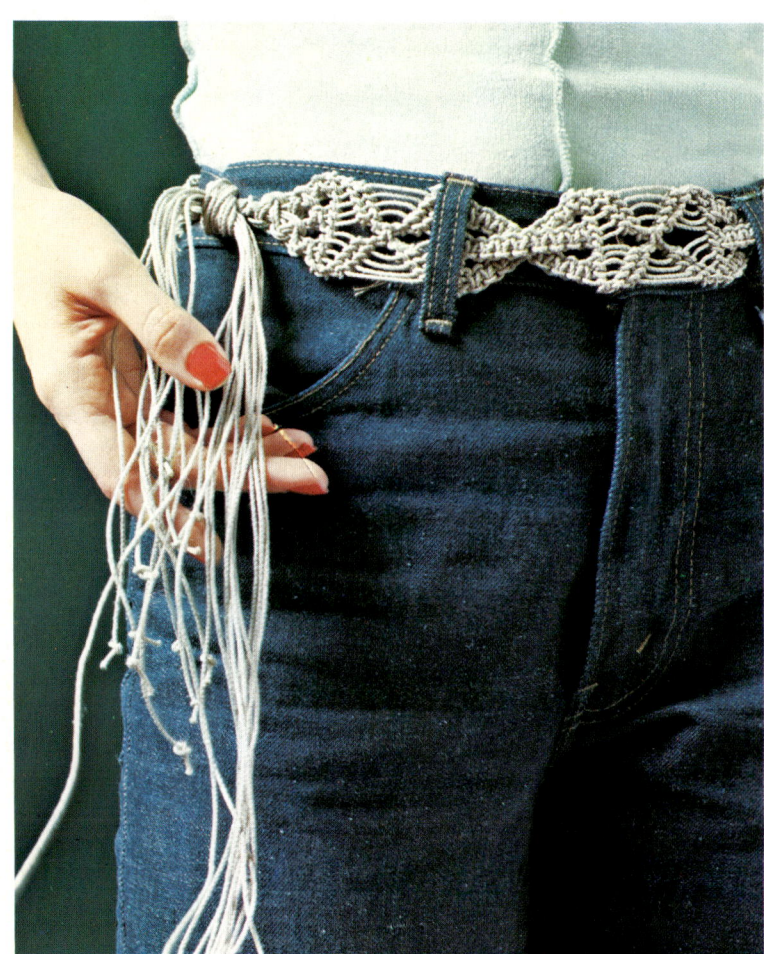

secure.** Untie the knot at the beginning and repeat from ** to **. Cut the strips into irregular lengths and make a knot at the end of each strand.

White belt

Materials 1 ball white string – approx 56m; knotting board; pin or tack for holding work.

TO MAKE
Cut 14 lengths of string, each about 4m in length. About 50cm [20 in] from one end join the strands together with an overhand knot. This knot will be untied at the finish. Pin the strands by the overhand knot to the knotting board to facilitate work. *Divide the lengths of string into two sets of 7 strands each. Take the first thread to the right-hand side of the left-hand set and work in diagonal cording from the centre towards the left (outside) edge. Beginning from the centre, work another cord parallel to the first, omitting to knot the leader cord of the previous row. Beginning always from the centre, continue in this way with parallel rows of diagonal cording, omitting to knot the leader cord of the previous row until 1 strand remains.

Now, working on the right-hand set of strands, beginning at the centre, work in diagonal cording in the reverse direction – ie, from left to right – and omitting to knot the leader cord of the previous row, until 1 strand remains. Two adjacent triangles have now been formed. Using the centre 4 strands only, join the triangles with a flat knot.*

Repeat from * to * until the desired length has been worked. Knot the strands in twos at irregular distances. Undo the overhand knot made at the beginning and join the first two triangles with a flat knot, then knot these strands also in twos.

Tie the belt as shown in the picture.

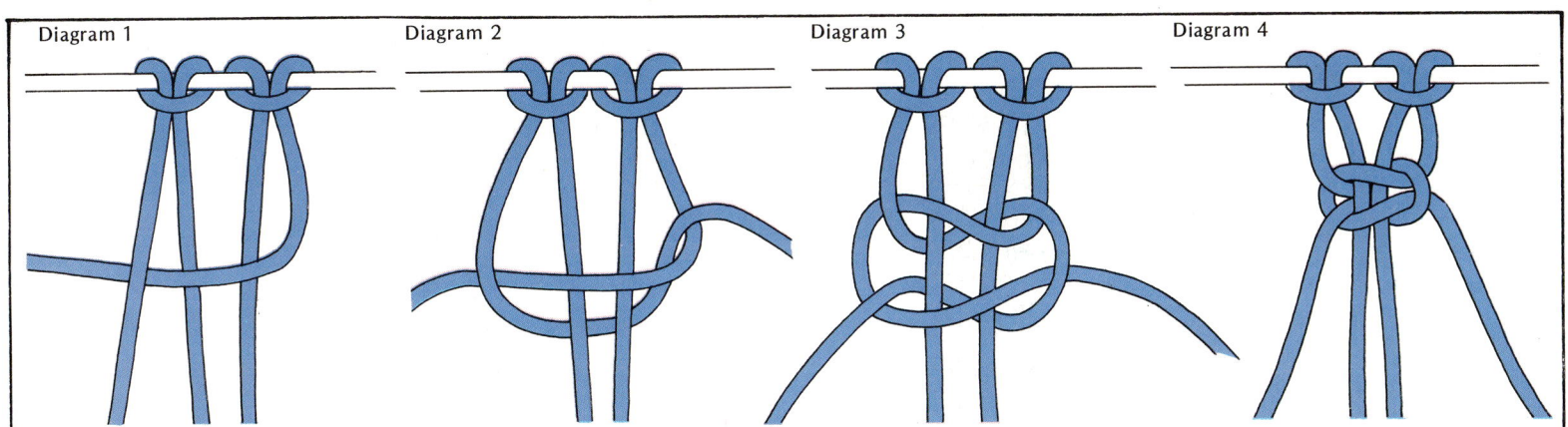

FLAT KNOT
Diagram 1 You can either do this in the usual way with 4 threads or you can use 6 or more threads. Start the knot on the leader cord and make two knots. Hold the two central threads firmly, then, with the right-hand thread, make a loop and pass it over the 2 central threads and under the left-hand thread.
Diagram 2 Then pass the left thread under the 2 central threads and through the first loop coming from the bottom to the front. Pull the knot up towards the top.

Diagram 3 Take the left-hand thread and make a loop passing over the threads in the centre and under the right-hand thread. Pass the right-hand thread. Pass the right-hand thread over the end of the left-hand loop, under the central threads and through the left-hand loop.
Diagram 4 Pull the 2 outside threads simultaneously and pull knot up to the top. Many different combinations can be made by varying the arrangements of the knots.

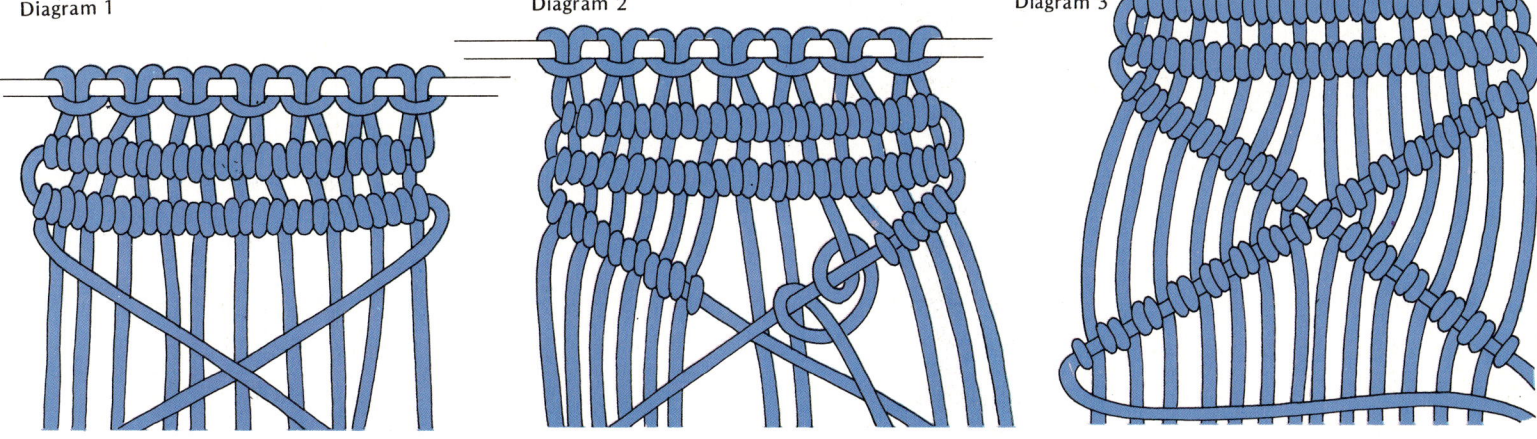

HORIZONTAL BRAID
One of the first principles of macrame.
After starting several threads, tie each one with a simple knot by using 2 turns using the first thread on the left as a through thread if you're moving from left to right or use the right-hand thread if you're moving from right to left. The through thread must be kept perfectly horizontal. It may be a good idea to nail it down. Each knot must be kept tight, so keep hold of the free end of the through thread at all times.
Diagram 1 Wrap the 2 threads for each knot round the through thread as in first pic. When you come to the end of a row, go back the other way.
Diagram 2 Then continue wrapping the threads round the through thread but this time holding it at 45°. Move from left to right and then when you reach the middle thread – stop – and take the far right-hand thread across the opposite way at 45° and wrap the threads around it until you reach the centre.
Diagram 3 Continue the one from left to right and when you reach the end, finish off the one from right to left.

Smocking

Smocking is a craft that has been popular for a long time and makes frequent appearances in fashion. It is nothing more than embroidery created over a series of folds which are made by gathering the fabric first – yet it can have many different looks simply because of the fabric it's worked on and the thread it's worked with.

Example 1 If you use a checked fabric such as gingham, you can follow the pattern as a guide for the gathering. If you want to use a plain fabric buy a sheet of smocking dots and iron them on so you have a guide for the various embroideries.

Example 2 You can also use squared paper and an indelible pencil to mark the dots.

Example 3 To work one row of gathering stitches, take a long length of machine twist and knot it at one end. Pick up a tiny stitch on each square (or dot) of the pattern across the width of the fabric, leaving a length of thread at the end. Work rows of stitches to the depth you require. Pull up the rows of gathering in pairs, not too tightly but leaving just enough room to insert the needle between the folds, then tie off the threads in pairs. The embroidery, worked on the reverse side of the fabric (that with the deepest folds), can be done in cotton wool, high-gloss silk or matt thread, even lurex.

> As smocking takes up to three times as much fabric across the width, remember to take this into account when working out how much fabric you will need for any garment that you intend to smock.

Smocking over pleats

You prepare the fabric with lines of gathering stitches, but instead of working over the folds of the fabric, press them all flat in one direction to make pleats.

The stitches most suitable for this embroidery are cross stitch and herringbone fan as they are firm and hold the pleats well. When working cross stitch, work an extra overcast stitch at the base of each cross to secure the stitch and hold the pleat in place. A good result can be obtained if you use this method of embroidery over a checked fabric such as gingham. The stitches pick up the fabric in such a way that different colours will show through. Try working on a sample first to see the different effects you can achieve.

Example 4 is cross stitch which is worked from right to left between two horizontal rows of gathering. Bring the needle and thread out from the back of the work just left of the fourth fold on the

second row of gathering. With thread above needle, take needle up to first row of gathering and insert just to the right of the first fold, taking needle through work and bringing it out to the left of the fourth fold on the same row. To work the second stage of cross stitch, take needle back down to the second line of gathering and insert to the right of the first fold, taking needle through work and bringing it out where you first started the stitch. To join the stitches up, between each cross stitch work a small horizontal stitch between the folds, bringing needle out four folds further along, ready to work the next stitch.

Example 5 is stab stitch, a firm stitch which holds the folds in shape. Working from right to left, bring the needle up from the back of work to the right of the second fold. Take needle back and insert just to the right of the first fold, taking needle through and bringing it up to the left of the fourth fold. Repeat the

Example 1: with gingham follow the pattern as a guide for the gathering

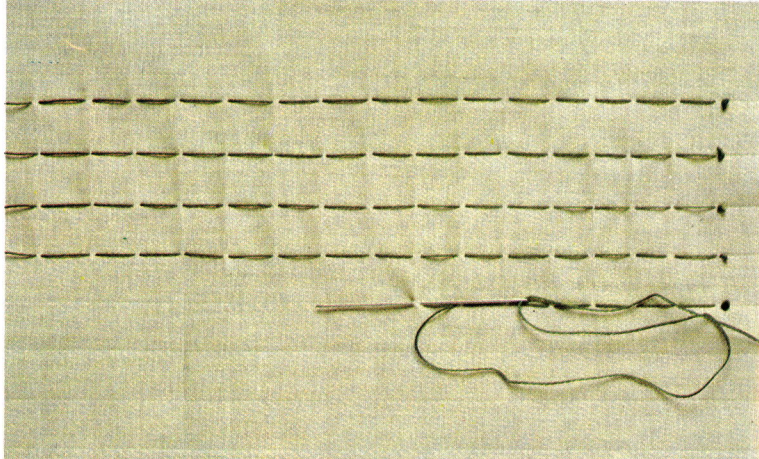

Example 3: gathering stitches are worked with a long thread knotted at one end

Example 2: use squared paper and an indelible pencil to mark the dots evenly

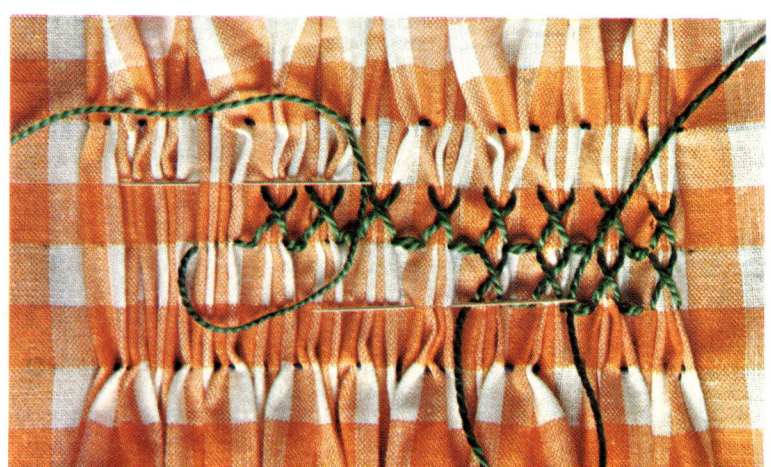

Example 4: cross stitch worked from left to right between two horizontal rows

method all along line. As this stitch only catches in every other fold, when working more than one row, work alternately so that the stitches do not fall directly under one another.

Example 6 is herringbone fan, a long stitch worked over three rows of gathering. Working from left to right, bring needle up from back of work to the left of the first fold on the first line of gathering. With thread above needle, work six equally spaced overcast stitches down to the third row of gathering, taking the sixth stitch through to catch in the next fold. To secure these folds together, take another overcast stitch over the last one. With thread below needle, work six corresponding stitches up the second fold, taking last stitch through to catch second and third folds together. Secure with an overcast stitch.

Example 7 shows surface honeycomb which is worked over two horizontal rows of gathers. Bring

the needle through from the back and oversew the first two pleats together bringing the needle out between the pleats. Take needle down to second row of gathers and oversew the second and third pleats together, inserting and bringing it out as before. Now go up to the first line of stitching and sew the third and fourth pleats together in the same way.

Example 8 shows honeycomb which is different from Example 7 in that the thread is taken behind the gathers, the needle is brought out to the left of the pleat and the pleats are sewn together twice with an overcast stitch.

Example 9 shows checked fabric worked with (from top to bottom) stem stitch, surface honeycomb, surface honeycomb with a gap left between rows, honeycomb and stem stitch.

Continued on next page

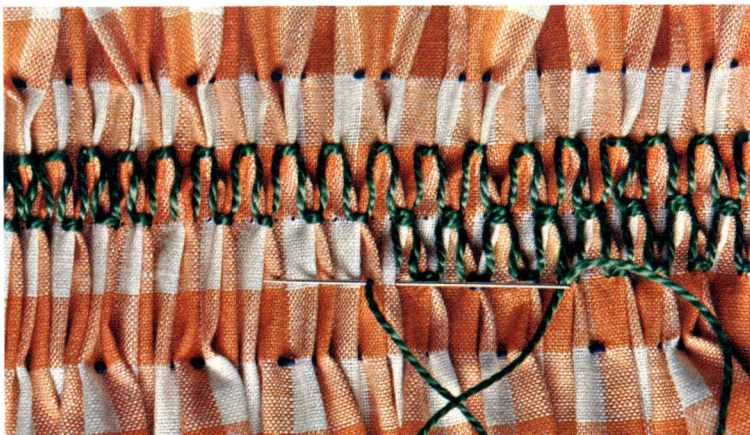
Example 7: surface honeycomb worked from right to left over two horizontal rows

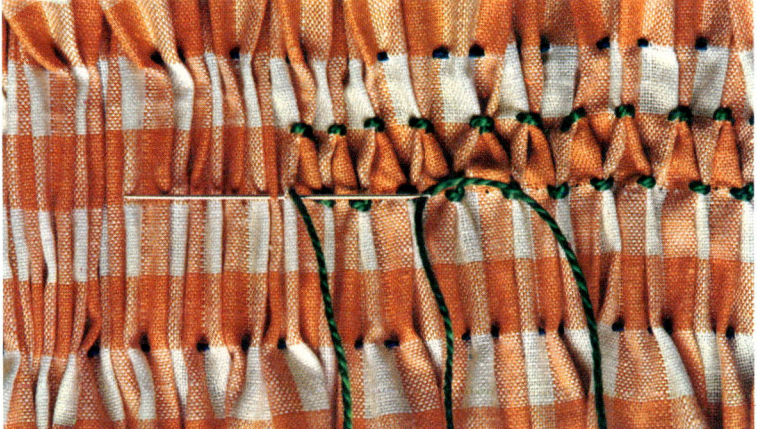
Example 8: honeycomb which has little on the surface as the threads are taken behind

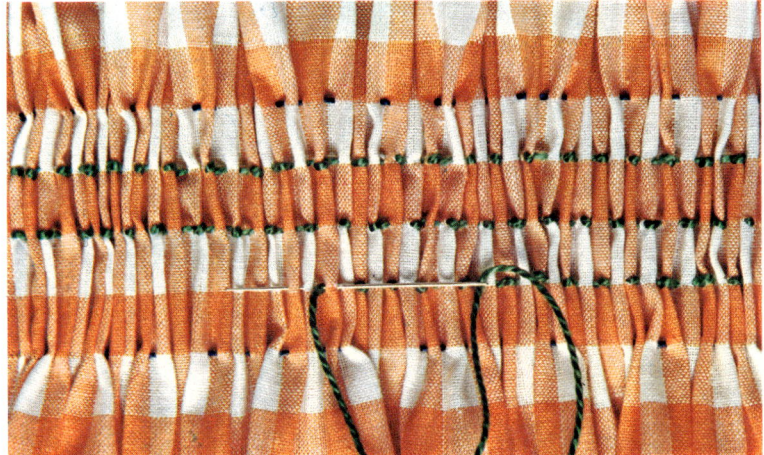
Example 5: stab stitch is a firm stitch which is worked from right to left

Example 6: herringbone fan is worked from left to right over three rows of gathering

Example 9: a selection of honeycomb stitches that shows the effectiveness of smocking on a checked fabric. The top and bottom rows are worked in stem stitch

Smocking . . . continued

Example 10

A: stem stitch. Also known as outline and rope stitch, this is worked along the same row of dots all the time. Bring the needle through from the back and just to the left of the first pleat. With the thread under the needle take a stitch through the second pleat. Take thread through to back and come up just to left of second pleat, take a stitch through third pleat. Stem can also be worked over two pleats.

B: cable stitch. This is worked from left to right on the same row all the time. It's worked by joining together two pleats and the second pleat becomes the first pleat of the next stitch. Bring the needle through to left of first pleat. With thread above needle take a

stitch through the second pleat coming out between the pleats. Move thread below needle and take another stitch through third pleat.

C: wavy stem stitch. This is also known as vandyke or diamond when it's worked in reverse as well to join up two triangles. It is worked between two horizontal rows of gathers and over a variable number of pleats. Bring the needle through to the left of the first pleat on the second row of gathers. With thread below needle take a stitch through the second pleat at a slightly higher level. Work thus up to height required then work top stitch with thread above needle. Keeping thread above, work down slope to match.

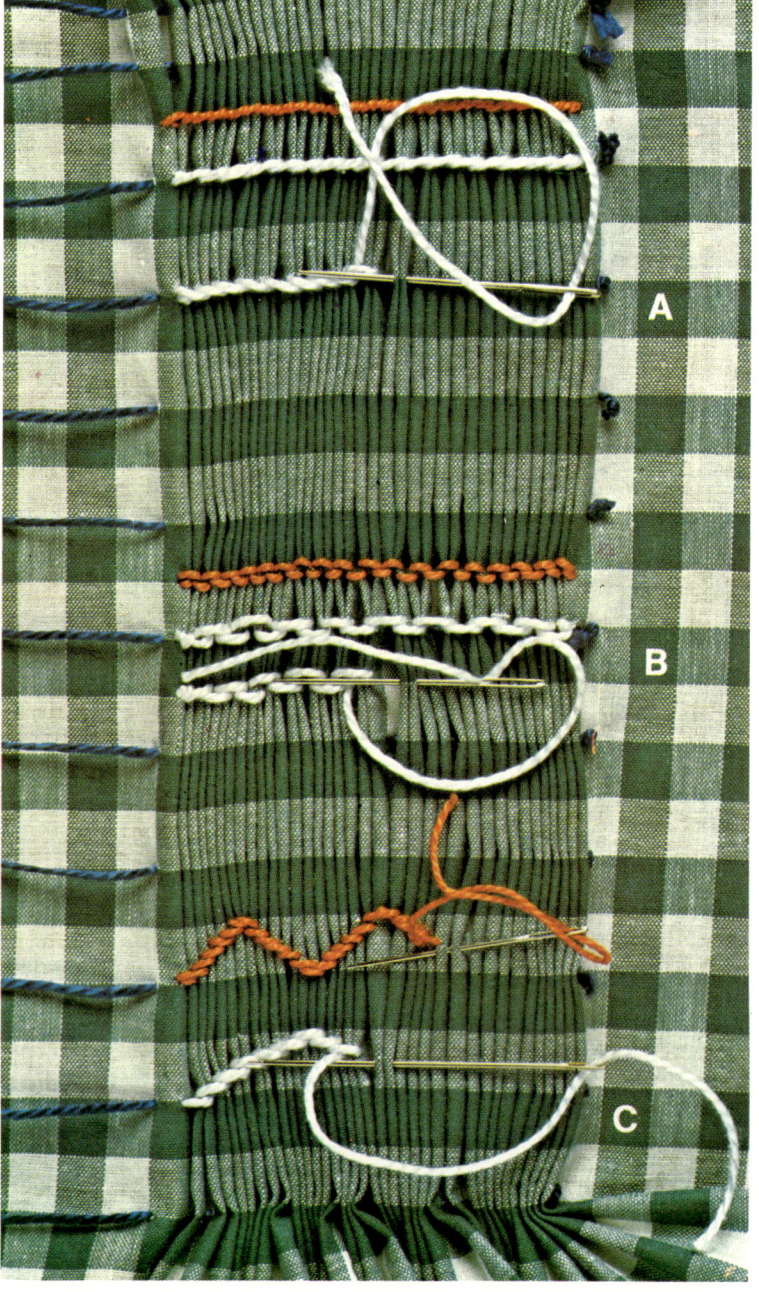

Smocked babyclothes

Clothes for a new baby are often decorated with smocking – an attractive way of giving shape to simple garments.

The rounded look at necklines is created by working in different tensions. Near the neck, the embroidery is tight and establishes the gathers. As you work downwards in rounds you gradually slacken the tension so that even though you're covering the same area as at the neckline, it appears wider. In the picture below you can see the technique. The first three rows are different tensions of stem stitch; the second two rows honeycomb. When working the honeycomb take care not to pull the thread at the back of the work too tight or you will bring the rows in again giving a "waisted" look. if you're not too certain about your ability to judge distance or keep rows straight without guidelines, before you start mark in your lines with ordinary cotton and a running stitch and you can make the gathers as tight or loose as you want.

Angel tops

Materials 60cm [24 in] of 90cm [35½ in] wide fabric; matching machine twist; embroidery cotton; matching or contrasting bias binding; 2 press-studs or two buttons.

TO MAKE

1. Using squared paper (1 square = 5cm) make patterns following Diagram 1. Separate front from back by cutting at dotted line.
2. Fold fabric in half lengthways and place centre front and centre back pieces to fold and sleeve piece on remaining fabric. Cut out each piece adding 15mm [⅝ in] at top and side (not hems) for seams.
3. Cut opening at centre back and bind edges with bias binding. Mark press-stud positions (or buttons and buttonholes if you prefer) and sew.
4. Sew side seams and press open. Sew sleeve seams and press open. Sew sleeves to body. Turn to right side.
5. Now work the smocking, beginning and ending each row either side of the back opening. Using a long enough thread to complete a whole row and starting with a knot, work one tight and close round of stem stitch (do make sure the opening will fit over a baby's head comfortably). Continue to work down for about 5cm [2 in] choosing any design you like but on each row lessen the tension a little to create the yoke effect.
6. Work two rows of smocking at the wrists. Make small rolled hems at bottom edge of body and sleeves then oversew with embroidery thread (see picture). Bind the neckline with bias binding leaving 12.5cm [5 in] at both ends for ties.

More smocking on page 214

Below: the rounded look worked on a striped material – the stripes act as guidelines

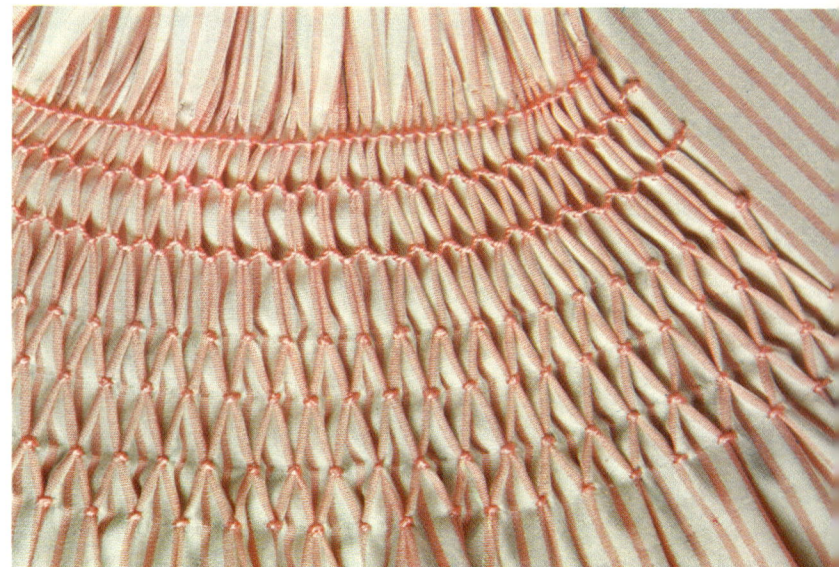

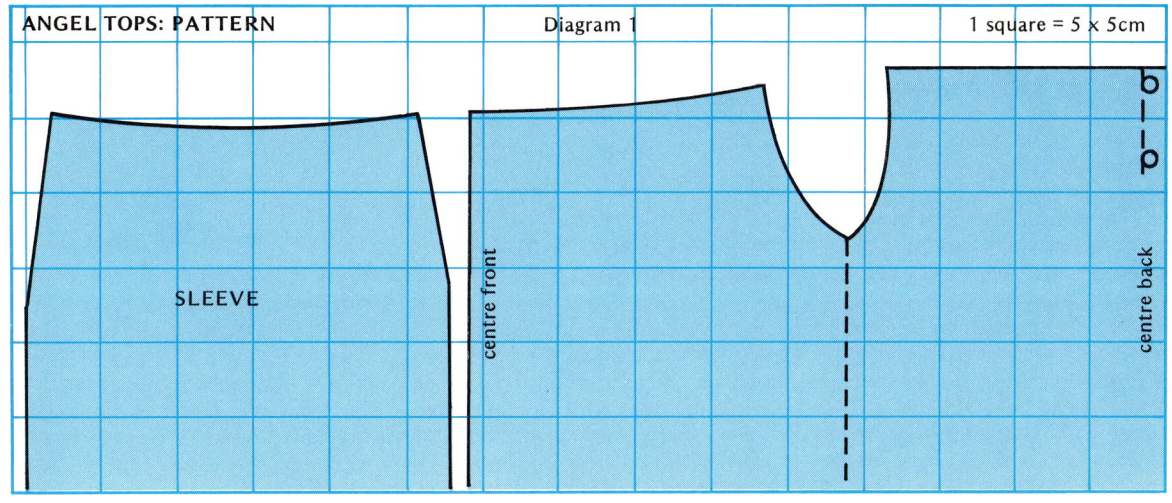

ANGEL TOPS: PATTERN	Diagram 1	1 square = 5 x 5cm

SLEEVE

centre front

centre back

Left: the pattern which you'll need for the Angel Tops
Below: smocking stitches are worked in different colours on the three tops. Note that the hems are rolled then oversewn with embroidery thread or silk

Dresses and pantaloons

Bands of smocking are worked at the top of the skirt and pants and this is then joined to the bodice. If you choose an easy-care cotton like piqué you'll have the extra benefit of the natural lines in the fabric to help you when smocking.

Materials For both: 1m [39 in] of 90cm [35½ in] wide fabric; matching machine twist; matching bias binding if liked; 2 buttons; embroidery thread; 3mm [⅛ in] elastic and press-studs for pantaloons.

TO MAKE

1. Using squared paper (1 square = 5cm) make patterns following Diagrams 1 or 2.

2. Fold fabric in half lengthways. Place centre front on fold and back on remaining material. Cut out adding 5cm [2 in] at bottom edges and 15mm [⅝ in] at gathering edges and sides for seams.

3. Rearrange remaining fabric and cut out front (placed on fold) and back bodice, adding 15mm [⅝ in] all round for seams. From rest of material cut out gusset (for pantaloons) and strips cut on the bias (if not using bias binding) for armholes and neckline of both.

4. Run a line of gathering stitches along front and back skirt pieces where shown in diagram. Make a second row of gathering stitches 4cm [1½ in] below first. Draw in the gathers to the same width as lower edge of front and back bodice pieces.

5. Work the embroidery in the 4cm [1½ in] band. The outer rows are worked in cable stitch, the triangles in wavy stem stitch, and the area between is filled in with tiny cross stitches or rows of stem stitch. The tiny flowers are worked from a central hole over four gathers. When the smocking is completed on front and both backs, make up the garments as step 6 or step 7.

6. **Dress** Pin, tack and stitch skirt front to bodice front, matching A's. Pin, tack and stitch skirt back to bodice matching B's and dotted lines. Join front to back at shoulders and sides. Bind armholes and neck (continue the binding to both buttonhole edges at back). Turn under and stitch small hem at back (BC). Make two buttonholes and sew on two buttons (the backs cross over each other and are closed by the buttons). Pin, tack and slip-stitch hem at bottom edge. Press.

7. **Pantaloons** Pin, tack and stitch skirt front to bodice front. Pin, tack and stitch skirt back to bodice back, matching unbroken and broken lines. Pin, tack and stitch front to back at shoulders and sides. Turn under small hem on edge of facing at back, stitch. Right sides of backs together, pin, tack and stitch XY. Fold facings back and catch-stitch on wrong side. On front, pin, tack and stitch gusset in place on right side, turning under a small hem all round. On wrong side of back make small hem just below where buttons will be sewn. Make one long casing for elastic on both sides at bottom edges of pants. Insert elastic, securing both ends with stitching. Bind armholes and neck, securing facing with the binding. Sew on press-studs to close back. Sew on buttons and make buttonholes to correspond above gusset at front. Press.

Right: the smocked dresses and pantaloons, and below them, the smocking in closer detail

Below: the patterns you'll need

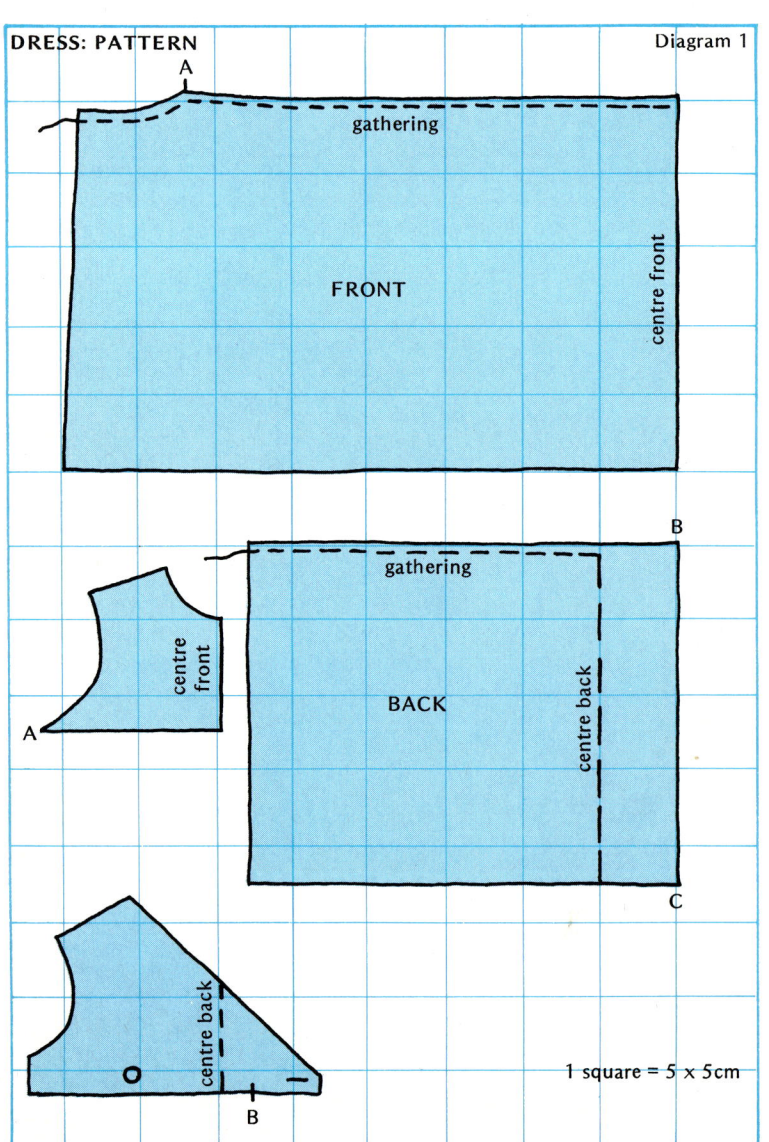

DRESS: PATTERN — Diagram 1

1 square = 5 x 5cm

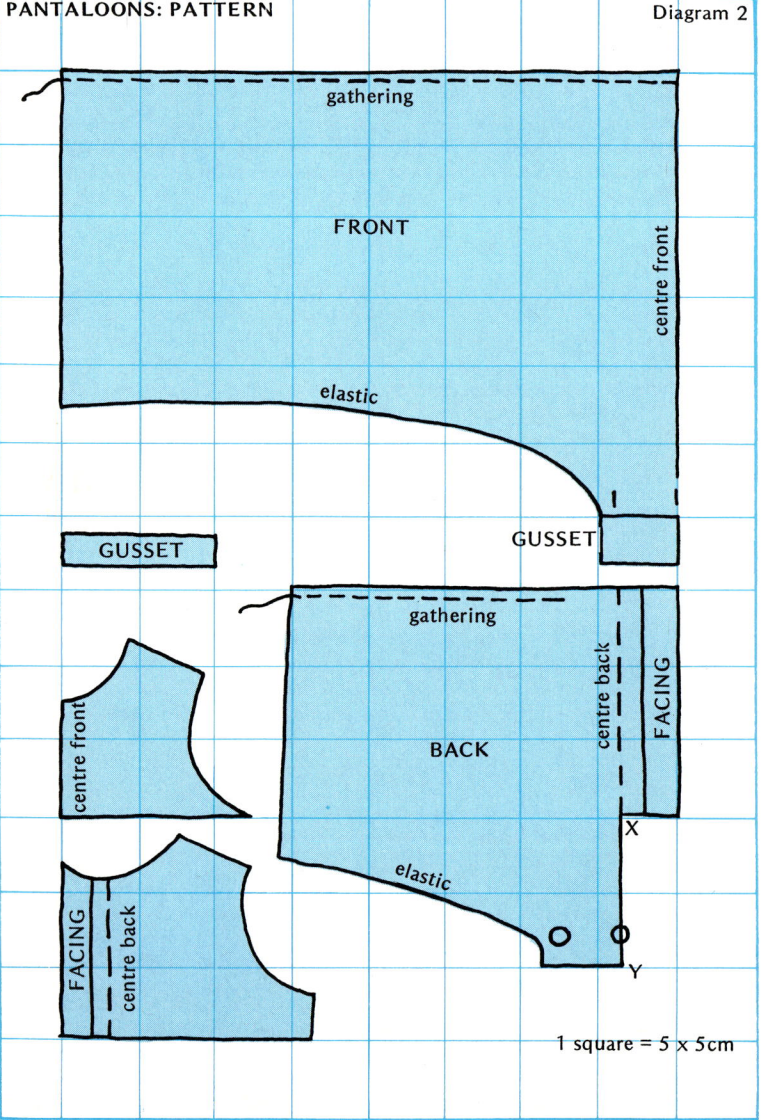

PANTALOONS: PATTERN — Diagram 2

1 square = 5 x 5cm

Tie dyeing

This process of adding bursts of colour to cloth not only cheers up yesterday's fashion but with a little practice will give you the popular designs of the current one – though the results are not always predictable! Of course this could be the reason why it is such a popular craft – garments dyed in this way have an individuality that's very hard to repeat.

It is most important that colourfast dyes are used – and you must have a separate dyebath (old large saucepans or old metal buckets) for each new colour. You'll need rubber gloves, an apron to keep you undyed and a lot of newspaper to protect the work surface. The other essentials look like a selection from a schoolboy's pocket: bits of string, cord or raffia, buttons, marbles, pebbles, screws, rubber bands and even paperclips.

The secret of tie dyeing is to protect certain parts of the fabric while the rest is soaking in dye. The protected parts become the patterns once the fabric is dry. How much protection you give those areas is all wrapped up in the tieing and fine fabrics especially require more knots, and tighter ones, than cotton does. The various shapes of the added-in buttons, marbles or screws help create the unusual designs.

Whatever material you're using, it must be washed to remove any finish or dressing and then dried. If you're dyeing a piece of cloth for a sarong or to be made up later into a top or skirt, mark the cloth with pencil first so that you know which areas are going to have what on them. To achieve the striped effect of the yellow and white sarong, for example, you must work out first how far apart you want the white areas – for these are the ones that will be tied while the yellow is being dyed.

You can buy paint-on fabric dyes and these expand the horizon for anyone interested in tie dyeing. By placing a little colour here and there around and between the ties you can enhance the designs as you can see in both the sarongs (this page) and the two T-shirts (see next page).

Yellow and white sarong

1. Divide the cloth so you know exactly where you want the stripes. Mark with pencil. Now pull the fabric between forefinger and thumb like an accordian.

2. Wind the string round the required width of the stripe and knot it securely.

3. This is how the stripe should be tied and knotted – a solid band of binding.

4. To protect the knots you can wrap around a piece of plastic or tape – cut piece to required width and set aside for the moment.

5. Use an eyedropper to mark the outside edges of the stripes with a contrasting paint-on fabric dye.

6. Wrap the plastic round the stripe so it covers the painted bit then secure in place with plastic bands.

Repeat these steps along the length of the fabric, attaching one long length of string to the last stripe. This will help you remove the cloth from the dye bath, and can also be tied to the clothesline while the cloth dries. Follow the directions on the dye packet (remember they must be colourfast) and prepare the dye. Dip the knotted cloth into the bath, pressing it down (you *do* have your gloves on) so that the whole cloth is covered. After the required length of time, remove fabric, squeeze it out and hang out to dry.

The dye must be completely dry before the knots are untied.

Do remember to wash all tie-dyed garments separately – just in case the colour should run!

Opposite page: sarongs, so practical for hot summer days in the garden or on the beach, can be tie dyed in the colours of your choice

Below: how the fabric is rolled and tied to create the panelled look of the yellow and white sarong

Step 1

Step 2

Step 3

Step 4

Step 5

Step 6

Colour burst T-shirt

This is the same technique used on the red sarong. A piece of the cloth is bunched up and tied, leaving a little space between each tie. Extra colour can be added with paint-on fabric dyes. Tie again over the top of the painted area, then dye as for Yellow and White Sarong (see previous pages).

Striped T-shirt

Work out just where you want the stripes to be – this is important if you are to get anywhere like a regular looking pattern. Mark with chalk. Tie as shown in the diagrams below.

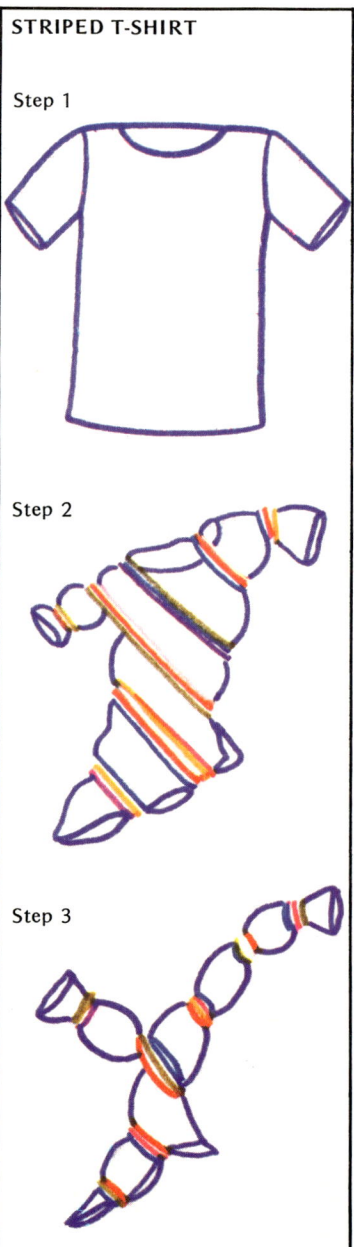

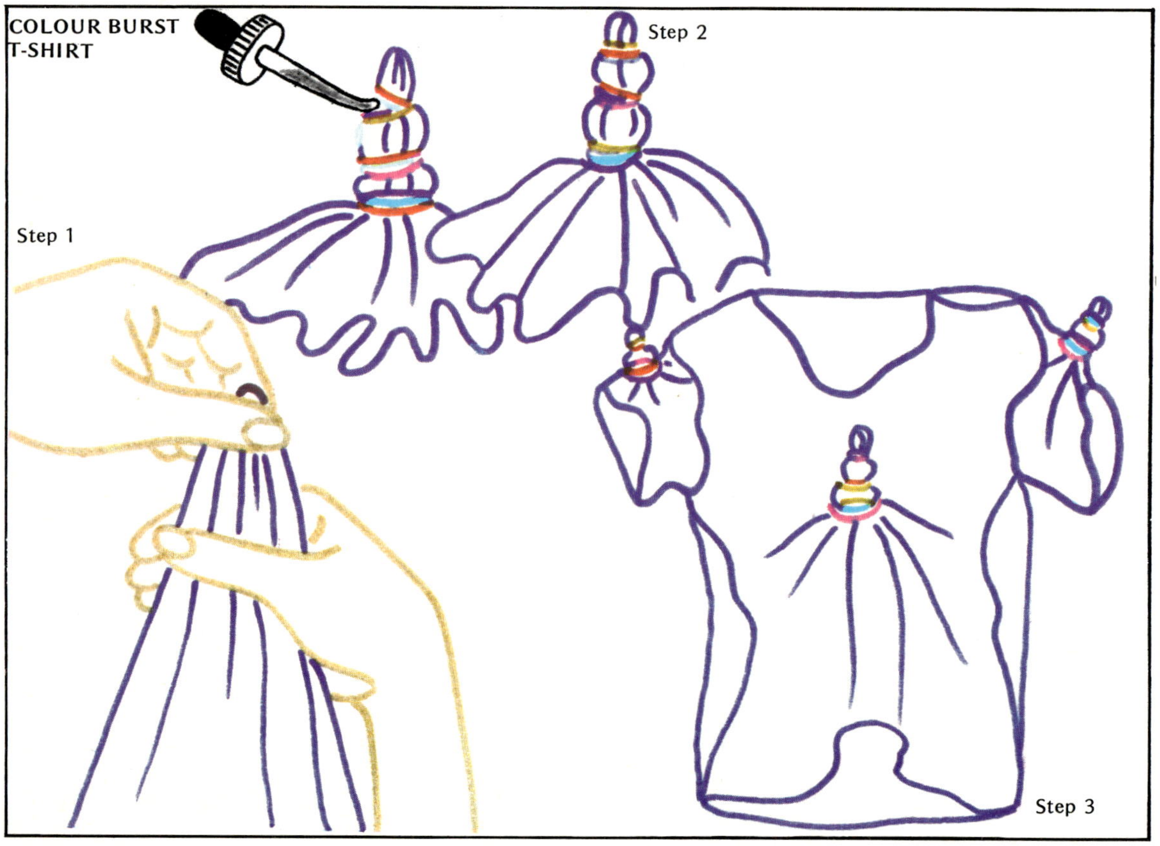

STRIPED T-SHIRT

Step 1

Step 2

Step 3

COLOUR BURST T-SHIRT

Step 1

Step 2

Step 3

Batik

Batik, apart from its worldwide popularity, has a fashion significance in that clothes can be given a new look almost overnight when the need arises. As it's hard to imagine a time when T-shirts won't be in style, we've chosen them to illustrate the techniques involved.

Though the origins of batik are unknown, it has been used for many centuries to decorate cloth. The Javanese were mainly responsible for developing the art, and it is their superbly ornate yet delicate designs that have inspired many. But batik doesn't have to be complicated. In its simplest form it is merely a way of using dye effectively by a technique that's known as "resist". By covering parts of the cloth with wax you prevent the dye from reaching that area, and so a contrast is created. The waxing and dyeing process can be repeated as many times as you like till you have the design you want.

The wax you use can either be paraffin or beeswax, though art and craft suppliers do sell what's called "batik wax" which is a mixture of the two. Paraffin wax is more brittle and it is the one to use if light veins and marbling effect is desired – the wax breaks into irregular cracks when tightly crushed in the dye bath. To melt the wax but to prevent overheating, you must use an indirect heat – eg, a double boiler, or a saucepan over an asbestos mat, even a can placed in a saucepan of constantly simmering water. The wax is applied with a fine paintbrush or the batik tool, the tjanting which has a bowl to hold the wax, and a fine nib or tube; bigger areas can be filled in with a thicker paintbrush.

The dyes have to be cold water ones (hot water would melt the wax) and salt (not iodised) must be added to "fix" the colour. You'll need a large plastic bowl or bucket (not metal – it will stain) and a small heatproof glass bowl or jug in which to mix the powdered dye. Rubber gloves are necessary, tongs are helpful for lifting the fabric and moving it around in the dyebath, and an apron will keep splashes off your clothes.

Most of all you need lots of space, and lots of time and patience because if batik is anything, it isn't quick – between each waxing and dyeing the cloth must be rinsed in lukewarm water until the water runs clear, and must be left to dry naturally (but not in direct sun) before the processes are repeated or the wax is ironed off.

You'll also need a knife to scrape off the wax after the dyeing's done, an iron (not a steam iron – the vents will get clogged), some unprinted absorbent paper (eg, paper towels), and a couple of weeks newspapers (to protect the floor if working indoors, and also to absorb the melting wax). On an ironing board first place a thick layer of newspaper then a layer of absorbent paper; place more newspaper inside the shirt, cover with another layer of absorbent paper then a final thick layer of newspaper. The iron's setting should be one lower than that normally used for that fabric. This is the stage that's considered most tedious as you have to keep ironing until all the wax has been absorbed by the paper – this usually means many changes of paper till it has all gone. Any stiffness or waxy smell that remains can be washed away in very hot water plus a fabric softener and conditioner.

Now for the T-shirt, or whatever it is you want to decorate: the fabric should be smooth and a natural fibre (synthetics don't dye well). It is most important, especially if using a new garment or fabric, to wash it well to remove any manufacturer's finish or dressing. The final rinse should be in cold water without any added softener. Dry the garment well then iron it so you start from a smooth base.

The washed T-shirts are hung out to dry naturally before they are ironed and ready to decorate. Dyeing one colour over another produces a third colour so if, for example, a marine blue dye is used the shirt, from left to right, will become dark blue, green, purple and greeny-blue. It is the pink one which is about to be transformed . . . please turn the page

Batik . . . continued

Step 1

Step 2

Step 3

1. Place a piece of perspex or thick, greaseproof covered cardboard inside the washed and ironed T-shirt to keep it taut and to separate the front from the back.

2. The bowl of the tjanting holds the hot wax which is placed on to the shirt through the fine nib used to draw the heart-shaped outlines.

3. A thicker brush fills in the hearts with wax so that the area beneath will remain the original colour.

Have a piece of rag handy to catch any drips.

4. Wet the T-shirt then put it into the prepared dye in the bath. Move it around gently every few minutes. Rinse till the water runs clear then hang out to dry. Keep dye in case you want to repeat process.

5. Place lots of newspapers under and inside the shirt then iron at one setting lower than usual for the fabric. Change the paper often. Wash in hot water plus fabric softener and conditioner.

Right: the T-shirt and its new look – the pink of the hearts was the original colour

Step 4

Step 5

Index